Economics Today

The Micro View

Economics Today

THE MICRO VIEW

Fifteenth Edition

Roger LeRoy Miller

Institute for University Studies, Arlington, Texas

Addison-Wesley

Boston San Francisco New York
London Toronto Sydney Tokyo Singapore Madrid
Mexico City Munich Paris Cape Town Hong Kong Montreal

Dedication

To Bill Stryker

Thanks for your years of hard work on my many projects. You've been able to have every book come out on time, no matter what. I greatly appreciate your dedication and continuing professionalism. —R. L. M.

Editor in Chief: Donna Battista
Acquisitions Editor: Noel Kamm Seibert
Development Editor: Julie Z. Lindstrom
Assistant Editor: Courtney E. Schinke
Editorial Assistant: Carolyn Terbush
Managing Editor: Nancy H. Fenton
Senior Production Supervisor: Kathryn Dinovo
Digital Assets Manager: Marianne Groth
Supplements Production Coordinator: Alison Eusden
Senior Author Support/Technology Specialist: Joe Vetere
Rights and Permissions Advisor: Shannon Barbe

Director of Media: Susan Schoenberg
Senior Media Producer: Melissa Honig
Content Lead, MyEconLab: Douglas Ruby
Executive Marketing Manager: Roxanne McCarley
Marketing Assistant: Kendra Bassi
Senior Manufacturing Buyer: Carol Melville
Senior Media Buyer: Ginny Michaud
Senior Cover Designer: Beth Paquin
Text Designer: Geri Davis, The Davis Group, Inc.
Production Coordinator: Orr Book Services
Compositor: Nesbitt Graphics, Inc.
Art Studio: ElectraGraphics, Inc.

Photo credits appear on page C-1, which constitutes a continuation of the copyright page.

Library of Congress Cataloging-in-Publication Data
Miller, Roger LeRoy.
 Economics today / Roger LeRoy Miller. -- 15th ed.
  p. cm. -- (The Addison-Wesley series in economics)
 Includes index.
 ISBN 978-0-321-57131-1 (main volume; chapters 1-34) -- ISBN 978-0-321-59453-2
   (macro view; chapters 1-19 and 33-34) -- ISBN 978-0-321-59452-5 (micro view;
   chapters 1-6 and 20-34)
 1. Economics. 2. Microeconomics. 3. Macroeconomics. I. Title.

HB171.5.M642 2010
330--dc22

2008049775

1 2 3 4 5 6 7 8 9 10—CRK—12 11 10 09 08

Addison-Wesley
is an imprint of

www.pearsonhighered.com

ISBN-10: 0-321-59452-5
ISBN-13: 978-0-321-59452-5

The Addison-Wesley Series in Economics

Abel/Bernanke/Croushore
Macroeconomics*

Bade/Parkin
Foundations of Economics*

Bierman/Fernandez
Game Theory with Economic Applications

Binger/Hoffman
Microeconomics with Calculus

Boyer
Principles of Transportation Economics

Branson
Macroeconomic Theory and Policy

Bruce
Public Finance and the American Economy

Byrns/Stone
Economics

Carlton/Perloff
Modern Industrial Organization

Caves/Frankel/Jones
World Trade and Payments: An Introduction

Chapman
Environmental Economics: Theory, Application, and Policy

Cooter/Ulen
Law & Economics

Downs
An Economic Theory of Democracy

Ehrenberg/Smith
Modern Labor Economics

Ekelund/Ressler/Tollison
Economics*

Fusfeld
The Age of the Economist

Gerber
International Economics

Ghiara
Learning Economics

Gordon
Macroeconomics

Gregory
Essentials of Economics

Gregory/Stuart
Russian and Soviet Economic Performance and Structure

Hartwick/Olewiler
The Economics of Natural Resource Use

Hoffman/Averett
Women and the Economy: Family, Work, and Pay

Holt
Markets, Games and Strategic Behavior

Hubbard
Money, the Financial System, and the Economy

Hughes/Cain
American Economic History

Husted/Melvin
International Economics

Jehle/Reny
Advanced Microeconomic Theory

Johnson-Lans
A Health Economics Primer

Klein
Mathematical Methods for Economics

Krugman/Obstfeld
International Economics: Theory & Policy*

Laidler
The Demand for Money

Leeds/von Allmen
The Economics of Sports

Leeds/von Allmen/Schiming
Economics*

Lipsey/Ragan/Storer
Economics*

Melvin
International Money and Finance

Miller
Economics Today*

Miller
Understanding Modern Economics

Miller/Benjamin
The Economics of Macro Issues

Miller/Benjamin/North
The Economics of Public Issues

Mills/Hamilton
Urban Economics

Mishkin
The Economics of Money, Banking, and Financial Markets*

Mishkin
The Economics of Money, Banking, and Financial Markets, Business School Edition*

Murray
Econometrics: A Modern Introduction

Parkin
Economics*

Perloff
Microeconomics*

Perloff
Microeconomics: Theory and Applications with Calculus

Perman/Common/McGilvray/Ma
Natural Resources and Environmental Economics

Phelps
Health Economics

Riddell/Shackelford/Stamos/Schneider
Economics: A Tool for Critically Understanding Society

Ritter/Silber/Udell
Principles of Money, Banking & Financial Markets*

Rohlf
Introduction to Economic Reasoning

Ruffin/Gregory
Principles of Economics

Sargent
Rational Expectations and Inflation

Scherer
Industry Structure, Strategy, and Public Policy

Sherman
Market Regulation

Stock/Watson
Introduction to Econometrics

Stock/Watson
Introduction to Econometrics, Brief Edition

Studenmund
Using Econometrics: A Practical Guide

Tietenberg/Lewis
Environmental and Natural Resource Economics

Tietenberg
Environmental Economics and Policy

Todaro/Smith
Economic Development

Waldman
Microeconomics

Waldman/Jensen
Industrial Organization: Theory and Practice

Weil
Economic Growth

Williamson
Macroeconomics

Brief Contents

Contents

Part Six   Market Structure, Resource Allocation, and Regulation

Preface

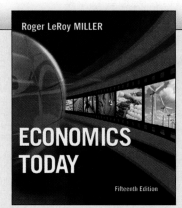

Generating the Motivation to Learn with Current News and Applications

We as professional economists find so much of what is happening around us exciting because we use the tools of economic analysis to analyze and investigate issues. As educators, we have the ability to persuade our students that economics is relevant, that it is a powerful tool for analysis, and that it represents a tool for managing one's life.

Throughout the years, I have found that the single most effective way to motivate students to learn more about economics is to present them with current and relevant examples. The new edition has a wide range of student-oriented examples—domestic, global, policy, and e-commerce—that demonstrate how relevant our discipline is in everyday life.

You will notice a new feature in every chapter called *You Are There*. These new features are all drawn from real-world experiences of real people making real policy and business decisions. Students can thereby see the importance and application of some of the theory that they have learned in each chapter.

Students learn most effectively when they can apply the concepts to their everyday lives.

As with each new edition, I have revised significant sections of this text. For instance, you will find that the content of Chapters 15 through 17 has been restructured and updated to provide more details about policymaking by today's Federal Reserve System. Elasticity and consumer choice (Chapters 20 and 21) have been reversed to better present these topics to students. Chapter 27 applies game theory to the issue of product compatibility, and Chapter 32 examines the European Union's system of emissions caps and tradable permits. Of course, all chapters have also been thoroughly updated to incorporate the latest developments, data, and policy debates.

The latest developments, data, and policy debates allow students to be on the cutting edge of economic theory and research.

Assessment has become an important topic on many campuses, and I aim to foster that type of learning. Students can continue to utilize the *Quick Quizzes* throughout each chapter, and Clicker/Personal Response Systems questions banks are available to instructors. Addison-Wesley and I continue to expand the assessment aspect of *MyEconLab*, our online course management and tutorial system. Now 100 percent of the end-of-chapter exercises are assignable in *MyEconLab* for greater flexibility in assessing students. We also strive to continue to provide students with current events coverage and analysis through weekly news and ABC News clips.

My goal in the Fifteenth Edition of *Economics Today* is to empower students to be able to analyze the way economics is involved in every aspect of their lives. Once they arrive at this realization, they can appreciate the relevance of economic principles.

— Roger LeRoy Miller

New to This Edition

This new edition of *Economics Today* tackles the most recent issues while keeping in mind key hurdles to student learning. The primary objectives, as ever, are to show students how economics is relevant to *them* and to give them many opportunities in each chapter to verify their understanding of fundamental concepts.

Cutting-edge developments have been incorporated throughout this new edition. These include:

- *Federal Reserve Interest-Rate-Based Policymaking and Assistance to Banks During the **Subprime Crisis***: Chapters 15 through 17 have been restructured to include expanded discussions of the monetary policy procedure the Fed utilizes in determining and adhering to an **interest rate target.** Chapter 17 includes a clear explanation of the temporary assistance program that the Fed implemented beginning in 2007 and 2008 to cushion the impact of the subprime-mortgage "mess" on the U.S. banking industry.
- *Developments in **New Keynesian Macroeconomics***: In addition to enhanced discussion of the sticky-price theory and policy analysis, Chapter 18 evaluates policy implications of the New Keynesian theory of the Phillips curve.
- *Application of **Game Theory***: Chapter 27 applies game theory to the issue of product compatibility for those firms utilizing electronic technologies.
- *Containing **Greenhouse Gas Emissions** via Caps and Permit Trading*: Chapter 32 explains how Europe's program operates and evaluates the experience to date.

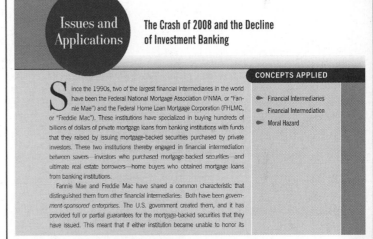

An all new Issues and Applications in Chapter 15 examines the Wall Street and investment banking crisis.

In the macro portion of the text, I've added analyses of the following:

- Chapter 7 delves into causes of a recent drop-off in U.S. labor force participation.
- Chapter 11 discusses the surprisingly muted economic impacts of **jumps in oil prices** during the 2000s.
- In Chapter 13, potential crowding-out effects of growing government **health care spending** are explored.
- In Chapter 14, the relationship between the **growing federal budget deficit** and expanding U.S. trade deficits is scrutinized.

In the micro portion, I've included the following:

- Chapters 20 and 21 have been reversed so that elasticity is now covered before consumer choice, a sequence that helps students better understand these important concepts.
- Chapter 21 examines efforts by **behavioral economists** to compare levels of satisfaction across individuals and groups.
- Chapter 26 describes the important role of product differentiation and trademarks in today's **auto industry**.
- Chapter 29 seeks to explain the difference in **earnings of male and female workers** in the United States.

Making the Connection— from the Classroom to the Real World

Today's students need to connect and apply economic theory to their diverse interests and lives. *Economics Today* speaks to students of all backgrounds, providing relentlessly current examples that effectively demonstrate economic principles. For this edition, **95 percent** of the examples are new.

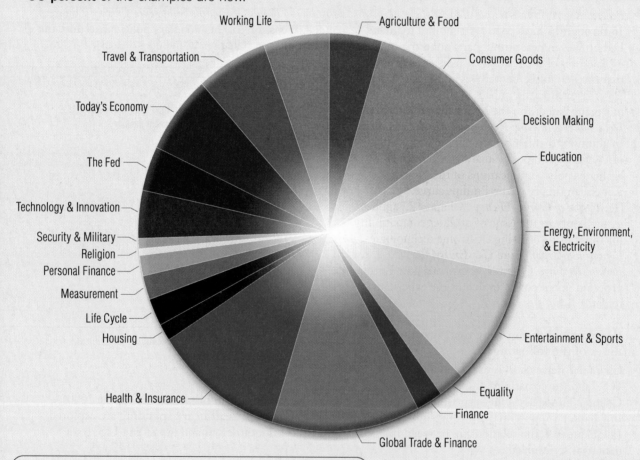

Working Life — Agriculture & Food
Travel & Transportation — Consumer Goods
Today's Economy — Decision Making
The Fed — Education
Technology & Innovation
Security & Military — Energy, Environment, & Electricity
Religion
Personal Finance
Measurement
Life Cycle
Housing — Entertainment & Sports
Health & Insurance — Equality
— Finance
— Global Trade & Finance

Domestic topics and events are presented through thought-provoking discussions, such as:

- Why Women Are Confronting Higher Inflation Than Men
- Zero-Priced Seats at Graduation Ceremonies Become Hot Items
- Explaining the Low U.S. "Saving Rate"

EXAMPLE
The Rising Price of Using Old Songs as Video Background Music

As video content pours onto televisions, cellphones, and computers, producers of videos are scrambling for background music. Indeed, an increasing number of video creators are producing videos carefully synchronized with music, in some cases with videos scripted to fit storylines in song lyrics. The result has been a significant increase in the demand for background music, often purchased for these specific uses from catalogs of long-retired or deceased songwriters. As more producers seek to include hit songs from the past in their video productions, the prices of the rights to use the songs have increased, too. Nearly forgotten songs once available for a few hundred dollars now cost as much as $50,000.

FOR CRITICAL ANALYSIS
What do you suppose has happened to the market clearing price of copyrighted songs newly written for use as background music for video productions?

Important policy questions help students see how they can evaluate public debates, such as:

- Incentives Coax Senior Citizens from Behind the Wheel
- The U.S. Military Confronts a Trade-Off
- Why It Can Pay to Form a Partnership Instead of a Corporation

POLICY EXAMPLE
How Empirical Evidence Aids in Thwarting Terrorism

Since 1968, there have been more than 13,000 incidents of "transnational" terrorism, or violent attacks in nations where the attackers do not reside. These data suggest predictable cycles in terrorist attacks. When terrorists launch a complex large-scale operation, such as an attack aimed at the destruction of high-rise buildings, public pressure to thwart such attacks remains high for a long time afterwards. Consequently, government countermeasures also remain in place for a lengthy period. Knowing this, terrorists lie low and begin long-term planning for a future large-scale attack. Thus, there are predictably long lulls between large-scale attacks. In contrast, public pressure to prevent simple small-scale attacks, such as bus bombings, wanes more

quickly. Government prevention efforts also dissipate more rapidly, thereby tempting terrorists to launch more small-scale attacks. Thus, there tend to be predictably short pauses between smaller-scale attacks.

Recognition of empirical regularities in terrorism has assisted governments in predicting terrorism upsurges. Governments can utilize these predictions to determine how to allocate their antiterrorism resources more effectively.

FOR CRITICAL ANALYSIS
Why do you suppose that when making predictions to help thwart terrorism, economists typically assume that terrorists behave rationally?

Global and international policy examples emphasize the continued importance of international perspectives and policy decisions, including:

- In a Global Economy, World Saving Equals World Investment
- A French Handbag Manufacturer Opts for Multitasking
- Struggling to Boost Government Spending in Peru
  - EU Governments Get Serious About Emissions —Or Do They?

INTERNATIONAL EXAMPLE
For Greenland, a Warming Climate Is Good Economic News

Greenland is the world's largest island by surface area, but its population is only about 60,000. The island nation is located at the meeting point of the Atlantic and Arctic oceans. Greenland owes its name to the fact that when it was discovered Medieval Warm Period wa and willows lined its sho slightly in later centuries, the country is covered w however, the nation's ave degrees Fahrenheit. Some land's average temperatu

tional degrees by the end of this century. Warmer days allow farmers to take advantage of the extended sunlight and raise more crops and animals, and fishermen have begun catching large numbers of warm-water cod that previously had been

INTERNATIONAL POLICY EXAMPLE
Greece Pays a Price for Broadening Its GDP Definition

The government of Greece recently announced that its official tabulation of GDP would now include the total estimated value of production in black market industries, such as illegal gambling and prostitution. Consequently, the Greek government revised upward by about 25 percent its official GDP figures for every year since 2000. This change in GDP measurement came at a price, however. The European Union (EU), of which Greece is a member nation, makes regular payments to governments of the lowest-income EU mem-

bers. As a result of the big jump in its annual GDP figures, Greece was no longer officially as "poor" in the eyes of the EU, which reduced its annual payments to the Greek government by almost $600 million.

FOR CRITICAL ANALYSIS
Why do you suppose that economists now have a harder time comparing Greek GDP to the levels of GDP in other nations, such as the United States?

Information technology is presented in relevant e-commerce examples, such as:

- The New Online Dating Incentive: Health Insurance
- Digital Imaging Boosts the Supply of Dentistry Services
- Help, I'm Shopping, and I Can't Stop!

E-COMMERCE EXAMPLE
Moviemakers Try to Avoid Projecting Negative Marginal Utility

In an average week during 1948, when the U.S. population was less than half its present level, 90 million people paid to view a motion picture at a movie theater. Today, the average weekly number of moviegoers is only 30 million. Since the late 1940s, a steady wave of close substitutes—television, videocassettes, DVDs, digital movie downloads—has reduced the number of movies that people choose to see at theaters. One way that moviemakers hope to lure people back to theaters is by producing more movies in digital three-dimensional (3D) formats. More than 2,000 U.S. theaters are now equipped with 3D digital projection systems, and some directors have indicated that they plan to make only digital 3D movies.

Hollywood's newfound fascination with digital 3D has one drawback, however: viewing digital 3D movies for much longer than 90 minutes causes some viewers to experience headaches, dizziness, or even nausea. Thus, a key objective of today's designers of digital 3D projection systems is to minimize the potential for some moviegoers to derive negative marginal utility from viewing 3D motion pictures.

FOR CRITICAL ANALYSIS
Why do you suppose that some in Hollywood are predicting that initially most digital 3D movies will be action packed and relatively short?

Helping Students Focus and Think Critically

New and revised pedagogical tools in each chapter engage students and help them focus on the central ideas in economics today.

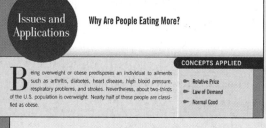

Demand and Supply   3

Three decades ago, about 45 percent of U.S. residents were classified as "overweight." Today, estimates indicate that as many as 67 percent of U.S. residents fall into this category. About 31 percent of the U.S. population is classified as extremely overweight, or obese, which is more than double the percentage of 30 years ago. One explanation for higher body weights is that people are exercising less, and thus the calories they consume are being transformed into body mass instead of energy. Another is that people are simply choosing to consume more food than in years past. Determining why individuals are opting to eat more requires an understanding, which you will develop by reading this chapter, of how two key factors—price and income—influence desired consumption of an item such as food.

LEARNING OBJECTIVES

After reading this chapter, you should be able to:

- Explain the law of demand
- Discuss the difference between money prices and relative prices
- Distinguish between changes in demand and changes in quantity demanded
- Explain the law of supply
- Distinguish between changes in supply and changes in quantity supplied
- Understand how the interaction of the demand for and supply of a commodity determines the market price of the commodity and the equilibrium quantity of the commodity that is produced and consumed

51

Chapter Openers tie to the **Issues and Applications** feature at the end of each chapter.

The current applications in the book—all new to this edition—get students' attention right at the beginning of the chapter, then follow through at the end of the chapter with an Issues and Applications feature that presents a more in-depth discussion of the issue.

Issues and Applications — Why Are People Eating More?

Being overweight or obese predisposes an individual to ailments such as arthritis, diabetes, heart disease, high blood pressure, respiratory problems, and strokes. Nevertheless, about two-thirds of the U.S. population is overweight. Nearly half of these people are classified as obese.

CONCEPTS APPLIED

- Relative Price
- Law of Demand
- Normal Good

Each **Issues and Applications** concludes by encouraging students to visit **MyEconLab** for additional news coverage of this topic. Critical Analysis questions, Web Resources, and a Suggested Research Project give students opportunities for in-depth discussion and exploration of the application. Suggested answers to critical analysis questions appear in the *Instructor's Manual*.

Some food items, such as canned beans and packaged macaroni and cheese, are inferior goods, so higher incomes have reduced consumption of these and similar foods. The vast majority of food items, however, are normal goods. Hence, the substantial rise in individual incomes has tended to raise the demand for foods as well as for other normal goods, such as personal computers and video games.

A Double-Whammy Effect on Food Consumption

Thus, two key factors have contributed to greater food consumption: the lower relative price of food and higher incomes. Increases in incomes have boosted demands for most food items, and declines in the relative prices have induced people to buy even more foods. Hence, people have been consuming more food and, with it, more calories. Without additional exercise, they have also been gaining more weight.

Test your understanding of this chapter by going online to **MyEconLab**.
In the Study Plan for this chapter, select Section N: News.

For Critical Analysis

1. If the demands for most food items have been rising as incomes have increased, what must have happened to the supplies of most food items to account for the declining relative price of food?

2. What factors might have accounted for the changes in food supplies discussed in Question 1? (Hint: What *ceteris paribus* conditions affect the position of a supply curve?)

Web Resources

1. For a review of the worldwide trend toward higher body masses, go to www.econtoday.com/chapter03.

2. To learn about various ways states and the federal government are trying to combat childhood obesity,

click on the link to the National Center for Chronic Disease Prevention and Health Promotion, available at www.econtoday.com/chapter03.

Research Project

One way that the federal government seeks to assist low-income people is by issuing them food stamps, which they can use to purchase food items. Some observers have suggested that the government's food stamp program contributes to the higher obesity rates observed among low-income people as compared with rates observed among middle- and high-income individuals. Evaluate this argument. (Hint: Many of the least-expensive food items are often the highest-fat foods containing the most calories per unit of food.)

Quick Quizzes encourage students' interaction with the text, providing them the opportunity to quickly judge their understanding of a section through fill-in-the-blank concept checks. Answers to Quick Quizzes at the end of each chapter provide immediate feedback. To further test their understanding of the concepts covered, students are encouraged to go to **MyEconLab**.

QUICK QUIZ See page 50 for the answers. Review concepts from this section in MyEconLab.

_____ is the situation in which human wants always exceed what can be produced with the limited resources and time that nature makes available.

We use scarce resources, such as _____, _____, _____ and _____ capital, and _____, to produce economic goods—goods that are desired but are not directly obtainable from nature to the extent demanded or desired at a zero price.

_____ are unlimited; they include all material desires and all nonmaterial desires, such as love, affection, power, and prestige.

The concept of _____ is difficult to define objectively for every person; consequently, we simply consider every person's wants to be unlimited. In a world of **scarcity**, satisfaction of one want necessarily means non-satisfaction of one or more other wants.

How does marginal utility derived from a music download influence the quantity of music downloads consumed?

Critical Thinking Captions
New to this edition, margin photos illustrate key concepts underlying current issues. Captions pose critical thinking questions to engage students' analyses of the topic. Suggested answers to all captions appear on the Companion Web site at www.econtoday.com.

INTERNATIONAL EXAMPLE
Evidence of a More Unequal Distribution of Income in China

In addition to using Lorenz curves to measure the degree of income inequality, economists sometimes calculate an index measure of inequality known as the *Gini coefficient*, which has a value varying between 0 and 1. A Gini-coefficient value of 0 represents complete equality of income, and a value of 1 represents complete income inequality in which one person receives all income. In the late 1970s, the value of the Gini coefficient for China was 0.15,

indicating considerable income equality. Today, it is estimated to be closer to 0.60, indicating that income in China has become much more unequal during the past three decades.

FOR CRITICAL ANALYSIS
Based on the change in value of the Gini coefficient since the late 1970s, has the Lorenz curve for China likely become more or less outward bowed?

For Critical Analysis questions
At the end of each boxed example, students are asked to "think like economists" as they answer For Critical Analysis questions. These probing questions are effective tools for sharpening students' analytical skills. Suggested answers to all questions are found in the *Instructor's Manual*.

ECONOMICS ON THE NET

Looking at the Unemployment and Inflation Data This chapter reviewed key concepts relating to unemployment and inflation. In this application, you get a chance to examine U.S. unemployment and inflation data on your own.

Title: Bureau of Labor Statistics: Employment and Unemployment

Navigation: Use the link at www.econtoday.com/chapter07 to visit the "Employment & Unemployment" page of the Bureau of Labor Statistics (BLS). Click on *Labor Force Statistics from the Current Population Survey*.

Application Perform the indicated operations, and answer the following questions.

1. Click checkmarks in the boxes for Civilian Labor Force Level, Employment Level, and Unemployment Level. Retrieve the data, and click a checkmark next to "include graphs." Can you identify periods of sharp cyclical swings? Do they show up in data for the labor force, employment, or unemployment?

2. Are cyclical factors important?

For Group Study and Analysis Divide the class into groups, and assign a price index to each group. Ask each group to take a look at the index for All Years at the link to the BLS statistics on inflation at www.econtoday.com/chapter07. Have each group identify periods during which their index accelerated or decelerated (or even fell). Do the indexes ever provide opposing implications about inflation and deflation?

Economics on the Net activities are designed to build student research skills and reinforce key concepts. The activities guide students to a Web site and provide structured assignments for both individual and group work.

The **end-of-chapter summary** makes *Economics Today* an efficient study tool by integrating chapter contents with online learning resources available in **MyEconLab**. A thorough summary of the key concepts—What You Should Know—is directly linked with the text and online resources—Where to Go to Practice.

A variety of **end-of-chapter problems** offer students opportunities to test their knowledge and review chapter concepts. These problem sets have been heavily revised for this edition. Answers for all odd-numbered questions are provided in the back of the text, and **all** questions are assignable in **MyEconLab**.

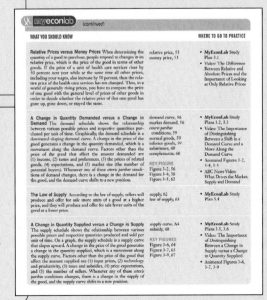

Economic Concepts in Today's News

Economics Today strives to bring the latest news and current events into the classroom, keeping students engaged and interested.

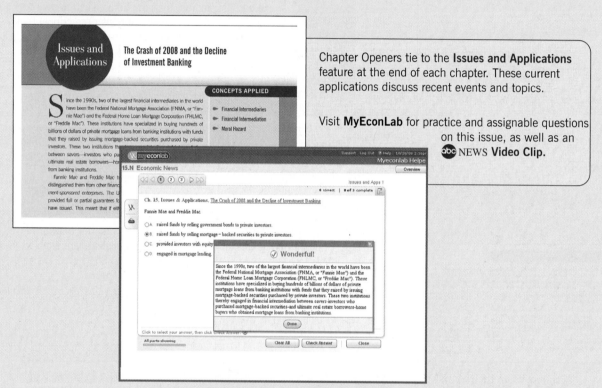

Chapter Openers tie to the **Issues and Applications** feature at the end of each chapter. These current applications discuss recent events and topics.

Visit **MyEconLab** for practice and assignable questions on this issue, as well as an abc NEWS **Video Clip.**

Each week, new microeconomic and macroeconomic current events are updated in **MyEconLab**'s **Weekly News** feature. Discussion questions, also posted weekly, test students' knowledge of the issues and ask them to apply the economic concepts.

You Are There

New to this edition, margin notes lead students to the You Are There feature at the conclusion of the text of each chapter. This feature, which depicts events involving **actual people confronting specific concepts** covered in the text, helps students see the relevance of those concepts in daily life. Topics include:

- An Invention Becomes a Market Innovation—By Accident
- In a Cold Twist, a Millionaire Bequeaths His Wealth to Himself
- Why Pouring Vegetable Oil into a Car Is Illegal in Illinois

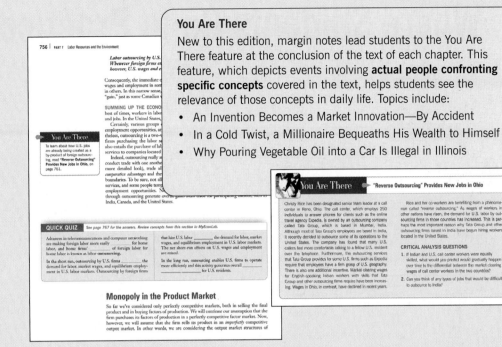

Economics Videos featuring abc NEWS

A series of videos covering core economic concepts including ABC News footage and commentary by economists can be found in **MyEconLab**. New **assessment questions** have been added for optional instructor assignment.

Videos in this series include:

- *Coca Cola in India,* which examines international trade, incentives, causation, and externalities.
- *The Ripple Effects of Oil Prices,* which discusses equilibrium and inflation.
- *Big Government: Who Is Going to Pay the Bill?* which discusses concepts such as taxes, budget, GDP, and fiscal policy.

MyEconLab now offers RSS feed for up-to-the-minute coverage of economic news. Please see page **xxxi** for additional news and issues options.

Where Students Go to Practice

 is the premier student and instructor tool, integrating lessons from the text into a powerful online learning and teaching resource.

PROBLEMS

All problems are assignable in MyEconLab. Answers to odd-numbered problems appear at the back of the book.

3-1. Suppose that in a recent market period, the following relationship existed between the price of prerecorded movie DVDs and the quantity supplied and quantity demanded.

Price	Quantity Demanded	Quantity Supplied
$19	100 million	40 million
$20	90 million	60 million
$21	80 million	80 million
$22	70 million	100 million
$23	60 million	120 million

Graph the supply and demand curves for movie DVDs given the information in the table. What are the equilibrium price and quantity? If the industry price is $20, is there a shortage or surplus of DVDs? How much is the shortage or surplus?

New in MyEconLab for *Economics Today*

- **100% of all end-of-chapter problems** are now assignable.

- For most chapters, **additional, instructor-only questions** are available to provide a larger pool of assignable options. A selection of these questions is algorithmic for additional learning opportunity. Instructors can also always choose from end-of-chapter problems, select test bank problems, or create their own exercises.

- Each chapter includes **questions for the Issues and Applications feature** found in the text, along with a related ⓐⓑⓒ NEWS **Video Clip** and critical thinking questions. All questions in this section are paired, so half are visible for student practice and half are instructor-only for assignable options.

Students control their learning through a variety of features unique to MyEconLab.

- **Sample Tests,** two for every chapter, ask students to test their understanding of the concepts. The powerful graphing application allows students to draw graphs themselves, and **MyEconLab** evaluates and grades them automatically.

- **Personalized Study Plans** analyze students' performance on Sample Tests, identify areas where they need further study, and offer additional exercises to reinforce learning. Tutorial instruction provides targeted learning aids and step-by-step explanations.

- **An integrated eText** allows access to the textbook on any computer.

- **Learning aids** such as animated graphs with audio explanations for each step, video clips of author Roger LeRoy Miller reviewing key points in every chapter, and glossary flashcards allow review of important terms.

Students can get additional help and resources.

- **Weekly News updates** feature new micro and macro current events. Discussion questions posted online each week by Andrew J. Dane of Angelo State University test students' knowledge of relevant issues and their ability to apply economic concepts. Instructor answer keys are available. The Weekly News is now **archived for easy searching and reference.**

- A subscription to **MyEconLab** includes complimentary access to a tutoring service provided by **Pearson Tutor Services**, powered by SMARTHINKING, Inc. Highly qualified tutors use whiteboard technology and feedback tools to help students understand and master the major concepts of economics. Students can receive real-time, one-on-one instruction, submit questions for response within 24 hours, and view archives of past sessions.

- **Economic Videos featuring ABC News** provide students with a glimpse of economics behind the news. Each video presents an issue using ABC News footage and includes commentary by economists.

- **Research Navigator** develops students' research skills by offering exclusive access to databases of *The New York Times*, the *Financial Times*, and peer-reviewed journals. This is available with **MyEconLab in CourseCompass.**

Instructors save time and gain flexibility.

- Instructors can design their own quizzes, tests, or homework assignments from the significant bank of questions or assign pre-loaded Sample Tests. All problems in **MyEconLab** are directly correlated to the text.

- **MyEconLab** automatically grades tests, quizzes, or homework— including graphing questions— and tracks the results in an online gradebook.

- For more information about **MyEconLab,** or to request an Instructor Access code, visit www.myeconlab.com.

Supplemental Resources

Student and instructor materials provide tools for success.

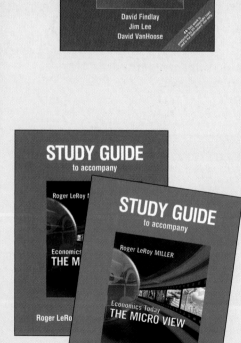

Meticulously Revised and Updated! Test Banks 1, 2, and 3 offer over 10,000 multiple choice and short answer questions, all of which are available in computerized format in the TestGen software. A selection of questions is also in **MyEconLab**. The significant revision process by authors David Findlay of Colby College and Jim Lee of Texas A&M–Corpus Christi and reviewer David VanHoose of Baylor University ensures the accuracy of problems and solutions in these heavily revised and updated test banks.

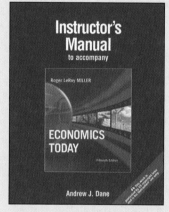

The Instructor's Manual, prepared by Andrew J. Dane of Angelo State University and reviewed by Victoria L. Figiel of Troy University, offers instructors materials to make the course successful. Features include lecture-ready examples; chapter overviews, objectives, and outlines; points to emphasize; answers to all critical analysis questions; answers to end-of-chapter problems; suggested answers to *You Are There* questions; and selected references.

The Instructor's Resource Disk offers instructors electronic supplements conveniently packaged on a CD-ROM. **PowerPoint lecture presentations** for each chapter, revised by Dennis Kovach of the Community College of Allegheny County and reviewed by Pete Mavrokordatos of Tarrant County College, include graphs from the text and outline key terms, concepts, and figures from the text. The entire **Instructor's Manual** is included as Microsoft Word files, and all three **Computerized Test Banks** are offered with TestGen software for simple test preparation.

Clicker PowerPoint Slides allow professors to instantly quiz students in class and receive immediate feedback through Clicker Response System technology.

The Instructor Resource Center puts supplements right at instructors' fingertips. By registering for the Instructor Resource Center, instructors can download supplements directly from the Internet. Visit www.pearsonhighered.com/irc to register.

The Study Guide offers the practice and review students need to excel. Written by Roger LeRoy Miller and updated by David VanHoose, the study guide has been thoroughly revised to take into account changes to the Fifteenth Edition.

PearsonChoices

A variety of options for students and instructors provide convenience and flexibility.

Books à la Carte Plus Edition is created for the student who wants a more flexible portable text. Students who use this three-hole punched version of *Economics Today* can take only what they need to class, incorporate their own notes, and save money. This version is packaged with a laminated study card and comes with access to MyEconLab.

CourseSmart improves teaching and learning through the availability of a lower-cost fully electronic alternative to the traditional textbook, in a reliable Web application. For additional information, log on to www.coursesmart.com.

Standalone Access to MyEconLab and the Complete eText may be purchased online at www.myeconlab.com or through the campus bookstore. This access to MyEconLab includes online access to the complete, searchable eText.

MyEconLab access may be purchased online at www.myeconlab.com. Students gain full access to MyEconLab's assessment and learning resources. Partial access to the eText is included, which links practice problems to relevant sections of the text.

Print Upgrade to the à la Carte Edition from within MyEconLab may be purchased at any point following students' online purchase of MyEconLab.

Pearson Custom Business Resourcees offers instructors the option of building their own book by selecting just the chapters they want and ordering them to fit their syllabus. Professors can also select chapters of the accompanying Study Guide as well as readings from Miller/Benjamin/North's *The Economics of Public Issues* and Miller/Benjamin's *The Economics of Macro Issues*. For more information, please contact your local Pearson sales representative.

Economist.com provides your students with the premier online source of news analysis, insight, and opinion on current economic events. When packaged with the text, students receive a low-cost subscription to Economist.com for three months, including the complete text of the current issue and access to searchable archives. Professors receive a complimentary one-year subscription to Economist.com.

The *Wall Street Journal* can be packaged with the text, and a 15-week subscription to the print and interactive editions of the *Wall Street Journal* is available at a reduced cost to students. Professors receive a complimentary one-year subscription to the print and interactive editions.

The *Financial Times* features international news and analysis from journalists in more than 50 countries. For a small charge, a 15-week student subscription to the *Financial Times* can be included with the text. Professors will receive a complimentary one-year print subscription, as well as access to the online edition at FT.com.

Acknowledgments

I am the most fortunate of economics textbook writers, for I receive the benefit of literally hundreds of suggestions from those of you who use *Economics Today*. I continue to be fully appreciative of the constructive criticisms that you offer. There are some professors who have been asked by my publisher to participate in a more detailed reviewing process of this edition. I list them below. I hope that each one of you so listed accepts my sincere appreciation for the fine work that you have done.

Ali A. Ataiifar, *Delaware County Community College*
Emil Berendt, *Siena Heights University*
John Bockino, *Suffolk County Community College*
Patrick M. Crowley, *Texas A&M University–Corpus Christi*
Diana Denison, *Red Rocks Community College*
Victoria L. Figiel, *Troy University*
Timothy S. Fuerst, *Bowling Green State University*
Peter A. Groothuis, *Appalachian State University*
Michael J. Haupert, *University of Wisconsin–La Crosse*
George Hughes, *University of Hartford*
Nancy Jianakoplos, *Colorado State University*
Brian Kench, *University of Tampa*

Dennis Lee Kovach, *Community College of Allegheny County–North Campus*
Dan Marburger, *Arkansas State University*
Pete Mavrokordatos, *Tarrant County College*
William H. Moon, *Georgia Perimeter College–Lawrenceville*
Ronald M. Nate, *Brigham Young University–Idaho*
Joan Osborne, *Palo Alto College*
Leila J. Pratt, *University of Tennessee at Chattanooga*
Basel Saleh, *Radford University*
Phil Smith, *Georgia Perimeter College*
Sharmila Vishwasrao, *Florida Atlantic University*
Ethel Weeks, *Nassau Community College*
George K. Zestos, *Christopher Newport University*

I also thank the reviewers of previous editions:

Rebecca Abraham
Cinda J. Adams
Esmond Adams
John Adams
Bill Adamson
Carlos Aguilar
John R. Aidem
John W. Allen
Mohammed Akacem
E. G. Aksoy
M. C. Alderfer
John Allen
Ann Al-Yasiri
Charles Anderson
Leslie J. Anderson
Fatma W. Antar
Rebecca Arnold
Mohammad Ashraf
Aliakbar Ataiifar
Leonard Atencio
John M. Atkins
Glen W. Atkinson
Thomas R. Atkinson
James Q. Aylesworth
John Baffoe-Bonnie
Kevin Baird
Charley Ballard
Maurice B. Ballabon
G. Jeffrey Barbour
Daniel Barszcz
Robin L. Bartlett
Kari Battaglia
Robert Becker
Charles Beem
Glen Beeson
Bruce W. Bellner
Daniel K. Benjamin
Charles Berry
Abraham Bertisch
John Bethune

R.A. Blewett
Scott Bloom
M. L. Bodnar
Mary Bone
Karl Bonnhi
Thomas W. Bonsor
John M. Booth
Wesley F. Booth
Thomas Borcherding
Melvin Borland
Tom Boston
Barry Boyer
Maryanna Boynton
Ronald Brandolini
Fenton L. Broadhead
Elba Brown
William Brown
Michael Bull
Maureen Burton
Conrad P. Caligaris
Kevin Carey
James Carlson
Robert Carlsson
Dancy R. Carr
Scott Carson
Doris Cash
Thomas H. Cate
Richard J. Cebula
Catherine Chanbers
K. Merry Chambers
Richard Chapman
Ronald Cherry
Young Back Choi
Marc Chopin
Carol Cies
Joy L. Clark
Curtis Clarke
Gary Clayton
Marsha Clayton
Dale O. Cloninger

Warren L. Coats
Ed Coen
Pat Conroy
James Cox
Stephen R. Cox
Eleanor D. Craig
Peggy Crane
Jerry Crawford
Joanna Cruse
John P. Cullity
Will Cummings
Thomas Curtis
Margaret M. Dalton
Andrew J. Dane
Mahmoud Davoudi
Diana Denison
Edward Dennis
Julia G. Derrick
Carol Dimamro
William Dougherty
Barry Duman
Diane Dumont
Floyd Durham
G. B. Duwaji
James A. Dyal
Ishita Edwards
Robert P. Edwards
Alan E. Ellis
Mike Ellis
Steffany Ellis
Frank Emerson
Carl Enomoto
Zaki Eusufzai
Sandy Evans
John L. Ewing-Smith
Frank Falero
Frank Fato
Abdollah Ferdowsi
Grant Ferguson
Mitchell Fisher

David Fletcher
James Foley
John Foreman
Diana Fortier
Ralph G. Fowler
Arthur Friedberg
Peter Frost
Tom Fullerton
E. Gabriel
James Gale
Byron Gangnes
Steve Gardner
Peter C. Garlick
Neil Garston
Alexander Garvin
Joe Garwood
Doug Gehrke
J. P. Gilbert
Otis Gilley
Frank Glesber
Jack Goddard
Michael G. Goode
Allen C. Goodman
Richard J. Gosselin
Paul Graf
Anthony J. Greco
Edward Greenberg
Gary Greene
Philip J. Grossman
Nicholas Grunt
William Gunther
Kwabena Gyimah-
   Brempong
Demos Hadjiyanis
Martin D. Haney
Mehdi Haririan
Ray Harvey
E. L. Hazlett
Sanford B. Helman
William Henderson

John Hensel
Robert Herman
Gus W. Herring
Charles Hill
John M. Hill
Morton Hirsch
Benjamin Hitchner
Charles W. Hockert
R. Bradley Hoppes
James Horner
Grover Howard
Nancy Howe-Ford
Yu-Mong Hsiao
Yu Hsing
James Hubert
Joseph W. Hunt Jr.
Scott Hunt
John Ifediora
R. Jack Inch
Christopher Inya
Tomotaka Ishimine
E. E. Jarvis
Parvis Jenab
Allan Jenkins
Mark Jensen
S. D. Jevremovic
J. Paul Jewell
Frederick Johnson
David Jones
Lamar B. Jones
Paul A. Joray
Daniel A. Joseph
Craig Justice
M. James Kahiga
Septimus Kai Kai
Devajyoti Kataky
Timothy R. Keely
Ziad Keilany
Norman F. Keiser
Randall G. Kesselring

Alan Kessler
E. D. Key
Saleem Khan
M. Barbara Killen
Bruce Kimzey
Philip G. King
Terrence Kinal
E. R. Kittrell
David Klingman
Charles Knapp
Jerry Knarr
Faik Koray
Janet Koscianski
Marie Kratochvil
Peter Kressler
Paul J. Kubik
Michael Kupilik
Larry Landrum
Margaret Landman
Richard LaNear
Keith Langford
Theresa Laughlin
Anthony T. Lee
Loren Lee
Bozena Leven
Donald Lien
George Lieu
Stephen E. Lile
Lawrence W. Lovick
Marty Ludlum
G. Dirk Mateer
Robert McAuliffe
James C. McBrearty
Howard J. McBride
Bruce McClung
John McDowell
E. S. McKuskey
James J. McLain
John L. Madden
Mary Lou Madden

John Marangos
Glen Marston
John M. Martin
Paul J. Mascotti
James D. Mason
Paul M. Mason
Tom Mathew
Warren Matthews
Warren T. Matthews
Akbar Marvasti
G. Hartley Mellish
Mike Melvin
Diego Mendez-Carbajo
Dan C. Messerschmidt
Michael Metzger
Herbert C. Milikien
Joel C. Millonzi
Glenn Milner
Daniel Mizak
Khan Mohabbat
Thomas Molloy
Margaret D. Moore
William E. Morgan
Stephen Morrell
Irving Morrissett
James W. Moser
Thaddeaus Mounkurai
Martin F. Murray
Densel L. Myers
George L. Nagy
Solomon Namala

Jerome Neadly
James E. Needham
Claron Nelson
Douglas Nettleton
William Nook
Gerald T. O'Boyle
Greg Okoro
Richard E. O'Neill
Lucian T. Orlowski
Diane S. Osborne
Melissa A. Osborne
James O'Toole
Jan Palmer
Zuohong Pan
Gerald Parker
Ginger Parker
Randall E. Parker
Kenneth Parzych
Norm Paul
Wesley Payne
Raymond A. Pepin
Martin M. Perline
Timothy Perri
Jerry Petr
Bruce Pietrykowski
Maurice Pfannesteil
James Phillips
Raymond J. Phillips
I. James Pickl
Dennis Placone
Mannie Poen

William L. Polvent
Robert Posatko
Greg Pratt
Reneé Prim
Robert W. Pulsinelli
Rod D. Raehsler
Kambriz Raffiee
Sandra Rahman
Jaishankar Raman
John Rapp
Richard Rawlins
Gautam Raychaudhuri
Ron Reddall
Mitchell Redlo
Charles Reichhelu
Robert S. Rippey
Charles Roberts
Ray C. Roberts
Richard Romano
Judy Roobian-Mohr
Duane Rosa
Richard Rosenberg
Larry Ross
Barbara Ross-Pfeiffer
Philip Rothman
John Roufagalas
Stephen Rubb
Henry Ryder
Patricia Sanderson
Thomas N. Schaap
William A. Schaeffer

William Schaniel
David Schauer
A. C. Schlenker
David Schlow
Scott J. Schroeder
William Scott
Dan Segebarth
Paul Seidenstat
Swapan Sen
Augustus Shackelford
Richard Sherman Jr.
Liang-rong Shiau
David Shorow
Vishwa Shukla
R. J. Sidwell
David E. Sisk
Alden Smith
Garvin Smith
Howard F. Smith
Lynn A. Smith
Phil Smith
Steve Smith
William Doyle Smith
Lee Spector
George Spiva
Richard L. Sprinkle
Alan Stafford
Amanda Stallings-Wood
Herbert F. Steeper
Diane L. Stehman
Columbus Stephens

William Stine
Allen D. Stone
Osman Suliman
J. M. Sullivan
Rebecca Summary
Joseph L. Swaffar
Thomas Swanke
Frank D. Taylor
Daniel Teferra
Lea Templer
Gary Theige
Dave Thiessen
Robert P. Thomas
Deborah Thorsen
Richard Trieff
George Troxler
William T. Trulove
William N. Trumbull
Arianne K. Turner
Kay Unger
Anthony Uremovic
John Vahaly
Jim Van Beek
David VanHoose
Lee J. Van Scyoc
Roy Van Til
Craig Walker
Robert F. Wallace
Henry C. Wallich
Milledge Weathers
Roger E. Wehr

Robert G. Welch
Terence West
James Wetzel
Wylie Whalthall
James H. Wheeler
Everett E. White
Michael D. White
Mark A. Wilkening
Raburn M. Williams
James Willis
George Wilson
Travis Wilson
Mark Wohar
Ken Woodward
Tim Wulf
Peter R. Wyman
Whitney Yamamura
Donald Yankovic
Alex Yguado
Paul Young
Shik Young
Mohammed Zaheer
Ed Zajicek
Sourushe Zandvakili
Paul Zarembka
William J. Zimmer Jr.

Revising *Economics Today* this time around was one of the biggest challenges I've faced with this textbook, given that changes in the economy within the United States and the world were so rapid. I believe that I was up to the task, but only because I had help along the way from not only the reviewers mentioned above, but my fantastic editorial team at Addison-Wesley. I was pushed hard by two unrelenting members of that team: Noel Seibert, my editor, and Julie Lindstrom, my developmental editor. In addition to managing this major project, they came up with numerous ideas "on the fly," which they suggested I incorporate into this new edition. Furthermore, all of us were dependent on Courtney Schinke, the assistant editor on this project. Courtney was great at coordination and making sure all aspects of the project moved along quickly.

On the production side of this revision, I was again fortunate enough to have as my production supervisor Kathryn Dinovo at Addison-Wesley. The designer, Geri Davis, succeeded in creating a new look that still kept the traditional feel of this text. As always, I benefited from the years of experience of John Orr of Orr Book Services. He has always faced the daunting task of putting this book together in a minimum amount of time—and he does it extremely well. I appreciate the fabulous copyediting and proofing services that Pat Lewis again provided. For this edition on the print supplements side, Marianne Groth and Alison Eusden did the job in a singularly professional matter, guaranteeing revised error-free ancillaries. I would also like to thank Roxanne McCarley for continued marketing and promotional efforts.

As you can imagine, more emphasis for each edition has been placed on online and other media materials. Melissa Honig and Susan Schoenberg worked overtime to make sure that MyEconLab was fully functional and without bugs. I also was lucky to have the services of Douglas Ruby who helped develop new content for MyEconLab.

This time around, I had some extremely talented colleagues who created a fully revised supplements package. Jim Lee of Texas A&M–Corpus Christi and David Findlay of Colby College authored the three test banks, and David VanHoose of Baylor University ensured they were error-free. He also continued to create not only accurate, but useful study guides. Similarly, Andrew J. Dane of Angelo State University has kept the *Instructor's Manual* in sync with the latest revisions, while Dennis Kovach of the Community College of Allegheny County provided the PowerPoint presentations. I would also like to thank the superb eagle-eyed professors who reviewed the text for accuracy: Victoria L. Figiel from Troy University, Ethel Weeks from Nassau Community College, Pete Mavrokordatos from Tarrant County College, and Leila J. Pratt from the University of Tennessee at Chattanooga.

Finally, there are two individuals I must thank for their work above and beyond the call of duty. The first is Professor Dan Benjamin of Clemson University, who continues to act as my "super reviewer" and "super proofreader." He again helped make this edition the best ever. Finally, Sue Jasin, my long-time assistant, could probably teach a course in economics after all of the typing and retyping of various drafts of this revision.

I welcome comments and ideas from professors and students alike and hope you enjoy the new edition of *Economics Today*.

R. L. M.

Economics Today

The Micro View

The Nature of Economics

1

Just a few years ago, a passenger on a commuter train in Mumbai, India (formerly known as Bombay), rarely had difficulty finding an empty seat even during peak commuting hours. Today, a Mumbai commuter train's passenger car built to hold a maximum of 200 people often carries as many as 550 passengers—some of whom hang out of the doors of the car or even cling to its exterior. Falls from train cars and other accidents are common events. As a consequence, at least 3,000 people are killed each year in the Mumbai commuter-rail system, and many more experience injuries. Why is Mumbai's rail system so overloaded? Why do people risk life and limb to ride the city's overcrowded trains? This chapter will equip you to contemplate the answers to these questions.

LEARNING OBJECTIVES

myeconlab

MyEconLab helps you master each objective and study more efficiently. See end of chapter for details.

After reading this chapter, you should be able to:

➤ Discuss the difference between microeconomics and macroeconomics

➤ Evaluate the role that rational self-interest plays in economic analysis

➤ Explain why economics is a science

➤ Distinguish between positive and normative economics

? Did you know that economics is one of the fastest-growing college majors? During the past 10 years, the number of students majoring in economics at U.S. colleges and universities has increased by nearly 40 percent. Certainly, a key factor motivating many students to opt for extensive study of economics is that they find the subject fascinating. Nevertheless, another important factor is self-interest. The fact that economics majors typically land higher-paying jobs than other majors—for instance, at least 10 percent more than business management majors and 75 percent more than psychology majors—provides a strong incentive to consider majoring in economics.

In this chapter, you will learn why contemplating the nature of self-interested responses to **incentives** is the starting point for analyzing choices people make in all walks of life. After all, how much time you devote to studying economics in this introductory course depends in part on the incentives established by your instructor's grading system. As you will see, self-interest and incentives are the underpinnings for all the decisions you and others around you make each day.

Incentives
Rewards for engaging in a particular activity.

The Power of Economic Analysis

Simply knowing that self-interest and incentives are central to any decision-making process is not sufficient for predicting the choices that people will actually make. You also have to develop a framework that will allow you to analyze solutions to each economic problem—whether you are trying to decide how much to study, which courses to take, whether to finish school, or whether the U.S. government should provide more grants to universities or raise taxes. The framework that you will learn in this text is the *economic way of thinking*.

This framework gives you power—the power to reach informed judgments about what is happening in the world. You can, of course, live your life without the power of economic analysis as part of your analytical framework. Indeed, most people do. But economists believe that economic analysis can help you make better decisions concerning your career, your education, financing your home, and other important matters. In the business world, the power of economic analysis can help you increase your competitive edge as an employee or as the owner of a business. As a voter, for the rest of your life you will be asked to make judgments about policies that are advocated by political parties. Many of these policies will deal with questions related to international economics, such as whether the U.S. government should encourage or discourage immigration, prevent foreign residents and firms from investing in port facilities or domestic banks, or restrict other countries from selling their goods here.

Finally, just as taking an art, music, or literature appreciation class increases the pleasure you receive when you view paintings, listen to concerts, or read novels, taking an economics course will increase your understanding and pleasure when watching the news on TV or reading articles in the newspaper or on the Internet.

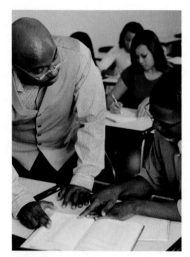

What determines how much time you decide to devote to studying one particular subject?

Defining Economics

Economics is part of the social sciences and as such seeks explanations of real events. All social sciences analyze human behavior, as opposed to the physical sciences, which generally analyze the behavior of electrons, atoms, and other nonhuman phenomena.

Economics
The study of how people allocate their limited resources to satisfy their unlimited wants.

Economics is the study of how people allocate their limited resources in an attempt to satisfy their unlimited wants. As such, economics is the study of how people make choices.

To understand this definition fully, two other words need explaining: *resources* and *wants*. **Resources** are things that have value and, more specifically, are used to produce goods and services that satisfy people's wants. **Wants** are all of the items that people would purchase if they had unlimited income.

Whenever an individual, a business, or a nation faces alternatives, a choice must be made, and economics helps us study how those choices are made. For example, you have to choose how to spend your limited income. You also have to choose how to spend your limited time. You may have to choose how much of your company's limited funds to spend on advertising and how much to spend on new-product research. In economics, we examine situations in which individuals choose how to do things, when to do things, and with whom to do them. Ultimately, the purpose of economics is to explain choices.

Resources
Things used to produce goods and services to satisfy people's wants.

Wants
What people would buy if their incomes were unlimited.

Microeconomics versus Macroeconomics

Economics is typically divided into two types of analysis: **microeconomics** and **macroeconomics.**

> *Microeconomics is the part of economic analysis that studies decision making undertaken by individuals (or households) and by firms. It is like looking through a microscope to focus on the small parts of our economy.*

> *Macroeconomics is the part of economic analysis that studies the behavior of the economy as a whole. It deals with economywide phenomena such as changes in unemployment, in the general price level, and in national income.*

Microeconomics
The study of decision making undertaken by individuals (or households) and by firms.

Macroeconomics
The study of the behavior of the economy as a whole, including such economywide phenomena as changes in unemployment, the general price level, and national income.

Microeconomic analysis, for example, is concerned with the effects of changes in the price of gasoline relative to that of other energy sources. It examines the effects of new taxes on a specific product or industry. If price controls were reinstituted in the United States, how individual firms and consumers would react to them would be in the realm of microeconomics. The effects of higher wages brought about by an effective union strike would also be analyzed using the tools of microeconomics.

In contrast, issues such as the rate of inflation, the amount of economywide unemployment, and the yearly growth in the output of goods and services in the nation all fall into the realm of macroeconomic analysis. In other words, macroeconomics deals with **aggregates,** or totals—such as total output in an economy.

Be aware, however, of the blending of microeconomics and macroeconomics in modern economic theory. Modern economists are increasingly using microeconomic analysis—the study of decision making by individuals and by firms—as the basis of macroeconomic analysis. They do this because even though macroeconomic analysis focuses on aggregates, those aggregates are the result of choices made by individuals and firms.

Aggregates
Total amounts or quantities; aggregate demand, for example, is total planned expenditures throughout a nation.

The Economic Person: Rational Self-Interest

Economists assume that individuals act *as if* motivated by self-interest and respond predictably to opportunities for gain. This central insight of economics was first clearly articulated by Adam Smith in 1776. Smith wrote in his most famous book, *An Inquiry into the Nature and Causes of the Wealth of Nations*, that "it is not from the benevolence of the butcher, the brewer, or the baker that we expect our dinner, but from their regard to their own interest." Thus, the typical person about whom economists make behavioral predictions is assumed to act *as though* motivated by self-interest. Because monetary benefits and costs of actions are often the most easily measured, economists make behavioral predictions about individuals' responses to opportunities to increase their wealth, measured in money terms.

Is it possible to apply the theory of rational self-interest to help in explaining regular church attendance?

EXAMPLE
Earthly Rewards of Religiosity

Undoubtedly, most people who attend church regularly do so because they feel an innate desire to participate actively in their chosen religious faith. Nevertheless, habitual church attendance has concrete rewards as well, in the form of more education, a lower chance of divorce, and even higher income. A 10 percent increase in church attendance boosts a typical individual's income by nearly 1 percent.

Why might churchgoing lead to higher income? One possible explanation is that attending church helps people establish trust within a social network and find more business opportunities. Another is that church membership provides a type of insurance that helps people recover emotionally and even financially following life setbacks such as illnesses or job losses. Finally, religious faith may reduce personal stresses, thereby making churchgoers more productive and employable. Thus, there are several channels by which greater church involvement can contribute to higher incomes.

FOR CRITICAL ANALYSIS
How might the fact that many churches sponsor schools help to boost incomes of families that maintain their church memberships over a generation or more? (Hint: People who are better educated possess more skills and hence are more employable.)

The Rationality Assumption

Rationality assumption
The assumption that people do not intentionally make decisions that would leave them worse off.

The **rationality assumption** of economics, simply stated, is as follows:

> *We assume that individuals do not intentionally make decisions that would leave them worse off.*

The distinction here is between what people may think—the realm of psychology and psychiatry and perhaps sociology—and what they do. Economics does *not* involve itself in analyzing individual or group thought processes. Economics looks at what people actually do in life with their limited resources. It does little good to criticize the rationality assumption by stating, "Nobody thinks that way" or "I never think that way" or "How unrealistic! That's as irrational as anyone can get!"

Take the example of driving. When you consider passing another car on a two-lane highway with oncoming traffic, you have to make very quick decisions: You must estimate the speed of the car that you are going to pass, the speed of the oncoming cars, the distance between your car and the oncoming cars, and your car's potential rate of acceleration. If we were to apply a model to your behavior, we would use the rules of calculus. In actual fact, you and most other drivers in such a situation do not actually think of using the rules of calculus, but to predict your behavior, we could make the prediction *as if* you understood those rules.

How might regular church attendance lead to higher income?

How can magnetic resonance imaging (MRI) scans aid in assessing the rationality assumption?

EXAMPLE
"Neuroeconomics" Evaluates Rational Choice

Neuroeconomics is a field of study aimed at determining how the human brain makes choices. Researchers in neuroeconomics have found that three parts of the brain typically interact in decision making. The *nucleus accumbens* processes emotions regarding the desirability of an item, and the *insular cortex* responds to the potential for a monetary loss associated with paying for the item. The *prefrontal cortex* handles rational calculation.

MRI scans reveal that when a person's brain is evaluating a purchase, the prefrontal cortex synthesizes conflicting positive feelings in the nucleus accumbens and negative emotions associated with payment in the insular cortex. Thus, there is evidence that the human brain naturally attempts to factor in reasoned calculations aimed at making a choice consistent with the "best" overall outcome. This conclusion, of course, supports the rationality assumption.

FOR CRITICAL ANALYSIS
Why might a person rationally pass up a choice that would yield a significant immediate gain in favor of a choice that would yield a series of smaller future gains? (Hint: The sum of many small numbers can exceed a single large number.)

Responding to Incentives

If it can be assumed that individuals never intentionally make decisions that would leave them worse off, then almost by definition they will respond to changes in incentives. Indeed, much of human behavior can be explained in terms of how individuals respond to changing incentives over time.

Schoolchildren are motivated to do better by a variety of incentive systems, ranging from gold stars and certificates of achievement when they are young, to better grades with accompanying promises of a "better life" as they get older. Of course, negative incentives affect our behavior, too. Penalties, punishments, and other forms of negative incentives can raise the cost of engaging in various activities.

What do you suppose is now a commonplace incentive at online dating sites?

You Are There

To contemplate how tax changes can provide incentives for people to alter their choices, consider **Herding Alpacas Toward a Tax Break,** on pages 11 and 12.

E-COMMERCE EXAMPLE
The New Online Dating Incentive: Health Insurance

"I'm looking for a woman who knows what she wants and isn't afraid to ask for it—one with a nice smile and a healthy attitude who is open and honest . . . and health insurance wouldn't hurt, either." So reads an ad at an online dating site. Another ad states: "Are you strong, smart and sophisticated, confident and kind, without being too uppity and conceited? Do you make at least $75,000 a year and have health insurance?" One ad is particularly straightforward: "My ideal man will have health insurance."

These ads reflect a growing trend at online dating sites. Alongside a winning personality, good looks, and other traditional attributes, another incentive that may induce an individual to agree to a date is a potential dating partner's access to health insurance.

FOR CRITICAL ANALYSIS
How might efforts by many U.S. companies to drastically reduce health insurance benefits influence the incentive effects of health insurance at online dating services?

Defining Self-Interest

Self-interest does not always mean increasing one's wealth measured in dollars and cents. We assume that individuals seek many goals, not just increased wealth measured in monetary terms. Thus, the self-interest part of our economic-person assumption includes goals relating to prestige, friendship, love, power, helping others, creating works of art, and many other matters. We can also think in terms of enlightened self-interest, whereby individuals, in the pursuit of what makes them better off, also achieve the betterment of others around them. In brief, individuals are assumed to want the ability to further their goals by making decisions about how things around them are used. The head of a charitable organization usually will not turn down an additional contribution, because accepting the funds yields control over how they are used, even though it is for other people's benefit.

Thus, self-interest does not rule out doing charitable acts. Giving gifts to relatives can be considered a form of charity that is nonetheless in the self-interest of the giver. But how efficient is such gift giving?

EXAMPLE
The Perceived Value of Gifts

Every holiday season, aunts, uncles, grandparents, mothers, and fathers give gifts to their college-aged loved ones. Joel Waldfogel, an economist at Yale University, surveyed several thousand college students after Christmas to find out the value of holiday gifts. He found that recorded music and outerwear (coats and jackets) had a perceived intrinsic value about equal to their actual cash equivalent. By the time he got down the list to socks, underwear, and cosmetics, the students' valuation was only about 85 percent of the cash value of the gift. He found out that aunts, uncles, and grandparents gave the "worst" gifts and friends, siblings, and parents gave the "best."

FOR CRITICAL ANALYSIS
What argument could you use against the idea of substituting cash or gift cards for physical gifts?

QUICK QUIZ See page 17 for the answers. Review concepts from this section in MyEconLab.

Economics is a social science that involves the study of how individuals choose among alternatives to satisfy their _____, which are what people would buy if their incomes were _____.

_____, the study of the decision-making processes of individuals (or households) and firms, and _____, the study of the performance of the economy as a whole, are the two main branches into which the study of economics is divided.

In economics, we assume that people do not intentionally make decisions that will leave them worse off. This is known as the _____ assumption.

_____ is not confined to material well-being but also involves any action that makes a person feel better off, such as having more friends, love, power, or affection or providing more help to others.

Economics as a Science

Economics is a social science that employs the same kinds of methods used in other sciences, such as biology, physics, and chemistry. Like these other sciences, economics uses models, or theories. Economic **models,** or **theories,** are simplified representations of the real world that we use to help us understand, explain, and predict economic phenomena in the real world. There are, of course, differences between sciences. The social sciences—especially economics—make little use of laboratory experiments in which changes in variables are studied under controlled conditions. Rather, social scientists, and especially economists, usually have to test their models, or theories, by examining what has already happened in the real world.

Models, or theories
Simplified representations of the real world used as the basis for predictions or explanations.

Models and Realism

At the outset it must be emphasized that no model in *any* science, and therefore no economic model, is complete in the sense that it captures *every* detail or interrelationship that exists. Indeed, a model, by definition, is an abstraction from reality. It is conceptually impossible to construct a perfectly complete realistic model. For example, in physics we cannot account for every molecule and its position and certainly not for every atom and subatomic particle. Not only is such a model impossibly expensive to build, but working with it would be impossibly complex.

The nature of scientific model building is that the model should capture only the *essential* relationships that are sufficient to analyze the particular problem or answer the particular question with which we are concerned. *An economic model cannot be faulted as unrealistic simply because it does not represent every detail of the real world.* A map of a city that shows only major streets is not faulty if, in fact, all you need to know is how to pass through the city using major streets. As long as a model is able to shed light on the *central* issue at hand or forces at work, it may be useful.

A map is the quintessential model. It is always a simplified representation. It is always unrealistic. But it is also useful in making predictions about the world. If the model—the map—predicts that when you take Campus Avenue to the north, you always run into the campus, that is a prediction. If a simple model can explain observed behavior in repeated settings just as well as a complex model, the simple model has some value and is probably easier to use.

Assumptions

Every model, or theory, must be based on a set of assumptions. Assumptions define the array of circumstances in which our model is most likely to be applicable. When some people predicted that sailing ships would fall off the edge of the earth, they used the *assumption* that the earth was flat. Columbus did not accept the implications of such a model because he did not accept its assumptions. He assumed that the world was round. The real-world test of his own model refuted the flat-earth model. Indirectly, then, it was a test of the assumption of the flat-earth model.

Is it possible to use our knowledge about assumptions to understand why driving directions sometimes contain very few details?

EXAMPLE
Getting Directions

Assumptions are a shorthand for reality. Imagine that you have decided to drive from your home in San Diego to downtown San Francisco. Because you have never driven this route, you decide to use a travel-planner device such as global-positioning-system equipment.

When you ask for directions, the electronic travel planner could give you a set of detailed maps that shows each city through which you will travel—Oceanside, San Clemente, Irvine, Anaheim, Los Angeles, Bakersfield, Modesto, and so on—and then, opening each map, show you exactly how the freeway threads through each of these cities. You would get a nearly complete description of reality because the AAA travel planner will not have used many simplifying assumptions. It

is more likely, however, that the travel planner will simply say, "Get on Interstate 5 going north. Stay on it for about 500 miles. Follow the signs for San Francisco. After crossing the toll bridge, take any exit marked 'Downtown.'" By omitting all of the trivial details, the travel planner has told you all that you really need and want to know. The models you will be using in this text are similar to the simplified directions on how to drive from San Diego to San Francisco—they focus on what is relevant to the problem at hand and omit what is not.

FOR CRITICAL ANALYSIS
In what way do small talk and gossip represent the use of simplifying assumptions?

Ceteris paribus [KAY-ter-us PEAR-uh-bus] assumption
The assumption that nothing changes except the factor or factors being studied.

THE *CETERIS PARIBUS* ASSUMPTION: ALL OTHER THINGS BEING EQUAL
Everything in the world seems to relate in some way to everything else in the world. It would be impossible to isolate the effects of changes in one variable on another variable if we always had to worry about the many other variables that might also enter the analysis. Similar to other sciences, economics uses the *ceteris paribus* **assumption.** *Ceteris paribus* means "other things constant" or "other things equal."

Consider an example taken from economics. One of the most important determinants of how much of a particular product a family buys is how expensive that product is relative to other products. We know that in addition to relative prices, other factors influence decisions about making purchases. Some of them have to do with income, others with tastes, and yet others with custom and religious beliefs. Whatever these other factors are, we hold them constant when we look at the relationship between changes in prices and changes in how much of a given product people will purchase.

Deciding on the Usefulness of a Model

We generally do not attempt to determine the usefulness, or "goodness," of a model merely by evaluating how realistic its assumptions are. Rather, we consider a model "good" if it yields usable predictions that are supported by real-world observations. In other words, can we use the model to predict what will happen in the world around us? Does the model provide useful implications about how things happen in our world?

Once we have determined that the model does predict real-world phenomena, the scientific approach to the analysis of the world around us requires that we consider evidence. Evidence is used to test the usefulness of a model. This is why we call economics an **empirical** science. *Empirical* means that evidence (data) is looked at to see whether we are right. Economists are often engaged in empirically testing their models.

How can empirical data help in combating terrorism?

Empirical
Relying on real-world data in evaluating the usefulness of a model.

POLICY EXAMPLE
How Empirical Evidence Aids in Thwarting Terrorism

Since 1968, there have been more than 13,000 incidents of "transnational" terrorism, or violent attacks in nations where the attackers do not reside. These data suggest predictable cycles in terrorist attacks. When terrorists launch a complex large-scale operation, such as an attack aimed at the destruction of high-rise buildings, public pressure to thwart such attacks remains high for a long time afterwards. Consequently, government countermeasures also remain in place for a lengthy period. Knowing this, terrorists lie low and begin long-term planning for a future large-scale attack. Thus, there are predictably long lulls between large-scale attacks. In contrast, public pressure to prevent simple small-scale attacks, such as bus bombings, wanes more quickly. Government prevention efforts also dissipate more rapidly, thereby tempting terrorists to launch more small-scale attacks. Thus, there tend to be predictably short pauses between smaller-scale attacks.

Recognition of empirical regularities in terrorism has assisted governments in predicting terrorism upsurges. Governments can utilize these predictions to determine how to allocate their antiterrorism resources more effectively.

FOR CRITICAL ANALYSIS
Why do you suppose that when making predictions to help thwart terrorism, economists typically assume that terrorists behave rationally?

Models of Behavior, Not Thought Processes

Take special note of the fact that economists' models do not relate to the way people *think*; they relate to the way people *act*, to what they do in life with their limited resources. Normally, the economist does not attempt to predict how people will think about a particular topic, such as a higher price of oil products, accelerated inflation, or higher taxes. Rather, the task at hand is to predict how people will behave, which may be quite different from what they *say* they will do (much to the consternation of poll takers and market researchers). The people involved in examining thought processes are psychologists and psychiatrists, not typically economists.

Behavioral Economics and Bounded Rationality

In recent years, some economists have proposed paying more attention to psychologists and psychiatrists. They have suggested an alternative approach to economic analysis. Their approach, which is known as **behavioral economics,** examines consumer behavior in the face of psychological limitations and complications that may interfere with rational decision making.

Behavioral economics
An approach to the study of consumer behavior that emphasizes psychological limitations and complications that potentially interfere with rational decision making.

BOUNDED RATIONALITY   Proponents of behavioral economics suggest that traditional economic models assume that people exhibit three "unrealistic" characteristics:

1. *Unbounded selfishness.* People are interested only in their own satisfaction.
2. *Unbounded willpower.* Their choices are always consistent with their long-term goals.
3. *Unbounded rationality.* They are able to consider every relevant choice.

Instead, advocates of behavioral economics have proposed replacing the rationality assumption with the assumption of **bounded rationality,** which assumes that people cannot examine and think through every possible choice they confront. As a consequence, behavioral economists suggest, people cannot always pursue their long-term

Bounded rationality
The hypothesis that people are *nearly,* but not fully, rational, so that they cannot examine every possible choice available to them but instead use simple rules of thumb to sort among the alternatives that happen to occur to them.

personal interests. From time to time, they must also rely on other people and take into account other people's interests as well as their own.

RULES OF THUMB A key behavioral implication of the bounded rationality assumption is that people should use so-called *rules of thumb*: Because every possible choice cannot be considered, an individual will tend to fall back on methods of making decisions that are simpler than trying to sort through every possibility.

A problem confronting advocates of behavioral economics is that people who *appear* to use rules of thumb may in fact behave *as if* they are fully rational. For instance, if a person faces persistently predictable ranges of choices for a time, the individual may rationally settle into repetitive behaviors that an outside observer might conclude to be consistent with a rule of thumb. The bounded rationality assumption indicates that the person should continue to rely on a rule of thumb even if there is a major change in the environment that the individual faces. Time and time again, however, economists find that people respond to altered circumstances by fundamentally changing their behaviors. Economists also generally observe that people make decisions that are consistent with their own self-interest and long-term objectives.

BEHAVIORAL ECONOMICS: A WORK IN PROGRESS It remains to be seen whether the application of the assumption of bounded rationality proposed by behavioral economists will truly alter the manner in which economists construct models intended to better predict human decision making. So far, proponents of behavioral economics have not conclusively demonstrated that paying closer attention to psychological thought processes can improve economic predictions.

As a consequence, the bulk of economic analysis continues to rely on the rationality assumption as the basis for constructing economic models. As you will learn in Chapter 20, advocates of behavioral economics continue to explore ways in which psychological elements might improve analysis of decision making by individual consumers.

Positive versus Normative Economics

Economics uses *positive analysis*, a value-free approach to inquiry. No subjective or moral judgments enter into the analysis. Positive analysis relates to statements such as "If A, then B." For example, "If the price of gasoline goes up relative to all other prices, then the amount of it that people buy will fall." That is a positive economic statement. It is a statement of *what is*. It is not a statement of anyone's value judgment or subjective feelings.

Distinguishing Between Positive and Normative Economics

Positive economics
Analysis that is *strictly* limited to making either purely descriptive statements or scientific predictions; for example, "If A, then B." A statement of *what is*.

Normative economics
Analysis involving value judgments about economic policies; relates to whether things are good or bad. A statement of *what ought to be*.

For many problems analyzed in the "hard" sciences such as physics and chemistry, the analyses are considered to be virtually value-free. After all, how can someone's values enter into a theory of molecular behavior? But economists face a different problem. They deal with the behavior of individuals, not molecules. That makes it more difficult to stick to what we consider to be value-free or **positive economics** without reference to our feelings.

When our values are interjected into the analysis, we enter the realm of **normative economics,** involving *normative analysis*. A positive economic statement is "If the price of gas rises, people will buy less." If we add to that analysis the statement "so we should not allow the price to go up," we have entered the realm of normative economics—we have expressed a value judgment. In fact, any time you see the word *should*, you will know that values are entering into the discussion. Just remember that positive statements are concerned with *what is*, whereas normative statements are concerned with *what ought to be*.

Each of us has a desire for different things. That means that we have different values. When we express a value judgment, we are simply saying what we prefer, like, or desire. Because individual values are diverse, we expect—and indeed observe—people expressing widely varying value judgments about how the world ought to be.

A Warning: Recognize Normative Analysis

It is easy to define positive economics. It is quite another matter to catch all unlabeled normative statements in a textbook, even though an author goes over the manuscript many times before it is printed. Therefore, do not get the impression that a textbook author will be able to keep all personal values out of the book. They will slip through. In fact, the very choice of which topics to include in an introductory textbook involves normative economics. There is no value-free way to decide which topics to use in a textbook. The author's values ultimately make a difference when choices have to be made. But from your own standpoint, you might want to be able to recognize when you are engaging in normative as opposed to positive economic analysis. Reading this text will help equip you for that task.

What might motivate U.S. residents to breed more llamas?

QUICK QUIZ   *See page 17 for the answers. Review concepts from this section in MyEconLab.*

A _____, or _____, uses assumptions and is by nature a simplification of the real world. The usefulness of a _____ can be evaluated by bringing empirical evidence to bear on its predictions.

Most models use the _____ _____ assumption that all other things are held constant, or equal.

_____ economics emphasizes psychological constraints and complexities that potentially interfere with rational

decision making. This approach utilizes the _____ _____ hypothesis that people are not quite rational, because they cannot study every possible alternative but instead use simple rules of thumb to decide among choices.

_____ economics is value-free and relates to statements that can be refuted, such as "If A, then B."

_____ economics involves people's values and typically uses the word *should*.

You Are There ▶ Herding Alpacas Toward a Tax Break

Recently, Claudia Weiner, a teacher in Ventura, California, was looking for a way to shelter a portion of household income from federal taxation. She found that in 2003, Congress passed the Jobs and Growth Tax Relief Reconciliation Act, which authorizes a 100 percent tax deduction for an asset purchased by a small business. One asset that qualifies

under the law is an alpaca, a small, long-necked South American llama that yields fleece prized by some clothing designers.

Weiner learned that raising several alpacas requires only about an acre of land and a direct annual expense of about $300. On any property designated as an "alpaca farm,"

You Are There (cont.)

tax-deductible expenses include purchases of food, water, fences, land upkeep, and under some circumstances even additions to homes.

Weiner and her husband ultimately decided to reclassify their home as an alpaca farm, which they call "As You Like It Alpacas." By responding in this way to the tax incentive Congress created, she and her husband joined nearly 2,500 new entrants into the U.S. alpaca-farming industry, which increased to about 4,500 farms. Few of these alpaca farmers have earned significant profits from selling alpaca fleece. Many of them, however, have succeeded in reducing the total taxes they must pay to the federal government each year.

CRITICAL ANALYSIS QUESTIONS

1. *How would a steep decline in the price of alpaca fleece, the main product of alpaca farmers, likely affect the incentive to raise alpacas?*

2. *Unless Congress takes action to renew the 2003 legislation, it will no longer be in force beginning in 2010. How might this affect the incentive to be an alpaca farmer?*

Risking Life and Limb on Mumbai Commuter Trains

Issues and Applications

CONCEPTS APPLIED

- Incentives
- Self-Interest
- Rationality Assumption

Every day, the commuter-rail network in Mumbai, India, carries more than 32,000 passengers per mile, a passenger rate 175 percent greater than the rail system was originally designed to transport. During peak hours, Mumbai rail commuters push their way across platforms and pack themselves into what they call the "super-dense crush load" of a typical passenger car—about 350 more passengers than the intended capacity of 200.

On a typical day, two or three people are killed when the surging crowd causes them to lose their footing on the platform and tumble onto the tracks. Two or three others die when they lose their grips on exterior handholds of passenger cars and fall from moving trains. Occasionally, someone is killed when he sticks his head out an open window or door to gasp for fresh air at an inopportune time, such as when the train is passing a pole near the tracks. Others die when they rush to catch a train and dart across the tracks in front of a locomotive. All told, 13 people on average are killed each working day in what media commentators have called the world's most dangerous train commute.

Incentives to Cram onto Mumbai Commuter Trains

Why do 6 million people per day wish to travel via Mumbai's commuter-rail system? To answer this question, we must consider the incentives faced by the 18 million residents of the Mumbai metropolitan area.

India's economy is growing rapidly. Most of the nation's highest-paying jobs are within its cities. Large numbers of people seeking to fill these positions are relocating from rural areas to the outskirts of metropolitan areas such as Mumbai. The government does not permit private autos to enter Mumbai's downtown interior, and taxi service into that area is sparse and relatively expensive. Reaching the central city from the city's outer edges by bus can take several hours, whereas commuter trains transit the same distance in 60 minutes or less. Furthermore, India's government, which operates the nation's rail systems, sets fares—typically little more than 25 cents for a one-hour ride—well below the levels that private operators would charge.

Self-Interest, Rationality, and Super-Dense Crush Loads

Clearly, higher-paying employment inside the city, lack of substitute transportation of equal quality, and low ticket prices are all strong positive incentives for the residents of Mumbai to choose rail transport. These incentives help to explain why so many self-interested people continue to brave the Mumbai rail commute.

At the same time, though, the discomfort of being packed into passenger cars or perhaps even having to hang to the outside of the cars is certainly a negative incentive to train travel in Mumbai. So is the average daily toll of 13 people killed in accidents. This overall death toll, however, implies an average daily death *rate* of about 2 per million passengers. The injury rate in the Mumbai commuter-rail system is somewhat higher than the death rate. Nevertheless, the overall chance of experiencing an injury to life or limb on a given day is still less than 1 out of 200,000.

Under the rationality assumption, people do not intentionally make decisions that make themselves worse off. Someone who resides on the outskirts of Mumbai typically can double her annual income by commuting into the city. In most cases, taking a commuter train to her place of employment is her only reasonable option, and the price of this mode of transport is very low. She must weigh these positive incentives against the disincentives of a cramped commute and a relatively low individual likelihood of injury or death. On net, a resident on the outer edge of Mumbai is unlikely to perceive the decision to make the "world's most dangerous commute" as inconsistent with her own self-interest. Thus, each working day she and 6 million others are likely to continue to traverse Mumbai's 813-mile commuter-rail system.

Test your understanding of this chapter by going online to **MyEconLab**.
In the Study Plan for this chapter, select Section N: News.

For Critical Analysis

1. Under Indian law, the family of a commuter killed in an accident is entitled to a government death benefit. Why do you suppose that India's government imposes fines on people caught crossing tracks or riding on top of trains?

2. What do you think would happen to Mumbai's average daily rail passenger totals if a private company were to manage the system and charge higher fares?

Web Resources

1. For a description of the Mumbai passenger rail system, go to www.econtoday.com/chapter01.

2. Read an Indian court's directions for trying to reduce Mumbai's rail death toll at www.econtoday.com/chapter01.

Research Project

Suppose that you have been appointed to a commission that the Indian government has charged with making recommendations about how to reduce the death toll on Mumbai's commuter-rail system. The Indian government states that it already plans to lay 113 miles of new track, thereby extending the Mumbai rail network by 13 percent. It also plans to add 147 more trains, which will increase the number of passenger cars by more than 70 percent. Based on what you have learned about incentives, self-interest, and rational behavior, what other recommendations do you have for the Indian government?

Here is what you should know after reading this chapter. **MyEconLab** will help you identify what you know, and where to go when you need to practice.

WHAT YOU SHOULD KNOW		WHERE TO GO TO PRACTICE
Microeconomics versus Macroeconomics In general, economics is the study of how individuals make choices to satisfy wants. Economics is usually divided into microeconomics, which is the study of decision making by individual households and individual firms, and macroeconomics, which is the study of nationwide phenomena, such as inflation and unemployment.	incentives, 2 economics, 2 resources, 3 wants, 3 microeconomics, 3 macroeconomics, 3 aggregates, 3	• **MyEconLab** Study Plans 1.1, 1.2, 1.3 • Audio introduction to Chapter 1 • Video: The Difference Between Microeconomics and Macroeconomics
Self-Interest in Economic Analysis Rational self-interest is the assumption that people never intentionally make decisions that would leave them worse off. Instead, they are motivated mainly by their self-interest, which can relate to monetary and nonmonetary goals, such as love, prestige, and helping others.	rationality assumption, 4	• **MyEconLab** Study Plan 1.4 • Video: The Economic Person: Rational Self-Interest
Economics as a Science Economic models, or theories, are simplified representations of the real world. Economic models are never completely realistic because by definition they are simplifications using assumptions that are not directly testable. Nevertheless, economists can subject the predictions of economic theories to empirical tests in which real-world data are used to decide whether or not to reject the predictions.	models, or theories, 7 *ceteris paribus* assumption, 8 empirical, 8 behavioral economics, 9 bounded rationality, 9	• **MyEconLab** Study Plan 1.5 • ABC News Video: Coca-Cola in India

(continued)

PROBLEMS

All problems are assignable in ⟨ myeconlab *. Answers to odd-numbered problems appear at the back of the book.*

1-1. Define economics. Explain briefly how the economic way of thinking—in terms of rational, self-interested people responding to incentives—relates to each of the following situations.

  a. A student deciding whether to purchase a textbook for a particular class

  b. Government officials seeking more funding for mass transit through higher taxes

  c. A municipality taxing hotel guests to obtain funding for a new sports stadium

1-2. Some people claim that the "economic way of thinking" does not apply to issues such as health care. Explain how economics does apply to this issue by developing a "model" of an individual's choices.

1-3. Does the phrase "unlimited wants and limited resources" apply to both a low-income household and a middle-income household? Can the same phrase be applied to a very high-income household?

1-4. In a single sentence, contrast microeconomics and macroeconomics. Next, categorize each of the following issues as either a microeconomic issue, a macroeconomic issue, or not an economic issue.

  a. The national unemployment rate

  b. The decision of a worker to work overtime or not

  c. A family's choice to have a baby

  d. The rate of growth of the money supply

  e. The national government's budget deficit

  f. A student's allocation of study time across two subjects

1-5. One of your classmates, Sally, is a hardworking student, serious about her classes, and conscientious about her grades. Sally is also involved, however, in volunteer activities and an extracurricular sport. Is Sally displaying rational behavior? Based on what you read in this chapter, construct an argument supporting the conclusion that she is.

1-6. Recently, a bank was trying to decide what fee to charge for "expedited payments"—payments that the bank would transmit extra speedily to enable customers to avoid late fees on cable TV bills, electric bills, and the like. To try to determine what fee customers were willing to pay for expedited payments, the bank conducted a survey. It was able to determine that many of the people surveyed already paid fees for expedited payment services that *exceeded* the maximum fees that they said they were willing to pay. How does the bank's finding relate to economists' traditional focus on what people do, rather than what they *say* they will do?

1-7. Explain, in your own words, the rationality assumption, and contrast it with the assumption of bounded rationality proposed by adherents of behavioral economics.

1-8. Why does the assumption of bounded rationality suggest that people might use rules of thumb to guide their decision making instead of considering every possible choice available to them?

1-9. Under what circumstances might people appear to use rules of thumb, as suggested by the assumption of bounded rationality, even though they really were behaving in a manner suggested by the rationality assumption?

1-10. Which of the following predictions appears to follow from a model based on the assumption that rational, self-interested individuals respond to incentives?

    a. For every 10 exam points Myrna must earn in order to pass her economics course and meet her graduation requirements, she will study one additional hour for her economics test next week.

    b. A coin toss will best predict Leonardo's decision about whether to purchase an expensive business suit or an inexpensive casual outfit to wear next week when he interviews for a high-paying job he is seeking.

    c. Celeste, who uses earnings from her regularly scheduled hours of part-time work to pay for her room and board at college, will decide to buy a newly released DVD this week only if she is able to work two additional hours.

1-11. Consider two models for estimating, in advance of an election, the shares of votes that will go to rival candidates. According to one model, pollsters' surveys of a randomly chosen set of registered voters before an election can be used to forecast the percentage of votes that each candidate will receive. This first model relies on the assumption that unpaid survey respondents will give truthful responses about how they will vote and that they will actually cast a ballot in the

election. The other model uses prices of financial assets (legally binding IOUs) issued by the Iowa Electronic Markets, operated by the University of Iowa, to predict electoral outcomes. The final payments received by owners of these assets, which can be bought or sold during the weeks and days preceding an election, depend on the shares of votes the candidates actually end up receiving. This second model assumes that owners of these assets wish to earn the highest possible returns, and it indicates that the market prices of these assets provide an indication of the percentage of votes that each candidate will actually receive on the day of the election.

    a. Which of these two models for forecasting electoral results is more firmly based on the rationality assumption of economics?

    b. How would an economist evaluate which is the better model for forecasting electoral outcomes?

1-12. Write a sentence contrasting positive and normative economic analysis.

1-13. Based on your answer to Problem 1–12, categorize each of the following conclusions as being the result of positive analysis or normative analysis.

    a. A higher minimum wage will reduce employment opportunities for minimum wage workers.

    b. Increasing the earnings of minimum wage employees is desirable, and raising the minimum wage is the best way to accomplish this.

    c. Everyone should enjoy open access to health care.

    d. Heath care subsidies will increase the consumption of health care.

1-14. Consider the following statements, based on a positive economic analysis that assumes that all other things remain constant. For each, list one other thing that might change and thus offset the outcome stated.

    a. Increased demand for laptop computers will drive up their price.

    b. Falling gasoline prices will result in additional vacation travel.

    c. A reduction of income tax rates will result in more people working.

ECONOMICS ON THE NET

The Usefulness of Studying Economics This application helps you see how accomplished people benefited from their study of economics. It also explores ways in which these people feel others of all walks of life can gain from learning more about the economics field.

Title: How Taking an Economics Course Can Lead to Becoming an Economist

Navigation: Go to **www.econtoday.com/chapter01** to visit the Federal Reserve Bank of Minneapolis publication, *The Region*. Select the last article of the issue, "Economists in *The Region* on Their Student Experiences and the Need for Economic Literacy."

Application Read the interviews of the six economists, and answer the following questions.

1. Based on your reading, which economists do you think other economists regard as influential? What educational institutions do you think are the most influential in economics?

2. Which economists do you think were attracted to microeconomics and which to macroeconomics?

For Group Study and Analysis Divide the class into three groups, and assign the groups the Blinder, Yellen, and Rivlin interviews. Have each group use the content of its assigned interview to develop a statement explaining why the study of economics is important, regardless of a student's chosen major.

ANSWERS TO QUICK QUIZZES

p. 6: (i) wants . . . unlimited; (ii) Microeconomics . . . macroeconomics; (iii) rationality; (iv) Self-interest
p. 11: (i) model . . . theory . . . model; (ii) *ceteris paribus*; (iii) Behavioral . . . bounded rationality; (iv) Positive . . . Normative

Reading and Working with Graphs

Independent variable
A variable whose value is determined independently of, or outside, the equation under study.

Dependent variable
A variable whose value changes according to changes in the value of one or more independent variables.

TABLE A-1

Gas Mileage as a Function of Driving Speed

Miles per Hour	Miles per Gallon
45	25
50	24
55	23
60	21
65	19
70	16
75	13

Direct relationship
A relationship between two variables that is positive, meaning that an increase in one variable is associated with an increase in the other and a decrease in one variable is associated with a decrease in the other.

A graph is a visual representation of the relationship between variables. In this appendix, we'll deal with just two variables: an **independent variable,** which can change in value freely, and a **dependent variable,** which changes only as a result of changes in the value of the independent variable. For example, even if nothing else is changing in your life, your weight depends on your intake of calories. The independent variable is caloric intake, and the dependent variable is weight.

A table is a list of numerical values showing the relationship between two (or more) variables. Any table can be converted into a graph, which is a visual representation of that list. Once you understand how a table can be converted to a graph, you will understand what graphs are and how to construct and use them.

Consider a practical example. A conservationist may try to convince you that driving at lower highway speeds will help you conserve gas. Table A-1 shows the relationship between speed—the independent variable—and the distance you can go on a gallon of gas at that speed—the dependent variable. This table does show a pattern. As the data in the first column get larger in value, the data in the second column get smaller.

Now let's take a look at the different ways in which variables can be related.

Direct and Inverse Relationships

Two variables can be related in different ways, some simple, others more complex. For example, a person's weight and height are often related. If we measured the height and weight of thousands of people, we would surely find that taller people tend to weigh more than shorter people. That is, we would discover that there is a **direct relationship** between height and weight. By this we simply mean that an *increase* in one variable is usually associated with an *increase* in the related variable. This can easily be seen in panel (a) of Figure A-1.

FIGURE A-1

Direct and Inverse Relationships

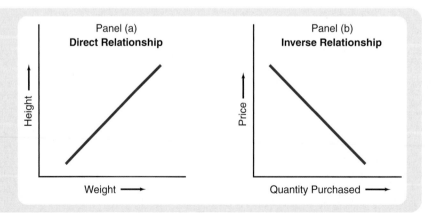

Let's look at another simple way in which two variables can be related. Much evidence indicates that as the price of a specific commodity rises, the amount purchased decreases—there is an **inverse relationship** between the variable's price per unit and quantity purchased. Such a relationship indicates that for higher and higher prices, smaller and smaller quantities will be purchased. We see this relationship in panel (b) of Figure A-1.

Inverse relationship
A relationship between two variables that is negative, meaning that an increase in one variable is associated with a decrease in the other and a decrease in one variable is associated with an increase in the other.

Constructing a Graph

Let us now examine how to construct a graph to illustrate a relationship between two variables.

A Number Line

The first step is to become familiar with what is called a **number line.** One is shown in Figure A-2. You should know two things about it:

Number line
A line that can be divided into segments of equal length, each associated with a number.

1. The points on the line divide the line into equal segments.
2. The numbers associated with the points on the line increase in value from left to right; saying it the other way around, the numbers decrease in value from right to left. However you say it, what you're describing is formally called an *ordered set of points*.

On the number line, we have shown the line segments—that is, the distance from 0 to 10 or the distance between 30 and 40. They all appear to be equal and, indeed, are each equal to $\frac{1}{2}$ inch. When we use a distance to represent a quantity, such as barrels of oil, graphically, we are *scaling* the number line. In the example shown, the distance between 0 and 10 might represent 10 barrels of oil, or the distance from 0 to 40 might represent 40 barrels. Of course, the scale may differ on different number lines. For example, a distance of 1 inch could represent 10 units on one number line but 5,000 units on another. Notice that on our number line, points to the left of 0 correspond to negative numbers and points to the right of 0 correspond to positive numbers.

Of course, we can also construct a vertical number line. Consider the one in Figure A-3 on the next page. As we move up this vertical number line, the numbers increase in value; conversely, as we descend, they decrease in value. Below 0 the numbers are negative, and above 0 the numbers are positive. And as on the horizontal number line, all the line segments are equal. This line is divided into segments such that the distance between −2 and −1 is the same as the distance between 0 and 1.

Combining Vertical and Horizontal Number Lines

By drawing the horizontal and vertical lines on the same sheet of paper, we are able to express the relationships between variables graphically. We do this in Figure A-4 on the next page. We draw them (1) so that they intersect at each other's 0 point and (2) so that they are perpendicular to each other. The result is a set of coordinate axes, where each line is called an *axis.* When we have two axes, they span a *plane.*

FIGURE A-2

Horizontal Number Line

FIGURE A-3

Vertical Number Line

FIGURE A-4

A Set of Coordinate Axes

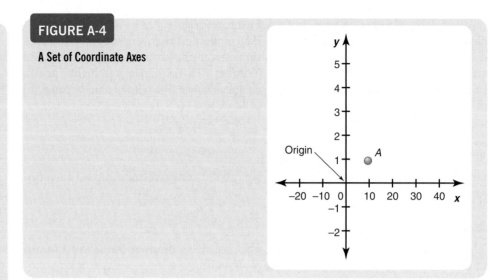

For one number line, you need only one number to specify any point on the line; equivalently, when you see a point on the line, you know that it represents one number or one value. With a coordinate value system, you need two numbers to specify a single point in the plane; when you see a single point on a graph, you know that it represents two numbers or two values.

The basic things that you should know about a coordinate number system are that the vertical number line is referred to as the **y axis,** the horizontal number line is referred to as the **x axis,** and the point of intersection of the two lines is referred to as the **origin.**

Any point such as A in Figure A-4 represents two numbers—a value of x and a value of y. But we know more than that: We also know that point A represents a positive value of y because it is above the x axis, and we know that it represents a positive value of x because it is to the right of the y axis.

Point A represents a "paired observation" of the variables x and y; in particular, in Figure A-4, A represents an observation of the pair of values $x = 10$ and $y = 1$. Every point in the coordinate system corresponds to a paired observation of x and y, which can be simply written (x, y)—the x value is always specified first and then the y value. When we give the values associated with the position of point A in the coordinate number system, we are in effect giving the coordinates of that point. A's coordinates are $x = 10, y = 1$, or $(10, 1)$.

Graphing Numbers in a Table

Consider Table A-2. Column 1 shows different prices for T-shirts, and column 2 gives the number of T-shirts purchased per week at these prices. Notice the pattern of these numbers. As the price of T-shirts falls, the number of T-shirts purchased per week increases. Therefore, an inverse relationship exists between these two variables, and as soon as we represent it on a graph, you will be able to see the relationship. We can graph this relationship using a coordinate number system—a vertical and horizontal number line for each of these two variables. Such a graph is shown in panel (b) of Figure A-5.

y axis
The vertical axis in a graph.

x axis
The horizontal axis in a graph.

Origin
The intersection of the y axis and the x axis in a graph.

In economics, it is conventional to put dollar values on the *y* axis and quantities on the horizontal axis. We therefore construct a vertical number line for price and a horizontal number line, the *x* axis, for quantity of T-shirts purchased per week. The resulting coordinate system allows the plotting of each of the paired observation points; in panel (a), we repeat Table A-2, with a column added expressing these points in paired-data (*x*, *y*) form. For example, point *J* is the paired observation (30, 9). It indicates that when the price of a T-shirt is $9, 30 will be purchased per week.

If it were possible to sell parts of a T-shirt ($\frac{1}{2}$ or $\frac{1}{20}$ of a shirt), we would have observations at every possible price. That is, we would be able to connect our paired observations, represented as lettered points. Let's assume that we can make T-shirts perfectly divisible so that the linear relationship shown in Figure A-5 also holds for fractions of dollars and T-shirts. We would then have a line that connects these points, as shown in the graph in Figure A-6 on the following page.

In short, we have now represented the data from the table in the form of a graph. Note that an inverse relationship between two variables shows up on a graph as a line or curve that slopes *downward* from left to right. (You might as well get used to the idea that economists call a straight line a "curve" even though it may not curve at all. Economists' data frequently turn out to be curves, so they refer to everything represented graphically, even straight lines, as curves.)

The Slope of a Line (A Linear Curve)

An important property of a curve represented on a graph is its *slope*. Consider Figure A-7 on page 22, which represents the quantities of shoes per week that a seller is willing to offer at different prices. Note that in panel (a) of Figure A-7, as in Figure A-5, we have expressed the coordinates of the points in parentheses in paired-data form.

TABLE A-2

T-Shirts Purchased

(1) Price of T-Shirts	(2) Number of T-Shirts Purchased per Week
$10	20
9	30
8	40
7	50
6	60
5	70

FIGURE A-5

Graphing the Relationship Between T-Shirts Purchased and Price

Panel (a)

Price per T-Shirt	T-Shirts Purchased per Week	Point on Graph
$10	20	*I* (20, 10)
9	30	*J* (30, 9)
8	40	*K* (40, 8)
7	50	*L* (50, 7)
6	60	*M* (60, 6)
5	70	*N* (70, 5)

FIGURE A-6

Connecting the Observation Points

Slope
The change in the *y* value divided by the corresponding change in the *x* value of a curve; the "incline" of the curve.

The **slope** of a line is defined as the change in the *y* values divided by the corresponding change in the *x* values as we move along the line. Let's move from point *E* to point *D* in panel (b) of Figure A-7. As we move, we note that the change in the *y* values, which is the change in price, is +$20, because we have moved from a price of $20 to a price of $40 per pair. As we move from *E* to *D*, the change in the *x* values is +80; the number of pairs of shoes willingly offered per week rises from 80 to 160 pairs.

FIGURE A-7

A Positively Sloped Curve

Panel (a)

Price per Pair	Pairs of Shoes Offered per Week	Point on Graph
$100	400	A (400,100)
80	320	B (320, 80)
60	240	C (240, 60)
40	160	D (160, 40)
20	80	E (80, 20)

Panel (b)

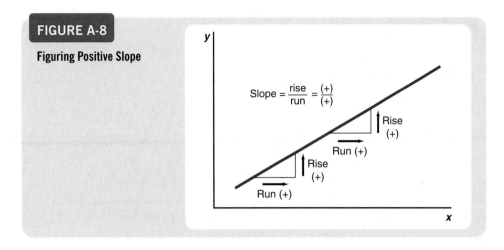

FIGURE A-8

Figuring Positive Slope

The slope, calculated as a change in the y values divided by the change in the x values, is therefore

$$\frac{20}{80} = \frac{1}{4}$$

It may be helpful for you to think of slope as a "rise" (movement in the vertical direction) over a "run" (movement in the horizontal direction). We show this abstractly in Figure A-8. The slope is the amount of rise divided by the amount of run. In the example in Figure A-8, and of course in Figure A-7, the amount of rise is positive and so is the amount of run. That's because it's a direct relationship. We show an inverse relationship in Figure A-9. The slope is still equal to the rise divided by the run, but in this case the rise and the run have opposite signs because the curve slopes downward. That means that the slope is negative and that we are dealing with an inverse relationship.

Now let's calculate the slope for a different part of the curve in panel (b) of Figure A-7. We will find the slope as we move from point B to point A. Again, we note that the slope, or rise over run, from B to A equals

$$\frac{20}{80} = \frac{1}{4}$$

A specific property of a straight line is that its slope is the same between any two points; in other words, the slope is constant at all points on a straight line in a graph.

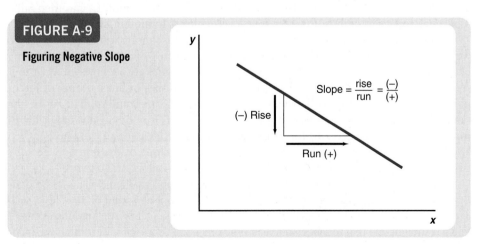

FIGURE A-9

Figuring Negative Slope

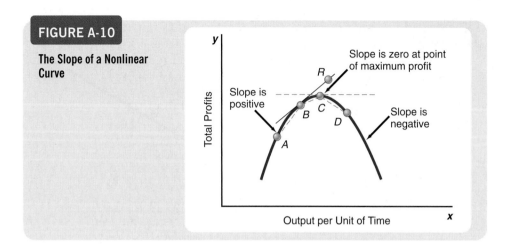

FIGURE A-10

The Slope of a Nonlinear Curve

We conclude that for our example in Figure A-7 on page 22, the relationship between the price of a pair of shoes and the number of pairs of shoes willingly offered per week is *linear*, which simply means "in a straight line," and our calculations indicate a constant slope. Moreover, we calculate a direct relationship between these two variables, which turns out to be an upward-sloping (from left to right) curve. Upward-sloping curves have positive slopes—in this case, the slope is $+\frac{1}{4}$.

We know that an inverse relationship between two variables shows up as a downward-sloping curve—rise over run will be negative because the rise and run have opposite signs, as shown in Figure A-9 on the previous page. When we see a negative slope, we know that increases in one variable are associated with decreases in the other. Therefore, we say that downward-sloping curves have negative slopes. Can you verify that the slope of the graph representing the relationship between T-shirt prices and the quantity of T-shirts purchased per week in Figure A-6 on page 22 is $-\frac{1}{10}$?

Slopes of Nonlinear Curves

The graph presented in Figure A-10 indicates a *nonlinear* relationship between two variables, total profits and output per unit of time. Inspection of this graph indicates that at first, increases in output lead to increases in total profits; that is, total profits rise as output increases. But beyond some output level, further increases in output cause decreases in total profits.

Can you see how this curve rises at first, reaches a peak at point *C*, and then falls? This curve relating total profits to output levels appears mountain-shaped.

Considering that this curve is nonlinear (it is obviously not a straight line), should we expect a constant slope when we compute changes in *y* divided by corresponding changes in *x* in moving from one point to another? A quick inspection, even without specific numbers, should lead us to conclude that the slopes of lines joining different points in this curve, such as between *A* and *B*, *B* and *C*, or *C* and *D*, will *not* be the same. The curve slopes upward (in a positive direction) for some values and downward (in a negative direction) for other values. In fact, the slope of the line between any two points on this curve will be different from the slope of the line between any two other points. Each slope will be different as we move along the curve.

Instead of using a line between two points to discuss slope, mathematicians and economists prefer to discuss the slope *at a particular point*. The slope at a point on the curve, such as point *B* in the graph in Figure A-10, is the slope of a line tangent to that point. A tangent line is a straight line that touches a curve at only one point. For example, it might be helpful to think of the tangent at *B* as the straight line that just "kisses" the curve at point *B*.

To calculate the slope of a tangent line, you need to have some additional information besides the two values of the point of tangency. For example, in Figure A-10, if we knew that the point *R* also lay on the tangent line and we knew the two values of that point, we could calculate the slope of the tangent line. We could calculate rise over run between points *B* and *R*, and the result would be the slope of the line tangent to the one point *B* on the curve.

myeconlab   Here is what you should know after reading this appendix. **MyEconLab** will help you identify what you know, and where to go when you need to practice.

WHAT YOU SHOULD KNOW		WHERE TO GO TO PRACTICE
Direct and Inverse Relationships In a direct relationship, a dependent variable changes in the same direction as the change in the independent variable. In an inverse relationship, the dependent variable changes in the opposite direction of the change in the independent variable.	independent variable, 18 dependent variable, 18 direct relationship, 18 inverse relationship, 19	• **MyEconLab** Study Plan 1.7
Constructing a Graph When we draw a graph showing the relationship between two economic variables, we are holding all other things constant (the Latin term for which is *ceteris paribus*).	number line, 19 *y* axis, 20 *x* axis, 20 origin, 20	• **MyEconLab** Study Plan 1.8
Graphing Numbers We obtain a set of coordinates by putting vertical and horizontal number lines together. The vertical line is called the *y* axis; the horizontal line, the *x* axis.		• **MyEconLab** Study Plan 1.9
The Slope of a Linear Curve The slope of any linear (straight-line) curve is the change in the *y* values divided by the corresponding change in the *x* values as we move along the line. Otherwise stated, the slope is calculated as the amount of rise over the amount of run, where rise is movement in the vertical direction and run is movement in the horizontal direction.	slope, 22 KEY FIGURES Figure A-8, 23 Figure A-9, 23	• **MyEconLab** Study Plan 1.10 • Animated Figures A-8, A-9
The Slope of a Nonlinear Curve The slope of a nonlinear curve changes; it is positive when the curve is rising and negative when the curve is falling. At a maximum or minimum point, the slope of the nonlinear curve is zero.	KEY FIGURE Figure A-10, 24	• **MyEconLab** Study Plan 1.10 • Animated Figure A-10

Log in to MyEconLab, take an appendix test, and get a personalized Study Plan that tells you which concepts you understand and which ones you need to review. From there, MyEconLab will give you further practice, tutorials, animations, videos, and guided solutions.
Log in to www.myeconlab.com

PROBLEMS

All problems are assignable in **myeconlab**. *Answers to odd-numbered problems appear at the back of the book.*

A-1. Explain which is the independent variable and which is the dependent variable for each of the following examples.

    a. Once you determine the price of a notebook at the college bookstore, you will decide how many notebooks to buy.

    b. You will decide how many credit hours to register for this semester once the university tells you how many work-study hours you will be assigned.

    c. You anticipate earning a higher grade on your next economics exam because you studied more hours in the weeks preceding the exam.

A-2. For each of the following items, state whether a direct or an inverse relationship is likely to exist.

    a. The number of hours you study for an exam and your exam score

    b. The price of pizza and the quantity purchased

    c. The number of games the university basketball team won last year and the number of season tickets sold this year

A-3. Review Figure A-4 on page 20, and then state whether each of the following paired observations is on, above, or below the x axis and on, to the left of, or to the right of the y axis.

    a. $(-10, 4)$

    b. $(20, -2)$

    c. $(10, 0)$

A-4. State whether each of the following functions specifies a direct or an inverse relationship.

    a. $y = 5x$

    b. $y = 10 - 2x$

    c. $y = 3 + x$

    d. $y = -3x$

A-5. Given the function $y = 5x$, complete the following schedule and plot the curve.

y	x
	-4
	-2
	0
	2
	4

A-6. Given the function $y = 8 - 2x$, complete the following schedule and plot the curve.

y	x
	-4
	-2
	0
	2
	4

A-7. Calculate the slope of the function you graphed in Problem A-5.

A-8. Calculate the slope of the function you graphed in Problem A-6.

Scarcity and the World of Trade-Offs

2

The employer of seven former college athletes requires them to practice five days per week. Each day, they lift weights to maintain their muscle strength, and they sprint through obstacle courses to reduce their reaction time. To improve their footwork and hand speed, they watch videos of previous performances. They consider themselves to be professional athletes, but thousands of people with the opportunity to observe them at work pay little heed to their exertions. These seven individuals constitute a pit crew at a motor speedway. Each crew member performs a very specific task, and the crew's tasks are organized so as to attain maximum output from their combined resources. These aspects of the activities of a speedway pit crew conform to key economic concepts that are the subject of this chapter.

LEARNING OBJECTIVES

myeconlab

After reading this chapter, you should be able to:

- Evaluate whether even affluent people face the problem of scarcity
- Understand why economics considers individuals' "wants" but not their "needs"
- Explain why the scarcity problem induces individuals to consider opportunity costs
- Discuss why obtaining increasing increments of any particular good typically entails giving up more and more units of other goods
- Explain why society faces a trade-off between consumption goods and capital goods
- Distinguish between absolute and comparative advantage

?

Did you know that there are more than 105 million parking spaces in the United States? Although parking spaces vary in size, the typical space is about 19 feet long and 8 feet wide and takes up an area of about 152 square feet. Consequently, U.S. parking spaces occupy almost 16 billion square feet of space, or almost 575 square miles.

All of this land devoted to parking spaces could, of course, be allocated to numerous alternative uses, such as housing developments, office buildings, city parks, and green spaces. These alternative uses of land now occupied by parking spaces could yield benefits to numerous members of society. Because this land does not yield these benefits, the allocation of land to parking spaces entails costs. Land, like all other resources, is scarce.

Scarcity

Scarcity

A situation in which the ingredients for producing the things that people desire are insufficient to satisfy all wants at a zero price.

Whenever individuals or communities cannot obtain everything they desire simultaneously, they must make choices. Choices occur because of *scarcity*. **Scarcity** is the most basic concept in all of economics. Scarcity means that we do not ever have enough of everything, including time, to satisfy our *every* desire. Scarcity exists because human wants always exceed what can be produced with the limited resources and time that nature makes available.

What Scarcity Is Not

Scarcity is not a shortage. After a hurricane hits and cuts off supplies to a community, TV newscasts often show people standing in line to get minimum amounts of cooking fuel and food. A news commentator might say that the line is caused by the "scarcity" of these products. But cooking fuel and food are always scarce—we cannot obtain all that we want at a zero price. Therefore, do not confuse the concept of scarcity, which is general and all-encompassing, with the concept of shortages as evidenced by people waiting in line to obtain a particular product.

Scarcity is not the same thing as poverty. Scarcity occurs among the poor and among the rich. Even the richest person on earth faces scarcity. For instance, even the world's richest person has only limited time available. Low income levels do not create more scarcity. High income levels do not create less scarcity.

Scarcity is a fact of life, like gravity. And just as physicists did not invent gravity, economists did not invent scarcity—it existed well before the first economist ever lived. It has existed at all times in the past and will exist at all times in the future.

What underlying fact about parking spaces would motivate someone to buy a small car?

Scarcity and Resources

Scarcity exists because resources are insufficient to satisfy our every desire. Resources are the inputs used in the production of the things that we want. **Production** can be defined as virtually any activity that results in the conversion of resources into products that can be used in consumption. Production includes delivering things from one part of the country to another. It includes taking ice from an ice tray to put it in your soft-drink glass. The resources used in production are called *factors of production*, and some economists use the terms *resources* and *factors of production* interchangeably. The total quantity of all resources that an economy has at any one time determines what that economy can produce.

Production

Any activity that results in the conversion of resources into products that can be used in consumption.

Factors of production can be classified in many ways. Here is one such classification:

Land

The natural resources that are available from nature. Land as a resource includes location, original fertility and mineral deposits, topography, climate, water, and vegetation.

1. *Land.* **Land** encompasses all the nonhuman gifts of nature, including timber, water, fish, minerals, and the original fertility of land. It is often called the *natural resource*.

2. *Labor*. **Labor** is the *human resource*, which includes productive contributions made by individuals who work, such as Web page designers, ballet dancers, and professional football players.

3. *Physical capital*. **Physical capital** consists of the factories and equipment used in production. It also includes improvements to natural resources, such as irrigation ditches.

4. *Human capital*. **Human capital** is the economic characterization of the education and training of workers. How much the nation produces depends not only on how many hours people work but also on how productive they are, and that in turn depends in part on education and training. To become more educated, individuals have to devote time and resources, just as a business has to devote resources if it wants to increase its physical capital. Whenever a worker's skills increase, human capital has been improved.

5. *Entrepreneurship*. **Entrepreneurship** (actually a subdivision of labor) is the component of human resources that performs the functions of organizing, managing, and assembling the other factors of production to create and operate business ventures. Entrepreneurship also encompasses taking risks that involve the possibility of losing large sums of wealth on new ventures. It includes new methods of doing common things and generally experimenting with any type of new thinking that could lead to making more income. Without entrepreneurship, virtually no business organization could operate.

Why do you suppose that the U.S. Navy wants its top officers to develop entrepreneurial skills?

Labor
Productive contributions of humans who work.

Physical capital
All manufactured resources, including buildings, equipment, machines, and improvements to land that are used for production.

Human capital
The accumulated training and education of workers.

Entrepreneurship
The component of human resources that performs the functions of raising capital, organizing, managing, and assembling other factors of production, making basic business policy decisions, and taking risks.

POLICY EXAMPLE
Schooling Admirals in Entrepreneurship

The U.S. Navy regularly sends officers back to school for graduate courses in areas such as nuclear engineering and foreign policy analysis. In recent years, however, admirals are as likely to find themselves enrolling in graduate business courses with titles such as "Using Effects-Based Thinking" and "Organizational Innovation." The Secretary of the Navy has decided that top officers should know as much about supply-chain management, management delegation, and organizational behavior as they know about seaborne aviation and submarine technology. Acquainting admirals with entrepreneurial skills, those heading the Navy have concluded, will lead to wiser allocation and utilization of military resources.

FOR CRITICAL ANALYSIS
In what ways is a military organization such as the U.S. Navy like a business?

Goods versus Economic Goods

Goods are defined as all things from which individuals derive satisfaction or happiness. Goods therefore include air to breathe and the beauty of a sunset as well as food, cars, and iPods.

   Economic goods are a subset of all goods—they are scarce goods, about which we must constantly make decisions regarding their best use. By definition, the desired quantity of an economic good exceeds the amount that is available at a zero price. Virtually every example we use in economics concerns economic goods—cars, DVD players,

Goods
All things from which individuals derive satisfaction or happiness.

Economic goods
Goods that are scarce, for which the quantity demanded exceeds the quantity supplied at a zero price.

computers, socks, baseball bats, and corn. Weeds are a good example of *bads*—goods for which the desired quantity is much *less* than what nature provides at a zero price.

Sometimes you will see references to "goods and services." **Services** are tasks that are performed for someone else, such as laundry, Internet access, hospital care, restaurant meal preparation, car polishing, psychological counseling, and teaching. One way of looking at services is to think of them as *intangible goods*.

Wants and Needs

Wants are not the same as needs. Indeed, from the economist's point of view, the term *needs* is objectively undefinable. When someone says, "I need some new clothes," there is no way to know whether that person is stating a vague wish, a want, or a life-saving requirement. If the individual making the statement were dying of exposure in a northern country during the winter, we might argue that indeed the person does need clothes—perhaps not new ones, but at least some articles of warm clothing. Typically, however, the term *need* is used very casually in conversation. What people mean, usually, is that they desire something that they do not currently have.

Humans have unlimited wants. Just imagine that every single material want that you might have was satisfied. You could have all of the clothes, cars, houses, DVDs, yachts, and other items that you want. Does that mean that nothing else could add to your total level of happiness? Undoubtedly, you might continue to think of new goods and services that you could obtain, particularly as they came to market. You would also still be lacking in fulfilling all of your wants for compassion, friendship, love, affection, prestige, musical abilities, sports abilities, and so on.

In reality, every individual has competing wants but cannot satisfy all of them, given limited resources. This is the reality of scarcity. Each person must therefore make choices. Whenever a choice is made to produce or buy something, something else that is also desired is not produced or not purchased. In other words, in a world of scarcity, every want that ends up being satisfied causes one or more other wants to remain unsatisfied or to be forfeited.

Would you classify a flat-screen TV as a want or a need? What is the difference?

QUICK QUIZ   *See page 50 for the answers. Review concepts from this section in MyEconLab.*

_____ is the situation in which human wants always exceed what can be produced with the limited resources and time that nature makes available.

We use scarce resources, such as _____, _____, _____ and _____ capital, and _____, to produce economic goods—goods that are desired but are not directly obtainable from nature to the extent demanded or desired at a zero price.

_____ are unlimited; they include all material desires and all nonmaterial desires, such as love, affection, power, and prestige.

The concept of _____ is difficult to define objectively for every person; consequently, we simply consider every person's wants to be unlimited. In a world of **scarcity,** satisfaction of one want necessarily means non-satisfaction of one or more other wants.

Scarcity, Choice, and Opportunity Cost

The natural fact of scarcity implies that we must make choices. One of the most important results of this fact is that every choice made means that some opportunity must be sacrificed. Every choice involves giving up an opportunity to produce or consume something else.

Valuing Forgone Alternatives

Consider a practical example. Every choice you make to study economics for one more hour requires that you give up the opportunity to engage in any of the following activities: study more of another subject, listen to music, sleep, browse at a local store, read a novel, or work out at the gym. The most highly valued of these opportunities is forgone if you choose to study economics an additional hour.

Because there were so many alternatives from which to choose, how could you determine the value of what you gave up to engage in that extra hour of studying economics? First of all, no one else can tell you the answer because only *you* can put a value on the alternatives forgone. Only you know the value of another hour of sleep or of an hour looking for the latest digital music downloads—whatever one activity *you* would have chosen if you had not opted to study economics for that hour. That means that only you can determine the highest-valued, next-best alternative that you had to sacrifice in order to study economics one more hour. Only you can determine the value of the next-best alternative.

Opportunity Cost

The value of the next-best alternative is called **opportunity cost.** The opportunity cost of any action is the value of what is given up—the next-highest-ranked alternative—because a choice was made. When you study one more hour, there may be many alternatives available for the use of that hour, but assume that you can do only one other thing in that hour—your next-highest-ranked alternative. What is important is the choice that you would have made if you hadn't studied one more hour. Your opportunity cost is the *next-highest-ranked* alternative, not *all* alternatives.

> *In economics, cost is always a forgone opportunity.*

One way to think about opportunity cost is to understand that when you choose to do something, you lose something else. What you lose is being able to engage in your next-highest-valued alternative. The cost of your chosen alternative is what you lose, which is by definition your next-highest-valued alternative. This is your opportunity cost.

What is the opportunity cost of precisely synchronizing the world's clocks?

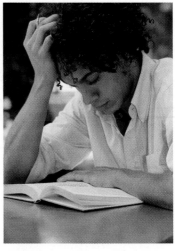

What is your next-highest alternative when you study an extra hour?

Opportunity cost
The highest-valued, next-best alternative that must be sacrificed to obtain something or to satisfy a want.

INTERNATIONAL EXAMPLE
The Significant Opportunity Cost of a Second of Time

The tug of the moon's gravity slows the earth's rotation, so the length of a day on earth is always increasing a tiny bit. At intervals averaging about 18 months, astronomers notify a United Nations group charged with regulating global timekeeping that the world's day has gained another second. Telecommunications companies, satellite operators, and governments then add an extra, "leap" second to the planet's atomic clocks.

Many computers, however, are not equipped with software that can handle the 61-second minute that results when a leap second is added. Particularly vulnerable are programs that manage the global positioning systems (GPS) utilized by surveyors, engineers, surgeons, and navigators, among others. The last time a leap second was added, GPS breakdowns created snafus that temporarily idled equipment and workers on every continent.

The U.S. government has proposed adding a "leap minute" every century instead of leap seconds every 18 months. In this way, the world's economies might avoid a significant opportunity cost—that is, forgoing productive activities—in order to keep the earth's time precisely synchronized with its rotation.

FOR CRITICAL ANALYSIS
If leap seconds are not added, astronomical observatories would have to devote some of their budgets to paying $10,000 to $500,000 per facility for telescope realignments to take into account the extra seconds not appearing on clocks. Why do astronomers argue that they would bear opportunity costs if the U.S. government's "leap minute" proposal is adopted?

The World of Trade-Offs

Whenever you engage in any activity using any resource, even time, you are *trading off* the use of that resource for one or more alternative uses. The extent of the trade-off is represented by the opportunity cost. The opportunity cost of studying economics has already been mentioned—it is the value of the next-best alternative. When you think of any alternative, you are thinking of trade-offs.

Let's consider a hypothetical example of a trade-off between the results of spending time studying economics and mathematics. For the sake of this argument, we will assume that additional time studying either economics or mathematics will lead to a higher grade in the subject to which additional study time is allocated. One of the best ways to examine this trade-off is with a graph. (If you would like a refresher on graphical techniques, study Appendix A at the end of Chapter 1 before going on.)

Graphical Analysis

In Figure 2-1, the expected grade in mathematics is measured on the vertical axis of the graph, and the expected grade in economics is measured on the horizontal axis. We simplify the world and assume that you have a maximum of 12 hours per week to spend studying these two subjects and that if you spend all 12 hours on economics, you will get an A in the course. You will, however, fail mathematics. Conversely, if you spend all of your 12 hours studying mathematics, you will get an A in that subject, but you will flunk economics. Here the trade-off is a special case: one to one. A one-to-one trade-off means that the opportunity cost of receiving one grade higher in economics (for example, improving from a C to a B) is one grade lower in mathematics (falling from a C to a D).

The Production Possibilities Curve (PPC)

The graph in Figure 2-1 illustrates the relationship between the possible results that can be produced in each of two activities, depending on how much time you choose to devote to each activity. This graph shows a representation of a **production possibilities curve (PPC).**

Production possibilities curve (PPC)
A curve representing all possible combinations of maximum outputs that could be produced assuming a fixed amount of productive resources of a given quality.

Consider that you are producing a grade in economics when you study economics and a grade in mathematics when you study mathematics. Then the line that goes from A on one axis to A on the other axis therefore becomes a production possibilities curve. It is defined as the maximum quantity of one good or service that can be produced, given that a specific quantity of another is produced. It is a curve that shows the possibilities available for increasing the output of one good or service by reducing the amount of another. In the example in Figure 2-1, your time for studying was limited to 12 hours per week. The two possible outputs were your grade in mathematics and your grade in economics. The particular production possibilities curve presented in Figure 2-1 is a graphical representation of the opportunity cost of studying one more hour in one subject. It is a *straight-line production possibilities curve*, which is a spe-

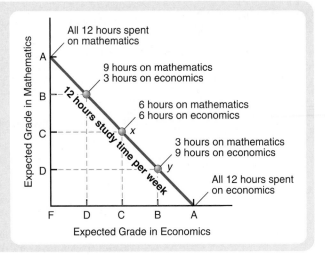

FIGURE 2-1

Production Possibilities Curve for Grades in Mathematics and Economics (Trade-Offs)

We assume that only 12 hours can be spent per week on studying. If the student is at point *x*, equal time (6 hours a week) is spent on both courses, and equal grades of C will be received. If a higher grade in economics is desired, the student may go to point *y*, thereby receiving a B in economics but a D in mathematics. At point *y*, 3 hours are spent on mathematics and 9 hours on economics.

cial case. (The more general case will be discussed next.) If you decide to be at point *x* in Figure 2-1, you will devote 6 hours of study time to mathematics and 6 hours to economics. The expected grade in each course will be a C. If you are more interested in getting a B in economics, you will go to point *y* on the production possibilities curve, spending only 3 hours on mathematics but 9 hours on economics. Your expected grade in mathematics will then drop from a C to a D.

Note that these trade-offs between expected grades in mathematics and economics are the result of *holding constant* total study time as well as all other factors that might influence your ability to learn, such as computerized study aids. Quite clearly, if you were able to spend more total time studying, it would be possible to have higher grades in both economics and mathematics. In that case, however, we would no longer be on the specific production possibilities curve illustrated in Figure 2-1. We would have to draw a new curve, farther to the right, to show the greater total study time and a different set of possible trade-offs.

What trade-off have the U.S. armed forces recently confronted as a result of the continuing military operations in Iraq and Afghanistan?

POLICY EXAMPLE
The U.S. Military Confronts a Trade-Off

Recently, U.S. military leaders decided to allocate an extra $1 billion in resources to expanding ground operations by troops in Iraq and Afghanistan. Given their available resources, the U.S. armed forces could undertake this expansion of troop operations only by forgoing the allocation of $1 billion in resources to a program known as Transformational Satellite Communications, or TSAT. The TSAT program would have involved development of space-based lasers and satellite-based Internet connections to facilitate ultrafast and highly secure data and video transmissions among military planes, ships, and troops. Thus, for the U.S. armed forces, the opportunity cost of maintaining troop levels in Iraq and Afghanistan was the forgone production of better military communications networks.

FOR CRITICAL ANALYSIS
How could Congress and taxpayers have made it possible for the U.S. armed forces to maintain their Iraq and Afghanistan operations without forgoing the allocation of resources to the TSAT program?

QUICK QUIZ *See page 50 for the answers. Review concepts from this section in MyEconLab.*

Scarcity requires us to choose. Whenever we choose, we lose the _____-_____-valued alternative.

Cost is always a forgone _____.

Another way to look at **opportunity cost** is the trade-off that occurs when one activity is undertaken rather than the _____-_____ alternative activity.

A _____ _____ curve graphically shows the trade-off that occurs when more of one output is obtained at the sacrifice of another. This curve is a graphical representation of, among other things, opportunity cost.

The Choices Society Faces

The straight-line production possibilities curve presented in Figure 2-1 can be generalized to demonstrate the related concepts of scarcity, choice, and trade-offs that our entire nation faces. As you will see, the production possibilities curve is a simple but powerful economic model because it can demonstrate these related concepts.

A Two-Good Example

The example we will use is the choice between the production of computer servers and high-definition televisions (HDTVs). We assume for the moment that these are the only two goods that can be produced in the nation.

Panel (a) of Figure 2-2 gives the various combinations of servers and HDTVs that are possible. If all resources are devoted to server production, 50 million per year can be produced. If all resources are devoted to production of HDTVs, 60 million per year can be produced. In between are various possible combinations.

Production Trade-Offs

The nation's production combinations are plotted as points *A*, *B*, *C*, *D*, *E*, *F*, and *G* in panel (b) of Figure 2-2. If these points are connected with a smooth curve, the nation's production possibilities curve (PPC) is shown, demonstrating the trade-off between the production of servers and HDTVs. These trade-offs occur *on* the PPC.

Notice the major difference in the shape of the production possibilities curves in Figure 2-1 on the previous page and Figure 2-2 on the facing page. In Figure 2-1, there is a constant trade-off between grades in economics and in mathematics. In Figure 2-2, the trade-off between production of computer servers and HDTV production is not constant, and therefore the PPC is a *bowed* curve. To understand why the production possibilities curve for a society is typically bowed outward, you must understand the assumptions underlying the PPC.

Go to www.econtoday.com/chapter02 for one perspective, offered by the National Center for Policy Analysis, on whether society's production decisions should be publicly or privately coordinated.

Assumptions Underlying the Production Possibilities Curve

When we draw the curve that is shown in Figure 2-2, we make the following assumptions:

1. Resources are fully employed.
2. Production takes place over a specific time period—for example, one year.
3. The resource inputs, in both quantity and quality, used to produce computer servers or HDTVs are fixed over this time period.
4. Technology does not change over this time period.

FIGURE 2-2

Society's Trade-Off Between Computer Servers and HDTVs

The production of computer servers and HDTVs is measured in millions of units per year. The various combinations are given in panel (a) and plotted in panel (b). Connecting the points A–G with a relatively smooth line gives society's production possibilities curve for servers and HDTVs. Point R lies outside the production possibilities curve and is therefore unattainable at the point in time for which the graph is drawn. Point S lies inside the production possibilities curve and therefore entails unemployed or underemployed resources.

Panel (a)

Combination	Servers (millions per year)	HDTVs (millions per year)
A	50.0	0
B	48.0	10
C	45.0	20
D	40.0	30
E	33.0	40
F	22.5	50
G	0.0	60

Technology is defined as society's pool of applied knowledge concerning how goods and services can be produced by managers, workers, engineers, scientists, and artisans, using land, physical and human capital, and entrepreneurship. You can think of technology as the formula or recipe used to combine factors of production. (When better formulas are developed, more production can be obtained from the same amount of resources.) The level of technology sets the limit on the amount and types of goods and services that we can derive from any given amount of resources. The production possibilities curve is drawn under the assumption that we use the best technology that we currently have available and that this technology doesn't change over the time period under study.

The land available to a town with established borders is an example of a fixed resource that is fully employed and used with available technology along a production possibilities curve. Why do you suppose that deciding how to allocate a fixed amount of land recently posed "grave" problems for a town in France?

Technology
Society's pool of applied knowledge concerning how goods and services can be produced.

INTERNATIONAL EXAMPLE
Making Death Illegal—At Least, Inside City Limits

Le Lavandou, France, a Riviera community known for breathtaking views of a rocky coastline along a clear-blue section of the Mediterranean Sea, recently drew international ridicule when it passed a law that appeared aimed at regulating death. Specifically, the law stated, "It is forbidden without a cemetery plot to die on the territory of the commune."

Of course, it is not possible for a law to prevent someone from dying inside a town. The purpose of the law was to indicate a permissible choice along a production possibilities curve. Land is a scarce resource with many alternative uses, so trade-offs involving different productive uses of land arise everywhere on the planet where people establish communities. Le Lavandou is no exception. The town's cemetery filled up, and the townspeople had to decide whether to allocate more land to cemetery plots, thereby providing a service for deceased individuals and for their family and friends, or to continue allocating remaining land resources to the production of other goods and services. The point of the legal requirement was to emphasize that the town had decided not to incur an opportunity cost by allocating more space to cemetery plots.

Nonetheless, it was still true that someone who happened to die in Le Lavandou without first buying an existing cemetery plot was technically breaking the law.

FOR CRITICAL ANALYSIS
What is likely to happen to the opportunity cost of cemetery space as the world's population continues to increase and spread over available land resources?

Being off the Production Possibilities Curve

Look again at panel (b) of Figure 2-2 on the previous page. Point *R* lies *outside* the production possibilities curve and is *impossible* to achieve during the time period assumed. By definition, the PPC indicates the *maximum* quantity of one good, given the quantity produced of the other good.

It is possible, however, to be at point *S* in Figure 2-2. That point lies beneath the production possibilities curve. If the nation is at point *S*, it means that its resources are not being fully utilized. This occurs, for example, during periods of relatively high unemployment. Point *S* and all such points inside the PPC are always attainable but imply unemployed or underemployed resources.

Efficiency

The production possibilities curve can be used to define the notion of efficiency. Whenever the economy is operating on the PPC, at points such as *A*, *B*, *C*, or *D*, we say that its production is efficient. Points such as *S* in Figure 2-2, which lie beneath the PPC, are said to represent production situations that are not efficient.

Efficiency
The case in which a given level of inputs is used to produce the maximum output possible. Alternatively, the situation in which a given output is produced at minimum cost.

Efficiency can mean many things to many people. Even in economics, there are different types of efficiency. Here we are discussing *productive efficiency*. An economy is productively efficient whenever it is producing the maximum output with given technology and resources.

A simple commonsense definition of efficiency is getting the most out of what we have. Clearly, we are not getting the most out of what we have if we are at point *S* in panel (b) of Figure 2-2. We can move from point *S* to, say, point *C*, thereby increasing the total quantity of servers produced without any decrease in the total quantity of HDTVs produced. Alternatively, we can move from point *S* to point *E*, for example, and have both more servers and more HDTVs. Point *S* is called an **inefficient point,** which is defined as any point below the production possibilities curve.

Inefficient point
Any point below the production possibilities curve, at which the use of resources is not generating the maximum possible output.

The Law of Increasing Relative Cost

In the example in Figure 2-1 on page 33, the trade-off between a grade in mathematics and a grade in economics was one to one. The trade-off ratio was constant. That is, the production possibilities curve was a straight line. The curve in Figure 2-2 is a more general case. We have re-created the curve in Figure 2-2 as Figure 2-3. Each combination, *A* through *G*, of computer servers and HDTVs is represented on the production

FIGURE 2-3

The Law of Increasing Relative Cost

Consider equal increments of production of HDTVs, as measured on the horizontal axis. All of the horizontal arrows—*aB, bC,* and so on—are of equal length (10 million). In contrast, the length of each vertical arrow—*Aa, Bb,* and so on—increases as we move down the production possibilities curve. Hence, the opportunity cost of going from 50 million HDTVs per year to 60 million (*Ff*) is much greater than going from zero units to 10 million (*Aa*). The opportunity cost of each additional equal increase in production of HDTVs rises.

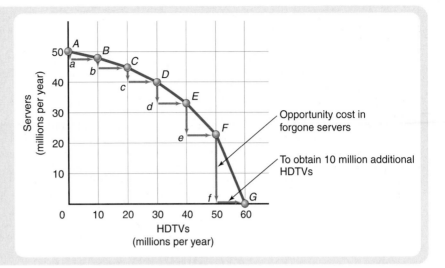

possibilities curve. Starting with the production of zero HDTVs, the nation can produce 50 million servers with its available resources and technology.

INCREASING RELATIVE COSTS   When we increase production of HDTVs from zero to 10 million per year, the nation has to give up in servers an amount shown by that first vertical arrow, *Aa.* From panel (a) of Figure 2-2 on page 35 you can see that this is 2 million per year (50 million minus 48 million). Again, if we increase production of HDTVs by another 10 million units per year, we go from *B* to *C*. In order to do so, the nation has to give up the vertical distance *Bb,* or 3 million servers per year. By the time we go from 50 million to 60 million HDTVs, to obtain that 10 million increase, we have to forgo the vertical distance *Ff,* or 22.5 million servers. In other words, we see that the opportunity cost of the last 10 million HDTVs has increased to 22.5 million servers, compared to 2 million servers for the same increase in HDTVs when we started with none at all being produced.

What we are observing is called the **law of increasing relative cost.** When society takes more resources and applies them to the production of any specific good, the opportunity cost increases for each additional unit produced.

EXPLAINING THE LAW OF INCREASING RELATIVE COST   The reason that as a nation we face the law of increasing relative cost (shown as a production possibilities curve that is bowed outward) is that certain resources are better suited for producing some goods than they are for other goods. Generally, resources are not *perfectly* adaptable for alternative uses. When increasing the output of a particular good, producers must use less suitable resources than those already used in order to produce the additional output. Hence, the cost of producing the additional units increases.

With respect to our hypothetical example here, at first the computing specialists at server firms would shift over to producing HDTVs. After a while, though, networking technicians, workers who normally design servers, and others would be asked to help design and manufacture HDTV components. Clearly, they would be less effective at making HDTVs than the people who previously specialized in this task.

In general, *the more specialized the resources, the more bowed the production possibilities curve.* At the other extreme, if all resources are equally suitable for server production or production of HDTVs, the curves in Figures 2-2 and 2-3 would approach the straight line shown in our first example in Figure 2-1 on page 33.

Law of increasing relative cost
The fact that the opportunity cost of additional units of a good generally increases as society attempts to produce more of that good. This accounts for the bowed-out shape of the production possibilities curve.

Economic Growth and the Production Possibilities Curve

At any particular point in time, a society cannot be outside the production possibilities curve. *Over time*, however, it is possible to have more of everything. This occurs through economic growth. (An important reason for economic growth, capital accumulation, is discussed next. A more complete discussion of why economic growth occurs appears in Chapter 9.) Figure 2-4 shows the production possibilities curve for computer servers and HDTVs shifting outward. The two additional curves shown represent new choices open to an economy that has experienced economic growth. Such economic growth occurs because of many things, including increases in the number of workers and productive investment in equipment.

Scarcity still exists, however, no matter how much economic growth there is. At any point in time, we will always be on some production possibilities curve; thus, we will always face trade-offs. The more we have of one thing, the less we can have of others.

If a nation experiences economic growth, the production possibilities curve between servers and HDTVs will move outward, as shown in Figure 2-4. This takes time and does not occur automatically. One reason it will occur involves the choice about how much to consume today.

FIGURE 2-4

Economic Growth Allows for More of Everything

If the nation experiences economic growth, the production possibilities curve between computer servers and HDTVs will move out as shown. This takes time, however, and it does not occur automatically. This means, therefore, that we can have more of both computer servers and HDTVs only after a period of time during which we have experienced economic growth.

The Trade-Off Between the Present and the Future

The production possibilities curve and economic growth can be combined to examine the trade-off between present **consumption** and future consumption. When we consume today, we are using up what we call consumption or consumer goods—food and clothes, for example.

Consumption
The use of goods and services for personal satisfaction.

Why We Make Capital Goods

Why would we be willing to use productive resources to make things—capital goods—that we cannot consume directly? For one thing, capital goods enable us to produce larger quantities of consumer goods or to produce them less expensively than we otherwise could. Before fish are "produced" for the market, equipment such as fishing boats, nets, and poles is produced first. Imagine how expensive it would be to obtain fish for market without using these capital goods. Catching fish with one's hands is not an easy task. The cost per fish would be very high if capital goods weren't used.

Forgoing Current Consumption

Whenever we use productive resources to make capital goods, we are implicitly forgoing current consumption. We are waiting for some time in the future to consume the rewards that will be reaped from the use of capital goods. In effect, when we forgo current consumption to invest in capital goods, we are engaging in an economic activity that is forward-looking—we do not get instant utility or satisfaction from our activity.

The Trade-Off Between Consumption Goods and Capital Goods

To have more consumer goods in the future, we must accept fewer consumer goods today, because resources must be used in producing capital goods instead of consumer goods. In other words, an opportunity cost is involved. Every time we make a choice of more goods today, we incur an opportunity cost of fewer goods tomorrow, and every time we make a choice of more goods in the future, we incur an opportunity cost of fewer goods today. With the resources that we don't use to produce consumer goods for today, we invest in capital goods that will produce more consumer goods for us later. The trade-off is shown in Figure 2-5 on the following page. On the left in panel (a), you can see this trade-off depicted as a production possibilities curve between capital goods and consumption goods.

Assume that we are willing to give up $1 trillion worth of consumption today. We will be at point *A* in the left-hand diagram of panel (a). This will allow the economy to grow. We will have more future consumption because we invested in more capital goods today. In the right-hand diagram of panel (a), we see two goods represented, food and entertainment. The production possibilities curve will move outward if we collectively decide to restrict consumption now and invest in capital goods.

In panel (b), we show the results of our willingness to forgo even more current consumption. We move to point *C* in the left-hand side, where we have many fewer consumer goods today but produce many more capital goods. This leads to more future growth in this simplified model, and thus the production possibilities curve in the right-hand side of panel (b) shifts outward more than it did in the right-hand side of panel (a). In other words, the more we give up today, the more we can have tomorrow, provided, of course, that the capital goods are productive in future periods.

FIGURE 2-5

Capital Goods and Growth

In panel (a), the nation chooses not to consume $1 trillion, so it invests that amount in capital goods. As a result, more of all goods may be produced in the future, as shown in the right-hand diagram in panel (a). In panel (b), society chooses even more capital goods (point C). The result is that the production possibilities curve (PPC) moves even more to the right on the right-hand diagram in panel (b).

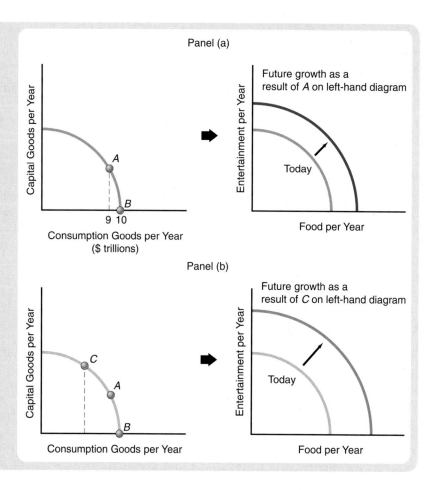

Panel (a)

Future growth as a result of A on left-hand diagram

Panel (b)

Future growth as a result of C on left-hand diagram

QUICK QUIZ   *See page 50 for the answers. Review concepts from this section in MyEconLab.*

_____ goods are goods that will later be used to produce consumer goods.

A trade-off is involved between current consumption and capital goods or, alternatively, between current consumption and future consumption. The _____ we invest in capital goods today, the greater the amount of consumer goods we can produce in the future and the _____ the amount of consumer goods we can produce today.

Specialization and Greater Productivity

Specialization
The organization of economic activity so that what each person (or region) consumes is not identical to what that person (or region) produces. An individual may specialize, for example, in law or medicine. A nation may specialize in the production of coffee, computers, or digital cameras.

Specialization involves working at a relatively well-defined, limited endeavor, such as accounting or teaching. It involves the organization of economic activity among different individuals and regions. Most individuals do specialize. For example, you could change the oil in your car if you wanted to. Typically, though, you take your car to a garage and let the mechanic change the oil. You benefit by letting the garage mechanic specialize in changing the oil and in doing other repairs on your car. The specialist normally will get the job finished sooner than you could and has the proper equipment to make the job go more smoothly. Specialization usually leads to greater productivity, not only for each individual but also for the nation.

Comparative Advantage

Specialization occurs because different individuals experience different costs when they engage in the same activities. Some individuals can accurately solve mathematical problems at lower cost than others who might try to solve the same problems. Thus, those who solve math problems at lower cost sacrifice production of fewer alternative items. Some people can develop more high-quality computer programs than others while giving up less production of other items, such as clean houses and neatly manicured yards.

Comparative advantage is the ability to perform an activity *at a lower opportunity cost*. You have a comparative advantage in one activity whenever you have a lower opportunity cost of performing that activity. Comparative advantage is always a *relative* concept. You may be able to change the oil in your car; you might even be able to change it faster than the local mechanic. But if the opportunity cost you face by changing the oil exceeds the mechanic's opportunity cost, the mechanic has a comparative advantage in changing the oil. The mechanic faces a lower opportunity cost for that activity.

You may be convinced that everybody can do more of everything than you can during the same period of time and using the same resources. In this extreme situation, do you still have a comparative advantage? The answer is yes. You do not have to be a mathematical genius to figure this out. The market tells you so very clearly by offering you the highest income for the job for which you have a comparative advantage. Stated differently, to find your comparative advantage, simply find the job that maximizes your income.

Comparative advantage
The ability to produce a good or service at a lower opportunity cost compared to other producers.

Absolute Advantage

Suppose that, conversely, you have a job at a firm and are convinced that you have the ability to do every job in that company at a lower cost than everyone else who works there. You might be able to keyboard documents into a computer faster than any of the other employees, file documents in order in a file cabinet faster than any of the file clerks, and wash windows faster than any of the window washers. Indeed, you might even be able to manage the firm in less time just as effectively as the current company president—and in less time than you would have to spend in any alternative function.

If all of these self-perceptions were really true, then you would have an **absolute advantage** in all of these endeavors. In other words, if you were to spend a given amount of time in any one of them, you could produce more than anyone else in the company. Nonetheless, you would not spend your time doing these other activities. Why not? Because your advantage in undertaking the president's managerial duties is even greater. Therefore, you would find yourself specializing in that particular task even though you have an *absolute* advantage in all these other tasks. Indeed, absolute advantage is irrelevant in predicting how you will allocate your time. Only *comparative advantage* matters in determining how you will allocate your time.

The coaches of sports teams often have to determine the comparative advantage of an individual player who has an absolute advantage in every aspect of the sport in question. Babe Ruth, who could hit more home runs and pitch more strikeouts per game than other players on the Boston Red Sox, was a pitcher on that professional baseball team. After he was traded to the New York Yankees, the owner and the manager decided to make him an outfielder, even though he could also hurl more strikeouts per game than other Yankees. They wanted "The Babe" to concentrate on his hitting because a home-run king would bring in more fans than a good pitcher would. Babe Ruth had an absolute advantage in both aspects of the game of baseball, but his

Absolute advantage
The ability to produce more units of a good or service using a given quantity of labor or resource inputs. Equivalently, the ability to produce the same quantity of a good or service using fewer units of labor or resource inputs.

comparative advantage was clearly in hitting homers rather than in practicing and developing his pitching game.

The opportunity cost of buying groceries is higher for some people than for others. How has this given entrepreneurs an opportunity to profit from taking grocery orders online?

E-COMMERCE EXAMPLE
A Comparative Advantage in Grocery Shopping

Traveling to a grocery store, grabbing a shopping cart, and searching through the store's aisles for items are time-consuming activities. Individuals who want a very particular grocery item, such as steak or salmon marinated with specific spices or herbs, may have to devote considerable time going to several grocery stores.

Increasingly, people are concluding that grocery shopping is a next-best alternative. These individuals allocate their time to other activities, such as earning more income, and pay others to shop for items on their grocery lists. FreshDirect is a company that takes online grocery orders from finicky eaters in New York City. Each year FreshDirect's trucks fulfill 2 million grocery orders for $200 million worth of food by transporting 60 million items packed into 8 million boxes. The Web-based company has a comparative advantage in tracking down gourmet steaks, salmon, and a wide variety of other grocery items, so it specializes in this activity.

FOR CRITICAL ANALYSIS
Why do you suppose that people who frequently consume hard-to-find gourmet foods are among FreshDirect's most regular customers?

You Are There

For an example of how the concepts of comparative advantage and specialization can matter in a realistic business context, read **Specializing in Providing Baggage-Free Business Trips,** on page 44.

Scarcity, Self-Interest, and Specialization

In Chapter 1, you learned about the assumption of rational self-interest. To repeat, for the purposes of our analyses we assume that individuals are rational in that they will do what is in their own self-interest. They will not consciously carry out actions that will make them worse off. In this chapter, you learned that scarcity requires people to make choices. We *assume* that they make choices based on their self-interest. When they make these choices, they attempt to maximize benefits net of opportunity cost. In so doing, individuals choose their comparative advantage and end up specializing.

The Division of Labor

In any firm that includes specialized human and nonhuman resources, there is a **division of labor** among those resources. The best-known example comes from Adam Smith, who in *The Wealth of Nations* illustrated the benefits of a division of labor in the making of pins, as depicted in the following example:

Division of labor
The segregation of resources into different specific tasks; for example, one automobile worker puts on bumpers, another doors, and so on.

> One man draws out the wire, another straightens it, a third cuts it, a fourth points it, a fifth grinds it at the top for receiving the head; to make the head requires two or three distinct operations; to put it on is a peculiar business, to whiten the pins is another; it is even a trade by itself to put them into the paper.

Making pins this way allowed 10 workers without very much skill to make almost 48,000 pins "of a middling size" in a day. One worker, toiling alone, could have made perhaps 20 pins a day; therefore, 10 workers could have produced 200. Division of labor allowed for an increase in the daily output of the pin factory from 200 to 48,000! (Smith did not attribute all of the gain to the division of labor but credited also the use of machinery and the fact that less time was spent shifting from task to task.)

What we are discussing here involves a division of the resource called labor into different uses of labor. The different uses of labor are organized in such a way as to increase the amount of output possible from the fixed resources available. We can therefore talk about an organized division of labor within a firm leading to increased output.

Comparative Advantage and Trade Among Nations

Most of our analysis of absolute advantage, comparative advantage, and specialization has dealt with individuals. Nevertheless, it is equally applicable to nations.

This automobile assembly line is a good example of what concept in economics?

Trade Among Regions

Consider the United States. The Plains states have a comparative advantage in the production of grains and other agricultural goods. Relative to the Plains states, the states to the east tend to specialize in industrialized production, such as automobiles. Not surprisingly, grains are shipped from the Plains states to the eastern states, and automobiles are shipped in the reverse direction. Such specialization and trade allow for higher incomes and standards of living.

If both the Plains states and the eastern states were separate nations, the same analysis would still hold, but we would call it international trade. Indeed, the European Union (EU) is comparable to the United States in area and population, but instead of one nation, the EU has 27. What U.S. residents call *interstate* trade, Europeans call *international* trade. There is no difference, however, in the economic results—both yield greater economic efficiency and higher average incomes.

International Aspects of Trade

Political problems that normally do not occur within a particular nation often arise between nations. For example, if California avocado growers develop a cheaper method of producing a tastier avocado than growers in southern Florida use, the Florida growers will lose out. They cannot do much about the situation except try to lower their own costs of production or improve their product.

If avocado growers in Mexico, however, develop a cheaper method of producing better-tasting avocados, both California and Florida growers can (and likely will) try to raise political barriers that will prevent Mexican avocado growers from freely selling their product in the United States. U.S. avocado growers will use such arguments as "unfair" competition and loss of U.S. jobs. Certainly, avocado-growing jobs may decline in the United States, but there is no reason to believe that U.S. jobs will decline overall. Instead, former U.S. avocado workers will move into alternative employment—something that 1 million people do every *week* in the United States. If the argument of U.S. avocado growers had any validity, every time a region in the United States developed a better way to produce a product manufactured somewhere else in the country, U.S. employment would decline. That has never happened and never will.

When nations specialize where they have a comparative advantage and then trade with the rest of the world, the average standard of living in the world rises. In effect, international trade allows the world to move from inside the global production possibilities curve toward the curve itself, thereby improving worldwide economic efficiency. Thus, all countries that engage in trade can benefit from comparative advantage, just as regions in the United States benefit from interregional trade.

Go to www.econtoday.com/chapter02 to find out from the World Trade Organization how much international trade takes place. Under "Resources," click on "Trade statistics" and then click on "International Trade Statistics" for the most recent year.

QUICK QUIZ See page 50 for the answers. Review concepts from this section in MyEconLab.

With a given set of resources, specialization results in _____ output; in other words, there are gains to specilization in terms of greater material well-being.

Individuals and nations specialize in their areas of _____ advantage in order to reap the gains of specialization.

Comparative advantages are found by determining which activities have the _____ opportunity cost—that is,

which activities yield the highest return for the time and resources used.

A _____ of labor occurs when different workers are assigned different tasks. Together, the workers produce a desired product.

You Are There ▸ Specializing in Providing Baggage-Free Business Trips

When Steve Zilinek was working as an investment adviser, he noticed something about traveling businesspeople. Although many of these individuals possess considerable financial resources, they must expend another key resource when they travel—namely, time that they could otherwise devote to other activities. Zilinek estimated that packing bags, waiting at airport check-in, security, and baggage stations, and laundering clothing takes about three hours per trip—time that otherwise could be devoted to alternative pursuits.

Zilinek decided that he might have a comparative advantage in providing baggage services to frequent travelers. He founded FlyLite, a company that specializes in storing, caring for, and shipping all the items that individuals desire to have with them on business trips, such as clothing and toiletries. FlyLite's customers send the items they regularly take on business trips to the company, which places them in storage. Before a trip, a client fills out and submits a Web

form indicating which items she will require at her destination. FlyLite then arranges for the items to be shipped to her hotel. When her business trip concludes, the customer sends the items back to FlyLite, which dry cleans the clothing and then re-stores all items until her next trip. For FlyLite's clients, paying about $100 per trip for its services is the next-best alternative to devoting three hours to handling baggage on their own.

CRITICAL ANALYSIS QUESTIONS

1. *What is the approximate minimum opportunity cost of three hours of time per trip for the typical FlyLite customer?*

2. *How do you suppose that an increase in the average amount of time that people must spend dealing with baggage at airports affects the number of people utilizing FlyLite's services?*

Issues and Applications

Specialization and Division of Labor at the Speedway

T he driver wheels his high-performance racecar around the track at speeds up to 200 miles per hour. After the next turn, he decelerates down a side track to a pre-assigned location. As soon as his car comes to a halt, seven individuals rapidly converge around it: front- and rear-tire carriers, front- and rear-tire changers, an individual who jacks up the car, and two others carrying 11-gallon cans of fuel. These seven people together produce a combined service without which no auto race could long continue: the motor speedway "pit stop."

CONCEPTS APPLIED

➤ Production
➤ Specialization
➤ Division of Labor

Achieving Speedy Production of Auto Services

Racing a car around an oval track at high speeds for a few hours consumes two key resources. The most obvious resource is the high-performance fuel required to keep racecar engine components spinning at thousands of revolutions per second. Another resource is tire tread, which must remain above a minimum threshold if the driver is to be able to safely accelerate, decelerate, and round turns.

Thus, the purpose of a pit stop is to refuel and change tires. From the moment that auto racing was born, racecar drivers began wrestling with how best to perform and organize these services. Obviously, at various points during a race, one person could perform the required tasks of pouring fuel, jacking up the racecar, and changing its four tires. Using a single person would never do, however, because in an auto race, speed is truly the name of the game. Racers recognized that several people could refuel a car and change its tires much faster than one person, and the idea of the speedway pit crew was born.

Division of Labor in the Pit

In gauging the production of pit services at a motor speedway, the fundamental unit of measurement is the rate at which refueling and tire-changing services are performed per unit of time. The involvement of several people is required to perform these services most rapidly. Hence, motor speedway pit crews have a natural division of labor: refueling, jacking up the car, carrying and changing front and rear tires.

After years of trial and error, racecar drivers settled on pit crews of seven members each. They found that given the technology involved in the provision of pit services, this division of labor yields the fastest rate of production.

Specialization Breeds Production Improvements in the Pits

Attaining the speediest possible pit stop requires each pit crew member's function to be highly specialized. Today, the person who jacks up a racecar aims to haul a 25-pound aluminum jack from the car's right side to the left within 3.8 seconds. Tire changers do their best to get five lug nuts off a car's wheel within 1.2 seconds. Tire carriers aim to raise 60-pound tires from the pavement to mounted positions on the car within 0.7 second. While five crew members carry out these activities with the car's body and wheels, the two crew members responsible for refueling are punching the necks of fuel cans into tank openings.

Twenty years ago, pit crews were doing well to complete a pit stop in fewer than 30 seconds. Today, a pit crew that takes more than 16 seconds to complete a stop is regarded as having failed to deliver a timely service to the driver. Thus, two decades of careful attention to division of labor and specialization have reduced by nearly 50 percent the time that a racecar driver typically spends obtaining pit services instead of racing in pursuit of prize money.

Test your understanding of this chapter by going online to **MyEconLab**.
In the Study Plan for this chapter, select Section N: News.

For Critical Analysis

1. Why do you suppose that having more than seven members tends to reduce a pit crew's service output per unit of time? (Hint: In a service pit area at a racetrack, there is limited physical space beside or beneath a racecar.)

2. Why do you suppose that there is a school, called 5 Off 5 On, that trains individuals in the fine art of rapidly removing and replacing the five lug nuts that attach tires to the wheels of racecars?

Web Resources

1. For information about a pit crew training program provided by the National Association for Stock Car Auto Racing (NASCAR), go to www.econtoday.com/chapter02.

2. To learn more about characteristics that NASCAR teams desire in their pit crew members, go to www.econtoday.com/chapter02.

Research Project

Compare the above description of the activities of a speedway pit crew with those of pin makers as described by Adam Smith (see page 42). In addition, compare the division of labor in the provision of pit services and eighteenth-century pin making to the division of labor in the production of educational services at your college or university (or, if you prefer, another production process with which you are familiar). Is the division of labor a fundamental aspect of production of goods and services?

Here is what you should know after reading this chapter. **MyEconLab** will help you identify what you know, and where to go when you need to practice.

WHAT YOU SHOULD KNOW

WHERE TO GO TO PRACTICE

The Problem of Scarcity, Even for the Affluent   Scarcity is very different from poverty. No one can obtain all one desires from nature without sacrifice. Thus, even the richest people face scarcity because they have to make choices among alternatives. Despite their high levels of income or wealth, affluent people, like everyone else, want more than they can have (in terms of goods, power, prestige, and so on).

scarcity, 28
production, 28
land, 28
labor, 29
physical capital, 29
human capital, 29
entrepreneurship, 29
goods, 29
economic goods, 29
services, 30

- **MyEconLab** Study Plan 2.1
- Audio introduction to Chapter 2
- Video: Scarcity, Resources, and Production

(continued)

(continued)

WHAT YOU SHOULD KNOW		WHERE TO GO TO PRACTICE
Why Economists Consider Individuals' Wants but Not Their "Needs" Goods are all things from which individuals derive satisfaction. Economic goods are those for which the desired quantity exceeds the amount that is directly available from nature at a zero price. To economists, the term *need* is undefinable, whereas humans have unlimited *wants*, which are defined as the goods and services on which we place a positive value.		• **MyEconLab** Study Plan 2.2
Why Scarcity Leads People to Evaluate Opportunity Costs Opportunity cost is the highest-valued alternative that one must give up to obtain an item. The trade-offs that we face as individuals and as a society can be represented by a production possibilities curve (PPC), and moving from one point on a PPC to another entails incurring an opportunity cost. Along a PPC, all currently available resources and technology are being used, so obtaining more of one good requires shifting resources to production of that good and away from production of another. That is, there is an opportunity cost of allocating scarce resources toward producing one good instead of another good.	opportunity cost, 31 production possibilities curve (PPC), 32 **KEY FIGURE** Figure 2-1, 33	• **MyEconLab** Study Plans 2.3, 2.4 • Animated Figure 2-1 • ABC News Video: Incentives for Perfect Attendance
Why Obtaining Increasing Increments of a Good Requires Giving Up More and More Units of Other Goods Typically, resources are specialized. Thus, when society allocates additional resources to producing more units of a good, it must increasingly employ resources that would be better suited for producing other goods. As a result, the law of increasing relative cost holds. Each additional unit of a good can be obtained only by giving up more and more of other goods, which means that the production possibilities curve is bowed outward.	technology, 35 efficiency, 36 inefficient point, 36 law of increasing relative cost, 37 **KEY FIGURES** Figure 2-3, 37 Figure 2-4, 38	• **MyEconLab** Study Plan 2.5 • Animated Figures 2-3, 2-4
The Trade-Off Between Consumption Goods and Capital Goods If we allocate more resources to producing capital goods today, then, other things being equal, the economy will grow faster than it would have otherwise. Thus, the production possibilities curve will shift outward by a larger amount in the future, which means that we can have more consumption goods in the future. The trade-off, however, is that producing more capital goods today entails giving up consumption goods today.	consumption, 39	• **MyEconLab** Study Plans 2.6, 2.7

(continued)

(continued)

PROBLEMS

All problems are assignable in myeconlab. *Answers to odd-numbered problems appear at the back of the book.*

2-1. Define opportunity cost. What is your opportunity cost of attending a class at 11:00 A.M.? How does it differ from your opportunity cost of attending a class at 8:00 A.M.?

2-2. If you receive a ticket to a concert at no charge, what, if anything, is your opportunity cost of attending the concert? How does your opportunity cost change if miserable weather on the night of the concert requires you to leave much earlier for the concert hall and greatly extends the time it takes to get home afterward?

2-3. Recently, a woman named Mary Krawiec attended an auction in Troy, New York. At the auction, a bank was seeking to sell a foreclosed property: a large Victorian house suffering from years of neglect in a neighborhood in which many properties had been on the market for years yet remained unsold. Her $10 offer was the highest bid in the auction, and she handed over a $10 bill for a title to ownership. Once she acquired the house, however, she became responsible for all taxes on the property and for an overdue water bill of $2,000. In addition, to make the house habitable, she and her husband devoted months of time and unpaid labor to renovating the property. In the process, they incurred explicit expenses totaling $65,000.

Why do you suppose that the bank was willing to sell the house to Ms. Krawiec for only $10? (Hint: Contemplate the bank's expected gain, net of all explicit and opportunity costs, if it had attempted to make the house habitable.)

2-4. The following table illustrates the points a student can earn on examinations in economics and biology if the student uses all available hours for study.

Economics	Biology
100	40
90	50
80	60
70	70
60	80
50	90
40	100

Plot this student's production possibilities curve. Does the PPC illustrate the law of increasing relative cost?

2-5. Based on the information provided in Problem 2-4, what is the opportunity cost to this student of allocating enough additional study time on economics to move her grade up from a 90 to a 100?

2-6. Consider a change in the table in Problem 2-4. The student's set of opportunities is now as follows:

Economics	Biology
100	40
90	60
80	75
70	85
60	93
50	98
40	100

Does the PPC illustrate the law of increasing relative cost? What is the opportunity cost to this student for the additional amount of study time on economics required to move her grade from 60 to 70? From 90 to 100?

2-7. Construct a production possibilities curve for a nation facing increasing opportunity costs for producing food and video games. Show how the PPC changes given the following events.

a. A new and better fertilizer is invented.

b. Immigration occurs, and immigrants' labor can be employed in both the agricultural sector and the video game sector.

c. A new programming language is invented that is less costly to code and is more memory-efficient, enabling the use of smaller game cartridges.

d. A heat wave and drought result in a 10 percent decrease in usable farmland.

Consider the following diagram when answering Problems 2-8, 2-9, and 2-10.

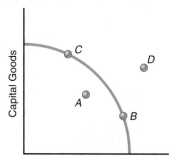

2-8. During a debate on the floor of the U.S. Senate, Senator Creighton states, "Our nation should not devote so many of its fully employed resources to producing capital goods because we already are not producing enough consumption goods for our citizens." Compared with the other labeled points on the diagram, which one could be con-

sistent with the *current* production combination choice that Senator Creighton believes the nation has made?

2-9. In response to Senator Creighton's statement reported in Problem 2-8, Senator Long replies, "We must remain at our current production combination if we want to be able to produce more consumption goods in the future." Of the labeled points on the diagram, which one could depict the *future* production combination Senator Long has in mind?

2-10. Senator Borman interjects the following comment after the statements by Senators Creighton and Long reported in Problems 2-8 and 2-9: "In fact, both of my esteemed colleagues are wrong, because an unacceptably large portion of our nation's resources is currently unemployed." Of the labeled points on the diagram, which one is consistent with Senator Borman's position?

2-11. A nation's residents can allocate their scarce resources either to producing consumption goods or to producing human capital—that is, providing themselves with training and education. The following table displays the production possibilities for this nation:

Production Combination	Units of Consumption Goods	Units of Human Capital
A	0	100
B	10	97
C	20	90
D	30	75
E	40	55
F	50	30
G	60	0

a. Suppose that the nation's residents currently produce combination A. What is the opportunity cost of increasing production of consumption goods by 10 units? By 60 units?

b. Does the law of increasing relative cost hold true for this nation? Why or why not?

2-12. Like physical capital, human capital produced in the present can be applied to the production of future goods and services. Consider the table in Problem 2-11, and suppose that the nation's residents are trying to choose between combination C and combination F. Other things being equal, will the future production possibilities curve for this nation be located farther outward if the nation chooses combination F instead of combination C? Explain.

2-13. You can wash, fold, and iron a basket of laundry in two hours and prepare a meal in one hour. Your roommate can wash, fold, and iron a basket of laundry in three hours and prepare a meal in one hour. Who has the absolute advantage in laundry, and who has an absolute advantage in meal preparation? Who has the comparative advantage in laundry, and who has a comparative advantage in meal preparation?

2-14. Based on the information in Problem 2-13, should you and your roommate specialize in a particular task? Why? And if so, who should specialize in which task? Show how much labor time you save if you choose to "trade" an appropriate task with your roommate as opposed to doing it yourself.

2-15. Using only the concept of comparative advantage, evaluate this statement: "A professor with a Ph.D. in physics should never mow his or her own lawn, because this would fail to take into account the professor's comparative advantage."

2-16. Country A and country B produce the same consumption goods and capital goods and currently have *identical* production possibilities curves. They also have the same resources at present, and they have access to the same technology.

a. At present, does either country have a comparative advantage in producing capital goods? Consumption goods?

b. Currently, country A has chosen to produce more consumption goods, compared with country B. Other things being equal, which country will experience the larger outward shift of its PPC during the next year?

ECONOMICS ON THE NET

Opportunity Cost and Labor Force Participation Many students choose to forgo full-time employment to concentrate on their studies, thereby incurring a sizable opportunity cost. This application explores the nature of this opportunity cost.

Title: College Enrollment and Work Activity of High School Graduates

Navigation: Go to www.econtoday.com/chapter02 to visit the Bureau of Labor Statistics (BLS) home page. Select A–Z Index and then click on *Educational attainment (Statistics)*. Finally, under the heading "Economic News Releases," click on "Annual," and then click on *College Enrollment and Work Activity of High School Graduates*.

Application Read the abbreviated report on college enrollment and work activity of high school graduates. Then answer the following questions.

1. Based on the article, explain who the BLS considers to be in the labor force and who it does not view as part of the labor force.

2. What is the difference in labor force participation rates between high school students entering four-year universities and those entering two-year universities? Using the concept of opportunity cost, explain the difference.

3. What is the difference in labor force participation rates between part-time college students and full-time college students? Using the concept of opportunity cost, explain the difference.

For Group Study and Analysis Read the last paragraph of the article. Then divide the class into two groups. The first group should explain, based on the concept of opportunity cost, the difference in labor force participation rates between youths not in school but with a high school diploma and youths not in school and without a high school diploma. The second group should explain, based on opportunity cost, the difference in labor force participation rates between men and women not in school but with a high school diploma and men and women not in school and without a high school diploma.

ANSWERS TO QUICK QUIZZES

p. 30: (i) Scarcity; (ii) land . . . labor . . . physical . . . human . . . entrepreneurship; (iii) Wants; (iv) need

p. 34: (i) next-highest; (ii) opportunity; (iii) next-best; (iv) production possibilities

p. 38: (i) production possibilities; (ii) fixed; (iii) outside . . . inside; (iv) outward

p. 40: (i) Capital; (ii) more . . . smaller

p. 44: (i) higher; (ii) comparative; (iii) lowest; (iv) division

Demand and Supply

3

Three decades ago, about 45 percent of U.S. residents were classified as "overweight." Today, estimates indicate that as many as 67 percent of U.S. residents fall into this category. About 31 percent of the U.S. population is classified as extremely overweight, or obese, which is more than double the percentage of 30 years ago. One explanation for higher body weights is that people are exercising less, and thus the calories they consume are being transformed into body mass instead of energy. Another is that people are simply choosing to consume more food than in years past. Determining why individuals are opting to eat more requires an understanding, which you will develop by reading this chapter, of how two key factors—price and income—influence desired consumption of an item such as food.

LEARNING OBJECTIVES

After reading this chapter, you should be able to:

➤ Explain the law of demand

➤ Discuss the difference between money prices and relative prices

➤ Distinguish between changes in demand and changes in quantity demanded

➤ Explain the law of supply

➤ Distinguish between changes in supply and changes in quantity supplied

➤ Understand how the interaction of the demand for and supply of a commodity determines the market price of the commodity and the equilibrium quantity of the commodity that is produced and consumed

? DID YOU KNOW THAT no new oil refineries—facilities that refine crude oil into transportation fuels such as gasoline—have been built in the United States since 1976? Recently, however, Hyperion, a Dallas-based company, announced its intention to build a new refinery at Elk Point, South Dakota, which would refine about 400,000 barrels of heavy Canadian crude oil per day. Hyperion indicated that the key factor motivating its decision was a significant, sustained increase in the U.S. price of gasoline during the preceding years.

If we use the economist's primary set of tools, *demand* and *supply,* we can develop a better understanding of why we sometimes observe relatively large increases in the price of gasoline. We can also better understand why a persistent increase in the price of gasoline ultimately induces an increase in gasoline production. Demand and supply are two ways of categorizing the influences on the prices of goods that you buy and the quantities available. Indeed, demand and supply characterize much economic analysis of the world around us.

As you will see throughout this text, the operation of the forces of demand and supply takes place in *markets*. A **market** is an abstract concept summarizing all of the arrangements individuals have for exchanging with one another. Goods and services are sold in markets, such as the automobile market, the health care market, and the market for Internet DSL services. Workers offer their services in the labor market. Companies, or firms, buy workers' labor services in the labor market. Firms also buy other inputs in order to produce the goods and services that you buy as a consumer. Firms purchase machines, buildings, and land. These markets are in operation at all times. One of the most important activities in these markets is the determination of the prices of all of the inputs and outputs that are bought and sold in our complicated economy. To understand the determination of prices, you first need to look at the law of demand.

Demand

Demand has a special meaning in economics. It refers to the quantities of specific goods or services that individuals, taken singly or as a group, will purchase at various possible prices, other things being constant. We can therefore talk about the demand for microprocessor chips, french fries, multifunction printer-copiers, children, and criminal activities.

The Law of Demand

Associated with the concept of demand is the **law of demand,** which can be stated as follows:

> *When the price of a good goes up, people buy less of it, other things being equal. When the price of a good goes down, people buy more of it, other things being equal.*

The law of demand tells us that the quantity demanded of any commodity is inversely related to its price, other things being equal. In an inverse relationship, one variable moves up in value when the other moves down. The law of demand states that a change in price causes a change in the quantity demanded in the *opposite* direction.

Notice that we tacked on to the end of the law of demand the statement "other things being equal." We referred to this in Chapter 1 as the *ceteris paribus* assumption. It means, for example, that when we predict that people will buy fewer DVD players if their price goes up, we are holding constant the price of all other goods in the economy as well as people's incomes. Implicitly, therefore, if we are assuming that no other

Market
All of the arrangements that individuals have for exchanging with one another. Thus, for example, we can speak of the labor market, the automobile market, and the credit market.

Demand
A schedule showing how much of a good or service people will purchase at any price during a specified time period, other things being constant.

Law of demand
The observation that there is a negative, or inverse, relationship between the price of any good or service and the quantity demanded, holding other factors constant.

How does the law of demand affect how much gas people buy?

prices change when we examine the price behavior of DVD players, we are looking at the *relative* price of DVD players.

The law of demand is supported by millions of observations of people's behavior in the marketplace. Theoretically, it can be derived from an economic model based on rational behavior, as was discussed in Chapter 1. Basically, if nothing else changes and the price of a good falls, the lower price induces us to buy more over a certain period of time because we can enjoy additional net gains that were unavailable at the higher price. If you examine your own behavior, you will see that it generally follows the law of demand.

Relative Prices versus Money Prices

The **relative price** of any commodity is its price in terms of another commodity. The price that you pay in dollars and cents for any good or service at any point in time is called its **money price.** You might hear from your grandparents, "My first new car cost only fifteen hundred dollars." The implication, of course, is that the price of cars today is outrageously high because the average new car may cost $32,000. But that is not an accurate comparison. What was the price of the average house during that same year? Perhaps it was only $12,000. By comparison, then, given that the average price of houses today is close to $270,000, the price of a new car today doesn't sound so far out of line, does it?

How much have both the price of attending college and the relative price of textbooks increased in recent years?

Relative price
The money price of one commodity divided by the money price of another commodity; the number of units of one commodity that must be sacrificed to purchase one unit of another commodity.

Money price
The price that we observe today, expressed in today's dollars; also called the *absolute* or *nominal price*.

EXAMPLE
College Students Face Higher Relative Prices

If you feel that you are paying relatively high prices for your college training, you are correct. During the past 20 years, average tuition and fees at U.S. colleges and universities have increased by 67 percent more than the average prices of other goods and services. The price of an average college textbook has risen about 60 percent compared with the average prices of other items. Thus,

the relative prices of college enrollment and reading materials have increased substantially.

FOR CRITICAL ANALYSIS
In the past two decades, has the average price of attending college increased or decreased relative to the average price of a textbook?

The point is that money prices during different time periods don't tell you much. You have to calculate relative prices. Consider an example of the price of 4-gigabyte flash memory drives versus the price of 4 gigabytes of rewritable DVDs from last year and this year. In Table 3-1 on page 54, we show the money prices of flash memory drives and rewritable DVDs for two years during which they have both gone down. That means that in today's dollars we have to pay out less for both flash memory drives and rewritable DVDs. If we look, though, at the relative prices of flash memory drives and rewritable DVDs, we find that last year, 4-gigabyte flash memory drives were four times as expensive as 4-gigabytes of rewritable DVDs, whereas this year they are only three and a half times as expensive. Conversely, if we compare rewritable DVDs to flash memory drives, last year the price of rewritable DVDs was 25 percent of the price of flash memory drives, but today the price of flash memory drives is about

TABLE 3-1

Money Price versus Relative Price

The money prices of both 4-gigabyte flash memory drives and 4 gigabytes of rewritable DVDs have fallen. But the relative price of rewritable DVDs has risen (or conversely, the relative price of flash memory drives has fallen).

	Money Price		Relative Price	
	Price Last Year	Price This Year	Price Last Year	Price This Year
4-Gigabyte flash memory drives	$20	$14	$\dfrac{\$20}{\$5} = 4.0$	$\dfrac{\$14}{\$4} = 3.50$
4 Gigabytes of rewritable DVDs	$5	$4	$\dfrac{\$5}{\$20} = 0.25$	$\dfrac{\$4}{\$14} = 0.29$

29 percent of the price of flash memory drives. In the one-year period, although both prices have declined in money terms, the relative price of rewritable DVDs has risen relative to that of flash memory drives.

Sometimes relative price changes occur because the quality of a product improves, thereby bringing about a decrease in the item's effective *price per constant-quality unit*. The price of an item may decrease simply because producers have reduced the item's quality. Thus, when evaluating the effects of price changes, we must always compare *price per constant-quality unit*.

For many Web surfers, speed defines quality. What difference does it make when the speed of Internet access is taken into account in comparisons of monthly prices for Internet broadband access?

E-COMMERCE EXAMPLE
Adjusting the Price of Broadband Service for Quality

In most U.S. locales, basic broadband Internet service is priced at about $15 per month. This appears to compare favorably with most locations in France, where the price of basic broadband Internet access is about $36 per month.

U.S. providers, however, typically offer broadband speeds of less than 0.77 megabit per second, implying a speed-adjusted price as high as $20 per megabit in most U.S. locales. In contrast, French service providers offer speeds as high as 20 megabits per second, yielding a

speed-adjusted price as low as $1.80 per megabit. Thus, the U.S. speed-adjusted price is nearly 10 times higher than the French price.

FOR CRITICAL ANALYSIS
In some U.S. locales, broadband access service with a speed of 20 megabits per second is now available at a price of about $50 per month. How does this price compare with the speed-adjusted price in France?

QUICK QUIZ

See page 81 for the answers. Review concepts from this section in MyEconLab.

The **law of demand** posits a(n) _____ relationship between the quantity demanded of a good and its price, other things being equal.

The law of _____ applies when other things, such as income and the prices of all other goods and services, are held constant.

The Demand Schedule

Let's take a hypothetical demand situation to see how the inverse relationship between the price and the quantity demanded looks (holding other things equal). We will consider the quantity of 256-megabyte secure digital cards (also known as "SD cards," used in cameras and other digital devices) demanded *per year*. Without stating the *time dimension*, we could not make sense out of this demand relationship because the numbers would be different if we were talking about the quantity demanded per month or the quantity demanded per decade.

In addition to implicitly or explicitly stating a time dimension for a demand relationship, we are also implicitly referring to *constant-quality units* of the good or service in question. Prices are always expressed in constant-quality units in order to avoid the problem of comparing commodities that are in fact not truly comparable.

In panel (a) of Figure 3-1, we see that if the price is $1 apiece, 50 secure digital (SD) cards will be bought each year by our representative individual, but if the price is $5 apiece, only 10 SD cards will be bought each year. This reflects the law of demand. Panel (a) is also called simply demand, or a *demand schedule*, because it gives a schedule of alternative quantities demanded per year at different possible prices.

The Demand Curve

Tables expressing relationships between two variables can be represented in graphical terms. To do this, we need only construct a graph that has the price per constant-quality secure digital card on the vertical axis and the quantity measured in constant-quality SD

FIGURE 3-1

The Individual Demand Schedule and the Individual Demand Curve

In panel (a), we show combinations *A* through *E* of the quantities of secure digital (SD) cards demanded, measured in constant-quality units at prices ranging from $5 down to $1 apiece. These combinations are points on the demand schedule. In panel (b), we plot combinations *A* through *E* on a grid. The result is the individual demand curve for SD cards.

Panel (a)

Combination	Price per Constant-Quality Secure Digital Card	Quantity of Constant-Quality Secure Digital Cards per Year
A	$5	10
B	4	20
C	3	30
D	2	40
E	1	50

Demand curve

A graphical representation of the demand schedule; a negatively sloped line showing the inverse relationship between the price and the quantity demanded (other things being equal).

Market demand

The demand of all consumers in the marketplace for a particular good or service. The summation at each price of the quantity demanded by each individual.

cards per year on the horizontal axis. All we have to do is take combinations *A* through *E* from panel (a) of Figure 3-1 and plot those points in panel (b). Now we connect the points with a smooth line, and *voilà*, we have a **demand curve.** It is downward sloping (from left to right) to indicate the inverse relationship between the price of SD cards and the quantity demanded per year. Our presentation of demand schedules and curves applies equally well to all commodities, including dental floss, bagels, textbooks, credit, and labor. Remember, the demand curve is simply a graphical representation of the law of demand.

Individual versus Market Demand Curves

The demand schedule shown in panel (a) of Figure 3-1 on the previous page and the resulting demand curve shown in panel (b) are both given for an individual. As we shall see, the determination of price in the marketplace depends on, among other things, the

---

FIGURE 3-2

The Horizontal Summation of Two Demand Curves

Panel (a) shows how to sum the demand schedule for one buyer with that of another buyer. In column 2 is the quantity demanded by buyer 1, taken from panel (a) of Figure 3-1 on page 55. Column 4 is the sum of columns 2 and 3.

We plot the demand curve for buyer 1 in panel (b) and the demand curve for buyer 2 in panel (c). When we add those two demand curves horizontally, we get the market demand curve for two buyers, shown in panel (d).

Panel (a)

(1) Price per Secure Digital Card	(2) Buyer 1's Quantity Demanded	(3) Buyer 2's Quantity Demanded	(4) = (2) + (3) Combined Quantity Demanded per Year
$5	10	10	20
4	20	20	40
3	30	40	70
2	40	50	90
1	50	60	110

market demand for a particular commodity. The way in which we measure a market demand schedule and derive a market demand curve for secure digital cards or any other good or service is by summing (at each price) the individual quantities demanded by all buyers in the market. Suppose that the market demand for SD cards consists of only two buyers: buyer 1, for whom we've already shown the demand schedule, and buyer 2, whose demand schedule is displayed in column 3 of panel (a) of Figure 3-2 on the facing page. Column 1 shows the price, and column 2 shows the quantity demanded by buyer 1 at each price. These data are taken directly from Figure 3-1 on page 55. In column 3, we show the quantity demanded by buyer 2. Column 4 shows the total quantity demanded at each price, which is obtained by simply adding columns 2 and 3. Graphically, in panel (d) of Figure 3-2, we add the demand curves of buyer 1 [panel (b)] and buyer 2 [panel (c)] to derive the market demand curve.

There are, of course, numerous potential consumers of SD cards. We'll simply assume that the summation of all of the consumers in the market results in a demand schedule, given in panel (a) of Figure 3-3, and a demand curve, given in panel (b). The quantity demanded is now measured in millions of units per year. Remember, panel (b) in Figure 3-3 shows the market demand curve for the millions of users of SD cards. The "market" demand curve that we derived in Figure 3-2 was undertaken assuming that there were only two buyers in the entire market. That's why we assume that the "market" demand curve for two buyers in panel (d) of Figure 3-2 is not a smooth line, whereas the true market demand curve in panel (b) of Figure 3-3 is a smooth line with no kinks.

FIGURE 3-3

The Market Demand Schedule for Secure Digital Cards

In panel (a), we add up the existing demand schedules for secure digital cards. In panel (b), we plot the quantities from panel (a) on a grid; connecting them produces the market demand curve for secure digital cards.

Panel (a)

Price per Constant-Quality Secure Digital Card	Total Quantity Demanded of Constant-Quality Secure Digital Cards per Year (millions)
$5	2
4	4
3	6
2	8
1	10

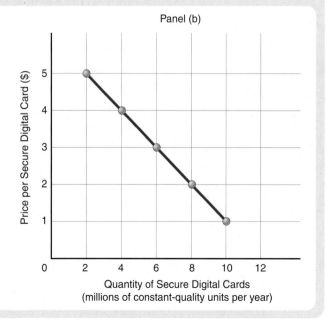

QUICK QUIZ   *See page 81 for the answers. Review concepts from this section in MyEconLab.*

We measure the **demand schedule** in terms of a time dimension and in _____-quality units.

The _____ _____ curve is derived by summing the quantity demanded by individuals at each price. Graphically, we add the individual demand curves horizontally to derive the total, or market, demand curve.

Shifts in Demand

Assume that the federal government gives every student registered in a college, university, or technical school in the United States a laptop computer with a slot for secure digital cards. The demand curve presented in panel (b) of Figure 3-3 on the preceding page would no longer be an accurate representation of total market demand for SD cards. What we have to do is shift the curve outward, or to the right, to represent the rise in demand that would result from this program. There will now be an increase in the number of SD cards demanded at *each and every possible price*. The demand curve shown in Figure 3-4 will shift from D_1 to D_2. Take any price, say, $3 per SD card. Originally, before the federal government giveaway of laptop computers, the amount demanded at $3 was 6 million SD cards per year. After the government giveaway of laptop computers, however, the new amount demanded at the $3 price is 10 million SD cards per year. What we have seen is a shift in the demand for SD cards.

Under different circumstances, the shift can also go in the opposite direction. What if colleges uniformly prohibited the use of laptop computers by any of their students? Such a regulation would cause a shift inward—to the left—of the demand curve for SD cards. In Figure 3-4, the demand curve would shift to D_3; the number demanded would now be less at each and every possible price.

The Other Determinants of Demand

The demand curve in panel (b) of Figure 3-3 is drawn with other things held constant, specifically all of the other factors that determine how many SD cards will be bought.

FIGURE 3-4

A Shift in the Demand Curve

If some factor other than price changes, we can show its effect by moving the entire demand curve, say, from D_1 to D_2. We have assumed in our example that this move was precipitated by the government's giving a laptop computer to every registered college student in the United States. Thus, at *all* prices, a larger number of secure digital cards would be demanded than before. Curve D_3 represents reduced demand compared to curve D_1, caused by a prohibition of laptop computers on campus.

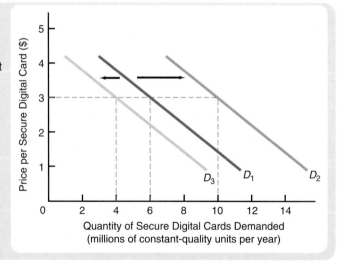

There are many such determinants. We refer to these determinants as *ceteris paribus* **conditions,** and they include consumers' income; tastes and preferences; the prices of related goods; expectations regarding future prices and future incomes; and market size (number of potential buyers). Let's examine each of these determinants more closely.

INCOME For most goods, an increase in income will lead to an increase in demand. That is, an increase in income will lead to a rightward shift in the position of the demand curve from, say, D_1 to D_2 in Figure 3-4. You can avoid confusion about shifts in curves by always relating a rise in demand to a rightward shift in the demand curve and a fall in demand to a leftward shift in the demand curve. Goods for which the demand rises when consumer income rises are called **normal goods.** Most goods, such as shoes, computers, and flash memory drives, are "normal goods." For some goods, however, demand *falls* as income rises. These are called **inferior goods.** Beans might be an example. As households get richer, they tend to purchase fewer and fewer beans and purchase more and more meat. (The terms *normal* and *inferior* are merely part of the economist's lexicon; no value judgments are associated with them.)

Remember, a shift to the left in the demand curve represents a decrease in demand, and a shift to the right represents an increase in demand.

TASTES AND PREFERENCES A change in consumer tastes in favor of a good can shift its demand curve outward to the right. When Pokémon trading cards became the rage, the demand curve for them shifted outward to the right; when the rage died out, the demand curve shifted inward to the left. Fashions depend to a large extent on people's tastes and preferences. Economists have little to say about the determination of tastes; that is, they don't have any "good" theories of taste determination or why people buy one brand of product rather than others. Advertisers, however, have various theories that they use to try to make consumers prefer their products over those of competitors.

How has "Web buzz" influenced preferences regarding remote-controlled toy helicopters and hence the demand for these items?

Ceteris paribus **conditions**
Determinants of the relationship between price and quantity that are unchanged along a curve; changes in these factors cause the curve to shift.

Normal goods
Goods for which demand rises as income rises. Most goods are normal goods.

Inferior goods
Goods for which demand falls as income rises.

E-COMMERCE EXAMPLE
Video Bloggers Generate a Takeoff in Toy Helicopter Demand

During the past couple of years, video bloggers on YouTube and Internet viral-network participants have directed Web viewers to creative videos of remote-controlled toy helicopters in action. Kids of all ages, including adults rediscovering the "child within," have been captivated by videos of toy helicopters rumbling above rough terrain, gliding over lakes, and being chased by housecats. Many have decided that they wish to have one of the toys to control on their own. As a consequence, the number of toy helicopters demanded at prevailing prices has risen by hundreds of thousands of units per year. The demand curve for remote-controlled toy helicopters has shifted outward and to the right.

FOR CRITICAL ANALYSIS
What do you suppose has happened in recent years to the demand for toy helicopters that are incapable of flying under their own power via remote control?

PRICES OF RELATED GOODS: SUBSTITUTES AND COMPLEMENTS Demand schedules are always drawn with the prices of all other commodities held constant. That is to say, when deriving a given demand curve, we assume that only the price of the good under study changes. For example, when we draw the demand curve for butter, we assume that the price of margarine is held constant. When we draw the demand curve for home cinema speakers, we assume that the price of surround-sound amplifiers is held constant. When we refer to *related goods*, we are talking about goods for which demand is interdependent. If a change in the price of one good shifts the demand for another good, those two goods have interdependent demands. There are two types of demand interdependencies: those in which goods are *substitutes* and those in which goods are *complements*. We can define and distinguish between substitutes and complements in terms of how the change in price of one commodity affects the demand for its related commodity.

Butter and margarine are **substitutes.** Either can be consumed to satisfy the same basic want. Let's assume that both products originally cost $2 per pound. If the price of butter remains the same and the price of margarine falls from $2 per pound to $1 per pound, people will buy more margarine and less butter. The demand curve for butter shifts inward to the left. If, conversely, the price of margarine rises from $2 per pound to $3 per pound, people will buy more butter and less margarine. The demand curve for butter shifts outward to the right. In other words, an increase in the price of margarine will lead to an increase in the demand for butter, and an increase in the price of butter will lead to an increase in the demand for margarine. For substitutes, a change in the price of a substitute will cause a change in demand *in the same direction*.

How do you suppose that laboratory techniques that replicate natural geologic processes are contributing to a decrease in the demand for diamonds extracted from the earth's interior?

Substitutes
Two goods are substitutes when a change in the price of one causes a shift in demand for the other in the same direction as the price change.

EXAMPLE
Diamonds May Not Really Be Forever

The day that sellers of diamonds have long dreaded has arrived. Several professionals who have each spent more than 700 hours in classrooms to become certified experts on precious stones examine three gems. The first gem is a real diamond, created by natural geologic processes beneath the earth's surface. The second is cubic zirconia, a fake diamond commonly used in costume jewelry. The third is something new—a "synthetic" diamond. It is a gem-quality diamond produced in a laboratory by machines that exert pressures 58,000 times that of the earth's at temperatures exceeding 2,300 degrees Fahrenheit. The jewelry experts readily distinguish cubic zirconia from the true diamond. But when they view the synthetic diamond, they cannot tell that it is not a real diamond until they examine it under a microscope and spot its inscribed serial number. Yet the experts have already pronounced the synthetic gem the highest quality of the three.

A number of U.S. jewelry retailers are utilizing synthetic diamonds, which are available at lower prices than real diamonds. At the same time, they are purchasing fewer real diamonds. Thus, the availability of the lower-priced substitute gems is reducing the demand for true gems.

FOR CRITICAL ANALYSIS
In what direction has the demand curve for real diamonds shifted as lower-priced synthetic diamonds have become available?

Complements
Two goods are complements when a change in the price of one causes an opposite shift in the demand for the other.

For **complements,** goods typically consumed together, the situation is reversed. Consider desktop computers and printers. We draw the demand curve for printers with the price of desktop computers held constant. If the price per constant-quality unit of computers decreases from, say, $700 to $500, that will encourage more people to purchase computer peripheral devices. They will now buy more printers, at any given printer price, than before. The demand curve for printers will shift outward to the right. If, by contrast, the price of desktop computers increases from $550 to $750, fewer people will purchase computer peripheral devices. The demand curve for printers will shift inward to the left. To summarize, a decrease in the price of computers leads to an increase in the demand for printers. An increase in the price of computers leads to a decrease in the demand for printers. Thus, for complements, a change in the price of a product will cause a change in demand *in the opposite direction* for the other good.

EXPECTATIONS Consumers' expectations regarding future prices and future incomes will prompt them to buy more or less of a particular good without a change in its current money price. For example, consumers getting wind of a scheduled 100 percent increase in the price of secure digital cards next month will buy more of them today at today's prices. Today's demand curve for SD cards will shift from D_1 to D_2 in Figure 3-4 on page 58. The opposite would occur if a decrease in the price of SD cards were scheduled for next month (from D_1 to D_3).

Expectations of a rise in income may cause consumers to want to purchase more of everything today at today's prices. Again, such a change in expectations of higher future income will cause a shift in the demand curve from D_1 to D_2 in Figure 3-4.

Finally, expectations that goods will not be available at any price will induce consumers to stock up now, increasing current demand.

MARKET SIZE (NUMBER OF POTENTIAL BUYERS) An increase in the number of potential buyers (holding buyers' incomes constant) at any given price shifts the market demand curve outward. Conversely, a reduction in the number of potential buyers at any given price shifts the market demand curve inward.

Changes in Demand versus Changes in Quantity Demanded

We have made repeated references to demand and to quantity demanded. It is important to realize that there is a difference between a *change in demand* and a *change in quantity demanded*.

Demand refers to a schedule of planned rates of purchase and depends on a great many *ceteris paribus* conditions, such as incomes, expectations, and the prices of substitutes or complements. Whenever there is a change in a *ceteris paribus* condition, there will be a change in demand—a shift in the entire demand curve to the right or to the left.

A quantity demanded is a specific quantity at a specific price, represented by a single point on a demand curve. When price changes, quantity demanded changes according to the law of demand, and there will be a movement from one point to another along the same demand curve. Look at Figure 3-5 on the following page. At a price of $3 per secure digital card, 6 million SD cards per year are demanded. If the price falls to $1, quantity demanded increases to 10 million per year. This movement occurs because the current market price for the product changes. In Figure 3-5, you can see the arrow pointing down the given demand curve D.

When you think of demand, think of the entire curve. Quantity demanded, in contrast, is represented by a single point on the demand curve.

> ***A change or shift in demand is a movement of the entire curve. The only thing that can cause the entire curve to move is a change in a determinant other than its own price.***

If the price of iPods goes down, what will happen to the demand for amplified speaker systems for iPods?

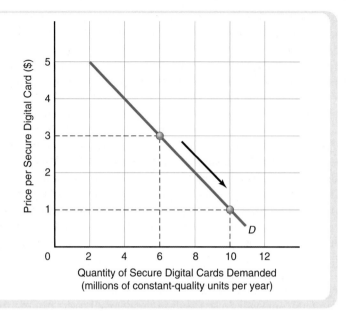

FIGURE 3-5

Movement Along a Given Demand Curve

A change in price changes the quantity of a good demanded. This can be represented as movement along a given demand schedule. If, in our example, the price of secure digital cards falls from $3 to $1 apiece, the quantity demanded will increase from 6 million to 10 million units per year.

In economic analysis, we cannot emphasize too much the following distinction that must constantly be made:

A change in a good's own price leads to a change in quantity demanded for any given demand curve, other things held constant. This is a movement along *the curve.*

A change in any of the ceteris paribus *conditions for demand leads to a change in demand. This causes a* shift *of the curve.*

Demand curves are drawn with determinants other than the price of the good held constant. These other determinants, called *ceteris paribus* **conditions,** are (1) _____; (2) _____; (3) _____; (4) _____; and (5) _____ at any given price. If any one of these determinants changes, the demand curve will shift to the right or to the left.

A change in demand comes about only because of a change in the _____ _____ conditions of demand. This change in demand is a shift in the demand curve to the left or to the right.

A change in the quantity demanded comes about when there is a change in the price of the good (other things held constant). Such a change in quantity demanded involves _____ _____ a given demand curve.

The Law of Supply

Supply
A schedule showing the relationship between price and quantity supplied for a specified period of time, other things being equal.

The other side of the basic model in economics involves the quantities of goods and services that firms will offer for sale to the market. The **supply** of any good or service is the amount that firms will produce and offer for sale under certain conditions during a specified time period. The relationship between price and quantity supplied, called the **law of supply,** can be summarized as follows:

> *At higher prices, a larger quantity will generally be supplied than at lower prices, all other things held constant. At lower prices, a smaller quantity will generally be supplied than at higher prices, all other things held constant.*

There is generally a direct relationship between price and quantity supplied. For supply, as the price rises, the quantity supplied rises; as price falls, the quantity supplied also falls. Producers are normally willing to produce and sell more of their product at a higher price than at a lower price, other things being constant. At $5 per secure digital card, manufacturers would almost certainly be willing to supply a larger quantity than at $1 per SD card, assuming, of course, that no other prices in the economy had changed.

As with the law of demand, millions of instances in the real world have given us confidence in the law of supply. On a theoretical level, the law of supply is based on a model in which producers and sellers seek to make the most gain possible from their activities. For example, as a manufacturer attempts to produce more and more SD cards over the same time period, it will eventually have to hire more workers, pay overtime wages (which are higher), and overutilize its machines. Only if offered a higher price per SD card will the manufacturer be willing to incur these higher costs. That is why the law of supply implies a direct relationship between price and quantity supplied.

How do you suppose that producers of minerals responded when prices of minerals rose during the 2000s?

> **Law of supply**
> The observation that the higher the price of a good, the more of that good sellers will make available over a specified time period, other things being equal.

EXAMPLE
Mining Production's Direct Response to Higher Prices for Minerals

Prices of minerals have jumped significantly during the 2000s. For instance, the price of uranium oxide, a mineral used as a key ingredient in fuel for nuclear power plants, has risen from just over $7 per pound in 2001 to more than $40 per pound today. Prices of other minerals, including nickel, zinc, copper, iron ore, and gold, have climbed as well. In response, mining companies have unveiled plans to carve out more mines. For instance, global minerals-producing firms such as BHP Billiton, Anglo American PLC, and OAO Rusal have indicated that they intend to nearly double their mining production by 2011.

FOR CRITICAL ANALYSIS
Some observers of markets for minerals suggest that prices of minerals may decline during the 2010s. Other things being equal, how would you expect mining production to respond if this prediction holds true?

The Supply Schedule

Just as we were able to construct a demand schedule, we can construct a *supply schedule*, which is a table relating prices to the quantity supplied at each price. A supply schedule can also be referred to simply as *supply*. It is a set of planned production rates that depends on the price of the product. We show the individual supply schedule for a hypothetical producer in panel (a) of Figure 3-6 on the next page. At a price of $1 per secure digital card, for example, this producer will supply 20,000 SD cards per year. At a price of $5 per SD card, this producer will supply 55,000 SD cards per year.

FIGURE 3-6

The Individual Producer's Supply Schedule and Supply Curve for Secure Digital Cards

Panel (a) shows that at higher prices, a hypothetical supplier will be willing to provide a greater quantity of secure digital cards. We plot the various price-quantity combinations in panel (a) on the grid in panel (b). When we connect these points, we create the individual supply curve for SD cards. It is positively sloped.

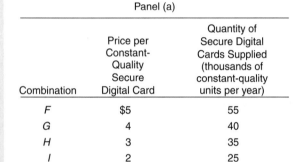

Panel (a)

Combination	Price per Constant-Quality Secure Digital Card	Quantity of Secure Digital Cards Supplied (thousands of constant-quality units per year)
F	$5	55
G	4	40
H	3	35
I	2	25
J	1	20

The Supply Curve

We can convert the supply schedule from panel (a) of Figure 3-6 into a **supply curve,** just as we earlier created a demand curve in Figure 3-1 on page 55. All we do is take the price-quantity combinations from panel (a) of Figure 3-6 and plot them in panel (b). We have labeled these combinations F through J. Connecting these points, we obtain an upward-sloping curve that shows the typically direct relationship between price and quantity supplied. Again, we have to remember that we are talking about quantity supplied *per year*, measured in constant-quality units.

The Market Supply Curve

Just as we summed the individual demand curves to obtain the market demand curve, we sum the individual producers' supply curves to obtain the market supply curve. Look at Figure 3-7, in which we horizontally sum two typical supply curves for manufacturers of SD cards. Supplier 1's data are taken from Figure 3-6. Supplier 2 is added. The numbers are presented in panel (a). The graphical representation of supplier 1 is in panel (b), of supplier 2 in panel (c), and of the summation in panel (d). The result, then, is the supply curve for SD cards, for suppliers 1 and 2. We assume that there are more suppliers of SD cards, however. The total market supply schedule and total market supply curve for SD cards are represented in Figure 3-8 on page 66, with the curve in panel (b) obtained by adding all of the supply curves such as those shown in panels (b) and (c) of Figure 3-7. Notice the difference between the market supply curve with only two suppliers in Figure 3-7 and the one with many suppliers—the entire true market—in panel (b) of Figure 3-8. (For simplicity, we assume that the true total market supply curve is a straight line.)

You Are There

To learn how the law of supply applies to the production of specialized insects, read **Beetle Factories Respond to Higher Demand for Weed-Eating Bugs,** on page 75.

FIGURE 3-7

Horizontal Summation of Supply Curves

In panel (a), we show the data for two individual suppliers of secure digital cards. Adding how much each is willing to supply at different prices, we come up with the combined quantities supplied in column 4. When we plot the values in columns 2 and 3 on grids from panels (b) and (c) and add them horizontally, we obtain the combined supply curve for the two suppliers in question, shown in panel (d).

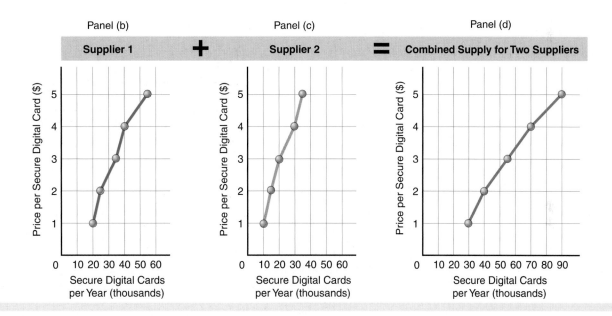

Panel (a)

(1) Price per Secure Digital Card	(2) Supplier 1's Quantity Supplied (thousands)	(3) Supplier 2's Quantity Supplied (thousands)	(4) = (2) + (3) Combined Quantity Supplied per Year (thousands)
$5	55	35	90
4	40	30	70
3	35	20	55
2	25	15	40
1	20	10	30

Note what happens at the market level when price changes. If the price is $3, the quantity supplied is 6 million. If the price goes up to $4, the quantity supplied increases to 8 million per year. If the price falls to $2, the quantity supplied decreases to 4 million per year. Changes in quantity supplied are represented by movements along the supply curve in panel (b) of Figure 3-8 on the following page.

QUICK QUIZ *See page 81 for the answers. Review concepts from this section in MyEconLab.*

There is normally a _____ relationship between price and quantity of a good supplied, other things held constant.

The _____ curve normally shows a direct relationship between price and quantity supplied. The _____

_____ curve is obtained by horizontally adding individual supply curves in the market.

FIGURE 3-8

The Market Supply Schedule and the Market Supply Curve for Secure Digital Cards

In panel (a), we show the summation of all the individual producers' supply schedules; in panel (b), we graph the resulting supply curve.

It represents the market supply curve for secure digital cards and is upward sloping.

Panel (a)

Price per Constant-Quality Secure Digital Card	Quantity of Secure Digital Cards Supplied (millions of constant-quality units per year)
$5	10
4	8
3	6
2	4
1	2

Panel (b)

Shifts in Supply

When we looked at demand, we found out that any change in anything relevant besides the price of the good or service caused the demand curve to shift inward or outward. The same is true for the supply curve. If something besides price changes and alters the willingness of suppliers to produce a good or service, we will see the entire supply curve shift.

Consider an example. There is a new method of manufacturing SD cards that significantly reduces the cost of production. In this situation, producers of SD cards will supply more product at *all* prices because their cost of so doing has fallen dramatically. Competition among manufacturers to produce more at each and every price will shift the supply curve outward to the right from S_1 to S_2 in Figure 3-9. At a price of $3, the number supplied was originally 6 million per year, but now the amount supplied (after the reduction in the costs of production) at $3 per SD card will be 9 million a year. (This is similar to what has happened to the supply curve of personal computers and cellphones in recent years as computer memory chip prices have fallen.)

Consider the opposite case. If the cost of making SD cards increases, the supply curve in Figure 3-9 will shift from S_1 to S_3. At each and every price, the quantity of SD cards supplied will fall due to the increase in the price of raw materials.

The Other Determinants of Supply

When supply curves are drawn, only the price of the good in question changes, and it is assumed that other things remain constant. The other things assumed constant are the *ceteris paribus* conditions of supply. They include the prices of resources (inputs)

FIGURE 3-9

A Shift in the Supply Curve

If the cost of producing secure digital cards were to fall dramatically, the supply curve would shift rightward from S_1 to S_2 such that at all prices, a larger quantity would be forthcoming from suppliers. Conversely, if the cost of production rose, the supply curve would shift leftward to S_3.

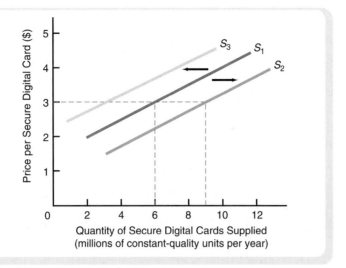

used to produce the product, technology and productivity, taxes and subsidies, producers' price expectations, and the number of firms in the industry. If *any* of these *ceteris paribus* conditions changes, there will be a shift in the supply curve.

COST OF INPUTS USED TO PRODUCE THE PRODUCT   If one or more input prices fall, production costs fall, and the supply curve will shift outward to the right; that is, more will be supplied at each and every price. The opposite will be true if one or more inputs become more expensive. For example, when we draw the supply curve of new laptop computers, we are holding the price of microprocessors (and other inputs) constant. When we draw the supply curve of blue jeans, we are holding the cost of cotton fabric fixed.

How has a fall in an input price affected the supply of dentistry services?

E-COMMERCE EXAMPLE

Digital Imaging Boosts the Supply of Dentistry Services

To design a cap, crown, or denture, dentists use three-dimensional (3D) maps of the tooth that is to be restored. Traditionally, they have relied on 3D models that required 50 million wax and plaster impressions to be submitted each year to the dental labs that fabricate dental appliances such as crowns. Imperfections in impressions and damage to impressions in transit to labs were common. Consequently, U.S. dentists typically had to ask patients to return to their offices to redo about half of the impressions that they submitted to dental labs. Time devoted to redoing impressions could otherwise have been allocated to performing services for other patients. Hence, considering the opportunity costs the dentists incurred, the input prices of 3D models of teeth were relatively high.

Now, however, 3D maps of teeth can be produced at a much lower per-unit price using a technique called digital imaging. A dentist uses a wand about the size and shape of an electric toothbrush to scan a patient's tooth in order to create a detailed, lifelike 3D digital image stored in a computer file. The dentist then transmits this computer file, via the Internet, to a dental lab, where a technician can view the 3D tooth map from a variety of different angles for purposes of producing the appliance the dentist has ordered. Dentists utilizing this lower-priced input are already reporting soaring daily service output in their offices.

FOR CRITICAL ANALYSIS

Now that dentistry has entered the digital era, how are falling prices of computers, software, and Internet access likely to affect the supply of dentistry services?

TECHNOLOGY AND PRODUCTIVITY   Supply curves are drawn by assuming a given technology, or "state of the art." When the available production techniques change, the supply curve will shift. For example, when a better production technique for SD cards becomes available, production costs decrease, and the supply curve will shift to the right. A larger quantity will be forthcoming at each and every price because the cost of production is lower.

How have new techniques utilizing poisonous venoms contributed to increased production of pharmaceuticals?

EXAMPLE
Integrating Poisons into Pharmaceuticals Production

The utilization of venomous secretions of reptiles has contributed to higher rates of production of pharmaceuticals used to treat multiple sclerosis, diabetes, and arterial disease. Technological advances have allowed the venom of cobras to be utilized in producing drugs for treatment of multiple sclerosis. In addition, a new technique employing the poisonous saliva of Gila monsters has given rise to drugs that help diabetics control their blood sugar levels. Furthermore, the use of the venom of the African saw-scaled viper has contributed to the development of new anticlotting heart medications. These and other efforts by drug companies to turn poisons into profits have boosted the amounts of pharmaceuticals produced.

FOR CRITICAL ANALYSIS
How are efforts to breed reptiles that produce larger amounts of venom likely to affect the supply of poison-based pharmaceuticals?

Subsidy
A negative tax; a payment to a producer from the government, usually in the form of a cash grant per unit.

TAXES AND SUBSIDIES   Certain taxes, such as a per-unit tax, are effectively an addition to production costs and therefore reduce the supply. If the supply curve is S_1 in Figure 3-9 on the previous page, a per-unit tax increase would shift it to S_3. A per-unit **subsidy** would do the opposite; it would shift the curve to S_2. Every producer would get a "gift" from the government for each unit produced.

How has the creation of a rail freight subsidy by European Union governments affected the supply of rail freight services in Europe?

INTERNATIONAL POLICY EXAMPLE
Government Subsidies Generate More Train Traffic in Europe

Recently, governments of nations that are members of the European Union (EU) decided to shoulder most of the regular expenses associated with maintaining railroad track networks, thereby providing a significant subsidy per kilometer of track traversed by rail freight. European railroad companies have responded by increasing the amounts of freight transport services they provide. Hence, the provision of government subsidies has brought about an increase in the supply of European rail freight services.

FOR CRITICAL ANALYSIS
Have the EU governments' subsidies induced a movement along the rail freight supply curve or a shift in the supply curve?

PRICE EXPECTATIONS A change in the expectation of a future relative price of a product can affect a producer's current willingness to supply, just as price expectations affect a consumer's current willingness to purchase. For example, suppliers of SD cards may withhold from the market part of their current supply if they anticipate higher prices in the future. The current amount supplied at each and every price will decrease.

How is one company profiting from helping producers form expectations of the weather's influence on the prices of various items?

EXAMPLE
Keeping Price Expectations Updated with Forecasts of Forecasts

The prices of certain products often vary with the weather. The price of oranges, for instance, climbs whenever a cold snap grips Florida. Prices of natural gas drop when springlike weather settles into place during winter months. Consequently, forming accurate expectations of future prices of such items requires forecasting the weather.

The propensity for meteorologists to constantly revise weather forecasts complicates the process of forming expectations about future prices of products such as oranges or natural gas. To assist those producers who wish to continually update expectations about future prices of such products, WSI, the company that owns the Weather Channel, offers a new service. At a price of $90,000 per year, it sells subscriptions to its prediction about the daily weather

forecast provided by the National Oceanic and Atmospheric Administration (NOAA). Each day, one hour before NOAA meteorologists issue a weather forecast for the next several days, WSI provides its subscribers with a prediction of how the NOAA's forecast will change from its forecast the previous day. Then subscribing firms can use WSI's forecast of the NOAAs forecast to adjust their own expectations of the weather's likely effects on prices in the following days.

FOR CRITICAL ANALYSIS
If an item's price typically increases on days with good weather and decreases on days with bad weather, how would a producer of the item adjust today's output in light of an expectation of improved weather during the next few days?

NUMBER OF FIRMS IN THE INDUSTRY In the short run, when firms can change only the number of employees they use, we hold the number of firms in the industry constant. In the long run, the number of firms may change. If the number of firms increases, supply will increase, and the supply curve will shift outward to the right. If the number of firms decreases, supply will decrease, and the supply curve will shift inward to the left.

Changes in Supply versus Changes in Quantity Supplied

We cannot overstress the importance of distinguishing between a movement along the supply curve—which occurs only when the price changes for a given supply curve—and a shift in the supply curve—which occurs only with changes in *ceteris paribus* conditions. A change in the price of the good in question always (and only) brings about a change in the quantity supplied along a given supply curve. We move to a different point on the existing supply curve. This is specifically called a *change in quantity supplied*. When price changes, quantity supplied changes—there is a movement from one point to another along the same supply curve.

When you think of *supply*, think of the entire curve. Quantity supplied is represented by a single point on the supply curve.

Why are these people waiting in line for the new iPhone?

*A change, or shift, in supply is a movement of the entire curve. The **only** thing that can cause the entire curve to move is a change in one of the **ceteris paribus** conditions.*

Consequently,

*A change in price leads to a change in the quantity supplied, other things being constant. This is a movement **along** the curve.*

*A change in any **ceteris paribus** condition for supply leads to a change in supply. This causes a **shift** of the curve.*

QUICK QUIZ | *See page 81 for the answers. Review concepts from this section in MyEconLab.*

If the price changes, we _____ _____ a curve—there is a change in quantity demanded or supplied. If some other determinant changes, we _____ a curve—there is a change in demand or supply.

The **supply curve** is drawn with other things held constant. If these *ceteris paribus* conditions of supply change, the supply curve will shift. The major *ceteris paribus* conditions are (1) _____, (2) _____, (3) _____, (4) _____, and (5) _____.

Putting Demand and Supply Together

In the sections on demand and supply, we tried to confine each discussion to demand or supply only. But you have probably already realized that we can't view the world just from the demand side or just from the supply side. There is interaction between the two. In this section, we will discuss how they interact and how that interaction determines the prices that prevail in our economy and other economies in which the forces of demand and supply are allowed to work.

Let's first combine the demand and supply schedules and then combine the curves.

Demand and Supply Schedules Combined

Go to www.econtoday.com/chapter03 to see how the U.S. Department of Agriculture seeks to estimate demand and supply conditions for major agricultural products.

Let's place panel (a) from Figure 3-3 (the market demand schedule) on page 57 and panel (a) from Figure 3-8 (the market supply schedule) on page 66 together in panel (a) of Figure 3-10. Column 1 shows the price; column 2, the quantity supplied per year at any given price; and column 3, the quantity demanded. Column 4 is the difference between columns 2 and 3, or the difference between the quantity supplied and the quantity demanded. In column 5, we label those differences as either excess quantity supplied (called a *surplus*, which we shall discuss shortly) or excess quantity demanded (commonly known as a *shortage*, also discussed shortly). For example, at a price of $1, only 2 million secure digital cards would be supplied, but the quantity demanded would be 10 million. The difference would be −8 million, which we label excess quantity demanded (a shortage). At the other end, a price of $5 would elicit 10 million in quantity supplied, but quantity demanded would drop to 2 million, leaving a difference of +8 million units, which we call excess quantity supplied (a surplus).

Now, do you notice something special about the price of $3? At that price, both the quantity supplied and the quantity demanded per year are 6 million. The difference then is zero. There is neither excess quantity demanded (shortage) nor excess quantity

FIGURE 3-10

Putting Demand and Supply Together

In panel (a), we see that at the price of $3, the quantity supplied and the quantity demanded are equal, resulting in neither an excess quantity demanded nor an excess quantity supplied. We call this price the equilibrium, or market clearing, price. In panel (b), the intersection of the supply and demand curves is at E, at a price of $3 and a quantity of 6 million per year. At point E, there is neither an excess quantity demanded nor an excess quantity supplied. At a price of $1, the quantity supplied will be only 2 million per year, but the quantity demanded will be 10 million. The difference is excess quantity demanded at a price of $1. The price will rise, so we will move from point A up the supply curve and from point B up the demand curve to point E. At the other extreme, a price of $5 elicits a quantity supplied of 10 million but a quantity demanded of only 2 million. The difference is excess quantity supplied at a price of $5. The price will fall, so we will move down the demand curve and the supply curve to the equilibrium price, $3 per SD card.

Panel (a)

(1) Price per Constant-Quality Secure Digital Card	(2) Quantity Supplied (secure digital cards per year)	(3) Quantity Demanded (secure digital cards per year)	(4) Difference (2) − (3) (secure digital cards per year)	(5) Condition
$5	10 million	2 million	8 million	Excess quantity supplied (surplus)
4	8 million	4 million	4 million	Excess quantity supplied (surplus)
3	6 million	6 million	0	Market clearing price—equilibrium (no surplus, no shortage)
2	4 million	8 million	−4 million	Excess quantity demanded (shortage)
1	2 million	10 million	−8 million	Excess quantity demanded (shortage)

Panel (b)

Market clearing, or **equilibrium, price**
The price that clears the market, at which quantity demanded equals quantity supplied; the price where the demand curve intersects the supply curve.

supplied (surplus). Hence the price of $3 is very special. It is called the **market clearing price**—it clears the market of all excess quantities demanded or supplied. There are no willing consumers who want to pay $3 per SD card but are turned away by sellers, and there are no willing suppliers who want to sell SD cards at $3 who cannot sell all they want at that price. Another term for the market clearing price is the **equilibrium price,** the price at which there is no tendency for change. Consumers are able to get all they want at that price, and suppliers are able to sell all they want at that price.

Equilibrium

Equilibrium
The situation when quantity supplied equals quantity demanded at a particular price.

We can define **equilibrium** in general as a point at which quantity demanded equals quantity supplied at a particular price. There tends to be no movement of the price or the quantity away from this point unless demand or supply changes. Any movement away from this point will set into motion forces that will cause movement back to it. Therefore, equilibrium is a stable point. Any point that is not an equilibrium is unstable and will not persist.

The equilibrium point occurs where the supply and demand curves intersect. The equilibrium price is given on the vertical axis directly to the left of where the supply and demand curves cross. The equilibrium quantity is given on the horizontal axis directly underneath the intersection of the demand and supply curves.

Panel (b) in Figure 3-3 and panel (b) in Figure 3-8 are combined as panel (b) in Figure 3-10 on the previous page. The demand curve is labeled *D*, the supply curve *S*. We have labeled the intersection of the supply curve with the demand curve as point *E*, for equilibrium. That corresponds to a market clearing price of $3, at which both the quantity supplied and the quantity demanded are 6 million units per year. There is neither excess quantity supplied nor excess quantity demanded. Point *E*, the equilibrium point, always occurs at the intersection of the supply and demand curves. This is the price *toward which* the market price will automatically tend to gravitate, because there is no outcome better than this price for both consumers and producers.

Shortages

The price of $3 depicted in Figure 3-10 represents a situation of equilibrium. If there were a non-market-clearing, or disequilibrium, price, this would put into play forces that would cause the price to change toward the market clearing price at which equilibrium would again be sustained. Look again at panel (b) in Figure 3-10. Suppose that instead of being at the equilibrium price of $3, for some reason the market price is $1. At this price, the quantity demanded of 10 million per year exceeds the quantity supplied of 2 million per year. We have a situation of excess quantity demanded at the price of $1. This is usually called a **shortage.** Consumers of SD cards would find that they could not buy all that they wished at $1 apiece. But forces will cause the price to rise: Competing consumers will bid up the price, and suppliers will increase output in response. (Remember, some buyers would pay $5 or more rather than do without SD cards. They do not want to be left out.) We would move from points *A* and *B* toward point *E*. The process would stop when the price again reached $3 per SD card.

Shortage
A situation in which quantity demanded is greater than quantity supplied at a price below the market clearing price.

At this point, it is important to recall a distinction made in Chapter 2:

> ***Shortages and scarcity are not the same thing.***

A shortage is a situation in which the quantity demanded exceeds the quantity supplied at a price that is somehow kept *below* the market clearing price. Our definition of scarcity was much more general and all-encompassing: a situation in which the resources available for producing output are insufficient to satisfy all wants. Any choice necessarily costs an opportunity, and the opportunity is lost. Hence, we will always live in a world of scarcity because we must constantly make choices, but we do not necessarily have to live in a world of shortages.

In what field is there currently a significant shortage of skilled workers?

EXAMPLE
In Nursing, Quantity Demanded Exceeds Quantity Supplied

At present, there are about 2.6 million positions filled or available for nurses at hospitals, physicians' offices, and other health care facilities across the land. Only about 2.2 million nurses are employed, however. Thus, at this time there is an excess quantity demanded—that is, a shortage—of nurses that is equal to approximately 0.4 million (at current wage rates, of course).

FOR CRITICAL ANALYSIS
What do you predict is likely to happen to the average hourly price of nurses' services—the average wage rate earned by nurses—within the next few years?

Surpluses

Now let's repeat the experiment with the market price at $5 rather than at the market clearing price of $3. Clearly, the quantity supplied will exceed the quantity demanded at that price. The result will be an excess quantity supplied at $5 per unit. This excess quantity supplied is often called a **surplus.** Given the curves in panel (b) in Figure 3-10 on page 71, however, there will be forces pushing the price back down toward $3 per SD card: Competing suppliers will cut prices and reduce output, and consumers will purchase more at these new lower prices. If the two forces of supply and demand are unrestricted, they will bring the price back to $3 per SD card.

Shortages and surpluses are resolved in unfettered markets—markets in which price changes are free to occur. The forces that resolve them are those of competition: In the case of shortages, consumers competing for a limited quantity supplied drive up the price; in the case of surpluses, sellers compete for the limited quantity demanded, thus driving prices down to equilibrium. The equilibrium price is the only stable price, and the (unrestricted) market price tends to gravitate toward it.

What happens when the price is set below the equilibrium price? Here come the scalpers.

Surplus
A situation in which quantity supplied is greater than quantity demanded at a price above the market clearing price.

POLICY EXAMPLE
Should Shortages in the Ticket Market Be Solved by Scalpers?

If you have ever tried to get tickets to a playoff game in sports, a popular Broadway play, or a superstar's rap concert, you know about "shortages." The standard Super Bowl ticket situation is shown in Figure 3-11 on the next page. At the face-value price of Super Bowl tickets ($800), the quantity demanded (175,000) greatly exceeds the quantity supplied

POLICY EXAMPLE (cont.)

(80,000). Because shortages last only as long as prices and quantities do not change, markets tend to exhibit a movement out of this disequilibrium toward equilibrium. Obviously, the quantity of Super Bowl tickets cannot change, but the price can go as high as $6,000.

Enter the scalper. This colorful term is used because when you purchase a ticket that is being resold at a price higher than face value, the seller is skimming an extra profit off the top ("taking your scalp"). If an event sells out and people who wished to purchase tickets at current prices were unable to do so, ticket prices by definition were lower than market clearing prices. People without tickets may be willing to buy high-priced tickets because they place a greater value on the entertainment event than the face value of the ticket. Without scalpers, those individuals would not be able to attend the event. In the case of the Super Bowl, various forms of scalping occur nationwide. Tickets for a seat on the 50-yard line have been sold for as much as $6,000 apiece. In front of every Super Bowl arena, you can find ticket scalpers hawking their wares.

In most states, scalping is illegal. In Pennsylvania, convicted scalpers are either fined $5,000 or sentenced to two years behind bars. For an economist, such legislation seems strange. As one New York ticket broker said, "I look at scalping like working as a stockbroker, buying low and selling high. If people are willing to pay me the money, what kind of problem is that?"

FOR CRITICAL ANALYSIS

What happens to ticket scalpers who are still holding tickets after an event has started?

FIGURE 3-11

Shortages of Super Bowl Tickets

The quantity of tickets for a Super Bowl game is fixed at 80,000. At the price per ticket of $800, the quantity demanded is 175,000. Consequently, there is an excess quantity demanded at the below-market clearing price. In this example, prices can go as high as $6,000 in the scalpers' market.

You Are There

Beetle Factories Respond to Higher Demand for Weed-Eating Bugs

Dan Palmer, production chief at the Phillip Alampi Beneficial Insect Rearing Laboratory in New Jersey, is struggling to handle new orders for one of the lab's products: *Galerucella,* which are brown beetles smaller than ladybugs. In the past, his lab mainly received daily orders for the beetles from private landowners and municipal governments in New Jersey, but now he is receiving numerous out-of-state orders as well.

The *Galerucella* beetles eat purple loosestrife, a weed imported from Europe 200 years ago that has spread throughout much of the United States and Canada. During the 1980s, environmentalists discovered that purple loosestrife chokes out native American flora and fills in spaces around lakes where wildlife such as ducks and turtles otherwise would thrive. Numerous landowners are now striving to halt and, if possible, reverse the spread of purple loosestrife. Weed-eating beetles such as *Galerucella* are increasingly regarded as a fundamental part of this effort—hence, the growing volume of orders placed for the beetles bred at labs such as Palmer's.

Dan Palmer contemplates the stack of orders that have arrived today. He concludes that the 12 people in his lab cannot possibly breed beetles in sufficient volumes to meet all his new orders. To increase daily beetle output, the lab must expand its staff, but to do that, it requires higher revenues and therefore must receive a higher price for each unit of beetles it ships. Otherwise, some of the orders that have been received today and that are likely to arrive in the days and weeks to come must go unfilled. He knows that the same situation exists at other labs that produce *Galerucella* and other weed-eating beetles. At current prices, these labs are simply unable to produce as many beetles as landowners would like to purchase.

CRITICAL ANALYSIS QUESTIONS

1. If the price of weed-eating beetles remains unchanged in the face of the recent rise in demand for these insects, what situation will exist in the market for the beetles?

2. If the price of the beetles increases, will there be a movement along the market supply curve, or will the market supply curve shift?

Issues and Applications

Why Are People Eating More?

Being overweight or obese predisposes an individual to ailments such as arthritis, diabetes, heart disease, high blood pressure, respiratory problems, and strokes. Nevertheless, about two-thirds of the U.S. population is overweight. Nearly half of these people are classified as obese.

CONCEPTS APPLIED

- Relative Price
- Law of Demand
- Normal Good

Undoubtedly, a generally more sedentary lifestyle helps to explain the increase in the body mass of the average U.S. resident. Panel (a) of Figure 3-12 suggests, however, that increased calorie consumption has contributed as well. Why are people ingesting so many more calories? To answer this question, one needs to look no further than two fundamental developments: (1) a falling relative price of food that has increased the quantity of food demanded and (2) rising incomes that have contributed to a higher demand for food.

FIGURE 3-12

U.S. Calorie Consumption and the Relative Price of Food

Panel (a) shows that the average U.S. resident's daily calorie consumption has surged since the late 1970s. Panel (b) shows that the price of food relative to the average price of all other items has declined since the 1970s. *Sources:* U.S. Department of Agriculture; U.S. Department of Labor.

(a)

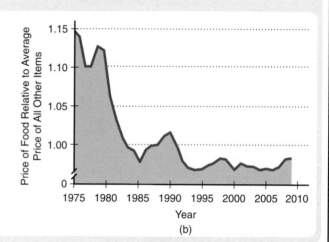

(b)

Moving Along the Food Demand Curve: Falling Relative Prices

Panel (b) of Figure 3-12 displays an index measure of the price of food relative to the average price of all other goods and services. This relative price measure indicates that the relative price of food has declined by almost 0.5 percent per year, which over the past three decades translates into an overall drop exceeding 17 percent.

The law of demand states that a decline in the relative price of an item leads to an increase in the quantity demanded of that item. With other things being equal, therefore, the significant decline in the relative price of food boosted desired food consumption. Hence, one reason that people today buy and eat more food is simply that food is cheaper than it used to be.

A Shift in the Food Demand Curve: Higher Incomes

Of course, other things have not remained unchanged since the mid-1970s. A key factor that has changed is incomes. The average inflation-adjusted income of a U.S. resident has increased by about 2 percent per year since the mid-1970s. The overall rise during the period has been more than 100 percent.

Some food items, such as canned beans and packaged macaroni and cheese, are inferior goods, so higher incomes have reduced consumption of these and similar foods. The vast majority of food items, however, are normal goods. Hence, the substantial rise in individual incomes has tended to raise the demand for foods as well as for other normal goods, such as personal computers and video games.

A Double-Whammy Effect on Food Consumption

Thus, two key factors have contributed to greater food consumption: the lower relative price of food and higher incomes. Increases in incomes have boosted demands for most food items, and declines in the relative prices have induced people to buy even more foods. Hence, people have been consuming more food and, with it, more calories. Without additional exercise, they have also been gaining more weight.

Test your understanding of this chapter by going online to **MyEconLab**.
In the Study Plan for this chapter, select Section N: News.

For Critical Analysis

1. If the demands for most food items have been rising as incomes have increased, what must have happened to the supplies of most food items to account for the declining relative price of food?

2. What factors might have accounted for the changes in food supplies discussed in Question 1? (Hint: What *ceteris paribus* conditions affect the position of a supply curve?)

Web Resources

1. For a review of the worldwide trend toward higher body masses, go to www.econtoday.com/chapter03.

2. To learn about various ways states and the federal government are trying to combat childhood obesity,

click on the link to the National Center for Chronic Disease Prevention and Health Promotion, available at www.econtoday.com/chapter03.

Research Project

One way that the federal government seeks to assist low-income people is by issuing them food stamps, which they can use to purchase food items. Some observers have suggested that the government's food stamp program contributes to the higher obesity rates observed among low-income people as compared with rates observed among middle- and high-income individuals. Evaluate this argument. (Hint: Many of the least-expensive food items are often the highest-fat foods containing the most calories per unit of food.)

   Here is what you should know after reading this chapter. **MyEconLab** will help you identify what you know, and where to go when you need to practice.

WHAT YOU SHOULD KNOW		WHERE TO GO TO PRACTICE
The Law of Demand According to the law of demand, other things being equal, individuals will purchase fewer units of a good at a higher price, and they will purchase more units of a good at a lower price.	market, 52 demand, 52 law of demand, 52	• **MyEconLab** Study Plan 3.1 • Audio introduction to Chapter 3

(continued)

(continued)

WHAT YOU SHOULD KNOW		WHERE TO GO TO PRACTICE
Relative Prices versus Money Prices When determining the quantity of a good to purchase, people respond to changes in its relative price, which is the price of the good in terms of other goods. If the price of a unit of health care services rises by 50 percent next year while at the same time all other prices, including your wages, also increase by 50 percent, then the relative price of the health care services has not changed. Thus, in a world of generally rising prices, you have to compare the price of one good with the general level of prices of other goods in order to decide whether the relative price of that one good has gone up, gone down, or stayed the same.	relative price, 53 money price, 53	• **MyEconLab** Study Plan 3.1 • Video: The Difference Between Relative and Absolute Prices and the Importance of Looking at Only Relative Prices
A Change in Quantity Demanded versus a Change in Demand The demand schedule shows the relationship between various possible prices and respective quantities purchased per unit of time. Graphically, the demand schedule is a downward-sloping demand curve. A change in the price of the good generates a change in the quantity demanded, which is a movement along the demand curve. Factors other than the price of the good that affect the amount demanded are (1) income, (2) tastes and preferences, (3) the prices of related goods, (4) expectations, and (5) market size (the number of potential buyers). Whenever any of these *ceteris paribus* conditions of demand changes, there is a change in the demand for the good, and the demand curve shifts to a new position.	demand curve, 56 market demand, 56 *ceteris paribus* conditions, 59 normal goods, 59 inferior goods, 59 substitutes, 60 complements, 60 **KEY FIGURE** Figure 3-2, 56 Figure 3-4, 58 Figure 3-5, 62	• **MyEconLab** Study Plans 3.2, 3.3 • Video: The Importance of Distinguishing Between a Shift in a Demand Curve and a Move Along the Demand Curve • Animated Figures 3-2, 3-4, 3-5 • ABC News Video: What Drives the Market: Supply and Demand
The Law of Supply According to the law of supply, sellers will produce and offer for sale more units of a good at a higher price, and they will produce and offer for sale fewer units of the good at a lower price.	supply, 62 law of supply, 63	• **MyEconLab** Study Plan 3.4
A Change in Quantity Supplied versus a Change in Supply The supply schedule shows the relationship between various possible prices and respective quantities produced and sold per unit of time. On a graph, the supply schedule is a supply curve that slopes upward. A change in the price of the good generates a change in the quantity supplied, which is a movement along the supply curve. Factors other than the price of the good that affect the amount supplied are (1) input prices, (2) technology and productivity, (3) taxes and subsidies, (4) price expectations, and (5) the number of sellers. Whenever any of these *ceteris paribus* conditions changes, there is a change in the supply of the good, and the supply curve shifts to a new position.	supply curve, 64 subsidy, 68 **KEY FIGURES** Figure 3-6, 64 Figure 3-7, 65 Figure 3-9, 67	• **MyEconLab** Study Plans 3.5, 3.6 • Video: The Importance of Distinguishing Between a Change in Supply versus a Change in Quantity Supplied • Animated Figures 3-6, 3-7, 3-9

(*continued*)

PROBLEMS

All problems are assignable in myeconlab *. Answers to odd-numbered problems appear at the back of the book.*

3-1. Suppose that in a recent market period, the following relationship existed between the price of prerecorded movie DVDs and the quantity supplied and quantity demanded.

Price	Quantity Demanded	Quantity Supplied
$19	100 million	40 million
$20	90 million	60 million
$21	80 million	80 million
$22	70 million	100 million
$23	60 million	120 million

Graph the supply and demand curves for movie DVDs given the information in the table. What are the equilibrium price and quantity? If the industry price is $20, is there a shortage or surplus of DVDs? How much is the shortage or surplus?

3-2. Suppose that in a later market period, the quantities supplied in the table in Problem 3-1 are unchanged. The quantity demanded, however, has increased by 30 million at each price. Construct the resulting demand curve in the illustration you made for Problem 3-1. Is this an increase or a decrease in demand? What are the new equilibrium quantity and the new market price? Give two examples of changes in *ceteris paribus* conditions that might cause such a change.

3-3. Consider the market for DSL high-speed Internet access service, which is a normal good. Explain whether the following events would cause an increase or a decrease in demand or an increase or a decrease in the quantity demanded.

    a. Firms providing cable (an alternative to DSL) Internet access services reduce their prices.

    b. Firms providing DSL high-speed Internet access services reduce their prices.

c. There is a decrease in the incomes earned by consumers of DSL high-speed Internet access services.

d. Consumers of DSL high-speed Internet access services anticipate a decline in the future price of these services.

3-4. In the market for flash memory drives (a normal good), explain whether the following events would cause an increase or a decrease in demand or an increase or a decrease in the quantity demanded. Also explain what happens to the equilibrium quantity and the market clearing price.

a. There are increases in the prices of storage racks and boxes for flash memory drives.

b. There is a decrease in the price of computer drives that read the information contained on flash memory drives.

c. There is a dramatic increase in the price of secure digital cards that, like flash memory drives, can be used to store digital data.

d. A booming economy increases the income of the typical buyer of flash memory drives.

e. Consumers of flash memory drives anticipate that the price of this good will decline in the future.

3-5. Give an example of a complement and a substitute in consumption for each of the following items.

a. Bacon

b. Tennis racquets

c. Coffee

d. Automobiles

3-6. At the beginning of the 2000s, the United States imposed high import taxes on a number of European goods due to a trade dispute. One of these goods was Roquefort cheese. Show how this tax affects the market for Roquefort cheese in the United States, shifting the appropriate curve and indicating a new equilibrium quantity and market price.

3-7. Consider the following diagram of a market for one-bedroom rental apartments in a college community.

a. At a rental rate of $1,000 per month, is there an excess quantity supplied, or is there an excess quantity demanded? What is the amount of the excess quantity supplied or demanded?

b. If the present rental rate of one-bedroom apartments is $1,000 per month, through what mechanism will the rental rate adjust to the equilibrium rental rate of $800?

c. At a rental rate of $600 per month, is there an excess quantity supplied, or is there an excess quantity demanded? What is the amount of the excess quantity supplied or demanded?

d. If the present rental rate of one-bedroom apartments is $600 per month, through what mechanism will the rental rate adjust to the equilibrium rental rate of $800?

3-8. Consider the market for economics textbooks. Explain whether the following events would cause an increase or a decrease in supply or an increase or a decrease in the quantity supplied.

a. The market price of paper increases.

b. The market price of economics textbooks increases.

c. The number of publishers of economics textbooks increases.

d. Publishers expect that the market price of economics textbooks will increase next month.

3-9. Consider the market for laptop computers. Explain whether the following events would cause an increase or a decrease in supply or an increase or a decrease in the quantity supplied. Illustrate each, and show what would happen to the equilibrium quantity and the market price.

a. The price of memory chips used in laptop computers declines.

b. The price of machinery used to produce laptop computers increases.

c. The number of manufacturers of laptop computers increases.

d. There is a decrease in the demand for laptop computers.

3-10. The U.S. government offers significant per-unit subsidy payments to U.S. sugar growers. Describe the effects of the introduction of such subsidies on the market for sugar and the market for artificial sweeteners. Explain whether the demand curve or the supply curve shifts in each market, and if so, in which direction. Also explain what happens to the equilibrium quantity and the market price in each market.

3-11. Platinum's white luster has made the rare metal the chic look in engagement rings and wedding bands. Recently, however, the price of palladium, a more abundant metal with virtually identical characteristics, has declined considerably. Explain the likely effects that the drop in the price of palladium will have on the market for platinum.

3-12. Ethanol is a motor fuel manufactured from corn, barley, or wheat, and it can be used to power the engines of many autos and trucks. Suppose that the government decides to provide a large per-

unit subsidy to ethanol producers. Explain the effects in the markets for the following items:

a. Corn

b. Gasoline

c. Automobiles

3-13. If the price of processor chips used in manufacturing personal computers decreases, what will happen in the market for personal computers? How will the equilibrium price and equilibrium quantity of personal computers change?

3-14. Assume that the cost of aluminum used by soft-drink companies increases. Which of the following correctly describes the resulting effects in the market for soft drinks distributed in aluminum cans? (More than one statement may be correct.)

a. The demand for soft drinks decreases.

b. The quantity of soft drinks demanded decreases.

c. The supply of soft drinks decreases.

d. The quantity of soft drinks supplied decreases.

ECONOMICS ON THE NET

The U.S. Nursing Shortage For some years media stories have discussed a shortage of qualified nurses in the United States. This application explores some of the factors that have caused the quantity of newly trained nurses demanded to tend to exceed the quantity of newly trained nurses supplied.

Title: Nursing Shortage Resource Web Link

Navigation: Go to the Nursing Shortage Resource Web Link at **www.econtoday.com/chapter03**, and click on *Enrollment Increase Insufficient to Meet the Projected Increase in Demand for New Nurses.*

Application Read the discussion, and answer the following questions.

1. What has happened to the demand for new nurses in the United States? What has happened to the supply of new nurses? Why has the result been a shortage?

2. If there is a free market for the skills of new nurses, what can you predict is likely to happen to the wage rate earned by individuals who have just completed their nursing training?

For Group Study and Analysis Discuss the pros and cons of high schools and colleges trying to factor predictions about future wages into student career counseling. How might this potentially benefit students? What problems might high schools and colleges face in trying to assist students in evaluating the future earnings prospects of various jobs?

ANSWERS TO QUICK QUIZZES

p. 54: (i) inverse; (ii) demand
p. 58: (i) constant; (ii) market demand
p. 62: (i) income . . . tastes and preferences . . . prices of related goods . . . expectations about future prices and incomes . . . market size (the number of potential buyers in the market); (ii) *ceteris paribus*; (iii) movement along
p. 65: (i) direct; (ii) supply; (iii) market supply
p. 70: (i) move along . . . shift; (ii) input prices . . . technology and productivity . . . taxes and subsidies . . . expectations of future relative prices . . . the number of firms in the industry
p. 74: (i) intersection . . . equilibrium; (ii) greater; (iii) less

4

Extensions of Demand and Supply Analysis

About 100,000 U.S. residents possessing a malfunctioning organ, such as a liver, heart, or lung, are on waiting lists for transplants from deceased or living donors. A majority of the people waiting for organ transplants are individuals who are suffering from kidney failure. As they wait for donations of compatible kidneys, most people with failed kidneys must undergo years of dialysis, which is an artificial means of cleaning their bloodstreams of harmful toxins. Many never receive a kidney transplant, and a number of these individuals die each year. Why do people suffering from kidney failure have to wait for years to obtain transplants? Why are so many individuals never able to obtain transplants? By the end of this chapter, you will understand the answer to these questions.

LEARNING OBJECTIVES

After reading this chapter, you should be able to:

➤ Discuss the essential features of the price system

➤ Evaluate the effects of changes in demand and supply on the market price and equilibrium quantity

➤ Understand the rationing function of prices

➤ Explain the effects of price ceilings

➤ Explain the effects of price floors

➤ Describe various types of government-imposed quantity restrictions on markets

? **DID YOU KNOW THAT** when the owner of a Wisconsin gasoline station recently offered a 2-cent-per-gallon price discount to senior citizens, the state's Department of Agriculture, Trade, and Consumer Protection objected? The state government agency informed the station owner that the price he had offered senior citizens was too low. Under state law, the station owner could not offer to sell gasoline to anyone at a price below a permissible minimum price, or price *floor*.

What effects can a price floor have on production and consumption of a good or service? As you will learn in this chapter, we can use the supply and demand analysis developed in Chapter 3 to answer this question. You will find that when a government sets a price floor above the equilibrium price, the result will be a surplus, in which quantity supplied remains above quantity demanded. Similarly, you will learn about how we can use supply and demand analysis to examine the "surplus" of various agricultural products, the "shortage" of apartments in certain cities, and many other phenomena. All of these examples are part of our economy, which we characterize as a *price system*.

The Price System and Markets

In a **price system,** otherwise known as a *market system*, relative prices are constantly changing to reflect changes in supply and demand for different commodities. The prices of those commodities are the signals to everyone within the system as to what is relatively scarce and what is relatively abundant. In this sense, prices provide information.

Indeed, it is the *signaling* aspect of the price system that provides the information to buyers and sellers about what should be bought and what should be produced. In a price system, there is a clear-cut chain of events in which any changes in demand and supply cause changes in prices that in turn affect the opportunities that businesses and individuals have for profit and personal gain. Such changes influence our use of resources.

Price system
An economic system in which relative prices are constantly changing to reflect changes in supply and demand for different commodities. The prices of those commodities are signals to everyone within the system as to what is relatively scarce and what is relatively abundant.

Exchange and Markets

The price system features **voluntary exchange,** acts of trading between individuals that make both parties to the trade subjectively better off. The **terms of exchange**— the prices we pay for the desired items—are determined by the interaction of the forces underlying supply and demand. In our economy, exchanges take place voluntarily in markets. A market encompasses the exchange arrangements of both buyers and sellers that underlie the forces of supply and demand. Indeed, one definition of a market is that it is a low-cost institution for facilitating exchange. A market increases incomes by helping resources move to their highest-valued uses.

Voluntary exchange
An act of trading, done on an elective basis, in which both parties to the trade expect to be better off after the exchange.

Terms of exchange
The conditions under which trading takes place. Usually, the terms of exchange are equal to the price at which a good is traded.

Transaction Costs

Individuals turn to markets because markets reduce the cost of exchanges. These costs are sometimes referred to as **transaction costs,** which are broadly defined as the costs associated with finding out exactly what is being transacted as well as the cost of enforcing contracts. If you were Robinson Crusoe and lived alone on an island, you would never incur a transaction cost. For everyone else, transaction costs are just as real as the costs of production. Today, high-speed computers have allowed us to reduce transaction costs by increasing our ability to process information and keep records.

How have real-time dating services via cellphone reduced the transaction costs of searching for a date?

Transaction costs
All of the costs associated with exchange, including the informational costs of finding out the price and quality, service record, and durability of a product, plus the cost of contracting and enforcing that contract.

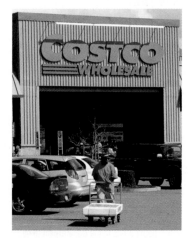

In what way does Costco reduce transaction costs?

Consider some simple examples of transaction costs. A club warehouse such as Sam's Club or Costco reduces the transaction costs of having to go to numerous specialty stores to obtain the items you desire. Financial institutions, such as commercial banks, have reduced the transaction costs of directing funds from savers to borrowers. In general, the more organized the market, the lower the transaction costs. Among those who constantly attempt to lower transaction costs are the much maligned middlemen.

The Role of Middlemen

As long as there are costs of bringing together buyers and sellers, there will be an incentive for intermediaries, normally called middlemen, to lower those costs. This means that middlemen specialize in lowering transaction costs. Whenever producers do not sell their products directly to the final consumer, by definition, one or more middlemen are involved. Farmers typically sell their output to distributors, who are usually called wholesalers, who then sell those products to retailers such as supermarkets.

As videos flood the Internet, are there profitable opportunities for middlemen?

Changes in Demand and Supply

A key function of middlemen is to reduce transaction costs of buyers and sellers in markets for goods and services, and it is in markets that we see the results of changes in demand and supply. Market equilibrium can change whenever there is a *shock* caused by a change in a *ceteris paribus* condition for demand or supply. A shock to the supply and demand system can be represented by a shift in the supply curve, a shift in the demand curve, or a shift in both curves. Any shock to the system will result in a new set of supply and demand relationships and a new equilibrium. Forces will come into play to move the system from the old price-quantity equilibrium (now a disequilibrium situation) to the new equilibrium, where the new demand and supply curves intersect.

Effects of Changes in Either Demand or Supply

In many situations, it is possible to predict what will happen to both equilibrium price and equilibrium quantity when demand or supply changes. Specifically, whenever one curve is stable while the other curve shifts, we can tell what will happen to both price and quantity. Consider the possibilities in Figure 4-1. In panel (a), the supply curve remains unchanged, but demand increases from D_1 to D_2. Note that the results are an increase in the market clearing price from P_1 to P_2 and an increase in the equilibrium quantity from Q_1 to Q_2.

FIGURE 4-1

Shifts in Demand and in Supply: Determinate Results

In panel (a), the supply curve is unchanged at S. The demand curve shifts outward from D_1 to D_2. The equilibrium price and quantity rise from P_1, Q_1 to P_2, Q_2, respectively. In panel (b), again the supply curve is unchanged at S. The demand curve shifts inward to the left, showing a decrease in demand from D_1 to D_3. Both equilibrium price and equilibrium quantity fall. In panel (c), the demand curve now remains unchanged at D. The supply curve shifts from S_1 to S_2. The equilibrium price falls from P_1 to P_2. The equilibrium quantity increases, however, from Q_1 to Q_2. In panel (d), the demand curve is unchanged at D. Supply decreases as shown by a leftward shift of the supply curve from S_1 to S_3. The market clearing price increases from P_1 to P_3. The equilibrium quantity falls from Q_1 to Q_3.

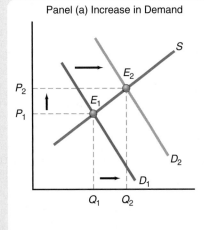

Panel (a) Increase in Demand

Panel (b) Decrease in Demand

Panel (c) Increase in Supply

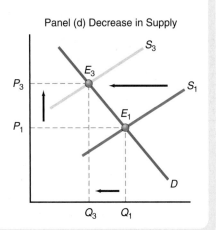

Panel (d) Decrease in Supply

In panel (b) on the previous page, there is a decrease in demand from D_1 to D_3. This results in a decrease in both the equilibrium price of the good and the equilibrium quantity. Panels (c) and (d) show the effects of a shift in the supply curve while the demand curve is unchanged. In panel (c), the supply curve has shifted rightward. The equilibrium price of the product falls; the equilibrium quantity increases. In panel (d), supply has shifted leftward—there has been a supply decrease. The product's equilibrium price increases, and the equilibrium quantity decreases.

Why has the demand for decades-old music recently risen and pushed up the prices of hit songs from the past?

EXAMPLE
The Rising Price of Using Old Songs as Video Background Music

As video content pours onto televisions, cellphones, and computers, producers of videos are scrambling for background music. Indeed, an increasing number of video creators are producing videos carefully synchronized with music, in some cases with videos scripted to fit storylines in song lyrics. The result has been a significant increase in the demand for background music, often purchased for these specific uses from catalogs of long-retired or deceased songwriters. As more producers seek to include hit songs from the past in their video productions, the prices of the rights to use the songs have increased, too. Nearly forgotten songs once available for a few hundred dollars now cost as much as $50,000.

FOR CRITICAL ANALYSIS
What do you suppose has happened to the market clearing price of copyrighted songs newly written for use as background music for video productions?

Situations in Which Both Demand and Supply Shift

The examples in Figure 4-1 show a theoretically determinate outcome of a shift either in the demand curve, holding the supply curve constant, or in the supply curve, holding the demand curve constant. When both the supply and demand curves change, the outcome is indeterminate for either equilibrium price or equilibrium quantity.

When both demand and supply increase, the equilibrium quantity unambiguously rises, because the increase in demand and the increase in supply *both* tend to generate a rise in quantity. The change in the equilibrium price is uncertain without more information, because the increase in demand tends to increase the equilibrium price, whereas the increase in supply tends to decrease the equilibrium price. Decreases in both demand and supply tend to generate a fall in quantity, so the equilibrium quantity falls. Again, the effect on the equilibrium price is uncertain without additional information, because a decrease in demand tends to reduce the equilibrium price, whereas a decrease in supply tends to increase the equilibrium price.

We can be certain that when demand decreases and supply increases at the same time, the equilibrium price will fall, because *both* the decrease in demand and the increase in supply tend to push down the equilibrium price. The change in the equilibrium quantity is uncertain without more information, because the decrease in demand tends to reduce the equilibrium quantity, whereas the increase in supply tends to increase the equilibrium quantity. If demand increases and supply decreases at the same time, both occurrences tend to push up the equilibrium price, so the equilibrium price definitely rises. The change in the equilibrium quantity cannot be determined without more information, because the increase in demand tends to raise the equilibrium quantity, whereas the decrease in supply tends to reduce the equilibrium quantity.

Why is one of the most common physical elements in the universe selling at a higher price here on planet Earth?

EXAMPLE
A Hot Market for a Cooling Element

The element helium is utilized by manufacturers of electronic components because its inert nature helps prevent other gases or impurities from lodging on microchips. In addition, helium readily absorbs heat, so it is very useful for cooling hot substances. Indeed, it can be used to cool metals to such low temperatures that they become superconductors. Even though helium is the second-most-abundant element in the known universe, on our world it is primarily found as a trace component of natural gas. Helium is extracted from natural gas by cooling it to the point at which component gases other than helium liquefy, leaving only helium gas.

The expanding range of industrial applications of helium has led to a rapidly expanding demand for the element. Thus, there has been a rightward shift in the demand curve

for helium, as shown in Figure 4-2. At the same time, however, breakdowns in aging equipment at natural gas fields in locales such as Qatar and Algeria have resulted in significant cutbacks in helium production. Thus, there has been a leftward shift in the helium supply curve. On net, the equilibrium quantity of helium produced and consumed has risen slightly, and the market clearing price of helium has also increased. Indeed, since early 2007 the world price of helium has risen by more than 20 percent.

FOR CRITICAL ANALYSIS
How do you suppose that the recent completion of a number of many new Asian factories that utilize helium as an input will affect the global price of helium?

FIGURE 4-2

The Effects of a Simultaneous Decrease in Helium Supply and Increase in Helium Demand

In the mid-2000s, various factors contributed to a reduction in the global supply of helium, depicted by the leftward shift in the helium supply curve from S_1 to S_2. At the same time, there was an increase in the demand for helium, as shown by the shift in the helium demand curve from D_1 to D_2. On net, the equilibrium quantity of helium produced and consumed rose slightly, from 100 million cubic feet per year at point E_1 to 110 million cubic feet per year at point E_2, and the equilibrium price of helium increased from about $0.04 per cubic foot to about $0.05 per cubic foot.

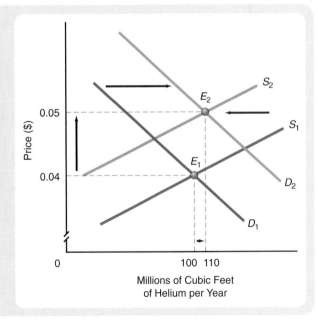

Price Flexibility and Adjustment Speed

We have used as an illustration for our analysis a market in which prices are quite flexible. Some markets are indeed like that. In others, however, price flexibility may take the form of subtle adjustments such as hidden payments or quality changes. For example, although the published price of bouquets of flowers may stay the same, the freshness of the flowers may change, meaning that the price per constant-quality unit changes. The published price of French bread might stay the same, but the quality could go up or down, perhaps through use of a different recipe, thereby changing the price per constant-quality unit. There are many ways to implicitly change prices without actually changing the published price for a *nominal* unit of a product or service.

We must also note that markets do not always return to equilibrium immediately. There may be a significant adjustment time. A shock to the economy in the form of an oil embargo, a drought, or a long strike will not be absorbed overnight. This means that even in unfettered market situations, in which there are no restrictions on changes in prices and quantities, temporary excess quantities supplied or excess quantities demanded may appear. Our analysis simply indicates what the market clearing price and equilibrium quantity ultimately will be, given a demand curve and a supply curve. Nowhere in the analysis is there any indication of the speed with which a market will get to a new equilibrium after a shock. The price may even temporarily overshoot the new equilibrium level. Remember this warning when we examine changes in demand and in supply due to changes in their *ceteris paribus* conditions.

QUICK QUIZ *See page 106 for the answers. Review concepts from this section in MyEconLab.*

The _____ of _____ in a voluntary exchange are determined by the interaction of the forces underlying demand and supply. These forces take place in markets, which tend to minimize _____ costs.

When the _____ curve shifts outward or inward with an unchanged _____ curve, equilibrium price and quantity increase or decrease, respectively. When the

_____ curve shifts outward or inward given an unchanged _____ curve, equilibrium price moves in the direction opposite to equilibrium quantity.

When there is a shift in demand or supply, the new equilibrium price is not obtained _____. Adjustment takes _____.

The Rationing Function of Prices

The synchronization of decisions by buyers and sellers that leads to equilibrium is called the *rationing function of prices*. Prices are indicators of relative scarcity. An equilibrium price clears the market. The plans of buyers and sellers, given the price, are not frustrated. It is the free interaction of buyers and sellers that sets the price that eventually clears the market. Price, in effect, rations a good to demanders who are willing and able to pay the highest price. Whenever the rationing function of prices is frustrated by government-enforced price ceilings that set prices below the market clearing level, a prolonged shortage results.

Methods of Nonprice Rationing

There are ways other than price to ration goods. *First come, first served* is one method. *Political power* is another. *Physical force* is yet another. Cultural, religious, and physical differences have been and are used as rationing devices throughout the world.

RATIONING BY WAITING Consider first come, first served as a rationing device. We call this *rationing by queues*, where *queue* means "line." Whoever is willing to wait in line the longest obtains the good that is being sold at less than the market clearing price. All who wait in line are paying a higher *total* price than the money price paid for the good. Personal time has an opportunity cost. To calculate the total price of the good, we must add up the money price plus the opportunity cost of the time spent waiting.

Rationing by waiting may occur in situations in which entrepreneurs are free to change prices to equate quantity demanded with quantity supplied but choose not to do so. This results in queues of potential buyers. It may seem that the price in the market is being held below equilibrium by some noncompetitive force. That is not true, however. Such queuing may arise in a free market when the demand for a good is subject to large or unpredictable fluctuations, and the additional costs to firms (and ultimately to consumers) of constantly changing prices or of holding sufficient inventories or providing sufficient excess capacity to cover peak demands are greater than the costs to consumers of waiting for the good. Common examples are waiting in line to purchase a fast-food lunch and queuing to purchase a movie ticket a few minutes before the next show.

RATIONING BY RANDOM ASSIGNMENT OR COUPONS *Random assignment* is another way to ration goods. You may have been involved in a rationing-by-random-assignment scheme in college if you were assigned a housing unit. Sometimes rationing by random assignment is used to fill slots in popular classes.

Rationing by *coupons* has also been used, particularly during wartime. In the United States during World War II, families were allotted coupons that allowed them to purchase specified quantities of rationed goods, such as meat and gasoline. To purchase such goods, they had to pay a specified price *and* give up a coupon.

The Essential Role of Rationing

In a world of scarcity, there is, by definition, competition for what is scarce. After all, any resources that are not scarce can be had by everyone at a zero price in as large a quantity as everyone wants, such as air to burn in internal combustion engines. Once scarcity arises, there has to be some method to ration the available resources, goods, and services. The price system is one form of rationing; the others that we mentioned are alternatives. Economists cannot say which system of rationing is "best." They can, however, say that rationing via the price system leads to the most efficient use of available resources. This means that generally in a freely functioning price system, all of the gains from mutually beneficial trade will be captured.

How is it that a number of summer internships for college students are now being rationed by the price system?

What are some alternative rationing methods to the ususal rationing-by-random-assignment schemes used for college housing units?

EXAMPLE
Summer Internships for Sale

Traditionally, college students have obtained summer internships with prestigious companies in two ways. One way is to apply for an internship administered through a school program and wait for university administrators to ration available internships to the students they deem most meritorious. Another is to apply to the companies directly and hope to be rated among the most desirable candidates.

In recent years, however, college students and their families have discovered a third method of securing a summer internship with a top firm: buy one at an auction. An increasing

EXAMPLE (cont.)

number of companies are now donating summer internships to charities, which raise funds by auctioning the internships to parents of college students looking for ways to obtain marketable experience for their children. Thus, a growing percentage of available summer college internships with highly regarded companies are now rationed by a freely functioning price system.

FOR CRITICAL ANALYSIS
How do you suppose that the auction price of a summer internship with investment bank Morgan Stanley would compare with the auction price of a summer internship with a small community bank?

QUICK QUIZ   *See page 106 for the answers. Review concepts from this section in MyEconLab.*

Prices in a market economy perform a rationing function because they reflect relative scarcity, allowing the market to clear. Other ways to ration goods include _____ _____, _____ _____; _____ _____; _____ _____; _____

_____; and _____.

Even when businesspeople can change prices, some rationing by waiting may occur. Such _____ arises when there are large changes in demand coupled with high costs of satisfying those changes immediately.

The Policy of Government-Imposed Price Controls

Price controls
Government-mandated minimum or maximum prices that may be charged for goods and services.

The rationing function of prices is prevented when governments impose price controls. **Price controls** often involve setting a **price ceiling**—the maximum price that may be allowed in an exchange. The world has had a long history of price ceilings applied to product prices, wages, rents, and interest rates. Occasionally, a government will set a **price floor**—a minimum price below which a good or service may not be sold. Price floors have most often been applied to wages and agricultural products. Let's first consider price ceilings.

Price ceiling
A legal maximum price that may be charged for a particular good or service.

Price floor
A legal minimum price below which a good or service may not be sold. Legal minimum wages are an example.

Price Ceilings and Black Markets

As long as a price ceiling is below the market clearing price, imposing a price ceiling creates a shortage, as can be seen in Figure 4-3. At any price below the market clearing, or equilibrium, price of $1,000, there will always be a larger quantity demanded than quantity supplied—a shortage, as you will recall from Chapter 3. Normally, whenever quantity demanded exceeds quantity supplied—that is, when a shortage exists—there is a tendency for the price to rise to its equilibrium level. But with a price ceiling, this tendency cannot be fully realized because everyone is forbidden to trade at the equilibrium price.

Nonprice rationing devices
All methods used to ration scarce goods that are price-controlled. Whenever the price system is not allowed to work, nonprice rationing devices will evolve to ration the affected goods and services.

The result is fewer exchanges and **nonprice rationing devices**. Figure 4-3 illustrates the situation for portable electricity generators after a natural disaster: the equilibrium quantity of portable generators demanded and supplied (or traded) would be 10,000 units, and the market clearing price would be $1,000 per generator. But, if the government essentially imposes a price ceiling by requiring the price of portable

FIGURE 4-3

Black Markets

The demand curve is *D*. The supply curve is *S*. The equilibrium price is $1,000. The government, however, steps in and imposes a maximum price of $600. At that lower price, the quantity demanded will be 15,000, but the quantity supplied will be only 5,000. There is a "shortage." The implicit price (including time costs) tends to rise to $1,400. If black markets arise, as they generally will, the equilibrium black market price will end up somewhere between $600 and $1,400. The actual quantity transacted will be between 5,000 and 10,000.

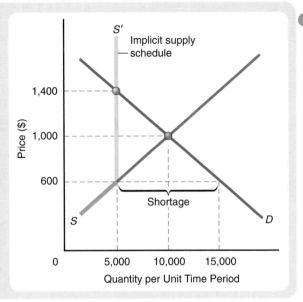

You Are There

To consider the problems faced by government-sponsored public schools confronting salary scales that effectively create a ceiling on teachers' wages, read **Finding a Spanish Instructor in the Midst of a Teacher Shortage,** on page 99.

generators to remain at the predisaster level, which the government determines was a price of $600, the equilibrium quantity offered is only 5,000. Because frustrated consumers will be able to purchase only 5,000 units, there is a shortage. The most obvious nonprice rationing device to help clear the market is queuing, or physical lines, which we have already discussed. To avoid physical lines, waiting lists may be established.

Typically, an effective price ceiling leads to a **black market.** A black market is a market in which the price-controlled good is sold at an illegally high price through various methods. For example, if the price of gasoline is controlled at lower than the market clearing price, drivers who wish to fill up their cars may offer the gas station attendant a cash payment on the side (as happened in the United States in the 1970s and in China and India in the mid-2000s during price controls on gasoline). If the price of beef is controlled at below its market clearing price, a customer who offers the butcher good tickets to an upcoming football game may be allocated otherwise unavailable beef. Indeed, the true implicit price of a price-controlled good or service can be increased in an infinite number of ways, limited only by the imagination. (Black markets also occur when goods are made illegal.)

In what black market have long-distance runners been known to participate?

Black market

A market in which goods are traded at prices above their legal maximum prices or in which illegal goods are sold.

INTERNATIONAL EXAMPLE
The Global Black Market for Marathon Entry Numbers

The world's top marathons are held in Amsterdam, Berlin, Boston, Chicago, Honolulu, London, New York, Paris, Rotterdam, and Stockholm. When runners register for a marathon in one of these cities, they receive "bibs," or officially authorized paper numbers, which must be worn on their shirts

during the event. Marathon organizers typically set registration fees between $80 and $120, well below the equilibrium price. As a result, every year there are shortages of bibs. Even though most marathon organizers say that they ban the reselling of bibs, each year hundreds of individuals who have no intention of participating in marathons register to run, obtain bibs, and put them up for sale on Web auction sites. Some black market bibs have fetched prices as high as $1,000.

FOR CRITICAL ANALYSIS
How could marathon organizers prevent bib shortages from occurring?

QUICK QUIZ   *See page 106 for the answers. Review concepts from this section in MyEconLab.*

Governments sometimes impose **price controls** in the form of price _____ and price _____.

An effective price _____ is one that sets the legal price below the market clearing price and is enforced.

Effective price _____ lead to nonprice rationing devices and black markets.

The Policy of Controlling Rents

Rent control
Price ceilings on rents.

More than 200 U.S. cities and towns, including Berkeley, California, and New York City, operate under some kind of rent control. **Rent control** is a system under which the local government tells building owners how much they can charge their tenants for rent. In the United States, rent controls date back to at least World War II. The objective of rent control is to keep rents below levels that would be observed in a freely competitive market.

The Functions of Rental Prices

In any housing market, rental prices serve three functions: (1) to promote the efficient maintenance of existing housing and stimulate the construction of new housing, (2) to allocate existing scarce housing among competing claimants, and (3) to ration the use of existing housing by current demanders. Rent controls interfere with all of these functions.

RENT CONTROLS AND CONSTRUCTION Rent controls discourage the construction of new rental units. Rents are the most important long-term determinant of profitability, and rent controls artificially depress them. Consider some examples. In a recent year in Dallas, Texas, with a 16 percent rental vacancy rate but no rent control laws, 11,000 new rental housing units were built. In the same year in San Francisco, California, only 2,000 units were built, despite a mere 1.6 percent vacancy rate. The major difference? San Francisco has had stringent rent control laws. In New York City, until changes in the law in 1997 and 2003, the only rental units being built were luxury units, which were exempt from controls.

EFFECTS ON THE EXISTING SUPPLY OF HOUSING When rental rates are held below equilibrium levels, property owners cannot recover the cost of maintenance, repairs, and capital improvements through higher rents. Hence, they curtail these activities. In the extreme situation, taxes, utilities, and the expenses of basic repairs exceed rental receipts. The result is abandoned buildings from Santa Monica, California, to New York City. Some owners have resorted to arson, hoping to collect the insurance on their empty buildings before the city claims them for back taxes.

RATIONING THE CURRENT USE OF HOUSING Rent controls also affect the current use of housing because they restrict tenant mobility. Consider a family whose children have gone off to college. That family might want to live in a smaller apartment. But in a rent-controlled environment, giving up a rent-controlled unit can entail a substantial cost. In most rent-controlled cities, rents can be adjusted only when a tenant leaves. That means that a move from a long-occupied rent-controlled apartment to a smaller apartment can involve a hefty rent hike. In New York, this artificial preservation of the status quo came to be known as "housing gridlock."

Attempts to Evade Rent Controls

The distortions produced by rent controls lead to efforts by both property owners and tenants to evade the rules. This leads to the growth of expensive government bureaucracies whose job it is to make sure that rent controls aren't evaded. In New York City, because rent on an apartment can be raised only if the tenant leaves, property owners have had an incentive to make life unpleasant for tenants in order to drive them out or to evict them on the slightest pretext. The city has responded by making evictions extremely costly for property owners. Eviction requires a tedious and expensive judicial proceeding. Tenants, for their part, routinely try to sublet all or part of their rent-controlled apartments at fees substantially above the rent they pay to the owner. Both the city and the property owners try to prohibit subletting and often end up in the city's housing courts—an entire judicial system developed to deal with disputes involving rent-controlled apartments. The overflow and appeals from the city's housing courts sometimes clog the rest of New York's judicial system.

How have universities' policies of providing students' family members with tickets to graduation ceremonies at no charge provided some students with a profit incentive?

Go to www.econtoday.com/chapter04 to learn more about New York City's rent controls from Tenant.net.

EXAMPLE
Zero-Priced Seats at Graduation Ceremonies Become Hot Items

Whenever you purchase a ticket to a concert or sporting event, you are effectively renting from the owner of the concert hall or sports center the space where you will sit during the time of the scheduled event. Likewise, a ticket to a college graduation ceremony grants the bearer the right to utilize space owned by the college for the duration of that particular occasion.

Colleges typically extend a few tickets at no charge to each graduating student to pass along for use by family members who wish to attend the student's graduation ceremony. Some students have more loved ones who would like to attend their graduation ceremonies than their allotments of no-charge tickets. Other students do not even wish to

attend their own graduation ceremonies, let alone ask family members to attend. The latter students recognize, however, that some students are willing to pay positive prices for access to seats for loved ones lacking tickets. Many colleges threaten to discipline students who sell their graduation seating tickets, but to no avail. Each year at colleges across the nation, tickets to graduation ceremonies sell at prices ranging from as low as $5 per ticket to as high as $100 per ticket.

FOR CRITICAL ANALYSIS
Does anyone "lose out" as a result of black market exchanges of tickets to college graduation ceremonies?

Who Gains and Who Loses from Rent Controls?

The big losers from rent controls are clearly property owners. But there is another group of losers—low-income individuals, especially single mothers, trying to find their first apartment. Some observers now believe that rent controls have worsened the problem of homelessness in cities such as New York.

Often, owners of rent-controlled apartments charge "key money" before allowing a new tenant to move in. This is a large up-front cash payment, usually illegal but demanded nonetheless—just one aspect of the black market in rent-controlled apartments. Poor individuals have insufficient income to pay the hefty key money payment, nor can they assure the owner that their rent will be on time or even paid each month. Because controlled rents are usually below market clearing levels, apartment owners have little incentive to take any risk on low-income individuals as tenants. This is particularly true when a prospective tenant's chief source of income is a welfare check. Indeed, a large number of the litigants in the New York housing courts are welfare mothers who have missed their rent payments due to emergency expenses or delayed welfare checks. Their appeals often end in evictions and a new home in a temporary public shelter—or on the streets.

Who benefits from rent control? Ample evidence indicates that upper-income professionals benefit the most. These people can use their mastery of the bureaucracy and their large network of friends and connections to exploit the rent control system. Consider that in New York, actresses Mia Farrow and Cicely Tyson live in rent-controlled apartments, paying well below market rates. So do the former director of the Metropolitan Museum of Art and singer and children's book author Carly Simon.

QUICK QUIZ See page 106 for the answers. Review concepts from this section in MyEconLab.

_____ prices perform three functions: (1) allocating existing scarce housing among competing claimants, (2) promoting efficient maintenance of existing houses and stimulating new housing construction, and (3) rationing the use of existing houses by current demanders.

Effective rent _____ impede the functioning of rental prices. Construction of new rental units is discouraged. Rent _____ decrease spending on maintenance of existing ones and also lead to "housing gridlock."

There are numerous ways to evade rent controls; _____ _____ is one.

Price Floors in Agriculture

Another way that government can affect markets is by imposing price floors or price supports. In the United States, price supports are most often associated with agricultural products.

Price Supports

During the Great Depression, the federal government swung into action to help farmers. In 1933, it established a system of price supports for many agricultural products. Since then, there have been price supports for wheat, feed grains, cotton, rice, soybeans, sorghum, and dairy products, among other foodstuffs. The nature of the supports is quite simple: The government simply chooses a *support price* for an agricultural product

FIGURE 4-4

Agricultural Price Supports

Free market equilibrium occurs at *E*, with an equilibrium price of $250 per ton and an equilibrium quantity of 1.4 million tons. When the government sets a support price at $350 per ton, the quantity demanded is 1.0 million tons, and the quantity supplied is 2.2 million tons. The difference is the surplus, which the government buys. Farmers' income from consumers equals $350 × 1.0 million = $350 million. Farmers' additional income from taxpayers equals $350 × (2.2 million − 1.0 million) = $420 million.

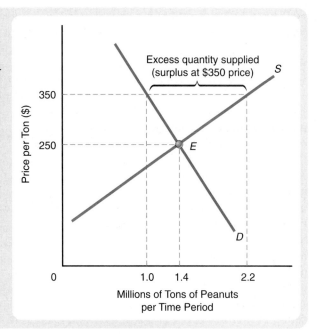

and then acts to ensure that the price of the product never falls below the support level. Figure 4-4 shows the market demand for and supply of peanuts. Without a price-support program, competitive forces would yield an equilibrium price of $250 per ton and an equilibrium quantity of 1.4 million tons per year. Clearly, if the government were to set the support price at or below $250 per ton, the quantity of peanuts demanded would equal the quantity of peanuts supplied at point *E*, because farmers could sell all they wanted at the market clearing price of $250 per ton.

But what happens when the government sets the support price *above* the market clearing price, at $350 per ton? At a support price of $350 per ton, the quantity demanded is only 1.0 million tons, but the quantity supplied is 2.2 million tons. The 1.2-million-ton difference between them is called the *excess quantity supplied*, or *surplus*. As simple as this program seems, its existence creates a fundamental question: How can the government agency charged with administering the price-support program prevent market forces from pushing the actual price down to $250 per ton?

If production exceeds the amount that consumers want to buy at the support price, what happens to the surplus? Quite simply, if the price-support program is to work, the government has to buy the surplus—the 1.2-million-ton difference. As a practical matter, the government acquires the 1.2-million-ton surplus indirectly through a government agency. The government either stores the surplus or sells it to foreign countries at a greatly reduced price (or gives it away free of charge) under the Food for Peace program.

Who Benefits from Agricultural Price Supports?

Although agricultural price supports have traditionally been promoted as a way to guarantee decent earnings for low-income farmers, most of the benefits have in fact gone to the owners of very large farms. Price-support payments are made on a per-bushel basis, not on a per-farm basis. Thus, traditionally, the larger the farm, the bigger

If this wheat farmer is guaranteed a high price, will he grow more or less wheat?

the benefit from agricultural price supports. In addition, *all* of the benefits from price supports ultimately accrue to *landowners* on whose land price-supported crops grow.

KEEPING PRICE SUPPORTS ALIVE UNDER A NEW NAME Back in the early 1990s, Congress indicated an intention to phase out most agricultural subsidies by the early 2000s. What Congress actually *did* throughout the 1990s, however, was to pass a series of "emergency laws" keeping farm subsidies alive. Some of these laws aimed to replace agricultural price supports with payments to many farmers for growing no crops at all, thereby boosting the market prices of crops by reducing supply. Nevertheless, the federal government and a number of state governments have continued to support prices of a number of agricultural products, such as peanuts, through "marketing loan" programs. These programs advance funds to farmers to help them finance the storage of some or all of their crops. The farmers can then use the stored produce as collateral for borrowing or sell it to the government and use the proceeds to repay debts. Marketing loan programs raise the effective price that farmers receive for their crops and commit federal and state governments to purchasing surplus production. Consequently, they lead to outcomes similar to traditional price-support programs.

How does the federal government's marketing loan program operate for U.S. cotton growers?

POLICY EXAMPLE
King Cotton Receives Royal Government Subsidies

Every year, before a U.S. cotton farmer plants a crop, the federal government extends a direct payment, based on the average size of the farmer's past planting, which the farmer uses to help finance the coming year's planting expenses. After the crop is planted, the farmer can borrow from the government, using the newly sown cotton as collateral. If the world price of cotton falls below a price floor of 65 cents per pound, the grower receives a payment from the government—effectively compensating the farmer for surplus cotton the farmer has planted—equal to 13 cents per pound. The world price of cotton has been less than 65 cents per pound for some time, so the government funds the production of surplus cotton in this manner every year. If the world price of cotton falls below 52 cents per pound, farmers turn their cotton over to the govern-

ment, which sells the cotton at the world price and absorbs the loan losses. In this way, the government effectively buys increased surpluses of cotton caused by unexpected drops in cotton prices well below the 65 cent price floor.

All told, total payments to cotton growers by the federal government amount to more than $3 billion per year. The entire U.S. cotton crop typically generates revenues to farmers of about $5 billion per year. Thus, the government usually provides at least 50 percent of all revenues received by cotton producers.

FOR CRITICAL ANALYSIS
What would happen to cotton farmers' revenues if the government raised the price floor?

The Main Beneficiaries of Agricultural Subsidies

In 2002, Congress enacted the Farm Security Act, which has perpetuated marketing loan programs and other subsidy and price-support arrangements for such farm products as wheat, corn, rice, peanuts, and soybeans. All told, the more than $9 billion in U.S. government payments for these and other products amounts to about 25 percent of the annual market value of all U.S. farm production.

The government seeks to cap the annual subsidy payment that an individual farmer can receive at $360,000 per year, but some farmers are able to garner higher annual amounts by exploiting regulatory loopholes. The greatest share of total agricultural subsidies goes to the owners of the largest farming operations. At present, 10 percent of U.S. farmers receive more than 70 percent of agricultural subsidies.

The 2007 Food, Security, and Bioenergy Act expanded on the 2002 legislation by giving farmers raising a number of crops a choice between federal subsidy programs. On the one hand, farmers can opt to participate in traditional programs involving a mix of direct payments and marketing loan programs. On the other hand, farmers can choose a program offering guaranteed revenues. If market clearing crop prices end up higher than those associated with the government's revenue guarantee, farmers sell their crops at the higher prices instead of collecting government subsidies. But if equilibrium crop prices end up below a level consistent with the government guarantee, farmers receive direct subsidies to bring their total revenues up to the guaranteed level.

Price Floors in the Labor Market

The **minimum wage** is the lowest hourly wage rate that firms may legally pay their workers. Proponents favor higher minimum wages to ensure low-income workers a "decent" standard of living. Opponents counter that higher minimum wages cause increased unemployment, particularly among unskilled minority teenagers.

Minimum wage
A wage floor, legislated by government, setting the lowest hourly rate that firms may legally pay workers.

Minimum Wages in the United States

The federal minimum wage started in 1938 at 25 cents an hour, about 40 percent of the average manufacturing wage at the time. Typically, its level has stayed at about 40 to 50 percent of average manufacturing wages. After holding the minimum wage at $5.15 per hour from 1997 to 2007, Congress enacted a series of phased increases in the hourly minimum wage, effective on July 24 of each year, to $5.85 in 2007, $6.55 in 2008, and $7.25 in 2009.

Many states and cities have their own minimum wage laws that exceed the federal minimum. A number of municipalities refer to their minimum wage rules as "living wage" laws. Governments of these municipalities seek to set minimum wages consistent with living standards they deem to be socially acceptable—that is, overall wage income judged to be sufficient to purchase basic items such as housing and food.

Go to **www.econtoday.com/chapter04** for information from the U.S. Department of Labor about recent developments concerning the federal minimum wage.

Economic Effects of a Minimum Wage

What happens when the government establishes a floor on wages? The effects can be seen in Figure 4-5 on the next page. We start off in equilibrium with the equilibrium wage rate of W_e and the equilibrium quantity of labor equal to Q_e. A minimum wage, W_m, higher than W_e, is imposed. At W_m, the quantity demanded for labor is reduced to Q_d, and some workers now become unemployed. Some workers will become unemployed as a result of the minimum wage, but others will move to sectors where minimum wage laws do not apply; wages will be pushed down in these uncovered sectors.

Note that the reduction in employment from Q_e to Q_d, or the distance from B to A, is less than the excess quantity of labor supplied at wage rate W_m. This excess quantity supplied is the distance between A and C, or the distance between Q_d and Q_s. The reason the reduction in employment is smaller than the excess quantity of labor supplied at the minimum wage is that the excess quantity of labor supplied also includes the *additional* workers who would like to work more hours at the new, higher minimum wage.

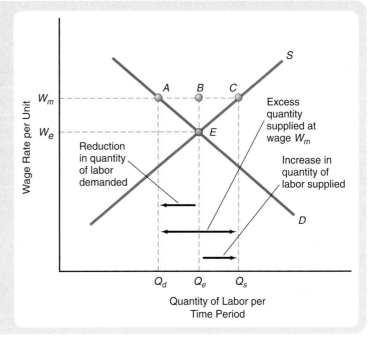

FIGURE 4-5

The Effect of Minimum Wages

The market clearing wage rate is W_e. The market clearing quantity of employment is Q_e, determined by the intersection of supply and demand at point E. A minimum wage equal to W_m is established. The quantity of labor demanded is reduced to Q_d. The reduction in employment from Q_e to Q_d is equal to the distance between B and A. That distance is smaller than the excess quantity of labor supplied at wage rate W_m. The distance between B and C is the increase in the quantity of labor supplied that results from the higher minimum wage rate.

In the long run (a time period that is long enough to allow for full adjustment by workers and firms), some of the reduction in the quantity of labor demanded will result from a reduction in the number of firms, and some will result from changes in the number of workers employed by each firm. Economists estimate that a 10 percent increase in the minimum wage relative to the average prices of goods and services decreases total employment of those affected by 1 to 2 percent.

We can conclude from application of demand and supply analysis that a minimum wage established above the equilibrium wage rate typically has two fundamental effects. On the one hand, it boosts the wage earnings of those people who obtain employment. On the other hand, the minimum wage results in unemployment for other individuals. Thus, demand and supply analysis implies that the minimum wage makes some people better off while making others much worse off.

Quantity Restrictions

Governments can impose quantity restrictions on a market. The most obvious restriction is an outright ban on the ownership or trading of a good. It is currently illegal to buy and sell human organs. It is also currently illegal to buy and sell certain psychoactive drugs such as cocaine, heroin, and marijuana. In some states, it is illegal to start a new hospital without obtaining a license for a particular number of beds to be offered to patients. This licensing requirement effectively limits the quantity of hospital beds in some states. From 1933 to 1973, it was illegal for U.S. citizens to own gold except for manufacturing, medicinal, or jewelry purposes.

Some of the most common quantity restrictions exist in the area of international trade. The U.S. government, as well as many foreign governments, imposes import quotas on a variety of goods. An **import quota** is a supply restriction that prohibits

Import quota

A physical supply restriction on imports of a particular good, such as sugar. Foreign exporters are unable to sell in the United States more than the quantity specified in the import quota.

the importation of more than a specified quantity of a particular good in a one-year period. The United States has had import quotas on tobacco, sugar, and immigrant labor. For many years, there were import quotas on oil coming into the United States. There are also "voluntary" import quotas on certain goods. For instance, in 2005 the Chinese government agreed to "voluntarily" restrict the amount of textile products China sends to the United States and the European Union.

QUICK QUIZ   *See page 106 for the answers. Review concepts from this section in MyEconLab.*

With a price-_____ system, the government sets a minimum price at which, say, qualifying farm products can be sold. Any farmers who cannot sell at that price in the market can "sell" their surplus to the government. The only way a price-_____ system can survive is for the government or some other entity to buy up the excess quantity supplied at the support price.

When a _____ is placed on wages at a rate that is above market equilibrium, the result is an excess quantity of labor supplied at that minimum wage.

Quantity restrictions may take the form of _____ _____, which are limits on the quantity of specific foreign goods that can be brought into the United States for resale purposes.

You Are There

Finding a Spanish Instructor in the Midst of a Teacher Shortage

This year, average starting salaries for all college graduates have increased 5 percent. But the good news for college graduates only magnifies the problem faced by Jill Rogers, superintendent of schools in Martinsville, Illinois.

Like most public school superintendents across the land, Rogers must deal with what promises to be a wave of retirements by experienced teachers who entered the profession in the 1960s and 1970s. As schools scramble to replace these teachers, the demand for new teachers in sciences and languages is rising rapidly. On this late summer day, finding a Spanish teacher is the challenge that Rogers confronts. Classes begin in a week, and so far she has been unable to hire a qualified person to fill an open position. The source of her difficulty is a dollar figure—$28,352, the maximum permissible salary for an inexperienced teacher mandated under the government-sponsored school system's salary scale. As the day begins, Rogers is among the hundreds of public school superintendents nationwide trying to hire Spanish teachers at a salary at least $3,000 below the market clearing salary for new liberal arts graduates.

Fortunately, good news arrives before the end of the day. Rogers finally has landed a Spanish teacher. The new hire is a native Spanish-speaking woman from Argentina. She lacks teaching credentials, so Rogers quickly arranges for her to begin an accelerated teaching certification program at a local university. Rogers realizes that her school district is now among the fortunate few that will manage to hire a new Spanish teacher this year.

CRITICAL ANALYSIS QUESTIONS

1. Average nonteaching salaries for college graduates in the sciences are almost $20,000 higher than those for graduates in languages and other liberal arts fields. Given that teachers in all fields are paid similar salaries, how does this help to explain why the shortage of public school science teachers is particularly acute?

2. During the coming years, barring changes in public school salary structures, what is likely to happen to shortages of teachers in various fields as more experienced teachers retire?

Effects of the $0 Price Ceiling in the Market for Kidneys

CONCEPTS APPLIED

- Price Ceilings
- Nonprice Rationing Devices
- Black Markets

At any given moment, about 76,000 U.S. residents are waiting for kidneys for transplant from donors. Even though so many people suffering from kidney failure would like to obtain a transplant, there are only about 16,000 kidney transplants per year. Most people with two healthy kidneys could get by with only one without shortening their lives. In principle, almost any willing individual with a compatible kidney could provide it to someone on the kidney-transplant waiting list who has the same blood type. Nevertheless, nearly all transplanted kidneys obtained from living donors are donated by relatives or friends of the recipients. There are two key reasons for this. One is that relatives are more likely to have compatible kidneys. Another is that a person who cares about a recipient is more likely to be willing to incur the explicit and implicit costs associated with donating a kidney at the legal price ceiling of $0.

The Predictable Result of a $0 Price Ceiling: A Shortage

In the United States and most other nations, it is illegal to pay someone to provide an organ for transplantation. Hence, the only price at which an organ can be obtained is $0. Effectively, this is a price ceiling for organs such as kidneys.

Figure 4-6 provides a graphical representation of the market for kidneys for transplant. The quantity of kidneys demanded at the ceiling price of $0, at the point at which the demand curve touches the horizontal axis, is about 76,000. For most goods and services, a positive price is required to induce a positive quantity supplied, so supply curves usually touch the vertical axis. In the market for kidneys for transplantation, however, some people

are willing to provide kidneys at the legal price of $0, as evidenced by the fact that donors now provide an average of about 16,000 kidneys per year at this price. Thus, there is an excess quantity demanded equal to about 60,000 kidneys per year—that is, 60,000 people suffering from kidney failure and languishing on the transplant list.

Predictable Consequences of a Kidney Shortage

Because elimination of the kidney shortage through the price system is illegal, nonprice rationing devices are the main focus of efforts to direct available kidneys to people with failed kidneys. Most medical centers utilize three key criteria. First, the donor kidney must be compatible with the recipient's blood type and other

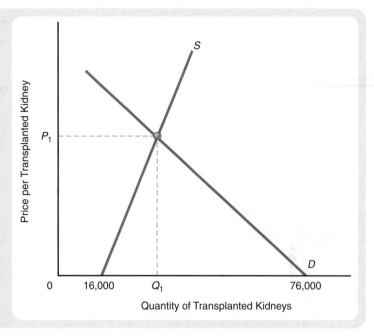

FIGURE 4-6

The Shortage of Kidneys for Transplantation at a Ceiling Price of $0

If kidneys for transplantation could be exchanged at an unregulated price, the equilibrium price would be equal to P_1, and the equilibrium quantity of transplants per year would be Q_1. At present, however, payments for organ transplants are illegal. Hence, there is a ceiling price of $0. At this price, about 16,000 kidneys for transplantation are supplied by donors each year. Approximately 76,000 kidneys for transplantation are demanded by people suffering from failed kidneys. Thus, there is a shortage of kidneys for transplantation equal to about 60,000 per year.

physical requirements. Second, a living donor must have a documented relationship—as a family member or friend—with a specially designated recipient. Third, if there is no clear relationship between a donor and a potential recipient, transplants take place strictly on a first-come, first-served basis.

For people with failed kidneys who are far down on the waiting list, the only legal option is to continue waiting. An illegal option is the black market. At fees starting at about $150,000, so-called organ brokers offer to locate a donor willing to provide a compatible kidney and a surgeon willing to perform a transplant (but often only for an additional fee). An estimated 6,000 kidney transplants worldwide are arranged by black market brokers.

Kidney Exchanges?

Economists have come up with a legal approach that may help reduce the size of the kidney shortage: organized "kidney exchanges" involving loved ones of people awaiting transplants. For instance, if a father with blood type A cannot donate a kidney to his daughter with blood type B, he may be amenable to donating a kidney to a young man with blood type A, whose sister with blood type B in turn donates a kidney to the father's daughter. Several medical centers are already utilizing kidney-exchange programs aimed at increasing the number of lifesaving transplants.

Test your understanding of this chapter by going online to **MyEconLab**.
In the Study Plan for this chapter, select Section N: News.

For Critical Analysis

1. Given normally shaped demand and supply curves, why does the maximum possible shortage of a good or service exist at a ceiling price of $0?

2. In recent years, an increasing number of medical facilities have struggled to prevent surgery patients from contracting infections caused by drug-resistant bacteria.

How do you suppose that the shortage of kidneys for transplantation would be affected if potential kidney donors become more fearful of such infections?

Web Resources

1. Read a description of the New England Program for Kidney Exchange at www.econtoday.com/chapter04.

2. To learn about the system of organized kidney exchange utilized by Johns Hopkins Medicine, go to www.econtoday .com/chapter04.

Research Project

Abstracting from normative issues relating to morals or ethics, what positive economic prediction can you make about the likely effect of legalized payments for transplanted kidneys on the size of the kidney shortage? Refer to Figure 4-6 on the previous page in explaining your answer.

 Here is what you should know after reading this chapter. **MyEconLab** will help you identify what you know, and where to go when you need to practice.

WHAT YOU SHOULD KNOW		WHERE TO GO TO PRACTICE
Essential Features of the Price System The price system, otherwise called the market system, allows prices to respond to changes in supply and demand for different commodities. Consumers' and business managers' decisions on resource use depend on what happens to prices. In the price system, exchange takes place in markets. The terms of exchange are communicated by prices in the marketplace, where middlemen reduce transaction costs by bringing buyers and sellers together.	price system, 83 voluntary exchange, 83 terms of exchange, 83 transaction costs, 83	• **MyEconLab** Study Plan 4.1 • Audio introduction to Chapter 4
How Changes in Demand and Supply Affect the Market Price and Equilibrium Quantity With a given supply curve, an increase in demand causes a rise in the market price and an increase in the equilibrium quantity, and a decrease in demand induces a fall in the market price and a decline in the equilibrium quantity. With a given demand curve, an increase in supply causes a fall in the market price and an increase in the equilibrium quantity, and a decrease in supply causes a rise in the market price and a decline in the equilibrium quantity. When both demand and supply shift at the same time, indeterminate results may occur. We must know the direction and degree of each shift in order to predict the change in the market price and the equilibrium quantity.	KEY FIGURE Figure 4-1, 85	• **MyEconLab** Study Plan 4.2 • Animated Figure 4-1 • ABC News Video: What Drives the Market: Supply and Demand
The Rationing Function of Prices In the market system, prices perform a rationing function—they ration scarce goods and services. Other ways of rationing include first come, first served; political power; physical force; random assignment; and coupons.		• **MyEconLab** Study Plan 4.3 • Video: Price Flexibility, the Essential Role of Rationing via Price and Alternative Rationing Systems

(continued)

(continued)

WHAT YOU SHOULD KNOW		WHERE TO GO TO PRACTICE
The Effects of Price Ceilings Government-imposed price controls that require prices to be no higher than a certain level are price ceilings. If a government sets a price ceiling below the market price, then at the ceiling price the quantity of the good demanded will exceed the quantity supplied. There will be a shortage of the good at the ceiling price. For instance, rent controls place a ceiling on permitted rental prices and create shortages in housing markets. Price ceilings can lead to nonprice rationing devices and black markets.	price controls, 90 price ceiling, 90 price floor, 90 nonprice rationing devices, 90 black market, 91 rent control, 92 **KEY FIGURE** Figure 4-3, 91	• **MyEconLab** Study Plans 4.4, 4.5 • Animated Figure 4-3
The Effects of Price Floors Government-mandated price controls that require prices to be no lower than a certain level are price floors. If a government sets a price floor above the market price, then at the floor price the quantity of the good supplied will exceed the quantity demanded. There will be a surplus of the good at the floor price. For instance, minimum wage laws that establish a price floor in the labor market and government price-support policies that set price floors in markets for agricultural goods often generate surpluses in these markets.	minimum wage, 97 **KEY FIGURES** Figure 4-4, 95 Figure 4-5, 98	• **MyEconLab** Study Plans 4.6, 4.7 • Video: Minimum Wages • Animated Figures 4-4, 4-5
Government-Imposed Restrictions on Market Quantities Quantity restrictions can take the form of outright government bans on the sale of certain goods, such as human organs or various psychoactive drugs. They can also arise from licensing requirements that limit the number of producers and thereby restrict the amount supplied of a good or service. Another example is an import quota, which limits the number of units of a foreign-produced good that can legally be sold domestically.	import quota, 98	• **MyEconLab** Study Plan 4.8

Log in to MyEconLab, take a chapter test, and get a personalized Study Plan that tells you which concepts you understand and which ones you need to review. From there, MyEconLab will give you further practice, tutorials, animations, videos, and guided solutions.
Log in to www.myeconlab.com

PROBLEMS

All problems are assignable in myeconlab . *Answers to odd-numbered problems appear at the back of the book.*

4-1. In recent years, technological improvements have greatly reduced the costs of producing music CDs, and a number of new firms have entered the music CD industry. At the same time, prices of substitutes for music CDs, such as Internet downloads and music DVDs, have declined considerably. Construct a supply and demand diagram of the market for music CDs. Illustrate the impacts of these developments, and evaluate the effects on the market price and equilibrium quantity.

4-2. Advances in research and development in the pharmaceutical industry have enabled manufacturers to identify potential cures more quickly and therefore at lower cost. At the same time, the aging of our society has increased the demand for new drugs. Construct a supply and demand diagram of the market for pharmaceutical drugs. Illustrate the impacts of these developments, and evaluate the effects on the market price and the equilibrium quantity.

4-3. The following table depicts the quantity demanded and quantity supplied of studio apartments in a small college town.

Monthly Rent	Quantity Demanded	Quantity Supplied
$600	3,000	1,600
$650	2,500	1,800
$700	2,000	2,000
$750	1,500	2,200
$800	1,000	2,400

What are the market price and equilibrium quantity of apartments in this town? If this town imposes a rent control of $650 per month, how many studio apartments will be rented?

4-4. The U.S. government imposes a price floor for U.S. sugar that is above the market clearing price. Illustrate the U.S. sugar market with the price floor in place. Discuss the effects of the price floor on conditions in the market for sugar in the United States.

4-5. The Canadian sugar industry has complained that U.S. sugar manufacturers "dump" sugar surpluses in the Canadian market. U.S. chocolate manufacturers have also complained about the high U.S. price of sugar. Explain how the imposition of a price floor for U.S. sugar, as described in Problem 4-4, affects each of these markets. What are the changes in equilibrium quantities and market prices due to the price floor?

4-6. Suppose that the U.S. government places a ceiling on the price of Internet access.

   a. Show why there is a shortage of Internet access at the legal price.

   b. Suppose that a black market for Internet providers arises, with Internet service providers developing hidden connections. Illustrate the black market for Internet access, including the implicit supply schedule, the legal price, the black market supply and demand, and the highest feasible black market price.

4-7. The table below illustrates the demand and supply schedules for seats on air flights between two cities:

Price	Quantity Demanded	Quantity Supplied
$200	2,000	1,200
$300	1,800	1,400
$400	1,600	1,600
$500	1,400	1,800
$600	1,200	2,000

What are the market price and equilibrium quantity in this market? Now suppose that federal authorities limit the number of flights between the two cities to ensure that no more than 1,200 passengers can be flown. Evaluate the effects of this quota if price adjusts. (Hint: How much are the 1,200 passengers willing to pay for their flights?)

4-8. The consequences of decriminalizing illegal drugs have long been debated. Some claim that legalization will lower the price of these drugs and reduce related crime. Others claim that more people will use these drugs. Suppose that some of these drugs are legalized so that anyone may sell them and use them. Now consider the two claims—that price will fall and quantity demanded will increase. Based on positive economic analysis, are these claims sound?

4-9. In recent years, the government of Pakistan has established a support price for wheat of about $0.20 per kilogram of wheat. At this price, consumers are willing to purchase 10 billion kilograms of wheat per year, while Pakistani farmers are willing to grow and harvest 18 billion kilograms of wheat per year. The government purchases and stores all surplus wheat.

   a. What are annual consumer expenditures on the Pakistani wheat crop?

   b. What are annual government expenditures on the Pakistani wheat crop?

   c. How much, in total, do Pakistani wheat farmers receive for the wheat they produce?

4-10. Consider the information in Problem 4-9 and your answers to that question. Suppose that the market clearing price of Pakistani wheat in the absence of price supports is equal to $0.10 per kilogram. At this price, the quantity of wheat demanded is 12 billion kilograms. Under the government wheat price-support program, how much more is spent each year on wheat harvested in Pakistan than otherwise would have been spent in an unregulated market for Pakistani wheat?

4-11. Consider the diagram below, which depicts the labor market in a city that has adopted a "living wage law" requiring employers to pay a minimum wage rate of $9 per hour. Answer the questions that follow.

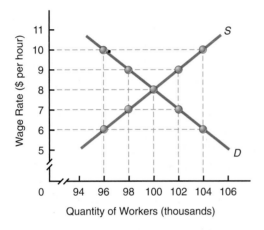

a. What condition exists in this city's labor market at the present minimum wage of $9 per hour? How many people are unemployed at this wage?

b. A city councilwoman has proposed amending the living wage law. She suggests reducing the minimum wage to $6 per hour. Assuming that the labor demand and supply curves were to remain in their present positions, how many people would be unemployed at a $6 minimum wage?

c. A councilman has offered a counterproposal. In his view, the current minimum wage is too low and should be increased to $10 per hour. Assuming that the labor demand and supply curves remain in their present positions, how

many people would be unemployed at a $10 minimum wage?

4-12. Suppose that owners of high-rise office buildings are the main employers of custodial workers in a city. The city has decided to impose rent controls, and it has established a rent ceiling below the previous equilibrium rental rate for offices throughout the city.

a. How will the quantity of offices the building owners lease change?

b. How will the market wage and equilibrium quantity of labor services provided by custodial workers be affected by the imposition of rent controls?

4-13. In 2007, the government of a nation established a price support for wheat. The government's support price has been above the equilibrium price each year since, and the government has purchased all wheat over and above the amounts that consumers have bought at the support price. Every year since 2007, there has been an increase in the number of wheat producers in the market. No other factors affecting the market for wheat have changed. Predict what has happened every year since 2007 to each of the following:

a. Amount of wheat supplied by wheat producers

b. Amount of wheat demanded by wheat consumers

c. Amount of wheat purchased by the government

4-14. In advance of the recent increase in the U.S. minimum wage rate, the government of the state of Arizona decided to boost its own minimum wage by $1.60 per hour. This pushed the wage rate earned by Arizona teenagers above the equilibrium wage rate in the teen labor market. What is the predicted effect of this action by Arizona's government on each of the following?

a. The quantity of labor supplied by Arizona teenagers

b. The quantity of labor demanded by employers of Arizona teenagers

c. The number of unemployed Arizona teenagers

ECONOMICS ON THE NET

The Floor on Milk Prices At various times, the U.S. government has established price floors for milk. This application gives you an opportunity to apply what you have learned in this chapter to this real-world issue.

Title: Northeast Dairy Compact Commission

Navigation: Go to **www.econtoday.com/chapter04** to visit the Web site of the Northeast Dairy Compact Commission.

Application Read the contents and answer these questions.

1. Based on the government-set price control concepts discussed in Chapter 4, explain the Northeast Dairy Compact that was once in place in the northeastern United States.

2. Draw a diagram illustrating the supply of and demand for milk in the Northeast Dairy Compact and the supply of and demand for milk outside the Northeast Dairy Compact. Illustrate how the compact affected the quantities demanded and supplied for participants in the compact. In addition, show how this affected the market for milk produced by those producers outside the dairy compact.

3. Economists have found that while the Northeast Dairy Compact functioned, midwestern dairy farmers lost their dominance of milk production and sales. In light of your answer to Question 2, explain how this occurred.

For Group Discussion and Analysis Discuss the impact of congressional failure to reauthorize the compact based on your above answers. Identify which arguments in your debate are based on positive economic analysis and which are normative arguments.

ANSWERS TO QUICK QUIZZES

p. 88: (i) terms . . . exchange . . . transaction; (ii) demand . . . supply . . . supply . . . demand; (iii) immediately . . . time

p. 90: (i) first come, first served . . . political power . . . physical force . . . random assignment . . . coupons; (ii) queuing

p. 92: (i) ceilings . . . floors; (ii) ceiling . . . controls

p. 94: (i) Rental; (ii) controls . . . controls; (iii) key money

p. 99: (i) support . . . support; (ii) floor; (iii) import quotas

Public Spending and Public Choice

I t is a clear, colorless liquid with a distinctive, sickly sweet odor. Chemists refer to it as an example of a "hydroxyl compound." To most of the rest of us, however, it is *ethanol*, a substance typically manufactured in the United States using corn as a key input. Combining 1 part ethanol with 9 parts gasoline yields a motor fuel, known as "E10," that can be used to power most existing vehicles. Many observers suggest that ethanol-based motor fuel offers a win–win situation: less reliance on gasoline derived largely from foreign oil and reduced carbon pollution from auto emissions. The U.S. government currently agrees—to the tune of more than $8 billion in annual government subsidies for ethanol production. In this chapter, you will learn about rationales for this and other government subsidies.

LEARNING OBJECTIVES

After reading this chapter, you should be able to:

➤ Explain how market failures such as externalities might justify economic functions of government

➤ Distinguish between private goods and public goods and explain the nature of the free-rider problem

➤ Describe political functions of government that entail its involvement in the economy

➤ Analyze how Medicare affects the incentives to consume medical services

➤ Explain why increases in government spending on public education have not been associated with improvements in measures of student performance

➤ Discuss the central elements of the theory of public choice

? DID YOU KNOW THAT an auditor recently discovered that a New Jersey public school district had been transmitting salary payments totaling $130,000 per year to the account of an employee who had been deceased for more than 30 years? The same audit found that the school district had paid a company $953,000 for copy equipment even though the purchase order was for equipment valued only at $55,000. A media report quoted a local resident's complaint that the school district "needs to learn how to function like a private business" and "should care about taxpayers as much as companies care about their owners." As you will learn in this chapter, the incentives and institutional arrangements that condition the behavior of private firms and governments differ in some fundamental respects. One key distinction is that while firms function within the price system, a key rationale for the operations of government is to perform functions that the price system does not do well.

What a Price System Can and Cannot Do

Throughout the book so far, we have alluded to the advantages of a price system. High on the list is economic efficiency. In its ideal form, a price system allows all resources to move from lower-valued uses to higher-valued uses via voluntary exchange, by which mutually advantageous trades take place. In a price system, consumers are sovereign; that is to say, they have the individual freedom to decide what they wish to purchase. Politicians and even business managers do not ultimately decide what is produced; consumers decide. Some proponents of the price system argue that this is its most important characteristic. Competition among sellers protects consumers from coercion by one seller, and sellers are protected from coercion by one consumer because other consumers are available.

Sometimes, though, the price system does not generate these results, and too few or too many resources go to specific economic activities. Such situations are called **market failures.** Market failures prevent the price system from attaining economic efficiency and individual freedom. Market failures offer one of the strongest arguments in favor of certain economic functions of government, which we now examine.

Market failure
A situation in which the market economy leads to too few or too many resources going to a specific economic activity.

Correcting for Externalities

In a pure market system, competition generates economic efficiency only when individuals know and must bear the true opportunity cost of their actions. In some circumstances, the price that someone actually pays for a resource, good, or service is higher or lower than the opportunity cost that all of society pays for that same resource, good, or service.

Externalities

What externality is this family attempting to avoid?

Consider a hypothetical world in which there is no government regulation against pollution. You are living in a town that until now has had clean air. A steel mill moves into town. It produces steel and has paid for the inputs—land, labor, capital, and entrepreneurship. The price the mill charges for the steel reflects, in this example, only the costs that it incurs. In the course of production, however, the mill utilizes one input—clean air—by simply using it. This is indeed an input because in making steel, the furnaces emit smoke. The steel mill doesn't have to pay the cost of dirtying the air. Rather, it is the people in the community who incur that cost in the form of dirtier clothes, dirtier cars and houses, and more respiratory illnesses. The effect is similar to what would happen if the steel mill could take coal or oil or workers' services without paying for them. There is an **externality,** an external cost. Some of the costs associated with the production of the steel have "spilled over" to affect **third parties,** parties other than the buyer and the seller of the steel.

A fundamental reason that air pollution creates external costs is that the air belongs to everyone and hence to no one in particular. Lack of clearly assigned **property rights,** or the rights of an owner to use and exchange property, prevents market prices from reflecting all the costs created by activities that generate spillovers onto third parties.

Why do some observers contend that negative externalities are associated with the growing use of digital billboards?

Externality
A consequence of an economic activity that spills over to affect third parties. Pollution is an externality.

Third parties
Parties who are not directly involved in a given activity or transaction.

Property rights
The rights of an owner to use and to exchange property.

EXAMPLE
Billboards That Catch Drivers' Eyes, Sometimes for Too Long

Outdoor advertising is now the second-fastest-growing form of advertising after Internet ads. Increasingly, advertisers are returning to old-fashioned roadside billboards. Not all billboards are so old-fashioned, however. Of the 500,000 billboards lining U.S. highways and city streets, approximately 2,000 are digital billboards. The number of digital billboards is likely to grow considerably in coming years, because the $500,000 cost of installing a digital billboard is more than outweighed by the ability to sell advertising space to multiple advertisers simultaneously.

For years, critics have regarded old-fashioned billboards as a form of visual pollution blocking views of scenery. In 1965, the federal Highway Beautification Act called for a reduction in the number of billboards but failed to provide sufficient funds to pay owners to remove them. Now, critics

deride billboards for more than just blocking scenic views. They suggest that the bright, eye-catching digital billboards are diverting drivers' eyes from roadways and causing accidents. The digital billboards' bright messages distract drivers, they argue, and thereby create a negative externality by making the roads less safe for drivers and for their passengers and occupants of other cars as well.

FOR CRITICAL ANALYSIS
Why might an owner of a digital billboard respond that assignment of property rights already solves the negative externality "problem" alleged by critics? (Hint: In most states, drivers must obtain liability insurance, and laws typically hold drivers solely responsible for accidents resulting from their being distracted while driving.)

External Costs in Graphical Form

To consider how market prices fail to take into account external costs in situations in which third-party spillovers exist without a clear assignment of property rights, look at panel (a) in Figure 5-1 on the following page. Here we show the demand curve for steel as D. The supply curve is S_1. The supply curve includes only the costs that the firms have to pay. Equilibrium occurs at point E, with a price of $500 per ton and a quantity equal to 110 million tons per year. But producing steel also involves externalities—the external costs that you and your neighbors pay in the form of dirtier clothes, cars, and houses and increased respiratory disease due to the air pollution emitted from the steel mill. In this case, the producers of steel use clean air without having to pay for it. Let's include these external costs in our graph to find out what the full cost of steel production would really be if property rights to the air around the steel mill could generate payments for "owners" of that air. We do this by imagining that steel producers have to pay the "owners" of the air for the input—clean air—that the producers previously used at a zero price.

FIGURE 5-1

External Costs and Benefits

In panel (a), we show a situation in which the production of steel generates external costs. If the steel mills ignore pollution, at equilibrium the quantity of steel will be 110 million tons. If the steel mills had to pay for the external costs that are caused by the mills' production but are currently borne by nearby residents, the supply curve would shift the vertical distance $A–E_1$, to S_2. If consumers of steel were forced to pay a price that reflected the spillover costs, the quantity demanded would fall to 100 million tons. In panel (b), we show a situation in which inoculations against communicable diseases generate external benefits to those individuals who may not be inoculated but who will benefit because epidemics will not occur. If each individual ignores the external benefit of inoculations, the market clearing quantity will be 150 million. If external benefits were taken into account by purchasers of inoculations, however, the demand curve would shift to D_2. The new equilibrium quantity would be 200 million inoculations, and the price of an inoculation would rise from $10 to $15.

Panel (a)

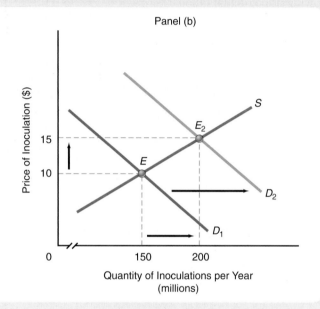

Panel (b)

Recall from Chapter 3 that an increase in input prices shifts the supply curve up and to the left. Thus, in panel (a) of the figure, the supply curve shifts from S_1 to S_2. External costs equal the vertical distance between A and E_1. In this example, if steel firms had to take into account these external costs, the equilibrium quantity would fall to 100 million tons per year, and the price would rise to $600 per ton. Equilibrium would shift from E to E_1. In contrast, if the price of steel does not account for external costs, third parties bear those costs—represented by the distance between A and E_1—in the form of dirtier clothes, houses, and cars and increased respiratory illnesses.

External Benefits in Graphical Form

Externalities can also be positive. To demonstrate external benefits in graphical form, we will use the example of inoculations against communicable disease. In panel (b) of Figure 5-1, we show the demand curve as D_1 (without taking account of any external benefits) and the supply curve as S. The equilibrium price is $10 per inoculation, and the equilibrium quantity is 150 million inoculations.

We assume, however, that inoculations against communicable diseases generate external benefits to individuals who may not be inoculated but will benefit nevertheless because epidemics will not break out. If such external benefits were taken into account by those who purchase inoculations, the demand curve would shift from D_1 to D_2.

As a consequence of this shift in demand at point E_2, the new equilibrium quantity would be 200 million inoculations, and the new equilibrium price would be $15 per inoculation. If people who consider getting inoculations fail to take external benefits into account, this society is not devoting enough resources to inoculations against communicable diseases.

How do inoculations generate positive externalities?

Resource Misallocations of Externalities

When there are external costs, the market will tend to *overallocate* resources to the production of the good or service in question, for those goods or services are implicitly priced deceptively low. In the steel example, too many resources will be allocated to steel production, because the steel mill owners and managers are not required to take account of the external cost that steel production is imposing on the rest of society. In essence, the full cost of production is not borne by the owners and managers, so the price they charge the public for steel is lower than it would otherwise be. And, of course, the lower price means that buyers are willing and able to buy more. More steel is produced and consumed than if the sellers were to bear external costs.

In contrast, when there are external benefits, the price is too low to induce suppliers to allocate resources to the production of that good or service (because the demand, which fails to reflect the external benefits, is relatively too low). Thus, the market *underallocates* resources to producing the good or service. Hence, in a market system, too many of the goods that generate external costs are produced, and too few of the goods that generate external benefits are produced.

How the Government Can Correct Negative Externalities

In theory, the government can take action to try to correct situations in which a lack of property rights allows third-party spillovers to create an externality. In the case of negative externalities, at least two avenues are open to the government: special taxes and legislative regulation or prohibition.

SPECIAL TAXES In our example of the steel mill, the externality problem arises because using the air for waste disposal is costless to the firm but not to society. The government could attempt to tax the steel mill commensurate with the cost to third parties from smoke in the air. This, in effect, would be a pollution tax or an **effluent fee.** The ultimate effect would be to reduce the supply of steel and raise the price to consumers, ideally making the price equal to the full cost of production to society.

Effluent fee
A charge to a polluter that gives the right to discharge into the air or water a certain amount of pollution; also called a *pollution tax*

REGULATION Alternatively, to correct a negative externality arising from steel production, the government could specify a maximum allowable rate of pollution. This regulation would require that the steel mill install pollution abatement equipment at its facilities, reduce its rate of output, or some combination of the two. Note that the government's job would not be simple, for it would have to determine the appropriate level of pollution, which would require extensive knowledge of both the benefits and the costs of pollution control.

Go to www.econtoday.com/chapter05 to learn more about how the Environmental Protection Agency uses regulations to try to protect the environment.

How the Government Can Correct Positive Externalities

What can the government do when the production of one good spills *benefits* over to third parties? It has several policy options: financing the production of the good or producing the good itself, subsidies (negative taxes), and regulation.

GOVERNMENT FINANCING AND PRODUCTION If the positive externalities seem extremely large, the government has the option of financing the desired additional production facilities so that the "right" amount of the good will be produced. Again consider inoculations against communicable diseases. The government could—and often does—finance campaigns to inoculate the population. It could (and does) even produce and operate inoculation centers where inoculations are given at no charge.

SUBSIDIES A subsidy is a negative tax; it is a payment made either to a business or to a consumer when the business produces or the consumer buys a good or a service. To generate more inoculations against communicable diseases, the government could subsidize everyone who obtains an inoculation by directly reimbursing those inoculated or by making payments to private firms that provide inoculations. Subsidies reduce the net price to consumers, thereby causing a larger quantity to be demanded.

How are governments seeking to help society capture the external benefits of transportation services that keep elderly drivers off the roads?

POLICY EXAMPLE
Incentives Coax Senior Citizens from Behind the Wheel

Many people continue driving even after their skills and senses falter. Drivers age 75 and older have higher crash rates per mile traveled than all age groups except 16- and 18-year-olds. Drivers age 85 and older are at fault in accidents more than twice as often as younger drivers. Members of the baby boom generation are already reaching the age of 65, when driving capabilities begin to falter, and many more will reach this age during the coming two decades. The Insurance Institute for Highway Safety estimates that if current U.S. population trends continue, by 2030 these drivers will account for 16 percent of all auto accidents and 25 percent of all fatal crashes.

Governments are already working to make roadways safer by providing incentives for aging baby boomers to park their cars and choose alternative modes of transportation. Many state governments are easing regulations that impede efforts by private firms to offer elderly people transportation. Some municipal governments, such as those in Atlanta and Oklahoma City, are providing vouchers that help cover most of the price of public transportation. A few cities, such as Portland, Maine, are supporting efforts by nonprofit organizations to provide transportation services to seniors. One Portland-supported nonprofit organization even accepts car trade-ins from seniors in return for credit toward future transportation services. Thus, governments are promoting alternative modes of transportation for seniors in an effort to attain the external benefit of getting more elderly residents out from behind the wheel.

FOR CRITICAL ANALYSIS
How do government subsidies for alternative modes of transportation affect seniors' demands for these alternative transportation services?

REGULATION In some cases involving positive externalities, the government can require by law that individuals in the society undertake a certain action. For example, regulations require that all school-age children be inoculated before entering public and private schools. Some people believe that a basic school education itself generates positive externalities. Perhaps as a result of this belief, we have regulations—laws—that require all school-age children to be enrolled in a public or private school.

The Other Economic Functions of Government

Besides correcting for externalities, the government performs many other economic functions that affect the way exchange is carried out. In contrast, the political functions of government have to do with deciding how income should be redistributed among households and selecting which goods and services have special merits and should therefore be treated differently. The economic and political functions of government can and do overlap.

Let's look at four more economic functions of government.

Providing a Legal System

The courts and the police may not at first seem like economic functions of government. Their activities nonetheless have important consequences for economic activities in any country. You and I enter into contracts constantly, whether they be oral or written, expressed or implied. When we believe that we have been wronged, we seek redress of our grievances through our legal institutions. Moreover, consider the legal system that is necessary for the smooth functioning of our economic system. Our system has defined quite explicitly the legal status of businesses, the rights of private ownership, and a method of enforcing contracts. All relationships among consumers and businesses are governed by the legal rules of the game. In its judicial function, then, the government serves as the referee for settling disputes in the economic arena. In this role, the government often imposes penalties for violations of legal rules.

Much of our legal system is involved with defining and protecting property rights. One might say that property rights are really the rules of our economic game. When property rights are well defined, owners of property have an incentive to use that property efficiently. Any mistakes in their decisions about the use of property have negative consequences that the owners suffer. Furthermore, when property rights are well defined, owners of property have an incentive to maintain that property so that if they ever desire to sell it, it will fetch a better price.

Promoting Competition

Many people believe that the only way to attain economic efficiency is through competition. One of the roles of government is to serve as the protector of a competitive economic system. Congress and the various state governments have passed **antitrust legislation.** Such legislation makes illegal certain (but not all) economic activities that might restrain trade—that is, that might prevent free competition among actual and potential rival firms in the marketplace. The avowed aim of

Antitrust legislation
Laws that restrict the formation of monopolies and regulate certain anticompetitive business practices.

Monopoly
A firm that can determine the market price of a good. In the extreme case, a monopoly is the only seller of a good or service.

antitrust legislation is to reduce the power of **monopolies**—firms that can determine the market price of the goods they sell. A large number of antitrust laws have been passed that prohibit specific anticompetitive actions. Both the Antitrust Division of the Department of Justice and the Federal Trade Commission attempt to enforce these antitrust laws. Various state judicial agencies also expend efforts at maintaining competition.

Providing Public Goods

Private goods
Goods that can be consumed by only one individual at a time. Private goods are subject to the principle of rival consumption.

The goods used in our examples up to this point have been **private goods.** When I eat a cheeseburger, you cannot eat the same one. So you and I are rivals for that cheeseburger, just as much as contenders for the title of world champion are. When I use a DVD player, you cannot play some other disc at the same time. When I use the services of an auto mechanic, that person cannot work at the same time for you. That is the distinguishing feature of private goods—their use is exclusive to the people who purchase or rent them. The **principle of rival consumption** applies to all private goods by definition. Rival consumption is easy to understand. Either you use a private good or I use it.

Principle of rival consumption
The recognition that individuals are rivals in consuming private goods because one person's consumption reduces the amount available for others to consume.

There is an entire class of goods that are not private goods. These are called **public goods.** The principle of rival consumption does not apply to them. They can be consumed *jointly* by many individuals simultaneously, and no one can be excluded from consuming these goods even if they fail to pay to do so. National defense, police protection, and the legal system are examples of public goods.

Public goods
Goods for which the principle of rival consumption does not apply; they can be jointly consumed by many individuals simultaneously at no additional cost and with no reduction in quality or quantity. Also no one who fails to help pay for the good can be denied the benefit of the good.

CHARACTERISTICS OF PUBLIC GOODS Two fundamental characteristics of public goods set them apart from all other goods:

1. *Public goods can be used by more and more people at no additional opportunity cost and without depriving others of any of the services of the goods.* Once funds have been spent on national defense, the defense protection you receive does not reduce the amount of protection bestowed on anyone else. The opportunity cost of your receiving national defense once it is in place is zero because once national defense is in place to protect you, it also protects others.

2. *It is difficult to design a collection system for a public good on the basis of how much individuals use it.* Nonpayers can often utilize a public good without incurring any monetary cost, because the cost of excluding them from using the good is so high. Those who provide the public good find that it is not cost-effective to prevent nonpayers from utilizing it. For instance, taxpayers who pay to provide national defense typically do not incur the costs that would be entailed in excluding nonpayers from benefiting from national defense.

One of the problems of public goods is that the private sector has a difficult, if not impossible, time providing them. Individuals in the private sector have little or no incentive to offer public goods. It is difficult for them to make a profit doing so, because nonpayers cannot be excluded. Consequently, true public goods must necessarily be provided by government. Note, though, that economists do not categorize something as a public good simply because the government provides it.

When it comes to public goods, what's new about "dot-nu" on the Internet?

E-COMMERCE EXAMPLE
Is the "Nu" Internet Domain a Public Good?

With its closest neighbor, Tonga, more than 350 miles distant, the South Pacific island nation of Niue (pronounced "new-ay") is among the earth's most remote locales. Nevertheless, a key national objective is to be one of the most Web-connected countries on the planet. Niue's residents were the first to possess nationwide wireless Internet access; hence, Niue's self-proclaimed nickname—the "WiFi nation." Complete wireless access is provided by a private company based in Medfield, Massachusetts. In return, Niue's government has granted to that company most legal rights to the Internet domain name "dot-nu." Of course, "nu" sounds like "new" in English, and in Swedish "nu" happens to mean "now." Thus, firms in English-speaking nations and in Sweden have been rushing to purchase Web addresses with the "nu" domain name.

Now many residents are objecting to this arrangement. If the Niue government had retained control over Web addresses within the "nu" domain, they contend, the nation could have reaped benefits, such as a steady stream of registration fees that more and more of its residents could have received at no additional opportunity cost. Furthermore, they argue, none of Niue's residents could have been denied such benefits, even if they had not paid for them. Hence, critics of the deal with the U.S. company suggest that residents of Niue have been cheated out of control over what ought to be a public good—at least, by their logic.

FOR CRITICAL ANALYSIS

Is the "nu" domain on the Internet really a public good? (Hint: Is the "nu" domain name currently subject to the principle of rival consumption? Does possession of only one *of the two characteristics of a public good mean that an item* is *a public good?)*

FREE RIDERS The nature of public goods leads to the **free-rider problem,** a situation in which some individuals take advantage of the fact that others will assume the burden of paying for public goods such as national defense. Suppose that citizens were taxed directly in proportion to how much they tell an interviewer that they value national defense. Some people who actually value national defense will probably tell interviewers that it has no value to them—they don't want any of it. Such people are trying to be free riders. We may all want to be free riders if we believe that someone else will provide the commodity in question that we actually value.

The free-rider problem often arises in connection with sharing the burden of international defense. A country may choose to belong to a multilateral defense organization, such as the North Atlantic Treaty Organization (NATO), but then consistently attempt to avoid contributing funds to the organization. The nation knows it would be defended by others in NATO if it were attacked but would rather not pay for such defense. In short, it seeks a free ride.

Free-rider problem
A problem that arises when individuals presume that others will pay for public goods so that, individually, they can escape paying for their portion without causing a reduction in production.

Ensuring Economywide Stability

Our economy sometimes faces the problems of undesired unemployment and rising prices. The government, especially the federal government, has made an attempt to solve these problems by trying to stabilize the economy by smoothing out the ups and downs in overall business activity. The notion that the federal government should undertake actions to stabilize business activity is a relatively new idea in the United States, encouraged by high unemployment rates during the Great Depression of the 1930s and subsequent theories about possible ways that government could reduce unemployment. In 1946, Congress passed the Full-Employment Act, a landmark law concerning government responsibility for economic performance. It established three goals for government stabilization policy: full employment, price stability, and economic growth. These goals have provided the justification for many government economic programs during the post–World War II period.

The Political Functions of Government

At least two functions of government are political or normative functions rather than economic ones like those discussed in the first part of this chapter. These two areas are (1) the provision and regulation of government-sponsored and government-inhibited goods and (2) income redistribution.

Government-Sponsored and Government-Inhibited Goods

Government-sponsored good
A good that has been deemed socially desirable through the political process. Museums are an example.

Government-inhibited good
A good that has been deemed socially undesirable through the political process. Heroin is an example.

Through political processes, governments often determine that certain goods possess special merit and seek to promote their production and consumption. A **government-sponsored good** is defined as any good that the political process has deemed socially desirable. (Note that nothing inherent in any particular good makes it a government-sponsored good. The designation is entirely subjective.) Examples of government-sponsored goods in our society are sports stadiums, museums, ballets, plays, and concerts. In these areas, the government's role is the provision of these goods to the people in society who would not otherwise purchase them at market clearing prices or who would not purchase an amount of them judged to be sufficient. This provision may take the form of government production and distribution of the goods. It can also take the form of reimbursement for spending on government-sponsored goods or subsidies to producers or consumers for part of the goods' costs. Governments do indeed subsidize such goods as professional sports, concerts, ballets, museums, and plays. In most cases, those goods would not be so numerous without subsidization.

Government-inhibited goods are the opposite of government-sponsored goods. They are goods that, through the political process, have been deemed socially undesirable. Heroin, cigarettes, gambling, and cocaine are examples. The government exercises its role with respect to these goods by taxing, regulating, or prohibiting their manufacture, sale, and use. Governments justify the relatively high taxes on alcohol and tobacco by declaring that they are socially undesirable. The best-known example of governmental exercise of power in this area is the stance against certain psychoactive drugs. Most psychoactives (except nicotine, caffeine, and alcohol) are either expressly prohibited, as is the case for heroin, cocaine, and opium, or heavily regulated, as in the case of prescription psychoactives.

This drug bust represents what type of government activity?

What item is a government-inhibited good in the United States but a government-sponsored good in China?

INTERNATIONAL POLICY EXAMPLE
China's Government Struggles with How to Regard Tobacco

About 36 percent of all adults in China smoke, whereas only 21 percent of adults in the United States do. An estimated 10 percent of Chinese middle school students smoke, which is nearly double the U.S. rate. All told, the number of smokers in China—about 350 million—exceeds the entire U.S. population.

For China's government, the good news is that it owns the nation's cigarette manufacturing company, China National Tobacco Corporation. The government plows earnings from the firm's tobacco sales into a variety of activities, including constructing highways, hydroelectric dams, and railroads. The bad news is that all the smoking that the China National Tobacco Corporation has promoted in advertising campaigns is creating an epidemic of diseases, including lung cancer,

emphysema, and oral cancer. At present, more than 1 million Chinese residents die of tobacco-related diseases each year. The rate of growth of smoking is so high that this death toll is projected to more than double by 2025.

Consequently, even as the Chinese government sponsors tobacco production, the government's Center for Disease Control and Prevention has declared tobacco use to be the nation's biggest public health problem. China's government has regarded cigarettes as a government-sponsored good for 50 years. Now it is beginning to reconsider this designation.

FOR CRITICAL ANALYSIS
Who stands to lose if China's government ends tobacco's status as a government-sponsored good?

Income Redistribution

Another relatively recent political function of government has been the explicit redistribution of income. This redistribution uses two systems: the progressive income tax (described in Chapter 6) and transfer payments. **Transfer payments** are payments made to individuals for which no services or goods are rendered in return. The two primary money transfer payments in our system are Social Security old-age and disability benefits and unemployment insurance benefits. Income redistribution also includes a large amount of income **transfers in kind,** rather than money transfers. Some income transfers in kind are food stamps, Medicare and Medicaid, government health care services, and subsidized public housing.

The government has also engaged in other activities as a form of redistribution of income. For example, the provision of public education is at least in part an attempt to redistribute income by making sure that the poor have access to education.

Transfer payments
Money payments made by governments to individuals for which no services or goods are rendered in return. Examples are Social Security old-age and disability benefits and unemployment insurance benefits.

Transfers in kind
Payments that are in the form of actual goods and services, such as food stamps, subsidized public housing, and medical care, and for which no goods or services are rendered in return.

QUICK QUIZ | *See page 133 for the answers. Review concepts from this section in MyEconLab.*

Political, or normative, activities of the government include the provision and regulation of _____-_____ and _____-_____ goods and _____ redistribution.

Government-sponsored and government-inhibited goods do not have any inherent characteristics that qualify them as such; rather, collectively, through the _____ process,

we make judgments about which goods and services are "good" for society and which are "bad."

Income redistribution can be carried out by a system of progressive taxation, coupled with _____ payments, which can be made in money or in kind, such as food stamps and Medicare.

Public Spending and Transfer Programs

The size of the public sector can be measured in many different ways. One way is to count the number of public employees. Another is to look at total government outlays. Government outlays include all government expenditures on employees, rent, electricity, and the like. In addition, total government outlays include transfer payments, such as welfare and Social Security. In Figure 5-2, you see that government outlays prior to World War I did not exceed 10 percent of annual national income. There was a spike during World War I, a general increase during the Great Depression, and then a huge spike during World War II. Contrary to previous postwar periods, after World War II government outlays as a percentage of total national income rose steadily before dropping in the 1990s and rising again in the 2000s.

How do federal and state governments allocate their spending? A typical federal government budget is shown in panel (a) of Figure 5-3. The three largest categories are Medicare and other health-related spending, Social Security and other income-security programs, and national defense, which together constitute 78.4 percent of the total federal budget.

The makeup of state and local expenditures is quite different. As panel (b) shows, education is the biggest category, accounting for 34.2 percent of all expenditures.

Publicly Subsidized Health Care: Medicare

Figure 5-3 shows that health-related spending is a significant portion of total government expenditures. Certainly, medical expenses are a major concern for many elderly people. Since 1965, that concern has been reflected in the existence of the Medicare program, which pays hospital and physicians' bills for U.S. residents over the age of 65 (and for those younger than 65 in some instances). In return for paying a tax on their earnings while in the workforce (currently set at 2.9 percent of wages and salaries), retirees are assured that the majority of their hospital and physicians' bills will be paid for with public monies.

Go to www.econtoday.com/chapter05 to visit the U.S. government's official Medicare Web site.

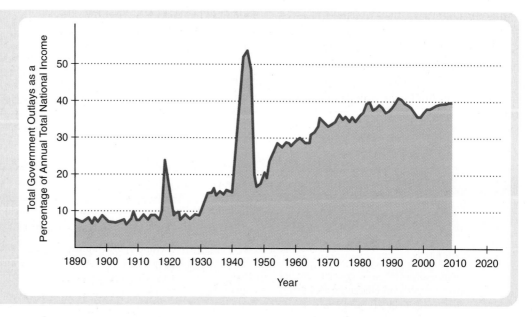

FIGURE 5-2

Total Government Outlays over Time

Total government outlays (federal, state, and local combined) remained small until the 1930s, except during World War I. Since World War II, government outlays have not fallen back to their historical average.

Sources: Facts and Figures on Government Finance, various issues; Economic Indicators, various issues.

FIGURE 5-3

Federal Government Spending Compared to State and Local Spending

The federal government's spending habits are quite different from those of the states and cities. In panel (a), you can see that the most important categories in the federal budget are Medicare and other health-related spending, Social Security and other income-security programs, and national defense, which make up 78.4 percent. In panel (b), the most important category at the state and local level is education, which makes up 34.2 percent. "Other" includes expenditures in such areas as waste treatment, garbage collection, mosquito abatement, and the judicial system.

Sources: Budget of the United States government; government finances.

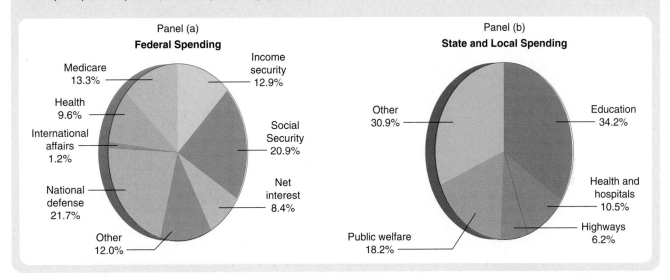

Panel (a)
Federal Spending

- Medicare 13.3%
- Health 9.6%
- International affairs 1.2%
- National defense 21.7%
- Other 12.0%
- Income security 12.9%
- Social Security 20.9%
- Net interest 8.4%

Panel (b)
State and Local Spending

- Other 30.9%
- Education 34.2%
- Health and hospitals 10.5%
- Highways 6.2%
- Public welfare 18.2%

THE SIMPLE ECONOMICS OF MEDICARE To understand how, in less than 40 years, Medicare became the second-biggest domestic government spending program in existence, a bit of economics is in order. Consider Figure 5-4 on the following page, which shows the demand for and supply of medical care.

The initial equilibrium price is P_0 and equilibrium quantity is Q_0. Perhaps because the government believes that Q_0 is not enough medical care for these consumers, suppose that the government begins paying a subsidy that eventually is set at M for each unit of medical care consumed. This will simultaneously tend to raise the price per unit of care received by providers (physicians, hospitals, and the like) and lower the perceived price per unit that consumers see when they make decisions about how much medical care to consume. As presented in the figure, the price received by providers rises to P_s, while the price paid by consumers falls to P_d. As a result, consumers of medical care want to purchase Q_m units, and suppliers are quite happy to provide it for them.

MEDICARE INCENTIVES AT WORK We can now understand the problems that plague the Medicare system today. First, one of the things that people observed during the 20 years after the founding of Medicare was a huge upsurge in physicians' incomes and medical school applications, the spread of private for-profit hospitals, and the rapid proliferation of new medical tests and procedures. All of this was being encouraged by the rise in the price of medical services from P_0 to P_s, which encouraged entry into this market.

Second, government expenditures on Medicare have routinely turned out to be far in excess of the expenditures forecast at the time the program was put in place or was

How has the existence of Medicare changed seniors' consumption of medical services?

FIGURE 5-4

The Economic Effects of Medicare Subsidies

When the government pays a per-unit subsidy M for medical care, consumers pay the price of services P_d for the quantity of services Q_m. Providers receive the price P_s for supplying this quantity. Originally, the federal government projected that its total spending on Medicare would equal an amount such as the area $Q_0 \times (P_0 - P_d)$. Because actual consumption equals Q_m, however, the government's total expenditures equal $Q_m \times M$.

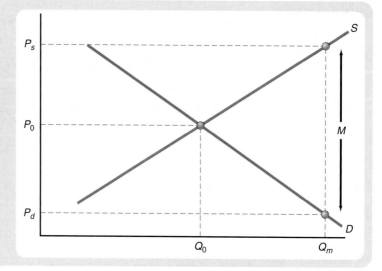

expanded. The reasons for this are easy to see. Bureaucratic planners often fail to recognize the incentive effects of government programs. On the demand side, they fail to account for the huge increase in consumption (from Q_0 to Q_m) that will result from a subsidy like Medicare. On the supply side, they fail to recognize that the larger amount of services can only be extracted from suppliers at a higher price, P_s. Consequently, original projected spending on Medicare was an area like $Q_0 \times (P_0 - P_d)$, because original plans for the program only contemplated consumption of Q_0 and assumed that the subsidy would have to be only $P_0 - P_d$ per unit. In fact, consumption rises to Q_m, and the additional cost per unit of service rises to P_s, implying an increase in the per-unit subsidy to M. Hence, actual expenditures turn out to be the far larger number $Q_m \times M$. Every expansion of the program, including the 2004 broadening of Medicare to cover obesity as a new illness eligible for coverage and the extension of Medicare to cover patients' prescription drug expenses beginning in 2006, has followed the same pattern.

Third, total spending on medical services soars, consuming far more income than initially expected. Originally, total spending on medical services was $P_0 \times Q_0$. In the presence of Medicare, spending rises to $P_s \times Q_m$.

HEALTH CARE SUBSIDIES CONTINUE TO GROW Just how fast are Medicare subsidies growing? Medicare's cost has risen from 0.7 percent of U.S. national income in 1970 to more than 2.8 percent today, which amounts to nearly $400 billion per year. Because Medicare spending is growing much faster than total employer and employee contributions, future spending guarantees far outstrip the taxes to be collected in the future to pay for the system. (The current Medicare tax rate is 2.9 percent on all earnings, with 1.45 percent paid by the employee and 1.45 percent paid by the employer.) Today, unfunded guarantees of Medicare spending in the future are estimated at more than $25 trillion (in today's dollars).

These amounts fail to reflect the costs of another federal health program called Medicaid. The Medicaid program is structured similarly to Medicare, in that the government also pays per-unit subsidies for health care to qualifying patients. Medicaid, however, provides subsidies only to people who qualify because they have lower incomes. At present, about 50 million people, or about one out of every six U.S. residents, qualify for Medicaid coverage. Medicaid is administered by state governments, but the federal government pays about 57 percent of the program's total cost from general tax revenues. The current cost of the program is more than $400 billion per year. In recent years, Medicaid spending has grown even faster than expenditures on Medicare, rising by more than 75 percent since 2000 alone. Current estimates indicate that spending on Medicaid is likely to increase at an annual rate of nearly 8 percent for the foreseeable future.

How have government health care subsidy programs such as Medicare contributed to a preference by physicians for expensive face-to-face communications with patients instead of less costly phone and e-mail consultations?

POLICY EXAMPLE
If the Government Doesn't Pay for It, Physicians Don't Do It

Lawyers, accountants, and most other professionals regard telephone and e-mail as indispensable tools for communicating with clients. In contrast, phone consultations with physicians are very rare, and only 2 percent of patients have regular e-mail contact with their physicians. Medicare pays for about 7,500 specific health-care-related services, including face-to-face visits with physicians. The program does not, however, recompense physicians for time they devote to telephone or e-mail consultations with patients. Hence, Medicare gives physicians incentives to schedule appointments with patients in their offices but provides no incentives to utilize modes of communication that would be more efficient in a number of situations. Physicians, in turn, have responded to these incentives by scheduling steady streams of office visits with patients and avoiding phone calls and e-mail communications.

FOR CRITICAL ANALYSIS
Who pays for the fact that Medicare's payment rules promote higher-priced, face-to-face physician-patient communications instead of lower-priced, remote communications?

Economic Issues of Public Education

In the United States, government involvement in health care is a relatively recent phenomenon. In contrast, state and local governments have assumed primary responsibility for public education for many years. Currently, these governments spend more than $700 billion on education—more than 4 percent of total U.S. national income. State and local sales, excise, property, and income taxes finance the bulk of these expenditures. In addition, each year the federal government provides tens of billions of dollars of support for public education through grants and other transfers to state and local governments.

THE NOW-FAMILIAR ECONOMICS OF PUBLIC EDUCATION State and local governments around the United States have developed a variety of complex mechanisms for funding public education. What all public education programs have in common, however, is the provision of educational services to primary, secondary, and college students at prices well below those that would otherwise prevail in the marketplace for these services.

So how do state and local governments accomplish this? The answer is that they operate public education programs that share some of the features of government-subsidized health care programs such as Medicare. Analogously to Figure 5-4, public schools provide educational services at a price below the market price. They are willing to produce the quantity of educational services demanded at this below-market price as long as they receive a sufficiently high per-unit subsidy from state and local governments.

THE INCENTIVE PROBLEMS OF PUBLIC EDUCATION Since the 1960s, various measures of the performance of U.S. primary and secondary students have failed to increase even as public spending on education has risen. Some measures of student performance have even declined.

Many economists argue that the incentive effects that have naturally arisen with higher government subsidies for public education help to explain this lack of improvement in student performance. A higher per-pupil subsidy creates a difference between the relatively high per-unit costs to schools of providing the amount of educational services that parents and students are willing to purchase and the relatively lower valuations of those services. As a consequence, some schools have provided services, such as after-school babysitting and various social services, that have contributed relatively little to student learning.

A factor that complicates efforts to assess the effects of education subsidies is that the public schools often face little or no competition from unsubsidized providers of educational services. In addition, public schools rarely compete against each other. In most locales, therefore, parents who are unhappy with the quality of services provided at the subsidized price cannot transfer their child to a different public school.

Have subsidies intended to promote public schools' Internet connectivity improved student learning outcomes?

You Are There

To contemplate the operation of a college as a private business, read **Aiming to Prevent Cost from Exceeding Value per Dollar in Higher Education,** on page 126.

E-COMMERCE EXAMPLE
The Minuscule Payoff from Public School Internet Subsidies

Among other things, the U.S. Telecommunications Act of 1996 created a program known as E-Rate, which provides subsidies to public schools for use in connecting classrooms to the Web. Under the E-Rate program, about $2 billion per year goes to subsidize between 20 and 90 percent of recipient schools' Internet-related telecommunications spending, depending on the schools' qualifying characteristics. On average, the E-Rate subsidy amounts to about $100 per pupil.

Although the immediate objective of this subsidy was to ensure that more students would have access to the Internet, E-Rate's creators also predicted that the program would improve student learning. Nevertheless, studies of student performances in two of the most populous states, Texas and California, find no concrete evidence that the program has improved outcomes. A decade after E-Rate was established, performances on standardized tests were virtually unchanged, as were student enrollments in advanced courses. High school dropout and graduation rates also remained the same. The E-Rate program has boosted Web access in the nation's public schools, but there is little evidence that more Internet connectivity has improved learning.

FOR CRITICAL ANALYSIS
Why might the $100-per-student E-Rate subsidy provide a minuscule learning payoff for students who already have Internet access at home?

QUICK QUIZ *See page 133 for the answers. Review concepts from this section in MyEconLab.*

Medicare subsidizes the consumption of medical care by the elderly, thus increasing the amount of such care consumed. People tend to purchase large amounts of _____-value, _____-cost services in publicly funded health care programs such as Medicare, because they do not directly bear the full cost of their decisions.

Basic economic analysis indicates that higher subsidies for public education have widened the differential between parents' and students' relatively _____ per-unit valuations of the educational services of public schools and the _____ costs that schools incur in providing those services.

Collective Decision Making: The Theory of Public Choice

Governments consist of individuals. No government actually thinks and acts; rather, government actions are the result of decision making by individuals in their roles as elected representatives, appointed officials, and salaried bureaucrats. Therefore, to understand how government works, we must examine the incentives of the people in government as well as those who would like to be in government—avowed or would-be candidates for elective or appointed positions—and special-interest lobbyists attempting to get government to do something. At issue is the analysis of **collective decision making.** Collective decision making involves the actions of voters, politicians, political parties, interest groups, and many other groups and individuals. The analysis of collective decision making is usually called the **theory of public choice.** It has been given this name because it involves hypotheses about how choices are made in the public sector, as opposed to the private sector. The foundation of public-choice theory is the assumption that individuals will act within the political process to maximize their *individual* (not collective) well-being. In that sense, the theory is similar to our analysis of the market economy, in which we also assume that individuals act as though they are motivated by self-interest.

To understand public-choice theory, it is necessary to point out other similarities between the private market sector and the public, or government, sector; then we will look at the differences.

Collective decision making
How voters, politicians, and other interested parties act and how these actions influence nonmarket decisions.

Theory of public choice
The study of collective decision making.

Similarities in Market and Public-Sector Decision Making

In addition to the assumption of self-interest being the motivating force in both sectors, there are other similarities.

OPPORTUNITY COST Everything that is spent by all levels of government plus everything that is spent by the private sector must add up to the total income available at any point in time. Hence, every government action has an opportunity cost, just as in the market sector.

COMPETITION Although we typically think of competition as a private-market phenomenon, it is also present in collective action. Given the scarcity constraint government faces, bureaucrats, appointed officials, and elected representatives will always be in competition for available government funds. Furthermore, the individuals within any government agency or institution will act as individuals do in the private sector: They will try to obtain higher wages, better working conditions, and higher job-level classifications. We assume that they will compete and act in their own interest, not society's.

SIMILARITY OF INDIVIDUALS Contrary to popular belief, the types of individuals working in the private sector and working in the public sector are not inherently different. The difference, as we shall see, is that the individuals in government face a different **incentive structure** than those in the private sector. For example, the costs and benefits of being efficient or inefficient differ in the private and public sectors.

One approach to predicting government bureaucratic behavior is to ask what incentives bureaucrats face. Take the United States Postal Service (USPS) as an example. The bureaucrats running that government corporation are human beings with

Incentive structure
The system of rewards and punishments individuals face with respect to their own actions.

IQs not dissimilar to those possessed by workers in similar positions at Microsoft or American Airlines. Yet the USPS does not function like either of these companies. The difference can be explained in terms of the incentives provided for managers in the two types of institutions. When the bureaucratic managers and workers at Microsoft make incorrect decisions, work slowly, produce shoddy products, and are generally "inefficient," the profitability of the company declines. The owners—millions of shareholders—express their displeasure by selling some of their shares of company stock. The market value, as tracked on the stock exchange, falls. This induces owners of shares of stock to pressure managers to pursue strategies more likely to boost revenues and reduce costs.

But what about the USPS? If a manager, a worker, or a bureaucrat in the USPS gives shoddy service, the organization's owners—the taxpayers—have no straightforward mechanism for expressing their dissatisfaction. Despite the postal service's status as a "government corporation," taxpayers as shareholders do not really own shares of stock in the organization that they can sell.

Thus, to understand purported inefficiency in the government bureaucracy, we need to examine incentives and institutional arrangements—not people and personalities.

Differences Between Market and Collective Decision Making

There are probably more dissimilarities between the market sector and the public sector than there are similarities.

GOVERNMENT GOODS AND SERVICES AT ZERO PRICE The majority of goods that governments produce are furnished to the ultimate consumers without payment required. **Government,** or **political, goods** can be either private or public goods. The fact that they are furnished to the ultimate consumer free of charge does *not* mean that the cost to society of those goods is zero, however. It only means that the price *charged* is zero. The full opportunity cost to society is the value of the resources used in the production of goods produced and provided by the government.

For example, none of us pays directly for each unit of consumption of defense or police protection. Rather, we pay for all these items indirectly through the taxes that support our governments—federal, state, and local. This special feature of government can be looked at in a different way. There is no longer a one-to-one relationship between consumption of government-provided goods and services and payment for these items. Indeed, most taxpayers will find that their tax bill is the same whether or not they consume government-provided goods.

USE OF FORCE All governments can resort to using force in their regulation of economic affairs. For example, governments can use *expropriation*, which means that if you refuse to pay your taxes, your bank account and other assets may be seized by the Internal Revenue Service. In fact, you have no choice in the matter of paying taxes to governments. Collectively, we decide the total size of government through the political process, but individually, we cannot determine how much service we pay for during any one year.

VOTING VERSUS SPENDING In the private market sector, a dollar voting system is in effect. This dollar voting system is not equivalent to the voting system in the public sector. There are at least three differences:

1. In a political system, one person gets one vote, whereas in the market system, each dollar a person spends counts separately.

Government, or political, goods
Goods (and services) provided by the public sector; they can be either private or public goods.

2. The political system is run by **majority rule,** whereas the market system is run by **proportional rule.**

3. The spending of dollars can indicate intensity of want, whereas because of the all-or-nothing nature of political voting, a vote cannot.

Ultimately, the main distinction between political votes and dollar votes is that political outcomes may differ from economic outcomes. Remember that economic efficiency is a situation in which, given the prevailing distribution of income, consumers obtain the economic goods they want. There is no corresponding situation when political voting determines economic outcomes. Thus, a political voting process is unlikely to lead to the same decisions that a dollar voting process would yield in the marketplace.

Indeed, consider the dilemma every voter faces. Usually, a voter is not asked to decide on a single issue (although this happens); rather, a voter is asked to choose among candidates who present a large number of issues and state a position on each of them. Just consider the average U.S. senator, who has to vote on several thousand different issues during a six-year term. When you vote for that senator, you are voting for a person who must make thousands of decisions during the next six years.

How are economic outcomes in the world oil market affected by governmental involvement in extraction and distribution?

Majority rule
A collective decision-making system in which group decisions are made on the basis of more than 50 percent of the vote. In other words, whatever more than half of the electorate votes for, the entire electorate has to accept.

Proportional rule
A decision-making system in which actions are based on the proportion of the "votes" cast and are in proportion to them. In a market system, if 10 percent of the "dollar votes" are cast for blue cars, 10 percent of automobile output will be blue cars.

INTERNATIONAL EXAMPLE
Why a Synonym for "Big Oil" Is "Big Government"

Politicians and pundits commonly blame "big oil"—their shorthand for private oil companies—for higher oil prices. In fact, one factor contributing to the upward creep of inflation-adjusted oil prices is that an ever-greater share of oil is produced under government direction. In the early days of oil production, private firms produced the bulk of the world's oil. In contrast, today private companies such as Chevron, British Petroleum, ConocoPhillips, and ExxonMobil directly manage oil production from only 5 percent of the world's known reserves. Governments and government-owned companies coordinate production from the remaining 95 percent of reserves. To the extent that political

factors influence governmentally managed oil production, output and price outcomes differ from those that privately directed production would have produced. Indeed, there is evidence that government-coordinated oil extraction and distribution is more costly than private oil production. These higher costs, in turn, lead to depressed oil output and higher oil prices.

FOR CRITICAL ANALYSIS
Why might dictators in totalitarian regimes make different oil production choices than private companies would have made?

QUICK QUIZ   *See page 133 for the answers. Review concepts from this section in MyEconLab.*

The theory of _____ _____ examines how voters, politicians, and other parties collectively reach decisions in the public sector of the economy.

As in private markets, _____ _____ and _____ have incentive effects that influence public-sector

decision making. In contrast to private market situations, however, there is not a one-to-one relationship between consumption of a publicly provided good and the payment for that good.

You Are There

Aiming to Prevent Cost from Exceeding Value per Dollar in Higher Education

In 2001, Graham Doxey, Scott McKinley, and Marlow Einelund pooled their resources to start a new business: a private computer engineering college called Neumont University. Salt Lake City–based Neumont, which has operated since 2004, has no summer breaks. Instead, it offers students a year-round curriculum with a daily class schedule that stretches from 8 AM to 5 PM, thereby enabling students to graduate after two years instead of four years. Unlike a traditional university with a sprawling—and costly-to-maintain—campus, Neumont is housed in a glass-and-steel executive office building. Rather than residing in dorms, fraternities, or sororities on a campus quad, students live in nearby apartments.

These are not, however, the most dramatic differences between Neumont and other U.S. institutions of higher learning. Neumont's single goal is to provide students with training geared to meet the desires of employers. In contrast to students in computer engineering programs at most other universities, Neumont's students spend 30 percent of their time on theory and 70 percent on applications—essentially a reversal of the percentages in traditional programs. Most Neumont students obtain professional certification as well as a bachelor's degree, which makes them both more employable and highly valued. Consequently, virtually all Neumont graduates obtain jobs, and most earn starting salaries 20 percent above the average for computer science graduates. In essence, Neumont seeks to ensure that the per-dollar cost of higher education is not higher than the per-dollar valuation that its graduates place on the tuition bills they pay for their education.

CRITICAL ANALYSIS QUESTIONS

1. Why might a university that is operated as a private firm be more likely than a traditional university to produce educational services at a cost per dollar that does not exceed students' per-dollar valuation of those services?

2. How could the entry of a number of other business-oriented universities such as Neumont induce traditional universities to alter their modes of operation?

An Ethanol Bonanza, or an Ethanol Boondoggle?

Issues and Applications

CONCEPTS APPLIED

- External Costs
- Government-Sponsored Good
- Subsidies

From the U.S. government's point of view, the use of gasoline as a motor fuel presents two problems. First, many reserves of the key input for refining gasoline, oil, are located in the politically unstable Middle East. Second, the utilization of gasoline as a motor fuel entails an external cost, because the burning of gasoline releases carbon dioxide and other pollutants into the air. In contrast, the key ingredients for manufacturing ethanol—corn and other grains—are readily grown domestically. Furthermore, burning ethanol may create a somewhat smaller "carbon footprint" in the atmosphere. These facts help to explain the government's fascination with ethanol-based fuel as a substitute for gasoline. What is unclear is whether there is a true economic rationale for government subsidies for ethanol.

Ethanol Is a Bonanza for Some

Motor fuels blended with ethanol, such as E10 (10 percent ethanol and 90 percent gasoline) and the more concentrated E85 (85 percent ethanol and 15 percent gasoline), have been available for a number of years. The U.S. government, however, had shown little interest in ethanol until the recent increase in gasoline prices and heightened worries over the potential global-warming impact of gasoline emissions.

Now, the government has effectively designated ethanol as a government-sponsored good. U.S. law currently requires U.S. refiners to blend 8 billion gallons of ethanol into motor fuels annually. The government provides a per-unit subsidy to ethanol producers of about $1 per gallon, or nearly half of the fuel's per-gallon production cost. Thus, annual government ethanol subsidies are about $8 billion. In phases through 2012, the ethanol requirement for U.S. refineries will rise to 36 billion gallons per year. Thus, total subsidies to ethanol producers are slated to increase to more than $36 billion.

All these government-generated revenues have certainly been a bonanza for ethanol manufacturers. Grain farmers have also been beneficiaries. The increased demand for corn as an ethanol input has boosted the market demand for corn and contributed to a nearly 40 percent increase in its inflation-adjusted price.

Others See Ethanol as a Boondoggle

The U.S. government's ethanol subsidies have certainly boosted production of ethanol. The cost is arguably very high relative to the benefits, however. Even if the 2012 target of 36 billion gallons of ethanol displaces an equal amount of gasoline, annual U.S. gasoline consumption will drop by less than 20 percent. As a consequence, U.S. dependence on volatile oil-producing nations will be reduced only slightly, and decreases in vehicular carbon emissions will be minor at best.

In fact, the ethanol production process releases pollutants into the atmosphere and fills the air surrounding ethanol refineries with a sickly sweet odor. One more implicit subsidy that the U.S. government has granted ethanol producers is looser air pollution regulations than those faced by other companies. The Environmental Protection Agency permits ethanol refineries to release 150 percent more emissions than other producers. Thus, emissions of pollutants from the nearly 200 ethanol refineries already operating or set to begin are likely to increase significantly during coming years.

Finally, some critics of ethanol subsidies suggest that producing ethanol from corn actually requires *more* energy than the ethanol ultimately creates. Whether or not this particular claim is correct, there is widespread agreement that given the energy expended to produce ethanol, the fuel is not the least costly source of energy for powering vehicles. This fact ultimately explains why the U.S. government requires its use and transmits billions of dollars of subsidies to producers each year to render ethanol a viable substitute for gasoline.

Test your understanding of this chapter by going online to **MyEconLab**.
In the Study Plan for this chapter, select Section N: News.

For Critical Analysis

1. In principle, could a higher per-unit tax on gasoline accomplish the U.S. government's objective of reducing gasoline consumption and related carbon emissions?

2. Who unambiguously benefits from the U.S. government's interventions in the ethanol market?

Web Resources

1. To contemplate a discussion of the pros and cons of ethanol and other so-called biofuels, go to www.econtoday.com/chapter05.

2. For information about vehicles equipped to operate using fuels with high concentrations of ethanol, go to www.econtoday.com/chapter05.

Research Project

Why is ethanol more appropriately classified as a government-sponsored good than as a public good? In your view, is there a strong *economic* argument for the government to continue to treat ethanol as a government-sponsored good and to promote ethanol output via explicit production requirements and subsidies? (Hint: In what situation does society underallocate resources to consumption of a good? Does this situation apply in the market for ethanol?)

Here is what you should know after reading this chapter. **MyEconLab** will help you identify what you know, and where to go when you need to practice.

WHAT YOU SHOULD KNOW

How Market Failures Such as Externalities Might Justify Economic Functions of Government A market failure is a situation in which an unhindered free market gives rise to too many or too few resources being directed to a specific form of economic activity. One market failure is an externality, which is a spillover effect on third parties not directly involved in producing or purchasing a good or service. In the case of a negative externality, firms do not pay for the costs arising from spillover effects that their production of a good imposes on others, so they produce too much of the good in question. Government may be able to improve the situation by restricting production or by imposing fees on producers. In the case of a positive externality, buyers fail to take into account the benefits that their consumption of a good yields to others, so they purchase too little of the good. Government may be able to induce more consumption of the good by regulating the market or subsidizing consumption. It can also provide a legal system to adjudicate disagreements about property rights, conduct antitrust policies to discourage monopoly and promote competition, provide public goods, and engage in policies designed to promote economic stability.

market failure, 108
externality, 109
third parties, 109
property rights, 109
effluent fee, 111
antitrust legislation, 113
monopoly, 114

KEY FIGURE
Figure 5-1, 110

WHERE TO GO TO PRACTICE

- **MyEconLab** Study Plans 5.1, 5.2
- Audio introduction to Chapter 5
- Animated Figure 5-1

(continued)

(Continued)

WHAT YOU SHOULD KNOW		WHERE TO GO TO PRACTICE
Private Goods versus Public Goods and the Free-Rider Problem Private goods are subject to the principle of rival consumption, meaning that one person's consumption of such a good reduces the amount available for another person to consume. This is not so for public goods, which can be consumed by many people simultaneously at no additional opportunity cost and with no reduction in the quality or quantity of the good. In addition, no individual can be excluded from the benefits of a public good even if that person fails to help pay for it. This leads to the free-rider problem, which occurs when a person who thinks that others will pay for a public good seeks to avoid contributing to financing its production.	private goods, 114 principle of rival consumption, 114 public goods, 114 free-rider problem, 115	• **MyEconLab** Study Plan 5.3 • Video: Private Goods and Public Goods
Political Functions of Government That Lead to Its Involvement in the Economy Through the political process, government may determine that certain goods are deemed socially desirable and seek to promote their production and consumption. These are called government-sponsored goods. The government may also seek to restrict or even ban the production and sale of other goods that have been deemed socially undesirable through the political process, called government-inhibited goods. In addition, the political process may determine that income redistribution is socially desirable, and governments may become involved in supervising transfer payments or in-kind transfers in the form of nonmoney payments.	government-sponsored good, 116 government-inhibited good, 116 transfer payments, 117 transfers in kind, 117	• **MyEconLab** Study Plan 5.4
The Effect of Medicare on the Incentives to Consume Medical Services Medicare subsidizes the consumption of medical services by the elderly. As a result, the quantity consumed is higher, as is the price sellers receive per unit of those services. Medicare also encourages people to consume medical services that are very low in per-unit value relative to the cost of providing them. Medicare thereby places a substantial tax burden on other sectors of the economy.	KEY FIGURES Figure 5-2, 118 Figure 5-4, 120	• **MyEconLab** Study Plan 5.5 • Video: Medicare • Animated Figures 5-2, 5-4
Why Bigger Subsidies for Public Schools Do Not Necessarily Translate into Improved Student Performance When governments subsidize public schools, the last unit of educational services provided by public schools costs more than its valuation by parents and students. Thus, public schools provide services in excess of those best suited to promoting student learning. This helps explain why overall U.S. student performance has stagnated even as per-pupil subsidies have increased.		• MyEconLab Study Plan 5.5

(continued)

WHAT YOU SHOULD KNOW		WHERE TO GO TO PRACTICE
Central Elements of the Theory of Public Choice The theory of public choice applies to collective decision making, or the process through which voters and politicians interact to influence nonmarket choices. Public-choice theory emphasizes the incentive structures, or system of rewards or punishments, that affect the provision of government goods by the public sector. This theory points out that certain aspects of public-sector decision making, such as scarcity and competition, are similar to those that affect private-sector choices. Others, however, such as legal coercion and majority-rule decision making, differ from those involved in the market system.	collective decision making, 123 theory of public choice, 123 incentive structure, 123 government, or political, goods, 124 majority rule, 125 proportional rule, 125	• **MyEconLab** Study Plan 5.6

Log in to MyEconLab, take a chapter test, and get a personalized Study Plan that tells you which concepts you understand and which ones you need to review. From there, MyEconLab will give you further practice, tutorials, animations, videos, and guided solutions.
Log in to www.myeconlab.com

PROBLEMS

All problems are assignable in myeconlab. *Answers to odd-numbered problems appear at the back of the book.*

5-1. Many people who do not smoke cigars are bothered by the odor of cigar smoke. In the absence of any government involvement in the market for cigars, will too many or too few cigars be produced and consumed? From society's point of view, will the market price of cigars be too high or too low?

5-2. Suppose that repeated application of a pesticide used on orange trees causes harmful contamination of groundwater. The pesticide is applied annually in virtually all of the orange groves throughout the world. Most orange growers regard the pesticide as a key input in their production of oranges.

    a. Use a diagram of the market for the pesticide to illustrate the implications of a failure of orange producers' costs to reflect the social costs of groundwater contamination.

    b. Use your diagram from part (a) to explain a government policy that might be effective in achieving the amount of orange production that fully reflects all social costs.

5-3. Now draw a diagram of the market for oranges. Explain how the government policy you discussed in part (b) of Problem 5-2 is likely to affect the market price and equilibrium quantity in the orange market. In what sense do consumers of oranges now "pay" for dealing with the spillover costs of pesticide production?

5-4. Suppose that the U.S. government determines that cigarette smoking creates social costs not reflected in the current market price and equilibrium quantity of cigarettes. A study has recommended that the government can correct for the externality effect of cigarette consumption by paying farmers *not* to plant tobacco used to manufacture cigarettes. It also recommends raising the funds to make these payments by increasing taxes on cigarettes. Assuming that the government is correct that cigarette smoking creates external costs, evaluate whether the study's recommended policies might help correct this negative externality.

5-5. The government of a major city in the United States has determined that mass transit, such as bus lines, helps alleviate traffic congestion, thereby benefiting both individual auto commuters and companies that desire to move products and factors of production speedily along streets and highways. Nevertheless, even though several private bus lines are in service, commuters in the city are failing to take the social benefits of the use of mass transit into account.

   a. Discuss, in the context of demand-supply analysis, the essential implications of commuters' failure to take into account the social benefits associated with bus ridership.

   b. Explain a government policy that might be effective in achieving the socially efficient use of bus services.

5-6. Draw a diagram of the market for automobiles, which are a substitute for buses. Explain how the government policy you discussed in part (b) of Problem 5-5 is likely to affect the market price and equilibrium quantity in the auto market. How are auto consumers affected by this policy to attain the spillover benefits of bus transit?

5-7. Displayed in the next column are conditions in the market for residential Internet access in a small U.S. state. The government of this state has determined that access to the Internet improves the learning skills of children, which it has concluded is an external benefit of Internet access. The government has also concluded that if these external benefits were to be taken into account, 3 million residences would have Internet access. Suppose that the state government's judgments about the benefits of Internet access are correct and that it wishes to offer a per-unit subsidy just sufficient to increase total Internet access to 3 million residences. What per-unit subsidy should it offer? Use the diagram to explain how providing this subsidy would affect conditions in the state's market for residential Internet access.

5-8. The French government recently allocated the equivalent of more than $120 million in public funds to *Quaero* (Latin for "I search"), an Internet search engine analogous to Google or Yahoo. Does an Internet search engine satisfy the key characteristics of a public good? Why or why not? Based on your answer, is a publicly funded Internet search engine a public good or a government-sponsored good?

5-9. To promote increased use of port facilities in a major coastal city, a state government has decided to construct a state-of-the-art lighthouse at a projected cost of $10 million. The state proposes to pay half this cost and asks the city to raise the additional funds. Rather than raise its $5 million in funds via an increase in city taxes and fees, however, the city's government asks major businesses in and near the port area to contribute voluntarily to the project. Discuss key problems that the city is likely to face in raising the funds.

5-10. Governments of country A and country B spend the same amount each year. Spending on functions relating to dealing with market externalities and public goods accounts for 25 percent of government expenditures in country A but makes up 75 percent of government expenditures in country B. Funding to provide government-sponsored goods and efforts to restrict the production of government-inhibited goods account for 75 percent of government expenditures in country A but only 25 percent of government expenditures in country B. Which country's government is more heavily involved in the economy through economic functions of government as opposed to political functions? Explain.

5-11. A government offers to let a number of students at a public school transfer to a private school under two conditions: It will transmit to the private school the same per-pupil subsidy it provides the public school, and the private school will be required to admit the students at a below-market net tuition rate. Will the economic outcome be the same as the one that would have arisen if the government instead simply provided students with grants to cover the current market tuition rate at the private school? (Hint: Does it matter if schools receive payments directly from the government or from consumers?)

5-12. After a government implements a voucher program, granting funds that families can spend at schools of their choice, numerous students in public schools switch to private schools. Parents' and students' valuations of the services provided at both private and public schools adjust to equality with the true market price of educational services. Is anyone likely to lose out nonetheless? If so, who?

5-13. Suppose that the current price of a DVD drive is $100 and that people are buying 1 million drives per year. In order to improve computer literacy, the government decides to begin subsidizing the purchase of new DVD drives. The government believes that the appropriate price is $60 per drive, so the program offers to send people cash for the difference between $60 and whatever the people pay for each drive they buy.

   a. If no consumers change their DVD-drive-buying behavior, how much will this program cost the taxpayers?

   b. Will the subsidy cause people to buy more, fewer, or the same number of drives? Explain.

   c. Suppose that people end up buying 1.5 million drives once the program is in place. If the market price of drives does not change, how much will this program cost the taxpayers?

   d. Under the assumption that the program causes people to buy 1.5 million drives and also causes the market price of drives to rise to $120, how much will this program cost the taxpayers?

5-14. Scans of internal organs using magnetic resonance imaging (MRI) devices are often covered by subsidized health insurance programs such as Medicare. Consider the following table illustrating hypothetical quantities of individual MRI testing procedures demanded and supplied at various prices, and then answer the questions that follow.

Price	Quantity Demanded	Quantity Supplied
$100	100,000	40,000
$300	90,000	60,000
$500	80,000	80,000
$700	70,000	100,000
$900	60,000	120,000

   a. In the absence of a government-subsidized health plan, what is the equilibrium price of MRI tests? What is the amount of society's total spending on MRI tests?

   b. Suppose that the government establishes a health plan guaranteeing that all qualified participants can purchase MRI tests at an effective price (that is, out-of-pocket cost) to the individual of $100 per test. How many MRI tests will people consume?

   c. What is the per-unit price that induces producers to provide the amount of MRI tests demanded at the government-guaranteed price of $100? What is society's total spending on MRI tests?

   d. Under the government's coverage of MRI tests, what is the per-unit subsidy it provides? What is the total subsidy that the government pays to support MRI testing at its guaranteed price?

5-15. Suppose that, as part of an expansion of its State Care health system, a state government decides to offer a $50 subsidy to all people who, according to their physicians, should have their own blood pressure monitoring devices. Prior to this governmental decision, the market clearing price of blood pressure monitors in this state was $50, and the equilibrium quantity purchased was 20,000 per year.

   a. After the government expands its State Care plan, people in this state desire to purchase 40,000 devices each year. Manufacturers of blood pressure monitors are willing to provide 40,000 devices at a price of $60 per device. What out-of-pocket price does each consumer pay for a blood pressure monitor?

   b. What is the dollar amount of the increase in total expenditures on blood pressure monitors in this state following the expansion in the State Care program?

   c. Following the expansion of the State Care program, what *percentage* of total expenditures on blood pressure monitors is paid by the government? What percentage of total expenditures is paid by consumers of these devices?

5-16. A government agency is contemplating launching an effort to expand the scope of its activities. One rationale for doing so is that another government agency might make the same effort and, if successful, receive larger budget allocations in future years. Another rationale for expanding the agency's activities is that this will make the jobs of its workers more interesting, which may help the agency attract better-qualified employees. Nevertheless, to broaden its legal mandate, the agency will have to convince more than half of the House of Representatives and the Senate to approve a formal proposal to expand its activities. In addition, to expand its activities, the agency must have the authority to force private companies it does not currently regulate to be officially licensed by agency personnel. Identify which aspects of this problem are similar to those faced by firms that operate in private markets and which aspects are specific to the public sector.

ECONOMICS ON THE NET

Putting Tax Dollars to Work In this application, you will learn about how the U.S. government allocates its expenditures. This will enable you to conduct an evaluation of the current functions of the federal government.

Title: Historical Tables: Budget of the United States Government

Navigation: Go to **www.econtoday.com/chapter05** to visit the home page of the U.S. Government Printing Office. Select the most recent budget available, and then click on *Historical Tables*.

Application After the document downloads, examine Section 3, Federal Government Outlays by Function, and in particular Table 3.1, Outlays by Superfunction and Function. Then answer the following questions.

1. What government functions have been capturing growing shares of government spending in recent years? Which of these do you believe are related to the problem of addressing externalities, providing public goods, or dealing with other market failures? Which appear to be related to political functions instead of economic functions?

2. Which government functions are receiving declining shares of total spending? Are any of these related to the problem of addressing externalities, providing public goods, or dealing with other market failures? Are any related to political functions instead of economic functions?

For Group Study and Analysis Assign groups to the following overall categories of government functions: national defense, health, income security, and Social Security. Have each group prepare a brief report concerning long-term and recent trends in government spending on its category. Each group should take a stand on whether specific spending on items in its category is likely to relate to resolving market failures, public funding of government-sponsored goods, regulating the sale of government-inhibited goods, and so on.

ANSWERS TO QUICK QUIZZES

p. 113: (i) costs . . . taxation . . . regulation; (ii) benefits . . . financing . . . subsidizing . . . regulation
p. 116: (i) externalities . . . legal system . . . competition . . . public . . . economywide stability; (ii) rival consumption; (iii) opportunity cost . . . charged
p. 117: (i) government-sponsored . . . government-inhibited . . . income; (ii) political; (iii) transfer
p. 122: (i) low . . . high; (ii) low . . . higher
p. 125: (i) public choice; (ii) opportunity cost . . . competition

Funding the Public Sector

Ever since the U.S. federal income tax was established in 1913, there has been disagreement about how much income tax rates should differ across households based on their incomes. In recent years, various U.S. politicians and pundits have called for boosts in tax rates for higher-income individuals and cuts in tax rates for middle- and lower-income individuals. "The rich should pay their fair share" and "The middle class deserves a break" are typical rallying cries you may have encountered in media reports. Are tax rates currently low for higher-income households relative to those faced by lower-income households? To evaluate this question, you must understand more about the structure of tax systems, which is one issue that governments confront in paying for their operations.

LEARNING OBJECTIVES

After reading this chapter, you should be able to:

- Distinguish between average tax rates and marginal tax rates

- Explain the structure of the U.S. income tax system

- Understand the key factors influencing the relationship between tax rates and the tax revenues governments collect

- Explain how the taxes governments levy on purchases of goods and services affect market prices and equilibrium quantities

- Understand how the Social Security system works and explain the nature of the problems it poses for today's students

myeconlab

MyEconLab helps you master each objective and study more efficiently. See end of chapter for details.

? DID YOU KNOW THAT since 1986, Congress has added 14,000 amendments containing 3 million words to U.S. tax laws? In addition, Congress has added 6 million words to regulations designed to implement all these amendments.

To obtain the funds required to finance their operations, governments collect taxes from many different sources—hence, the multitude of words written into a variety of legal statutes governing taxation. State and local governments assess sales taxes, property taxes, income taxes, hotel occupancy taxes, and electricity, gasoline, water, and sewage taxes. At the federal level, there are income taxes, Social Security taxes, Medicare taxes, and so-called excise taxes. When a person dies, state and federal governments also collect estate and inheritance taxes. Clearly, governments give considerable attention to their roles as tax collectors.

Paying for the Public Sector

There are three sources of funding available to governments. One source is explicit fees, called user *charges*, for government services. The second and main source of government funding is taxes. Nevertheless, sometimes federal, state, and local governments spend more than they collect in taxes. To do this, they must rely on a third source of financing, which is borrowing. During a specific interval, the **government budget constraint** expresses the key limitation on public expenditures. It states that the sum of public spending on goods, services, and transfer payments during a given period cannot exceed the sum of user charges, tax revenues, and borrowed funds.

A government cannot borrow unlimited amounts, however. After all, a government, like an individual or a firm, can convince others to lend it funds only if it can provide evidence that it will repay its debts. A government must ultimately rely on taxation and user charges, the sources of its own current and future revenues, to repay its debts. Over the long run, therefore, taxes and user charges are any government's *fundamental* sources of revenues. This long-term constraint indicates that the total amount that a government plans to spend and transfer today and into the future cannot exceed the total taxes and user charges that it currently earns and can reasonably anticipate collecting in future years. Taxation dwarfs user charges as a source of government resources, so let's begin by looking at taxation from a government's perspective.

Why are some states that rely on gasoline taxes to finance highway maintenance and construction contemplating a switch to "mileage taxes"?

Government budget constraint
The limit on government spending and transfers imposed by the fact that every dollar the government spends, transfers, or uses to repay borrowed funds must ultimately be provided by the user charges and taxes it collects.

POLICY EXAMPLE
States Consider Shifting Tax Gears to Satisfy Budget Constraints

A number of U.S. states earmark gasoline tax revenues to finance highway expansion and maintenance expenditures. Governments of these states are concerned that gasoline tax receipts will shrink as people respond to higher gasoline prices by switching from gas-guzzling sport utility vehicles to more fuel-efficient cars. State governments in North Carolina and Oregon are contemplating an alternative to taxing gasoline purchases: mileage taxation. Experiments are already under way in these states to equip autos with electronic odometers that record their mileage at gasoline stations. When drivers pump gasoline, specially equipped pumps read the mileage and charge taxes based on miles driven. To ensure that drivers pay only for miles driven within state borders, the tax systems under consideration include global-positioning-system devices and automatically deduct out-of-state miles traveled. In this way, the states seek to raise funds to finance work on highways from drivers who traverse them the most.

FOR CRITICAL ANALYSIS
What is a one-sentence statement of the budget constraint for highway financing in states in which highway work is financed exclusively by gasoline taxes?

Systems of Taxation

In light of the government budget constraint, a major concern of any government is how to collect taxes. Jean-Baptiste Colbert, the seventeenth-century French finance minister, said the art of taxation was in "plucking the goose so as to obtain the largest amount of feathers with the least possible amount of hissing." In the United States, governments have designed a variety of methods of plucking the private-sector goose.

The Tax Base and the Tax Rate

Tax base
The value of goods, services, wealth, or incomes subject to taxation.

Tax rate
The proportion of a tax base that must be paid to a government as taxes.

To collect a tax, a government typically establishes a **tax base,** which is the value of goods, services, wealth, or incomes subject to taxation. Then it assesses a **tax rate,** which is the proportion of the tax base that must be paid to the government as taxes.

Federal, state, and local governments have established a number of tax bases and tax rates. How does a "dual-bracket" tax system with two different tax bases function?

POLICY EXAMPLE
The Same Tax Rate, but Different Tax Bases for Different People

Like municipalities in most states, city and county governments in Florida collect property taxes by applying a tax rate to assessed valuations of structures and surrounding properties. Unlike most states, Florida permits municipalities to establish a "dual-bracket" property tax system, meaning that municipalities can set the taxable values of properties at lower levels for permanent residents than for seasonal residents. To determine the property taxes owed, a municipality multiplies the differently assessed property values by the same property tax rate.

In some Florida communities, assessed values of properties owned by seasonal residents are up to 10 times higher than assessed values of virtually identical properties that permanent residents own on the same streets. Thus, the property taxes paid by seasonal residents are as much as 10 times higher than those paid by permanent residents.

FOR CRITICAL ANALYSIS
Why do you suppose that democratically elected municipal governments in Florida choose to value properties of permanent residents lower than properties of seasonal residents for purposes of establishing tax bases for property tax payments? (Hint: Seasonal residents typically register to vote in the cities and counties in which they reside most of the year.)

As we discuss shortly, for the federal government and many state governments, incomes are key tax bases. Therefore, to discuss tax rates and the structure of taxation systems in more detail, let's focus for now on income taxation.

Marginal and Average Tax Rates

If somebody says, "I pay 28 percent in taxes," you cannot really tell what that person means unless you know whether he or she is referring to average taxes paid or the tax rate on the last dollars earned. The latter concept refers to the **marginal tax rate,** where the word *marginal* means "incremental."

The marginal tax rate is expressed as follows:

Marginal tax rate
The change in the tax payment divided by the change in income, or the percentage of additional dollars that must be paid in taxes. The marginal tax rate is applied to the highest tax bracket of taxable income reached.

$$\text{Marginal tax rate} = \frac{\text{change in taxes due}}{\text{change in taxable income}}$$

It is important to understand that the marginal tax rate applies only to the income in the highest **tax bracket** reached, where a tax bracket is defined as a specified range of taxable income to which a specific and unique marginal tax rate is applied.

The marginal tax rate is not the same thing as the **average tax rate,** which is defined as follows:

$$\text{Average tax rate} = \frac{\text{total taxes due}}{\text{total taxable income}}$$

Taxation Systems

No matter how governments raise revenues—from income taxes, sales taxes, or other taxes—all of those taxes fit into one of three types of taxation systems: proportional, progressive, or regressive, according to the relationship between the tax rate and income. To determine whether a tax system is proportional, progressive, or regressive, we simply ask, What is the relationship between the average tax rate and the marginal tax rate?

PROPORTIONAL TAXATION **Proportional taxation** means that regardless of an individual's income, taxes comprise exactly the same proportion. In a proportional taxation system, the marginal tax rate is always equal to the average tax rate. If every dollar is taxed at 20 percent, then the average tax rate is 20 percent, and so is the marginal tax rate.

Under a proportional system of taxation, taxpayers at all income levels end up paying the same *percentage* of their income in taxes. With a proportional tax rate of 20 percent, an individual with an income of $10,000 pays $2,000 in taxes, while an individual making $100,000 pays $20,000. Thus, the identical 20 percent rate is levied on both taxpayers.

PROGRESSIVE TAXATION Under **progressive taxation,** as a person's taxable income increases, the percentage of income paid in taxes increases. In a progressive system, the marginal tax rate is above the average tax rate. If you are taxed 5 percent on the first $10,000 you earn, 10 percent on the next $10,000 you earn, and 30 percent on the last $10,000 you earn, you face a progressive income tax system. Your marginal tax rate is always above your average tax rate.

REGRESSIVE TAXATION With **regressive taxation,** a smaller percentage of taxable income is taken in taxes as taxable income increases. The marginal rate is *below* the average rate. As income increases, the marginal tax rate falls, and so does the average tax rate. The U.S. Social Security tax is regressive. Once the legislative maximum taxable wage base is reached, no further Social Security taxes are paid. Consider a simplified hypothetical example: Suppose that every dollar up to $100,000 is taxed at 10 percent. After $100,000 there is no Social Security tax. Someone making $200,000 still pays only $10,000 in Social Security taxes. That person's average Social Security tax is 5 percent. The person making $100,000, by contrast, effectively pays 10 percent. The person making $1 million faces an average Social Security tax rate of only 1 percent in our simplified example.

What form of voluntary yet regressive taxation is spreading throughout the U.S. states?

Tax bracket
A specified interval of income to which a specific and unique marginal tax rate is applied.

Average tax rate
The total tax payment divided by total income. It is the proportion of total income paid in taxes.

You Are There

To contemplate how marginal income tax rates can affect a person's job decisions, read **For This Physician, the Tax Rate Is Too High to Justify Working,** on pages 151 and 152.

Proportional taxation
A tax system in which, regardless of an individual's income, the tax bill comprises exactly the same proportion.

Progressive taxation
A tax system in which, as income increases, a higher percentage of the additional income is paid as taxes. The marginal tax rate exceeds the average tax rate as income rises.

Regressive taxation
A tax system in which as more dollars are earned, the percentage of tax paid on them falls. The marginal tax rate is less than the average tax rate as income rises.

POLICY EXAMPLE
State-Sponsored Gambling—Voluntary but Regressive Taxation

Increasingly, state governments are raising funds over and above traditional taxes and fees by operating lotteries and other legalized games of chance. State governments that supervise lotteries and other profitable gambling mechanisms regard them as forms of voluntary taxation. Economists have concluded that lower-income individuals usually pay larger percentages of their incomes to participate in state-run games of chance than do higher-income individuals. Thus, most state gambling operations involve *regressive* voluntary taxation.

FOR CRITICAL ANALYSIS
Why do you suppose that economists have found that slot-machine operations are among the most regressive forms of voluntary taxation conducted via state-run gambling operations? (Hint: Although each individual slot-machine bet is very small, people are equally tempted regardless of their incomes to feed large numbers of coins into the slots.)

QUICK QUIZ
See page 158 for the answers. Review concepts from this section in MyEconLab.

Governments collect taxes by applying a tax _____ to a tax _____, which refers to the value of goods, services, wealth, or incomes. Income tax rates are applied to tax brackets, which are ranges of income over which the tax rate is constant.

The _____ tax rate is the total tax payment divided by total income, and the _____ tax rate is the change in the tax payment divided by the change in income.

Tax systems can be _____, _____, or _____, depending on whether the marginal tax rate is the same as, greater than, or less than the average tax rate as income rises.

The Most Important Federal Taxes

What types of taxes do federal, state, and local governments collect? The two pie diagrams in Figure 6-1 show the percentages of receipts from various taxes obtained by the federal government and by state and local governments. For the federal government, key taxes are individual income taxes, corporate income taxes, Social Security taxes, and excise taxes on items such as gasoline and alcoholic beverages. For state and local governments, sales taxes, property taxes, and personal and corporate income taxes are the main types of taxes.

State-sponsored games of chance create what type of voluntary tax system?

The Federal Personal Income Tax

The most important tax in the U.S. economy is the federal personal income tax, which, as Figure 6-1 indicates, accounts for about 46.6 percent of all federal revenues. All U.S. citizens, resident aliens, and most others who earn income in the United States are required to pay federal income taxes on all taxable income, including income earned abroad.

The rates that are paid rise as income increases, as can be seen in Table 6-1 on page 140. Marginal income tax rates at the federal level have ranged from as low as 1 percent after the 1913 passage of the Sixteenth Amendment, which made the individual

FIGURE 6-1

Sources of Government Tax Receipts

As panel (a) shows, about 80 percent of federal revenues comes from income and Social Security and other social insurance taxes. State government revenues, shown in panel (b), are spread more evenly across sources, with less emphasis on taxes based on individual income.

Source: U.S. Department of Commerce, Bureau of Economic Analysis.

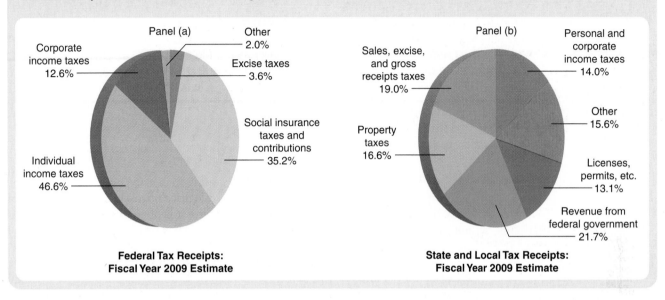

Panel (a)

- Corporate income taxes 12.6%
- Other 2.0%
- Excise taxes 3.6%
- Social insurance taxes and contributions 35.2%
- Individual income taxes 46.6%

Federal Tax Receipts: Fiscal Year 2009 Estimate

Panel (b)

- Sales, excise, and gross receipts taxes 19.0%
- Personal and corporate income taxes 14.0%
- Other 15.6%
- Licenses, permits, etc. 13.1%
- Revenue from federal government 21.7%
- Property taxes 16.6%

State and Local Tax Receipts: Fiscal Year 2009 Estimate

income tax constitutional, to as high as 94 percent (reached in 1944). There were 14 separate tax brackets prior to the Tax Reform Act of 1986, which reduced the number to three (now six, as shown in Table 6-1 on the following page.).

Why is it somewhat surprising that many people among one particular group of U.S. residents pay federal income taxes?

Go to www.econtoday.com/chapter06 to learn from the National Center for Policy Analysis about what distinguishes recent flat tax proposals from a truly proportional income tax system. Click on "Flat Tax Proposals."

INTERNATIONAL POLICY EXAMPLE
Defying One Agency, Illegal Immigrants Pay Taxes to Another

No one knows exactly how many illegal immigrants reside in the United States, but most estimates put the number somewhere between 10 million and 15 million. As many as 1 out of every 20 U.S. workers may be in the country in defiance of efforts by the Department of Homeland Security to keep them out. Another U.S. government agency, the Department of the Treasury's Internal Revenue Service (IRS), makes it easy for these illegally residing but gainfully employed individuals to pay federal income taxes. All they have to do is obtain a special taxpayer identification number that begins with a "9" and indicates that they are unable to qualify for a Social Security number. Each year, the IRS collects an estimated $50 million in income taxes from illegal immigrants who obtain an identification number and pay income taxes through regular deductions from their wages.

FOR CRITICAL ANALYSIS

What is the marginal income tax rate for illegal workers who fail to report taxable earnings to the IRS because they fear their illegal status will be discovered?

TABLE 6-1

Federal Marginal Income Tax Rates

These rates became effective in 2008.

Single Persons		Married Couples	
Marginal Tax Bracket	Marginal Tax Rate	Marginal Tax Bracket	Marginal Tax Rate
$0–$8,025	10%	$0–$16,050	10%
$8,026–$32,550	15%	$16,051–$65,100	15%
$32,551–$78,850	25%	$65,101–$131,450	25%
$78,851–$164,550	28%	$131,451–$300,300	28%
$164,551–$357,700	33%	$300,301–$357,700	33%
$357,701 and up	35%	$357,701 and up	35%

Source: U.S. Department of the Treasury.

The Treatment of Capital Gains

Capital gain

A positive difference between the purchase price and the sale price of an asset. If a share of stock is bought for $5 and then sold for $15, the capital gain is $10.

Capital loss

A negative difference between the purchase price and the sale price of an asset.

The difference between the purchase price and sale price of an asset, such as a share of stock or a plot of land, is called a **capital gain** if it is a profit and a **capital loss** if it is not. The federal government taxes capital gains, and as of 2009, there were several capital gains tax rates.

What appear to be capital gains are not always real gains. If you pay $100,000 for a financial asset in one year and sell it for 50 percent more 10 years later, your nominal capital gain is $50,000. But what if during those 10 years inflation has driven average asset prices up by 50 percent? Your *real* capital gain would be zero, but you would still have to pay taxes on that $50,000. To counter this problem, many economists have argued that capital gains should be indexed to the rate of inflation. This is exactly what is done with the marginal tax brackets in the federal income tax code. Tax brackets for the purposes of calculating marginal tax rates each year are expanded at the rate of inflation, that is, the rate at which the average of all prices is rising. So, if the rate of inflation is 10 percent, each tax bracket is moved up by 10 percent. The same concept could be applied to capital gains and financial assets. So far, Congress has refused to enact such a measure.

The Corporate Income Tax

Figure 6-1 on page 139 shows that corporate income taxes account for about 12.6 percent of all federal taxes collected and about 2 percent of all state and local taxes collected. Corporations are generally taxed on the difference between their total revenues and their expenses. The federal corporate income tax structure is given in Table 6-2.

Retained earnings

Earnings that a corporation saves, or retains, for investment in other productive activities; earnings that are not distributed to stockholders.

DOUBLE TAXATION Because individual stockholders must pay taxes on the dividends they receive, and those dividends are paid out of *after-tax* profits by the corporation, corporate profits are taxed twice. If you receive $1,000 in dividends, you have to declare them as income, and you must normally pay taxes on them. Before the corporation was able to pay you those dividends, it had to pay taxes on all its profits, including any that it put back into the company or did not distribute in the form of dividends. Eventually, the new investment made possible by those **retained earnings**—profits not given out to stockholders—along with borrowed funds will be reflected in the value of the stock in that company. When you sell your stock in that company, you will have to pay taxes on the difference between what you paid for the stock and what you sold it for. In both cases, dividends and retained earnings (corporate profits) are taxed

TABLE 6-2

Federal Corporate Income Tax Schedule

These corporate tax rates were in effect through 2009.

Corporate Taxable Income	Corporate Tax Rate
$0–$50,000	15%
$50,001–$75,000	25%
$75,001–$100,000	34%
$100,001–$335,000	39%
$335,001–$10,000,000	34%
$10,000,001–$15,000,000	35%
$15,000,001–$18,333,333	38%
$18,333,334 and up	35%

Source: Internal Revenue Service.

twice. In 2003, Congress reduced the double taxation effect somewhat by enacting legislation that allowed most dividends to be taxed at lower rates than are applied to regular income, with this provision up for renewal in 2010.

WHO REALLY PAYS THE CORPORATE INCOME TAX? Corporations can function only as long as consumers buy their products, employees make their goods, stockholders (owners) buy their shares, and bondholders buy their bonds. Corporations per se do not do anything. We must ask, then, who really pays the tax on corporate income? This is a question of **tax incidence.** (The question of tax incidence applies to all taxes, including sales taxes and Social Security taxes.) The incidence of corporate taxation is the subject of considerable debate. Some economists suggest that corporations pass their tax burdens on to consumers by charging higher prices. Other economists argue that it is the stockholders who bear most of the tax. Still others contend that employees pay at least part of the tax by receiving lower wages than they would otherwise. Because the debate is not yet settled, we will not hazard a guess here as to what the correct conclusion may be. Suffice it to say that you should be cautious when you advocate increasing corporation income taxes. *People*—whether owners, consumers, or workers—ultimately end up paying the increase.

Tax incidence
The distribution of tax burdens among various groups in society.

Social Security and Unemployment Taxes

Each year, taxes levied on payrolls account for an increasing percentage of federal tax receipts. These taxes, which are distinct from personal income taxes, are for Social Security, retirement, survivors' disability, and old-age medical benefits (Medicare). Today, the Social Security tax is imposed on earnings up to roughly $105,000 at a rate of 6.2 percent on employers and 6.2 percent on employees. That is, the employer matches your "contribution" to Social Security. (The employer's contribution is really paid by the employees, at least in part, in the form of a reduced wage rate.) As Chapter 5 explained, a Medicare tax is imposed on all wage earnings at a combined rate of 2.9 percent. These taxes and the base on which they are levied are slated to rise in the next decade. Social Security taxes came into existence when the Federal Insurance Contributions Act (FICA) was passed in 1935. The future of Social Security is addressed later in this chapter.

There is also a federal unemployment tax, which helps pay for unemployment insurance. This tax rate is 0.6 percent on the first $7,000 of annual wages of each employee who earns more than $1,500. Only the employer makes this tax payment. This tax covers the costs of the unemployment insurance system. In addition to this federal tax, some states with an unemployment system impose their own tax of up to about 3 percent, depending on the past record of the particular employer. An employer who frequently lays off workers typically will have a slightly higher state unemployment tax rate than an employer who never lays off workers.

Tax Rates and Tax Revenues

For most state and local governments, income taxes yield fewer revenues than taxes imposed on sales of goods and services. Figure 6-1 on page 139 shows that sales taxes, gross receipts taxes, and excise taxes generate almost one-fifth of the total funds available to state and local governments. Thus, from the perspective of many state and local governments, a fundamental issue is how to set tax rates on sales of goods and services to extract desired total tax payments.

Sales Taxes

Sales taxes
Taxes assessed on the prices paid on most goods and services.

Ad valorem taxation
Assessing taxes by charging a tax rate equal to a fraction of the market price of each unit purchased.

Governments levy **sales taxes** on the prices that consumers pay to purchase each unit of a broad range of goods and services. Sellers collect sales taxes and transmit them to the government. Sales taxes are a form of ***ad valorem*** **taxation,** which means that the tax is applied "to the value" of the good. Thus, a government using a system of *ad valorem* taxation charges a tax rate equal to a fraction of the market price of each unit that a consumer buys. For instance, if the tax rate is 8 percent and the market price of an item is $100, then the amount of the tax on the item is $8.

A sales tax is therefore a proportional tax. The total amount of sales taxes a government collects equals the sales tax rate times the sales tax base, which is the market value of total purchases.

Static Tax Analysis

Static tax analysis
Economic evaluation of the effects of tax rate changes under the assumption that there is no effect on the tax base, meaning that there is an unambiguous positive relationship between tax rates and tax revenues.

There are two approaches to evaluating how changes in tax rates affect government tax collections. **Static tax analysis** assumes that changes in the tax rate have no effect on the tax base. Thus, this approach implies that if a state government desires to increase its sales tax collections, it can simply raise the tax rate. Multiplying the higher tax rate by the tax base thereby produces higher tax revenues.

Governments often rely on static tax analysis. Sometimes this yields unpleasant surprises. Consider, for instance, what happened in 1992 when Congress implemented a federal "luxury tax" on purchases of new pleasure boats priced at $100,000 or more. Applying the 10 percent luxury tax rate to the anticipated tax base—sales of new boats during previous years—produced a forecast of hundreds of million of dollars in revenues from the luxury tax. What actually happened, however, was an 80 percent plunge in sales of new luxury boats. People postponed boat purchases or bought used boats instead. Consequently, the tax base all but disappeared, and the federal government collected only a few tens of millions of dollars in taxes on boat sales. Congress repealed the tax a year later.

Dynamic Tax Analysis

The problem with static tax analysis is that it ignores incentive effects created by new taxes or hikes in existing tax rates. According to **dynamic tax analysis,** a likely response to an increase in a tax rate is a decrease in the tax base. When a government pushes up its sales tax rate, for example, consumers have an incentive to cut back on their purchases of goods and services subjected to the higher rate, perhaps by buying them in a locale where there is a lower sales tax rate or perhaps no tax rate at all. As shown in Figure 6-2 on the following page, the maximum sales tax rate varies considerably from state to state. Consider someone who lives in a state bordering Oregon. In such a border state, the sales tax rate can be as high as 8 percent, so a resident of that state has a strong incentive to buy higher-priced goods and services in Oregon, where there is no sales tax. Someone who lives in a high-tax county in Alabama has an incentive to buy an item online from an out-of-state firm to avoid paying sales taxes. Such shifts in expenditures in response to higher relative tax rates will reduce a state's sales tax base and thereby result in lower sales tax collections than the levels predicted by static tax analysis.

Dynamic tax analysis recognizes that increasing the tax rate could actually cause the government's total tax collections to *decline* if a sufficiently large number of consumers react to the higher sales tax rate by cutting back on purchases of goods and services included in the state's tax base. Some residents who live close to other states with lower sales tax rates might, for instance, drive across the state line to do more of their shopping. Other residents might place more orders with catalog companies or online firms located in other legal jurisdictions where their state's sales tax does not apply.

Why will the Connecticut state government probably receive less in estate tax revenues than state legislators anticipated?

Dynamic tax analysis
Economic evaluation of tax rate changes that recognizes that the tax base eventually declines with ever-higher tax rates, so that tax revenues may eventually decline if the tax rate is raised sufficiently.

If sales taxes are greatly increased only for luxury items, will anticipated tax revenues be fully realized?

POLICY EXAMPLE
Connecticut's "Death Tax" May Induce Changes in Residency

The Connecticut legislature recently passed a law imposing taxes on deceased individuals' estates valued in excess of $2 million. Under this law, an estate valued at $10 million typically will owe about $1 million in taxes to the state government. Based on estimates of the annual death rate among individuals with estates valued at more than $2 million, legislators anticipated that the law would generate an additional $150 million in annual tax revenues for Connecticut.

This static analysis, however, ignores the fact that thousands of wealthy Connecticut residents already own second homes in states without estate taxes. A Connecticut resident who anticipates an estate valued at $10 million when she dies

and already owns a second home in a state without an estate tax can save $1 million for her heirs by changing her residency. Economists cannot predict how many Connecticut residents may alter their state of residency to avoid the new estate tax. Economists agree, however, that dynamic tax analysis suggests that the tax law will generate fewer revenues than Connecticut legislators anticipated.

FOR CRITICAL ANALYSIS
Why would reducing Connecticut estate tax rates tend to decrease the likelihood of residency changes by people with second homes in other states?

FIGURE 6-2

States with the Highest and Lowest Sales Tax Rates

A number of states allow counties and cities to collect their own sales taxes in addition to state sales taxes. This figure shows the maximum sales tax rates for selected states, including county and municipal taxes. Delaware, Montana, New Hampshire, and Oregon have no sales taxes. All other states besides those in the figure and the District of Columbia have maximum sales tax rates between the 4 percent rate of Hawaii and the 9.875 percent rate in Arkansas.

Source: U.S. Department of Commerce.

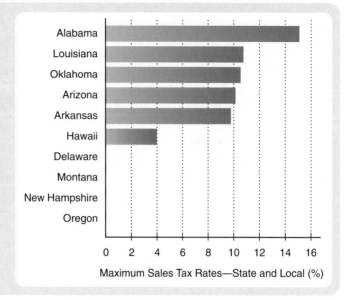

Maximizing Tax Revenues

Dynamic tax analysis indicates that whether a government's tax revenues ultimately rise or fall in response to a tax rate increase depends on exactly how much the tax base declines in response to the higher tax rate. On the one hand, the tax base may decline by a relatively small amount following an increase in the tax rate, or perhaps even imperceptibly, so that tax revenues rise. For instance, in the situation we imagine a government facing in Figure 6-3, a rise in the tax rate from 5 percent to 6 percent causes tax revenues to increase. Along this range, static tax analysis can provide a good approximation of the revenue effects of an increase in the tax rate. On the other hand, the tax base may decline so much that total tax revenues decrease. In Figure 6-3, for example, increasing the tax rate from 6 percent to 7 percent causes tax revenues to *decline*.

What is most likely is that when the tax rate is already relatively low, increasing the tax rate causes relatively small declines in the tax base. Within a range of relatively low sales tax rates, therefore, increasing the tax rate generates higher sales tax revenues, as illustrated along the upward-sloping portion of the curve depicted in Figure 6-3. If the government continues to push up the tax rate, however, people increasingly have an incentive to find ways to avoid purchasing taxable goods and services. Eventually, the tax base decreases sufficiently that the government's tax collections decline with ever-higher tax rates.

Consequently, governments that wish to maximize their tax revenues should not necessarily assess a high tax rate. In the situation illustrated in Figure 6-3, the government maximizes its tax revenues at T_{max} by establishing a sales tax rate of 6 percent. If the government were to raise the rate above 6 percent, it would induce a sufficient decline in the tax base that its tax collections would decline. If the government wishes to collect more than T_{max} in revenues to fund various government programs, it must somehow either expand its sales tax base or develop another tax.

How did Iceland discover that its corporate tax rates were above the revenue-maximizing level?

FIGURE 6-3

Maximizing the Government's Sales Tax Revenues

Dynamic tax analysis predicts that ever-higher tax rates bring about declines in the tax base, so that at sufficiently high tax rates the government's tax revenues begin to fall off. This implies that there is a tax rate, 6 percent in this example, at which the government can collect the maximum possible revenues, T_{max}.

INTERNATIONAL POLICY EXAMPLE
How Iceland Slashed a Tax Rate and Boosted Tax Revenues

During the 1990s and 2000s, the Icelandic government phased in cuts in its corporate income tax rate from an initial rate of 45 percent to the current rate of 18 percent. In the process, the government's inflation-adjusted revenues from corporate income taxation more than doubled. Some in the Icelandic government suggest that the revenue-maximizing tax rate may be still lower, and a proposal to cut the rate to as low as 10 percent is under consideration. In any event, it is now apparent to the government that the revenue-maximizing corporate income tax rate is considerably lower than 45 percent.

FOR CRITICAL ANALYSIS

What must have happened to the tax base relevant to Iceland's corporate income taxation system during the 1990s and 2000s?

QUICK QUIZ   *See page 158 for the answers. Review concepts from this section in MyEconLab.*

The _____ view of the relationship between tax rates and tax revenues implies that higher tax rates always generate increased government tax collections.

According to _____ tax analysis, higher tax rates cause the tax base to decrease. Tax collections will rise less than predicted by _____ tax analysis.

Dynamic tax analysis indicates that there is a tax rate that maximizes the government's tax collections. Setting the tax rate any higher would cause the tax base to _____ sufficiently that the government's tax revenues will _____.

Taxation from the Point of View of Producers and Consumers

Governments collect taxes on product sales at the source. They require producers to charge these taxes when they sell their output. This means that taxes on sales of goods and services affect market prices and quantities. Let's consider why this is so.

Taxes and the Market Supply Curve

Imposing taxes on final sales of a good or service affects the position of the market supply curve. To see why, consider panel (a) of Figure 6-4, which shows a gasoline market supply curve S_1 in the absence of taxation. At a price of $4.35 per gallon, gasoline producers are willing and able to supply 180,000 gallons of gasoline per week. If the price increases to $4.45 per gallon, firms increase production to 200,000 gallons of gasoline per week.

Excise tax
A tax levied on purchases of a particular good or service.

Unit tax
A constant tax assessed on each unit of a good that consumers purchase.

Both federal and state governments assess **excise taxes**—taxes on sales of particular commodities—on sales of gasoline. They levy gasoline excise taxes as a **unit tax,** or a constant tax per unit sold. On average, combined federal and state excise taxes on gasoline are about $0.40 per gallon.

Let's suppose, therefore, that a gasoline producer must transmit a total of $0.40 per gallon to federal and state governments for each gallon sold. Producers must

FIGURE 6-4

The Effects of Excise Taxes on the Market Supply and Equilibrium Price and Quantity of Gasoline

Panel (a) shows what happens if the government requires gasoline sellers to collect and transmit a $0.40 unit excise tax on gasoline. To be willing to continue supplying a given quantity, sellers must receive a price that is $0.40 higher for each gallon they sell, so the market supply curve shifts vertically by the amount of the tax. As illustrated in panel (b), this decline in market supply causes a reduction in the equilibrium quantity of gasoline produced and purchased. It also causes a rise in the market clearing price, to $4.75, so that consumers pay part of the tax. Sellers pay the rest in lower profits.

continue to receive a net amount of $4.35 per gallon to induce them to supply 180,000 gallons each week, so they must now receive $4.75 per gallon to supply that weekly quantity. Likewise, gasoline producers now will be willing to supply 200,000 gallons each week only if they receive $0.40 more per gallon, or a total amount of $4.85 per gallon.

As you can see, imposing the combined $0.40 per gallon excise taxes on gasoline shifts the supply curve vertically by exactly that amount to S_2 in panel (a). Thus, the effect of levying excise taxes on gasoline is to shift the supply curve vertically by the total per-unit taxes levied on gasoline sales. Hence, there is a decrease in supply. (In the case of an *ad valorem* sales tax, the supply curve would shift vertically by a proportionate amount equal to the tax rate.)

How Taxes Affect the Market Price and Equilibrium Quantity

Panel (b) of Figure 6-4 shows how imposing $0.40 per gallon in excise taxes affects the market price of gasoline and the equilibrium quantity of gasoline produced and sold. In the absence of excise taxes, the market supply curve S_1 crosses the demand curve D at a market price of $4.45 per gallon. At this market price, the equilibrium quantity of gasoline is 200,000 gallons of gasoline per week.

The excise tax levy of $0.40 per gallon shifts the supply curve to S_2. At the original $4.45 per gallon price, there is now an excess quantity of gasoline demanded, so the market price of gasoline rises to $4.75 per gallon. At this market price, the equilibrium quantity of gasoline produced and consumed each week is 180,000 gallons.

What factors determine how much the equilibrium quantity of a good or service declines in response to taxation? The answer to this question depends on how responsive quantities demanded and supplied are to changes in price.

Who Pays the Tax?

In our example, imposing excise taxes of $0.40 per gallon of gasoline causes the market price to rise to $4.75 per gallon from $4.45 per gallon. Thus, the price that each consumer pays is $0.30 per gallon higher. Consumers pay three-fourths of the excise tax levied on each gallon of gasoline produced and sold.

Gasoline producers must pay the rest of the tax. Their profits decline by $0.10 per gallon because costs have increased by $0.40 per gallon while consumers pay $0.30 more per gallon.

In the gasoline market, as in other markets for products subject to excise taxes and other taxes on sales, the shapes of the market demand and supply curves determine who pays most of a tax. The reason is that the shapes of these curves reflect the responsiveness to price changes of the quantity demanded by consumers and of the quantity supplied by producers.

In the example illustrated in Figure 6-4, the fact that consumers pay most of the excise taxes levied on gasoline reflects a relatively low responsiveness of quantity demanded by consumers to a change in the price of gasoline. Consumers pay most of the excise taxes on each gallon produced and sold because in this example the amount of gasoline they desire to purchase is relatively (but not completely) unresponsive to a change in the market price induced by excise taxes. We will revisit the issue of who pays excise taxes in Chapter 20.

If a state government increases the tax on a pack of cigarettes, who pays the tax?

QUICK QUIZ *See page 158 for the answers. Review concepts from this section in MyEconLab.*

When the government levies a tax on sales of a particular product, firms must receive a higher price to continue supplying the same quantity as before, so the supply curve shifts _____. If the tax is a unit excise tax, the supply curve shifts _____ by the amount of the tax.

Imposing a tax on sales of an item _____ the equilibrium quantity produced and consumed and _____ the market price.

When a government assesses a unit excise tax, the market price of the good or service typically rises by an amount _____ than the per-unit tax. Hence, consumers pay a portion of the tax, and firms pay the remainder.

Financing Social Security

In Chapter 5, you learned about Medicare, which is one of two major federal transfer programs. The other is Social Security, the federal system that transfers portions of the incomes of working-age people to elderly and disabled individuals. If current laws are maintained, Medicare's share of total national income will double over the next 20 years, as will the number of "very old" people—those over 85 and most in need of care. When Social Security is also taken into account, probably *half* of all federal government spending will go to the elderly by 2025. In a nutshell, senior citizens are the beneficiaries of an expensive and rapidly growing share of all federal spending.

Good Times for the First Retirees

The Social Security system was founded in 1935, as the United States was recovering from the Great Depression. The decision was made to establish Social Security as a means of guaranteeing a minimum level of pension benefits to all residents. Today, many people regard Social Security as a kind of "social compact"—a national promise to successive generations that they will receive support in their old age.

Social Security contributions
The mandatory taxes paid out of workers' wages and salaries.

Rate of return
The proportional annual benefit that results from making an investment.

Inflation-adjusted return
A rate of return that is measured in terms of real goods and services; that is, after the effects of inflation have been factored out.

BIG PAYOFFS FOR THE EARLIEST RECIPIENTS The first Social Security taxes (called "contributions") were collected in 1937, but it was not until 1940 that the first retirement benefits were paid. Ida May Fuller was the first person to receive a regular Social Security pension. She had paid a total of $25 in **Social Security contributions** before she retired. By the time she died in 1975 at age 100, she had received benefits totaling $23,000. Although Fuller perhaps did better than most, for the average retiree of 1940, the Social Security system was still more generous than any private investment plan anyone is likely to devise: After adjusting for inflation, the implicit **rate of return** on their contributions was an astounding 135 percent. (Roughly speaking, every $100 of combined employer and employee contributions yielded $135 *per year* during each and every year of that person's retirement. This is also called the **inflation-adjusted return.**)

Ever since the early days of Social Security, however, the implicit rate of return has decreased. Nonetheless, Social Security was an excellent deal for most retirees during the twentieth century. Figure 6-5 shows the implicit rate of return for people retiring in different years.

Given that the inflation-adjusted long-term rate of return on the stock market is about 7 to 9 percent, it is clear that for retirees, Social Security was a good deal until

FIGURE 6-5

Private Rates of Return on Social Security Contributions, by Year of Retirement

The rate of return on Social Security contributions has steadily declined.

Sources: Social Security Administration and author's estimates.

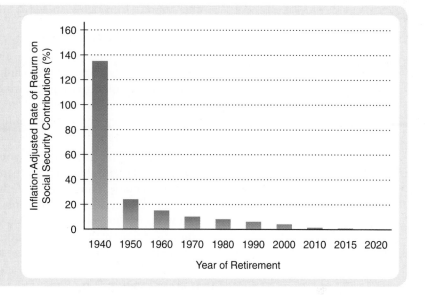

at least 1970. In fact, because Social Security benefits are a lot less risky than stocks, Social Security actually remained a pretty good "investment" for many people until around 1990.

SLOWING GROWTH IN WORKERS' CONTRIBUTIONS Social Security has managed to pay such high returns because at each point in time, current retirees are paid benefits out of the contributions of individuals who are currently working. (The contributions of today's retirees were long ago used to pay the benefits of previous retirees.) As long as Social Security was pulling in growing numbers of workers, either through a burgeoning workforce or by expanding its coverage of individuals in the workforce, the impressive rates of return during the early years of the program were possible.

But as birthrates declined beginning in the mid-1960s and the post–World War II baby boom generation began to reach retirement age, membership growth slowed, and the rate of return fell. Moreover, because the early participants received more than they contributed, it follows that if the number of participants stops growing, later participants must receive less—and that ultimately means a *negative* rate of return. And for today's college students—indeed for most people now under the age of 50 or so—that negative rate of return is what lies ahead, unless reforms are implemented.

What Will It Take to Salvage Social Security?

The United States now finds itself with a social compact—the Social Security system—that entails a flow of promised benefits that could exceed the inflow of taxes sometime between 2010 and 2015. What, if anything, might be done about this? There are five relevant options to consider.

1. **Raise Taxes**. The history of Social Security has been one of steadily increasing tax rates applied to an ever-larger portion of workers' wages. In 1935, a Social Security payroll tax rate of 2 percent was applied to the first $3,000 of an individual's earnings (more than $40,000 in today's dollars). Now the Social Security payroll tax rate is 10.4 percentage points higher, and the government applies

Go to www.econtoday.com/chapter06 to learn more about Social Security at the official Web site of the Social Security Administration.

this tax rate to roughly an additional $65,000 of a worker's wages measured in today's dollars.

One prominent proposal promises an $80 billion increase in contributions via a 2.2 percentage-point hike in the payroll tax rate, to an overall rate of 14.6 percent. Another proposal is to eliminate the current cap on the level of wages to which the payroll tax is applied, which would also generate about $80 billion per year in additional tax revenues. Nevertheless, even a combined policy of eliminating the wage cap and implementing a 2.2 percentage-point tax increase would not, by itself, keep tax collections above benefit payments over the long run.

2. **Reduce Retirement Benefit Payouts**. Proposals are on the table to increase the age of full benefit eligibility, perhaps to as high as 70. Another option is to cut benefits to nonworking spouses. A third proposal is to impose "means testing" on some or all Social Security benefits. As things stand now, all individuals covered by the system collect benefits when they retire, regardless of their assets or other sources of retirement income. Under a system of means testing, individuals with substantial amounts of alternative sources of retirement income would receive reduced Social Security benefits.

3. **Reduce Disability Benefits**. In addition to old-age pension payments, the U.S. Social Security system also offers benefits to people with various types of disabilities. In 1984, Congress greatly liberalized the definition of "disability" for purposes of qualifying for these benefits, and the result has been a near doubling of disability beneficiaries, from 2.6 million to more than 5 million today. One way to help shore up Social Security's financial situation would be to tighten requirements for this program or perhaps separate it from the Social Security system.

4. **Reform Immigration Policies**. Many experts believe that significant changes in U.S. immigration laws could offer the best hope of dealing with the tax burdens and workforce shrinkage of the future. Currently, however, more than 90 percent of new immigrants are admitted on the basis of a selection system unchanged since 1952. This system ties immigration rights to family preference. That is why most people admitted to the United States happen to be the spouses, children, or siblings of earlier immigrants. Unless Congress makes skills or training that are highly valued in the U.S. workplace a criterion in the U.S. immigration preference system, new immigrants are unlikely to contribute significant payments to Social Security, because their incomes will remain relatively low. Without reforms, it is unlikely that immigration will relieve much of the pressure building due to our aging population.

5. **Find a Way to Increase Social Security's Implicit Rate of Return**. As noted earlier, a major current problem for Social Security is a low implicit rate of return. Looking into the future, however, the situation appears even worse. As Figure 6-6 indicates, implicit rates of return for the system will be *negative* by 2020.

The long-term inflation-adjusted return available in the stock market has been 7 to 9 percent since the 1930s. It is not surprising, therefore, that some observers have advocated that the Social Security system purchase stocks rather than Treasury bonds with the current excess of payroll taxes over current benefit payments. (Because this would necessitate the Treasury's borrowing more from the public, this amounts to having the government borrow from the public for purposes of investing in the stock market.)

Although the added returns on stock investments could help stave off tax increases or benefit cuts, there are a few potential problems with this proposal. Despite the stock market's higher long-term returns, the inherent uncertainty of those returns is not entirely

FIGURE 6-6

Projected Social Security Rates of Return for Future Retirees

Whereas workers who paid into Social Security in earlier years got a good deal, those who are now paying in and those who will pay in the future are facing low or negative implicit rates of return.

Sources: Social Security Administration and author's estimates.

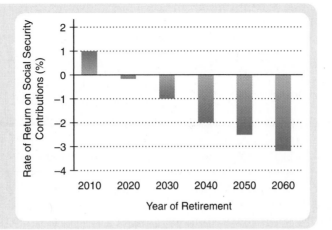

consistent with the function of Social Security as a source of *guaranteed* retirement income. Another issue is which stocks would be purchased. Political pressure to invest in companies that happened to be politically popular and to refrain from investing in those that were unpopular, regardless of their returns, would reduce the expected returns from the government's stock portfolio—possibly even below the returns on Treasury bonds.

QUICK QUIZ   *See page 158 for the answers. Review concepts from this section in MyEconLab.*

Social Security and Medicare payments are using up a large and _____ portion of the federal budget. Because of a shrinking number of workers available to support each retiree, the per capita expense for future workers to fund these programs will _____ rapidly unless reforms are made.

During the early years of the Social Security system, taxes were _____ relative to benefits, resulting in a

_____ implicit rate of return for retirees. As taxes have risen relative to benefits, the implicit rate of return on Social Security has _____ steadily.

There are only five options—or combinations of these five options—for preserving the current social compact: _____ taxes, _____ retirement benefit payouts, _____ disability benefits, reform _____ policies, or _____ Social Security's rate of return.

You Are There ▶ For This Physician, the Tax Rate Is Too High to Justify Working

John McGoldrick and his wife are physicians living in Brunswick, Maine. Their combined income puts them among higher-income U.S. households. Thus, every dollar that John earns over and above his wife's income is normally taxed at an effective top marginal income tax rate of 51.1 percent (including Medicare, Social Security, and state taxes). Today,

though, John has completed a tax worksheet indicating that the couple also owes the *alternative minimum tax (AMT)*. Congress created the AMT in 1969 to prevent very-high-income taxpayers from using numerous special deductions and credits to reduce their tax liabilities. When Congress created the AMT, however, it failed to take inflation into account.

You Are There (cont.)

Since 1969, inflation has pushed up current-dollar incomes. Hence, current-dollar incomes that were "very high" in 1969 are just "high" or even "middle" today. In addition, since then Congress has added numerous deductions and exemptions intended to benefit middle-income taxpayers. Both factors have had the effect of imposing the AMT on more households, including the McGoldricks', thereby pushing John's effective marginal income tax rate even higher.

John realizes that after he and his wife pay all federal taxes including the AMT, state and local taxes, malpractice insurance premiums, and the like, his net earnings do not cover expenses he and his wife incur for child care. The time has come, he decides, to quit his job as an emergency room physician and care for their children himself.

CRITICAL ANALYSIS QUESTIONS

1. How does John McGoldrick know that his effective marginal income tax rate for his year of labor has turned out to be higher than 51.1 percent?

2. Why does the AMT's existence make it difficult for someone contemplating employment or more hours of wage-earning work in her current job to assess her marginal income tax rate? (Hint: Individuals often do not know whether they face the AMT in a given year until after the year-end when they calculate their federal tax liability.)

Progressive Income Taxation in the United States

Issues and Applications

CONCEPTS APPLIED

➤ Progressive Taxation

➤ Tax Rate

➤ Average Tax Rate

On a regular basis, a number of members of the U.S. Congress propose decreasing income tax rates for middle- and lower-income households and increasing income tax rates for higher-income households. They argue that the federal income tax system places a disproportionate burden on middle- and lower-income households and that higher-income taxpayers do not pay "their fair share" of income taxes.

Just how progressive is the *current* U.S. income tax system? One way to evaluate this question is to look at the tax rates—percentages of incomes transmitted to the federal government as income taxes—that apply to different income groups. Another is to compare different income groups' shares of income to their shares of total tax payments.

FIGURE 6-7

Average Tax Rates and Shares of U.S. Federal Income Taxes for Different Income Groups

As panel (a) shows, average tax rates increase for groups with higher incomes. In addition, panel (b) indicates that among those who pay federal income taxes, lower-income taxpayers account for a much smaller portion of payments than higher-income taxpayers. These patterns indicate that the U.S. federal income tax system is progressive.

Source: Internal Revenue Service.

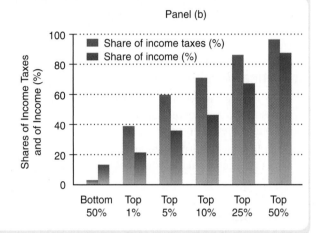

Average Tax Rates for Different Income Groups

Figure 6-7 displays the average federal income tax rates paid by various income groups in the United States. As you can see in panel (a), the average tax rate for all taxpayers in the lower half of the income distribution of taxpayers is about 3 percent. The average tax rate paid by those in the top half of income earners paying taxes is more than 10 percentage points higher.

Also shown in panel (a) are the average tax rates for those in the top 25, 10, 5, and 1 percent of income earners. The tax rate rises as incomes increase, so the U.S. income tax system is clearly progressive throughout the upper range of incomes.

The Distribution of Federal Income Tax Payments

Naturally, even if lower-income individuals faced the same income tax rates as higher-income individuals, the former group would pay a smaller share of total income taxes because they earn lower incomes. In a progressive income tax system, however, lower-income individuals also pay lower tax rates than those assessed against incomes of higher earners. Thus, under progressive taxation lower-income people typically pay a very small share of total tax payments.

Panel (b) of Figure 6-7 verifies that this is currently true in the United States. Taxpayers among the bottom 50 percent of income earners, who earn about 14 percent of all income, account for less than 4 percent of federal income taxes. Thus, the share of taxes paid by the lowest-income individuals is considerably less than their share of total income. Furthermore, panel (b) shows that the bulk of income tax payments is concentrated among the highest-income taxpayers. The top 10 percent of taxpaying income earners, who earn just about 45 percent of all income, pay almost 66 percent of federal income taxes. Those among the top 1 percent earn about 20 percent of all income but account for more than 38 percent of the government's total receipts.

In summary, U.S. income tax rates increase as incomes rise. Consequently, the highest-income taxpayers pay considerably larger shares of the nation's overall income tax bill than lower-income taxpayers.

The highest-income taxpayers also pay proportionately higher shares of taxes than their own shares of total income. Clearly, the United States has a progressive tax system.

Test your understanding of this chapter by going online to **MyEconLab**.
In the Study Plan for this chapter, select Section N: News.

For Critical Analysis

1. If the income tax system were made more progressive across all income groups, how would panel (a) of Figure 6-7 on the previous page change?

2. If the income tax system were made more progressive across all income groups, how would panel (b) of Figure 6-7 change?

Web Resources

1. To see the latest Internal Revenue Service statistics on U.S. income tax rates paid by different income groups, go to www.econtoday.com/chapter06.

2. For information about the increasing share of income earners who owe no federal income taxes at all, go to www.econtoday.com/chapter06.

Research Project

Figure 6-7 includes data only for U.S. income earners who actually paid taxes. Each year, a slightly larger portion—currently about one-third—of income earners in the United States owes zero federal income taxes. Other things being equal, does this trend tend to make the U.S. tax system more progressive? Explain. (Hint: Recall that by definition, 50 percent of all income earners are below the middle-income level.)

Here is what you should know after reading this chapter. **MyEconLab** will help you identify what you know, and where to go when you need to practice.

WHAT YOU SHOULD KNOW

WHERE TO GO TO PRACTICE

Average Tax Rates versus Marginal Tax Rates The average tax rate is the ratio of total tax payments to total income. In contrast, the marginal tax rate is the change in tax payments induced by a change in total taxable income. Thus, the marginal tax rate applies to the last dollar that a person earns.

government budget
  constraint, 135
tax base, 136
tax rate, 136
marginal tax rate, 136
tax bracket, 137
average tax rate, 137
proportional taxation,
  137
progressive taxation, 137
regressive taxation, 137

- **MyEconLab** Study Plans 6.1, 6.2
- Audio introduction to Chapter 6
- Video: Types of Tax Systems
- ABC News Video: Big Government: Who Is Going to Pay the Bill?

(continued)

(continued)

WHAT YOU SHOULD KNOW		WHERE TO GO TO PRACTICE
The U.S. Income Tax System The U.S. income tax system assesses taxes against both personal and business income. It is designed to be a progressive tax system, in which the marginal tax rate increases as income rises, so that the marginal tax rate exceeds the average tax rate. This contrasts with a regressive tax system, in which higher-income people pay lower marginal tax rates, resulting in a marginal tax rate that is less than the average tax rate. The marginal tax rate equals the average tax rate only under proportional taxation, in which the marginal tax rate does not vary with income.	capital gain, 140 capital loss, 140 retained earnings, 140 tax incidence, 141	• **MyEconLab** Study Plan 6.3 • Video: The Corporate Income Tax
The Relationship Between Tax Rates and Tax Revenues Static tax analysis assumes that the tax base does not respond significantly to an increase in the tax rate, so it seems to imply that a tax rate hike must always boost a government's total tax collections. Dynamic tax analysis reveals, however, that increases in tax rates cause the tax base to decline. Thus, there is a tax rate that maximizes the government's tax revenues. If the government pushes the tax rate higher, tax collections decline.	sales taxes, 142 *ad valorem* taxation, 142 static tax analysis, 142 dynamic tax analysis, 143 **KEY FIGURE** Figure 6-3, 145	• **MyEconLab** Study Plan 6.4 • Animated Figure 6-3
How Taxes on Purchases of Goods and Services Affect Market Prices and Quantities When a government imposes a per-unit tax on a good or service, a seller is willing to supply any given quantity only if the seller receives a price that is higher by exactly the amount of the tax. Hence, the supply curve shifts vertically by the amount of the tax per unit. In a market with typically shaped demand and supply curves, this results in a fall in the equilibrium quantity and an increase in the market price. To the extent that the market price rises, consumers pay a portion of the tax on each unit they buy. Sellers pay the remainder in lower profits.	excise tax, 146 unit tax, 146 **KEY FIGURE** Figure 6-4, 146	• **MyEconLab** Study Plan 6.5 • Animated Figure 6-4
How Social Security Works and Why It Poses Problems for Today's Students Since its inception, Social Security benefits have been paid out of taxes. Because of the growing mismatch between elderly and younger citizens, future scheduled benefits vastly exceed future scheduled taxes, so some combination of higher taxes and lower benefits will have to be implemented to maintain the current system. The situation might also be eased a bit if more skilled workers were permitted to immigrate and if Social Security contributions were invested in the stock market, where they could earn higher rates of return.	Social Security contributions, 148 rate of return, 148 inflation-adjusted return, 148 **KEY FIGURE** Figure 6-6, 151	• **MyEconLab** Study Plan 6.6 • Animated Figure 6-6

Log in to MyEconLab, take a chapter test, and get a personalized Study Plan that tells you which concepts you understand and which ones you need to review. From there, MyEconLab will give you further practice, tutorials, animations, videos, and guided solutions.
Log in to www.myeconlab.com

PROBLEMS

All problems are assignable in myeconlab *. Answers to odd-numbered problems appear at the back of the book.*

6-1. A senior citizen gets a part-time job at a fast-food restaurant. She earns $8 per hour for each hour she works, and she works exactly 25 hours per week. Thus, her total pretax weekly income is $200. Her total income tax assessment each week is $40, but she has determined that she is assessed $3 in taxes for the final hour she works each week.

    a. What is this person's average tax rate each week?

    b. What is the marginal tax rate for the last hour she works each week?

6-2. For purposes of assessing income taxes, there are three official income levels for workers in a small country: high, medium, and low. For the last hour on the job during a 40-hour workweek, a high-income worker pays a marginal income tax rate of 15 percent, a medium-income worker pays a marginal tax rate of 20 percent, and a low-income worker is assessed a 25 percent marginal income tax rate. Based only on this information, does this nation's income tax system appear to be progressive, proportional, or regressive?

6-3. Suppose that a state has increased its sales tax rate every other year since 2001. Assume that the state collected all sales taxes that residents legally owed. The following table summarizes its experience. What were total taxable sales in this state during each year displayed in the table?

Year	Sales Tax Rate	Sales Tax Collections
2001	0.03 (3 percent)	$9.0 million
2003	0.04 (4 percent)	$14.0 million
2005	0.05 (5 percent)	$20.0 million
2007	0.06 (6 percent)	$24.0 million
2009	0.07 (7 percent)	$29.4 million

6-4. The sales tax rate applied to all purchases within a state was 0.04 (4 percent) throughout 2008 but increased to 0.05 (5 percent) during all of 2009. The state government collected all taxes due, but its tax revenues were equal to $40 million each year. What happened to the sales tax base between 2008 and 2009? What could account for this result?

6-5. A city government imposes a proportional income tax on all people who earn income within its city limits. In 2008, the city's income tax rate was 0.05 (5 percent), and it collected $20 million in income taxes. In 2009, it raised the income tax rate to 0.06 (6 percent), and its income tax collections declined to $19.2 million. What happened to the city's income tax base between 2008 and 2009? How could this have occurred?

6-6. An obscure subsidiary of Microsoft Corporation, Ireland-based Round Island One Limited, has only about 1,000 employees. Nevertheless, Microsoft has gradually been shifting more income-generating activities to Ireland, which has a lower corporate tax rate than nations such as the United States and the United Kingdom. In one year alone, shifting more of its operations to Ireland allowed Microsoft to reduce its worldwide corporate income tax rate by 6 percentage points. What has happened to Ireland's tax base as a result? What has happened to tax bases in nations such as the United States and the United Kingdom?

6-7. The British government recently imposed a unit excise tax of about $154 per ticket on airline tickets applying to flights to or from London airports. In answering the following questions, assume normally shaped demand and supply curves.

    a. Use an appropriate diagram to predict effects of the ticket tax on the market clearing price of London airline tickets and on the equilibrium number of flights into and out of London.

    b. What do you predict is likely to happen to the equilibrium price of tickets for air flights into and out of cities that are in close proximity to London but are not subject to the new ticket tax? Explain your reasoning.

6-8. To raise funds aimed at providing more support for public schools, a state government has just imposed a unit excise tax equal to $4 for each monthly unit of telephone services sold by each telephone company operating in the state. The diagram on the next page depicts the positions of the demand and supply curves for telephone services *before* the unit excise tax was imposed. Use this diagram to determine the position of the new market supply curve now that the tax hike has gone into effect.

Quantity of Telephone Services
(million of units per month)

a. Does imposing the $4-per-month unit excise tax cause the market price of telephone services to rise by $4 per month? Why or why not?

b. What portion of the $4-per-month unit excise tax is paid by consumers? What portion is paid by providers of telephone services?

6-9. Suppose that the federal government imposes a unit excise tax of $2 per month on the monthly rates that Internet service providers charge for providing DSL high-speed Internet access to households and businesses. Draw a diagram of normally shaped market demand and supply curves for DSL Internet access services. Use this diagram to predict how the Internet service tax is likely to affect the market price and market quantity.

6-10. Consider the $2-per-month tax on DSL Internet access in Problem 6-9. Suppose that in the market for DSL Internet access services provided to households, the market price increases by $2 per month after the unit excise tax is imposed. If the market supply curve slopes upward, what can you say about the shape of the market demand curve over the relevant ranges of prices and quantities? Who pays the excise tax in this market?

6-11. Consider once more the DSL Internet access tax of $2 per month discussed in Problem 6-9. Suppose that in the market for DSL Internet access services provided to businesses, the market price does not change after the unit excise tax is imposed. If the market supply curve slopes upward, what can you say about the shape of the

market demand curve over the relevant ranges of prices and quantities? Who pays the excise tax in this market?

6-12. The following information applies to the market for a particular item in the *absence* of a unit excise tax:

Price ($ per unit)	Quantity Supplied	Quantity Demanded
4	50	200
5	75	175
6	100	150
7	125	125
8	150	100
9	175	75

a. According to the information above, in the *absence* of a unit excise tax, what is the market price? What is the equilibrium quantity?

b. Suppose that the government decides to subject producers of this item to a unit excise tax equal to $2 per unit sold. What is the new market price? What is the new equilibrium quantity?

c. What portion of the tax is paid by producers? What portion of the tax is paid by consumers?

6-13. In the following situations, what is the rate of return on the investment? (Hint: In each case, what is the percentage by which next year's benefit exceeds—or falls short of—this year's cost?)

a. You invest $100 today and receive in return $150 exactly one year from now.

b. You invest $100 today and receive in return $80 exactly one year from now.

6-14. Suppose that the following Social Security reform became law: All current Social Security recipients will continue to receive their benefits, but no increase will be made other than cost-of-living adjustments; U.S. citizens between age 40 and retirement not yet receiving Social Security can opt to continue with the current system; those who opt out can place what they would have contributed to Social Security into one or more government-approved investments; and those under 40 must place their contributions into one or more government-approved investments.

Now answer the following questions:

a. Who will be in favor of this reform and why?

b. Who will be against this reform and why?

c. What might happen to stock market indexes?

d. What additional risk is involved for those who end up in the private system?

e. What additional benefits are possible for the people in the private system?

f. Which firms in the investment industry might not be approved by the federal government and why?

ECONOMICS ON THE NET

Social Security Privatization There are many proposals for reforming Social Security, but only one fundamentally alters the nature of the current system: privatization. The purpose of this exercise is to learn more about what would happen if Social Security were privatized.

Title: Social Security Privatization

Navigation: Go to **www.econtoday.com/chapter06** to learn about Social Security privatization. Click on *FAQ on Social Security* in the left-hand column.

Application For each of the three entries noted here, read the entry and answer the question.

1. Click on *Is there really a Social Security crisis?* According to this article, when will the system begin to experience difficulties? Why?

2. Click on *What about raising the tax cap?* What does this article contend are the likely consequences of applying the Social Security payroll tax to more of a person's income? Why?

3. Click on *What about personal accounts in addition to Social Security?* Why does this article argue that simply adding personal accounts will not solve Social Security's problems?

For Group Study and Analysis It will be worthwhile for those not nearing retirement age to examine what the "older" generation thinks about the idea of privatizing the Social Security system in the United States. So create two groups—one for and one against privatization. Each group will examine the following Web site and come up with arguments in favor of or against the ideas expressed on it.

Go to **www.econtoday.com/chapter06** to read a proposal for Social Security reform. Accept or rebut the proposal, depending on the side to which you have been assigned. Be prepared to defend your reasons with more than just your feelings. At a minimum, be prepared to present arguments that are logical, if not entirely backed by facts.

Taking into account the characteristics of your group as a whole, is it likely to be made better off or worse off if Social Security is privatized? Should your decision to support or oppose privatization be based solely on how it affects you personally? Or should your decision take into account how it might affect others in your group?

ANSWERS TO QUICK QUIZZES

p. 138: (i) rate . . . base; (ii) average . . . marginal; (iii) proportional . . . progressive . . . regressive

p. 142: (i) income . . . sales . . . property; (ii) double; (iii) Social Security . . . Medicare . . . unemployment

p. 145: (i) static; (ii) dynamic . . . static; (iii) fall . . . decline

p. 148: (i) vertically . . . vertically; (ii) reduces . . . raises; (iii) less

p. 151: (i) rising . . . grow; (ii) low . . . high . . . decreased; (iii) raise . . . reduce . . . reduce . . . immigration . . . increase

20 Demand and Supply Elasticity

Between 1981 and 1992, it appeared that one battle in the nationwide war against illicit drugs was being won. Marijuana use among both teens and adults was declining steadily. In the early 1990s, some optimists suggested that marijuana use was about to reach record-low levels and would remain subdued for years to come. These optimists were wrong. Between the mid-1990s and the mid-2000s, the number of U.S. residents using marijuana increased by an estimated 45 percent. During the same period, the number of drug users reporting that marijuana was their "primary problem drug" increased from 7 percent to 16 percent. Why did this dramatic shift in marijuana use and dependency occur? A big part of the answer surely has to do with the responsiveness of the quantity demanded to a change in price, which is a key topic of this chapter.

LEARNING OBJECTIVES

After reading this chapter, you should be able to:

➤ Express and calculate price elasticity of demand

➤ Understand the relationship between the price elasticity of demand and total revenues

➤ Discuss the factors that determine the price elasticity of demand

➤ Describe the cross price elasticity of demand and how it may be used to indicate whether two goods are substitutes or complements

➤ Explain the income elasticity of demand

➤ Classify supply elasticities and explain how the length of time for adjustment affects the price elasticity of supply

? DID YOU KNOW THAT estimates indicate that every 10 percent decline in earnings reduces the amount of health insurance coverage purchased by uninsured people by about 1.5 percent? In addition, every 10 percent increase in the price of health insurance generates an estimated 3.5 percent reduction in health insurance coverage by individuals without employer-provided health coverage. Together, these facts help to explain why the U.S. Census Bureau's estimate of the number of U.S. residents without health insurance coverage could be as high as 40 million. Most people without health insurance coverage have lower incomes, and they have responded to increases in the price of health insurance by reducing their purchases of insurance coverage. This is why politicians jockeying to solve what they perceive as a "health care problem" for lower-income individuals naturally focus on how to bring about reductions in the prices these individuals pay for health insurance.

Politicians trying to design changes in U.S. government health care policies are not the only ones who must recognize how individuals respond to changes in prices. Businesses must constantly take into account consumers' response to changing prices. If Dell reduces its prices by 10 percent, will consumers respond by buying so many more computers that the company's revenues rise? At the other end of the spectrum, can Ferrari dealers "get away" with a 2 percent increase in prices? That is, will Ferrari purchasers respond so little to the relatively small increase in price that the total revenues received for Ferrari sales will not fall and may actually rise? The only way to answer these questions is to know how responsive consumers in the real world will be to changes in prices. Economists have a special name for quantity responsiveness—*elasticity*, which is the subject of this chapter.

What are the main factors responsible for the large number of U.S. residents without health insurance coverage?

Price Elasticity

To begin to understand what elasticity is all about, just keep in mind that it means "responsiveness." Here we are concerned with the price elasticity of demand. We wish to know the extent to which a change in the price of, say, petroleum products will cause the quantity demanded to change, other things held constant. We want to determine the percentage change in quantity demanded in response to a percentage change in price.

Price Elasticity of Demand

We will formally define the **price elasticity of demand,** which we will label E_p, as follows:

$$E_p = \frac{\text{percentage change in quantity demanded}}{\text{percentage change in price}}$$

What will price elasticity of demand tell us? It will tell us the *relative* amount by which the quantity demanded will change in response to a change in the price of a particular good.

Consider an example in which a 10 percent rise in the price of oil leads to a reduction in quantity demanded of only 1 percent. Putting these numbers into the formula, we find that the price elasticity of demand for oil in this case equals the percentage change in quantity demanded divided by the percentage change in price, or

$$E_p = \frac{-1\%}{+10\%} = -0.1$$

An elasticity of −0.1 means that a 1 percent *increase* in the price would lead to a mere 0.1 percent *decrease* in the quantity demanded. If you were now told, in contrast, that

Price elasticity of demand (E_p)
The responsiveness of the quantity demanded of a commodity to changes in its price; defined as the percentage change in quantity demanded divided by the percentage change in price.

the price elasticity of demand for oil was −1, you would know that a 10 percent increase in the price of oil would lead to a 10 percent decrease in the quantity demanded.

RELATIVE QUANTITIES ONLY Notice that in our elasticity formula, we talk about *percentage* changes in quantity demanded divided by *percentage* changes in price. We focus on relative amounts of price changes, because percentage changes are independent of the units chosen. This means that it doesn't matter if we measure price changes in terms of cents, dollars, or hundreds of dollars. It also doesn't matter whether we measure quantity changes in ounces, grams, or pounds.

Go to **www.econtoday.com/chapter20** for additional review of the price elasticity of demand.

ALWAYS NEGATIVE The law of demand states that quantity demanded is *inversely* related to the relative price. An *increase* in the price of a good leads to a *decrease* in the quantity demanded. If a *decrease* in the relative price of a good should occur, the quantity demanded would *increase* by some percentage. The point is that price elasticity of demand will always be negative. By convention, however, *we will ignore the minus sign in our discussion from this point on*.

Basically, the greater the *absolute* price elasticity of demand (disregarding the sign), the greater the demand responsiveness to relative price changes—a small change in price has a great impact on quantity demanded. Conversely, the smaller the absolute price elasticity of demand, the smaller the demand responsiveness to relative price changes—a large change in price has little effect on quantity demanded.

QUICK QUIZ *See page 524 for the answers. Review concepts from this section in MyEconLab.*

Elasticity is a measure of the price _____ of the quantity demanded and the quantity supplied.

The **price elasticity of demand** is equal to the percentage change in _____ _____ divided by the percentage change in _____.

Price elasticity of demand is calculated in terms of _____ changes in quantity demanded and in price. Thus, it is expressed as a unitless, dimensionless number that is _____ of units of measurement.

The law of demand states that quantity demanded and price are _____ related. Therefore, the price elasticity of demand is always _____, because an increase in price will lead to a decrease in quantity demanded and a decrease in price will lead to an increase in quantity demanded. By convention, we ignore the negative sign in discussions of the price elasticity of demand.

Calculating Elasticity

To calculate the price elasticity of demand, we must compute percentage changes in quantity demanded and in price. For the percentage change in quantity demanded, we might divide the change in the quantity demanded by the original quantity demanded:

$$\frac{\text{change in quantity demanded}}{\text{original quantity demanded}}$$

To find the percentage change in price, we might divide the change in price by the original price:

$$\frac{\text{change in price}}{\text{original price}}$$

There is an arithmetic problem, though, when we calculate percentage changes in this manner. The percentage change, say, from 2 to 3—50 percent—is not the same as the percentage change from 3 to 2—$33\frac{1}{3}$ percent. In other words, it makes a difference where you start. One way out of this dilemma is simply to use average values.

To compute the price elasticity of demand, we take the average of the two prices and the two quantities over the range we are considering and compare the change with these averages. Thus, the formula for computing the price elasticity of demand is as follows:

$$E_p = \frac{\text{change in quantity}}{\text{sum of quantities}/2} \div \frac{\text{change in price}}{\text{sum of prices}/2}$$

We can rewrite this more simply if we do two things: (1) We can let Q_1 and Q_2 equal the two different quantities demanded before and after the price change and let P_1 and P_2 equal the two different prices. (2) Because we will be dividing a percentage by a percentage, we simply use the ratio, or the decimal form, of the percentages. Therefore,

$$E_p = \frac{\Delta Q}{(Q_1 + Q_2)/2} \div \frac{\Delta P}{(P_1 + P_2)/2}$$

where the Greek letter Δ (delta) stands for "change in."

How can we use actual changes in the price of oranges and associated changes in the quantity of oranges demanded to calculate the price elasticity of demand for oranges with this formula?

EXAMPLE
The Price Elasticity of Demand for Oranges

Between 2006 and 2007, the price of oranges increased from $1.56 per pound to $1.91 per pound. As a consequence, the total quantity of oranges consumed in the United States declined from 16.4 billion pounds to 13.8 billion pounds.

We can calculate the price elasticity of demand for oranges:

$$E_p = \frac{\text{change in } Q}{\text{sum of quantities}/2} \div \frac{\text{change in } P}{\text{sum of prices}/2}$$

$$= \frac{16.4 \text{ billion} - 13.8 \text{ billion}}{(16.4 \text{ billion} + 13.8 \text{ billion})/2} \div \frac{\$1.91 - \$1.56}{(\$1.91 + \$1.56)/2}$$

$$= \frac{2.6 \text{ billion}}{30.2 \text{ billion}/2} \div \frac{\$0.35}{\$3.47/2} = 0.85$$

The price elasticity of 0.85 means that a 1 percent increase in price generated a 0.85 percent decrease in the quantity of oranges demanded.

FOR CRITICAL ANALYSIS
Would the estimated price elasticity of demand for oranges have been different if we had not used the average-values formula? How?

Price Elasticity Ranges

We have names for the varying ranges of price elasticities, depending on whether a 1 percent change in price elicits more or less than a 1 percent change in the quantity demanded.

Elastic demand
A demand relationship in which a given percentage change in price will result in a larger percentage change in quantity demanded.

- We say that a good has an **elastic demand** whenever the price elasticity of demand is greater than 1. A change in price of 1 percent causes a greater than 1 percent change in the quantity demanded.

Unit elasticity of demand
A demand relationship in which the quantity demanded changes exactly in proportion to the change in price.

Inelastic demand
A demand relationship in which a given percentage change in price will result in a less than proportionate percentage change in the quantity demanded.

- In a situation of **unit elasticity of demand,** a change in price of 1 percent causes exactly a 1 percent change in the quantity demanded.
- In a situation of **inelastic demand,** a change in price of 1 percent causes a change of less than 1 percent in the quantity demanded.

When we say that a commodity's demand is elastic, we are indicating that consumers are relatively responsive to changes in price. When we say that a commodity's demand is inelastic, we are indicating that its consumers are relatively unresponsive to price changes. When economists say that demand is inelastic, it does not necessarily mean that quantity demanded is *totally* unresponsive to price changes. Remember, the law of demand implies that there will be some responsiveness in quantity demanded to a price change. The question is how much. That's what elasticity attempts to determine.

Extreme Elasticities

There are two extremes in price elasticities of demand. One extreme represents total unresponsiveness of quantity demanded to price changes, which is referred to as **perfectly inelastic demand,** or zero elasticity. The other represents total responsiveness, which is referred to as infinitely or **perfectly elastic demand.**

Perfectly inelastic demand
A demand that exhibits zero responsiveness to price changes; no matter what the price is, the quantity demanded remains the same.

Perfectly elastic demand
A demand that has the characteristic that even the slightest increase in price will lead to zero quantity demanded.

We show perfect inelasticity in panel (a) of Figure 20-1. Notice that the quantity demanded per year is 8 million units, no matter what the price. Hence, for any price change, the quantity demanded will remain the same, and thus the change in the quantity demanded will be zero. Look back at our formula for computing elasticity. If the change in the quantity demanded is zero, the numerator is also zero, and a nonzero number divided into zero results in a value of zero too. This is true at any point along the demand curve. Hence, there is perfect inelasticity.

At the opposite extreme is the situation depicted in panel (b) of Figure 20-1. Here we show that at a price of 30 cents, an unlimited quantity will be demanded. At a price that is only slightly above 30 cents, no quantity will be demanded. There is perfect, or infinite, responsiveness at each point along this curve, and hence we call the demand schedule in panel (b) perfectly elastic.

FIGURE 20-1

Extreme Price Elasticities

In panel (a), we show infinite price unresponsiveness. The demand curve is vertical at the quantity of 8 million units per year. This means that the price elasticity of demand is zero. In panel (b), we show complete price responsiveness. At a price of 30 cents, in this example, consumers will demand an unlimited quantity of the particular good in question. This is a case of infinite price elasticity of demand.

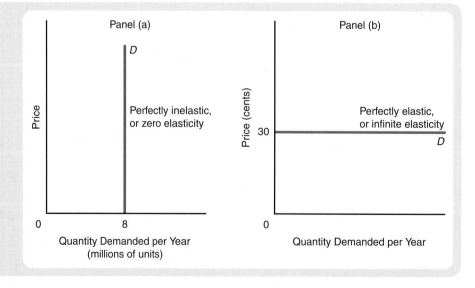

QUICK QUIZ   *See page 524 for the answers. Review concepts from this section in MyEconLab.*

One extreme elasticity occurs when a demand curve is vertical. It has _____ price elasticity of demand. It is completely_____.

Another extreme elasticity occurs when a demand curve is horizontal. It has completely _____ demand. Its price elasticity of demand is _____.

Elasticity and Total Revenues

Suppose that you are an employee of a firm in the cellular telephone service industry. How would you know when a rise in the market clearing price of cellular telephone services will result in an increase in total revenues, or the total receipts, of firms in the industry? It is commonly thought that the way for total receipts to rise is for the price per unit to increase. But is it possible that a rise in price per unit could lead to a decrease in total revenues? The answer to this question depends on the price elasticity of demand.

How does price elasticity of demand affect who pays taxes on beer?

POLICY EXAMPLE
Who Pays Higher Beer Taxes?

State governments impose taxes on beer, which are often assessed as a flat amount per unit sold. These taxes are paid by sellers of beer from the revenues they earn from their total sales. Thus, to receive the same effective price for selling a given quantity, a beer seller would have to receive a price that is higher by exactly the amount of the tax. As shown in panel (a) of Figure 20-2, imposing a tax on beer shifts the supply curve upward by the amount of the tax.

FIGURE 20-2

Price Elasticity and a Tax on Beer

Placing a per-unit tax on beer causes the supply curve to shift upward by the amount of the tax, as illustrated in panel (a). If the demand for beer were perfectly inelastic, as depicted in panel (b), imposing the tax would cause the market price of beer to rise by the amount of the tax, so that beer consumers would effectively pay all the tax. Conversely, if the demand for beer were perfectly elastic, as shown in panel (c), the market price would not change, and sellers would pay all the tax. The quantity demanded would fall to Q_2.

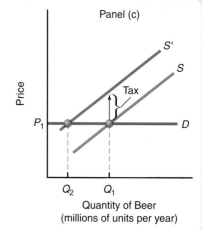

POLICY EXAMPLE (cont.)

Sellers supply a given quantity of beer at a price that is higher by the amount of the tax that they will transmit to the government.

Who *truly* pays the tax depends on the price elasticity of demand, however. Take a look at panel (b) of Figure 20-2 on page 505, which illustrates what would happen to the market price in the case of perfectly inelastic demand for beer. In this instance, the market price rises by the full amount that the supply curve shifts upward. This amount, of course, is the amount of the tax. Consequently, if beer consumers were to have a perfectly inelastic demand for beer, they would effectively pay the entire tax in the form of higher prices. Panel (c) illustrates the opposite case,

in which the demand for beer happens to be perfectly elastic. In this situation, the market price is unresponsive to a tax-induced shift in the supply curve, so sellers must pay all the tax.

Realistically, the price elasticity of demand for beer is relatively low—most beer price elasticity estimates indicate values of 0.3 to 0.7. Thus, the burden of taxes on beer falls mainly on beer consumers.

FOR CRITICAL ANALYSIS

Based on the information in this example, if taxes on beer increase by 10 percent, by what range of percentages will desired beer purchases decline?

Let's look at Figure 20-3. In panel (a), column 1 shows the price of cellular telephone service in cents per minute, and column 2 represents billions of minutes per year. In column 3, we multiply column 1 times column 2 to derive total revenue because total revenue is always equal to the number of units (quantity) sold times the price per unit. In column 4, we calculate values of elasticity. Notice what happens to total revenues throughout the schedule. They rise steadily as the price rises from 1 cent to 5 cents per minute. When the price rises further to 6 cents per minute, total revenues remain constant at $3 billion. At prices per minute higher than 6 cents, total revenues fall as price increases. Indeed, if prices are above 6 cents per minute, total revenues will increase only if the price *declines*, not if the price rises.

Labeling Elasticity

The relationship between price and quantity on the demand schedule is given in columns 1 and 2 of panel (a) in Figure 20-3. In panel (b), the demand curve, *D*, representing that schedule is drawn. In panel (c), the total revenue curve representing the data in column 3 is drawn. Notice first the level of these curves at small quantities. The demand curve is at a maximum height, but total revenue is zero, which makes sense according to this demand schedule—at a price of 11 cents per minute and above, no units will be purchased, and therefore total revenue will be zero. As price is lowered, we travel down the demand curve, and total revenues increase until price is 6 cents per minute, remain constant from 6 cents to 5 cents per minute, and then fall at lower unit prices. Corresponding to those three sections, demand is elastic, unit-elastic, and inelastic. Hence, we have three relationships among the three types of price elasticity and total revenues.

- *Elastic demand.* A negative relationship exists between changes in price and changes in total revenues. That is to say, when market demand for an item is elastic, total revenues will rise if the market price decreases. Total revenues will fall if the market price increases.

- *Unit-elastic demand.* Changes in price do not change total revenues. When market demand is unit-elastic and the market price increases, total revenues will not change, nor will total revenues change if the market price decreases.

FIGURE 20-3

The Relationship Between Price Elasticity of Demand and Total Revenues for Cellular Phone Service

In panel (a), we show the elastic, unit-elastic, and inelastic sections of the demand schedule according to whether a reduction in price increases total revenues, causes them to remain constant, or causes them to decrease, respectively. In panel (b), we show these regions graphically on the demand curve. In panel (c), we show them on the total revenue curve.

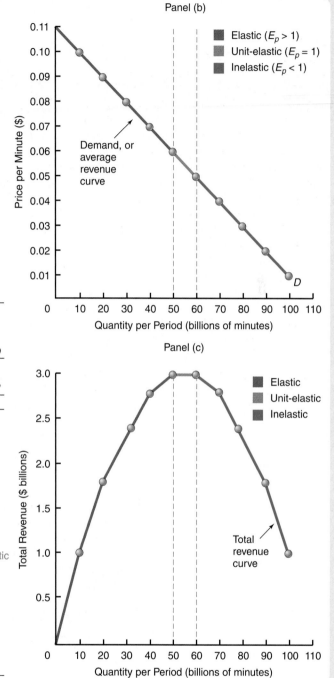

Panel (b)

Panel (c)

Panel (a)

(1) Price, P, per Minute of Cellular Phone Service	(2) Quantity Demanded, D (billions of minutes)	(3) Total Revenue ($ billions) = (1) x (2)	(4) Elasticity, $E_p = \dfrac{\text{Change in } Q}{(Q_1 + Q_2)/2} \div \dfrac{\text{Change in } P}{(P_1 + P_2)/2}$	
$0.11	0	0		
0.10	10	1.0	21.000	
0.09	20	1.8	6.330	
0.08	30	2.4	3.400	Elastic
0.07	40	2.8	2.143	
0.06	50	3.0	1.144	
0.05	60	3.0	1.000	Unit-elastic
0.04	70	2.8	.692	
0.03	80	2.4	.467	Inelastic
0.02	90	1.8	.294	
0.01	100	1.0	.158	

- *Inelastic demand.* A positive relationship exists between changes in price and total revenues. When market demand is inelastic and the market price increases, total revenues will go up. When the market price decreases, total revenues will fall. We therefore conclude that if demand is inelastic, price and total revenues move in the *same* direction.

Why have higher prices led to increased revenues in the global hearing aid industry?

INTERNATIONAL EXAMPLE
Why Hearing Aid Producers Settle for a Low Rate of "Market Penetration"

Most of the world's hearing aid producers are located outside the United States, in nations such as Denmark and Germany. For years, these international producers have worried about low rates of "market penetration"—that is, the relatively small percentages of people with hearing problems who actually use hearing aids. In the United States, for instance, more than 31 million people experience some form of hearing loss, but there are only about 7.3 million hearing aid users. Thus, the rate of market penetration in the United States is only 23.6 percent. Yet this rate is higher than the penetration rate in most other nations of the world.

One factor contributing to the relatively low rate of use of hearing aids is their high price, ranging from several hundred to several thousand dollars depending on the type of hearing aid. Furthermore, in recent years the average inflation-adjusted market price of a hearing aid has increased by about 5 percent per year. These steady price increases have tended to reduce the quantity of hearing aids demanded. The responsiveness of quantity demanded to higher prices has been subdued, however, because the estimated price elasticity of demand for hearing aids is about 0.5. That is, the demand for hearing aids is inelastic. This helps to explain why, even as global producers have worried about low market penetration rates, their inflation-adjusted worldwide revenues have increased in recent years, from about $8.4 billion in 2005 to more than $9 billion today.

FOR CRITICAL ANALYSIS
Why do you suppose that profit-seeking owners of hearing aid production firms are likely pleased by the fact that market hearing aid prices are higher even though the result is a continuing low rate of market penetration?

GRAPHIC PRESENTAION The elastic, unit-elastic, and inelastic areas of the demand curve are shown in Figure 20-3 on the preceding page. For prices from 11 cents per minute of cellular phone time to 6 cents per minute, as price decreases, total revenues rise from zero to $3 billion. Demand is elastic. When price changes from 6 cents to 5 cents, however, total revenues remain constant at $3 billion; demand is unit-elastic. Finally, when price falls from 5 cents to 1 cent, total revenues decrease from $3 billion to $1 billion; demand is inelastic. In panels (b) and (c) of Figure 20-3, we have labeled the sections of the demand curve accordingly, and we have also shown how total revenues first rise, then remain constant, and finally fall.

THE ELASTICITY-REVENUE RELATIONSHIP The relationship between price elasticity of demand and total revenues brings together some important microeconomic concepts. Total revenues, as we have noted, are the product of price per unit times number of units purchased. The law of demand states that along a given demand curve, price and quantity changes will move in opposite directions: One increases as the other decreases. Consequently, what happens to the product of price times quantity depends on which of the opposing changes exerts a greater force on total revenues. But this is just what price elasticity of demand is designed to measure—responsiveness of quantity demanded to a change in price. The relationship between price elasticity of demand and total revenues is summarized in Table 20-1.

TABLE 20-1

Relationship Between Price Elasticity of Demand and Total Revenues

Price Elasticity of Demand (E_p)		Effect of Price Change on Total Revenues (TR)	
		Price Decrease	Price Increase
Inelastic	($E_p < 1$)	TR ↓	TR ↑
Unit-elastic	($E_p = 1$)	No change in TR	No change in TR
Elastic	($E_p > 1$)	TR ↑	TR ↓

QUICK QUIZ *See page 524 for the answers. Review concepts from this section in MyEconLab.*

Price elasticity of demand is related to total _____.

When demand is *elastic*, the change in price elicits a change in total revenues in the _____ direction from the price change.

When demand is *unit-elastic*, a change in price elicits _____ change in total revenues (or in total consumer expenditures).

When demand is *inelastic*, a change in price elicits a change in total revenues (and in consumer expenditures) in the _____ direction as the price change.

Determinants of the Price Elasticity of Demand

We have learned how to calculate the price elasticity of demand. We know that theoretically it ranges numerically from zero (completely inelastic) to infinity (completely elastic). What we would like to do now is come up with a list of the determinants of the price elasticity of demand. The price elasticity of demand for a particular commodity at any price depends, at a minimum, on the following factors:

- The existence, number, and quality of substitutes
- The percentage of a consumer's total budget devoted to purchases of that commodity
- The length of time allowed for adjustment to changes in the price of the commodity

Existence of Substitutes

The closer the substitutes for a particular commodity and the more substitutes there are, the greater will be its price elasticity of demand. At the limit, if there is a perfect substitute, the elasticity of demand for the commodity will be infinity. Thus, even the slightest increase in the commodity's price will cause a dramatic reduction in the quantity demanded: Quantity demanded will fall to zero.

Keep in mind that in this extreme example, we are really talking about two goods that the consumer believes are exactly alike and equally desirable, like dollar bills whose only difference is their serial numbers. When we talk about less extreme examples, we can speak only in terms of the number and the similarity of substitutes that are available.

Thus, we will find that the more narrowly we define a good, the closer and greater will be the number of substitutes available. For example, the demand for diet soft drinks may be relatively elastic because consumers can switch to other low-calorie liquid refreshments. The demand for diet drinks in general, however, is relatively less elastic because there are fewer substitutes.

Share of Budget

We know that the greater the share of a person's total budget that is spent on a commodity, the greater that person's price elasticity of demand is for that commodity. A key reason that the demand for pepper is very inelastic is because individuals spend so little on it relative to their total budgets. In contrast, the demand for items such as transportation and housing is far more elastic because they occupy a large part of people's budgets—changes in their prices cannot easily be ignored without sacrificing a lot of other alternative goods that could be purchased.

Consider a numerical example. A household spends $40,000 a year. It purchases $4 of pepper per year and $4,000 of transportation services. Now consider the spending power of this family when the price of pepper and the price of transportation both double. If the household buys the same amount of pepper, it will now spend $8. It will thus have to reduce other expenditures by $4. This $4 represents only 0.01 percent of the entire household budget. By contrast, a doubling of transportation costs requires that the family spend $8,000, or $4,000 more on transportation, if it is to purchase the same quantity. That increased expenditure on transportation of $4,000 represents 10 percent of total expenditures that must be switched from other purchases. We would therefore predict that the household will react differently to the doubling of the price of pepper than it will for a doubling of transportation prices. It will reduce its transportation purchases by a proportionately greater amount.

Why might the price elasticity of demand for transportation be greater than the price elasticity of demand for, say, salt?

Time for Adjustment

When the price of a commodity changes and that price change persists, more people will learn about it. Further, consumers will be better able to revise their consumption patterns the longer the time period they have to do so. And in fact, the longer the time they do take, the less costly it will be for them to engage in this revision of consumption patterns. Consider a price decrease. The longer the price decrease persists, the greater will be the number of new uses that consumers will discover for the particular commodity, and the greater will be the number of new users of that particular commodity.

It is possible to make a very strong statement about the relationship between the price elasticity of demand and the time allowed for adjustment:

> ***The longer any price change persists, the greater the elasticity of demand, other things held constant. Elasticity of demand is greater in the long run than in the short run.***

SHORT-RUN VERSUS LONG-RUN ADJUSTMENTS Let's consider an example. Suppose that the price of electricity goes up 50 percent. How do you adjust in the short run? You can turn the lights off more often, you can stop using your personal computer as much as you usually do, and similar measures. Otherwise it's very difficult to cut back on your consumption of electricity.

In the long run, though, you can devise other methods to reduce your consumption. Instead of using only electric heaters, the next time you have a house built you will install solar panels. You will purchase fluorescent bulbs because they use less electricity. The more time you have to think about it, the more ways you will find to cut your electricity consumption.

DEMAND ELASTICITY IN THE SHORT RUN AND IN THE LONG RUN We would expect, therefore, that the short-run demand curve for electricity would be relatively less elastic (in the price range around P_e), as demonstrated by D_1 in Figure 20-4. However, the long-run demand curve will exhibit more elasticity (in the neighborhood of P_e), as demonstrated by D_3. Indeed, we can think of an entire family of demand curves such as those depicted in the figure. The short-run demand curve is for the period when there is little time for adjustment. As more time is allowed, the demand curve goes first to D_2 and then all the way to D_3. Thus, in the neighborhood of P_e, elasticity differs for each of these curves. It is greater for the less steep curves (but slope alone does not measure elasticity for the entire curve).

HOW TO DEFINE THE SHORT RUN AND THE LONG RUN We've mentioned the short run and the long run. Is the short run one week, two weeks, one month, two months? Is the long run three years, four years, five years? There is no single answer. The long run is the period of time necessary for consumers to make a full adjustment to a given price change, all other things held constant. In the case of the demand for electricity, the long run will be however long it takes consumers to switch over to cheaper sources of heating, to buy houses and appliances that are more energy-efficient, and so on. The long-run elasticity of demand for electricity therefore relates to a period of at least several years. The short run—by default—is any period less than the long run. What are estimated short- and long-run elasticities for common items? See the next page.

Does the addition of solar panels to a newly built house represent a short-run or a long-run response to an increase in the price of electricity?

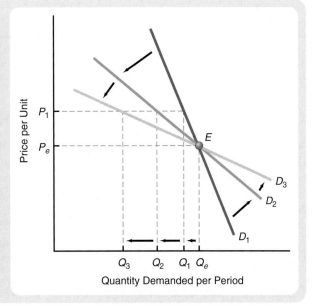

FIGURE 20-4

Short-Run and Long-Run Price Elasticity of Demand

Consider a situation in which the market price is P_e and the quantity demanded is Q_e. Then there is a price increase to P_1. In the short run, as evidenced by the demand curve D_1, we move from equilibrium quantity demanded, Q_e, to Q_1. After more time is allowed for adjustment, the demand curve rotates at original price P_e to D_2. Quantity demanded falls again, now to Q_2. After even more time is allowed for adjustment, the demand curve rotates at price P_e to D_3. At the higher price P_1 in the long run, the quantity demanded falls all the way to Q_3.

EXAMPLE
What Do Real-World Price Elasticities of Demand Look Like?

In Table 20-2, we present demand elasticities for selected goods. None of them is zero, and the largest is 4.6. Remember that even though we are leaving off the negative sign, there is an inverse relationship between price and quantity demanded, and the minus sign is understood. Also remember that these elasticities are measured over given price ranges. Choosing different price ranges could yield different elasticity estimates for these goods.

Economists have consistently found that estimated price elasticities of demand are greater in the long run than in the short run, as seen in Table 20-2. There you see that all available estimates indicate that the long-run price elasticity of demand for vacation air travel is 2.7, whereas the estimate for the short run is 1.1. Throughout the table, you see that all estimates of long-run price elasticities of demand exceed their short-run counterparts.

FOR CRITICAL ANALYSIS
Explain the intuitive reasoning behind the difference between long-run and short-run price elasticity of demand.

TABLE 20-2

Price Elasticities of Demand for Selected Goods

Here are estimated demand elasticities for selected goods. All of them are negative, although we omit the minus sign. We have given some estimates of the long-run price elasticities of demand. The long run is associated with the time necessary for consumers to adjust fully to any given price change. (Note: "N.A." indicates that no estimate is available.)

	Estimated Elasticity	
Category	Short Run	Long Run
Air travel (business)	0.4	1.2
Air travel (vacation)	1.1	2.7
Beef	0.6	N.A.
Cheese	0.3	N.A.
Electricity	0.1	1.7
Fresh tomatoes	4.6	N.A.
Gasoline	0.2	0.5
Hospital services	0.1	0.7
Intercity bus service	0.6	2.2
Physician services	0.1	0.6
Private education	1.1	1.9
Restaurant meals	2.3	N.A.
Tires	0.9	1.2

Cross Price Elasticity of Demand

In Chapter 3, we discussed the effect of a change in the price of one good on the demand for a related good. We defined substitutes and complements in terms of whether a reduction in the price of one caused a decrease or an increase, respectively, in the demand for the other. If the price of compact discs is held constant, the number of CDs purchased (at any price) will certainly be influenced by the price of a close substitute such as Internet digital music downloads. If the price of computer printers is held constant, the amount of computer printers demanded (at any price) will certainly be affected by changes in the price of computers. (These goods are complements.)

Measuring the Cross Price Elasticity of Demand

What we now need to do is come up with a numerical measure of the price responsiveness of demand to the prices of related goods. This is called the

cross price elasticity of demand (E_{xy}), which is defined as the percentage change in the demand for one good (a shift in the demand curve) divided by the percentage change in the price of the related good. In equation form, the cross price elasticity of demand between good X and good Y is

$$E_{xy} = \frac{\text{percentage change in demand for good X}}{\text{percentage change in price of good Y}}$$

Alternatively, the cross price elasticity of demand between good Y and good X would use the percentage change in the demand for good Y as the numerator and the percentage change in the price of good X as the denominator.

Substitutes and Complements

When two goods are substitutes, the cross price elasticity of demand will be positive. For example, when the price of rewritable DVD drives goes up, the demand for flash memory drives will rise—the demand curve for flash drives will shift horizontally rightward—in response as consumers shift away from the now relatively more expensive rewritable DVD drives to flash memory drives. A producer of flash memory drives could benefit from a numerical estimate of the cross price elasticity of demand between rewritable DVD drives and flash memory drives. For example, if the price of rewritable DVD drives goes up by 10 percent and the producer of flash memory drives knows that the cross price elasticity of demand is 1, the flash drive producer can estimate that the demand for flash memory drives will also go up by 10 percent at any given price. Plans for increasing production of flash memory drives can then be made.

When two related goods are complements, the cross price elasticity of demand will be negative (and we will *not* disregard the minus sign). For example, when the price of personal computers declines, the demand for computer printers will rise. This is because as prices of computers decrease, the number of printers purchased at any given price of printers will naturally increase, because computers and printers are often used together. Any manufacturer of computer printers must take this into account in making production plans.

If goods are completely unrelated, their cross price elasticity of demand will, by definition, be zero.

Why does the U.S. Postal Service have to take into account the cross price elasticity of demand each time it increases the price of first-class mail?

Cross price elasticity of demand (E_{xy})
The percentage change in the demand for one good (holding its price constant) divided by the percentage change in the price of a related good.

You Are There

To consider how to use cross price elasticities to assess consumer willingness to switch between different grocery product brands and stores, read **Using Cross Price Elasticities to Assess Brand and Supermarket "Loyalty,"** on page 518.

EXAMPLE
Sending Mail First Class or Second Class?

The U.S. Postal Service (USPS) has raised rates on first-class mail, which it aims to deliver more speedily than second-class mail, several times in the past few years. Each time it does so, it must take into account the cross price elasticity of demand between first-class mail and second-class mail. The estimated cross price elasticity of demand between first-class mail and second-class mail is about 0.3. Each 10 percent increase in the price of first-class mail induces USPS customers to increase the volume of mail that they send via second-class mail by about 3 percent. Thus, first-class mail and second-class mail are substitutes.

FOR CRITICAL ANALYSIS
In light of the positive cross elasticity of demand between first- and second-class mail, why does every 1 percent increase in the price of first-class mail tend to slow down the average USPS mail delivery time?

Income Elasticity of Demand

In Chapter 3, we discussed the determinants of demand. One of those determinants was income. We can apply our understanding of elasticity to the relationship between changes in income and changes in demand.

Measuring the Income Elasticity of Demand

Income elasticity of demand (E_i)
The percentage change in demand for any good, holding its price constant, divided by the percentage change in income; the responsiveness of demand to changes in income, holding the good's relative price constant.

We measure the responsiveness of quantity purchased to income changes by the **income elasticity of demand (E_i):**

$$E_i = \frac{\text{percentage change in demand}}{\text{percentage change in income}}$$

holding relative price constant.

Income elasticity of demand refers to a *horizontal shift* in the demand curve in response to changes in income, whereas price elasticity of demand refers to a *movement along* the curve in response to price changes. Thus, income elasticity of demand is calculated at a given price, and price elasticity of demand is calculated at a given income.

Calculating the Income Elasticity of Demand

To get the same income elasticity of demand over the same range of values regardless of the direction of change (increase or decrease), we can use the same formula that we used in computing the price elasticity of demand. When doing so, we have

$$E_i = \frac{\text{change in quantity}}{\text{sum of quantities}/2} \div \frac{\text{change in income}}{\text{sum of incomes}/2}$$

A simple example will demonstrate how income elasticity of demand can be computed. Table 20-3 gives the relevant data. The product in question is pre-recorded DVDs. We assume that the price of DVDs remains constant relative to other prices. In period 1, six DVDs per month are purchased. Income per month is $4,000. In period 2, monthly income increases to $6,000, and the number of DVDs demanded per month increases to eight. We can apply the following calculation:

$$E_i = \frac{2/[(6 + 8)/2]}{\$2,000/[(\$4,000 + \$6,000)/2]} = \frac{2/7}{2/5} = 0.71$$

Hence, measured income elasticity of demand for DVDs for the individual represented in this example is 0.7l.

TABLE 20-3			
How Income Affects Quantity of DVDs Demanded	Period	Number of DVDs Demanded per Month	Income per Month
	1	6	$4,000
	2	8	6,000

What can we infer from a negative income elasticity of demand for city bus travel in Finland?

INTERNATIONAL EXAMPLE
The Income Elasticity of Demand for Finnish City Bus Travel

Estimated values of the income elasticity of demand for city bus travel in Finland's 10 largest cities during the mid-2000s range from −0.4 to −1.1. Thus, a 10 percent increase in income induces Finnish interurban travelers to *reduce* their consumption of city bus services in these cities by between 4 and 11 percent. Because an income increase generates a decline in travel on city buses, interurban bus services are

what we call an *inferior good*—the demand for city bus travel declines as consumers' incomes rise.

FOR CRITICAL ANALYSIS
Given that recent studies estimate the income elasticity of demand for air travel to be about +1.5, is air travel an inferior good or a normal good? (See page 59 in Chapter 3.)

You have just been introduced to three types of elasticities. All three elasticities are important in influencing the consumption of most goods. Reasonably accurate estimates of these elasticities can go a long way toward making accurate forecasts of demand for goods or services.

QUICK QUIZ | *See page 524 for the answers. Review concepts from this section in MyEconLab.*

Some determinants of price elasticity of demand are (1) the existence, number, and quality of _____; (2) the _____ of the total budget spent on the good in question; and (3) the length of time allowed for _____ to a change in prices.

_____ price elasticity of demand measures one good's demand responsiveness to another's price changes.

For substitutes, it is _____; for complements, it is _____.

Income elasticity of demand tells you by what percentage _____ will change for a particular percentage change in _____.

Price Elasticity of Supply

The **price elasticity of supply** (E_s) is defined similarly to the price elasticity of demand. Supply elasticities are generally positive; this is because at higher prices, larger quantities will generally be forthcoming from suppliers. The definition of the price elasticity of supply is as follows:

$$E_s = \frac{\text{percentage change in quantity supplied}}{\text{percentage change in price}}$$

Price elasticity of supply (E_s)
The responsiveness of the quantity supplied of a commodity to a change in its price; the percentage change in quantity supplied divided by the percentage change in price.

Classifying Supply Elasticities

Just as with demand, there are different ranges of supply elasticities. They are similar in definition to the ranges of demand elasticities.

If a 1 percent increase in price elicits a greater than 1 percent increase in the quantity supplied, we say that at the particular price in question on the supply schedule, *supply is elastic*. The most extreme elastic supply is called **perfectly elastic supply**—the slightest reduction in price will cause quantity supplied to fall to zero.

If, conversely, a 1 percent increase in price elicits a less than 1 percent increase in the quantity supplied, we refer to that as an *inelastic supply*. The most extreme inelastic supply is called **perfectly inelastic supply**—no matter what the price, the quantity supplied remains the same.

If the percentage change in the quantity supplied is just equal to the percentage change in the price, we call this *unit-elastic supply*.

Figure 20-5 shows two supply schedules, *S* and *S'*. You can tell at a glance, even without reading the labels, which one is perfectly elastic and which one is perfectly inelastic. As you might expect, most supply schedules exhibit elasticities that are somewhere between zero and infinity.

Price Elasticity of Supply and Length of Time for Adjustment

We pointed out earlier that the longer the time period allowed for adjustment, the greater the price elasticity of demand. It turns out that the same proposition applies to supply. The longer the time for adjustment, the more elastic the supply curve. Consider why this is true:

1. The longer the time allowed for adjustment, the more resources can flow into (or out of) an industry through expansion (or contraction) of existing firms. As an example, suppose that there is a long-lasting, significant increase in the demand for gasoline. The result is a sustained rise in the market price of gasoline. Initially, gasoline refiners will be hampered in expanding their production with the operating refining equipment available to them. Over time, however, some refining companies might be able to recondition old equipment that had fallen into disuse. They can also place orders for construction of new gasoline-refining equipment, and once the equipment arrives, they can also put it into place to expand their gasoline production. Given sufficient time, therefore, existing gasoline refiners can eventually respond to higher gasoline prices by adding new refining operations.

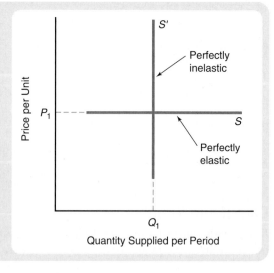

FIGURE 20-5

The Extremes in Supply Curves

Here we have drawn two extremes of supply schedules: *S* is a perfectly elastic supply curve; *S'* is a perfectly inelastic one. In the former, an unlimited quantity will be supplied at price P_1. In the latter, no matter what the price, the quantity supplied will be Q_1. An example of *S'* might be the supply curve for fresh (unfrozen) fish on the morning the boats come in.

2. The longer the time allowed for adjustment, the entry (or exit) of firms increases (or decreases) production in an industry. Consider what happens if the price of gasoline remains higher than before as a result of a sustained rise in gasoline demand. Even as existing refiners add to their capability to produce gasoline by retooling old equipment, purchasing new equipment, and adding new refining facilities, additional businesses may seek to earn profits at the now-higher gasoline prices. Over time, the entry of new gasoline-refining companies adds to the productive capabilities of the entire refining industry, and the quantity of gasoline supplied increases.

We therefore talk about short-run and long-run price elasticities of supply. The short run is defined as the time period during which full adjustment has not yet taken place. The long run is the time period during which firms have been able to adjust fully to the change in price.

Why is there a significant difference between the values of the short-run and long-run elasticities of housing supply?

EXAMPLE
Short-Run versus Long-Run Price Elasticities of Housing Supply

Constructing apartment buildings, condominium complexes, and houses typically requires time to coordinate various activities related to building construction, stretching from initial design to finished housing units. It is not particularly surprising, therefore, that estimated values of the short-run U.S. price elasticity of housing supply—with the short run defined to be one year—rarely exceed 0.1. Thus, within a one-year interval, a 10 percent increase in the price of housing generates a less than 1 percent increase in the quantity of housing supplied. When given a period of several years to adjust to a price change, however, builders' quantity responses are much greater. Recent estimates of the long-run U.S. price elasticity of housing supply—with the long run defined in this example to be 10 years—exceed 3.0. Consequently, if builders have 10 years to adjust to a 10 percent increase in the price of housing, the quantity of new housing supplied over the 10-year period rises by at least 30 percent.

FOR CRITICAL ANALYSIS
How would a technological development enabling builders to construct frames and walls more rapidly likely affect the short-run price elasticity of supply?

A GRAPHIC PRESENTATION We can show a whole set of supply curves similar to the ones we generated for demand. As Figure 20-6 on the following page shows, when nothing can be done in the immediate run, the supply curve is vertical, S_1. As more time is allowed for adjustment, the supply curve rotates to S_2 and then to S_3, becoming more elastic as it rotates.

QUICK QUIZ
See page 524 for the answers. Review concepts from this section in MyEconLab.

Price elasticity of supply is calculated by dividing the percentage change in _____ _____ by the percentage change in _____.

Usually, price elasticities of supply are_____ —higher prices yield _____ quantities supplied.

Long-run supply curves are _____ elastic than short-run supply curves because the _____ the time allowed, the more resources can flow into or out of an industry when price changes.

FIGURE 20-6

Short-Run and Long-Run Price Elasticity of Supply

Consider a situation in which the price is P_e and the quantity supplied is Q_e. In the immediate run, we hypothesize a vertical supply curve, S_1. With the price increase to P_1, therefore, there will be no change in the short run in quantity supplied; it will remain at Q_e. Given some time for adjustment, the supply curve will rotate to S_2. The new amount supplied will increase to Q_1. The long-run supply curve is shown by S_3. The amount supplied again increases to Q_2.

 You Are There ⟩ **Using Cross Price Elasticities to Assess Brand and Supermarket "Loyalty"**

Benaissa Chidmi of Texas Tech University and Rigoberto Lopez of the University of Connecticut recently sought to understand the distinction between "brand loyalty" and "supermarket loyalty." To do so, they tried to determine if consumers tend to purchase the same brands of breakfast cereals at the same Boston supermarkets even in the face of price increases.

Chidmi and Lopez first examined the price elasticities of demand for 37 brands of breakfast cereal. The absolute price elasticities ranged from 2.7 to just over 3.6. Thus, the demands for breakfast cereal brands were elastic: A 1 percent increase in the price of a particular brand of breakfast cereal caused the quantity of that breakfast cereal demanded to decline by more than 1 percent.

Chidmi and Lopez found that *within* a typical individual supermarket, the cross price elasticities for different pairings of breakfast cereals ranged from +0.02 to just over +0.04. Hence, a 10 percent increase in the price of a breakfast cereal brand would cause the amount of an alternative brand of breakfast cereal demanded to rise by 0.2 to 0.4 percent. The somewhat small values of the cross price elasticities within stores indicated that consumers were relatively loyal to cereal brands but nonetheless were sometimes willing to substitute to other brands when one brand's price increased.

To assess "supermarket loyalty," Chidmi and Lopez examined the cross price elasticities of demand for identical brands at different supermarkets. For instance, they estimated the cross price elasticity of Kellogg's Corn Flakes at Stop & Shop versus Shaw's Supermarket. They did the same for the other 36 cereals and obtained estimates of cross price elasticities for the same product at different stores ranging from as low as +0.005 to as high as almost +0.05. Thus, consumers sometimes responded to a higher price of, say, Corn Flakes at Stop & Shop by purchasing Corn Flakes at Shaw's instead. Nevertheless, the small values of these cross price elasticities of demand for the same cereal brands at different supermarkets imply relatively high loyalty to individual supermarkets. Apparently, not many Boston consumers go to the trouble to drive to another supermarket to buy Corn Flakes when the price of Corn Flakes at Stop & Shop rises by 10 percent.

CRITICAL ANALYSIS QUESTIONS

1. How would the price elasticity of demand for brands of breakfast cereals likely change if the number of substitute "quick breakfasts" available to consumers increased?

2. What do you think would happen to the cross price elasticities of demand for the same brands at Stop & Shop versus Shaw's if Shaw's were to locate all of its supermarkets immediately adjacent to Stop & Shop supermarkets?

Price Elasticity of Demand and the Upswing in Marijuana Use

In the early 1990s, studies of marijuana use indicated that the percentage of people buying marijuana declined by more than 50 percent between 1981 and 1992. Private groups and government agencies that provide education about the ill effects of using the illicit drug hailed this decline as evidence of success in fighting marijuana use. Today, however, more than 40 percent of high school seniors are reporting marijuana purchases, and marijuana use among adults has jumped. Indeed, the percentage of drug-using adults indicating that marijuana is the "primary problem drug" in their lives has more than doubled since the mid-1990s.

What happened between the early 1990s and today? The answer comes in two parts, both of which have to do with a change in the price of marijuana.

A Big Price Drop

When antidrug agencies first tried to determine why the upsurge in marijuana use has occurred, they distributed surveys to teens and adults who had tried marijuana or were using the drug regularly. They learned from answers to the survey questions that people had heard the agencies' messages about the drug's unhealthful effects. They also learned, however, that the market price of marijuana was dropping considerably and that people were responding by consuming more of the drug.

Since 1992, the estimated price of marijuana has fallen by more than 30 percent. At the same time, the potency of a typical ounce of marijuana sold on the street has increased by more than 50 percent. Combined, these two factors have translated into a decline in the constant-quality price per ounce of marijuana of more than 60 percent. Of course, a result of this significant fall in price has been a movement down along the marijuana demand curve and a corresponding increase in the quantity of marijuana demanded.

The Role of Price Elasticities in Marijuana Usage

When evaluating the sensitivity of illicit drug use to changes in drug prices, economists typically examine two different types of price elasticities. Naturally, one of these is the price elasticity of demand. Most estimates indicate that the absolute price elasticity of demand for regular users of marijuana is about 2.8. Thus, the demand for marijuana is elastic. A 1 percent decrease in price generates roughly a 2.8 percent increase in marijuana consumption. This means that the more than 60 percent decrease in the constant-quality price of marijuana may have boosted consumption by regular marijuana users by as much as 140 percent.

Another elasticity that economists look at when examining the usage of illicit drugs is the *price elasticity of participation*, which is the responsiveness of people's first experiments with drugs to observed price changes. For most drugs, this elasticity is typically higher than the price elasticity of demand. Estimates of the price elasticity of participation for marijuana range between about 3.1 and 4.5. This range of estimates implies that a 1 percent decrease in marijuana's price leads to a 3.1 percent to 4.5 percent increase in first tries of the drug. Thus, the nearly 60 percent drop in the price of marijuana since 1992 has likely increased first uses of the drug by somewhere between 155 percent and 225 percent.

Medical studies indicate that between 2 and 3 percent of those who try and continue to use marijuana become habitual users of the drug within two years. About 10 percent of all who try the drug eventually become regular users. Lower marijuana prices and high price elasticities of marijuana demand and of participation in use of the drug explain why so many more people now report that marijuana is their "primary problem drug." Because the price of marijuana has declined considerably and the price elasticity of participation is high, more people than ever are responding to the price drop by trying marijuana. The price elasticity of demand by regular users is high, so once people become regular users, they are responding to the price decrease by consuming much larger amounts of the drug.

Test your understanding of this chapter by going online to **MyEconLab**.
In the Study Plan for this chapter, select Section N: News.

For Critical Analysis

1. Why do you suppose that people who propose stiffer penalties for violations of laws prohibiting the sale and use of marijuana argue that toughened enforcement would push up the market price of marijuana and significantly reduce its use? (Hint: Tougher penalties push up suppliers' costs and reduce users' quantity demanded.)

2. Why do you think that economists interpret the high price elasticity of demand for marijuana by regular users to be consistent with the fact that 90 percent of users do not become habitual users of the drug?

Web Resources

1. For information about estimates of price elasticities of demand for marijuana and other illicit drugs, go to www.econtoday.com/chapter20.

2. To see a recent study of short-run and longer-term effects of changes in enforcement efforts against marijuana, go to www.econtoday.com/chapter20.

Research Project

In light of the information provided above, evaluate whether the total revenues of marijuana sellers have likely increased or decreased. Explain your reasoning.

Here is what you should know after reading this chapter. **MyEconLab** will help you identify what you know, and where to go when you need to practice.

WHAT YOU SHOULD KNOW		WHERE TO GO TO PRACTICE
Expressing and Calculating the Price Elasticity of Demand The price elasticity of demand is the responsiveness of the quantity demanded of a good to a change in the price of the good. It is the percentage change in quantity demanded divided by the percentage change in price. To calculate the price elasticity of demand for relatively small changes in price, the percentage change in quantity demanded is equal to the change in the quantity resulting from a price change divided by the average of the initial and final quantities, and the percentage change in price is equal to the price change divided by the average of the initial and final prices.	price elasticity of demand (E_p), 501	• **MyEconLab** Study Plan 20.1 • Audio introduction to Chapter 20
The Relationship Between the Price Elasticity of Demand and Total Revenues Demand is elastic when the price elasticity of demand exceeds 1, and over the elastic range of a demand curve, an increase in price reduces total revenues. Demand is inelastic when the price elasticity of demand is less than 1, and over this range of a demand curve, an increase in price raises total revenues. Finally, demand is unit-elastic when the price elasticity of demand equals 1, and over this range of a demand curve, an increase in price does not affect total revenues.	elastic demand, 503 unit elasticity of demand, 504 inelastic demand, 504 perfectly inelastic demand, 504 perfectly elastic demand, 504 **KEY FIGURES** Figure 20-1, 504 Figure 20-2, 505 Figure 20-3, 507 Figure 20-4, 511	• **MyEconLab** Study Plans 20.2, 20.3 • Animated Figures 20-1, 20-2, 20-3, 20-4
Factors That Determine the Price Elasticity of Demand Three factors affect the price elasticity of demand. If there are more close substitutes for a good, the price elasticity of demand increases. The price elasticity of demand for a good also tends to be higher when a larger portion of a person's budget is spent on the good. In addition, if people have a longer period of time to adjust to a price change and change their consumption patterns, the price elasticity of demand tends to be higher.		• **MyEconLab** Study Plan 20.4 • Video: The Determinants of the Price Elasticity of Demand
The Cross Price Elasticity of Demand and Using It to Determine Whether Two Goods Are Substitutes or Complements The cross price elasticity of demand for a good is the percentage change in the demand for that good divided by the percentage change in the price of a related good. If two goods are substitutes in consumption, an increase in the price of one of the goods induces an increase in the demand for the other good, so that the cross price elasticity of demand is positive. In contrast, if two goods are complements in consumption, an increase in the price of one of the goods brings about a decrease in the demand for the other good, so that the cross price elasticity of demand is negative.	cross price elasticity of demand (E_{xy}), 513	• **MyEconLab** Study Plan 20.5 • Video: Cross Price Elasticity of Demand

(continued)

(continued)

WHAT YOU SHOULD KNOW		WHERE TO GO TO PRACTICE
The Income Elasticity of Demand The income elasticity of demand for any good is the responsiveness of the demand for the good to a change in income, holding the good's relative price unchanged. It is equal to the percentage change in demand for the good divided by the percentage change in income.	income elasticity of demand (E_i), 514	• **MyEconLab** Study Plan 20.6 • Video: Income Elasticity of Demand
Classifying Supply Elasticities and How the Length of Time for Adjustment Affects the Price Elasticity of Supply The price elasticity of supply is equal to the percentage change in quantity supplied divided by the percentage change in price. If the price elasticity of supply is greater than 1, supply is elastic, and if the price elasticity of supply is less than 1, supply is inelastic. Supply is unit-elastic if the price elasticity of supply equals 1. Supply is more likely to be elastic when sellers have more time to adjust to price changes.	price elasticity of supply (E_s), 515 perfectly elastic supply, 516 perfectly inelastic supply, 516 **KEY FIGURE** Figure 20-6, 518	• **MyEconLab** Study Plan 20.7 • Animated Figure 20-6

Log in to MyEconLab, take a chapter test, and get a personalized Study Plan that tells you which concepts you understand and which ones you need to review. From there, MyEconLab will give you further practice, tutorials, animations, videos, and guided solutions. Log in to www.myeconlab.com

PROBLEMS

All problems are assignable in myeconlab. *Answers to odd-numbered problems appear at the back of the book.*

20-1. When the price of shirts emblazoned with a college logo is $10, consumers buy 150 per week. When the price declines to $9, consumers purchase 200 per week. Based on this information, calculate the price elasticity of demand for logo-emblazoned shirts.

20-2. Table 20-2 on page 512 indicates that the short-run price elasticity of demand for tires is 0.9. If an increase in the price of petroleum (used in producing tires) causes the market prices of tires to rise from $50 to $60, by what percentage would you expect the quantity of tires demanded to change?

20-3. The diagram alongside depicts the demand curve for "miniburgers" in a local fast-food market. Use the information in this diagram to answer the questions that follow.

a. What is the price elasticity of demand along the range of the demand curve between a price of $0.20 per miniburger and a price of $0.40 per miniburger? Is demand elastic or inelastic over this range?

b. What is the price elasticity of demand along the range of the demand curve between a price of $0.80 per miniburger and a price of $1.20 per miniburger? Is demand elastic or inelastic over this range?

c. What is the price elasticity of demand along the range of the demand curve between a price of $1.60 per miniburger and a price of $1.80 per miniburger? Is demand elastic or inelastic over this range?

20-4. In a local market, the monthly price of Internet access service decreases from $20 to $10, and the total quantity of monthly accounts across all Internet access providers increases from 100,000 to 200,000. What is the price elasticity of demand? Is demand elastic, unit-elastic, or inelastic?

20-5. At a price of $30.00 to play 18 holes on local golf courses, 1,200 consumers pay to play a game of golf each day. A rise in the price to $32.50 causes the number of consumers to decline to 800. What is the price elasticity of demand? Is demand elastic, unit-elastic, or inelastic?

20-6. It is very difficult to find goods with perfectly elastic or perfectly inelastic demand. We can, however, find goods that lie near these extremes. Characterize demands for the following goods as being near perfectly elastic or near perfectly inelastic.

a. Corn grown and harvested by a small farmer in Iowa

b. Heroin for a drug addict

c. Water for a desert hiker

d. One of several optional textbooks in a pass-fail course

20-7. In the market for hand-made guitars, when the price of guitars is $800, annual revenues are $640,000. When the price falls to $700, annual revenues decline to $630,000. Over this range of guitar prices, is the demand for hand-made guitars elastic, unit-elastic, or inelastic?

20-8. Suppose that over a range of prices, the price elasticity of demand varies from 15.0 to 2.5. Over another range of prices, the price elasticity of demand varies from 1.5 to 0.75. What can you say

about total revenues and the total revenues curve over these two ranges of the demand curve as price falls?

20-9. Based on the information provided alone, characterize the demands for the following goods as being more elastic or more inelastic.

a. A 45-cent box of salt that you buy once a year

b. A type of high-powered ski boat that you can rent from any one of a number of rental agencies

c. A specific brand of bottled water

d. Automobile insurance in a state that requires autos to be insured but has few insurance companies

e. A 75-cent guitar pick for the lead guitarist of a major rock band

20-10. The value of cross price elasticity of demand between goods X and Y is 1.25, while the cross price elasticity of demand between goods X and Z is −2.0. Characterize X and Y and X and Z as substitutes or complements.

20-11. Suppose that the cross price elasticity of demand between eggs and bacon is −0.5. What would you expect to happen to sales of bacon if the price of eggs rises by 10 percent?

20-12. Assume that the income elasticity of demand for hot dogs is −1.25 and that the income elasticity of demand for lobster is 1.25. Based on the fact that the measure for hot dogs is negative while that for lobster is positive, are these normal or inferior goods? (Hint: You may want to refer to the discussion of normal and inferior goods in Chapter 3.)

20-13. At a price of $25,000, producers of midsized automobiles are willing to manufacture and sell 75,000 cars per month. At a price of $35,000, they are willing to produce and sell 125,000 a month. Using the same type of calculation method used to compute the price elasticity of demand, what is the price elasticity of supply? Is supply elastic, unit-elastic, or inelastic?

20-14. The price elasticity of supply of a basic commodity that a nation imports from producers in other countries is 2. What would you expect to happen to the volume of imports if the price of this commodity rises by 10 percent?

20-15. A 20 percent increase in the price of skis induces ski manufacturers to increase production of skis by 10 percent in the short run. In the long run, other things being equal, the 20 percent price increase generates a production increase of 40 percent. What is the short-run price elasticity of supply? What is the long-run price elasticity of supply?

20-16. An increase in the market price of men's haircuts, from $15 per haircut to $25 per haircut, initially causes a local barbershop to have its employees work overtime to increase the number of daily haircuts provided from 35 to 45. When the $25 market price remains unchanged for several weeks and all other things remain equal as well, the barbershop hires additional employees and provides 65 haircuts per day. What is the short-run price elasticity of supply? What is the long-run price elasticity of supply?

ECONOMICS ON THE NET

Price Elasticity and Consumption of Illegal Drugs Making the use of certain drugs illegal drives up their market prices, so the price elasticity of demand is a key factor affecting the use of illegal drugs. This application applies concepts from this chapter to analyze how price elasticity of demand affects drug consumption.

Title: The Demand for Illicit Drugs

Navigation: Go to **www.econtoday.com/chapter20**, and follow the link to the summary of this paper published by the National Bureau of Economic Research.

Application Read the summary of the results of this study of price elasticities of participation in use of illegal drugs, and answer the following questions.

1. Based on the results of the study, is the demand for cocaine more or less price elastic than the demand for heroin? For which drug, therefore, will quantity demanded fall by a greater percentage in response to a proportionate increase in price?

2. The study finds that decriminalizing currently illegal drugs would bring about sizable increases both in overall consumption of heroin and cocaine and in the price elasticity of demand for both drugs. Why do you suppose that the price elasticity of demand would rise? (Hint: At present, users of cocaine and heroin are restricted to only a few illegal sources of the drugs, but if the drugs could legally be produced and sold, there would be many more suppliers providing a variety of different types of both drugs.)

For Group Study and Analysis Discuss ways that government officials might use information about the price elasticities of demand for illicit drugs to assist in developing policies intended to reduce the use of these drugs. Which of these proposed policies might prove most effective? Why?

ANSWERS TO QUICK QUIZZES

p. 502: (i) responsiveness; (ii) quantity demanded . . . price; (iii) percentage . . . independent; (iv) inversely . . . negative

p. 505: (i) zero . . . inelastic; (ii) elastic . . . infinite

p. 509: (i) revenues; (ii) opposite; (iii) zero; (iv) same

p. 515: (i) substitutes . . . share . . . adjustment; (ii) Cross . . . positive . . . negative; (iii) demand . . . income

p. 517: (i) quantity supplied . . . price; (ii) positive . . . greater; (iii) more . . . longer

Consumer Choice

21

"**T**aken all together, how would you say things are these days—would you say that you are very happy, pretty happy, or not too happy?" A social science research center at the University of Chicago has been posing this question to a sample of several thousand U.S. residents each year since 1972. Researchers now commonly address similar questions to people around the world. Then they compare expressed levels of satisfaction both within countries and across countries. For more than two centuries, economists have been contemplating how people seek to maximize their happiness levels when making choices. Nevertheless, until recently most economists doubted that answers to survey questions could yield measures of happiness that can be compared across individuals. In this chapter, you will learn about economists' traditional measure of happiness, called *utility*, which economists apply to developing an understanding of how people make choices.

LEARNING OBJECTIVES

After reading this chapter, you should be able to:

➤ Distinguish between total utility and marginal utility

➤ Discuss why marginal utility first rises but ultimately tends to decline as a person consumes more of a good or service

➤ Explain why an individual's optimal choice of how much to consume of each good or service entails equalizing the marginal utility per dollar spent across all goods and services

➤ Describe the substitution effect of a price change on the quantity demanded of a good or service

➤ Understand how the real-income effect of a price change affects the quantity demanded of a good or service

➤ Evaluate why the price of diamonds is so much higher than the price of water even though people cannot survive long without water

DID YOU KNOW THAT the human brain does its intelligent computing with 10^{11} (100,000,000,000) neurons? These neurons are interconnected in a complex network of about 10^{16} (10,000,000,000,000,000) electrochemical connections called synapses, each of which performs about 1,000 operations per second. Evidence indicates that all this computing power makes the human brain at least 10,000 times more intelligent than most artificially constructed supercomputers. Thus, there is general agreement that the human brain is thousands of times better at making choices among desirable alternatives than the computing machines available today. Human beings have considerable capability to evaluate choices and determine the quantities of different goods and services they wish to consume.

In Chapter 3, you learned that a determinant of the quantity demanded of any particular item is the price of that item. The law of demand implies that at a lower overall price, there will be a higher quantity demanded. Understanding the derivation of the law of demand is useful because it allows us to examine the relevant variables, such as price, income, and tastes, in such a way as to make better sense of the world and even perhaps generate predictions about it. One way of deriving the law of demand involves an analysis of the logic of consumer choice in a world of limited resources. In this chapter, therefore, we discuss what is called *utility analysis*.

What are some of the determinants of this consumer's decision to buy a new cell phone?

Utility
The want-satisfying power of a good or service.

Utility analysis
The analysis of consumer decision making based on utility maximization.

Utility Theory

When you buy something, you do so because of the satisfaction you expect to receive from having and using that good. For everything that you like to have, the more you have of it, the higher the level of total satisfaction you receive. Another term that can be used for satisfaction is **utility,** or want-satisfying power. This property is common to all goods that are desired. The concept of utility is purely subjective, however. There is no way that you or I can measure the amount of utility that a consumer might be able to obtain from a particular good, for utility does not imply "useful" or "utilitarian" or "practical." Thus, there can be no accurate scientific assessment of the utility that someone might receive by consuming a fast-food dinner or a movie relative to the utility that another person might receive from that same good or service.

The utility that individuals receive from consuming a good depends on their tastes and preferences. These tastes and preferences are normally assumed to be given and stable for a particular individual. An individual's tastes determine how much utility that individual derives from consuming a good, and this in turn determines how that individual allocates his or her income to purchases of that good. But we cannot explain why tastes are different between individuals. For example, we cannot explain why some people like yogurt but others do not.

We can analyze in terms of utility the way consumers decide what to buy, just as physicists have analyzed some of their problems in terms of what they call force. No physicist has ever seen a unit of force, and no economist has ever seen a unit of utility. In both cases, however, these concepts have proved useful for analysis.

Throughout this chapter, we will be discussing **utility analysis,** which is the analysis of consumer decision making based on utility maximization—that is, making choices with the aim of attaining the highest feasible satisfaction.

Utility and Utils

Economists once believed that utility could be measured. In fact, there is a philosophical school of thought based on utility theory called *utilitarianism*, developed by the English philosopher Jeremy Bentham (1748–1832). Bentham held that society should seek the greatest happiness for the greatest number. He sought to apply an arithmetic formula for measuring happiness. He and his followers developed the notion of measurable utility and invented the **util** to measure it. For the moment, we will also assume that we can measure satisfaction using this representative unit. Our assumption will allow us to quantify the way we examine consumer behavior. Thus, the first chocolate bar that you eat might yield you 4 utils of satisfaction; the first peanut cluster, 6 utils; and so on. Today, no one really believes that we can actually measure utils, but the ideas forthcoming from such analysis will prove useful in understanding how consumers choose among alternatives.

Util
A representative unit by which utility is measured.

Total and Marginal Utility

Consider the satisfaction, or utility, that you receive each time that you download and listen to digital music albums. To make the example straightforward, let's say that there are hundreds of downloadable music albums to choose from each year and that each of them is of the same quality. Let's say that you normally download and listen to one music album per week. You could, of course, download two, or three, or four per week. Presumably, each time you download and listen to another music album per week, you will get additional satisfaction, or utility. The question that we must ask though, is, given that you are already downloading and listening to one album per week, will the next one downloaded and listened to during that week give you the same amount of additional utility?

That additional, or incremental, utility is called **marginal utility,** where *marginal* means "incremental" or "additional." (Marginal changes also refer to decreases, in which cases we talk about *decremental* changes.) The concept of marginality is important in economics because we can think of people comparing additional (marginal) benefits with additional (marginal) costs.

Marginal utility
The change in total utility due to a one-unit change in the quantity of a good or service consumed.

Applying Marginal Analysis to Utility

The example in Figure 21-1 on the following page will clarify the distinction between total utility and marginal utility. The table in panel (a) shows the total utility and the marginal utility of downloading and listening to digital music albums each week. Marginal utility is the difference between total utility derived from one level of consumption and total utility derived from another level of consumption within a given time interval. A simple formula for marginal utility is this:

$$\text{Marginal utility} = \frac{\text{change in total utility}}{\text{change in number of units consumed}}$$

In our example, when a person has already downloaded and listened to two music albums in one week and then downloads and listens to another, total utility increases from 16 utils to 19 utils. Therefore, the marginal utility (of downloading and listening to one more album of Internet music after already having downloaded and listened to two in one week) is equal to 3 utils.

Graphical Analysis

We can transfer the information in panel (a) onto a graph, as we do in panels (b) and (c) of Figure 21-1 on the next page. Total utility, which is represented in column 2 of panel (a), is transferred to panel (b).

FIGURE 21-1

Total and Marginal Utility of Downloading and Listening to Digital Music Albums

If we were able to assign specific values to the utility derived from downloading and listening to digital music albums each week, we could obtain a marginal utility schedule similar in pattern to the one shown in panel (a). In column 1 is the number of music albums downloaded and listened to per week; in column 2, the total utility derived from each quantity; and in column 3, the marginal utility derived from each additional quantity, which is defined as the change in total utility due to a change of one unit of listening to downloaded albums per week. Total utility from panel (a) is plotted in panel (b). Marginal utility is plotted in panel (c), where you see that it reaches zero where total utility hits its maximum at between 4 and 5 units.

Panel (a)

(1) Number of Music Albums Downloaded and Listened to per Week	(2) Total Utility (utils per week)	(3) Marginal Utility (utils per week)
0	0	
		10 (10 − 0)
1	10	
		6 (16 − 10)
2	16	
		3 (19 − 16)
3	19	
		1 (20 − 19)
4	20	
		0 (20 − 20)
5	20	
		−2 (18 − 20)
6	18	

Panel (b)

Panel (c)

Total utility continues to rise until four digital music albums are downloaded and listened to per week. This measure of utility remains at 20 utils through the fifth album, and at the sixth album per week it falls to 18 utils; we assume that at some quantity consumed per unit time period, boredom with consuming more digital music albums begins to set in. Thus, at some quantity consumed, the additional utility from consuming an additional album begins to fall, so total utility first rises and then declines in panel (b).

Marginal Utility

If you look carefully at panels (b) and (c) of Figure 21-1, the notion of marginal utility becomes clear. In economics, the term *marginal* always refers to a *change* in the total. The marginal utility of listening to three downloaded digital music albums per week instead of two albums per week is the increment in total utility and is equal to 3 utils per week. All of the points in panel (c) are taken from column 3 of the table in panel (a). Notice that marginal utility falls throughout the graph. A special point occurs after four albums are downloaded and listened to per week because the total utility curve in panel (b) is unchanged after the consumption of the fourth album. That means that the consumer receives no additional (marginal) utility from downloading and listening to the fifth album. This is shown in panel (c) as *zero* marginal utility. After that point, marginal utility becomes negative.

In our example, when marginal utility becomes negative, it means that the consumer is tired of downloading and listening to digital music albums and would require some form of compensation to listen to any more. When marginal utility is negative, an additional unit consumed actually lowers total utility by becoming a nuisance. Rarely does a consumer face a situation of negative marginal utility. Whenever this point is reached, goods in effect become "bads." Consuming more units actually causes total utility to *fall* so that marginal utility is negative. A rational consumer will stop consuming at the point at which marginal utility becomes negative, even if the good is available at a price of zero.

Why is Hollywood concerned about the possibility that some viewers of motion pictures may soon begin to experience rapidly falling marginal utility?

E-COMMERCE EXAMPLE
Moviemakers Try to Avoid Projecting Negative Marginal Utility

In an average week during 1948, when the U.S. population was less than half its present level, 90 million people paid to view a motion picture at a movie theater. Today, the average weekly number of moviegoers is only 30 million. Since the late 1940s, a steady wave of close substitutes—television, videocassettes, DVDs, digital movie downloads—has reduced the number of movies that people choose to see at theaters. One way that moviemakers hope to lure people back to theaters is by producing more movies in digital three-dimensional (3D) formats. More than 2,000 U.S. theaters are now equipped with 3D digital projection systems, and some directors have indicated that they plan to make only digital 3D movies.

Hollywood's newfound fascination with digital 3D has one drawback, however: viewing digital 3D movies for much longer than 90 minutes causes some viewers to experience headaches, dizziness, or even nausea. Thus, a key objective of today's designers of digital 3D projection systems is to minimize the potential for some moviegoers to derive negative marginal utility from viewing 3D motion pictures.

FOR CRITICAL ANALYSIS
Why do you suppose that some in Hollywood are predicting that initially most digital 3D movies will be action packed and relatively short?

Diminishing Marginal Utility

Diminishing marginal utility

The principle that as more of any good or service is consumed, its extra benefit declines. Otherwise stated, increases in total utility from the consumption of a good or service become smaller and smaller as more is consumed during a given time period.

Notice that in panel (c) of Figure 21-1 on page 528, marginal utility is continuously declining. This property has been named the principle of **diminishing marginal utility.** There is no way that we can prove diminishing marginal utility. Nevertheless, diminishing marginal utility has even been called a law. This supposed law concerns a psychological, or subjective, utility that you receive as you consume more and more of a particular good. Stated formally, the law is as follows:

> *As an individual consumes more of a particular commodity, the total level of utility, or satisfaction, derived from that consumption usually increases. Eventually, however, the rate at which it increases diminishes as more is consumed.*

Take a hungry individual at a dinner table. The first serving is greatly appreciated, and the individual derives a substantial amount of utility from it. The second serving does not have quite as much pleasurable impact as the first one, and the third serving is likely to be even less satisfying. This individual experiences diminishing marginal utility of food until he or she stops eating, and this is true for most people. All-you-can-eat restaurants count on this fact; a second helping of ribs may provide some marginal utility, but the third helping would have only a little or even negative marginal utility.

Consider for a moment the opposite possibility—increasing marginal utility. Under such a situation, the marginal utility after consuming, say, one hamburger would increase. The second hamburger would be more valuable to you, and the third would be even more valuable yet. If increasing marginal utility existed, each of us would consume only one good or service! Rather than observing that "variety is the spice of life," we would see that monotony in consumption was preferred. We do not observe this, and therefore we have great confidence in the concept of diminishing marginal utility.

Can diminishing marginal utility explain why newspaper vending machines rarely prevent people from taking more than the one current issue they have paid to purchase?

EXAMPLE
Newspaper Vending Machines versus Candy Vending Machines

Have you ever noticed that newspaper vending machines nearly everywhere in the United States allow you to put in the correct change, lift up the door, and—if you were willing to violate the law—take as many newspapers as you want? Contrast this type of vending machine with candy machines. They are securely locked at all times. You must designate the candy that you wish, normally by using some type of keypad. The candy then drops down so that you can retrieve it but cannot grab any other candy.

EXAMPLE (cont.)

The difference between these two types of vending machines is explained by diminishing marginal utility. Newspaper companies dispense newspapers from coin-operated boxes that allow dishonest people to take more copies than they pay for. What would a dishonest person do with more than one copy of a newspaper, however? The marginal utility of a second newspaper is normally zero. The benefit of storing excessive newspapers is usually nil because yesterday's news has no value. But the same analysis does not hold for candy. The marginal utility of a second candy bar is certainly less than the first,

but it is normally not zero. Moreover, one can store candy for relatively long periods of time at relatively low cost. Consequently, food vending machine companies have to worry about dishonest users of their equipment and must make that equipment more theftproof than newspaper vending machines.

FOR CRITICAL ANALYSIS
Can you think of a circumstance under which a substantial number of newspaper purchasers might be inclined to take more than one newspaper out of a vending machine?

Optimizing Consumption Choices

Every consumer has a limited income, so choices must be made. When a consumer has made all of his or her choices about what to buy and in what quantities, and when the total level of satisfaction, or utility, from that set of choices is as great as it can be, we say that the consumer has *optimized*. When the consumer has attained an optimum consumption set of goods and services, we say that he or she has reached **consumer optimum.**

Consumer optimum
A choice of a set of goods and services that maximizes the level of satisfaction for each consumer, subject to limited income.

A Two-Good Example

Consider a simple two-good example. The consumer has to choose between spending income on downloads of digital music albums at $5 per download and on purchasing cappuccinos at $3 each. Let's say that when the consumer has spent all income on music album downloads and cappuccinos, the last dollar spent on a cappuccino yields 3 utils of utility but the last dollar spent on downloading music albums yields 10 utils. Wouldn't this consumer increase total utility if some dollars were taken away from consumption of cappuccinos and allocated to music album downloads? The answer is yes. More dollars spent downloading music albums will reduce marginal utility per last dollar spent, whereas fewer dollars spent on consumption of cappuccinos will increase marginal utility per last dollar spent. The loss in utility from spending fewer dollars purchasing fewer cappuccinos is more than made up by spending additional dollars on more album downloads. As a consequence, total utility increases. The consumer optimum—where total utility is maximized—occurs when the satisfaction per last dollar spent on both cappuccinos and music album downloads per week is equal for the two goods. Thus, the amount of goods consumed depends on the prices of the goods, the income of the consumer, and the marginal utility derived from the amounts of each good consumed.

Table 21-1 on the next page presents information on utility derived from consuming various quantities of music album downloads and cappuccinos. Columns 4 and 8 show the marginal utility per dollar spent on music downloads and cappuccinos, respectively. If the prices of both goods are zero, individuals will consume each as long as their respective marginal utility is positive (at least five units of each and probably much more). It is also true that a consumer with unlimited income will

How does marginal utility derived from a music download influence the quantity of music downloads consumed?

continue consuming goods until the marginal utility of each is equal to zero. When the price is zero or the consumer's income is unlimited, there is no effective constraint on consumption.

What happens when people are confronted with "too many" choices, or with too few?

EXAMPLE
Which Is Worse—Too Many Choices or No Choice?

Consider the following experiment, which is intended to illustrate that consumers can sometimes confront "too many choices." The experimenter asks groups of students to look inside boxes containing a variety of chocolates and to discuss which type of chocolate they might choose to buy based on its name and shape. Then the experimenter allows half of the people in each group to eat the chocolate they selected. Some students are shown a box containing 6 types of chocolates, but others view a box with 30 different selections. The students choosing from boxes containing 6 chocolates usually report higher levels of satisfaction from eating their selected chocolates than students who must choose from boxes with 30. Typically, students choosing from the boxes with 30 chocolates report that the larger array of choices caused them to worry that they might

not have selected the best chocolate. Hence, confronting too much choice appears to reduce overall satisfaction.

What about the students in the other half of each group, who are *not* allowed to eat the chocolate they selected? For these students, the *experimenter* selects the chocolate they receive. Consistently, students who are not allowed to make their own choices report less satisfaction than the students who are permitted to choose from boxes containing either 6 or 30 chocolates. Being denied the opportunity to choose yields the least satisfaction.

FOR CRITICAL ANALYSIS
Why is it that a choice that yields greatest utility to one person does not necessarily maximize the satisfaction of someone else?

TABLE 21-1

Total and Marginal Utility from Consuming Music Album Downloads and Cappuccinos on an Income of $26

(1) Music Album Downloads per Period	(2) Total Utility of Music Album Downloads per Period (utils)	(3) Marginal Utility (utils) MU_d	(4) Marginal Utility per Dollar Spent (MU_d/P_d) (price = $5)	(5) Cappuccinos per Period	(6) Total Utility of Cappuccinos per Period (utils)	(7) Marginal Utility (utils) MU_c	(8) Marginal Utility per Dollar Spent (MU_c/P_c) (price = $3)
0	0	–	–	0	0	–	–
1	50.0	50.0	10.0	1	25	25	8.3
2	95.0	45.0	9.0	2	47	22	7.3
3	135.0	40.0	8.0	3	65	18	6.0
4	171.5	36.5	7.3	4	80	15	5.0
5	200.0	28.5	5.7	5	89	9	3.0

A Two-Good Consumer Optimum

Consumer optimum is attained when the marginal utility of the last dollar spent on each good yields the same utility and income is completely exhausted. In the situation in Table 21-1, the individual's income is $26. From columns 4 and 8 of Table 21-1, equal marginal utilities per dollar spent occur at the consumption level of four music album downloads and two cappuccinos (the marginal utility per dollar spent equals 7.3). Notice that the marginal utility per dollar spent for both goods is also (approximately) equal at the consumption level of three music album downloads and one cappuccino, but here total income is not completely exhausted. Likewise, the marginal utility per dollar spent is (approximately) equal at five music album downloads and three cappuccinos, but the expenditures necessary for that level of consumption ($34) exceed the individual's income.

Table 21-2 shows the steps taken to arrive at consumer optimum. The first download of a music album from the Internet would yield a marginal utility per dollar of 10 (50 units of utility divided by $5 per music album download), while the first cappuccino would yield a marginal utility of only 8.3 per dollar (25 units of utility divided by $3 per cappuccino). Because it yields the higher marginal utility per dollar, the music album is downloaded. This leaves $21 of income. The second download of a music album yields a higher marginal utility per dollar (9, versus 8.3 for a cappuccino), so it is also purchased, leaving an unspent income of $16. At the third purchase, the first cappuccino now yields a higher marginal utility per dollar than the next download of a music album (8.3 versus 8), so the first cappuccino is purchased. This leaves income of $13 to spend. The process continues until all income is exhausted and the marginal utility per dollar spent is equal for both goods.

To restate, consumer optimum requires the following:

A consumer's money income should be allocated so that the last dollar spent on each good purchased yields the same amount of marginal utility (when all income is spent), because this rule yields the largest possible total utility.

TABLE 21-2

Steps to Consumer Optimum

In each purchase situation described here, the consumer always purchases the good with the higher marginal utility per dollar spent (MU/P). For example, at the time of the third purchase, the marginal utility per last dollar spent on downloads of music albums is 8, but it is 8.3 for cappuccinos, and $16 of income remains, so the next purchase will be a cappuccino. Here $P_d = \$5$, $P_c = \$3$, MU_d is the marginal utility of consumption of music album downloads, and MU_c is the marginal utility of consumption of cappuccinos.

	Music Album Downloads		Cappuccinos			
Purchase	Unit	MU_d/P_d	Unit	MU_c/P_c	Buying Decision	Remaining Income
1	First	10.0	First	8.3	First music album download	$26 − $5 = $21
2	Second	9.0	First	8.3	Second music album download	$21 − $5 = $16
3	Third	8.0	First	8.3	First cappuccino	$16 − $3 = $13
4	Third	8.0	Second	7.3	Third music album download	$13 − $5 = $8
5	Fourth	7.3	Second	7.3	Fourth music album download and second cappuccino	$8 − $5 = $3 $3 − $3 = $0

The header "Choices" spans Music Album Downloads and Cappuccinos.

A Little Math

We can state the rule of consumer optimum in algebraic terms by examining the ratio of marginal utilities and prices of individual products. The rule simply states that a consumer maximizes personal satisfaction when allocating money income in such a way that the last dollars spent on good A, good B, good C, and so on, yield equal amounts of marginal utility. Marginal utility (*MU*) from good A is indicated by "*MU* of good A." For good B, it is "*MU* of good B." Our algebraic formulation of this rule, therefore, becomes

$$\frac{MU \text{ of good A}}{\text{Price of good A}} = \frac{MU \text{ of good B}}{\text{Price of good B}} = \cdots = \frac{MU \text{ of good Z}}{\text{price of good Z}}$$

You Are There

To think about how consideration of the consumer optimum can influence an individual's decision about health insurance coverage, read **Opting Out of Company Health Plans**, on page 540.

The letters A, B, . . . , Z indicate the various goods and services that the consumer might purchase.

We know, then, that in order for the consumer to maximize utility, the marginal utility of good A divided by the price of good A must equal the marginal utility of any other good divided by its price. Note, though, that the application of the rule of equal marginal utility per dollar spent does not necessarily describe an explicit or conscious act on the part of consumers. Rather, this is a *model* of consumer optimum.

Does this model of a consumer optimum apply even to the poorest of the poor?

INTERNATIONAL EXAMPLE
A Consumer Optimum with One Inflation-Adjusted Dollar a Day

In 2000, the governments of 189 nations agreed to a so-called Millennium Development Goal of reducing by one-half the percentage of people who live on less than $1 per day. At the time, these nations were basing their estimates of the number of people living on less than $1 per day on global prices prevailing in the early 1990s. In today's dollars this translates into living on less than about $1.50 per day.

How do people get by on less than the equivalent of $1.50 per day? Studies of some of the world's poorest people in rural India reveal that half of them are anemic. About 14 percent have poor eyesight. Most are underweight. Nevertheless, nearly all of those in rural India who have less than $1.50 per day available for consumption manage to buy more than food. They also allocate these meager resources to expenditures on items such as alcohol, tobacco, weddings, funerals, and religious events. Thus, even the world's poorest people choose to consume a variety of goods and services. Instead of equating the marginal utility of the last *dollar* of purchasing power spent on each item, however, these people consume to the point at which the marginal utility per last *penny* spent is the same for all items.

FOR CRITICAL ANALYSIS
Why does the model of consumer optimum imply that the highest-price goods are unlikely to be consumed by the world's poorest people? (Hint: The last dollar, or penny, spent must be taken from funds actually available to a consumer.)

How a Price Change Affects Consumer Optimum

Consumption decisions are summarized in the law of demand, which states that the amount purchased is inversely related to price. We can now see why by using utility analysis.

A Consumer's Response to a Price Change

When a consumer has optimally allocated all her income to purchases, the marginal utility per dollar spent at current prices of goods and services is the same for each good or service she buys. No consumer will, when optimizing, buy 10 units of a good per unit of time when the marginal utility per dollar spent on the tenth unit of that good is less than the marginal utility per dollar spent on some other item.

If we start out at a consumer optimum and then observe a good's price decrease, we can predict that consumers will respond to the price decrease by consuming more of that good. This is because before the price change, the marginal utility per dollar spent on each good or service consumed was the same. Now, when a specific good's price is lower, it is possible to consume more of that good while continuing to equalize the marginal utility per dollar spent on that good with the marginal utility per dollar spent on other goods and services. The purchase and consumption of additional units of the lower-priced good will cause the marginal utility from consuming the good to fall. Eventually, it will fall to the point at which the marginal utility per dollar spent on the good is once again equal to the marginal utility per dollar spent on other goods and services. At this point, the consumer will stop buying additional units of the lower-priced good.

A hypothetical demand curve for music downloads per week for a typical consumer is presented in Figure 21-2. Suppose that at point A, at which the price per music download is $5, the marginal utility of the last music album downloaded per week is MU_A. At point B, at which the price is $4 per music download per week, the marginal utility is represented by MU_B. With the consumption of more downloaded digital music, the marginal utility of the last unit of these additional music downloads is lower—MU_B must be less than MU_A. What has happened is that at a lower price, the number of music album downloads per week increased from four to five; marginal utility must have fallen. At a higher consumption rate, the marginal utility falls in response to the rise in downloadable music consumption so that the marginal utility per dollar spent is equalized across all purchases.

FIGURE 21-2

Digital Music Download Prices and Marginal Utility

When consumers respond to a reduction in music download prices from $5 per download to $4 per download by increasing consumption, marginal utility falls. The movement from point A, at which marginal utility is MU_A, to point B, at which marginal utility is MU_B, which is less than MU_A. This brings about the equalization of the marginal utility per dollar spent across all purchases.

The Substitution Effect

Substitution effect
The tendency of people to substitute cheaper commodities for more expensive commodities.

What is happening as the price of music downloads falls is that consumers are substituting the now relatively cheaper music downloads for other goods and services, such as restaurant meals and live concerts. We call this the **substitution effect** of a change in the price of a good because it occurs when consumers substitute relatively cheaper goods for relatively more expensive ones.

We assume that people desire a variety of goods and pursue a variety of goals. That means that few, if any, goods are irreplaceable in meeting demand. We are generally able to substitute one product for another to satisfy demand. This is commonly referred to as the **principle of substitution.**

Principle of substitution
The principle that consumers shift away from goods and services that become priced relatively higher in favor of goods and services that are now priced relatively lower.

AN EXAMPLE Let's assume now that there are several goods, not exactly the same, and perhaps even very different from one another, but all contributing to consumers' total utility. If the relative price of one particular good falls, we will most likely substitute in favor of the now lower-priced good and against the other goods that we might have been purchasing. Conversely, if the price of that good rises relative to the price of the other goods, we will substitute in favor of them and not buy as much of the now higher-priced good. An example is the growth in purchases of personal computers since the late 1980s. As the relative price of computers has plummeted, people have substituted away from other, now relatively more expensive goods in favor of purchasing additional computers to use in their homes.

Purchasing power
The value of money for buying goods and services. If your money income stays the same but the price of one good that you are buying goes up, your effective purchasing power falls, and vice versa.

PURCHASING POWER AND REAL INCOME If the price of some item that you purchase goes down while your money income and all other prices stay the same, your ability to purchase goods goes up. That is to say, your effective **purchasing power** has increased, even though your money income has stayed the same. If you purchase 20 gallons of gas a week at $5 per gallon, your total outlay for gas is $100. If the price goes down by 50 percent, to $2.50 per gallon, you would have to spend only $50 a week to purchase the same number of gallons of gas. If your money income and the prices of other goods remain the same, it would be possible for you to continue purchasing 20 gallons of gas a week *and* to purchase more of other goods. You will feel richer and will indeed probably purchase more of a number of goods, including perhaps even more gasoline.

The converse will also be true. When the price of one good you are purchasing goes up, without any other change in prices or income, the purchasing power of your income will drop. You will have to reduce your purchases of either the now higher-priced good or other goods (or a combination).

Real-income effect
The change in people's purchasing power that occurs when, other things being constant, the price of one good that they purchase changes. When that price goes up, real income, or purchasing power, falls, and when that price goes down, real income increases.

In general, this **real-income effect** is usually quite small. After all, unless we consider broad categories, such as housing or food, a change in the price of one particular item that we purchase will have a relatively small effect on our total purchasing power. Thus, we expect that the substitution effect will be more important than the real-income effect in causing us to purchase more of goods that have become cheaper and less of goods that have become more expensive.

The Demand Curve Revisited

Linking the law of diminishing marginal utility and the rule of equal marginal utilities per dollar gives us a negative relationship between the quantity demanded of a good or service and its price. As the relative price of digital music downloads goes up, for example, the quantity demanded will fall; and as the relative price of music downloads goes down, the quantity demanded will rise. Figure 21-2 on page 535 showed this demand curve for music downloads. As the price of music downloads falls, the consumer can maximize total utility only by purchasing more digital music, and vice versa. In other words, the relationship between price and quantity desired is simply a downward-sloping demand curve. Note, though, that this downward-sloping demand curve (the law of demand) is derived under the assumption of constant tastes and incomes. You must remember that we are keeping these important determining variables constant when we look at the relationship between price and quantity demanded.

Marginal Utility, Total Utility, and the Diamond-Water Paradox

Even though water is essential to life and diamonds are not, water is relatively cheap and diamonds are relatively expensive. The economist Adam Smith in 1776 called this the "diamond-water paradox." The paradox is easily understood when we make the distinction between total utility and marginal utility. The total utility of water greatly exceeds the total utility derived from diamonds. What determines the price, though, is what happens on the margin. We have relatively few diamonds, so the marginal utility of the last diamond consumed is relatively high. The opposite is true for water. Total utility does not determine what people are willing to pay for a unit of a particular commodity; marginal utility does. Look at the situation graphically in Figure 21-3. We show the demand curve for diamonds, labeled D_{diamonds}. The demand curve for water is labeled D_{water}. We plot quantity in terms of kilograms per unit time period on the horizontal axis. On the vertical axis, we plot price in dollars per kilogram. We use kilograms as our common unit of measurement for water and for diamonds. We could just as well have used pounds or liters.

Notice that the demand for water is many, many times the demand for diamonds (even though we really can't show this in the diagram). We draw the supply curve of water as S_1 at a quantity of Q_{water}. The supply curve for diamonds is given as S_2 at quantity Q_{diamonds}. At the intersection of the supply curve of water with the demand curve of water, the price per kilogram is P_{water}. The intersection of the supply curve of diamonds with the demand curve of diamonds is at P_{diamonds}. Notice that P_{diamonds} exceeds P_{water}. Diamonds sell at a higher price than water.

FIGURE 21-3

The Diamond-Water Paradox

We pick kilograms as a common unit of measurement for both water and diamonds. To demonstrate that the demand for and supply of water are immense, we have put a break in the horizontal quantity axis. Although the demand for water is much greater than the demand for diamonds, the marginal valuation of water is given by the marginal value placed on the *last* unit of water consumed. To find that, we must know the supply of water, which is given as S_1. At that supply, the price of water is P_{water}. But the supply for diamonds is given by S_2. At that supply, the price of diamonds is P_{diamonds}. The total valuation that consumers place on water is tremendous relative to the total valuation consumers place on diamonds. What is important for price determination, however, is the marginal valuation, or the marginal utility received.

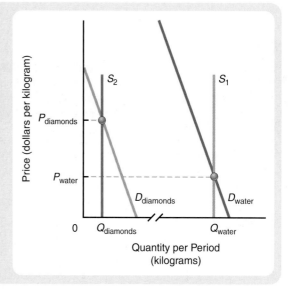

Behavioral Economics and Consumer Choice Theory

Utility analysis has long been appealing to economists because it makes clear predictions about how individuals will adjust their consumption of different goods and services based on the prices of those items and their incomes. Traditionally, another attraction of utility analysis to many economists has been its reliance on the assumption that consumers behave *rationally*, or that they do not intentionally make decisions that would leave them worse off. As we discussed in Chapter 1, proponents of behavioral economics have doubts about the rationality assumption, which causes them to question the utility-based theory of consumer choice.

Does Behavioral Economics Better Predict Consumer Choices?

Advocates of behavioral economics question whether utility theory is supported by the facts, which they argue are better explained by applying the assumption of *bounded rationality*. Recall from Chapter 1 that this assumption states that human limitations prevent people from examining every possible choice available to them and thereby thwart their efforts to effectively pursue long-term personal interests.

As evidence favoring the bounded rationality assumption, proponents of behavioral economics point to real-world examples that they claim violate rationality-based utility theory. For instance, economists have found that when purchasing electric appliances such as refrigerators, people sometimes buy the lowest-priced, energy-inefficient models even though the initial purchase-price savings often fail to compensate for higher future energy costs. There is also evidence that people who live in earthquake- or flood-prone regions commonly fail to purchase sufficient insurance against these events. In addition, experiments have shown that when people are placed in situations in which strong emotions come into play, they may be willing to pay different amounts for items than they would pay in calmer settings.

These and other observed behaviors, behavioral economists suggest, indicate that consumers do not behave as if they are rational. If the rationality assumption does not apply to actual behavior, they argue, it follows that utility-based consumer choice theory cannot, either.

Can behavioral economics explain why people who enjoy shopping for its own sake might later regret purchases they make on shopping excursions?

E-COMMERCE EXAMPLE
Help, I'm Shopping, and I Can't Stop!

Undoubtedly, you know someone who just loves to shop. Recent research indicates that much of the joy that such individuals derive from shopping can be traced to the brain chemical dopamine, which is associated with feelings of pleasure and satisfaction. The brain releases dopamine when a person experiences something novel or enjoyable, such as purchasing a new item at a retail outlet. By strapping portable electroencephalogram monitors to individuals and sending

them on shopping trips, researchers have measured what they believe to be the satisfaction that people receive from the act of shopping. Maps of brain activity while shopping show that for a number of people, simply looking forward to the pleasure they anticipate from purchasing an item generates an upswing in dopamine-induced satisfaction.

Behavioral economists argue that for many individuals, the short-term enjoyment of shopping for its own sake leads to

E-COMMERCE EXAMPLE (cont.)

purchases that the individuals later regret. That is, at least some consumers may get more satisfaction from the act of *choosing* among alternative items than they actually derive from the items they decide to purchase. The possibility that consumers make such impulse purchases, behavioral economists suggest, is not taken into account by traditional consumer choice theory. Of course, the utility-based theory of a consumer optimum hypothesizes that choices are always consistent with self-interest. Thus, the traditional theory suggests that what behavioral economists view as impulse buying is actually viewed by a consumer as the optimal outcome.

FOR CRITICAL ANALYSIS
How might traditional consumer choice theory explain why some people might choose to "buy" a shopping trip to a mall, inclusive of spending on items bought during the shopping excursion, as a bundled item alongside other items they might purchase? (Hint: If the act of shopping itself is treated as a good, how does consumer choice theory indicate that a consumer will decide how much to "spend" on shopping relative to other goods, such as housing and groceries?)

Consumer Choice Theory Remains Alive and Well

In spite of the doubts expressed by proponents of behavioral economics, most economists continue to apply the assumption that people behave *as if* they act rationally with an aim to maximize utility. These economists continue to utilize utility theory because of a fundamental strength of this approach: it yields clear-cut predictions regarding consumer choices.

In contrast, if the rationality assumption is rejected, any number of possible human behaviors might be considered. To proponents of behavioral economics, ambiguities about actual outcomes make the bounded rationality approach to consumer choice more realistic than utility-based consumer choice theory. Nevertheless, a major drawback is that no clearly testable predictions emerge from the many alternative behaviors that people might exhibit if they fail to behave *as if* they are rational.

Certainly, arguments among economists about the "reasonableness" of rational consumers maximizing utility are likely to continue. So far, however, the use of utility-based consumer choice theory has allowed economists to make a wide array of predictions about how consumers respond to changes in prices, incomes, and other factors. By and large, these key predictions continue to be supported by the actual choices that consumers make.

QUICK QUIZ *See page 545 for the answers. Review concepts from this section in MyEconLab.*

The principle of **diminishing marginal utility** tells us that each successive marginal unit of a good consumed adds _____ extra utility.

The consumer maximizes total utility by _____ the marginal utility of the last dollar spent on one good with the marginal utility per last dollar spent on all other goods. That is the state of consumer _____.

To remain in **consumer optimum**, a price decrease requires an _____ in consumption; a price increase requires a _____ in consumption.

Each change in price has a substitution effect and a real-income effect. When the price of a good _____, the consumer substitutes in favor of that relatively cheaper good. When price _____, the consumer's real purchasing power increases, causing the consumer to purchase more of most goods. Assuming that the principle of diminishing marginal utility holds, the demand curve must slope downward.

You Are There ▶ Opting Out of Company Health Plans

Sarah Landis, a nursing assistant at Children's Hospitals and Clinics of Minnesota, knows from experience that obtaining certain forms of health care can require paying high relative prices to providers. Nevertheless, she has opted not to participate in her employer's health plan, even though her husband is self-employed and has no health insurance coverage. Thus, to the chagrin of U.S. politicians who constantly bemoan the fact that millions have no health insurance, Ms. Landis and her husband have *chosen* not to buy coverage for themselves and their two children.

Why is health insurance not part of the consumer optimum in the Landis household? The answer relates to equating the marginal utility of the last dollar spent on each item in the family budget. Ms. Landis has a choice among three employer-provided health care plans with different *deductibles*—expense cutoffs below which she and her family would have to pay the costs of care from their own pockets. The lowest-deductible plan would provide the greatest expected marginal utility, because the deductible is sufficiently low that the insurance plan would pay most health care expenses that might arise. Paying the premiums for this plan, however, would require Ms. Landis and her husband to spend more than one-third of their household income on health insurance. Thus, Ms. Landis perceives that the expected marginal utility per dollar she might spend on this plan is too low relative to other allocations of their income to justify purchasing it.

Ms. Landis could purchase the highest-deductible plan at a price of about one-sixth of the household's income. The drawback of this option is that the deductible is so high that she anticipates receiving little benefit, given that she and her husband are both young and healthy and that their daughters have no health problems, either. Thus, the marginal utility per dollar she might spend on this plan is also too low to justify purchasing it. As for the third, middle-deductible option, her judgment is that the price is still too high and the expected benefit still too low. Hence, none of the options yields a marginal utility per last dollar that Ms. Landis might spend to justify purchasing health care coverage. At least for the time being, her family has opted to allocate available income to the point at which the marginal utility per dollar spent is equalized across *other* goods and services.

CRITICAL ANALYSIS QUESTIONS

1. How does Ms. Landis's calculation help to illustrate why one person's consumer optimum can differ considerably from the consumer optimum of another person, even if both people have the same income? (Hint: Contrast Ms. Landis's choice with a hypothetical choice made by a co-employee earning the same income but with a sick husband and two children experiencing chronic health problems.)

2. Why might Ms. Landis's choice change in a future year if her employer offers a fourth option with both a lower premium and a lower deductible?

A Renewed Interest in Measuring Utility

Issues and Applications

CONCEPTS APPLIED

▶ Utility

▶ Util

▶ Marginal Utility

In the early nineteenth century, the philosopher Jeremy Bentham and his followers sought to measure utility. They even developed an explicit unit of measurement, the "util," that they attempted to use as a yardstick. Economists of the late nineteenth and twentieth centuries generally concluded that utility—expressed as satisfaction, pleasure, happiness, and related concepts—could not be objectively measured.

Now, in the twenty-first century, behavioral economists have rejuvenated the idea of measuring utility. They aim to do so through the use of "happiness studies," which utilize surveys of people's subjective reporting of their level of happiness. Using these surveys, behavioral economists seek to gauge levels of satisfaction for society as a whole and across individual members of society. Eventually, they suggest, measuring changes in happiness ratings resulting from additional consumption of a good or service could provide information about marginal utility. Policymakers could use such information to assess the effects of policy-induced income changes on utility, and firms could apply happiness measures to assess consumers' satisfaction with their products.

Assessing the Happiness of Individual Workers and Consumers

Today, efforts to measure happiness include more than just surveys of samples taken from national populations. David's Bridal, the largest U.S. bridal-store chain, has employed happiness measures to assess approaches to keeping sales associates more cheery in the face of pressures of dealing with anxious brides. Sensory Logic, a Minnesota-based company, conducts studies for firms such as Whirlpool and Sherwin Williams, in which it examines videos of people's facial reactions to products. Based on incremental changes of expression that may last no longer than 0.03 second, Sensory Logic claims to be able to assess a customer's initial satisfaction with a new product.

Of course, implicit in the use of happiness surveys or careful studies of individuals' responses are two assumptions. One is that numerical ratings from surveys and information gleaned from facial expressions *truly* measure subjectively unobservable satisfaction levels so reliably that they can be treated as objective measures of happiness. The other is that it is reasonable to compare survey ratings or other measures of happiness *across* individuals. If one person, say, scores a "10" for happiness on a survey while another scores only a "7," does this unambiguously mean that the person with the higher score is the more satisfied of the two?

Where Happiness Research Is Headed

Not all economists are convinced that proposed happiness measures actually tell us anything about how to rate a *single* individual's satisfaction levels. In fact, most are uncomfortable with the idea that *any* objective happiness measure could be developed that would enable comparisons of satisfaction levels *across* individuals.

Nevertheless, considerable research is under way to evaluate whether satisfaction measures, such as numerical ratings derived from surveys, are consistent for individuals and among groups of people. One approach to evaluating life satisfaction surveys has been to utilize psychiatric measures of people's moods to check for the reliability of happiness measures. For instance, researchers have asked the same basic questions each year on a regular basis, such as every couple of weeks, over an extended period of time. At the time the questions are asked, researchers interview respondents in an effort to determine their *affect*, or mood as defined by psychiatric classification techniques. A tentative conclusion from such studies is that life satisfaction surveys may provide a measure of happiness that is at least as reliable as affect measures utilized by psychiatrists.

An alternative approach has been to look at hypertension (blood pressure) levels of people who participate in happiness surveys. Physicians have found that psychological well-being and blood pressure are inversely related. Examining the hypertension levels of people who provide happiness ratings in surveys indicates that people with higher happiness ratings tend to have lower blood pressure than people with lower happiness ratings. To proponents of happiness measures, this fact provides additional evidence that happiness studies can provide useful measures of satisfaction.

Test your understanding of this chapter by going online to **MyEconLab**.
In the Study Plan for this chapter, select Section N: News.

For Critical Analysis

1. Why would evidence of inconsistency of measured happiness levels for a single individual cast considerable doubt on the appropriateness of comparing happiness levels across individuals?

2. Why is the utility theory applied to consumer choice theory silent about comparing people's utility levels? (Hint: Does a consumer optimum for an individual typically depend on the utility levels of other consumers?)

Web Resources

1. To learn more details about the General Social Surveys, use the link at www.econtoday.com/chapter21.

2. To read a recent study by David Blanchflower and Andrew Oswald applying happiness measures derived from surveys to the United States and the United Kingdom, go to www.econtoday.com/chapter21.

Research Project

Discuss the pros and cons of attempting to use happiness survey questions to measure one individual's levels of happiness at different points in time, such as the beginning of every month, throughout the individual's life. Next, evaluate the pros and cons of trying to compare "happiness scores" based on posing the same questions to two people at the same points in time. What can you deduce about the pros and cons of applying results from such survey questions to compare measured happiness levels of thousands of people?

 Here is what you should know after reading this chapter. **MyEconLab** will help you identify what you know, and where to go when you need to practice.

WHAT YOU SHOULD KNOW		WHERE TO GO TO PRACTICE
Total Utility versus Marginal Utility Total utility is the total satisfaction that an individual derives from consuming a given amount of a good or service during a given period. Marginal utility is the additional satisfaction that a person gains by consuming an additional unit of the good or service.	utility, 526 utility analysis, 526 util, 527 marginal utility, 527 **KEY FIGURE** Figure 21-1, 528	• **MyEconLab** Study Plans 21.1, 21.2 • Audio introduction to Chapter 21 • Animated Figure 21-1
The Law of Diminishing Marginal Utility For at least the first unit of consumption of a good or service, a person's total utility increases with increased consumption. Eventually, however, the rate at which an individual's utility rises with greater consumption tends to fall. Thus, marginal utility ultimately declines as the person consumes more and more of the good or service.	diminishing marginal utility, 530	• **MyEconLab** Study Plan 21.3

(continued)

WHAT YOU SHOULD KNOW		WHERE TO GO TO PRACTICE
The Consumer Optimum An individual optimally allocates available income to consumption of all goods and services when the marginal utility per dollar spent on the last unit consumed of each good is equalized. Thus, a consumer optimum occurs when (1) the ratio of the marginal utility derived from an item to the price of that item is equal across all items that the person consumes and (2) when the person spends all available income.	consumer optimum, 531	• **MyEconLab** Study Plan 21.4 • Video: Optimizing Consumption Choices
The Substitution Effect of a Price Change One effect of a change in the price of a good or service is that the price change induces people to substitute among goods. For example, if the price of a good rises, the individual will tend to consume some other good that has become relatively less expensive as a result. In addition, the individual will tend to reduce consumption of the good whose price increased.	substitution effect, 536 principle of substitution, 536 **KEY FIGURE** Figure 21-2, 535	• **MyEconLab** Study Plan 21.5 • Animated Figure 21-2
The Real-Income Effect of a Price Change If the price of a good increases, a person responds to the loss of purchasing power of available income by reducing purchases of either the now higher-priced good or other goods (or a combination of both of these responses). Normally, we anticipate that the real-income effect is smaller than the substitution effect, so that when the price of a good or service increases, people will purchase more of goods or services that have lower relative prices as a result.	purchasing power, 536 real-income effect, 536 **KEY FIGURE** Figure 21-2, 535	• **MyEconLab** Study Plan 21.5 • Animated Figure 21-2
The Price of Diamonds versus the Price of Water and Behavioral Economics versus Consumer Choice Theory The typical consumer purchases a small number of diamonds, so the marginal utility derived from consuming a diamond is relatively high. People consume relatively large volumes of water, so the marginal utility of the last unit of water consumed is relatively low. Thus, at a consumer optimum, in which the marginal utility per dollar spent is equalized for diamonds and water, people are willing to pay a much higher price for diamonds. Proponents of behavioral economics suggest that people sometimes depart from adherence to a consumer optimum when emotions come into play or insufficient time or information is available. A difficulty with this perspective is that outside of a consumer optimum, many behaviors could be possible, yielding few testable predictions. Predictions of consumer choice theory, such as the price of diamonds will be higher than the price of a unit of water, are, in contrast, testable.	**KEY FIGURE** Figure 21-3, 537	• **MyEconLab** Study Plans 21.6, 21.7 • Animated Figure 21-3

Log in to MyEconLab, take a chapter test, and get a personalized Study Plan that tells you which concepts you understand and which ones you need to review. From there, MyEconLab will give you further practice, tutorials, animations, videos, and guided solutions.
Log in to www.myeconlab.com

PROBLEMS

All problems are assignable in 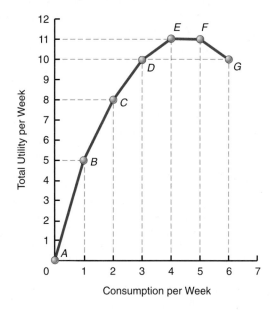 myeconlab *. Answers to odd-numbered problems appear at the back of the book.*

21-1. The campus pizzeria sells a single pizza for $12. If you order a second pizza, however, the pizzeria charges a price of only $5 for the additional pizza. Explain how an understanding of marginal utility helps to explain the pizzeria's pricing strategy.

21-2. As an individual consumes more units of an item, the person eventually experiences diminishing marginal utility. This means that to increase marginal utility, the person must consume less of an item. Explain the logic of this behavior using the example in Problem 21-1.

21-3. Where possible, complete the missing cells in the table.

Number of Cheeseburgers	Total Utility of Cheeseburgers	Marginal Utility of Cheeseburgers	Bags of French Fries	Total Utility of French Fries	Marginal Utility of French Fries
0	0	—	0	0	—
1	20	—	1	—	10
2	36	—	2	—	8
3	—	12	3	—	2
4	—	8	4	21	—
5	—	4	5	21	—

21-4. From the data in Problem 21-3, if the price of a cheeseburger is $2, the price of a bag of french fries is $1, and you have $6 to spend (and you spend all of it), what is the utility-maximizing combination of cheeseburgers and french fries?

21-5. Return to Problem 21-4. Suppose that the price of cheeseburgers falls to $1. Determine the new utility-maximizing combination of cheeseburgers and french fries.

21-6. Suppose that you observe that total utility rises as more of an item is consumed. What can you say for certain about marginal utility? Can you say for sure that it is rising or falling or that it is positive or negative?

21-7. After monitoring your daily consumption patterns, you determine that your daily consumption of soft drinks is 3 and your daily consumption of tacos is 4 when the prices per unit are 50 cents and $1, respectively. Explain what happens to your consumption bundle, the marginal utility of soft drinks, and the marginal utility of tacos when the price of soft drinks rises to 75 cents.

21-8. At a consumer optimum, for all goods purchased, marginal utility per dollar spent is equalized. A high school student is deciding between attending Western State University and Eastern State University. The student cannot attend both universities simultaneously. Both are fine universities, but the reputation of Western is slightly higher, as is the tuition. Use the rule of consumer optimum to explain how the student will go about deciding which university to attend.

21-9. Consider the movements that take place from one point to the next (*A* to *B* to *C* and so on) along the total utility curve below as the individual successively increases consumption by one more unit, and answer the questions that follow.

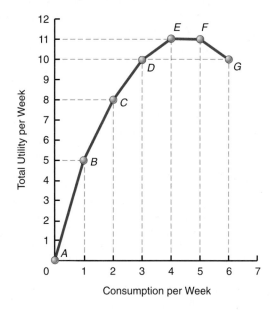

a. Which one-unit increase in consumption from one point to the next along the total utility curve generates the highest marginal utility?

b. Which one-unit increase in consumption from one point to the next along the total utility curve generates zero marginal utility?

c. Which one-unit increase in consumption from one point to the next along the total utility curve generates negative marginal utility?

21-10. Draw a marginal utility curve corresponding to the total utility curve depicted in Problem 21-9.

21-11. Refer to the following table. If the price of a fudge bar is $2, the price of a Popsicle is $1, and a student has $9 to spend on these two items, what quantity of each item will she purchase at a consumer optimum?

Quantity of Fudge Bars per Week	Marginal Utility (utils)	Quantity of Popsicles per Week	Marginal Utility (utils)
1	1,200	1	1,700
2	1,000	2	1,400
3	800	3	1,100
4	600	4	800
5	400	5	500
6	100	6	200

21-12. Refer to the table for a different consumer in the next column, and assume that each week this consumer buys only hot dogs and tickets to baseball games. The price of a hot dog is $2, and the price of a baseball game is $60. If the consumer's income is $128 per week, what quantity of each item will he purchase each week at a consumer optimum?

Quantity of Hot Dogs per Week	Total Utility (utils)	Quantity of Baseball Games per Week	Total Utility (utils)
1	40	1	400
2	60	2	700
3	76	3	850
4	86	4	950
5	91	5	1,000
6	93	6	1,025

21-13. In Problem 21-12, if the consumer's income rises to $190 per week, what new quantities characterize the new consumer optimum?

21-14. At a consumer optimum involving goods A and B, the marginal utility of good A is twice the marginal utility of good B. The price of good B is $3.50. What is the price of good A?

21-15. At a consumer optimum involving goods X and Y, the marginal utility of good X equals 3 utils. The price of good Y is three times the price of good X. What is the marginal utility of good Y?

ECONOMICS ON THE NET

Book Prices and Consumer Optimum This application helps you see how a consumer optimum can be attained when one engages in Internet shopping.

Title: Amazon.com Web site

Navigation: Go to **www.econtoday.com/chapter21** to start at Amazon.com's home page. Click on the *Books* tab.

Application

1. At the top of the page, find the list of the top books in the Amazon.com "Bestsellers" section. Click on the number one book. Record the price of the book. Then locate the Search window. Type in *Economics Today*. Scroll down until you find your class text listed. Record the price.

2. Suppose you are an individual who has purchased both the number one book and *Economics Today* through Amazon.com. Describe how economic analysis would explain this choice.

3. Using the prices you recorded for the two books, write an equation that relates the prices and your marginal utilities of the two books. Use this equation to explain verbally how you might quantify the magnitude of your marginal utility for the number one book relative to your marginal utility for your class text.

For Group Study and Analysis Discuss what changes might occur if the price of the number one book were lowered but the student remains enrolled in this course. Discuss what changes might take place regarding the consumer optimum if the student were not enrolled in this course.

ANSWERS TO QUICK QUIZZES

p. 530: (i) Utility; (ii) utils; (iii) Total . . . Marginal
p. 539: (i) less; (ii) equating . . . optimum; (iii) increase . . . decrease; (iv) falls . . . falls

More Advanced Consumer Choice Theory

It is possible to analyze consumer choice verbally, as we did for the most part in Chapter 21. The theory of diminishing marginal utility can be fairly well accepted on intuitive grounds and by introspection. If we want to be more formal and perhaps more elegant in our theorizing, however, we can translate our discussion into a graphical analysis with what we call *indifference curves* and the *budget constraint*. Here we discuss these terms and their relationship and demonstrate consumer equilibrium in geometric form.

On Being Indifferent

What does it mean to be indifferent? It usually means that you don't care one way or the other about something—you are equally disposed to either of two alternatives. With this interpretation in mind, we will turn to two choices, viewing films at theaters and consuming fast-food meals. In panel (a) of Figure E-1, we show several combinations of fast-food and movie tickets per week that a representative consumer considers equally satisfactory. That is to say, for each combination, *A*, *B*, *C*, and *D*, this consumer will have exactly the same level of total utility.

The simple numerical example that we have used happens to concern the consumption of fast-food meals and visits to movie theaters (both of which we assume this consumer enjoys) per week. This example is used to illustrate general features of indifference curves and related analytical tools that are necessary for deriving the demand curve. Obviously, we could have used any two commodities. Just remember that we are using a *specific* example to illustrate a *general* analysis.

FIGURE E-1

Combinations That Yield Equal Levels of Satisfaction

A, *B*, *C*, and *D* represent combinations of fast-food meals and movie tickets per week that give an equal level of satisfaction to this consumer. In other words, the consumer is indifferent among these four combinations.

Panel (b)

Panel (a)

Combination	Fast-Food Meals per Week	Movie Tickets per Week
A	7	1
B	4	2
C	2	3
D	1	4

We plot these combinations graphically in panel (b) of Figure E-1, with movie tickets per week on the horizontal axis and fast-food meals per week on the vertical axis. These are our consumer's indifference combinations—the consumer finds each combination as acceptable as the others. These combinations lie along a smooth curve that is known as the consumer's **indifference curve.** Along the indifference curve, every combination of the two goods in question yields the same level of satisfaction. Every point along the indifference curve is equally desirable to the consumer. For example, one fast-food meal per week and four movie tickets per week will give our representative consumer exactly the same total satisfaction as consuming four fast-food meals per week and viewing two movies per week.

Indifference curve
A curve composed of a set of consumption alternatives, each of which yields the same total amount of satisfaction.

Properties of Indifference Curves

Indifference curves have special properties relating to their slope and shape.

Downward Slope

The indifference curve shown in panel (b) of Figure E-1 slopes downward; that is, it has a negative slope. Now consider Figure E-2. Here we show two points, *A* and *B*. Point *A* represents four fast-food meals per week and two movie tickets per week. Point *B* represents five fast-food meals per week and six movie viewings per week. Clearly, *B* is always preferred to *A* for a consumer who enjoys both fast-food meals and movies, because *B* represents more of everything. If *B* is always preferred to *A*, it is impossible for points *A* and *B* to be on the same indifference curve because the definition of the indifference curve is a set of combinations of two goods that are preferred equally.

Curvature

The indifference curve that we have drawn in panel (b) of Figure E-1 is special. Notice that it is curved. Why didn't we just draw a straight line, as we have usually done for a demand curve?

FIGURE E-2

Indifference Curves: Impossibility of an Upward Slope

Point *B* represents a consumption of more movie tickets per week and more fast-food meals per week than point *A*. *B* is always preferred to *A*. Therefore, *A* and *B* cannot be on the same *positively* sloped indifference curve. An indifference curve shows *equally preferred* combinations of the two goods.

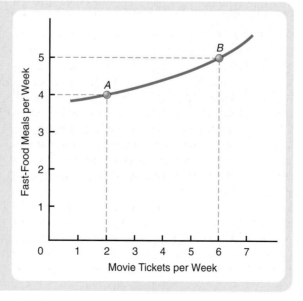

IMAGINING A STRAIGHT-LINE INDIFFERENCE CURVE To find out why we don't posit straight-line indifference curves, consider the implications. We show such a straight-line indifference curve in Figure E-3. Start at point *A*. The consumer has no movie tickets and five fast-food meals per week. Now the consumer wishes to go to point *B*. She is willing to give up only one fast-food meal in order to get one ticket to a movie. Now let's assume that the consumer is at point *C*, consuming one fast-food meal per week and viewing four movies at a theater per week. If the consumer wants to go to point *D*, she is again willing to give up one fast-food meal in order to get one more movie ticket per week.

In other words, no matter how many times the consumer consumes a fast-food meal, she is willing to give up one fast-food meal to get one movie viewing per week—which does not seem plausible. Doesn't it make sense to hypothesize that the more times the consumer consumes fast-food meals per week, the less she will value an *additional* fast-food meal that week? Presumably, when the consumer has five fast-food meals and no movie tickets per week, she should be willing to give up *more than* one fast-food meal in order to get one movie ticket. Therefore, a straight-line indifference curve as shown in Figure E-3 no longer seems plausible.

CONVEXITY OF THE INDIFFERENCE CURVE In mathematical jargon, an indifference curve is convex with respect to the origin. Let's look at this in panel (a) of Figure E-1 on page 546. Starting with combination *A*, the consumer has one movie ticket but seven fast-food meals per week. To remain indifferent, the consumer would have to be willing to give up three fast-food meals to obtain one more ticket to a movie (as shown in combination *B*). To go from combination *C* to combination *D*, however, notice that the consumer would have to be willing to give up only one fast-food meal for an additional movie ticket per week. The quantity of the substitute considered acceptable changes as the rate of consumption of the original item changes.

Consequently, the indifference curve in panel (b) of Figure E-1 will be convex when viewed from the origin.

FIGURE E-3

Implications of a Straight-Line Indifference Curve

This straight-line indifference curve indicates that the consumer will always be willing to give up the same number of fast-food meals to get one more movie ticket per week. For example, the consumer at point *A* consumes five fast-food meals and views no movies at theaters per week. She is willing to give up one fast-food meal in order to get one movie ticket per week. At point *C*, however, the consumer has only one fast-food meal and views four movies per week. Because of the straight-line indifference curve, this consumer is willing to give up the last fast-food meal in order to get one more movie ticket per week, even though she already has four.

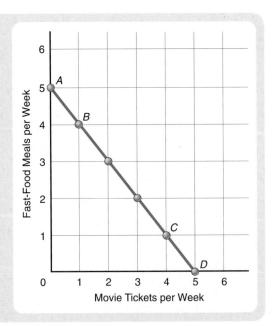

The Marginal Rate of Substitution

Instead of using marginal utility, we can talk in terms of the *marginal rate of substitution* between fast-food meals and movie tickets per week. We can formally define the consumer's marginal rate of substitution as follows:

> ***The marginal rate of substitution is equal to the change in the quantity of one good that just offsets a one-unit change in the consumption of another good, such that total satisfaction remains constant.***

We can see numerically what happens to the marginal rate of substitution in our example if we rearrange panel (a) of Figure E-1 on page 546 into Table E-1. Here we show fast-food meals in the second column and movie tickets in the third. Now we ask the question, what change in the number of movie tickets per week will just compensate for a three-unit change in the consumption of fast-food meals per week and leave the consumer's total utility constant? The movement from *A* to *B* increases the number of weekly movie tickets by one. Here the marginal rate of substitution is 3:1—a three-unit decrease in fast-food meals requires an increase of one movie ticket to leave the consumer's total utility unaltered. Thus, the consumer values the three fast-food meals as the equivalent of one movie ticket. We do this for the rest of the table and find that as fast-food meals decrease, the marginal rate of substitution goes from 3:1 to 2:1 to 1:1. The marginal rate of substitution of fast-food meals for movie tickets per week falls as the consumer views more films at theaters. That is, the consumer values successive movie viewings less and less in terms of fast-food meals. The first movie ticket is valued at three fast-food meals; the last (fourth) movie ticket is valued at only one fast-food meal. The fact that the marginal rate of substitution falls is sometimes called the *law of substitution*.

In geometric language, the slope of the consumer's indifference curve (actually, the negative of the slope of the indifference curve) measures the consumer's marginal rate of substitution.

The Indifference Map

Let's now consider the possibility of having both more movie tickets *and* more fast-food meals per week. When we do this, we can no longer stay on the same indifference curve that we drew in Figure E-1. That indifference curve was drawn for equally

TABLE E-1				
Calculating the Marginal Rate of Substitution	(1)	(2)	(3)	(4)
As we move from combination *A* to combination *B*, we are still on the same indifference curve. To stay on that curve, the number of fast-food meals decreases by three and the number of movie tickets increases by one. The marginal rate of substitution is 3:1. A three-unit decrease in fast-food meals requires an increase in one movie ticket to leave the consumer's total utility unaltered.	Combination	Fast-Food Meals per Week	Movie Tickets per Week	Marginal Rate of Substitution of Fast-Food Meals for Movie Tickets
	A	7	1	
	B	4	2	3:1
	C	2	3	2:1
	D	1	4	1:1

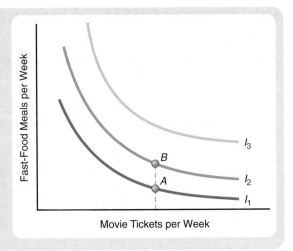

FIGURE E-4

A Set of Indifference Curves

An infinite number of indifference curves can be drawn. We show three possible ones. Realize that a higher indifference curve represents the possibility of higher rates of consumption of both goods. Hence, a higher indifference curve is preferred to a lower one because more is preferred to less. Look at points A and B. Point B represents more fast-food meals than point A; therefore, bundles on indifference curve I_2 have to be preferred over bundles on I_1 because the number of tickets for movie viewings per week is the same at points A and B.

satisfying combinations of movie tickets and fast-food meals per week. If the individual can now obtain more of both, a new indifference curve will have to be drawn, above and to the right of the one shown in panel (b) of Figure E-1 on page 546. Alternatively, if the individual faces the possibility of having less of both movie tickets and fast-food meals per week, an indifference curve will have to be drawn below and to the left of the one in panel (b) of Figure E-1. We can map out a whole set of indifference curves corresponding to these possibilities.

Figure E-4 shows three possible indifference curves. Indifference curves that are higher than others necessarily imply that for every given quantity of one good, more of the other good can be obtained on a higher indifference curve. Looked at another way, if one goes from curve I_1 to I_2, it is possible to view the same number of movies *and* be able to consume more fast-food meals each week. This is shown as a movement from point A to point B in Figure E-4. We could do it the other way. When we move from a lower to a higher indifference curve, it is possible to view the same number of movies *and* to consume more fast-food meals each week. Thus, the higher an indifference curve is for a consumer, the greater that consumer's total level of satisfaction.

The Budget Constraint

Budget constraint
All of the possible combinations of goods that can be purchased (at fixed prices) with a specific budget.

Our problem here is to find out how to maximize consumer satisfaction. To do so, we must consult not only our *preferences*—given by indifference curves—but also our *market opportunities*, which are given by our available income and prices, called our **budget constraint.** We might want more of everything, but for any given budget constraint, we have to make choices, or trade-offs, among possible goods. Everyone has a budget constraint; that is, everyone faces a limited consumption potential. How do we show this graphically? We must find the prices of the goods in question and determine the maximum consumption of each allowed by our budget. For example, let's assume that there is a $5 price for each fast-food meal and that a ticket to a movie costs $10. Let's also assume that our representative consumer has a total budget of $30 per week. What is the maximum number of fast-food meals this individual can consume? Six. And the maximum number of films per week she can view? Three. So now, as shown in Figure E-5, we have two points on our budget line, which is sometimes called the *consumption possibilities curve.* These anchor points of the

FIGURE E-5

The Budget Constraint

The line bb' represents this individual's budget constraint. Assuming that meals at fast-food restaurants cost $5 each, movie tickets cost $10 each, and the individual has a budget of $30 per week, a maximum of six fast-food meals or three movie tickets can be bought each week. These two extreme points are connected to form the budget constraint. All combinations within the colored area and on the budget constraint line are feasible.

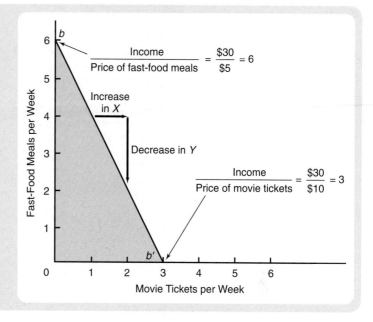

budget line are obtained by dividing money income by the price of each product. The first point is at *b* on the vertical axis; the second, at *b'* on the horizontal axis. The budget line is linear because prices are constant.

Any combination along line *bb'* is possible; in fact, any combination in the colored area is possible. We will assume, however, that the individual consumer completely uses up the available budget, and we will consider as possible only those points along *bb'*.

Slope of the Budget Constraint

The budget constraint is a line that slopes downward from left to right. The slope of that line has a special meaning. Look carefully at the budget line in Figure E-5. Remember from our discussion of graphs in Appendix A on page 23 that we measure a negative slope by the ratio of the decrease in Y over the run in X. In this case, Y is fast-food meals per week and X is movie tickets per week. In Figure E-5, the decrease in Y is -2 fast-food meals per week (a drop from 4 to 2) for an increase in X of one movie ticket per week (an increase from 1 to 2); therefore, the slope of the budget constraint is $-2/1$ or -2. This slope of the budget constraint represents the *rate of exchange* between meals at fast-food restaurants and tickets to movies.

Now we are ready to determine how the consumer achieves the optimum consumption rate.

Consumer Optimum Revisited

Consumers will try to attain the highest level of total utility possible, given their budget constraints. How can this be shown graphically? We draw a set of indifference curves similar to those in Figure E-4, and we bring in reality—the budget constraint *bb'*. Both are drawn in Figure E-6 on the following page. Because a higher level of total satisfaction is represented by a higher indifference curve, we know that the consumer will strive to be on the highest indifference curve possible. The consumer cannot get to indifference curve I_3, however, because the budget will be exhausted before any

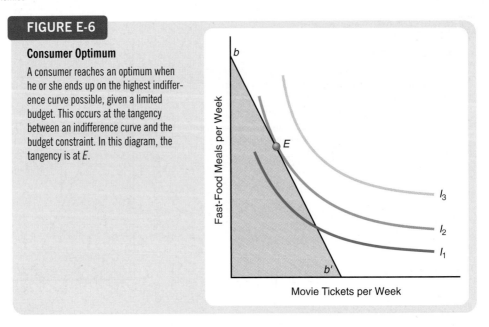

FIGURE E-6

Consumer Optimum

A consumer reaches an optimum when he or she ends up on the highest indifference curve possible, given a limited budget. This occurs at the tangency between an indifference curve and the budget constraint. In this diagram, the tangency is at E.

Go to www.econtoday.com/chapter21 for a numerical example illustrating the consumer optimum.

combination of fast-food meals and movie tickets represented on indifference curve I_3 is attained. This consumer can maximize total utility, subject to the budget constraint, only by being at point E on indifference curve I_2 because here the consumer's income is just being exhausted. Mathematically, point E is called the *tangency point* of the curve I_2 to the straight line bb'.

Consumer optimum is achieved when the marginal rate of substitution (which is subjective) is just equal to the feasible rate of exchange between meals at fast-food restaurants and tickets to movies. This rate is the ratio of the two prices of the goods involved. It is represented by the absolute value of the slope of the budget constraint (i.e., ignoring the negative signs). At point E, the point of tangency between indifference curve I_2 and budget constraint bb', the rate at which the consumer wishes to substitute fast-food meals for movie tickets (the numerical value of the slope of the indifference curve) is just equal to the rate at which the consumer *can* substitute fast-food meals for tickets to movies (the slope of the budget line).

Effects of Changes in Income

A change in income will shift the budget constraint bb' in Figure E-6. Consider only increases in income and no changes in price. The budget constraint will shift outward. Each new budget line will be parallel to the original one because we are not allowing a change in the relative prices of fast-food meals and movie tickets. We would now like to find out how an individual consumer responds to successive increases in income when relative prices remain constant. We do this in Figure E-7. We start out with an income that is represented by a budget line bb'. Consumer optimum is at point E, where the consumer attains the highest indifference curve I_1, given the budget constraint bb'. Now we let income increase. This is shown by a shift outward in the budget line to cc'. The consumer attains a new optimum at point E'. That is where a higher indifference curve, I_2, is reached. Again the consumer's income is increased so that the new budget line is dd'. The optimum now moves to E''. This is where indifference curve I_3 is reached. If we connect the three consumer optimum points, E, E', and E'', we have what is called an income-consumption curve.

FIGURE E-7

Income-Consumption Curve

We start off with income sufficient to yield budget constraint *bb'*. The highest attainable indifference curve is I_1, which is just tangent to *bb'* at *E*. Next we increase income. The budget line moves outward to *cc'*, which is parallel to *bb'*. The new highest indifference curve is I_2, which is just tangent to *cc'* at *E'*. We increase income again, which is represented by a shift in the budget line to *dd'*. The new tangency point of the highest indifference curve, I_3, with *dd'* is at point *E"*. When we connect these three points, we obtain the income-consumption curve.

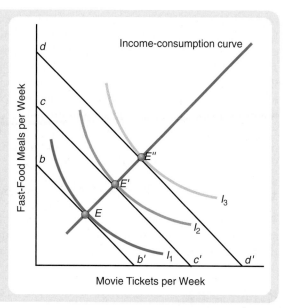

The **income-consumption curve** shows the optimum consumption points that would occur if income for that consumer were increased continuously, holding the prices of fast-food meals and movie tickets constant.

Income-consumption curve
The set of optimal consumption points that would occur if income were increased, relative prices remaining constant.

The Price-Consumption Curve

In Figure E-8, we hold money income and the price of fast-food meals constant while we lower the price of tickets to movies. As we keep lowering the price of movie tickets, the quantity of tickets that could be purchased if all income were spent on viewing movies increases; thus, the extreme points for the budget constraint keep moving outward to the right as the price of movie tickets falls. In other words, the budget line rotates

FIGURE E-8

Price-Consumption Curve

As we lower the price of movie tickets, income measured in terms of movie tickets per week increases. We show this by rotating the budget constraint from *bb'* to *bb"* and finally to *bb'''*. We then find the highest indifference curve that is attainable for each successive budget constraint. For budget constraint *bb'*, the highest indifference curve is I_1, which is tangent to *bb'* at point *E*. We do this for the next two budget constraints. When we connect the optimum points, *E*, *E'*, and *E"*, we derive the price-consumption curve, which shows the combinations of the two commodities that a consumer will purchase when money income and the price of one commodity remain constant while the other commodity's price changes.

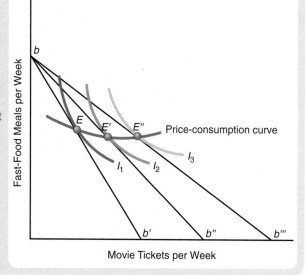

outward from bb' to bb'' and bb'''. Each time the price of movie tickets falls, a new budget line is formed. There has to be a new optimum point. We find it by locating on each new budget line the highest attainable indifference curve. This is shown at points E, E', and E''. We see that as price decreases for movie tickets, the consumer views more movies per week. We call the line connecting points E, E', and E'' the **price-consumption curve** in Figure E-8 on the previous page. It connects the tangency points of the budget constraints and indifference curves, thus showing the amounts of two goods that a consumer will buy when money income and the price of one commodity are held constant while the price of the remaining good changes.

Price-consumption curve
The set of consumer-optimum combinations of two goods that the consumer would choose as the price of one good changes while money income and the price of the other good remain constant.

Deriving the Demand Curve

We are now in a position to derive the demand curve using indifference curve analysis. In panel (a) of Figure E-9, we show what happens when the price of tickets to movies decreases, holding both the price of meals at fast-food restaurants and income

FIGURE E-9

Deriving the Demand Curve

In panel (a), we show the effects of a decrease in the price of movie tickets from $10 to $5. At $10, the highest indifference curve touches the budget line bb' at point E. The number of movies viewed is two. We transfer this combination—price, $10; quantity demanded, 2—down to panel (b). Next we decrease the price of movie tickets to $5. This generates a new budget line, or constraint, which is bb''. Consumer optimum is now at E'. The optimum quantity of movie tickets demanded at a price of $5 is five. We transfer this point—price, $5; quantity demanded, 5—down to panel (b). When we connect these two points, we have a demand curve, D, for tickets to movies.

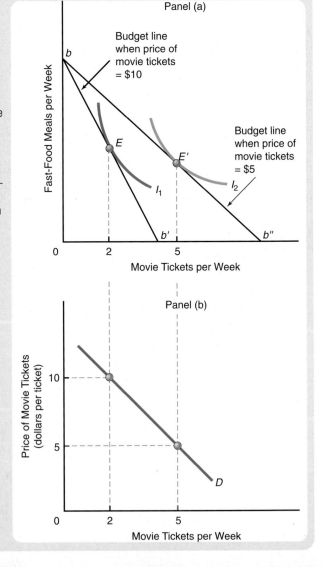

constant. If the price of movie tickets decreases, the budget line rotates from *bb'* to *bb''*. The two optimum points are given by the tangency at the highest indifference curve that just touches those two budget lines. This is at *E* and *E'*. But those two points give us two price-quantity pairs. At point *E*, the price of movie tickets is $10; the quantity demanded is 2. Thus, we have one point that we can transfer to panel (b) of Figure E-9. At point *E'*, we have another price-quantity pair. The price has fallen to $5; the quantity demanded has increased to 5. We therefore transfer this other point to panel (b). When we connect these two points (and all the others in between), we derive the demand curve for tickets to movies, which slopes downward.

myeconlab

Here is what you should know after reading this chapter. **MyEconLab** will help you identify what you know, and where to go when you need to practice.

WHAT YOU SHOULD KNOW		WHERE TO GO TO PRACTICE
On Being Indifferent Along an indifference curve, the consumer experiences equal levels of satisfaction. That is to say, along any indifference curve, every combination of the two goods in question yields exactly the same level of satisfaction.	indifference curve, 547	• **MyEconLab** Study Plan 21.8
Properties of Indifferent Curves Indifference curves typically slope downward and are usually convex to the origin.		• **MyEconLab** Study Plan 21.9
The Marginal Rate of Substitution To measure the marginal rate of substitution, we find out how much of one good has to be given up in order to allow the consumer to consume one more unit of the other good while still remaining on the same indifference curve. The marginal rate of substitution falls as one moves down an indifference curve.	KEY FIGURE Figure E-1, 546	• **MyEconLab** Study Plans 21.10
The Budget Constraint Indifference curves represent preferences. A budget constraint represents opportunities—how much can be purchased with a given level of income. Consumer optimum is obtained when the highest feasible indifference curve is just tangent to the budget constraint line; at that point, the consumer reaches the highest feasible indifference curve.	budget constraint, 550 KEY FIGURE Figure E-5, 551	• **MyEconLab** Study Plans 21.11, 21.12, 21.13
Slope of the Budget Constraint The slope of the budget constraint is the rate of exchange between two goods, which is the ratio of their dollar prices.	KEY FIGURE Figure E-5, 551	• **MyEconLab** Study Plan 21.12

(continued)

(continued)

WHAT YOU SHOULD KNOW		WHERE TO GO TO PRACTICE
The Income-Consumption Curve As income increases, the consumer optimum moves up to higher and higher indifference curves. When we connect those points with a line, we derive the income-consumption curve.	income-consumption curve, 553 **KEY FIGURE** Figure E-7, 553	• **MyEconLab** Study Plan 21.13
The Price-Consumption Curve As the price of one good decreases, the budget line rotates. When we connect the tangency points of the highest indifference curves to these new budget lines, we derive the price-consumption curve.	price-consumption curve, 554 **KEY FIGURE** Figure E-8, 553	• **MyEconLab** Study Plan 21.14
Deriving the Demand Curve A decrease in the price of an item causes the budget line to rotate outward. This generates a new consumer optimum, at which the individual chooses to consume more units of the item. Hence, a decrease in price generates an increase in quantity demanded, or a movement down along a derived demand curve.	**KEY FIGURE** Figure E-9, 554	• **MyEconLab** Study Plan 21.15

Log in to MyEconLab, take a chapter test, and get a personalized Study Plan that tells you which concepts you understand and which ones you need to review. From there, MyEconLab will give you further practice, tutorials, animations, videos, and guided solutions.
Log in to www.myeconlab.com

PROBLEMS

All problems are assignable in myeconlab *. Answers to odd-numbered problems appear at the back of the book.*

E-1. Consider the indifference curve illustrated in Figure E-1 on page 546. Explain, in economic terms, why the curve is convex to the origin.

E-2. Your classmate tells you that he is indifferent between three soft drinks and two hamburgers or two soft drinks and three hamburgers.

    a. Draw a rough diagram of an indifference curve containing your classmate's consumption choices.

    b. Suppose that your classmate states that he is also indifferent between two soft drinks and three hamburgers or one soft drink and four hamburgers, but that he prefers three soft drinks and two hamburgers to one soft drink and four ham-

burgers. Use your diagram from part (a) to reason out whether he can have these preferences.

E-3. The following table represents Sue's preferences for bottled water and soft drinks, the combination of which yields the same level of utility.

Combination of Bottled Water and Soft Drinks	Bottled Water per Month	Soft Drinks per Month
A	5	11
B	10	7
C	15	4
D	20	2
E	25	1

Calculate Sue's marginal rate of substitution of soft drinks for bottled water. Relate the marginal rate of substitution to marginal utility.

E-4. Using the information provided in Problem E-3, illustrate Sue's indifference curve, with water on the horizontal axis and soft drinks on the vertical axis.

E-5. Sue's monthly budget for bottled water and soft drinks is $23. The price of bottled water is $1 per bottle, and the price of soft drinks is $2 per bottle. Calculate the slope of Sue's budget constraint. Given this information and the information provided in Problem E-3, find the combination of goods that satisfies Sue's utility maximization problem in light of her budget constraint.

E-6. Using the indifference curve diagram you constructed in Problem E-4, add in Sue's budget constraint given the information in Problem E-5. Illustrate the utility-maximizing combination of bottled water and soft drinks.

E-7. Suppose that at a higher satisfaction level than in problem E-3, Sue's constant-utility preferences are as shown in the table on the right. Calculate the slope of Sue's new budget constraint using the information provided in Problem E-5, suppose

Combination of Bottled Water and Soft Drinks	Bottled Water per Month	Soft Drinks per Month
A	5	22
B	10	14
C	15	8
D	20	4
E	25	2

now that the price of a soft drink falls to $1, and find the combination of goods that satisfies Sue's utility maximization problem in light of her budget constraint.

E-8. Illustrate Sue's new budget constraint and indifference curve in the diagram you constructed for Problem E-6. Illustrate also the utility-maximizing combination of goods. Finally, draw the price-consumption curve.

E-9. Given your answers to Problems E-5 and E-7, are Sue's preferences for soft drinks consistent with the law of demand?

E-10. Using your answer to Problem E-8, draw Sue's demand curve for soft drinks.

22

Rents, Profits, and the Financial Environment of Business

They are known as Bowie bonds. The returns on the first Bowie bonds, which were issued in 1997, are based on royalties generated by sales of songs and albums by 1970s rock star David Bowie. Today, the term *Bowie bonds* encompasses similar bonds issued by many other artists who continue to earn royalties on works recorded in years past. Bowie bonds are just one particular type of bond traded in markets for *securities*, or legal claims on firms that most of us more commonly refer to as stocks and bonds. In this chapter, you will learn about how securities markets function. In addition, you will learn about economic rents, economic profits, and the allocative role of interest.

LEARNING OBJECTIVES

After reading this chapter, you should be able to:

➤ Understand the concept of economic rent

➤ Distinguish among the main organizational forms of business and explain the chief advantages and disadvantages of each

➤ Explain the difference between accounting profits and economic profits

➤ Discuss how the interest rate performs a key role in allocating resources

➤ Calculate the present discounted value of a payment to be received at a future date

➤ Identify the three main sources of corporate funds and differentiate between stocks and bonds

myeconlab

MyEconLab helps you master each objective and study more efficiently. See end of chapter for details.

? DID YOU KNOW THAT since 1897, nearly all the increase in the values of ownership shares of companies traded in U.S. stock markets has occurred when Congress has been in recess? Indeed, returns earned on shares of stock have been almost eight times higher on days when Congress has not been in session. The reason, most financial economists agree, is that when Congress is in session, representatives and senators propose numerous bills that might reduce firms' profits. The possibility that some of these bills may pass creates uncertainty about future profitability that tends to depress stock prices. How do firms measure their profits, and what factors determine profits? Why do anticipations of future profits of companies affect the prices of their ownership shares today? In this chapter, you will learn the answers to these questions. First, however, you must learn about the important function of *economic rent*.

Economic Rent

When you hear the term *rent*, you are accustomed to having it mean the payment made to property owners for the use of land or dwellings. The term *rent* has a different meaning in economics. **Economic rent** is payment to the owner of a resource in excess of its *opportunity cost*—that is, the minimum payment that would be necessary to call forth production of that amount of the resource.

Economic rent
A payment for the use of any resource over and above its opportunity cost.

Determining Land Rent

Economists originally used the term *rent* to designate payment for the use of land. What was thought to be important about land was that its supply was completely inelastic. That is, the supply curve for land was thought to be a vertical line, so that no matter what the prevailing market price for land, the quantity supplied would remain the same.

The concept of economic rent is associated with the British economist David Ricardo (1772–1823). Here is how Ricardo analyzed economic rent for land. He first simplified his model by assuming that all land is equally productive. Then Ricardo assumed that the quantity of land in a country is *fixed* so that land's opportunity cost is equal to zero. Graphically, then, in terms of supply and demand, we draw the supply curve for land vertically (zero price elasticity). In Figure 22-1 on the following page, the supply curve of land is represented by S. If the demand curve is D_1, it intersects the supply curve, S, at price P_1. The entire amount of revenues obtained, $P_1 \times Q_1$, is labeled "Economic rent." If the demand for land increases to D_2, the equilibrium price will rise to P_2. Additions to economic rent are labeled "More economic rent." Notice that the quantity of land remains insensitive to the change in price. Another way of stating this is that the supply curve is perfectly inelastic.

Economic Rent to Labor

Land and natural resources are not the only factors of production to which the analysis of economic rent can be applied. In fact, the analysis is probably more often applicable to labor. Here is a list of people who provide different labor services, some of whom probably receive large amounts of economic rent:

- Professional sports superstars
- Rock stars

- Movie stars
- World-class models
- Successful inventors and innovators
- World-famous opera stars

Just apply the definition of economic rent to the phenomenal earnings that these people make. They would undoubtedly work for considerably less than they earn. Therefore, much of their earnings constitutes economic rent (but not all, as we shall see). Economic rent occurs because specific resources cannot be replicated exactly. No one can duplicate today's most highly paid entertainment figures, and therefore they receive economic rent.

Economic Rent and the Allocation of Resources

Suppose that a highly paid movie star would make the same number of movies at half his or her current annual earnings. Why, then, does the superstar receive a higher income? Look again at Figure 22-1, but substitute *entertainment activities of the super-stars* for the word *land*. The high "price" received by the superstar is due to the demand for his or her services. If Reese Witherspoon announces that she will work for a million dollars per movie and do two movies a year, how is she going to know which production company values her services the most highly? Witherspoon and other movie stars let the market decide where their resources should be used. In this sense, we can say the following:

Economic rent allocates resources to their highest-valued use.

Otherwise stated, economic rent directs resources to the people who can use them most efficiently.

How much do top performers earn?

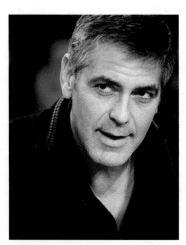

Do you think that actor George Clooney earns economic rent? Why or why not?

FIGURE 22-1

Economic Rent

If indeed the supply curve of land were completely price-inelastic in the long run, it would be depicted by S. The opportunity cost of land is zero, so the same quantity of land is forthcoming at any constant-quality price. Thus, at the quantity in existence, Q_1, any and all revenues are economic rent. If demand is D_1, the price will be P_1; if demand is D_2, price will rise to P_2. Economic rent would be $P_1 \times Q_1$ and $P_2 \times Q_1$, respectively.

EXAMPLE
Do Entertainment Superstars Make Super Economic Rents?

Superstars certainly do well financially. Table 22–1 shows the earnings of selected individuals in the entertainment industry as estimated by *Forbes* magazine. Earnings are totaled for a two-year period. How much of these earnings can be called economic rent? The question is not easy to answer, because an entertainment newcomer would almost certainly work for much less than he or she earns, implying that the newcomer is making high economic rent. The same cannot necessarily be said for entertainers who have been raking in millions for years. They probably have very high accumulated wealth and also a more jaded outlook about their work. It is therefore not clear how much they would work if they were not offered those huge sums of money.

FOR CRITICAL ANALYSIS
Even if some superstar entertainers would work for less, what forces cause them to make so much income anyway?

TABLE 22-1
Superstar Earnings

Name	Occupation	Two-Year Earnings
Oprah Winfrey	Talk show host and owner, author	$275,000,000
50 Cent	Hip-hop artist	150,000,000
Jerry Bruckheimer	Director, producer	145,000,000
Steven Spielberg	Director, producer	130,000,000
Tyler Perry	Director, producer	125,000,000
The Police	Rock group	115,000,000
Jerry Seinfeld	Actor, Comedian	85,000,000
Jay-Z	Hop-hop artist	82,000,000
Beyonce Knowles	Musician	80,000,000
Will Smith	Actor	80,000,000

Source: Forbes, 2008.

QUICK QUIZ
See page 582 for the answers. Review concepts from this section in MyEconLab.

Economic rent is defined as payment for a factor of production that is completely _____ in supply.

Economic rent _____ resources to their _____-valued use.

Firms and Profits

Firms or businesses, like individuals, seek to earn the highest possible returns. We define a **firm** as follows:

A firm is an organization that brings together factors of production—labor, land, physical capital, human capital, and entrepreneurial skill—to produce a product or service that it hopes can be sold at a profit.

Firm
A business organization that employs resources to produce goods or services for profit. A firm normally owns and operates at least one "plant" or facility in order to produce.

A typical firm will have an organizational structure consisting of an entrepreneur, managers, and workers. The entrepreneur is the person who takes the risks, mainly of losing his or her personal wealth. In compensation, the entrepreneur will get any profits that are made. Recall from Chapter 2 that entrepreneurs take the initiative in combining land, labor, and capital to produce a good or a service. Entrepreneurs are the ones who innovate in the form of new production and new products. The entrepreneur also decides whom to hire to manage the firm. Some economists maintain that the true quality of an entrepreneur becomes evident with his or her selection of managers.

Managers, in turn, decide who should be hired and fired and how the business should be operated on a day-to-day basis. The workers ultimately use the other inputs to produce the products or services that are being sold by the firm. Workers and managers are paid contractual wages. They receive a specified amount of income for a specified time period. Entrepreneurs are not paid contractual wages. They receive no reward specified in advance. The entrepreneurs make profits if there are any, for profits accrue to those who are willing to take risks. (Because the entrepreneur gets only what is left over after all expenses are paid, he or she is often referred to as a *residual claimant*. The entrepreneur lays claim to the residual—whatever is left.)

The Legal Organization of Firms

We all know that firms differ from one another. Some sell frozen yogurt, others make automobiles; some advertise, some do not; some have annual sales of a few thousand dollars, others have sales in the billions of dollars. The list of differences is probably endless. Yet for all this diversity, the basic organization of *all* firms can be thought of in terms of a few simple structures, the most important of which are the proprietorship, the partnership, and the corporation.

Proprietorship
A business owned by one individual who makes the business decisions, receives all the profits, and is legally responsible for the debts of the firm.

PROPRIETORSHIP The most common form of business organization is the **proprietorship.** As shown in Table 22-2, close to 72 percent of all firms in the United States are proprietorships. Each is owned by a single individual who makes the business decisions, receives all the profits, and is legally responsible for all the debts of the firm. Although proprietorships are numerous, they are generally rather small businesses, with annual sales averaging not much more than $56,000. For this reason, even though there are nearly 21 million proprietorships in the United States, they account for less than 5 percent of all business revenues.

Advantages of Proprietorships. Proprietorships offer several advantages as a form of business organization. First, they are *easy to form and to dissolve*. In the simplest case, all one must do to start a business is to start working; to dissolve the firm, one simply stops

TABLE 22-2

Forms of Business Organization

Type of Firm	Percentage of U.S. Firms	Average Size (annual sales in dollars)	Percentage of Total Business Revenues
Proprietorship	71.7	56,000	4.4
Partnership	8.9	1,234,000	12.1
Corporation	19.4	3,907,000	83.5

Sources: U.S. Bureau of the Census; *2008 Statistical Abstract.*

working. Second, *all decision-making power resides with the sole proprietor.* No partners, shareholders, or board of directors need be consulted. The third advantage is that its *profit is taxed only once.* All profit is treated by law as the net income of the proprietor and as such is subject only to personal income taxation.

Disadvantages of Proprietorships. The most important disadvantage of a proprietorship is that the proprietor faces **unlimited liability** *for the debts of the firm.* This means that the owner is personally responsible for all of the firm's debts. The second disadvantage is that many lenders are reluctant to lend large sums to a proprietorship. Consequently, a proprietorship may have a *limited ability to raise funds,* to expand the business or even simply to help it survive bad times. The third disadvantage of proprietorships is that they normally *end with the death of the proprietor,* which creates added uncertainty for prospective lenders or employees.

Unlimited liability
A legal concept whereby the personal assets of the owner of a firm can be seized to pay off the firm's debts.

PARTNERSHIP The second important form of business organization is the **partnership.** As shown in Table 22-2, partnerships are far less numerous than proprietorships but tend to be larger businesses—about 22 times greater on average. A partnership differs from a proprietorship chiefly in that there are two or more co-owners, called partners. They share the responsibilities of operating the firm and its profits, and they are *each* legally responsible for *all* of the debts incurred by the firm. In this sense, a partnership may be viewed as a proprietorship with more than one owner.

Partnership
A business owned by two or more joint owners, or partners, who share the responsibilities and the profits of the firm and are individually liable for all the debts of the partnership.

Advantages of Partnerships. The first advantage of a partnership is that it is *easy to form.* In fact, it is almost as easy to form as a proprietorship. Second, partnerships, like proprietorships, often help *reduce the costs of monitoring job performance.* This is particularly true when interpersonal skills are important for successful performance and in lines of business in which, even after the fact, it is difficult to measure performance objectively. Thus, attorneys and physicians often organize themselves as partnerships. A third advantage of the partnership is that it *permits more effective specialization* in occupations in which, for legal or other reasons, the multiple talents required for success are unlikely to be uniform across individuals. Finally, the income of the partnership is treated as personal income and thus is *subject only to personal taxation.*

Disadvantages of Partnerships. Partnerships also have their disadvantages. First, the *partners each have unlimited liability.* Thus, the personal assets of *each* partner are at risk due to debts incurred on behalf of the partnership by *any* of the partners. Second, *decision making is generally more costly* in a partnership than in a proprietorship; more people are involved in making decisions, and they may have differences of opinion that must be resolved before action is possible. Finally, *dissolution of the partnership* often occurs when a partner dies or voluntarily withdraws or when one or more partners wish to remove someone from the partnership. This creates potential uncertainty for creditors and employees.

CORPORATION A **corporation** is a legal entity that may conduct business in its own name just as an individual does. The owners of a corporation are called *shareholders* because they own shares of the profits earned by the firm. By law, shareholders enjoy **limited liability,** meaning that if the corporation incurs debts that it cannot pay, the shareholders' personal property is shielded from claims by the firm's creditors. As shown in Table 22-2, corporations are far less numerous than proprietorships, but because of their large size, they are responsible for more than 83 percent of all business revenues in the United States.

Corporation
A legal entity that may conduct business in its own name just as an individual does; the owners of a corporation, called shareholders, own shares of the firm's profits and enjoy the protection of limited liability.

Limited liability
A legal concept in which the responsibility, or liability, of the owners of a corporation is limited to the value of the shares in the firm that they own.

Advantages of Corporations. Perhaps the greatest advantage of corporations is that their owners (the shareholders) enjoy *limited liability*. The liability of shareholders is limited to the value of their shares. The second advantage is that, legally, the corporation *continues to exist* even if one or more owners cease to be owners. A third advantage of the corporation stems from the first two: Corporations are well positioned to *raise large sums of financial capital*. People are able to buy ownership shares or lend funds to the corporation knowing that their liability is limited to the amount of funds they invest and confident that the corporation's existence does not depend on the life of any one of the firm's owners.

Disadvantages of Corporations. The chief disadvantage of the corporation is that corporate income is subject to *double taxation*. The profits of the corporation are subject first to corporate taxation. Then, if any of the after-tax profits are distributed to shareholders as **dividends,** such payments are treated as personal income to the shareholders and subject to personal taxation, although the dividends may be taxed at lower rates than other personal income. Despite the lower tax rates on dividends, owners of corporations generally pay higher taxes on corporate income than on other forms of income because the corporate income is also taxed at the corporate level.

A second disadvantage of the corporation is that corporations are potentially subject to problems associated with the *separation of ownership and control*. The owners and managers of a corporation are typically different persons and may have different incentives. The problems that can result are discussed later in the chapter.

Have recently enacted U.S. government regulations created a new disadvantage of the corporate form of business organization?

Dividends
Portion of a corporation's profits paid to its owners (shareholders).

POLICY EXAMPLE
Why It Can Pay to Form a Partnership Instead of a Corporation

Each year between 1992 and 2002, an average of more than 135 new companies, called corporate *start-ups*, began issuing new ownership shares in U.S. stock markets. Since 2002, only about 40 start-ups have occurred on average per year. Most observers agree that a key reason for this big decline in corporate start-ups was the enactment of the Sarbanes-Oxley Act in 2002. This law imposes tougher internal auditing requirements on publicly traded companies and requires executives to certify a firm's financial statements. Corporate officers who fail to fully abide by these provisions can face

significant fines. The costs of complying with the Sarbanes-Oxley Act can be particularly burdensome for small companies. Thus, many more start-ups than in past years are opting for alternative business structures, such as limited liability companies and partnerships, instead of becoming publicly traded corporations.

FOR CRITICAL ANALYSIS
Why might the Sarbanes-Oxley Act help to explain why nearly 50 major corporations have opted to become private since 2002?

The Profits of a Firm

Most people think of a firm's profit as the difference between the amount of revenues the firm takes in and the amount it spends for wages, materials, and so on. In a bookkeeping sense, the following formula could be used:

$$\text{Accounting profit} = \text{total revenues} - \text{explicit costs}$$

Explicit costs
Costs that business managers must take account of because they must be paid; examples are wages, taxes, and rent.

Accounting profit
Total revenues minus total explicit costs.

where **explicit costs** are expenses that must actually be paid out by the firm. This definition of profit is known as **accounting profit.** It is appropriate when used by accountants to determine a firm's taxable income. Economists are more interested in how firm managers react not just to changes in explicit costs but also to changes in **implicit costs**, defined as expenses that business managers do not have to pay out of pocket but are costs to the firm nonetheless because they represent an opportunity cost. They do not involve any direct cash outlay by the firm and must therefore be measured by the *opportunity cost principle*. That is to say, they are measured by what the resources (land, capital) currently used in producing a particular good or service could earn in other uses. Therefore, a better definition of implicit cost is the opportunity cost of using factors that a producer does not buy or hire but already owns. Economists use the full opportunity cost of all resources (including both explicit and implicit costs) as the figure to subtract from revenues to obtain a definition of profit.

Implicit costs
Expenses that managers do not have to pay out of pocket and hence normally do not explicitly calculate, such as the opportunity cost of factors of production that are owned; examples are owner-provided capital and owner-provided labor.

Opportunity Cost of Capital

Firms enter or remain in an industry if they earn, at minimum, a **normal rate of return.** People will not invest their wealth in a business unless they obtain a positive normal (competitive) rate of return—that is, unless their invested wealth pays off. Any business wishing to attract capital must expect to pay at least the same rate of return on that capital as all other businesses (of similar risk) are willing to pay. Put another way, when a firm requires the use of a resource in producing a particular product, it must bid against alternative users of that resource. Thus, the firm must offer a price that is at least as much as other potential users are offering to pay. For example, if individuals can invest their wealth in almost any publishing firm and get a rate of return of 10 percent per year, each firm in the publishing industry must *expect* to pay 10 percent as the normal rate of return to present and future investors. This 10 percent is a *cost to the firm*, the **opportunity cost of capital.** The opportunity cost of capital is the amount of income, or yield, that could have been earned by investing in the next-best alternative. Capital will not stay in firms or industries in which the expected rate of return falls below its opportunity cost—that is, what could be earned elsewhere. If a firm owns some capital equipment, it can either use it or lease it and earn a return. If the firm uses the equipment for production, part of the cost of using that equipment is the forgone revenue that the firm could have earned had it leased out that equipment.

Normal rate of return
The amount that must be paid to an investor to induce investment in a business; also known as the *opportunity cost of capital*.

Opportunity cost of capital
The normal rate of return, or the available return on the next-best alternative investment. Economists consider this a cost of production, and it is included in our cost examples.

Opportunity Cost of Owner-Provided Labor and Capital

Single-owner proprietorships often grossly exaggerate their profit rates because they understate the opportunity cost of the labor that the proprietor provides to the business. Here we are referring to the opportunity cost of labor. For example, you may know people who run a small grocery store. These people will sit down at the end of the year and figure out what their "profits" are. They will add up all their sales and subtract what they had to pay to other workers, what they had to pay to their suppliers, what they had to pay in taxes, and so on. The end result they will call "profit." They normally will not, however, have figured into their costs the salary that they could have made if they had worked for somebody else in a similar type of job. By working for themselves, they become residual claimants—they receive what is left after all explicit costs have been accounted for. Part of the costs, however, should include the salary the owner-operator could have received working for someone else.

Consider a simple example of a skilled auto mechanic working 14 hours a day at his own service station, six days a week. Compare this situation to how much he could earn working 84 hours a week as a trucking company mechanic. This self-employed auto mechanic might have an opportunity cost of about $35 an hour. For his 84-hour week in his own service station, he is forfeiting $2,940. Unless his service station shows accounting profits of more than that per week, he is incurring losses in an economic sense.

Go to www.econtoday.com/chapter22 for a link to Internal Revenue Service reports on U.S. annual revenues and expenses of proprietorships, partnerships, and corporations based on tax returns. Click on recent quarters and choose relevant reports.

Another way of looking at the opportunity cost of running a business is that opportunity cost consists of all explicit and implicit costs. Accountants only take account of explicit costs. Therefore, accounting profit ends up being the residual after only explicit costs are subtracted from total revenues.

This same analysis can apply to owner-provided capital, such as land or buildings. The fact that the owner owns the building or the land with which he or she operates a business does not mean that it is "free." Rather, use of the building and land still has an opportunity cost—the value of the next-best alternative use for those assets.

Accounting Profits versus Economic Profits

Economic profits
Total revenues minus total opportunity costs of all inputs used, or the total of all implicit and explicit costs.

The term *profits* in economics means the income that entrepreneurs earn, over and above all costs including their own opportunity cost of time, plus the opportunity cost of the capital they have invested in their business. Profits can be regarded as total revenues minus total costs—which is how accountants think of them—but we must now include *all* costs. Our definition of **economic profits** will be the following:

$$\text{Economic profits} = \text{total revenues} - \text{total opportunity cost of all input used}$$

or

$$\text{Economic profits} = \text{total revenues} - (\text{explicit} + \text{implicit costs})$$

Remember that implicit costs include a normal rate of return on invested capital. We show this relationship in Figure 22-2.

The Goal of the Firm: Profit Maximization

When we examined the theory of consumer demand, utility (or satisfaction) maximization by the individual provided the basis for the analysis. In the theory of the firm and

FIGURE 22-2

Simplified View of Economic and Accounting Profit

We see on the right column that accounting profit is the difference between total revenues and total explicit accounting costs. Conversely, we see on the left column that economic profit is equal to total revenues minus economic costs. Economic costs equal explicit accounting costs plus all implicit costs, including a normal rate of return on invested capital.

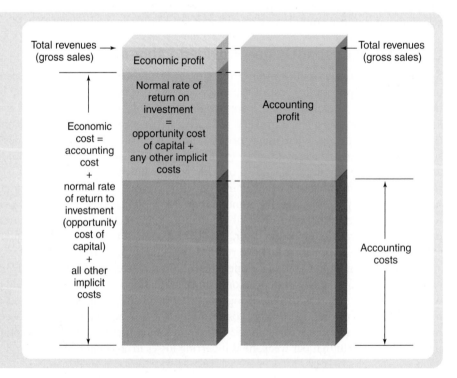

production, *profit maximization* is the underlying hypothesis of our predictive theory. The goal of the firm is to maximize economic profits, and the firm is expected to try to make the positive difference between total revenues and total costs as large as it can.

Our justification for assuming profit maximization by firms is similar to our assumption concerning utility maximization by individuals (see Chapter 21). To obtain labor, capital, and other resources required to produce commodities, firms must first obtain financing from investors. Although investors typically monitor managers' performances to ensure that the funds they provide are not misused, they are most interested in the earnings on these funds and the risk of obtaining lower returns or losing the funds they have invested. Firms that can provide relatively higher risk-corrected returns will therefore have an advantage in obtaining the financing needed to continue or expand production. Over time, we would expect a policy of profit maximization to become the dominant mode of behavior for firms that survive.

Why is it that in college sports, posting losses can be a profitable activity?

EXAMPLE
How Chalking Up Sports Losses Raises Schools' Profits

What do these pairings of college basketball opponents have in common: Texas Southern versus Illinois; Prairie View versus Texas; Chicago State versus Louisville; and State University of New York at Stony Brook versus Villanova? The answer is that in each of these matchups, the first opponent listed goes into the game almost certain of chalking up a mark in the season's loss column. Nevertheless, the teams' schools earn tens of thousands of dollars in revenues, paid by their opponents from ticket receipts, which more than cover the opportunity costs of playing top-rated opponents. Indeed, administrators at the colleges fielding underdog teams in such pairings sometimes worry that their teams might actually win stunning upsets. If so, the powerhouse schools looking for a few easy wins on their schedules may not want to play them in the future. Then the underdogs' revenues and profits would disappear.

FOR CRITICAL ANALYSIS
Why might colleges with top basketball programs determine that scheduling opponents that they anticipate their teams will defeat handily is a profit-maximizing strategy? (Hint: Why might colleges with powerhouse teams have a profit-maximizing motive to win a significant percentage of their games?)

QUICK QUIZ   *See page 582 for the answers. Review concepts from this section in MyEconLab.*

_____ are the most common form of business organization, comprising close to 72 percent of all firms. Each is owned by a single individual who makes all business decisions, receives all the profits, and has _____ liability for the firm's debts.

_____ are much like proprietorships, except that two or more individuals, or partners, share the decisions and the profits of the firm. In addition, each partner has _____ liability for the debts of the firm.

Corporations are responsible for the largest share of business revenues. The owners, called _____, share in the firm's profits but normally have little responsibility for the firm's day-to-day operations. They enjoy _____ liability for the debts of the firm.

Accounting profits differ from **economic profits**, which are defined as total revenues minus total costs, where costs include the full _____ cost of all of the factors of production plus all other implicit costs.

The full opportunity cost of capital invested in a business is generally not included as a cost when accounting profits are calculated. Thus, accounting profits often are _____ than economic profits. We assume throughout that the goal of the firm is to _____ economic profits.

Interest

Financial capital
Funds used to purchase physical capital goods, such as buildings and equipment, and patents and trademarks.

Interest is the price paid by debtors to creditors for the use of loanable funds. Often businesses go to credit markets to obtain so-called **financial capital** in order to invest in physical capital and rights to patents and trademarks from which they hope to make a satisfactory return. In other words, in our complicated society, the production of capital goods is often facilitated by the existence of credit markets. These are markets in which borrowing and lending take place.

Interest and Credit

Interest
The payment for current rather than future command over resources; the cost of obtaining credit.

When you obtain credit, you actually obtain funds to have command over resources today. We can say, then, that **interest** is the payment for current rather than future command over resources. Thus, interest is the payment for obtaining credit. If you borrow $100 from me, you have command over $100 worth of goods and services today. I no longer have that command. You promise to pay me back $100 plus interest at some future date. The interest that you pay is usually expressed as a percentage of the total loan, calculated on an annual basis. If at the end of one year you pay me back $105, the annual interest rate is $5 ÷ $100, or 5 percent. When you go out into the marketplace to obtain credit, you will find that the interest rate charged differs greatly. A loan to buy a house (a mortgage) may cost you 6 to 8 percent in annual interest. An installment loan to buy an automobile may cost you 7 to 9 percent in annual interest. The federal government, when it wishes to obtain credit (issue U.S. Treasury securities), may have to pay only 2 to 6 percent in annual interest. Variations in the rate of annual interest that must be paid for credit depend on the following factors.

FINANCIAL AID OFFICE

When you borrow to finance your college or university studies, what do the interest payments represent?

1. *Length of loan.* In many (but not all) cases, the longer the loan will be outstanding, other things being equal, the greater will be the interest rate charged.

2. *Risk.* The greater the risk of nonrepayment of the loan, other things being equal, the greater the interest rate charged. Risk is assessed on the basis of the creditworthiness of the borrower and whether the borrower provides collateral for the loan. Collateral consists of any asset that will automatically become the property of the lender should the borrower fail to comply with the loan agreement.

3. *Handling charges.* It takes resources to set up a loan. Papers have to be filled out and filed, credit references have to be checked, collateral has to be examined, and so on. The larger the amount of the loan, the smaller the handling (or administrative) charges as a percentage of the total loan. Therefore, we would predict that, other things being equal, the larger the loan, the lower the interest rate.

Go to www.econtoday.com/chapter22 for Federal Reserve data on U.S. interest rates.

Real versus Nominal Interest Rates

Nominal rate of interest
The market rate of interest expressed in today's dollars.

We have been assuming that there is no inflation. In a world of inflation—a persistent rise in an average of all prices—the **nominal rate of interest** will be higher than it would be in a world with no inflation. Nominal, or market, rates of interest rise to take account of the anticipated rate of inflation. If, for example, no inflation is expected, the nominal rate of interest might be 5 percent for home mortgages. If the rate of inflation goes to 4 percent a year and stays there, everybody will anticipate that inflation rate. The nominal rate of interest will rise to about 9 percent to take account of the anticipated rate of inflation. If the interest rate did not rise to 9 percent, the principal plus interest earned at 5 percent would have lower purchasing power in the future because inflation would have eroded its real value. We can therefore say that the nominal, or market, rate of interest is approximately equal to the real rate of interest plus the anticipated rate of inflation, or

$$i_n = i_r + \text{anticipated rate of inflation}$$

where i_n equals the nominal rate of interest and i_r equals the real rate of interest. In short, you can expect to see high nominal rates of interest in periods of high inflation rates. The **real rate of interest** may not necessarily be high, though. We must first correct the nominal rate of interest for the anticipated rate of inflation before determining whether the real interest rate is in fact higher than normal.

Real rate of interest
The nominal rate of interest minus the anticipated rate of inflation.

The Allocative Role of Interest

In Chapter 4, we talked about the price system and the role that prices play in the allocation of resources. Interest is a price that allocates loanable funds (credit) to consumers and to businesses. Within the business sector, interest allocates funds to different firms and therefore to different investment projects. An investment, or capital, project with a rate of return—an annual payoff as a percentage of the investment— higher than the market rate of interest in the credit market will be undertaken, given an unrestricted market for loanable funds. For example, if the expected rate of return on the purchase of a new factory or of intellectual property—patents or copyrights— in some industry is 10 percent and funds can be acquired for 6 percent, the investment project will proceed. If, however, that same project had an expected rate of return of only 4 percent, it would not be undertaken. In sum, the interest rate allocates funds to industries whose investments yield the highest (risk-adjusted) returns—where resources will be the most productive.

It is important to realize that the interest rate performs the function of allocating financial capital and that this ultimately allocates real physical capital to various firms for investment projects.

How has the Iranian government's policy regarding bank loan rates brought about a reallocation of financial capital in that nation?

INTERNATIONAL POLICY EXAMPLE
An Interest Rate Policy Reallocates Iranian Financial Capital

In Iran, the government sets limits on the interest rates that banks can charge on loans. Recently, it reduced the ceiling on bank loan rates to 12 percent per year. This rate is about 8 percentage points below the prevailing annual rate of inflation and hence less than the nominal loan rate banks otherwise would have charged. Owners of shares in Iranian banks have responded to the government's action by selling off their shares and using their financial capital to purchase gold and real estate instead.

FOR CRITICAL ANALYSIS
Why is the market loan rate that banks otherwise would charge borrowers in the absence of the Iranian government's legal limit likely to be higher than 20 percent?

Interest Rates and Present Value

Businesses make investments in which they often incur large costs today but don't make any profits until some time in the future. Somehow they have to be able to compare their investment cost today with a stream of future profits. How can they relate present cost to future benefits?

Interest rates are used to link the present with the future. After all, if you have to pay $105 at the end of the year when you borrow $100, that 5 percent interest rate gives you a measure of the premium on the earlier availability of goods and services. If you want to have things today, you have to pay the 5 percent interest rate in order to have current purchasing power.

The question could be put this way: What is the present value (the value today) of $105 that you could receive one year from now? That depends on the market rate of interest, or the rate of interest that you could earn in some appropriate savings institution, such as in a savings account. To make the arithmetic simple, let's assume that the rate of interest is 5 percent. Now you can figure out the **present value** of $105 to be received one year from now. You figure it out by asking, What sum must I put aside today at the market interest rate of 5 percent to receive $105 one year from now? Mathematically, we represent this equation as

$$(1 + 0.05)PV_1 = \$105$$

where PV_1 is the sum that you must set aside now.

Let's solve this simple equation to obtain PV_1:

$$PV_1 = \frac{\$105}{1.05} = \$100$$

That is, $100 will accumulate to $105 at the end of one year with a market rate of interest of 5 percent. Thus, the present value of $105 one year from now, using a rate of interest of 5 percent, is $100. The formula for present value of any sums to be received one year from now thus becomes

$$PV_1 = \frac{FV_1}{1 + i}$$

where

PV_1 = present value of a sum one year hence
FV_1 = future sum paid or received one year hence
i = market rate of interest

PRESENT VALUES FOR MORE DISTANT PERIODS The present-value formula for figuring out today's worth of dollars to be received at a future date can now be determined. How much would have to be put in the same savings account today to have $105 *two years* from now if the account pays a rate of 5 percent per year compounded annually?

After one year, the sum that would have to be set aside, which we will call PV_2, would have grown to $PV_2 \times 1.05$. This amount during the second year would increase to $PV_2 \times 1.05 \times 1.05$, or $PV_2 \times (1.05)^2$. To find the PV_2 that would grow to $105 over two years, let

$$PV_2 \times (1.05)^2 = \$105$$

and solve for PV_2:

$$PV_2 = \frac{\$105}{(1.05)^2} = \$95.24$$

Thus, the present value of $105 to be paid or received two years hence, discounted at an interest rate of 5 percent per year compounded annually, is equal to $95.24. In other words, $95.24 put into a savings account yielding 5 percent per year compounded interest would accumulate to $105 in two years.

Present value

The value of a future amount expressed in today's dollars; the most that someone would pay today to receive a certain sum at some point in the future.

Go to www.econtoday.com/chapter22 to utilize an MFM Communication Software, Inc., manual providing additional review of present value.

You Are There

To consider what a difference the rate of interest makes in present-value calculations involving sums to be received far into the future, contemplate **In a Cold Twist, a Millionaire Bequeaths His Wealth to Himself,** on pages 575 and 576.

TABLE 22-3

Present Value of a Future Dollar

This table shows how much a dollar received at the end of a certain number of years in the future is worth today. For example, at 5 percent a year, a dollar to be received 20 years in the future is worth 37.7 cents; if received in 50 years, it isn't even worth a dime today. To find out how much $10,000 would be worth a certain number of years from now, just multiply the figures in the table by 10,000. For example, $10,000 received at the end of 10 years discounted at a 5 percent rate of interest would have a present value of $6,140.

	Discounted Present Values of $1				
Year	3%	5%	8%	10%	20%
1	.971	.952	.926	.909	.833
2	.943	.907	.857	.826	.694
3	.915	.864	.794	.751	.578
4	.889	.823	.735	.683	.482
5	.863	.784	.681	.620	.402
6	.838	.746	.630	.564	.335
7	.813	.711	.583	.513	.279
8	.789	.677	.540	.466	.233
9	.766	.645	.500	.424	.194
10	.744	.614	.463	.385	.162
15	.642	.481	.315	.239	.0649
20	.554	.377	.215	.148	.0261
25	.478	.295	.146	.0923	.0105
30	.412	.231	.0994	.0573	.00421
40	.307	.142	.0460	.0221	.000680
50	.228	.087	.0213	.00852	.000109

Discounting
The method by which the present value of a future sum or a future stream of sums is obtained.

Rate of discount
The rate of interest used to discount future sums back to present value.

THE GENERAL FORMULA FOR DISCOUNTING   The general formula for **discounting** becomes

$$PV_t = \frac{FV_t}{(1 + i)^t}$$

where t refers to the number of periods in the future the money is to be paid or received.

Table 22-3 gives the present value of $1 to be received in future years at various interest rates. The interest rate used to derive the present value is called the **rate of discount.**

Why is General Motors Corporation installing virtual diagnostic components in many of its vehicles?

E-COMMERCE EXAMPLE
At GM, a Wireless Mechanic Helps Cut the Present Value of Future Warranty Costs

OnStar, a wireless satellite service, is a subsidiary of General Motors. The service appeals to owners of GM vehicles because it can open a car door when the owner is locked out and notify an ambulance when a vehicle's air bag deploys. Initially, OnStar charged about $17 per month for providing these and other services. Recently, GM has reduced this fee to induce more vehicle owners to utilize another feature: more than 1,600 diagnostic checks of a vehicle's operations that OnStar can process remotely. When OnStar identifies a problem in a vehicle, such as a minor malfunction in an electronic ventilation system, it automatically transmits an e-mail notification to the vehicle's owner. If the owner responds by taking the vehicle to a dealer for service, GM often benefits by incurring lower expenses for providing warranty services. Repairing such a small problem at an early stage is typically much less costly to GM than addressing it after it becomes a major malfunction. GM managers hope that a slight cut in OnStar's monthly fee today will induce more owners to utilize the service, thereby enabling the company to realize a significant present-value reduction in future warranty service costs.

FOR CRITICAL ANALYSIS
If the interest rate decreases, does GM have a larger or smaller incentive to cut the monthly fee for its OnStar service?

QUICK QUIZ *See page 582 for the answers. Review concepts from this section in MyEconLab.*

Interest is the price of obtaining credit. In the credit market, the rate of interest paid depends on the _____ of the loan, the _____, and the handling charges, among other things.

Nominal interest rates include a factor to take account of the _____ rate of inflation. Therefore, during periods of high _____ inflation, nominal interest rates will be relatively high.

Payments received or costs incurred in the future are worth less than those received or incurred today. The _____ _____ of any future sum is lower the farther it occurs in the future and the greater the discount rate used.

Corporate Financing Methods

When the Dutch East India Company was founded in 1602, it raised financial capital by selling shares of its expected future profits to investors. The investors thus became the owners of the company, and their ownership shares eventually became known as "shares of stock," or simply *stocks*. The company also issued notes of indebtedness, which involved borrowing funds in return for interest paid on the funds, plus eventual repayment of the principal amount borrowed. In modern parlance, these notes of indebtedness are called *bonds*. As the company prospered over time, some of its revenues were used to pay lenders the interest and principal owed them; of the profits that remained, some were paid to shareholders in the form of dividends, and some were retained by the company for reinvestment in further enterprises. The methods of financing used by the Dutch East India Company four centuries ago—stocks, bonds, and reinvestment—remain the principal methods of financing for today's corporations.

Stocks

Share of stock
A legal claim to a share of a corporation's future profits. If it is *common stock*, it incorporates certain voting rights regarding major policy decisions of the corporation. If it is *preferred stock*, its owners are accorded preferential treatment in the payment of dividends but do not have any voting rights.

A **share of stock** in a corporation is simply a legal claim to a share of the corporation's future profits. If there are 100,000 shares of stock in a company and you own 1,000 of them, you own the right to 1 percent of that company's future profits. If the stock you own is *common stock*, you also have the right to vote on major policy decisions affecting the company, such as the selection of the corporation's board of directors. Your 1,000 shares would entitle you to cast 1 percent of the votes on such issues.

If the stock you own is *preferred stock*, you own a share of the future profits of the corporation but do *not* have regular voting rights. You do, however, get something in return for giving up your voting rights: preferential treatment in the payment of dividends. Specifically, the owners of preferred stock generally must receive at least a certain amount of dividends in each period before the owners of common stock can receive *any* dividends.

Bonds

Bond
A legal claim against a firm, usually entitling the owner of the bond to receive a fixed annual coupon payment, plus a lump-sum payment at the bond's maturity date. Bonds are issued in return for funds lent to the firm.

A **bond** is a legal claim against a firm, entitling the owner of the bond to receive a fixed annual *coupon* payment, plus a lump-sum payment at the maturity date of the bond. Bonds are issued in return for funds lent to the firm; the coupon payments represent interest on the amount borrowed by the firm, and the lump-sum payment at maturity of the bond generally equals the amount originally borrowed by the firm.

Bonds are *not* claims on the future profits of the firm; legally, bondholders must be paid whether the firm prospers or not. To help ensure this, bondholders generally receive their coupon payments each year, along with any principal that is due, before *any* shareholders can receive dividend payments.

Reinvestment

Reinvestment takes place when the firm uses some of its profits to purchase new capital equipment rather than paying the profits out as dividends to shareholders. Although sales of stock are an important source of financing for new firms, reinvestment and borrowing are the primary means of financing for existing firms. Indeed, reinvestment by established firms is such an important source of financing that it dominates the other two sources of corporate finance, amounting to roughly 75 percent of new financial capital for corporations in recent years. Also, small businesses, which are the source of much current growth, often cannot rely on the stock market to raise investment funds.

Reinvestment
Profits (or depreciation reserves) used to purchase new capital equipment.

The Markets for Stocks and Bonds

Economists often refer to the "market for wheat" or the "market for labor," but these are concepts rather than actual places. For **securities** (stocks and bonds), however, there really are markets—centralized, physical locations where exchange takes place. The most prestigious of these markets are the New York Stock Exchange (NYSE) and the New York Bond Exchange, both located in New York City. More than 2,500 stocks are traded on the NYSE, which is sometimes called the "Big Board." Numerous other stock and bond markets, or exchanges, exist throughout the United States and in various financial capitals of the world, such as London and Tokyo.

Securities
Stocks and bonds.

What function does the New York Stock Exchange serve?

Although the exact process by which exchanges are conducted in these markets varies slightly from one to another, the process used on the NYSE is representative of the principles involved. Essentially, brokers attempt to earn commissions from volumes of shares traded, while dealers attempt to profit from "buying low and selling high."

Even though the NYSE is traditionally the most prestigious of U.S. stock exchanges, it is no longer the largest. Since the mid-2000s, this title has belonged to the National Association of Securities Dealers Automated Quotations (Nasdaq), which began in 1971 as a tiny electronic network linking about 100 securities firms. Today, the Nasdaq market links about 500 dealers, and Nasdaq is home to nearly 4,000 stocks, including those of such companies as Microsoft, Intel, and Cisco.

The Theory of Efficient Markets

At any point in time, there are tens of thousands, even millions, of persons looking for any bit of information that will enable them to forecast correctly the future prices of stocks. Responding to any information that seems useful, these people try to buy low and sell high. The result is that all publicly available information that might be used to forecast stock prices gets taken into account by those with access to the information and the knowledge and ability to learn from it, leaving no predictable profit opportunities. And because so many people are involved in this process, it occurs quite swiftly. Indeed, there is some evidence that *all* information entering the market is fully incorporated into stock prices within less than a minute of its arrival. One view is that any information about specific stocks will prove to have little value by the time it reaches you.

Consequently, stock prices tend to drift upward following a *random walk*, which is to say that the best forecast of tomorrow's price is today's price plus the effect of any upward drift. This is called the **random walk theory.** Although large values of the random component of stock price changes are less likely than small values, nothing else about the magnitude or direction of a stock price change can be predicted. Indeed,

Random walk theory
The theory that there are no predictable trends in securities prices that can be used to "get rich quick."

the random component of stock prices exhibits behavior much like what would occur if you rolled two dice and subtracted 7 from the resulting total. On average, the dice will show a total of 7, so after you subtract 7, the average result will be zero. It is true that rolling a 12 or a 2 (resulting in a total of + 5 or −5) is less likely than rolling an 8 or a 6 (yielding a total of +1 or −1). Nevertheless, positive and negative totals are equally likely, and the expected total is zero.

Why are doubts about whether markets utilize information as the efficient markets hypothesis implies important to a number of people currently serving prison terms?

EXAMPLE
Efficient Markets or Adaptive Markets?

In 1988, the U.S. Supreme Court endorsed a legal theory known as "fraud on the market," which in turn is based on the efficient markets hypothesis. The Supreme Court ruled that because the efficient markets hypothesis indicates that market prices reflect all available information, misleading statements affect the share price that investors use to assess a company's value. Thus, the Supreme Court decided, misleading statements about a firm's condition defraud those who buy the firm's stock even if they do not rely directly on such statements—indeed, even if they are not even aware of them. Under this reasoning, a number of corporate officers have been sentenced to prison terms ranging from several months to more than 20 years.

According to some behavioral economists, the Supreme Court may have relied on faulty economics. In place of the efficient markets hypothesis, they propose an *adaptive markets hypothesis*. They note that there is evidence that traders are guided by emotion and thus use trial and error to develop rules of thumb to guide their purchases and sales. If correct, the adaptive markets hypothesis implies that markets do not efficiently process information. Thus, movements in stock prices following the release of misleading statements may not actually reflect the information in such statements. Naturally, some convicted corporate managers are basing their legal appeals on this alternative theory of how stock prices are determined.

FOR CRITICAL ANALYSIS
Why might proponents of the efficient markets hypothesis contend that even traders influenced by emotion still respond fully to all available market information? (Hint: The efficient markets hypothesis relies on the assumption that traders behave as if *they are rational, not a claim that they behave like emotionless robots.)*

Inside Information

Inside information
Information that is not available to the general public about what is happening in a corporation.

Isn't there any way to "beat the market"? The answer is yes—but normally only if you have **inside information** that is not available to the public. Suppose that your best friend is in charge of new product development at the world's largest software firm, Microsoft Corporation. Your friend tells you that the company's smartest programmer has just come up with major new software that millions of computer users will want to buy. No one but your friend and the programmer—and now you—is aware of this. You could indeed make a killing using this information by purchasing shares of Microsoft and then selling them (at a higher price) as soon as the new product is publicly announced. There is one problem: Stock trading based on inside information such as this is illegal, punishable by substantial fines and even imprisonment. So, unless you happen to have a stronger-than-average desire for a long vacation in a federal prison, you might be better off investing in Microsoft after the new program is publicly announced.

Go to www.econtoday.com/chapter22 to explore how the U.S. Securities and Exchange Commission seeks to prevent the use of inside information.

It is, of course, possible for people to influence stock or bond prices through the accidental release of inside information. For instance, when the U.S. Treasury decided it would discontinue issuing 30-year bonds, it chose to announce its decision on October 31, 2001. Treasury officials told the media that the information of the bond's demise would be public as of 10 AM. Nevertheless, as a courtesy officials informed reporters in advance in an impromptu 9 AM meeting so that the reporters would have time to write stories to release at the later hour. Officials failed to check the credentials of everyone who attended the meeting, however, and one of those individuals was a financial consultant who did not understand that this early news of the bond's end was "embargoed" until 10 AM. After the news conference ended just before 9:30 AM, the consultant called some of his clients and told them of the media announcement. Within a very few minutes, word of the Treasury's plans had spread widely. Ten minutes before the Treasury's formal announcement, 30-year bond prices rose in response to higher demand for existing bonds.

QUICK QUIZ   See page 582 for the answers. Review concepts from this section in MyEconLab.

The three primary sources of corporate funds are _____, _____, and _____ of profits.

A **share of stock** is a share of _____ providing a legal claim to a corporation's future profits. A _____ is a legal claim entitling the owner to a fixed annual coupon payment and to a lump-sum payment on the date it matures.

Many economists believe that asset markets, especially the stock market, are _____, meaning that one cannot make a higher-than-normal rate of return without having inside information (information that the general public does not possess). Stock prices normally drift upward following a _____ _____, meaning that you cannot predict changes in future stock prices based on information about stock price behavior in the past.

You Are There ▶ In a Cold Twist, a Millionaire Bequeaths His Wealth to Himself

David Pizer, the operator of a resort in Arizona, plans to hold onto his wealth following his death—literally. When the end of his life arrives, his body will be added to the more than 150 bodies (or, in some cases, heads only) held in cold storage at two U.S. cryonics facilities.

Pizer anticipates that future technological developments will enable medical scientists to remove his body from cold storage and reanimate it hundreds or perhaps even thousands of years from now. Thus, he has taken advantage of a legal arrangement known as a *dynasty trust*. Normally, such trusts shield assets from estate taxes by making payments to children, grandchildren, and subsequent generations. Instead, Pizer has structured a dynasty trust that will make payments to him whenever the time might arrive that medical scientists are able to bring him back to life.

Pizer's dynasty trust will manage roughly $10 million in wealth that he anticipates he will have accumulated by the time of his death. He speculates that with these funds earning interest while he is frozen, he could wake up in 100 years the "richest man in the world." Of course, even if his optimism about future advances in medical science turns out to be well placed, much depends on the average rate of interest earned by his dynasty trust. At an annual interest rate of 5 percent, $10 million is the present value of about $1,315 million to be received 100 years from now. Hence, at a 5 percent annual interest rate, Pizer could anticipate reawakening with more than $1.3 billion in wealth. In contrast, at an annual interest rate of 8 percent, $10 million is the present value of about $21,998 million to be received in 100 years. Thus, if this higher interest rate were to prevail for a century, Pizer would have about $22 billion in wealth when he awakened. This is still less than half of Bill Gates's current wealth, however.

You Are There (cont.)

CRITICAL ANALYSIS QUESTIONS

1. Why does Pizer's present value of $10 million translate into such widely varying future sums a century hence depending on the assumed annual interest rate?

2. Based on Table 22-3 on page 571, if Pizer is "reanimated" 50 years after his death and finds that his dynasty trust is worth "only" $43.86 million, what rate of interest must have prevailed over the 50-year interval?

How Musicians Increasingly Rely on Stocks and Bonds

Issues and Applications

CONCEPTS APPLIED

➤ Markets for Stocks and Bonds

➤ Securities

➤ Discounted Present Value

Some musicians take courses in economics. A few, such as Mick Jagger of the Rolling Stones, even allocate time to serious study of the subject. Nevertheless, many musicians choose to concentrate almost exclusively on becoming more proficient at playing or singing. Perhaps these musicians should change their tune, however, because professional musicians increasingly are issuing stocks and bonds to finance their activities.

Raising Funds for the Instrument

What if you are a classical music performer and desire one of the best string instruments—say, a 1712 Guarneri *filius Andreae* cello or a Stradivarius violin in mint condition—for the sound that will propel you into the best concert halls? If so, you face a fundamental complication: such instruments fetch auction prices that can exceed $3 million.

One possible solution is to follow the path of a growing number of classical performers by selling shares in one of these string instruments. Since 1970, such instruments have seen price increases more than 200 percent higher than the average increase in the prices of shares trading in U.S. stock markets. Indeed, prices of the very best instruments have more than tripled during the past 15 years. Thus, it is usually not difficult to line up investors willing to purchase shares in instruments—though some contracts also require the artist using the instrument to present private performances for the investors.

Selling Shares in the Band

Challenges in financing musical endeavors are not limited to classical musicians. Rock bands trying to get a start in the recording industry often struggle to raise sufficient funds to pay a producer and marketing representative and to cover the cost of manufacturing their first few thousand CDs.

The German company SellaBand coordinates start-up funding efforts for more than 250 fledgling rock bands. Fans—or simply interested investors—can buy shares in promising bands online for $10 apiece. After a band raises $50,000, SellaBand arranges production, marketing, and CD manufacturing. Revenues from CD sales and advertising on SellaBand are then shared by the company, members of the band, and the investors.

Issuing Bonds Backed by Music Royalties

What about the artist who has already had a big career touring the world's top concert halls and stadiums and a stream of top 40 hits but who now wishes to obtain extra funds to settle down into a calmer lifestyle? One approach might be to follow the example of rock musician David Bowie, who in 1997 raised $55 million by issuing securities with returns derived from the stream of revenues generated by continuing sales of his albums. Other artists, such as Ashford & Simpson, (the late) James Brown, and the Isley Brothers, issued similar bonds, which are called "Bowie bonds" in honor of the first issuer of music-revenue-backed securities.

In the early 2000s, market clearing prices of Bowie bonds dropped considerably when the recording industry experienced an extended downturn. Prices have recovered in recent years with the growth of iTunes and other online digital-download platforms, which promise to boost earnings of royalties on recorded music. The growing use of recorded music for cellphone "rings" has also helped boost Bowie bond prices. Every song downloaded for this purpose generates more than 8 cents in royalties for the song's owner—and hence boosts the stream of revenues for owners of the bonds.

Test your understanding of this chapter by going online to **MyEconLab**.
In the Study Plan for this chapter, select Section N: News.

For Critical Analysis

1. Why might shares in a cello or a violin be less liquid than shares of stock in a major U.S. corporation?

2. How would the market value of the first Bowie bonds likely respond if David Bowie were to experience a comeback as a performer for a new generation of rock fans?

Web Resources

1. For a description of Bowie bonds, use the link available at www.econtoday.com/chapter22.

2. To learn more about SellaBand, go to www.econtoday.com/chapter22.

Research Project

Evaluate whether the theory of efficient markets would likely apply to shares of stock in cellos, violins, or rock bands, just as it is hypothesized to apply to ownership shares in companies. If so, how should stock prices vary over time? If not, why not?

WHAT YOU SHOULD KNOW

WHERE TO GO TO PRACTICE

Economic Rent and Resource Allocation Owners of a resource in fixed supply, meaning that the resource supply curve is perfectly inelastic, are paid economic rent. Originally, this term was used to refer to payment for the use of land or any other natural resource that is considered to be in fixed supply. More generally, however, economic rent is a payment for the use of any resource that exceeds the opportunity cost of the resource. The economic rents received by the owners of such a resource reflect the maximum market valuation of the resource's value. Thus, economic rent allocates resources to their highest-valued use.

economic rent, 559

KEY FIGURE
Figure 22-1, 560

- **MyEconLab** Study Plan 22.1
- Audio introduction to Chapter 22
- Animated Figure 22-1
- Video: Economic Rent and the Allocation of Resources

The Main Organizational Forms of Business and the Chief Advantages and Disadvantages of Each The primary organizational forms businesses take are the proprietorship, the partnership, and the corporation. The proprietorship is owned by a single person, who makes the business decisions, is entitled to all the profits, and is subject to unlimited liability. The partnership has two or more owners, who share the responsibility for decision making, share the firm's profits, and individually bear unlimited liability for the firm's debts. The corporation differs from proprietorships and partnerships in three important dimensions. Owners of corporations enjoy limited liability, so their responsibility for the debts of the corporation is limited to the value of their ownership shares. In addition, the income from corporations is subject to double taxation—corporate taxation when income is earned by the corporation and personal taxation when after-tax profits are paid as dividends to the owners. Finally, corporations do not legally cease to exist due to a change of ownership or the death of an owner.

firm, 561
proprietorship, 562
unlimited liability, 563
partnership, 563
corporation, 563
limited liability, 563
dividends, 564

- **MyEconLab** Study Plan 22.2
- Video: The Goal of the Firm Is Profit Maximization

Accounting Profits versus Economic Profits A firm's accounting profits equal its total revenues minus its total explicit costs, which are expenses directly paid out by the firm. Economic profits equal accounting profits minus implicit costs, which are expenses that managers do not have to pay out of pocket, such as the opportunity cost of factors of production dedicated to the firm's production process. Owners of a firm seek to maximize the firm's economic profits to ensure that they earn at least a normal rate of return, meaning that the firm's total revenues at least cover explicit costs and implicit opportunity costs.

explicit costs, 564
accounting profit, 564
implicit costs, 565
normal rate of return, 565
opportunity cost of capital, 565
economic profits, 566

KEY FIGURE
Figure 22-2, 566

- **MyEconLab** Study Plan 22.2
- Animated Figure 22-2
- Video: The Goal of the Firm Is Profit Maximization

(continued)

(continued)

WHAT YOU SHOULD KNOW		WHERE TO GO TO PRACTICE
Interest Rates Interest is a payment for the ability to use resources today instead of in the future. Factors that influence interest rates are the length of the term of a loan, the loan's risk, and handling charges. The nominal interest rate includes a factor that takes into account the anticipated inflation rate, so during periods of high anticipated inflation, current market (nominal) interest rates are high. Comparing the market interest rate with the rate of return on prospective capital investment projects enables owners of funds to determine the highest-valued uses of the funds. Thus, the interest rate allocates funds to industries whose investments yield the highest (risk-adjusted) returns, and available resources are put to their most productive uses.	financial capital, 568 interest, 568 nominal rate of interest, 568 real rate of interest, 569	• **MyEconLab** Study Plan 22.3 • Video: Interest Rates and Present Value
Calculating the Present Discounted Value of a Payment to Be Received at a Future Date The present value of a future payment is the value of the future amount expressed in today's dollars, and it is equal to the most that someone would pay today to receive that amount in the future. The method by which the present value of a future sum is calculated is called *discounting*. This method implies that the present value of a sum to be received a year from now is equal to the future amount divided by 1 plus the appropriate rate of interest, which is called the *rate of discount*.	present value, 570 discounting, 571 rate of discount, 571	• **MyEconLab** Study Plan 22.3 • Video: Interest Rates and Present Value
The Three Main Sources of Corporate Funds The main sources of financial capital for corporations are stocks, bonds, and reinvestment of profits. Stocks are ownership shares, promising a share of profits, sold to investors. Common stocks also embody voting rights regarding the major decisions of the firm; preferred stocks typically have no voting rights but enjoy priority status in the payment of dividends. Bonds are notes of indebtedness, issued in return for the loan of funds. They typically promise to pay interest in the form of annual coupon payments, plus repayment of the original principal amount upon maturity. Bondholders are generally promised payment before any payment of dividends to shareholders, and for this reason bonds are less risky than stocks. Reinvestment involves the purchase of assets by the firm, using retained profits or depreciation reserves it has set aside for this purpose. No new stocks or bonds are issued in the course of reinvestment, although the firm's value is fully reflected in the price of existing shares of stock.	share of stock, 572 bond, 572 reinvestment, 573 securities, 573 random walk theory, 573 inside information, 574	• **MyEconLab** Study Plans 22.4, 22.5 • Video: The Theory of Efficient Markets and Inside Information

Log in to MyEconLab, take a chapter test, and get a personalized Study Plan that tells you which concepts you understand and which ones you need to review. From there, MyEconLab will give you further practice, tutorials, animations, videos, and guided solutions.
Log in to www.myeconlab.com

PROBLEMS

All problems are assignable in **myeconlab** *. Answers to odd-numbered problems appear at the back of the book.*

22-1. Which of the following individuals would you expect to have a high level of economic rent, and which would you expect to have a low level of economic rent? Explain why for each.

    a. Bob has a highly specialized medical skill shared by very few individuals.

    b. Sally has never attended school. She is 25 years old and is an internationally known supermodel.

    c. Tim is a high school teacher and sells insurance part time.

22-2. Though he has retired as a professional football receiver, Jerry Rice still earns a sizable annual income from endorsements that advertisers view as closely tied to his "persona." Explain why, in economic terms, Rice's level of economic rent is so high.

22-3. Former professional basketball star Michael Jordan once left basketball to play baseball. As a result, his annual dollar income dropped from the millions to the thousands. Eventually, Jordan quit baseball and returned to basketball. What role did economic rents likely play in influencing his decision?

22-4. A British pharmaceutical company spent several years and considerable funds on the development of a treatment for HIV patients. Now, with the protection afforded by patent rights, the company has the potential to reap enormous gains. The government, in response, has threatened to tax away any rents the company may earn. Is this an advisable policy? Why or why not? (Hint: Contrast the short-run and long-run effects of taxing away the economic rents.)

22-5. Write a brief explanation of the differences among a sole proprietorship, a partnership, and a corporation. In addition, list one advantage and one disadvantage of a proprietorship, a partnership, and a corporation.

22-6. After graduation, you face a choice. One option is to work for a multinational consulting firm and earn a starting salary (benefits included) of $40,000. The other option is to use $5,000 in savings to start your own consulting firm. You could earn an interest return of 5 percent on your savings. You choose to start your own consulting firm. At the end of the first year, you add up all of your expenses and revenues. Your total includes $12,000 in rent, $1,000 in office supplies, $20,000 for office staff, and $4,000 in telephone expenses. What are your total explicit costs and total implicit costs?

22-7. Suppose, as in Problem 22-6, that you have now operated your consulting firm for a year. At the end of the first year, your total revenues are $77,250. Based on the information in Problem 22-6, what is the accounting profit, and what is your economic profit?

22-8. An individual leaves a college faculty, where she was earning $40,000 a year, to begin a new venture. She invests her savings of $10,000, which were earning 10 percent annually. She then spends $20,000 renting office equipment, hires two students at $30,000 a year each, rents office space for $12,000, and has other variable expenses of $40,000. At the end of the year, her revenues are $200,000. What are her accounting profit and her economic profit for the year?

22-9. Classify the following items as either financial capital or physical capital.

    a. A computer server owned by an information-processing company

    b. $100,000 set aside in an account to purchase a computer server

    c. Funds raised through a bond offer to expand plant and equipment

    d. A warehouse owned by a shipping company

22-10. Explain the difference between the dividends of a corporation and the profits of a proprietorship or partnership, particularly in their tax treatment.

22-11. The owner of WebCity is trying to decide whether to remain a proprietorship or to incorporate. Suppose that the corporate tax rate on profits is 20 percent and the personal income tax rate is 30 percent. For simplicity, assume that all corporate profits (after corporate taxes are paid) are distributed as dividends in the year they are earned and that such dividends are subject to tax at the personal income tax rate.

a. If the owner of WebCity expects to earn $100,000 in before-tax profits this year, regardless of whether the firm is a proprietorship or a corporation, which method of organization should be chosen?

b. What is the dollar value of the after-tax advantage of the form of organization determined in part (a)?

c. Suppose that the corporate form of organization has cost advantages that will raise before-tax profits by $50,000. Should the owner of WebCity incorporate?

d. By how much will after-tax profits change due to incorporation?

e. Suppose that tax policy is changed to completely exempt from personal taxation the first $40,000 per year in dividends. Would this change in policy affect the decision made in part (a)?

f. How can you explain the fact that even though corporate profits are subject to double taxation, most business in the United States is conducted by corporations rather than by proprietorships or partnerships?

22-12. Explain how the following events would likely affect the relevant interest rate.

a. A major bond-rating agency has improved the risk rating of a developing nation.

b. To regulate and to protect the public, the government has passed legislation that requires a considerable increase in the reporting paperwork when a bank makes a loan.

22-13. Suppose that the interest rate in Japan is only 2 percent, while the comparable rate in the United States is 4 percent. Japan's rate of inflation is 0.5 percent, while the U.S. inflation rate is 3 percent. Which economy has the higher real interest rate?

22-14. You expect to receive a payment of $104 one year from now.

a. Your discount rate is 4 percent. What is the present value of the payment to be received?

b. Suppose that your discount rate rises to 5 percent. What is the present value of the payment to be received?

22-15. Outline the differences between common stock and preferred stock.

22-16. Explain the basic differences between a share of stock and a bond.

22-17. Suppose that one of your classmates informs you that he has developed a method of forecasting stock market returns based on past trends. With a monetary investment by you, he claims that the two of you could profit handsomely from this forecasting method. How should you respond to your classmate?

22-18. Suppose that you are trying to decide whether to spend $1,000 on stocks issued by WildWeb or on bonds issued by the same company. There is a 50 percent chance that the value of the stock will rise to $2,200 at the end of the year and a 50 percent chance that the stock will be worthless at the end of the year. The bonds promise an interest rate of 20 percent per year, and it is certain that the bonds and interest will be repaid at the end of the year.

a. Assuming that your time horizon is exactly one year, will you choose the stocks or the bonds?

b. By how much is your expected end-of-year wealth reduced if you make the wrong choice?

c. Suppose the odds of success improve for WildWeb: Now there is a 60 percent chance that the value of the stock will be $2,200 at year's end and only a 40 percent chance that it will be worthless. Should you now choose the stocks or the bonds?

d. By how much did your expected end-of-year wealth rise as a result of the improved outlook for WildWeb?

ECONOMICS ON THE NET

How the New York Stock Exchange Operates This application gives you the chance to learn about how the New York Stock Exchange functions.

Title: The New York Stock Exchange: How a Stock Is Bought and Sold

Navigation: Follow the link at **www.econtoday.com/ chapter22** to visit the New York Stock Exchange. Click "About us" in the left margin for a pop-up menu, and then click on *Education*. Select the tab named *Educational Materials*. Under "Publications for Investors," click on *How a Stock Is Bought and Sold*. Read the article.

Application Answer the following questions.

1. Why might companies contemplating issuing stock value the relatively low costs of trading shares on the New York Stock Exchange?

2. Why might people who buy and sell stocks value the relatively faster speeds of trade execution that the NYSE has achieved in recent years?

For Group Study and Analysis Go back up to "Publications for Investors," click on *NYSE Indexes*, and read the article. Divide the class into groups, and assign each group to examine one of the six NYSE indexes discussed in the article. Ask each group to evaluate how stock traders might use the specific index as a "benchmark" when evaluating whether to buy or sell stocks.

ANSWERS TO QUICK QUIZZES

p. 561: (i) inelastic; (ii) allocates . . . highest

p. 567: (i) Proprietorships . . . unlimited; (ii) Partnerships . . . unlimited; (iii) shareholders . . . limited; (iv) opportunity; (v) greater . . . maximize

p. 572: (i) length . . . risk; (ii) anticipated . . . anticipated; (iii) present value

p. 575: (i) stocks . . . bonds . . . reinvestment; (ii) ownership . . . bond; (iii) efficient . . . random walk

The Firm: Cost and Output Determination

23

Y ou report to your first appointment with a new family physician whom a friend has recommended highly. On the way, you remember that when you called to make the appointment, the physician herself answered and set the appointment time. Now that you have arrived, you are surprised to find no waiting room, no receptionist or nurses, and no large suite of offices. Instead, the physician herself greets you and asks you to enter her small but comfortable office. What you are encountering is the latest trend in family medicine, called the "micropractice." This scenario is increasingly relevant in light of an altered cost structure in the provision of family medical services. In this chapter, you will learn why, for family physicians at least, it now pays to think small when it comes to operating a medical practice.

LEARNING OBJECTIVES

myeconlab

MyEconLab helps you master each objective and study more efficiently. See end of chapter for details.

After reading this chapter, you should be able to:

- Discuss the difference between the short run and the long run from the perspective of a firm

- Understand why the marginal physical product of labor eventually declines as more units of labor are employed

- Explain the short-run cost curves a typical firm faces

- Describe the long-run cost curves a typical firm faces

- Identify situations of economies and diseconomies of scale and define a firm's minimum efficient scale

? **DID YOU KNOW THAT** since 1997, openings of new U.S. manufacturing facilities as a percentage of existing factories have declined from more than 3.5 percent per year to about 2.5 percent per year? During the same period, U.S. companies have closed about 3.5 percent of existing factories each year. On net, therefore, the number of U.S. manufacturing facilities has shrunk by about 1 percent per year since 1997. Some politicians have worried that this negative growth rate in the number of factories suggests a decline in U.S. manufacturing capabilities. Many economists, however, point out that another trend since the late 1990s has been toward *larger* U.S. manufacturing facilities. Thus, even as the overall number of factories has declined, the scale of production of the average plant has increased.

How does a company determine the scale of its production? To find the answer to this question, we must consider how firms employ inputs in the production of goods and services. We must also consider the nature of the costs that firms incur in their productive endeavors. First, however, we must think about alternative time horizons over which firms make decisions regarding their costly productive activities.

Short Run versus Long Run

In Chapter 20, we discussed short-run and long-run price elasticities of supply and demand. As you will recall, for consumers, the long run means the time period during which all adjustments to a change in price can be made, and anything shorter than that is considered the short run. For suppliers, the long run is the time in which all adjustments can be made, and anything shorter than that is the short run.

Now that we are discussing firms only, we will maintain a similar distinction between the short and the long run, but we will be more specific. In the theory of the firm, the **short run** is defined as any time period that is so short that there is at least one input, such as current **plant size,** that the firm cannot alter. In other words, during the short run, a firm makes do with whatever big machines and factory size it already has, no matter how much more it wants to produce because of increased demand for its product. We consider the plant and heavy equipment, the size or amount of which cannot be varied in the short run, as fixed resources. In agriculture and in some other businesses, land may be a fixed resource.

There are, of course, variable resources that the firm can alter when it wants to change its rate of production. These are called *variable inputs* or *variable factors of production.* Typically, the variable inputs of a firm are its labor and its purchases of raw materials. In the short run, in response to changes in demand, the firm can, by definition, change only the amounts of its variable inputs.

The **long run** can now be considered the period of time in which *all* inputs can be varied. Specifically, in the long run, the firm can alter its plant size. How long is the long run? That depends on each individual industry. For Wendy's or McDonald's, the long run may be four or five months, because that is the time it takes to add new franchises. For a steel company, the long run may be several years, because that's how long it takes to plan and build a new plant. An electric utility might need more than a decade to build a new plant, as another example.

Short run and *long run* in our discussion are terms that apply to planning decisions made by managers. Managers routinely take account of both the short-run and the long-run consequences of their behavior. While always making decisions about what to do today, tomorrow, and next week—the short run as it were—they keep an eye on the long-run net benefits of all short-run actions. As an individual, you have long-run plans, such as going to graduate school or on vacation, and you make a series of short-run decisions with these long-run plans in mind.

Short run
The time period during which at least one input, such as plant size, cannot be changed.

Plant size
The physical size of the factories that a firm owns and operates to produce its output. Plant size can be defined by square footage, maximum physical capacity, and other physical measures.

Long run
The time period during which all factors of production can be varied.

The Relationship Between Output and Inputs

A firm takes numerous inputs, combines them using a technological production process, and ends up with an output. There are, of course, a great many factors of production, or inputs. Keeping the quantity of land fixed, we classify production inputs into two broad categories—capital and labor. The relationship between output and these two inputs is as follows:

Output per time period = some function of capital and labor inputs

We have used the word *production* but have not defined it. **Production** is any process by which resources are transformed into goods or services. Production includes not only making things but also transporting them, retailing, repackaging them, and so on. Notice that the production relationship tells nothing about the worth or value of the inputs or the output.

Production
Any activity that results in the conversion of resources into products that can be used in consumption.

The Production Function: A Numerical Example

The relationship between maximum physical output and the quantity of capital and labor used in the production process is sometimes called the **production function**. The production function is a technological relationship between inputs and output.

Production function
The relationship between inputs and maximum physical output. A production function is a technological, not an economic, relationship.

PROPERTIES OF THE PRODUCTION FUNCTION The production function specifies the maximum possible output that can be produced with a given amount of inputs. It also specifies the minimum amount of inputs necessary to produce a given level of output. Firms that are inefficient or wasteful in their use of capital and labor will obtain less output than the production function in theory will show. No firm can obtain more output than the production function allows, however. The production function also depends on the technology available to the firm. It follows that an improvement in technology that allows the firm to produce more output with the same amount of inputs (or the same output with fewer inputs) results in a new production function.

How has software that creates three-dimensional images allowed escalator manufacturers to produce the same output with fewer inputs?

E-COMMERCE EXAMPLE
Riding an Escalator to the Outer Edge of a Production Function

Since escalators were first invented back in 1891, figuring out how to put one together has been a highly labor-intensive process. Designers must determine how to mesh more than 4,500 different components. Essentially, developing a production process for an escalator is like assembling an incredibly complex three-dimensional jigsaw puzzle. Until very recently, working through the intricacies of a lower-cost process for escalator design and production took engineers more than one year. Today, the use of three-dimensional software, such as a widely used program called AutoCAD, enables engineers to devise production processes for producing escalators in less than 12 weeks.

FOR CRITICAL ANALYSIS
Why do you suppose that business managers regard the process of developing the best production procedures as a fundamental requirement of operating at a point on a firm's production function?

Panel (a) of Figure 23-1 shows a production function relating maximum output in column 2 to the quantity of labor in column 1. Zero workers per week produce no output. Five workers per week of input produce a total output of 50 computer printers per week. (Ignore for the moment the rest of that panel.) Panel (b) of Figure 23-1 displays this production function. It relates to the short run, because plant size is fixed, and it applies to a single firm.

TOTAL PHYSICAL PRODUCT Panel (b) shows a total physical product curve, or the maximum feasible output when we add successive equal-sized units of labor while holding all other inputs constant. The graph of the production function in panel (b) is not a straight line. It peaks at seven workers per week and then starts to go down.

Average and Marginal Physical Product

Average physical product
Total product divided by the variable input.

Marginal physical product
The physical output that is due to the addition of one more unit of a variable factor of production; the change in total product occurring when a variable input is increased and all other inputs are held constant; also called *marginal product*.

To understand the shape of the total physical product curve, let's examine columns 3 and 4 of panel (a) of Figure 23-1—that is, average and marginal physical products. **Average physical product** is the total product divided by the number of worker-weeks. You can see in column 3 of panel (a) of Figure 23-1 that the average physical product of labor first rises and then steadily falls after two workers are hired.

Marginal means "additional," so the **marginal physical product** of labor is the *change* in total product that occurs when a worker is added to a production process. (The term *physical* here emphasizes the fact that we are measuring in terms of material quantities of goods or tangible amounts of services, not in dollar terms.) The marginal physical product of labor therefore refers to the *change in output caused by a one-unit change in the labor input* as shown in column 4 of panel (a) of Figure 23-1. (Marginal physical product is also referred to as *marginal product*.)

Diminishing Marginal Product

Note that in Figure 23-1, after the second worker is employed, marginal product declines. The concept of diminishing marginal product applies to many situations. If you put a seat belt across your lap, a certain amount of safety is obtained. If you add another seat belt over your shoulder, some additional safety is obtained, but less than when the first belt was secured. When you add a third seat belt over the other shoulder, the amount of *additional* safety obtained is even smaller.

Measuring Diminishing Marginal Product

How do we measure diminishing marginal product? First, we limit the analysis to only one variable factor of production (or input)—let's say the factor is labor. Every other factor of production, such as machines, must be held constant. Only in this way can we calculate the marginal product from using more workers and know when we reach the point of diminishing marginal product.

SPECIALIZATION AND MARGINAL PRODUCT The marginal productivity of labor may increase rapidly at the very beginning. A firm starts with no workers, only machines. The firm then hires one worker, who finds it difficult to get the work

FIGURE 23-1

The Production Function and Marginal Product: A Hypothetical Case

Marginal product is the addition to the total product that results when one additional worker is hired. Thus, in panel (a), the marginal product of the fourth worker is eight computer printers. With four workers, 44 printers are produced, but with three workers, only 36 are produced; the difference is 8. In panel (b), we plot the numbers from columns 1 and 2 of panel (a). In panel (c), we plot the numbers from columns 1 and 4 of panel (a). When we go from 0 to 1, marginal product is 10. When we go from one worker to two workers, marginal product increases to 16. After two workers, marginal product declines, but it is still positive. Total product (output) reaches its peak at seven workers, so after seven workers, marginal product is negative. When we move from seven to eight workers, marginal product becomes −1 printer.

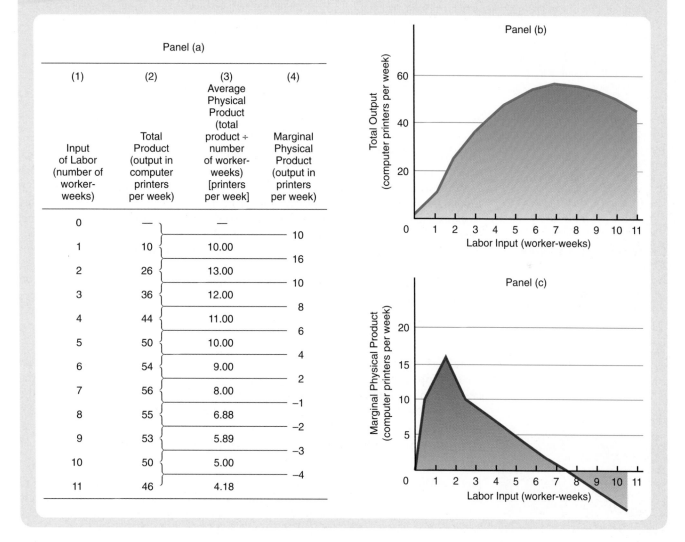

Panel (a)

(1) Input of Labor (number of worker-weeks)	(2) Total Product (output in computer printers per week)	(3) Average Physical Product (total product ÷ number of worker-weeks) [printers per week]	(4) Marginal Physical Product (output in printers per week)
0	—	—	
			10
1	10	10.00	
			16
2	26	13.00	
			10
3	36	12.00	
			8
4	44	11.00	
			6
5	50	10.00	
			4
6	54	9.00	
			2
7	56	8.00	
			−1
8	55	6.88	
			−2
9	53	5.89	
			−3
10	50	5.00	
			−4
11	46	4.18	

started. But when the firm hires more workers, each is able to *specialize* in performing different tasks, and the marginal product of those additional workers may actually be greater than the marginal product of the previous few workers.

Can firms sometimes discover that avoiding *overspecialization* can raise marginal product?

INTERNATIONAL EXAMPLE
A French Handbag Manufacturer Opts for Multitasking

Louis Vuitton, a firm that specializes in producing high-fashion handbags, has long built specialization into its production process. For years, every factory has had about 250 employees, each of whom has specialized in a specific task: cutting leather or canvas; preparing, gluing, or sewing leather or canvas; making pockets; stitching lining; or assembling the final components of a bag. Since the mid-2000s, however, Louis Vuitton has reorganized its production process by slightly reducing specialization of tasks among workers. It has opted for *multitasking*, a production approach first championed by Japanese companies such as Toyota.

With this approach, a worker typically performs two or more tasks. Thus, individual workers at Louis Vuitton now perform multiple tasks, such as gluing, stitching, *and* finishing a pocket flap. The company has found that each worker's marginal product is higher with this system of slightly expanded responsibilities than it was when each worker specialized in a *single* task.

FOR CRITICAL ANALYSIS
What has happened to Louis Vuitton's marginal physical product curve—similar to panel (b) in Figure 23-1?

DIMINISHING MARGINAL PRODUCT Beyond some point, diminishing marginal product must set in—*not* because new workers are less qualified but because each worker has, on average, fewer machines with which to work (remember, all other inputs are fixed). In fact, eventually the firm's plant will become so crowded that workers will start to get in each other's way. At that point, marginal physical product becomes negative, and total production declines.

Using these ideas, we can define the **law of diminishing marginal product:**

Law of diminishing marginal product
The observation that after some point, successive equal-sized increases in a variable factor of production, such as labor, added to fixed factors of production will result in smaller increases in output.

> *As successive equal increases in a variable factor of production are added to fixed factors of production, there will be a point beyond which the extra, or marginal, product that can be attributed to each additional unit of the variable factor of production will decline.*

Note that the law of diminishing marginal product is a statement about the *physical* relationships between inputs and outputs that we have observed in many firms. If the law of diminishing marginal product were not a fairly accurate statement about the world, what would stop firms from hiring additional workers forever?

An Example of the Law of Diminishing Marginal Product

Production of computer printers provides an example of the law of diminishing marginal product. With a fixed amount of factory space, assembly equipment, and quality-control diagnostic software, the addition of more workers eventually yields successively smaller increases in output. After a while, when all the assembly equipment and quality-control diagnostic software are being used, additional workers will have to start assembling and troubleshooting quality problems manually. They obviously won't be as productive as the first workers, who had access to other productive inputs. The marginal physical product of an additional worker, given a specified amount of capital, must eventually be less than that for the previous workers.

GRAPHING THE MARGINAL PRODUCT OF LABOR A hypothetical set of numbers illustrating the law of diminishing marginal product is presented in panel (a) of Figure 23-1 on the previous page. The numbers are presented graphically in panel (c). Marginal

How has Louis Vuitton benefited from less specialization in the production process?

productivity (returns from adding more workers) first increases, then decreases, and finally becomes negative.

When one worker is hired, total output goes from 0 to 10. Thus, marginal physical product is 10 computer printers per week. When the second worker is hired, total product goes from 10 to 26 printers per week. Marginal physical product therefore increases to 16 printers per week. When a third worker is hired, total product again increases, from 26 to 36 printers per week. This represents a marginal physical product of only 10 printers per week. Therefore, the point of diminishing marginal product occurs after two workers are hired.

THE POINT OF SATURATION Notice that after seven workers per week, marginal physical product becomes negative. That means that the hiring of an eighth worker would reduce total product. Sometimes this is called the *point of saturation*, indicating that given the amount of fixed inputs, there is no further positive use for more of the variable input. We have entered the region of negative marginal product.

QUICK QUIZ | *See page 609 for the answers. Review concepts from this section in MyEconLab.*

The technological relationship between output and inputs is called the _____ function. It relates _____ per time period to several inputs, such as capital and labor.

After some rate of output, the firm generally experiences diminishing marginal _____.

The law of diminishing marginal product states that if all factors of production are held constant except one, equal increments in that one variable factor will eventually yield _____ increments in _____.

Short-Run Costs to the Firm

You will see that costs are the extension of the production ideas just presented. Let's consider the costs the firm faces in the short run. To make this example simple, assume that there are only two factors of production, capital and labor. Our definition of the short run will be the time during which capital is fixed but labor is variable.

In the short run, a firm incurs certain types of costs. We label all costs incurred **total costs.** Then we break total costs down into total fixed costs and total variable costs, which we will explain shortly. Therefore,

Total costs
The sum of total fixed costs and total variable costs.

Total costs (TC) = total fixed costs (TFC) + total variable costs (TVC)

Remember that these total costs include both explicit and implicit costs, including the normal rate of return on investment.

After we have looked at the elements of total costs, we will find out how to compute average and marginal costs.

Total Fixed Costs

Let's look at an ongoing business such as Hewlett-Packard (HP). The decision makers in that corporate giant can look around and see big machines, thousands of parts, huge buildings, and a multitude of other components of plant and equipment that have already been bought and are in place. HP has to take into account expenses to replace some worn-out equipment, no matter how many computers it produces. The payments on the loans taken out to buy the equipment will all be exactly the same regardless of the rate of output. The opportunity costs of any land that HP owns will all be exactly the same. In the short run, these costs are more or less the same for HP no matter how many computers it produces.

We also have to point out that the opportunity cost (or normal rate of return) of capital must be included along with other costs. Remember that we are dealing in the short run, during which capital is fixed. If investors in HP have already put $100 million into a factory addition, the opportunity cost of that capital invested is now, in essence, a *fixed cost*. Why? Because in the short run, nothing can be done about that cost; the investment has already been made. This leads us to a very straightforward definition of fixed costs: All costs that do not vary—that is, all costs that do not depend on the rate of production—are called **fixed costs.**

Let's now take as an example the fixed costs incurred by a producer of secure digital (SD) cards, digital storage cards used with digital cameras, laptop computers, and other devices. This firm's total fixed costs will usually include the cost of the rent for its plant and equipment and the insurance it has to pay. We see in panel (a) of Figure 23-2 that total fixed costs per hour are $10. In panel (b), these total fixed costs are represented by the horizontal line at $10 per hour. They are invariant to changes in the daily output of these SD cards—no matter how many are produced, fixed costs will remain at $10 per hour.

Fixed costs
Costs that do not vary with output. Fixed costs typically include such expenses as rent on a building. These costs are fixed for a certain period of time (in the long run, though, they are variable).

Total Variable Costs

Total **variable costs** are costs whose magnitude varies with the rate of production. Wages are an obvious variable cost. The more the firm produces, the more labor it has to hire; therefore, the more wages it has to pay. Parts are another variable cost. To manufacture secure digital cards, for example, microchips must be bought. The more SD cards that are made, the greater the number of chips that must be bought. A portion of the rate of depreciation (wear and tear) on machines that are used in the assembly process can also be considered a variable cost if depreciation depends partly on how long and how intensively the machines are used. Total variable costs are given in column 3 in panel (a) of Figure 23-2. These are translated into the total variable cost curve in panel (b). Notice that the total variable cost curve lies below the total cost curve by the vertical distance of $10. This vertical distance represents, of course, total fixed costs.

Variable costs
Costs that vary with the rate of production. They include wages paid to workers and purchases of materials.

Short-Run Average Cost Curves

In panel (b) of Figure 23-2, we see total costs, total variable costs, and total fixed costs. Now we want to look at average cost. With the average cost concept, we are measuring cost per unit of output. It is a matter of simple arithmetic to figure the averages of these three cost concepts. We can define them as follows:

$$\text{Average total costs (ATC)} = \frac{\text{total costs (TC)}}{\text{output }(Q)}$$

$$\text{Average variable costs (AVC)} = \frac{\text{total variable costs (TVC)}}{\text{output }(Q)}$$

$$\text{Average fixed costs (AFC)} = \frac{\text{total fixed costs (TFC)}}{\text{output }(Q)}$$

FIGURE 23-2

Cost of Production: An Example

In panel (a), the derivations of columns 4 through 9 are given in parentheses in each column heading. For example, column 6, average variable costs, is derived by dividing column 3, total variable costs, by column 1, total output per hour. Note that marginal cost (MC) in panel (c) intersects average variable costs (AVC) at the latter's minimum point. Also, MC intersects average total costs (ATC) at that latter's minimum point. It is a little more difficult to see that MC equals AVC and ATC at their respective minimum points in panel (a) because we are using discrete one-unit changes. You can see, though, that the marginal cost of going from 4 units per hour to 5 units per hour is $2 and increases to $3 when we move to 6 units per hour. Somewhere in between it equals AVC of $2.60, which is in fact the minimum average variable cost. The same analysis holds for ATC, which hits minimum at 7 units per day at $4.28 per unit. MC goes from $4 to $5 and just equals ATC somewhere in between.

Panel (a)

(1) Total Output (Q/hour)	(2) Total Fixed Costs (TFC)	(3) Total Variable Costs (TVC)	(4) Total Costs (TC) (4) = (2) + (3)	(5) Average Fixed Costs (AFC) (5) = (2) ÷ (1)	(6) Average Variable Costs (AVC) (6) = (3) ÷ (1)	(7) Average Total Costs (ATC) (7) = (4) ÷ (1)	(8) Total Costs (TC) (4)	(9) Marginal Cost (MC) $(9) = \dfrac{\text{Change in (8)}}{\text{Change in (1)}}$
0	$10	$ 0	$10	—	—	—	$10	
1	10	5	15	$10.00	$5.00	$15.00	15	$5
2	10	8	18	5.00	4.00	9.00	18	3
3	10	10	20	3.33	3.33	6.67	20	2
4	10	11	21	2.50	2.75	5.25	21	1
5	10	13	23	2.00	2.60	4.60	23	2
6	10	16	26	1.67	2.67	4.33	26	3
7	10	20	30	1.43	2.86	4.28	30	4
8	10	25	35	1.25	3.12	4.38	35	5
9	10	31	41	1.11	3.44	4.56	41	6
10	10	38	48	1.00	3.80	4.80	48	7
11	10	46	56	.91	4.18	5.09	56	8

Panel (b)

Panel (c)

The arithmetic is done in columns 5, 6, and 7 in panel (a) of Figure 23-2 on the preceding page. The numerical results are translated into a graphical format in panel (c). Because total costs (TC) equal variable costs (TVC) plus fixed costs (TFC), the difference between average total costs (ATC) and average variable costs (AVC) will always be identical to average fixed costs (AFC). That means that average total costs and average variable costs move together as output expands.

Now let's see what we can observe about the three average cost curves in Figure 23-2.

Average fixed costs
Total fixed costs divided by the number of units produced.

AVERAGE FIXED COSTS (AFC) **Average fixed costs** continue to fall throughout the output range. In fact, if we were to continue panel (c) of Figure 23-2 farther to the right, we would find that average fixed costs would get closer and closer to the horizontal axis. That is because total fixed costs remain constant. As we divide this fixed number by a larger and larger number of units of output, the resulting AFC becomes smaller and smaller. In business, this is called "spreading the overhead."

Average variable costs
Total variable costs divided by the number of units produced.

AVERAGE VARIABLE COSTS (AVC) We assume a particular form of the curve for **average variable costs.** The form that it takes is U-shaped: First it falls; then it starts to rise. It is possible for the AVC curve to take other shapes in the long run.

Average total costs
Total costs divided by the number of units produced; sometimes called *average per-unit total costs.*

AVERAGE TOTAL COSTS (ATC) This curve has a shape similar to that of the AVC curve. Nevertheless, it falls even more dramatically in the beginning and rises more slowly after it has reached a minimum point. It falls and then rises because **average total costs** are the vertical summation of the AFC curve and the AVC curve. Thus, when AFC and AVC are both falling, ATC must fall too: At some point, however, AVC starts to increase while AFC continues to fall. Once the increase in the AVC curve outweighs the decrease in the AFC curve, the ATC curve will start to increase and will develop a U shape, just like the AVC curve.

Marginal Cost

Marginal costs
The change in total costs due to a one-unit change in production rate.

We have stated repeatedly that the basis of decisions is always on the margin—movement in economics is always determined at the margin. This dictum also holds true within the firm. Firms, according to the analysis we use to predict their behavior, are very concerned with their **marginal costs.** Because the term *marginal* means "additional" or "incremental" (or "decremental," too) here, *marginal costs* refer to costs that result from a one-unit change in the production rate. For example, if the production of 10 secure digital cards per hour costs a firm $48 and the production of 11 of these SD cards costs $56 per hour, the marginal cost of producing 11 rather than 10 SD cards per hour is $8.

Marginal costs can be measured by using the formula

$$\text{Marginal cost} = \frac{\text{change in total cost}}{\text{change in output}}$$

We show the marginal costs of production of SD cards per hour in column 9 of panel (a) in Figure 23-2 on the previous page, computed according to the formula just given. In our example, we have changed output by one unit every time, so the denominator in that particular formula always equals one.

This marginal cost schedule is shown graphically in panel (c) of Figure 23-2 on page 591. Just like average variable costs and average total costs, marginal costs first fall and then rise. The U shape of the marginal cost curve is a result of increasing and then diminishing marginal product. At lower levels of output, the marginal cost curve declines. The reasoning is that as marginal physical product increases with each addition of output, the marginal cost of this last unit of output must fall. Conversely, when diminishing marginal product sets in, marginal physical product decreases (and eventually becomes negative); it follows that the marginal cost must rise when the marginal product begins its decline. These relationships are clearly reflected in the geometry of panels (b) and (c) of Figure 23-2.

In summary:

As long as marginal physical product rises, marginal cost will fall, and when marginal physical product starts to fall (after reaching the point of diminishing marginal product), marginal cost will begin to rise.

The Relationship Between Average and Marginal Costs

Let us now examine the relationship between average costs and marginal costs. There is always a definite relationship between averages and marginals. Consider the example of 10 football players with an average weight of 250 pounds. An eleventh player is added. His weight is 300 pounds. That represents the marginal weight. What happens now to the average weight of the team? It must increase. That is, when the marginal player weighs more than the average, the average must increase. Likewise, if the marginal player weighs less than 250 pounds, the average weight will decrease.

AVERAGE VARIABLE COSTS AND MARGINAL COSTS There is a similar relationship between average variable costs and marginal costs. When marginal costs are less than average costs, the latter must fall. Conversely, when marginal costs are greater than average costs, the latter must rise. When you think about it, the relationship makes sense. The only way average variable costs can fall is if the extra cost of the marginal unit produced is less than the average variable cost of all the preceding units. For example, if the average variable cost for two units of production is $4.00 a unit, the only way for the average variable cost of three units to be less than that of two units is for the variable costs attributable to the last unit—the marginal cost—to be less than the average of the past units. In this particular case, if average variable cost falls to $3.33 a unit, total variable cost for the three units would be three times $3.33, or almost exactly $10.00. Total variable cost for two units is two times $4.00 (average variable cost), or $8.00. The marginal cost is therefore $10.00 minus $8.00, or $2.00, which is less than the average variable cost of $3.33.

A similar type of computation can be carried out for rising average variable costs. The only way average variable costs can rise is if the average variable cost of additional units is more than that for units already produced. But the incremental cost is the marginal cost. In this particular case, the marginal costs have to be higher than the average variable costs.

AVERAGE TOTAL COSTS AND MARGINAL COSTS There is also a relationship between marginal costs and average total costs. Remember that average total cost is equal to total costs divided by the number of units produced. Also remember that marginal cost does not include any fixed costs. Fixed costs are, by definition, fixed and cannot influence marginal costs. Our example can therefore be repeated substituting *average total costs* for *average variable costs*.

These rising and falling relationships can be seen in panel (c) of Figure 23-2 on page 591, where MC intersects AVC and ATC at their respective minimum points.

Minimum Cost Points

At what rate of output of secure digital cards per hour does our representative firm experience the minimum average total costs? Column 7 in panel (a) of Figure 23-2 shows that the minimum average total cost is $4.28, which occurs at an output rate of seven of these SD cards per hour. We can also find this minimum cost by finding the point in panel (c) of Figure 23-2 where the marginal cost curve intersects the average total cost curve. This should not be surprising. When marginal cost is below average total cost, average total cost falls. When marginal cost is above average total cost, average total cost rises. At the point where average total cost is neither falling nor rising, marginal cost must then be equal to average total cost. When we represent this graphically, the marginal cost curve will intersect the average total cost curve at the latter's minimum.

The same analysis applies to the intersection of the marginal cost curve and the average variable cost curve. When are average variable costs at a minimum? According to panel (a) of Figure 23-2, average variable costs are at a minimum of $2.60 at an output rate of five SD cards per hour. This is where the marginal cost curve intersects the average variable cost curve in panel (c) of Figure 23-2.

Why has Wal-Mart recently experienced problems with minimizing its distribution costs?

E-COMMERCE EXAMPLE
Wal-Mart Encounters Interference in Inventory Radio-Tracking

In 2005, Wal-Mart launched "Remix," a plan to reduce the costs of distributing goods to its huge network of stores. A key part of the cost-cutting program was the use of radio-frequency identification (RFID) tags that provide more detailed information about shipments than traditional bar codes. In addition to pricing information, RFID tags store information about a product's serial number, the location of the facility that manufactured the product, and when the product was made and sold. All this logistical information, the company anticipated, would reduce costs by enabling employees to avoid time-wasting distributional inefficiencies.

So far, however, Wal-Mart's costs have been drifting *higher*, not lower. Whereas traditional bar codes are printed on boxes and cases at factories, Wal-Mart suppliers must attach RFID tags in warehouses, which pushes up labor costs and slows shipments. Furthermore, installing RFID-reading equipment in Wal-Mart facilities has proceeded more slowly than planned. When RFID-tagged merchandise arrives from suppliers, Wal-Mart warehouses and stores are not always prepared to use the technology and end up relying on the old bar codes. Thus, instead of declining as anticipated, Wal-Mart's total expenses as a percentage of sales have risen from 16.2 percent in the early 2000s to nearly 18.5 percent today.

FOR CRITICAL ANALYSIS
Do you think that the distribution costs Wal-Mart incurs are fixed costs or variable costs? Explain your reasoning.

QUICK QUIZ   *See page 609 for the answers. Review concepts from this section in MyEconLab.*

Total costs equal total _____ costs plus total _____ costs. Fixed costs are those that do not vary with the rate of production; variable costs are those that do vary with the rate of production.

_____ total costs equal total costs divided by output (_____ = TC/Q).

Average _____ costs equal total variable costs divided by output (_____ = TVC/Q).

Average _____ costs equal total fixed costs divided by output (_____ = TFC/Q).

_____ cost equals the change in _____ cost divided by the change in output (_____ = Δ _____/ΔQ, where the Greek letter Δ, delta, means "change in").

The marginal cost curve intersects the _____ point of the average total cost curve and the _____ point of the average variable cost curve.

The Relationship Between Diminishing Marginal Product and Cost Curves

There is a unique relationship between output and the shape of the various cost curves we have drawn. Let's consider Internet service calls and the relationship between marginal cost and diminishing marginal physical product shown in panel (a) of Figure 23-3 on the next page. It turns out that if wage rates are constant, the shape of the marginal cost curve in panel (d) of Figure 23-3 is both a reflection of and a consequence of the law of diminishing marginal product.

Marginal Cost and Marginal Physical Product

Let's assume that each unit of labor can be purchased at a constant price. Further assume that labor is the only variable input. We see that as more workers are hired, marginal physical product first rises and then falls. Thus, the marginal cost of each extra unit of output will first fall as long as marginal physical product is rising, and then it will rise as long as marginal physical product is falling. Recall that marginal cost is defined as

$$MC = \frac{\text{change in total cost}}{\text{change in output}}$$

Because the price of labor is assumed to be constant, the change in total cost depends solely on the unchanged price of labor, W. The change in output is simply the marginal physical product (MPP) of the one-unit increase in labor. Therefore, we see that

$$\text{Marginal cost} = \frac{W}{\text{MPP}}$$

This means that initially, when marginal physical product is increasing, marginal cost falls (we are dividing W by increasingly larger numbers), and later, when marginal product is falling, marginal cost must increase (we are dividing W by smaller numbers). So, as marginal physical product increases, marginal cost decreases, and as marginal

Panel (a)

(1) Labor Input	(2) Total Product (number of Internet access accounts serviced)	(3) Average Physical Product (accounts per technician) (3) = (2) ÷ (1)	(4) Marginal Physical Product	(5) Average Variable Cost (5) = W ($1,000) ÷ (3)	(6) Marginal Cost (6) = W ($1,000) ÷ (4)
0	0	—	—	—	—
1	50	50	50	$20.00	$20.00
2	110	55	60	18.18	16.67
3	180	60	70	16.67	14.29
4	240	60	60	16.67	16.67
5	290	58	50	17.24	20.00
6	330	55	40	18.18	25.00
7	360	51	30	19.61	33.33

FIGURE 23-3

The Relationship Between Output and Costs

As the number of skilled technicians increases, the total number of Internet access accounts serviced each month rises, as shown in panels (a) and (b). In panel (c), marginal physical product (MPP) first rises and then falls. Average physical product (APP) follows. The near mirror image of panel (c) is shown in panel (d), in which MC and AVC first fall and then rise.

physical product decreases, marginal cost must increase. Thus, when marginal physical product reaches its maximum, marginal cost necessarily reaches its minimum.

An Illustration

To illustrate this, let's return to Figure 23-1 on page 587 and consider specifically panel (a). Assume that a skilled printer-assembly worker is paid $1,000 a week. When we go from zero labor input to one unit, output increases by 10 computer printers. Each of those 10 printers has a marginal cost of $100. Now the second unit of labor is hired, and this individual costs $1,000 per week. Output increases by 16. Thus, the marginal cost is $1,000 ÷ 16 = $62.50. We continue the experiment. We see that the next unit of labor yields only 10 additional computer printers, so marginal cost starts to rise again back to $100. The following unit of labor yields a marginal physical product of only 8, so marginal cost becomes $1,000 ÷ 8 = $125.

All of the foregoing can be restated in relatively straightforward terms:

Firms' short-run cost curves are a reflection of the law of diminishing marginal product. Given any constant price of the variable input, marginal costs decline as long as the marginal physical product of the variable resource is rising. At the point at which marginal product begins to diminish, marginal costs begin to rise as the marginal physical product of the variable input begins to decline.

The result is a marginal cost curve that slopes down, hits a minimum, and then slopes up.

Average Costs and Average Physical Product

Of course, the average total cost curve and average variable cost curve are affected. They will have their familiar U shape in the short run. Again, to see this, recall that

Can the marginal cost of computer printers decline forever? Why or why not?

$$AVC = \frac{\text{total variable costs}}{\text{total output}}$$

As we move from zero labor input to one unit in panel (a) of Figure 23-1 on page 587, output increases from zero to 10 computer printers. The total variable costs are the price per worker, W ($1,000), times the number of workers (1). Because the average product of one worker (column 3) is 10, we can write the total product, 10, as the average product, 10, times the number of workers, 1. Thus, we see that

$$AVC = \frac{\$1,000 \times 1}{10 \times 1} = \frac{\$1,000}{10} = \frac{W}{AP}$$

From column 3 in panel (a) of Figure 23-1, we see that the average product increases, reaches a maximum, and then declines. Because AVC = W/AP, average variable cost decreases as average product increases and increases as average product decreases. AVC reaches its minimum when average product reaches its maximum. Furthermore, because ATC = AVC + AFC, the average total cost curve inherits the relationship between the average variable cost and diminishing returns.

To illustrate, consider an Internet service provider that employs skilled technicians to provide access services within a given geographic area. Panel (a) of Figure 23-3 on the previous page presents in column 2 the total number of Internet access accounts serviced as the number of technicians increases. Notice that the total product first increases at an increasing rate and later increases at a decreasing rate. This is reflected in column 4, which shows that the marginal physical product increases at first and then falls. The average physical product too first rises and then falls. The marginal and average physical products are graphed in panel (c) of Figure 23-3 on page 596.

Our immediate interest here is the average variable and marginal costs. Because we can define average variable cost as $1,000/AP (assuming that the wage paid is constant at $1,000), as the average product rises from 50 to 55 to 60 Internet access accounts, the average variable cost falls from $20.00 to $18.18 to $16.67. Conversely, as average product falls from 60 to 51, average variable cost rises from $16.67 to $19.61. Likewise, because marginal cost can also be defined as W/MPP, we see that as marginal physical product rises from 50 to 70, marginal cost falls from $20.00 to $14.29. As marginal physical product falls to 30, marginal cost rises to $33.33. These relationships are also expressed in panels (b), (c), and (d) of Figure 23-3 on page 596.

Long-Run Cost Curves

Planning horizon
The long run, during which all inputs are variable.

The long run is defined as a time period during which full adjustment can be made to any change in the economic environment. Thus, in the long run, *all* factors of production are variable. Long-run curves are sometimes called *planning curves*, and the long run is sometimes called the **planning horizon.** We start our analysis of long-run cost curves by considering a single firm contemplating the construction of a single plant. The firm has three alternative plant sizes from which to choose on the planning horizon. Each particular plant size generates its own short-run average total cost curve. Now that we are talking about the difference between long-run and short-run cost curves, we will label all short-run curves with an S and long-run curves with an L; short-run average (total) costs will be labeled SAC; and long-run average cost curves will be labeled LAC.

Panel (a) of Figure 23-4 shows short-run average cost curves for three successively larger plants. Which is the optimal size to build, if we can only choose among these three? That depends on the anticipated normal, sustained rate of output per time period. Assume for a moment that the anticipated normal, sustained rate is approximately Q_1. If a plant of size 1 is built, average cost will be C_1. If a plant of size 2 is built, we see on SAC$_2$ that average cost will be C_2, which is greater than C_1. Thus, if the anticipated rate of output is Q_1, the appropriate plant size is the one from which SAC$_1$ was derived.

However, if the anticipated sustained rate of output per time period increases from approximately Q_1 to a higher level such as Q_2 and a plant of size 1 is selected, average cost will be C_4. If a plant of size 2 is chosen, average cost will be C_3, which is clearly less than C_4.

In choosing the appropriate plant size for a single-plant firm during the planning horizon, the firm will pick the size whose short-run average cost curve generates an average cost that is lowest for the expected rate of output.

Long-Run Average Cost Curve

Long-run average cost curve
The locus of points representing the minimum unit cost of producing any given rate of output, given current technology and resource prices.

If we now assume that the entrepreneur faces an infinite number of choices of plant sizes in the long run, we can conceive of an infinite number of SAC curves similar to the three in panel (a) of Figure 23-4. We are not able, of course, to draw an infinite number, but we have drawn quite a few in panel (b) of Figure 23-4. We then draw the "envelope" to all these various short-run average cost curves. The resulting envelope is the **long-run average cost curve.** This long-run average cost curve is sometimes

FIGURE 23-4

Preferable Plant Size and the Long-Run Average Cost Curve

If the anticipated sustained rate of output per unit time period is approximately Q_1, the optimal plant to build is the one corresponding to SAC$_1$ in panel (a) because average cost is lower. However, if the sustained rate of output increases toward the higher level Q_2, it will be more profitable to have a plant size

corresponding to SAC$_2$. If we draw all the possible short-run average cost curves that correspond to different plant sizes and then draw the envelope (a curve tangent to each member of a set of curves) to these various curves, SAC$_1$ – SAC$_8$, we obtain the long-run average cost (LAC) curve as shown in panel (b).

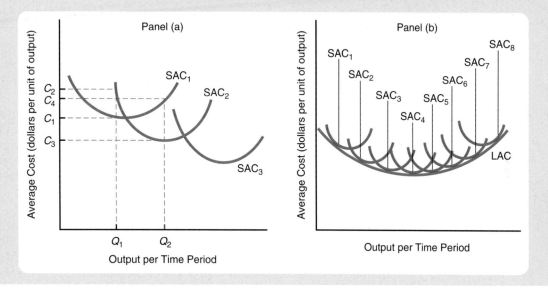

called the **planning curve,** for it represents the various average costs attainable at the planning stage of the firm's decision making. It represents the locus (path) of points giving the least unit cost of producing any given rate of output. Note that the LAC curve is *not* tangent to each individual SAC curve at the latter's minimum points, except at the minimum point of the LAC curve. Then and only then are minimum long-run average costs equal to minimum short-run average costs.

Planning curve
The long-run average cost curve.

Why the Long-Run Average Cost Curve Is U-Shaped

Notice that the long-run average cost curve, LAC, in panel (b) of Figure 23-4 is U-shaped, similar to the U shape of the short-run average cost curve developed earlier in this chapter. The reason behind the U shape of the two curves is not the same, however. The short-run average cost curve is U-shaped because of the law of diminishing marginal product. But the law cannot apply to the long run, because in the long run, all factors of production are variable; there is no point of diminishing marginal product because there is no fixed factor of production.

Why, then, do we see the U shape in the long-run average cost curve? The reasoning has to do with economies of scale, constant returns to scale, and diseconomies of scale. When the firm is experiencing **economies of scale,** the long-run average cost

Economies of scale
Decreases in long-run average costs resulting from increases in output.

Constant returns to scale
No change in long-run average costs when output increases.

Diseconomies of scale
Increases in long-run average costs that occur as output increases.

curve slopes downward—an increase in scale and production leads to a fall in unit costs. When the firm is experiencing **constant returns to scale,** the long-run average cost curve is at its minimum point, such that an increase in scale and production does not change unit costs. When the firm is experiencing **diseconomies of scale,** the long-run average cost curve slopes upward—an increase in scale and production increases unit costs. These three sections of the long-run average cost curve are broken up into panels (a), (b), and (c) in Figure 23-5.

Reasons for Economies of Scale

We shall examine three of the many reasons why a firm might be expected to experience economies of scale: specialization, the dimensional factor, and improvements in productive equipment.

SPECIALIZATION As a firm's scale of operation increases, the opportunities for specialization in the use of resource inputs also increase. This is sometimes called *increased division of tasks* or *operations*. Cost reductions generated by productivity enhancements from such division of labor or increased specialization are well known. When we consider managerial staffs, we also find that larger enterprises may be able to put together more highly specialized staffs.

DIMENSIONAL FACTOR Large-scale firms often require proportionately less input per unit of output simply because certain inputs do not have to be physically doubled in order to double the output. Consider an oil-storage firm's cost of storing oil. The cost of storage is related to the cost of steel that goes into building the storage container; however, the amount of steel required goes up less than in proportion to the volume (storage capacity) of the container (because the volume of a container increases more than proportionately with its surface area).

FIGURE 23-5

Economies of Scale, Constant Returns to Scale, and Diseconomies of Scale Shown with the Long-Run Average Cost Curve

The long-run average cost curve will fall when there are economies of scale, as shown in panel (a). It will be constant (flat) when the firm is experiencing constant returns to scale, as shown in panel (b). It will rise when the firm is experiencing diseconomies of scale, as shown in panel (c).

IMPROVEMENTS IN PRODUCTIVE EQUIPMENT The larger the scale of the enterprise, the more the firm is able to take advantage of larger-volume (output capacity) types of machinery. Small-scale operations may not be able to profitably use large-volume machines that can be more efficient per unit of output. Also, smaller firms often cannot use technologically more advanced machinery because they are unable to spread out the high cost of such sophisticated equipment over a large output.

For any of these reasons, the firm may experience economies of scale, which means that equal percentage increases in output result in a decrease in average cost. Thus, output can double, but total costs will less than double; hence, average cost falls. Note that the factors listed for causing economies of scale are all *internal* to the firm; they do not depend on what other firms are doing or what is happening in the economy.

Why are global cargo-shipping firms rushing to build dozens of massive new container ships?

INTERNATIONAL EXAMPLE
Global Cargo Shippers Pursue Scale Economies

For an international shipping firm, a "plant" is a cargo ship. In recent years, shippers have reduced their long-run average costs both by expanding the number of ships afloat and by increasing the absolute size of those ships. Worldwide, work is under way on more than 150 massive new cargo ships, several of which have recently put to sea. These ships are longer than three football fields and wider than the Panama Canal. Each ship has sufficient storage space for at least 8,000 20-foot-long cargo containers. Because the huge ships carry such large loads, the average transportation cost per ton of cargo is much lower than shippers incur by using traditional cargo ships. Thus, expanding scale through the use of additional larger ships has allowed global cargo shippers to experience economies of scale.

FOR CRITICAL ANALYSIS
What could you conclude if several years from now you noticed that shipping firms had stopped putting any additional massive container ships out to sea?

Why a Firm Might Experience Diseconomies of Scale

One of the basic reasons that a firm can expect to run into diseconomies of scale is that there are limits to the efficient functioning of management. This is so because larger levels of output imply successively larger *plant* size, which in turn implies successively larger *firm* size. Thus, as the level of output increases, more people must be hired, and the firm gets bigger. As this happens, however, the support, supervisory, and administrative staff and the general paperwork of the firm all increase. As the layers of supervision grow, the costs of information and communication grow more than proportionately; hence, the average unit cost will start to increase.

Some observers of corporate giants claim that many of them have been experiencing some diseconomies of scale. Witness the difficulties that firms such as Dell and General Motors have experienced in the 2000s. Some analysts say that the profitability declines they have encountered are at least partly a function of their size relative to their smaller, more flexible competitors, which can make decisions more quickly and then take advantage of changing market conditions more rapidly.

You Are There

To contemplate why airlines' efforts to achieve economies of scale might contribute to diseconomies of scale at the airports handling their flights, read **More Flights of Smaller Jets Translate into Higher Long-Run Average Costs at Airports,** on page 603.

Minimum Efficient Scale

Economists and statisticians have obtained actual data on the relationship between changes in all inputs and changes in average cost. It turns out that for many industries, the long-run average cost curve does not resemble the curve shown in panel (b) of Figure 23-4 on page 599. Rather, it more closely resembles Figure 23-6. What you observe there is a small portion of declining long-run average costs (economies of scale) and then a wide range of outputs over which the firm experiences relatively constant economies of scale. At the output rate when economies of scale end and constant economies of scale start, the **minimum efficient scale (MES)** for the firm is encountered. It occurs at point *A*. The minimum efficient scale is defined as the lowest rate of output at which long-run average costs are minimized. In any industry with a long-run average cost curve similar to the one in Figure 23-6, larger firms will have no cost-saving advantage over smaller firms as long as the smaller firms have at least obtained the minimum efficient scale at point *A*.

Why has Toyota decided to stop building new U.S. auto plants?

Minimum efficient scale (MES)
The lowest rate of output per unit time at which long-run average costs for a particular firm are at a minimum.

EXAMPLE
Toyota Finds Itself Just Beyond Its Minimum Efficient Scale

Since 2002, Japanese automaker Toyota has increased by more than 50 percent the number of vehicles it sells in the United States. This explains why the company has sharply increased the number of auto plants it operates in the United States. Recently, however, Toyota decided that it will build no more plants in the foreseeable future. The reason is that the company's long-run average cost of producing autos began to increase in the late 2000s. To avoid experiencing any further diseconomies and get back

to its minimum efficient scale, Toyota has cut back slightly on production of vehicles in portions of U.S. facilities built just a few years ago.

FOR CRITICAL ANALYSIS
In the long run, why might Toyota choose not to expand its production capabilities further even if it could sell more vehicles than it is currently producing? (Hint: Remember that the fundamental goal of a firm is to maximize profits.)

FIGURE 23-6

Minimum Efficient Scale

This long-run average cost curve reaches a minimum point at *A*. After that point, long-run average costs remain horizontal, or constant, and then rise at some later rate of output. Point *A* is called the minimum efficient scale for the firm because that is the point at which it reaches minimum costs. It is the lowest rate of output at which average long-run costs are minimized. At point *B*, diseconomies of scale arise, so long-run average cost begins to increase with further increases in output.

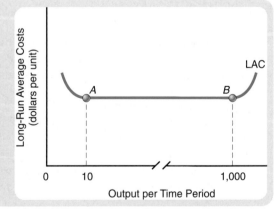

QUICK QUIZ *See page 609 for the answers. Review concepts from this section in MyEconLab.*

The _____ run is often called the **planning horizon.** The _____-run average cost curve is the planning curve. It is found by drawing a curve tangent to one point on a series of _____-run average cost curves, each corresponding to a different plant size.

The firm can experience **economies of scale, diseconomies of scale,** or **constant returns** to scale, all according to whether the long-run average cost curve slopes _____, slopes _____, or is _____. Economies of scale refer to what happens to average cost when all factors of production are increased.

We observe economies of scale for a number of reasons, including specialization, improved productive equipment, and the _____ factor, because large-scale firms require proportionately less input per unit of output. The firm may experience _____ of scale primarily because of limits to the efficient functioning of management.

The **minimum efficient scale** occurs at the _____ rate of output at which long-run average costs are _____.

You Are There   ⟩   More Flights of Smaller Jets Translate into Higher Long-Run Average Costs at Airports

Why has Marion Blakely, an administrator with the Federal Aviation Administration (FAA), unveiled a plan aimed at forcing airlines to increase the average size of the planes they land at New York's La Guardia Airport? The answer is that she and other FAA officials have concluded that too many flights by small planes are driving up average operating costs at this and other U.S. airports.

From the airlines' perspective, the use of smaller planes has permitted an expansion of scale that has pushed down the long-run average costs of transporting passengers among both major-city airports and smaller regional airports. Consequently, scheduling more flights by smaller planes has created economies of scale for the airlines. Transporting more passengers using a larger number of smaller planes, however, translates into many more flights that the nation's airports must handle. This has pushed up airports' labor costs as they have increased runway crews, air traffic control and security staffs, and ground transportation services. In addition, airports have incurred higher costs by adding more aeronautical capital in the form of runways, radar facilities, and sophisticated computer equipment, as well as software for tracking all the additional flights.

Thus, as airlines have sought to attain economies of scale through more flights by smaller planes, airports have experienced diseconomies of scale. This is why airlines have responded to Blakely's plan with howls of protest. Nevertheless, a number of airport operators are already arguing that her plan to limit flights into La Guardia by smaller planes should also be extended to their airports.

CRITICAL ANALYSIS QUESTIONS

1. Why do you suppose that the operators of some of the nation's busiest airports have argued that airlines should pay some of the costs of expanding the airports' scales of operation?

2. Why do you think that some economists have argued that the economies-of-scale benefits attained with smaller planes and more flights might still be obtainable if more airports were built instead of expanding operating scale at existing airports? (Hint: Is it possible that increasing overall production by expanding the number of "plants" could result in lower long-run average costs even if expanding the sizes of existing "plants" fails to reduce long-run average costs?)

Family Physicians Downsize
to Reduce Long-Run Average Costs

CONCEPTS APPLIED

- Diseconomies of Scale
- Long-Run Average Cost Curve
- Minimum Efficient Scale

Today, fewer medical school students are becoming family practitioners than in years past. As Figure 23-7 indicates, the number of medical school graduates opting for medical school residency positions in the area of family medicine has dropped by about one-half since 1997. The reason is simple: For most new physicians, a family medicine practice simply is not as lucrative as it once was. Even though revenues earned by family practitioners have held steady, the average costs of operating family practices have risen.

FIGURE 23-7

The Number of Medical Students Opting for Family Practice Residencies

Since 1997, there has been a steady decline in the number of students in medical schools who have chosen to specialize in providing family medical services.

Source: U.S. Department of Health and Human Services.

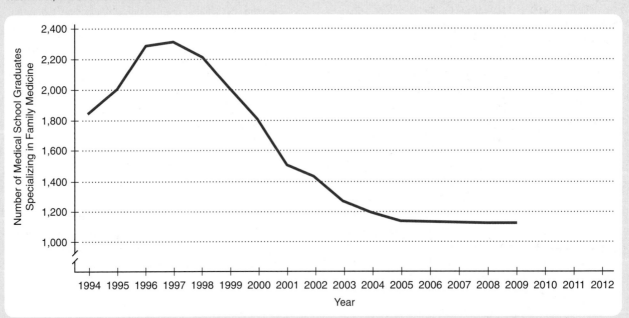

A More Skewed Long-Run Average Cost Curve

Many family physicians have discovered that trying to operate a family practice at the average scale that was typical in the 1990s now entails experiencing significant diseconomies of scale. Higher labor costs and increased capital expenses have boosted the long-run costs associated with operating family practices organized around large-scale operations.

In light of these changes, the long-run average cost curve faced by family physicians is bending upward at ever-smaller scales of operation. The minimum efficient scale in the provision of family medicine services has declined.

The New Trend in Family Medicine: Micropractices

The decline in the minimum efficient scale in family medicine explains why more of today's family physicians are opting to downsize their operations considerably.

For many family practitioners, the latest buzzword is "micropractice." Increasingly, family practice graduates from medical schools are not scouting out buildings with large amounts of office space and interviewing people for receptionist or nursing positions. Instead, these new physicians are leasing small offices and using their cellphones to take calls directly from patients. In addition, they are buying computer software. They use software programs to track patients' appointments, illnesses, and medications; to submit prescriptions and process insurance claims electronically; and to communicate with patients via e-mail.

Operating these high-tech micropractices allows family physicians to avoid the higher overhead expenses that they would incur if they attempted to operate a family practice at a yesteryear scale. Reducing the scale of operations to a micropractice level is enabling the new generation of family practitioners to attain the inflation-adjusted profit levels of years past. Ultimately, this should alter the incentives faced by coming generations of medical students. If so, the trend plotted in Figure 23-7 eventually should reverse.

Test your understanding of this chapter by going online to **MyEconLab**.
In the Study Plan for this chapter, select Section N: News.

For Critical Analysis

1. If a micropractice is the minimum efficient scale for a family practice, during the adjustment to this new minimum efficient scale, will there be a rightward or leftward movement along the long-run average cost curve?

2. Why do you suppose that most family practitioners who do *not* set up micropractices increasingly are opting to partner with numerous physicians in offices that previously would have been occupied by only one physician?

Web Resources

1. For a short summary of why some physicians might determine that they could benefit from a micropractice, go to www.econtoday.com/chapter23.

2. To learn about how physicians put micropractices into operation, go to www.econtoday.com/chapter23.

Research Project

Evaluate whether it is likely that the minimum efficient scale for physicians in other medical specialties is as small as the micropractices of many of today's family physicians. For instance, are practitioners of inpatient and outpatient surgery or radiology as likely to confront a long-run average cost curve that begins sloping upward at a micropractice scale of operations? (Hint: Could surgeons and radiologists function as efficiently without nurses, equipment that requires significant space, and other inputs requiring a larger overhead than is consistent with a micropractice?)

Here is what you should know after reading this chapter. **MyEconLab** will help you identify what you know, and where to go when you need to practice.

WHAT YOU SHOULD KNOW

WHERE TO GO TO PRACTICE

The Short Run versus the Long Run from a Firm's Perspective The short run for a firm is a period during which at least one input, such as plant size, cannot be altered. Inputs that cannot be changed in the short run are fixed inputs, whereas factors of production that may be adjusted in the short run are variable inputs. The long run is a period in which a firm may vary all factors of production.

short run, 584
plant size, 584
long run, 584

- **MyEconLab** Study Plan 23.1
- Audio introduction to Chapter 23
- ABC News Videos: The Space Shuttle: Cost vs. Benefit and Incentives for Perfect Attendance

The Law of Diminishing Marginal Product The production function is the relationship between inputs and the maximum physical output, or total product, that a firm can produce. Typically, a firm's marginal physical product—the physical output resulting from the addition of one more unit of a variable factor of production—increases with the first few units of the variable factor of production that it employs. Eventually, however, as the firm adds more and more units of the variable input, the marginal physical product begins to decline. This is the law of diminishing marginal product.

production, 585
production function, 585
average physical product, 586
marginal physical product, 586
law of diminishing marginal product, 588

KEY FIGURE
Figure 23-1, 587

- **MyEconLab** Study Plans 23.2, 23.3
- Animated Figure 23-1

A Firm's Short-Run Cost Curves The expenses for a firm's fixed inputs are its fixed costs, and the expenses for its variable inputs are variable costs. The total costs of a firm are the sum of its fixed costs and variable costs. Dividing fixed costs by various possible output levels traces out the firm's average fixed cost curve, which slopes downward because dividing fixed costs by a larger total product yields a lower average fixed cost. Average variable cost equals total variable cost divided by total product, and average total cost equals total cost divided by total product. For the latter two, doing these computations at various possible output levels yields U-shaped curves. Finally, marginal cost is the change in total cost resulting from a one-unit change in production. A firm's marginal costs typically decline as the firm produces the first few units of output, but at the point where marginal product begins to diminish, the marginal cost curve begins to slope upward. The marginal cost curve also intersects the minimum points of the average variable cost curve and average total cost curve.

total costs, 589
fixed costs, 590
variable costs, 590
average fixed costs, 592
average variable costs, 592
average total costs, 592
marginal costs, 592

KEY FIGURE
Figure 23-2, 591

- **MyEconLab** Study Plans 23.4, 23.5
- Animated Figure 23-2
- Video: Short-Run Costs to the Firm

A Firm's Long-Run Cost Curves Over a firm's long-run, or planning, horizon, it can choose all factors of production, including plant size. Thus, it can choose a long-run scale of production along a long-run average cost curve. The long-run average cost curve, which for most firms is U-shaped, is traced out by the short-run average cost curves corresponding to various plant sizes.

planning horizon, 598
long-run average cost curve, 598
planning curve, 599

KEY FIGURES
Figure 23-3, 596
Figure 23-4, 599

- **MyEconLab** Study Plans 23.6, 23.7
- Animated Figures 23-3, 23-4

(continued)

(continued)

WHAT YOU SHOULD KNOW		WHERE TO GO TO PRACTICE

Economies and Diseconomies of Scale and a Firm's Minimum Efficient Scale Along the downward-sloping range of a firm's long-run average cost curve, the firm experiences economies of scale, meaning that its long-run production costs decline as it increases its plant size and thereby raises its output scale. In contrast, along the upward-sloping portion of the long-run average cost curve, the firm encounters diseconomies of scale, so that its long-run costs of production rise as it increases its output scale. The minimum point of the long-run average cost curve occurs at the firm's minimum efficient scale, which is the lowest rate of output at which the firm can achieve minimum long-run average cost.

economies of scale, 599
constant returns to scale, 600
diseconomies of scale, 600
minimum efficient scale (MES), 602

KEY FIGURES
Figure 23-5, 600
Figure 23-6, 602

- **MyEconLab** Study Plans 23.7, 23.8
- Animated Figures 23-5, 23-6
- Video: Reasons for Economies of Scale

Log in to MyEconLab, take a chapter test, and get a personalized Study Plan that tells you which concepts you understand and which ones you need to review. From there, MyEconLab will give you further practice, tutorials, animations, videos, and guided solutions.
Log in to www.myeconlab.com

PROBLEMS

All problems are assignable in myeconlab. *Answers to odd-numbered problems appear at the back of the book.*

23-1. The academic calendar for a university is August 15 through May 15. A professor commits to a contract that binds her to a teaching position at this university for this period. Based on this information, explain the short run and long run that the professor faces.

23-2. The short-run production function for a manufacturer of flash memory drives is shown in the table below. Based on this information, answer the following questions.

Input of Labor (workers per week)	Total Output of Flash Memory Drives
0	0
1	25
2	60
3	85
4	105
5	115
6	120

a. Calculate the average physical product at each quantity of labor.

b. Calculate the marginal physical product of labor at each quantity of labor.

c. At what point does marginal product begin to diminish?

23-3. At the end of the year, a firm produced 10,000 laptop computers. Its total costs were $5 million, and its fixed costs were $2 million. What are the average variable costs of this firm?

23-4. The cost structure of a manufacturer of microchips is described in the following table. The firm's fixed

Output (microchips per day)	Total Cost of Output ($ thousands)
0	10
25	60
50	95
75	150
100	220
125	325
150	465

costs equal $10 per day. Calculate the average variable cost, average fixed cost, and average total cost at each output level.

23-5. The diagram below displays short-run cost curves for a facility that produces liquid crystal display (LCD) screens for cellphones:

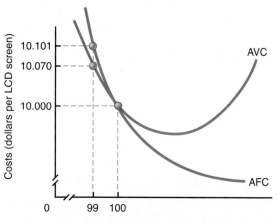

a. What are the daily total fixed costs of producing LCD screens?

b. What are the total variable costs of producing 100 LCD screens per day?

c. What are the total costs of producing 100 LCD screens per day?

d. What is the marginal cost of producing the hundredth LCD screen? (Hint: To answer this question, you must first determine the total costs—or, alternatively, the total variable costs—of producing 99 LCD screens.)

23-6. A watch manufacturer finds that at 1,000 units of output, its marginal costs are below average total costs. If it produces an additional watch, will its average total costs rise, fall, or stay the same?

23-7. At its current short-run level of production, a firm's average variable costs equal $20 per unit, and its average fixed costs equal $30 per unit. Its total costs at this production level equal $2,500.

a. What is the firm's current output level?

b. What are its total variable costs at this output level?

c. What are its total fixed costs?

23-8. In an effort to reduce their total costs, many companies are now replacing paychecks with payroll cards, which are stored-value cards onto which the companies can download employees' wages and salaries electronically. If the only factor of production that a company varies in the short run is the number of hours worked by people already on its payroll, would shifting from paychecks to payroll cards reduce the firm's total fixed costs or its total variable costs? Explain your answer.

23-9. During autumn months, passenger railroads across the globe deal with a condition called slippery rail. It results from a combination of water, leaf oil, and pressure from the train's weight, which creates a slippery black ooze that prevents trains from gaining traction.

a. One solution for slippery rail is to cut back trees from all of a rail firm's rail network on a regular basis, thereby helping prevent the problem from developing. If incurred, would this railroad expense be a better example of a fixed cost or a variable cost? Why?

b. Another way of addressing slippery rail is to wait until it begins to develop. Then the company purchases sand and dumps it on the slippery tracks so that trains already en route within the rail network can proceed. If incurred, would this railroad expense be a better example of a fixed cost or a variable cost? Why?

23-10. In the short run, a firm's total costs of producing 100 units of output equal $10,000. If it produces one more unit, its total costs will increase to $10,150.

a. What is the marginal cost of the 101st unit of output?

b. What is the firm's average total cost of producing 100 units?

c. What is the firm's average total cost of producing 101 units?

23-11. Suppose that a firm's only variable input is labor, and the constant hourly wage rate is $20 per hour. The last unit of labor hired enabled the firm to increase its hourly production from 250 units to 251 units. What was the marginal cost of the 251st unit of output?

23-12. Suppose that a firm's only variable input is labor. The firm increases the number of employees from four to five, thereby causing weekly output to rise by two units and total costs to increase from $3,000 per week to $3,300 per week.

a. What is the marginal physical product of the fifth worker?

b. What is the weekly wage rate earned by the fifth worker?

23-13. Suppose that a company currently employs 1,000 workers and produces 1 million units of output per month. Labor is its only variable input, and the company pays each worker the same monthly wage. The company's current total variable costs equal $2 million.

   a. What are average variable costs at this firm's current output level?

   b. What is the average physical product of labor?

   c. What monthly wage does the firm pay each worker?

23-14. A manufacturing firm with a single plant is contemplating changing its plant size. It must choose from among seven alternative plant sizes. In the table, plant size A is the smallest it might build, and size G is the largest. Currently, the firm's plant size is B.

Plant Size	Average Total Cost ($)
A (smallest)	4,250
B	3,600
C	3,100
D	3,100
E	3,100
F	3,250
G (largest)	4,100

   a. At plant site B, is this firm currently experiencing economies of scale or diseconomies of scale?

   b. What is the firm's minimum efficient scale?

23-15. An electricity-generating company confronts the following long-run average total costs associated with alternative plant sizes. It is currently operating at plant size G.

Plant Size	Average Total Cost ($)
A (smallest)	2,000
B	1,800
C	1,600
D	1,550
E	1,500
F	1,500
G (largest)	1,500

   a. What is this firm's minimum efficient scale?

   b. If damage caused by a powerful hurricane generates a reduction in the firm's plant size from its current size to B, would there be a leftward or rightward movement along the firm's long-run average total cost curve?

ECONOMICS ON THE NET

Industry-Level Capital Expenditures In this chapter, you learned about the explicit and implicit costs that firms incur in the process of producing goods and services. This Internet application gives you an opportunity to consider one type of cost—expenditures on capital goods.

Title: U.S. Census Bureau's Annual Capital Expenditures Survey

Navigation: Follow the link at **www.econtoday.com/ chapter23**, and select the most recent *Annual Capital Spending Report*.

Application Read the introductory summary of the report, and then answer the following questions.

1. What types of business expenditures does the Census Bureau include in this report?

2. Are the inputs that generate these business expenditures more likely to be inputs that firms can vary in the short run or in the long run?

3. Which inputs account for the largest portion of firms' capital expenditures? Why do you suppose this is so?

For Group Discussion and Analysis Review reports for the past several years. Do capital expenditures vary from year to year? What factors might account for such variations? Are there noticeable differences in capital expenditures from industry to industry?

ANSWERS TO QUICK QUIZZES

   p. 589: (i) production . . . output; (ii) product; (iii) decreasing . . . output
   p. 595: (i) fixed . . . variable; (ii) Average . . . ATC; (iii) variable . . . AVC; (iv) fixed . . . AFC; (v) Marginal . . . total . . . MC . . . TC; (vi) minimum . . . minimum
   p. 603: (i) long . . . long . . . short; (ii) downward . . . upward . . . horizontal; (iii) dimensional . . . diseconomies; (iv) lowest . . . minimized

24

Perfect Competition

S ince 2003, the total amount of stored digital data on planet Earth has increased from an estimated 5 exabytes (5,000,000,000,000,000,000 bytes of data) to more than 200 exabytes—enough data to fill the hard drives of about 200 billion personal computers. Naturally, this massive expansion of digital data has been accompanied by the development of a data-storage industry, with numerous companies providing essentially identical data-storage services. In spite of the considerable growth in demand for the services of such firms, the average price per byte of data stored has decreased over time. To understand how this has occurred, you must learn about the theory of perfect competition, the topic of this chapter.

LEARNING OBJECTIVES

myeconlab

MyEconLab helps you master each objective and study more efficiently. See end of chapter for details.

After reading this chapter, you should be able to:

- Identify the characteristics of a perfectly competitive market structure

- Discuss the process by which a perfectly competitive firm decides how much output to produce

- Understand how the short-run supply curve for a perfectly competitive firm is determined

- Explain how the equilibrium price is determined in a perfectly competitive market

- Describe what factors induce firms to enter or exit a perfectly competitive industry

- Distinguish among constant-, increasing-, and decreasing-cost industries based on the shape of the long-run industry supply curve

? DID YOU KNOW THAT on average 6,000 farms have ceased independent operations in the United States during each of the past 30 years? Ease of exit from the industry is a fundamental characteristic of the theory of *perfect competition*, the topic of this chapter. In common speech, *competition* simply means "rivalry." In an extreme perfectly competitive situation, individual buyers and sellers cannot affect the market price—it is determined by the market forces of demand and supply. In addition, firms in a perfectly competitive industry that have been earning economic losses for a time begin to return to profitability as other firms respond to these losses by leaving the industry. In this chapter, we examine these and other implications of the theory of perfect competition.

Characteristics of a Perfectly Competitive Market Structure

We are interested in studying how a firm acting within a perfectly competitive market structure makes decisions about how much to produce. In a situation of **perfect competition,** each firm is such a small part of the total industry that it cannot affect the price of the product in question. That means that each **perfectly competitive firm** in the industry is a **price taker**—the firm takes price as a given, something determined *outside* the individual firm.

This definition of a competitive firm is obviously idealized, for in one sense the individual firm *has* to set prices. How can we ever have a situation in which firms regard prices as set by forces outside their control? The answer is that even though every firm sets its own prices, a firm in a perfectly competitive situation will find that it will eventually have no customers at all if it sets its price above the competitive price. The best example is in agriculture. Although the individual farmer can set any price for a bushel of wheat, if that price doesn't coincide with the market price of a bushel of similar-quality wheat, no one will purchase the wheat at a higher price; nor would the farmer be inclined to reduce revenues by selling below the market price.

Let's examine why a firm in a perfectly competitive industry is a price taker.

1. *There are large numbers of buyers and sellers.* When this is the case, the quantity demanded by one buyer or the quantity supplied by one seller is negligible relative to the market quantity. No one buyer or seller has any influence on price.

2. *The product sold by the firms in the industry is homogeneous.* The product sold by each firm in the industry is a perfect substitute for the product sold by every other firm. Buyers are able to choose from a large number of sellers of a product that the buyers regard as being the same.

3. *Both buyers and sellers have access to all relevant information.* Consumers are able to find out about lower prices charged by competing firms. Firms are able to find out about cost-saving innovations that can lower production costs and prices, and they are able to learn about profitable opportunities in other industries.

4. *Any firm can enter or leave the industry without serious impediments.* Firms in a competitive industry are not hampered in their ability to get resources or reallocate resources. In pursuit of profit-making opportunities, they move labor and capital to whatever business venture gives them their highest expected rate of return on their investment.

How is the art of blogging becoming a highly competitive, profit-generating line of business?

Perfect competition
A market structure in which the decisions of *individual* buyers and sellers have no effect on market price.

Perfectly competitive firm
A firm that is such a small part of the total *industry* that it cannot affect the price of the product it sells.

Price taker
A perfectly competitive firm that must take the price of its product as given because the firm cannot influence its price.

E-COMMERCE EXAMPLE
Blogging Becomes a Business

There are an estimated 60 million Web blogs in existence. Most of them are personal diaries that happen to be online, have tiny audiences, and earn not a single penny in revenues. Nevertheless, a few blogs have emerged as essentially niche magazines run as businesses and published in an online format by companies such as Gawker Media, Weblogs, Inc., and Engadget. Increasingly, others are also entering the blogging business. With today's low-cost computers and software in hand, the main impediment to entering the blogging market that bloggers face is the opportunity cost of the time they devote to their blogs. Once bloggers attract a sufficient readership, they sell online ad space and begin generating revenues. Many, such as Heather Armstrong, author of a blog called Dooce, are now earning sufficient profits to account for the bulk of their family incomes. Effectively, Armstrong and other bloggers who have entered this market operate small proprietorships.

Surveys indicate that about 7 percent of bloggers post their blogs in hopes of earning revenues. With some 60 million bloggers on the Web, this implies that more than 4 million people are competing to operate blogs as profitable businesses.

FOR CRITICAL ANALYSIS
Why is entry into the blogging market not entirely "free"?

Why does the blog perezhilton.com, run by Mario Lavanderia, satisfy the criteria necessary for a highly competitive firm?

The Demand Curve of the Perfect Competitor

When we discussed substitutes in Chapter 20, we pointed out that the more substitutes there are and the more similar they are to the commodity in question, the greater is the price elasticity of demand. Here we assume that the perfectly competitive firm is producing a homogeneous commodity that has perfect substitutes. That means that if the individual firm raises its price one penny, it will lose all of its business. This, then, is how we characterize the demand schedule for a perfectly competitive firm: It is the going market price as determined by the forces of market supply and market demand—that is, where the market demand curve intersects the market supply curve. The demand curve for the product of an individual firm in a perfectly competitive industry is perfectly elastic at the going market price. Remember that with a perfectly elastic demand curve, any increase in price leads to zero quantity demanded.

We show the market demand and supply curves in panel (a) of Figure 24-1. Their intersection occurs at the price of $5. The commodity in question is secure digital (SD) cards used with digital cameras, laptop computers, and other digital devices. Assume for the purposes of this exposition that all of these SD cards are perfect substitutes for all others. At the going market price of $5 apiece, a hypothetical individual demand curve for a producer of SD cards who sells a very, very small part of total industry production is shown in panel (b). At the market price, this firm can sell all the output it wants. At the market price of $5 each, which is where the demand curve for the individual producer lies, consumer demand for the SD cards of that one producer is perfectly elastic. This can be seen by noting that if the firm raises its price, consumers, who are assumed to know that this supplier is charging more than other producers, will buy elsewhere, and the producer in question will have no sales at all. Thus, the demand curve for that producer is perfectly elastic. We label the individual producer's demand curve *d*, whereas the *market* demand curve is always labeled *D*.

FIGURE 24-1

The Demand Curve for a Producer of Secure Digital Cards

At $5—where market demand, *D*, and market supply, *S*, intersect—the individual firm faces a perfectly elastic demand curve, *d*. If the firm raises its price even one penny, it will sell no secure digital cards, measured from its point of view in hourly production, at all. Notice the difference in the quantities of SD cards represented on the horizontal axes of panels (a) and (b).

How Much Should the Perfect Competitor Produce?

As we have shown, a perfect competitor has to accept the price of the product as a given. If the firm raises its price, it sells nothing; if it lowers its price, it earns lower revenues per unit sold than it otherwise could. The firm has one decision left: How much should it produce? We will apply our model of the firm to this question to come up with an answer. We'll use the *profit-maximization model*, which assumes that firms attempt to maximize their total profits—the positive difference between total revenues and total costs. This also means that firms seek to minimize any losses that arise in times when total revenues may be less than total costs.

Total Revenues

Every firm has to consider its *total revenues*. **Total revenues** are defined as the quantity sold multiplied by the price per unit. (They are the same as total receipts from the sale of output.) The perfect competitor must take the price as a given.

Look at Figure 24-2 on the following page. The information in panel (a) comes from panel (a) of Figure 23-2 on page 591, but we have added some essential columns for our analysis. Column 3 is the market price, *P*, of $5 per SD card. Column 4 shows the total revenues, or TR, as equal to the market price, *P*, times the total output per hour, or *Q*. Thus, TR = *PQ*.

For the perfect competitor, price is also equal to average revenue (AR) because

$$AR = \frac{TR}{Q} = \frac{PQ}{Q} = P$$

where *Q* stands for quantity. If we assume that all units sell for the same price, it becomes apparent that another name for the demand curve is the *average revenue curve* (this is true regardless of the type of market structure under consideration).

Total revenues
The price per unit times the total quantity sold.

Panel (a)

(1) Total Output and Sales per Hour (Q)	(2) Total Costs (TC)	(3) Market Price (P)	(4) Total Revenues (TR) (4) = (3) x (1)	(5) Total Profit (TR − TC) (5) = (4) − (2)	(6) Average Total Cost (ATC) (6) = (2) ÷ (1)	(7) Average Variable Cost (AVC)	(8) Marginal Cost (MC) (8) = Change in (2) / Change in (1)	(9) Marginal Revenue (MR) (9) = Change in (4) / Change in (1)
0	$10	$5	$ 0	−$10	—	—		
							$5	$5
1	15	5	5	−10	$15.00	$5.00		
							3	5
2	18	5	10	−8	9.00	4.00		
							2	5
3	20	5	15	−5	6.67	3.33		
							1	5
4	21	5	20	−1	5.25	2.75		
							2	5
5	23	5	25	2	4.60	2.60		
							3	5
6	26	5	30	4	4.33	2.67		
							4	5
7	30	5	35	5	4.28	2.86		
							5	5
8	35	5	40	5	4.38	3.12		
							6	5
9	41	5	45	4	4.56	3.44		
							7	5
10	48	5	50	2	4.80	3.80		
							8	5
11	56	5	55	−1	5.09	4.18		

FIGURE 24-2

Profit Maximization

Profit maximization occurs where marginal revenue equals marginal cost. Panel (a) indicates that this point occurs at a rate of sales of between seven and eight secure digital cards per hour. In panel (b), we find maximum profits where total revenues exceed total costs by the largest amount. This occurs at a rate of production and sales per hour of seven or eight SD cards. In panel (c), the marginal cost curve, MC, intersects the marginal revenue curve at a rate of output and sales of somewhere between seven and eight SD cards per hour.

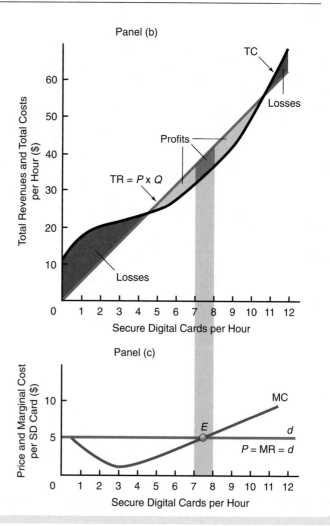

Panel (b)

Panel (c)

We are assuming that the market supply and demand schedules intersect at a price of $5 and that this price holds for all the firm's production. We are also assuming that because our maker of secure digital cards is a small part of the market, it can sell all that it produces at that price. Thus, panel (b) of Figure 24-2 shows the total revenue curve as a straight green line. For every additional SD card sold, total revenue increases by $5.

Comparing Total Costs with Total Revenues

Total costs are given in column 2 of panel (a) of Figure 24-2 and plotted in panel (b). Remember, the firm's costs always include a normal rate of return on investment. So, whenever we refer to total costs, we are talking not about accounting costs but about economic costs. When the total cost curve is above the total revenue curve, the firm is experiencing losses. When total costs are less than total revenues, the firm is making profits.

By comparing total costs with total revenues, we can figure out the number of SD cards the individual competitive firm should produce per hour. Our analysis rests on the assumption that the firm will attempt to maximize total profits. In panel (a) of Figure 24-2, we see that total profits reach a maximum at a production rate of between seven and eight SD cards per hour. We can see this graphically in panel (b) of the figure. The firm will maximize profits where the total revenue curve lies above the total cost curve by the greatest amount. That occurs at a rate of output and sales of between seven and eight SD cards per hour. This rate is called the **profit-maximizing rate of production.** (If output were continuously divisible or we were dealing with extremely large numbers of SD cards, we would get a unique profit-maximizing output.)

We can also find the profit-maximizing rate of production for the individual competitive firm by looking at marginal revenues and marginal costs.

Profit-maximizing rate of production
The rate of production that maximizes total profits, or the difference between total revenues and total costs; also, the rate of production at which marginal revenue equals marginal cost.

Using Marginal Analysis to Determine the Profit-Maximizing Rate of Production

It is possible—indeed, preferable—to use marginal analysis to determine the profit-maximizing rate of production. We end up with the same results derived in a different manner, one that focuses more on where decisions are really made—on the margin. Managers examine changes in costs and relate them to changes in revenues. In fact, whether the question is how much more or less to produce, how many more workers to hire or fire, or how much more to study or not study, we compare changes in costs with changes in benefits, where change is occurring at the margin.

Marginal Revenue

Marginal revenue represents the change in total revenues attributable to changing production of an item by one unit. Hence, a more formal definition of marginal revenue is

Marginal revenue
The change in total revenues resulting from a one-unit change in output (and sale) of the product in question.

$$\text{Marginal revenue} = \frac{\text{change in total revenues}}{\text{change in output}}$$

In a perfectly competitive market, the marginal revenue curve is exactly equivalent to the price line, which is the individual firm's demand curve. Each time the firm produces and sells one more unit, total revenues rise by an amount equal to the (constant) market price of the good. Thus, in Figure 24-1 on page 613, the demand curve, *d*, for the individual producer is at a price of $5—the price line is coincident with the demand curve. But so is the marginal revenue curve, for marginal revenue in this case also equals $5.

The marginal revenue curve for our competitive producer of secure digital cards is shown as a line at $5 in panel (c) of Figure 24-2 on page 614. Notice again that the marginal revenue curve is the price line, which is the firm's demand, or average revenue, curve, *d*. This equality of MR, *P*, AR, and *d* for an individual firm is a general feature of a perfectly competitive industry. The price line shows the quantity that consumers desire to purchase from this firm at each price—which is *any* quantity that the firm provides at the market price—and hence is the demand curve, *d*, faced by the firm. The market clearing price per unit does not change as the firm varies its output, so the average revenue and marginal revenue also are equal to this price. Thus, MR and AR are identically equal to *P* along the firm's demand curve.

When Are Profits Maximized?

Now we add the marginal cost curve, MC, taken from column 8 in panel (a) of Figure 24-2 on page 614. As shown in panel (c) of that figure, because of the law of diminishing marginal product, the marginal cost curve first falls and then starts to rise, eventually intersecting the marginal revenue curve and then rising above it. Notice that the numbers for both the marginal cost schedule, column 8 in panel (a), and the marginal revenue schedule, column 9 in panel (a), are printed *between* the rows on which the quantities appear. This indicates that we are looking at a *change* between one rate of output and the next rate of output.

EQUALIZING MARGINAL REVENUE AND MARGINAL COST In panel (c) of Figure 24-2 on page 614, the marginal cost curve intersects the marginal revenue curve somewhere between seven and eight SD cards per hour. The firm has an incentive to produce and sell until the amount of the additional revenue received from selling one more SD card just equals the additional costs incurred for producing and selling that SD card. This is how the firm maximizes profit. Whenever marginal cost is less than marginal revenue, the firm will always make more profit by increasing production.

Now consider the possibility of producing at an output rate of 10 SD cards per hour. The marginal cost at that output rate is higher than the marginal revenue. The firm would be spending more to produce that additional output than it would be receiving in revenues; it would be foolish to continue producing at this rate.

THE PROFIT-MAXIMIZING OUTPUT RATE But how much should the firm produce? It should produce at point *E* in panel (c) of Figure 24-2, where the marginal cost curve intersects the marginal revenue curve from below. The firm should continue production until the cost of increasing output by one more unit is just equal to the revenues obtainable from that extra unit. This is a fundamental rule in economics:

> *Profit maximization occurs at the rate of output at which marginal revenue equals marginal cost.*

For a perfectly competitive firm, this rate of output is at the intersection of the demand schedule, *d*, which is identical to the MR curve, and the marginal cost curve, MC. When MR exceeds MC, each additional unit of output adds more to total revenues than to total costs, so the additional unit should be produced. When MC is greater than MR, each unit produced adds more to total cost than to total revenues, so this unit should not be produced. Therefore, profit maximization occurs when MC equals MR. In our particular example, our profit-maximizing, perfectly competitive producer of secure digital cards will produce at a rate of between seven and eight SD cards per hour.

QUICK QUIZ   *See page 638 for the answers. Review concepts from this section in MyEconLab.*

Four fundamental characteristics of the market in **perfect competition** are (1) _____ numbers of buyers and sellers, (2) a _____ product, (3) good information in the hands of both buyers and sellers, and (4) _____ exit from and entry into the industry by other firms.

A perfectly competitive firm is a **price taker.** It has _____ control over price and consequently has to take price as a given, but it can sell _____ that it wants at the going market price.

The demand curve for a perfect competitor is perfectly elastic at the going market price. The demand curve is also

the perfect competitor's _____ revenue curve because _____ revenue is defined as the change in total revenue due to a one-unit change in output.

Profit is maximized at the rate of output at which the positive difference between total revenues and total costs is the greatest. This is the same level of output at which marginal _____ equals marginal _____. The perfectly competitive firm produces at an output rate at which marginal cost equals the _____ per unit of output, because MR is always equal to *P*.

Short-Run Profits

To find what our competitive individual producer of secure digital cards is making in terms of profits in the short run, we have to add the average total cost curve to panel (c) of Figure 24-2 on page 614. We take the information from column 6 in panel (a) and add it to panel (c) to get Figure 24-3 on the following page. Again the profit-maximizing rate of output is between seven and eight SD cards per hour. If we have production and sales of seven SD cards per hour, total revenues will be $35 per hour. Total costs will be $30 a day, leaving a profit of $5 per hour. If the rate of output and sales is eight SD cards per hour, total revenues will be $40 and total costs will be $35, again leaving a profit of $5 per hour.

A Graphical Depiction of Maximum Profits

In Figure 24-3, the lower boundary of the rectangle labeled "Profits" is determined by the intersection of the profit-maximizing quantity line represented by vertical dashes and the average total cost curve. Why? Because the ATC curve gives us the cost per unit, whereas the price ($5), represented by *d*, gives us the revenue per unit, or average revenue. The difference is profit per unit.

Thus, the height of the rectangular box representing profits equals profit per unit, and the length equals the amount of units produced. When we multiply these two quantities, we get total profits. Note, as pointed out earlier, that we are talking about *economic profits* because a normal rate of return on investment plus all opportunity costs is included in the average total cost curve, ATC.

Measuring Total Profits

Profits are represented by the blue-shaded area. The height of the profit rectangle is given by the difference between average total costs and price ($5), where price is also equal to average revenue. This is found by the vertical difference between the ATC curve and the price, or average revenue, line d, at the profit-maximizing rate of output of between seven and eight SD cards per hour.

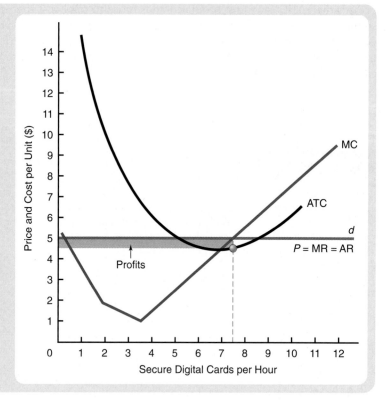

A Graphical Depiction of Minimum Losses

It is also certainly possible for the competitive firm to make short-run losses. We give an example in Figure 24-4, where we show the firm's demand curve shifting from d_1 to d_2. The going market price has fallen from $5 to $3 per secure digital card because of changes in market demand conditions. The firm will do the best it can by producing where marginal revenue equals marginal cost.

We see in Figure 24-4 that the marginal revenue (d_2) curve is intersected (from below) by the marginal cost curve at an output rate of about $5\frac{1}{2}$ SD cards per hour. The firm is clearly not making profits because average total costs at that output rate are greater than the price of $3 per SD card. The losses are shown in the shaded area. By producing where marginal revenue equals marginal cost, however, the firm is minimizing its losses; that is, losses would be greater at any other output.

The Short-Run Break-Even Price and the Short-Run Shutdown Price

In Figure 24-4, the firm is sustaining economic losses. Will it go out of business? In the long run it will, but in the short run the firm will not necessarily go out of business. In the short run, as long as the loss from staying in business is less than the loss from shutting down, the firm will remain in business and continue to produce. A firm *goes out of business* when the owners sell its assets to someone else. A firm temporarily *shuts down* when it stops producing, but it still is in business.

FIGURE 24-4

Minimization of Short-Run Losses

In situations in which average total costs exceed price, which in turn is greater than or equal to average variable cost, profit maximization is equivalent to loss minimization. This again occurs where marginal cost equals marginal revenue. Losses are shown in the red-shaded area.

Now how can a firm that is sustaining economic losses in the short run tell whether it is still worthwhile *not* to shut down? The firm must compare the loss incurred if it continues producing with the loss it incurs if it ceases production. Looking at the problem on a per-unit basis, as long as average variable cost (AVC) is covered by average revenues (price), the firm is better off continuing to produce. If average variable costs are exceeded even a little bit by the price of the product, staying in production produces some revenues in excess of variable costs. The logic is fairly straightforward:

As long as the price per unit sold exceeds the average variable cost per unit produced, the earnings of the firm's owners will be higher if it continues to produce in the short run than if it shuts down.

Calculating the Short-Run Break-Even Price

Look at demand curve d_1 in Figure 24-5 on the next page. It just touches the minimum point of the average total cost curve, which is exactly where the marginal cost curve intersects the average total cost curve. At that price, which is about $4.30, the firm will be making exactly zero short-run *economic* profits. That price is called the **short-run break-even price,** and point E_1 therefore occurs at the short-run break-even price for a competitive firm. It is the point at which marginal revenue, marginal cost, and average total cost are all equal (that is, at which $P = MC$ and $P = ATC$). The break-even price is the one that yields zero short-run *economic* profits or losses.

Calculating the Short-Run Shutdown Price

To calculate the firm's shutdown price, we must introduce the average variable cost (AVC) to our graph. In Figure 24-5, we have plotted the AVC values from column 7 in panel (a) of Figure 24-2 on page 614. For the moment, consider two possible demand

Short-run break-even price
The price at which a firm's total revenues equal its total costs. At the break-even price, the firm is just making a normal rate of return on its capital investment. (It is covering its explicit and implicit costs.)

FIGURE 24-5

Short-Run Break-Even and Shutdown Prices

We can find the short-run break-even price and the short-run shutdown price by comparing price with average total costs and average variable costs. If the demand curve is d_1, profit maximization occurs at output E_1, where MC equals marginal revenue (the d_1 curve). Because the ATC curve includes all relevant opportunity costs, point E_1 is the break-even point, and zero economic profits are being made. The firm is earning a normal rate of return. If the demand curve falls to d_2, profit maximization (loss minimization) occurs at the intersection of MC and MR (the d_2 curve), or E_2. Below this price, it does not pay for the firm to continue in operation because its average variable costs are not covered by the price of the product.

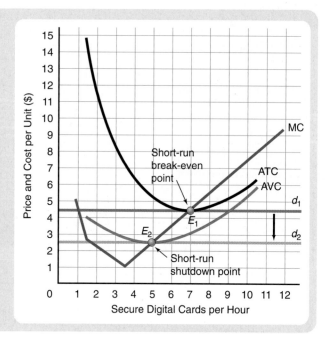

Short-run shutdown price

The price that covers average variable costs. It occurs just below the intersection of the marginal cost curve and the average variable cost curve.

curves, d_1 and d_2, which are also the firm's respective marginal revenue curves. If demand is d_1, the firm will produce at E_1, where that curve intersects the marginal cost curve. If demand falls to d_2, the firm will produce at E_2. The special feature of the hypothetical demand curve, d_2, is that it just touches the average variable cost curve at the latter's minimum point, which is also where the marginal cost curve intersects it. This price is the **short-run shutdown price.** Why? Below this price, the firm would be paying out more in variable costs than it is receiving in revenues from the sale of its product. Each unit it sold would generate losses that could be avoided if it shut down operations.

The intersection of the price line, the marginal cost curve, and the average variable cost curve is labeled E_2. The resulting short-run shutdown price is valid only for the short run because, of course, in the long run the firm will not stay in business if it is earning less than a normal rate of return (zero economic profits).

The Meaning of Zero Economic Profits

The fact that we labeled point E_1 in Figure 24-5 the break-even point may have disturbed you. At point E_1, price is just equal to average total cost. If this is the case, why would a firm continue to produce if it were making no profits whatsoever? If we again make the distinction between accounting profits and economic profits, you will realize that at that price, the firm has zero economic profits but positive accounting profits. Recall that accounting profits are total revenues minus total explicit costs. But such accounting ignores the reward offered to investors—the opportunity cost of capital—plus all other implicit costs.

In economic analysis, the average total cost curve includes the full opportunity cost of capital. Indeed, the average total cost curve includes the opportunity cost of *all* factors of production used in the production process. At the short-run break-even price, economic profits are, by definition, zero. Accounting profits at that price are not, however, equal to zero; they are positive. Consider an example. A baseball bat manufacturer sells bats at some price. The owners of the firm have supplied all the funds in the business. They have not borrowed from anyone else, and they explicitly pay the full opportunity cost to all factors of production, including any managerial labor that they themselves contribute to the business. Their salaries show up as a cost in the books and are equal to what they could have earned in the next-best alternative occupation. At the end of the year, the owners find that after they subtract all explicit costs from total revenues, accounting profits are $100,000. If their investment was $1 million, the rate of return on that investment is 10 percent per year. We will assume that this turns out to be equal to the market rate of return.

This $100,000, or 10 percent rate of return, is actually, then, a competitive, or normal, rate of return on invested capital in all industries with similar risks. If the owners had made only $50,000, or 5 percent on their investment, they would have been able to make higher profits by leaving the industry. The 10 percent rate of return is the opportunity cost of capital. Accountants show it as a profit; economists call it a cost. We include that cost in the average total cost curve, similar to the one shown in Figure 24-5. At the short-run break-even price, average total cost, including this opportunity cost of capital, will just equal that price. The firm will be making zero economic profits but a 10 percent *accounting profit*.

The Supply Curve for a Perfectly Competitive Industry

As you learned in Chapter 3, the relationship between a product's price and the quantity produced and offered for sale is a supply curve. Let's now examine the supply curve for a perfectly competitive industry.

The Perfect Competitor's Short-Run Supply Curve

What does the supply curve for the individual firm look like? Actually, we have been looking at it all along. We know that when the price of secure digital cards is $5, the firm will supply seven or eight of them per hour. If the price falls to $3, the firm will supply five or six SD cards per hour. And if the price falls below $3, the firm will shut down. Hence, in Figure 24-6, the firm's supply curve is the marginal cost curve above the short-run shutdown point. This is shown as the solid part of the marginal cost curve.

FIGURE 24-6

The Individual Firm's Short-Run Supply Curve

The individual firm's short-run supply curve is the portion of its marginal cost curve at and above the minimum point on the average variable cost curve.

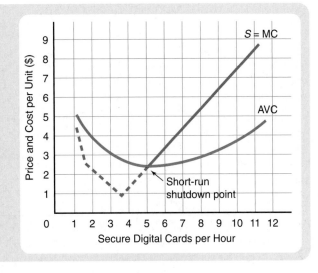

By definition, then, a firm's short-run supply curve in a competitive industry is its marginal cost curve at and above the point of intersection with the average variable cost curve.

The Short-Run Industry Supply Curve

In Chapter 3, we indicated that the market supply curve was the summation of individual supply curves. At the beginning of this chapter, we drew a market supply curve in Figure 24-1 on page 613. Now we want to derive more precisely a market, or industry, supply curve to reflect individual producer behavior in that industry. First we must ask, What is an industry? It is merely a collection of firms producing a particular product. Therefore, we have a way to figure out the total supply curve of any industry: As discussed in Chapter 3, we add the quantities that each firm will supply at every possible price. In other words, we sum the individual supply curves of all the competitive firms *horizontally*. The individual supply curves, as we just saw, are simply the marginal cost curves of each firm.

Consider doing this for a hypothetical world in which there are only two producers of SD cards in the industry, firm A and firm B. These two firms' marginal cost curves are given in panels (a) and (b) of Figure 24-7. The marginal cost curves for the two separate firms are presented as MC_A in panel (a) and MC_B in panel (b). Those two marginal cost curves are drawn only for prices above the minimum average variable cost for each respective firm. In panel (a), for firm A, at a price of $6 per unit, the quantity supplied would be 7 units. At a price of $10 per unit, the quantity supplied would be 12 units. In panel (b), we see the two different quantities that would be supplied by firm B corresponding to those two prices. Now, at a price of $6, we add horizontally the quantities 7 and 10 to obtain 17 units. This gives us one point, *F*, for our short-run **industry supply curve,** *S*. We obtain the other point, *G*, by doing the same

Industry supply curve
The locus of points showing the minimum prices at which given quantities will be forthcoming; also called the *market supply curve*.

FIGURE 24-7

Deriving the Industry Supply Curve

Marginal cost curves at and above minimum average variable cost are presented in panels (a) and (b) for firms A and B. We horizontally sum the two quantities supplied, 7 units by firm A and 10 units by firm B, at a price of $6. This gives us point *F* in panel (c). We do the same thing for the quantities supplied at a price of $10. This gives us point *G*. When we connect those points, we have the industry supply curve, *S*, which is the horizontal summation—represented by the Greek letter sigma (Σ)—of the firms' marginal cost curves above their respective minimum average variable costs.

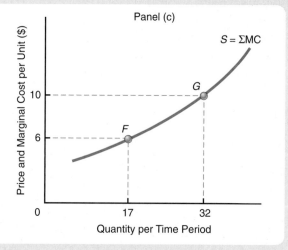

horizontal adding of quantities at a price of $10 per unit. When we connect all points such as *F* and *G*, we obtain the industry supply curve *S*, which is also marked ΣMC (where the capital Greek sigma, Σ, is the symbol for summation), indicating that it is the horizontal summation of the marginal cost curves (at and above the respective minimum average variable cost of each firm). Because the law of diminishing marginal product makes marginal cost curves rise, the short-run supply curve of a perfectly competitive industry must be upward sloping.

Factors That Influence the Industry Supply Curve

As you have just seen, the industry supply curve is the horizontal summation of all of the individual firms' marginal cost curves at and above their respective minimum average variable cost points. This means that anything that affects the marginal cost curves of the firm will influence the industry supply curve. Therefore, the individual factors that will influence the supply schedule in a competitive industry can be summarized as the factors that cause the variable costs of production to change. These are factors that affect the individual marginal cost curves, such as changes in the individual firm's productivity, in factor costs (such as wages paid to labor and prices of raw materials), in per-unit taxes, and in anything else that would influence the individual firm's marginal cost curve.

All of these are *ceteris paribus* conditions of supply (see page 66 in Chapter 3). Because they affect the position of the marginal cost curve for the individual firm, they affect the position of the industry supply curve. A change in any of these will shift the firms' marginal cost curves and thus shift the industry supply curve.

QUICK QUIZ   *See page 638 for the answers. Review concepts from this section in MyEconLab.*

Short-run average profits or losses are determined by comparing _____ total costs with _____ (average revenue) at the **profit-maximizing rate of output**. In the short run, the perfectly competitive firm can make economic profits or economic losses.

The perfectly competitive firm's short-run _____-_____ price equals the firm's minimum average total cost, which is at the point at which the _____ cost curve intersects the average total cost curve.

The perfectly competitive firm's short-run _____ price equals the firm's minimum average variable cost, which is at the point at which the _____ cost curve intersects the average variable cost curve. Shutdown will occur if price falls below average variable cost.

The firm will continue production at a price that exceeds average variable costs because revenues exceed total _____ costs of producing.

At the short-run break-even price, the firm is making _____ economic profits, which means that it is just making a _____ rate of return for industries with similar risks.

The firm's short-run supply curve is the portion of its marginal cost curve at and above its minimum average _____ cost. The industry short-run supply curve is a horizontal _____ of the individual firms' marginal cost curves at and above their respective minimum average _____ costs.

Price Determination Under Perfect Competition

How is the market, or "going," price established in a competitive market? This price is established by the interaction of all the suppliers (firms) and all the demanders (consumers).

The Market Clearing Price

The market demand schedule, *D*, in panel (a) of Figure 24-8 represents the demand schedule for the entire industry, and the supply schedule, *S*, represents the supply schedule for the entire industry. The market clearing price, P_e, is established by the forces of supply and demand at the intersection of *D* and the short-run industry supply curve, *S*. Even though each individual firm has no control or effect on the price of its product in a competitive industry, the interaction of *all* the producers and buyers determines the price at which the product will be sold.

We say that the price P_e and the quantity Q_e in panel (a) of Figure 24-8 constitute the competitive solution to the resource allocation problem in that particular industry. It is the equilibrium at which quantity demanded equals quantity supplied, and both suppliers and demanders are doing as well as they can. The resulting individual firm demand curve, *d*, is shown in panel (b) of Figure 24-8 at the price P_e.

Market Equilibrium and the Individual Firm

In a purely competitive industry, the individual producer takes price as a given and chooses the output level that maximizes profits. (This is also the equilibrium level of output from the producer's standpoint.) We see in panel (b) of Figure 24-8 that this is at q_e. If the producer's average costs are given by AC_1, the short-run break-even price arises at q_e (see Figure 24-5 on page 620). If its average costs are given by AC_2, then at q_e, AC exceeds price (average revenue), and the firm is incurring losses. Alternatively, if average costs are given by AC_3, the firm will be making economic profits at q_e. In the

---

FIGURE 24-8

Industry Demand and Supply Curves and the Individual Firm Demand Curve

The industry demand curve is represented by *D* in panel (a). The short-run industry supply curve is *S* and is equal to ΣMC. The intersection of the demand and supply curves at *E* determines the equilibrium or market clearing price at P_e. The demand curve faced by the individual firm in panel (b) is perfectly elastic at the market clearing price determined in panel (a). If the producer has a marginal cost curve MC, its profit-maximizing output level is at q_e. For AC_1, economic profits are zero; for AC_2, profits are negative; and for AC_3, profits are positive.

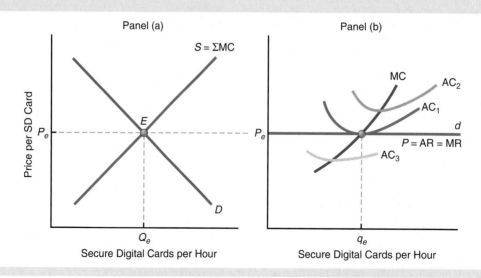

former case, we would expect, over time, that some firms will cease production (exit the industry), causing supply to shift inward, whereas in the latter case, we would expect new firms to enter the industry to take advantage of the economic profits, thereby causing supply to shift outward. We now turn to these long-run considerations.

The Long-Run Industry Situation: Exit and Entry

In the long run in a competitive situation, firms will be making zero economic profits. (Actually, this is true only for identical firms. Throughout the remainder of the discussion, we assume firms have the same cost structures.) We surmise, therefore, that in the long run a perfectly competitive firm's price (marginal and average revenue) curve will just touch its average total cost curve. How does this occur? It is through an adjustment process that depends on economic profits and losses.

Exit and Entry of Firms

Look back at Figure 24-3 on page 618 and Figure 24-4 on page 619. The existence of either profits or losses is a signal to owners of capital both inside and outside the industry. If the industry is characterized by firms showing economic profits as represented in Figure 24-3, this will signal owners of capital elsewhere in the economy that they, too, should enter this industry. If, by contrast, there are firms in the industry suffering economic losses as represented in Figure 24-4, this signals resource owners outside the industry to stay out. It also signals resource owners within the industry not to reinvest and if possible to leave the industry. It is in this sense that we say that profits direct resources to their highest-valued use. In the long run, capital will flow into industries in which profitability is highest and will flow out of industries in which profitability is lowest.

ALLOCATION OF CAPITAL AND MARKET SIGNALS The price system therefore allocates capital according to the relative expected rates of return on alternative investments. Hence, entry restrictions (such as limits on the numbers of taxicabs and banks permitted to enter the taxi service and banking industries) will hinder economic efficiency by not allowing resources to flow to their highest-valued use. Similarly, exit restrictions (such as laws that require firms to give advance notice of closings) will act to trap resources (temporarily) in sectors in which their value is below that in alternative uses. Such laws will also inhibit the ability of firms to respond to changes in both the domestic and international marketplaces.

Not every industry presents an immediate source of opportunity for every firm. In a brief period of time, it may be impossible for a firm that produces tractors to switch to the production of computers, even if there are very large profits to be made. Over the long run, however, we would expect to see owners of some other resources switch to producing computers. In a market economy, investors supply firms in the more profitable industry with more investment funds, which they take from firms in less profitable industries. (Also, positive economic profits induce existing firms to use internal investment funds for expansion.) Consequently, resources useful in the production of more profitable goods, such as labor, will be bid away from lower-valued opportunities. Investors and other suppliers of resources respond to market **signals** about their highest-valued opportunities.

Signals
Compact ways of conveying to economic decision makers information needed to make decisions. An effective signal not only conveys information but also provides the incentive to react appropriately. Economic profits and economic losses are such signals.

Why are farmers in the U.S. plains states selling off their farm implements and cattle and lodging thousands of human guests on their properties instead?

EXAMPLE
Sell the Livestock and Open the Farm to Pheasant Hunters!

Throughout the Great Plains, farmers who once grew wheat and raised cattle have opted for a new crop: pheasants. Hundreds of families whose lands have been farms for more than a century have sold off their tractors and livestock and converted barns and outbuildings into lodges for use by pheasant hunters. These ex-farming families have then given their farms new names, such as Medicine Creek Pheasant Ranch or Rooster Ridge Pheasant Lodge, and begun booking visits by hunters who roam their lands in search of game. Hunting lodge operators have found

that reallocating their lands from crops and livestock to pheasant hunting has yielded profits several times higher than they had earned as farmers. Naturally, this has sent a clear signal to other farmers to consider shifting resources to the booming pheasant-hunting industry.

FOR CRITICAL ANALYSIS
At what point would you anticipate that farmers in the Great Plains will no longer have an incentive to enter the pheasant-hunting market?

TENDENCY TOWARD EQUILIBRIUM Market adjustment to changes in demand will occur regardless of the wishes of the managers of firms in less profitable markets. They can either attempt to adjust their product line to respond to the new demands, be replaced by managers who are more responsive to new conditions, or see their firms go bankrupt as they find themselves unable to replace worn-out plant and equipment.

In addition, when we say that in a competitive long-run equilibrium situation firms will be making zero economic profits, we must realize that at a particular point in time it would be pure coincidence for a firm to be making *exactly* zero economic profits. Real-world information is not as precise as the curves we use to simplify our analysis. Things change all the time in a dynamic world, and firms, even in a very competitive situation, may for many reasons not be making exactly zero economic profits. We say that there is a *tendency* toward that equilibrium position, but firms are adjusting all the time to changes in their cost curves and in the market demand curves.

Long-Run Industry Supply Curves

In panel (a) of Figure 24-8 on page 624, we drew the summation of all of the portions of the individual firms' marginal cost curves at and above each firm's respective minimum average variable costs as the upward-sloping supply curve of the entire industry. We should be aware, however, that a relatively inelastic supply curve may be appropriate only in the short run. After all, one of the prerequisites of a competitive industry is freedom of entry.

Remember that our definition of the long run is a period of time in which all adjustments can be made. The **long-run industry supply curve** is a supply curve showing the relationship between quantities supplied by the entire industry at different prices after firms have been allowed to either enter or leave the industry, depending on whether there have been positive or negative economic profits. Also, the long-run industry supply curve is drawn under the assumption that firms are identical and that

You Are There

For practice thinking about how a perfect competitor responds to market signals in the form of market prices and economic profits, take a look at **Conflicting Signals in the Crocodile Market,** on page 631.

Long-run industry supply curve
A market supply curve showing the relationship between prices and quantities after firms have been allowed the time to enter into or exit from an industry, depending on whether there have been positive or negative economic profits.

entry and exit have been completed. This means that along the long-run industry supply curve, firms in the industry earn zero economic profits.

The long-run industry supply curve can take one of three shapes, depending on whether input prices stay constant, increase, or decrease as the number of firms in the industry changes. In Chapter 23, we assumed that input prices remained constant to the *firm* regardless of the firm's rate of output. When we look at the entire *industry*, however, when all firms are expanding and new firms are entering, they may simultaneously bid up input prices.

CONSTANT-COST INDUSTRIES In principle, there are industries that use such a small percentage of the total supply of inputs required for industrywide production that firms can enter the industry without bidding up input prices. In such a situation, we are dealing with a **constant-cost industry.** Its long-run industry supply curve is therefore horizontal and is represented by S_L in panel (a) of Figure 24-9.

We can work through the case in which constant costs prevail. We start out in panel (a) with demand curve D_1 and supply curve S_1. The equilibrium price is P_1. Market demand shifts rightward to D_2. In the short run, the equilibrium price rises to P_2. This generates positive economic profits for existing firms in the industry. Such economic profits induce capital to flow into the industry. The existing firms expand or new firms enter (or both). The short-run supply curve shifts outward to S_2. The new intersection with the new demand curve is at E_3. The new equilibrium price is again P_1. The long-run supply curve, labeled S_L, is obtained by connecting the intersections of the corresponding pairs of demand and supply curves, E_1 and E_3. In a constant-cost industry, long-run supply is perfectly elastic. Any shift in demand is eventually met by just enough entry or exit of suppliers that the long-run price is constant at P_1.

Retail trade is often given as an example of such an industry because output can be expanded or contracted without affecting input prices. Banking is another example.

Why have some farmers sold their farm equipment and transformed their farmlands into pheasant-hunting estates?

Constant-cost industry

An industry whose total output can be increased without an increase in long-run per-unit costs; its long-run supply curve is horizontal.

FIGURE 24-9

Constant-Cost, Increasing-Cost, and Decreasing-Cost Industries

In panel (a), we show a situation in which the demand curve shifts from D_1 to D_2. Price increases from P_1 to P_2. In time, the short-run supply curve shifts outward because positive profits are being earned, and the equilibrium shifts from E_2 to E_3. The market clearing price is again P_1. If we connect points such as E_1 and E_3, we come up with the long-run supply curve S_L. This is a constant-cost industry. In panel (b), costs are increasing for the industry, and therefore the long-run supply curve, S_L', slopes upward and long-run prices rise from P_1 to P_2. In panel (c), costs are decreasing for the industry as it expands, and therefore the long-run supply curve, S_L'', slopes downward such that long-run prices decline from P_1 to P_2.

Increasing-cost industry
An industry in which an increase in industry output is accompanied by an increase in long-run per-unit costs, such that the long-run industry supply curve slopes upward.

INCREASING-COST INDUSTRIES In an **increasing-cost industry,** expansion by existing firms and the addition of new firms cause the price of inputs specialized to that industry to be bid up. As costs of production rise, the ATC curve and the firms' MC curves shift upward, causing short-run supply curves (each firm's marginal cost curve) to shift upward. Hence, industry supply shifts out by less than in a constant-cost industry. The result is a long-run industry supply curve that slopes upward, as represented by S'_L in panel (b) of Figure 24-9 on the previous page. Examples are residential construction and coal mining—both use specialized inputs that cannot be obtained in ever-increasing quantities without causing their prices to rise.

What are the implications of this discussion for the future of the oil industry?

INTERNATIONAL EXAMPLE
Increasing Costs and Future Prices in the Oil Industry

During the 1950s, there were predictions that the world would run out of a fixed stock of available oil reserves by the 1980s. In the late 1970s, the predicted oil depletion date was pushed back to the 2000s. As Figure 24-10 indicates, however, the world's known reserves of oil actually continued to increase. Today, once again there are dire predictions that the world's stock of nonrenewable oil reserves will be consumed by the end of the 2030s.

The problem with recurring pessimistic forecasts that current *stocks* of known oil reserves may be depleted at future dates at current rates of oil production and consumption is that they ignore long-run *flow* adjustments. Many times in the past, producers faced short-run situations in which the stocks of oil reserves they were tapping began to dwindle. Each time, the price of oil increased, which encouraged oil producers to find novel ways to search for and extract oil located at ever-increasing depths beneath the planet's surface.

As the world demand for oil has increased, so have the prices of inputs required to find new reserves of oil and to tap these reserves. These input price increases, in turn, have boosted oil prices. Since 1998, the inflation-adjusted price of oil has increased by more than 800 percent, and the quantity of oil supplied by petroleum firms has also risen. Many energy economists suggest that this increase in price is an indication that the oil industry may be an increasing-cost industry. In the long run, as predicted, prices have increased, and so has production.

FOR CRITICAL ANALYSIS

Why are industries that specialize in extracting minerals such as coal and oil increasing-cost industries?

FIGURE 24-10

Proven Global Oil Reserves, 1983–2013

In spite of periodic predictions that known stocks of oil reserves will eventually shrink, proven global oil reserves have continued to increase over time.

Source: U.S. Department of Energy.

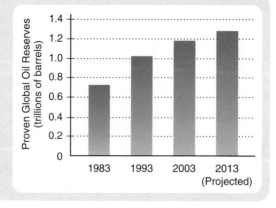

DECREASING-COST INDUSTRIES An expansion in the number of firms in an industry can lead to a reduction in input costs and a downward shift in the ATC and MC curves. When this occurs, the long-run industry supply curve will slope downward. An example, S_L'', is given in panel (c) of Figure 24-9. This is a **decreasing-cost industry.**

Decreasing-cost industry
An industry in which an increase in output leads to a reduction in long-run per-unit costs, such that the long-run industry supply curve slopes downward.

Long-Run Equilibrium

In the long run, the firm can change the scale of its plant, adjusting its plant size in such a way that it has no further incentive to change. It will do so until profits are maximized.

The Firm's Long-Run Situation

Figure 24-11 shows the long-run equilibrium of the perfectly competitive firm. Given a price of P and a marginal cost curve, MC, the firm produces at output q_e. Because profits must be zero in the long run, the firm's short-run average costs (SAC) must equal P at q_e, which occurs at minimum SAC. In addition, because we are in long-run equilibrium, any economies of scale must be exhausted, so we are on the minimum point of the long-run average cost curve (LAC). In other words, the long-run equilibrium position is where "everything is equal," which is at point E in Figure 24-11. There, *price* equals *marginal revenue* equals *marginal cost* equals *average cost* (minimum, short-run, and long-run).

Perfect Competition and Minimum Average Total Cost

Look again at Figure 24-11. In long-run equilibrium, the perfectly competitive firm finds itself producing at output rate q_e. At that rate of output, the price is just equal to the minimum long-run average cost as well as the minimum short-run average cost. In this sense, perfect competition results in the production of goods and services using the least costly combination of resources. This is an important attribute of a perfectly

FIGURE 24-11

Long-Run Firm Competitive Equilibrium

In the long run, the firm operates where price, marginal revenue, marginal cost, short-run minimum average cost, and long-run minimum average cost are all equal. This occurs at point E.

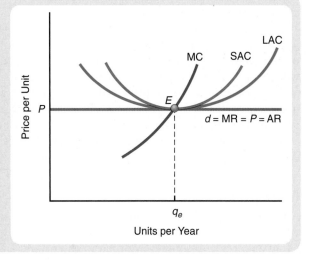

competitive long-run equilibrium, particularly when we wish to compare the market structure of perfect competition with other market structures that are less than perfectly competitive. We will examine these other market structures in later chapters.

Competitive Pricing: Marginal Cost Pricing

In a perfectly competitive industry, each firm produces where its marginal cost curve intersects its marginal revenue curve from below. Thus, perfectly competitive firms always sell their goods at a price that just equals marginal cost. This is said to be the optimal price of this good because the price that consumers pay reflects the opportunity cost to society of producing the good. Recall that marginal cost is the amount that a firm must spend to purchase the additional resources needed to expand output by one unit. Given competitive markets, the amount paid for a resource will be the same in all of its alternative uses. Thus, MC reflects relative resource input use; that is, if the MC of good 1 is twice the MC of good 2, one more unit of good 1 requires twice the resource input of one more unit of good 2.

Marginal Cost Pricing

Marginal cost pricing
A system of pricing in which the price charged is equal to the opportunity cost to society of producing one more unit of the good or service in question. The opportunity cost is the marginal cost to society.

The competitive firm produces up to the point at which the market price just equals the marginal cost. Herein lies the element of the optimal nature of a competitive solution. It is called **marginal cost pricing.** The competitive firm sells its product at a price that just equals the cost to society—the opportunity cost—for that is what the marginal cost curve represents. (But note here that it is the self-interest of firm owners that causes price to equal the marginal cost to society.) In other words, the marginal benefit to consumers, given by the price that they are willing to pay for the last unit of the good purchased, just equals the marginal cost to society of producing the last unit. (If the marginal benefit exceeds the marginal cost, that is, if $P > MC$, too little is being produced in that people value additional units more than the cost to society of producing them; if $P < MC$, the opposite is true.)

When an individual pays a price equal to the marginal cost of production, the cost to the user of that product is equal to the sacrifice or cost to society of producing that quantity of that good as opposed to more of some other good. (We are assuming that all marginal social costs are accounted for.) The competitive solution, then, is called *efficient*, in the economic sense of the word. Economic efficiency means that it is impossible to increase the output of any good without lowering the *value* of the total output produced in the economy. No juggling of resources, such as labor and capital, will result in an output that is higher in total value than the value of all of the goods and services already being produced. In an efficient equilibrium, it is impossible to make one person better off without making someone else worse off. All resources are used in the most advantageous way possible, and society therefore enjoys an efficient allocation of productive resources. All goods and services are sold at their opportunity cost, and marginal cost pricing prevails throughout.

Market Failure

Although perfect competition does offer many desirable results, situations arise when perfectly competitive markets cannot efficiently allocate resources. Either too many or too few resources are used in the production of a good or service. These situations are instances of **market failure.** Externalities arising from failures to fully assign property rights and public goods are examples. For reasons discussed in later chapters, perfectly competitive markets cannot efficiently allocate resources in these situations, and alternative allocation mechanisms are called for. In some cases, alternative market structures or government intervention *may* improve the economic outcome.

Market failure
A situation in which an unrestrained market operation leads to either too few or too many resources going to a specific economic activity.

QUICK QUIZ   *See page 638 for the answers. Review concepts from this section in MyEconLab.*

The perfectly competitive price is determined by the _____ of the market demand curve and the market supply curve; the market supply curve is equal to the horizontal summation of the portions of the individual marginal cost curves above their respective minimum average _____ costs.

In the long run, perfectly competitive firms make _____ economic profits because of entry and exit whenever there are industrywide economic profits or losses.

A constant-cost industry has a _____ long-run supply curve. An increasing-cost industry has an _____ -

sloping long-run supply curve. A decreasing-cost industry has a _____-sloping long-run supply curve.

In the long run, a perfectly competitive firm produces to the point at which price, marginal revenue, marginal cost, short-run minimum average cost, and long-run minimum average cost are all _____.

Perfectly competitive pricing is essentially _____ _____ pricing. Therefore, the perfectly competitive solution is called efficient because _____ _____ represents the social opportunity cost of producing one more unit of the good.

You Are There   ▶ Conflicting Signals in the Crocodile Market

In many parts of the world, the latest fashion in clothing and accessories is items made from the skins of exotic creatures, such as stingrays, anacondas and other snakes, and, especially, crocodiles. Crocodile shoes sell for around $300 a pair, and crocodile purses are priced at about $450. For Yingos Ratanakorn of the Suphan Buri province of Thailand, a big run-up in crocodile prices in the early 2000s was a signal that it was time to transform his farm into a crocodile ranch.

Today, however, Ratanakorn is contemplating going back to old-fashioned farming. The problem he faces is that too many others made the same decision he did. As a consequence, since the early 2000s, Thailand's population of captive crocodiles has nearly doubled, to more than 400,000 of the beasts. Thus, the market supply of crocodile hides has surged, and prices have declined. Indeed, the equilibrium price of crocodile hides started to fall as soon as

Ratanakorn opened his crocodile ranch in 2002. Initially, the market clearing price was sufficiently high that Ratanakorn was earning more than he did as a crop-raising farmer. Now, however, in most years the difference between his revenues and his costs is lower than he could be earning by planting, tending, and harvesting crops and raising less dangerous livestock.

CRITICAL ANALYSIS QUESTIONS

1. Are Ratanakorn's accounting profits currently positive or negative? What about his economic profits?

2. In 2002, did Ratanakorn's marginal revenue curve lie above or below his break-even point? What is the position of the marginal revenue curve today in relation to his break-even point?

The Data-Storage Industry Booms, and Price Declines

CONCEPTS APPLIED

- Perfect Competition
- Industry Supply Curve
- Decreasing-Cost Industry

Long a dull backwater of the computer industry, the data-storage business is now growing by leaps and bounds. It is also a highly competitive industry with characteristics consistent with the theory of perfect competition.

The Data-Storage Industry's Roots

Firms offering to store commercial data—records of financial firms such as banks and insurance companies and other corporations with large amounts of accounting information stored on mainframe computers—have been around since the 1960s. Originally, data-storage companies did little more than place huge reels of magnetic tape in nondescript warehouse storage boxes. At the end of every business week, an employee of a data-storage firm would pick up a new reel of tape from a client's headquarters. If the client suffered a computer crash or damage from a fire or flood, the latest reel of tape would be available, so the client would lose no more than a few days' worth of data.

As data-storage firms' clients became more reliant on up-to-the minute, digitized data, and as computers became more sophisticated, data-storage firms gradually became more "high tech." Today's data-storage machines, known as "plain vanilla boxes"—a term coined by IBM salespeople back in the early 1980s—have capacities of a few terabytes. (A terabyte is about 2,500 gigabytes, or the hard-drive space of about 25 personal computers, but only 2.5 millionths of an exabyte.) The data-storage business remains "plain vanilla." Each data-storage company provides essentially the same type of service: backing up data in storage boxes. Thus, the numerous firms in the data-storage industry offer to sell a homogeneous product to many customers, and entering the business requires only obtaining the latest data-storage and networking equipment.

A Downward-Sloping Long-Run Supply Curve for Data-Storage Services

Over time, an increasing number of businesses have determined that they possess more precious digital data that they wish to store. Oil companies, for instance, now consume 50 times more data-storage space for surveys of oil fields than they did just a decade ago. Professional sports teams possess game videos taken by cameras at multiple angles that require considerable storage space. Scientists store massive amounts of data. Even college students have computer hard drives filled with supplementary course materials assigned by professors, drafts of course research papers, and music and video downloads that they may be willing to pay to place in backup storage. Thus, since the mid-1990s the demand for data-storage services has increased dramatically.

Figure 24-12 examines the adjustments that have taken place in the data-storage industry as demand has risen over time. Panel (a) displays the short-run adjustments that have occurred as the demand for the services of data-storage firms has increased, from D_1 to D_2. A few years ago, the equilibrium amount of data flowing to data-storage firms was about 500 million gigabytes, and the price of storing data was about $3.50 per gigabyte per year. When the demand for data-storage services increased during the late 1990s and early 2000s, the equilibrium flow of data stored rose to about 1 billion gigabytes per year. The market clearing price of these services rose to about $4 per gigabyte per year. In addition, existing providers of data-storage services began to earn positive economic profits. Panel (b) displays the

FIGURE 24-12

Short-Run and Long-Run Adjustments in the Data-Storage Industry

Panel (a) shows that when the demand for data-storage services increased in the late 1990s and early 2000s, the market clearing price rose from about $3.50 per gigabyte of data per year at point E_1 to about $4 per gigabyte per year at point E_2. The equilibrium quantity of data-storage services also increased. Panel (b) displays the long-run adjustments that took place during the rest of the 2000s as numerous firms entered the industry, causing market supply to increase. The equilibrium quantity of data-storage services continued to rise, but the market clearing price declined, to about $3.20 per gigabyte per year at point E_3. Hence, the long-run supply curve in this industry sloped downward, indicating that this is a decreasing-cost industry.

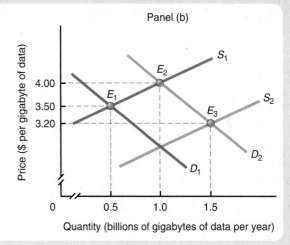

long-run effects of entry of new firms into the data-storage industry during the 2000s, which caused short-run market supply to increase. The equilibrium flow of data to data-storage firms rose to about 1.5 billion gigabytes per year. Accompanying the expansion of data-storage firms was a decrease in the prices of key inputs—data-storage and networking equipment. Consequently, the market price of data-storage services declined to about $3.20 per gigabyte per year. Thus, the data-storage industry is a decreasing-cost industry.

Test your understanding of this chapter by going online to **MyEconLab**.
In the Study Plan for this chapter, select Section N: News.

For Critical Analysis

1. What role might software improvements have played in helping reduce costs of employing other inputs in the provision of data-storage services, such as storage and networking equipment?

2. In the long run, what appears to have happened to the ATC and MC curves of firms that provide data-storage services?

Web Resources

1. To learn about the latest developments in the data-storage industry, go to www.econtoday.com/chapter24.

2. For links to information provided by data-storage trade associations, go to www.econtoday.com/chapter24.

Research Project

Suppose that a technological advance enables data-storage firms to squeeze even more data into their "plain vanilla box" storage machines. What short-run and long-run adjustments would then take place in the data-storage industry?

Here is what you should know after reading this chapter. **MyEconLab** will help you identify what you know, and where to go when you need to practice.

WHAT YOU SHOULD KNOW		WHERE TO GO TO PRACTICE
The Characteristics of a Perfectly Competitive Market Structure A perfectly competitive industry has four fundamental characteristics: (1) there are large numbers of buyers and sellers, (2) firms in the industry produce and sell a homogeneous product, (3) information is equally accessible to both buyers and sellers, and (4) there are insignificant barriers to industry entry or exit. These characteristics imply that each firm in a perfectly competitive industry is a price taker, meaning that the firm takes the market price as given and outside its control.	perfect competition, 611 perfectly competitive firm, 611 price taker, 611	• **MyEconLab** Study Plan 24.1 • Audio introduction to Chapter 24
How a Perfectly Competitive Firm Decides How Much to Produce Because a perfectly competitive firm sells the amount that it wishes at the market price, the additional revenue it earns from selling an additional unit of output is the market price. Thus, the firm's marginal revenue equals the market price, and its marginal revenue curve is the firm's own perfectly elastic demand curve. The firm maximizes economic profits when marginal cost equals marginal revenue, as long as the market price is not below the short-run shutdown price, where the marginal cost curve crosses the average variable cost curve.	total revenues, 613 profit-maximizing rate of production, 615 marginal revenue, 615 **KEY FIGURES** Figure 24-1, 613 Figure 24-2, 614	• **MyEconLab** Study Plans 24.2, 24.3 • Animated Figures 24-1, 24-2
The Short-Run Supply Curve of a Perfectly Competitive Firm If the market price is below the short-run shutdown price, the firm's total revenues fail to cover its variable costs. Then the firm would be better off halting production, thereby minimizing its economic loss in the short run. If the market price is above the short-run shutdown price, however, the firm produces the rate of output where marginal revenue, the market price, equals marginal cost. Thus, the range of the firm's marginal cost curve above the short-run shutdown price gives combinations of market prices and production choices of the perfectly competitive firm. This range of the firm's marginal cost curve is therefore the firm's short-run supply curve.	short-run break-even price, 619 short-run shutdown price, 620 industry supply curve, 622 **KEY FIGURES** Figure 24-3, 618 Figure 24-4, 619 Figure 24-5, 620 Figure 24-6, 621 Figure 24-7, 622	• **MyEconLab** Study Plans 24.4, 24.5, 24.6, 24.7 • Animated Figures 24-3, 24-4, 24-5, 24-6, 24-7 • Video: The Short-Run Shutdown Price • Video: The Meaning of Zero Economic Profits

(continued)

(continued)

WHAT YOU SHOULD KNOW		WHERE TO GO TO PRACTICE
The Equilibrium Price in a Perfectly Competitive Market The short-run supply curve for a perfectly competitive industry is obtained by summing the quantities supplied at each price by all firms in the industry. At the equilibrium market price, the total amount of output supplied by all firms is equal to the total amount of output demanded by all buyers.	KEY FIGURE Figure 24-8, 624	• **MyEconLab** Study Plan 24.8 • Animated Figure 24-8
Incentives to Enter or Exit a Perfectly Competitive Industry In the short run, a perfectly competitive firm will continue to produce output as long as the market price exceeds the short-run shutdown price. This is so even if the market price is below the short-run break-even point where the marginal cost curve crosses the firm's average total cost curve. Even though the firm earns an economic loss, it minimizes the amount of the loss by continuing to produce in the short run. In the long run, however, an economic loss is a signal that the firm is not engaged in the highest-value activity available to its owners, and continued economic losses in the long run will induce exit from the industry.	signals, 625	• **MyEconLab** Study Plan 24.9
The Long-Run Industry Supply Curve and Constant-, Increasing-, and Decreasing-Cost Industries The long-run industry supply curve in a perfectly competitive industry shows the relationship between prices and quantities after firms have the opportunity to enter or leave the industry in response to economic profits or losses. In a constant-cost industry, total output can increase without a rise in long-run per-unit production costs, so the long-run industry supply curve is horizontal. In an increasing-cost industry, however, per-unit costs increase with a rise in industry output, so the long-run industry supply curve slopes upward. In contrast, in a decreasing-cost industry per-unit costs decline as industry output increases, and the long-run industry supply curve slopes downward.	long-run industry supply curve, 626 constant-cost industry, 627 increasing-cost industry, 628 decreasing-cost industry, 629 marginal cost pricing, 630 market failure, 631 KEY FIGURE Figure 24-11, 629	• **MyEconLab** Study Plans 24.10, 24.11 • Animated Figure 24-11

Log in to MyEconLab, take a chapter test, and get a personalized Study Plan that tells you which concepts you understand and which ones you need to review. From there, MyEconLab will give you further practice, tutorials, animations, videos, and guided solutions.
Log in to www.myeconlab.com

PROBLEMS

All problems are assignable in 🗶 myeconlab *. Answers to odd-numbered problems appear at the back of the book.*

24-1. Explain why each of the following examples is *not* a perfectly competitive industry.

a. One firm produces a large portion of the industry's total output, but there are many firms in the industry, and their products are indistinguishable. Firms can easily exit and enter the industry.

b. There are many buyers and sellers in the industry. Consumers have equal information about the prices of firms' products, which differ slightly in quality from firm to firm.

c. Many taxicabs compete in a city. The city's government requires all taxicabs to provide identical service. Taxicabs are virtually identical, and all drivers must wear a designated uniform. The government also limits the number of taxicab companies that can operate within the city's boundaries.

24-2. Consider the market for DVD movie rentals, which is perfectly competitive. The market supply curve slopes upward, the market demand curve slopes downward, and the equilibrium rental price equals $3.50. Consider each of the following events, and discuss the effects they will have on the market clearing price and on the demand curve faced by the individual rental store.

a. People's tastes change in favor of going to see more movies at cinemas with their friends and family members.

b. National DVD-rental chains open a number of new stores in this market.

c. There is a significant increase in the price of downloading movies on the Internet.

24-3. Consider the diagram in the next column, which applies to a perfectly competitive firm, which at present faces a market clearing price of $20 per unit and produces 10,000 units of output per week.

a. What is the firm's current average revenue per unit?

b. What are the present economic profits of this firm? Is the firm maximizing economic profits? Explain.

c. If the market clearing price drops to $12.50 per unit, should this firm continue to produce in the short run if it wishes to maximize its economic profits (or minimize its economic losses)? Explain.

d. If the market clearing price drops to $7.50 per unit, should this firm continue to produce in the short run if it wishes to maximize its economic profits (or minimize its economic losses)? Explain.

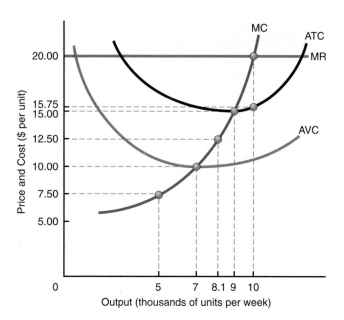

24-4. The following table represents the hourly output and cost structure for a local pizza shop. The market is perfectly competitive, and the market price of a pizza in the area is $10. Total costs include all opportunity costs.

Total Hourly Output and Sales of Pizzas	Total Hourly Cost ($)
0	5
1	9
2	11
3	12
4	14
5	18
6	24
7	32
8	42
9	54
10	68

a. Calculate the total revenue and total economic profit for this pizza shop at each rate of output.

b. Assuming that the pizza shop always produces and sells at least one pizza per hour, does this appear to be a situation of short-run or long-run equilibrium?

c. Calculate the pizza shop's marginal cost and marginal revenue at each rate of output. Based on marginal analysis, what is the profit-maximizing rate of output for the pizza shop?

d. Draw a diagram depicting the short-run marginal revenue and marginal cost curves for this pizza shop, and illustrate the determination of its profit-maximizing output rate.

24-5. Consider the information provided in Problem 24-4. Suppose the market price drops to only $5 per pizza. In the short run, should this pizza shop continue to make pizzas, or will it maximize its economic profits (that is, minimize its economic loss) by shutting down?

24-6. Yesterday, a perfectly competitive producer of construction bricks manufactured and sold 10,000 bricks per week at a market price that was just equal to the minimum average variable cost of producing each brick. Today, all the firm's costs are the same, but the market price of bricks has declined.

   a. Assuming that this firm has positive fixed costs, did the firm earn economic profits, economic losses, or zero economic profits yesterday?

   b. To maximize economic profits today, how many bricks should this firm produce today?

24-7. Suppose that a perfectly competitive firm faces a market price of $5 per unit, and at this price the upward-sloping portion of the firm's marginal cost curve crosses its marginal revenue curve at an output level of 1,500 units. If the firm produces 1,500 units, its average variable costs equal $5.50 per unit, and its average fixed costs equal 50 cents per unit. What is the firm's profit-maximizing (or loss-minimizing) output level? What is the amount of its economic profits (or losses) at this output level?

24-8. Suppose that the price of a service sold in a perfectly competitive market is $25 per unit. For a firm in this market, the output level corresponding to a marginal cost of $25 per unit is 2,000 units. Average variable costs at this output level equal $15 per unit, and average fixed costs equal $5 per unit. What is the firm's profit-maximizing (or loss-minimizing) output level? What is the amount of its economic profits (or losses) at this output level?

24-9. Suppose that a firm in a perfectly competitive industry finds that at its current output rate, marginal revenue exceeds the minimum average total cost of producing any feasible rate of output. Furthermore, the firm is producing an output rate at which marginal cost is less than the average total cost at that rate of output. Is the firm maximizing its economic profits? Why or why not?

24-10. A perfectly competitive industry is initially in a short-run equilibrium in which all firms are earning zero economic profits but in which firms are operating below their minimum efficient scale. Explain the long-run adjustments that will take place for the industry to attain long-run equilibrium with firms operating at their minimum efficient scale.

24-11. Two years ago, a large number of firms entered a market in which existing firms had been earning positive economic profits. By the end of last year, the typical firm in this industry had begun earning negative economic profits. No other events occurred in this market during the past two years.

   a. Explain the adjustment process that occurred last year.

   b. Predict what adjustments will take place in this market beginning this year, other things being equal.

24-12. Numerous "hookah bars," at which patrons can pay to utilize water pipes to smoke regular and flavored tobaccos, have popped up around the nation. Hookah bars are particularly popular with college students.

   a. Suppose that the market for the services of hookah bars is in long-run equilibrium. Then two events occur: (1) more cities end regulations that had generated fixed costs for hookah bars, and (2) many nonstudent adults discover previously unknown preferences for the services of hookah bars. Use diagrams to trace through the short-run effects on the market price of hookah-bar services, the marginal revenue and marginal cost of these services at a typical hookah bar, and the equilibrium quantity of services provided both by a typical hookah bar and by the hookah-bar industry.

   b. Redraw your diagrams showing the situation at the conclusion of your answer to part (a). Use these new diagrams to explain the long-run adjustments that will take place in this industry.

ECONOMICS ON THE NET

The Cost Structure of the Movie Theater Business A key idea in this chapter is that competition among firms in an industry can influence the long-run cost structure within the industry. Here you get a chance to apply this concept to a multinational company that owns movie theaters.

Title: AMC International

Navigation: Follow the link at **www.econtoday.com/chapter24** to visit American Multi-Cinema's home page.

Application Answer the following questions.

1. Click on *Investor Resources*. What is the average number of screens in an AMC theater? How many theaters does AMC own and manage?

2. Click on *Locations Worldwide*, and use the map to select the theater in Hong Kong. This is the largest megaplex theater in Hong Kong. How many screens does the megaplex have?

3. Based on the average number of screens at an AMC theater and the number of screens at the Hong Kong facility, what can you conclude about the cost structure of this industry? Illustrate the long-run average cost curve for this industry.

For Group Discussion and Analysis Is the Hong Kong facility the largest multiplex? What do you think constrains the size of a multiplex in Hong Kong? How does the location of AMC's headquarters affect the cost structure of the firm? Is it easier for AMC to have fewer facilities that are larger in size than to have many smaller facilities?

ANSWERS TO QUICK QUIZZES

p. 617: (i) large . . . homogeneous . . . unrestrained; (ii) no . . . all; (iii) marginal . . . marginal; (iv) revenue . . . cost . . . price

p. 623: (i) average . . . price; (ii) break-even . . . marginal; (iii) shutdown . . . marginal; (iv) variable; (v) zero . . . normal; (vi) variable . . . summation . . . variable

p. 631: (i) intersection . . . variable; (ii) zero; (iii) horizontal . . . upward . . . downward; (iv) equal; (v) marginal cost . . . marginal cost

Monopoly

Economists have found that when a nation's government proclaims that a single church denomination represents the "official" state religion, the church loses attendance equal to an average of about 15 percent of the nation's population. At first glance, it might appear that economics probably can tell us little about why attendance falls when a denomination is declared to be the official state religion. In fact, lower attendance at such churches is a prediction of the theory of *monopoly* applied to religious institutions. Granting monopoly status to a single religious denomination is likely to reduce "religious output," thereby giving people less reason to attend church. In this chapter, you will learn why a monopoly produces less output of a good or service than we would observe in a perfectly competitive market.

LEARNING OBJECTIVES

myeconlab

MyEconLab helps you master each objective and study more efficiently. See end of chapter for details.

After reading this chapter, you should be able to:

- Identify situations that can give rise to monopoly
- Describe the demand and marginal revenue conditions a monopolist faces
- Discuss how a monopolist determines how much output to produce and what price to charge
- Evaluate the profits earned by a monopolist
- Understand price discrimination
- Explain the social cost of monopolies

? DID YOU KNOW THAT many chefs are now patenting specific dishes? As the culinary world has become more interconnected with increased mobility of people and access to restaurant menus on the Internet, chefs have sought to protect their food-preparation inventions from duplication. Some chefs now have dozens of patents, all aimed at preventing other chefs from competing against them with copies of their own products.

In this chapter, you will learn about the consequences of allowing producers to patent their inventions, thereby giving only them authorization to sell all of the output of a particular patented good or service. These consequences stem from the fact that the holder of a patent faces the entire demand curve for its product. This creates a situation called *monopoly*.

Definition of a Monopolist

The word *monopoly* probably brings to mind notions of a business that gouges the consumer, sells faulty products, and gets unconscionably rich in the process. But if we are to succeed in analyzing and predicting the behavior of imperfectly competitive firms, we will have to be more objective in our definition. Although most monopolies in the United States are relatively large, our definition will be equally applicable to small businesses: A **monopolist** is the *single supplier* of a good or service for which there is no close substitute.

In a monopoly market structure, the firm (the monopolist) and the industry are one and the same. Occasionally, there may be a problem in identifying an industry and therefore determining if a monopoly exists. For example, should we think of aluminum and steel as separate industries, or should we define the industry in terms of basic metals? Our answer depends on the extent to which aluminum and steel can be substituted in the production of a wide range of products.

As we shall see in this chapter, a seller prefers to have a monopoly than to face competitors. In general, we think of monopoly prices as being higher than prices under perfect competition and of monopoly profits as being higher than profits under perfect competition (which are, in the long run, merely equivalent to a normal rate of return). How does a firm obtain a monopoly in an industry? Basically, there must be *barriers to entry* that enable firms to receive monopoly profits in the long run. Barriers to entry are restrictions on who can start a business or who can stay in a business.

Does it surprise you that the U.S. Department of Commerce oversees a global monopoly on the granting of names for Web addresses?

Monopolist
The single supplier of a good or service for which there is no close substitute. The monopolist therefore constitutes its entire industry.

INTERNATIONAL POLICY EXAMPLE
A Monopoly in the Assignment of Internet Addresses

In 1998, the U.S. Department of Commerce established the Internet Corporation for Assigned Names and Numbers (ICANN), which oversees names for Internet domains. Although ICANN has an international advisory board, the U.S. government, through the Commerce Department, exercises power over all decisions, including assignment of new Web domains and, in principle, specific Web addresses.

In the (perhaps mistaken) view of residents of many other nations, the U.S. government's effective control over Web addresses allows it to enforce restrictions on who can start a

Web-based business or stay in business on the Internet. Thus, these nations' residents worry that the U.S. government might use its control over ICANN to establish barriers to entry to Internet business on the part of non-U.S. firms. In this way, it could protect U.S. firms from foreign competition on the Web.

FOR CRITICAL ANALYSIS
How could U.S. restrictions on Web addresses protect U.S. firms from foreign competition?

Barriers to Entry

For any amount of monopoly power to continue to exist in the long run, the market must be closed to entry in some way. Either legal means or certain aspects of the industry's technical or cost structure may prevent entry. We will discuss several of the barriers to entry that have allowed firms to reap monopoly profits in the long run (even if they are not pure monopolists in the technical sense).

Ownership of Resources Without Close Substitutes

Preventing a newcomer from entering an industry is often difficult. Indeed, some economists contend that no monopoly acting without government support has been able to prevent entry into the industry unless that monopoly has had the control of some essential natural resource. Consider the possibility of one firm's owning the entire supply of a raw material input that is essential to the production of a particular commodity. The exclusive ownership of such a vital resource serves as a barrier to entry until an alternative source of the raw material input is found or an alternative technology not requiring the raw material in question is developed. A good example of control over a vital input is the Aluminum Company of America (Alcoa), a firm that prior to World War II owned most world stocks of bauxite, the essential raw material in the production of aluminum. Such a situation is rare, though, and is ordinarily temporary.

How do auto manufacturers use their control over production of diagnostic equipment to help their dealer networks try to maintain repair-service monopolies?

EXAMPLE
Keeping Customers Flowing to Mr. Goodwrench Instead of Independent Auto Mechanics

In 1996, under a federal mandate to reduce emissions from every vehicle sold, all auto manufacturers began installing small computers that closely monitor emission systems of autos and light-body trucks. When they designed these computers, the companies developed their own technologies for also monitoring nonemission systems. Today, such computers control virtually all information flows relating to a vehicle's internal functioning. Access to this information, which is required for a mechanic to diagnose most problems with a vehicle's operation, is only available through special equipment. This equipment is produced solely by vehicle manufacturers.

Hence, auto manufacturers have monopolies in the provision of diagnostic equipment for the vehicles they manufacture. Typically, they make such equipment available to independent mechanics at prices well above those charged to their own dealers. In a few cases, auto manufacturers have refused to sell the equipment to independent mechanics, thereby aiding their dealers in establishing monopolies in the provision of mechanical repair and maintenance services on the vehicles their companies produce.

FOR CRITICAL ANALYSIS
What incentives do independent auto mechanics have to try to join dealer repair-service networks?

Economies of Scale

Sometimes it is not profitable for more than one firm to exist in an industry. This is so if one firm would have to produce such a large quantity in order to realize lower unit costs that there would not be sufficient demand to warrant a second producer of the same product. Such a situation may arise because of a phenomenon we discussed in Chapter 23, economies of scale. When economies of scale exist, total costs increase less than proportionately to the increase in output. That is, proportional increases in output yield proportionately smaller increases in total costs, and per-unit costs drop. When economies of scale exist, larger firms (with larger output) have an advantage in that they have lower costs that enable them to charge lower prices and thereby drive smaller firms out of business.

When economies of scale occur over a wide range of outputs, a **natural monopoly** may develop. A natural monopoly is the first firm to take advantage of persistent declining long-run average costs as scale increases. The natural monopolist is able to underprice its competitors and eventually force all of them out of the market.

Figure 25-1 shows a downward-sloping long-run average cost curve (LAC). Recall that when average costs are falling, marginal costs are less than average costs. Thus, when the long-run average cost curve slopes downward, the long-run marginal cost curve (LMC) will be below the LAC.

In our example, long-run average costs are falling over such a large range of production rates that we would expect only one firm to survive in such an industry. That firm would be the natural monopolist. It would be the first one to take advantage of the decreasing average costs. That is, it would construct the large-scale facilities first. As its average costs fell, it would lower prices and get an ever-larger share of the market. Once that firm had driven all other firms out of the industry, it would set its price to maximize profits.

Natural monopoly

A monopoly that arises from the peculiar production characteristics in an industry. It usually arises when there are large economies of scale relative to the industry's demand such that one firm can produce at a lower average cost than can be achieved by multiple firms.

Legal or Governmental Restrictions

Governments and legislatures can also erect barriers to entry. These include licenses, franchises, patents, tariffs, and specific regulations that tend to limit entry.

In what nation does a law require that the government allocate about 8,000 geographic markets to monopolists?

INTERNATIONAL POLICY EXAMPLE
German Chimney-Sweep Competition Goes Up in Smoke

In 1937, the acting interior minister of Germany, the infamous Nazi leader Heinrich Himmler, decreed that chimney sweeps—people who specialize in cleaning chimneys—had to be German and would be assigned to "districts." The 8,000 districts were geographic regions in which only a single chimney sweep was allowed to practice the trade. In 1937, Himmler's rule was amended to permit non-Germans to qualify as chimney sweeps, but the requirement of only one chimney sweep per district remains in force today. Thus, within each district, a chimney sweep has a monopoly strictly enforced by German law.

FOR CRITICAL ANALYSIS
What is the basic shape of each of the demand curves faced by the 8,000 German chimney sweeps?

You Are There

For an example of how a government can go about enforcing restrictions on market competition, see **Why Pouring Vegetable Oil into a Car Is Illegal in Illinois,** on page 657.

LICENSES, FRANCHISES, AND CERTIFICATES OF CONVENIENCE It is illegal to enter many industries without a government license, or a "certificate of convenience and public necessity." For example, in some states you cannot form an electrical utility to compete with the electrical utility already operating in your area. You would first have to obtain a certificate of convenience and public necessity from the appropriate authority, which is usually the state's public utility commission. Yet public utility commissions in these states rarely, if ever, issue a certificate to a group of investors

FIGURE 25-1

The Cost Curves That Might Lead to a Natural Monopoly

Whenever long-run marginal costs (LMC) are less than long-run average costs (LAC), then long-run average costs will be falling. A natural monopoly might arise when this situation exists over most output rates. The first firm to establish low-unit-cost capacity would be able to take advantage of declining average total costs. This firm would drive out all rivals by charging a lower price than the others could sustain at their higher average costs.

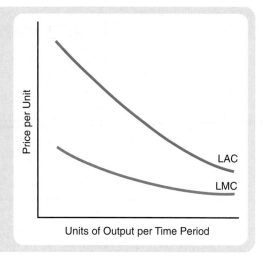

who want to compete directly in the same geographic area as an existing electrical utility. Hence, entry into the industry in a particular geographic area is prohibited, and long-run monopoly profits could conceivably be earned by the electrical utility already serving the area.

To enter interstate (and also many intrastate) markets for pipelines, television and radio broadcasting, and transmission of natural gas, to cite a few such industries, it is often necessary to obtain similar permits. Because these franchises or licenses are restricted, long-run monopoly profits might be earned by the firms already in the industry.

PATENTS A patent is issued to an inventor to provide protection from having the invention copied or stolen for a period of 20 years. Suppose that engineers working for Ford Motor Company discover a way to build an engine that requires half the parts of a regular engine and weighs only half as much. If Ford is successful in obtaining a patent on this discovery, it can (in principle) prevent others from copying it. The patent holder has a monopoly. It is the patent holder's responsibility to defend the patent, however. That means that Ford—like other patent owners—must expend resources to prevent others from imitating its invention. If the costs of enforcing a particular patent are greater than the benefits, though, the patent may not bestow any monopoly profits on its owner. The policing costs would be just too high.

Why does Hewlett-Packard incur the costs of policing its ink patents?

Go to **www.econtoday.com/chapter25** to learn more about patents and trademarks from the U.S. Patent and Trademark Office and to learn all about copyrights from the U.S. Copyright Office.

EXAMPLE
For Hewlett-Packard, Ink Patents Generate the Color of Money

Hewlett-Packard Company, the giant manufacturer of computers, peripherals, and accessories, owns more than 33,000 different patents. Of these, 4,000 patents cover the company's formulations of inks and cartridges used in printers, copiers, and fax machines.

In a typical year, Hewlett-Packard earns nearly $3 billion in profits from sales of ink and toner supplies—or more than half of its operating profits. To protect its patents from infringement by competitors, Hewlett-Packard maintains a team of scientists to analyze the inks produced by other companies.

EXAMPLE (cont.)

This group analyzes 20 to 25 different inks every week. They use machines that heat the ink into a gaseous form, and then they test the gases for the chemical solvents utilized to create the ink. If they find scientific evidence that a competitor has combined solvents in ways specified by one or more of Hewlett-Packard's patents, then the company files a lawsuit against the alleged patent violator. In most case, an admitted violator settles out of court by paying Hewlett-Packard a lump sum and promising to stop infringing on Hewlett-Packard's patented ink formulations.

FOR CRITICAL ANALYSIS

Why do you suppose that Hewlett-Packard also regularly has engineers check the design of competitors' toner cartridges for possible violations of company patents?

Tariffs
Taxes on imported goods.

What are some of the costs associated with Hewlett-Packard's continuing attempts to maintain its monopoly in ink cartridges for its printers?

TARIFFS **Tariffs** are special taxes that are imposed on certain imported goods. Tariffs make imports more expensive relative to their domestic counterparts, encouraging consumers to switch to the relatively cheaper domestically made products. If the tariffs are high enough, domestic producers may be able to act together like a single firm and gain monopoly advantage as the sole suppliers. Many countries have tried this protectionist strategy by using high tariffs to shut out foreign competitors.

REGULATIONS Throughout the twentieth century and to the present, government regulation of the U.S. economy has increased, especially along the dimensions of safety and quality. U.S. firms incur hundreds of billions of dollars in expenses each year to comply with federal, state, and local government regulations of business conduct relating to workplace conditions, environmental protection, product safety, and various other activities. Presumably, these large fixed costs of complying with regulations can be spread over a greater number of units of output by larger firms than by smaller firms, thereby putting the smaller firms at a competitive disadvantage. Entry will also be deterred to the extent that the scale of operation of a potential entrant must be sufficiently large to cover the average fixed costs of compliance. We examine regulation in more detail in Chapter 28.

QUICK QUIZ   *See page 663 for the answers. Review concepts from this section in MyEconLab.*

A **monopolist** is the single seller of a product or good for which there is no _____ substitute.

To maintain a monopoly, there must be barriers to entry. Barriers to entry include _____ of resources without close substitutes; economies of _____; legally required licenses, franchises, and certificates of convenience; patents; tariffs; and safety and quality regulations.

The Demand Curve a Monopolist Faces

A *pure monopolist* is the sole supplier of *one* product, good, or service. A pure monopolist faces a demand curve that is the demand curve for the entire market for that good.

The monopolist faces the industry demand curve because the monopolist is the entire industry.

Because the monopolist faces the industry demand curve, which is by definition downward sloping, its choice regarding how much to produce is not the same as for a perfect competitor. When a monopolist changes output, it does not automatically receive the same price per unit that it did before the change.

Profits to Be Made from Increasing Production

How do firms benefit from changing production rates? What happens to price in each case? Let's first review the situation among perfect competitors.

MARGINAL REVENUE FOR THE PERFECT COMPETITOR Recall that a firm in a perfectly competitive industry faces a perfectly elastic demand curve. That is because the perfectly competitive firm is such a small part of the market that it cannot influence the price of its product. It is a *price taker*. If the forces of supply and demand establish that the price per constant-quality pair of shoes is $50, the individual firm can sell all the pairs of shoes it wants to produce at $50 per pair. The average revenue is $50, the price is $50, and the marginal revenue is also $50.

Let us again define marginal revenue:

Marginal revenue equals the change in total revenue due to a one-unit change in the quantity produced and sold.

In the case of a perfectly competitive industry, each time a single firm changes production by one unit, total revenue changes by the going price, and price is unchanged. Marginal revenue always equals price, or average revenue. Average revenue was defined as total revenue divided by quantity demanded, or

$$\text{Average revenue} = \frac{\text{TR}}{Q} = \frac{PQ}{Q} = P$$

Hence, marginal revenue, average revenue, and price are all the same for the price-taking firm.

MARGINAL REVENUE FOR THE MONOPOLIST What about a monopoly firm? We begin by considering a situation in which a monopolist charges every buyer the same price for each unit of its product. Because a monopoly is the entire industry, the monopoly firm's demand curve is the market demand curve. The market demand curve slopes downward, just like the other demand curves that we have seen. Therefore, to induce consumers to buy more of a particular product, given the industry demand curve, the monopoly firm must lower the price. Thus, the monopoly firm moves *down* the demand curve. If all buyers are to be charged the same price, the monopoly must lower the price on *all* units sold in order to sell more. It cannot lower the price on just the *last* unit sold in any given time period in order to sell a larger quantity.

Put yourself in the shoes of a monopoly ferryboat owner. You have a government-bestowed franchise, and no one can compete with you. Your ferryboat goes between two islands. If you are charging $1 per crossing, a certain quantity of your services will be demanded. Let's say that you are ferrying 100 people a day each way at that price. If you decide that you would like to ferry more individuals, you must lower your price to all individuals—you must move *down* the existing demand curve for ferrying services. To calculate the marginal revenue of your change in price, you must first calculate the total revenues you received at $1 per passenger per crossing and then calculate the total revenues you would receive at, say, 90 cents per passenger per crossing.

FIGURE 25-2

Demand Curves for the Perfect Competitor and the Monopolist

The perfect competitor in panel (a) faces a perfectly elastic demand curve, *d*. The monopolist in panel (b) faces the entire industry demand curve, which slopes downward.

PERFECT COMPETITION VERSUS MONOPOLY It is sometimes useful to compare monopoly markets with perfectly competitive markets. The monopolist is constrained by the demand curve for its product, just as a perfectly competitive firm is constrained by its demand. The key difference is the nature of the demand curve each type of firm faces. We see this in Figure 25-2, which compares the demand curves of the perfect competitor and the monopolist.

Here we see the fundamental difference between the monopolist and the perfect competitor. The perfect competitor doesn't have to worry about lowering price to sell more. In a perfectly competitive situation, the perfectly competitive firm accounts for such a small part of the market that it can sell its entire output, whatever that may be, at the same price. The monopolist cannot. The more the monopolist wants to sell, the lower the price it has to charge on the last unit (and on *all* units put on the market for sale). To sell the last unit, the monopolist has to lower the price because it is facing a downward-sloping demand curve, and the only way to move down the demand curve is to lower the price. As long as this price must be the same for all units, the extra revenues the monopolist receives from selling one more unit are going to be smaller than the extra revenues received from selling the next-to-last unit.

The Monopolist's Marginal Revenue: Less Than Price

An essential point is that for the monopolist, marginal revenue is always less than price. To understand why, look at Figure 25-3, which shows a unit increase in output sold due to a reduction in the price of a commodity from P_1 to P_2. Price P_2 is the price received for the last unit, so selling this unit contributes P_2 to revenues. That is equal to the vertical column (area A). Area A is one unit wide by P_2 high.

But price times the last unit sold is *not* the net addition to *total* revenues received from selling that last unit. Why? Because price had to be reduced on all previous units sold (Q) in order to sell the larger quantity $Q + 1$. The reduction in price is represented by the vertical distance from P_1 to P_2 on the vertical axis. We must therefore subtract area B from area A to come up with the *change* in total revenues due to a one-unit increase in sales. Clearly, the change in total revenues—that is, marginal revenue—must be less than price because marginal revenue is always the

FIGURE 25-3

Marginal Revenue: Always Less Than Price

The price received for the last unit sold is equal to P_2. The revenues received from selling this last unit are equal to P_2 times one unit, or the orange-shaded area of the vertical column. However, if a single price is being charged for all units, total revenues do not go up by the amount of the area represented by that column. The price had to be reduced on all the previous Q units that were being sold at price P_1. Thus, we must subtract the green-shaded area B—the rectangle between P_1 and P_2 from the vertical axis to Q—from area A in order to derive marginal revenue. Marginal revenue is therefore always less than price.

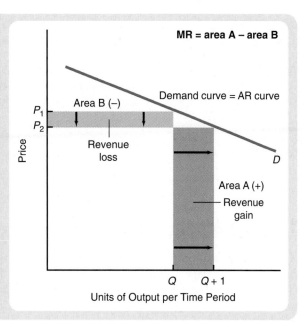

difference between areas A and B in Figure 25-3. For example, if the initial price is $8 and quantity demanded is 3, to increase quantity to 4 units, it is necessary to decrease price to $7, not just for the fourth unit, but on all three previous units as well. Thus, at a price of $7, marginal revenue is $7 − $3 = $4 because there is a $1 per unit price reduction on three previous units. Hence, marginal revenue, $4, is less than price, $7.

Elasticity and Monopoly

The monopolist faces a downward-sloping demand curve (its average revenue curve). That means that it cannot charge just *any* price with no changes in quantity (a common misconception) because, depending on the price charged, a different quantity will be demanded.

Earlier we defined a monopolist as the single seller of a well-defined good or service with no *close* substitute. This does not mean, however, that the demand curve for a monopoly is vertical or exhibits zero price elasticity of demand. After all, consumers have limited incomes and unlimited wants. The market demand curve, which the monopolist alone faces in this situation, slopes downward because individuals compare the marginal satisfaction they will receive to the cost of the commodity to be purchased. Take the example of telephone service. Even if miraculously there were absolutely no substitutes whatsoever for telephone service, the market demand curve would still slope downward. At lower prices, people will add more phones and separate lines for different family members.

Furthermore, the demand curve for telephone service slopes downward because there are at least several *imperfect* substitutes, such as letters, e-mail, in-person conversations, and Internet telephony. The more such substitutes there are, and the better these substitutes are, the more elastic will be the monopolist's demand curve, all other things held constant.

QUICK QUIZ *See page 663 for the answers. Review concepts from this section in MyEconLab.*

The monopolist estimates its marginal revenue curve, where marginal revenue is defined as the _____ in _____ revenues due to a one-unit change in quantity sold.

For the perfect competitor, price equals _____ revenue equals average revenue. For the monopolist,

_____ revenue is always less than price because price must be reduced on all units to sell more.

The price _____ of demand for the monopolist depends on the number and similarity of substitutes. The more numerous the imperfect substitutes, the greater the price _____ of the monopolist's demand curve.

Costs and Monopoly Profit Maximization

Price searcher

A firm that must determine the price-output combination that maximizes profit because it faces a downward-sloping demand curve.

To find the rate of output at which the perfect competitor would maximize profits, we had to add cost data. We will do the same thing now for the monopolist. We assume that profit maximization is the goal of the pure monopolist, just as it is for the perfect competitor. The perfect competitor, however, has only to decide on the profit-maximizing rate of output because price is given. The perfect competitor is a price taker. For the pure monopolist, we must seek a profit-maximizing *price-output combination* because the monopolist is a **price searcher.** We can determine this profit-maximizing price-output combination with either of two equivalent approaches—by looking at total revenues and total costs or by looking at marginal revenues and marginal costs. We shall examine both approaches.

The Total Revenues–Total Costs Approach

Suppose that the government of a small town located in a remote desert area grants a single satellite television company the right to offer services within its jurisdiction. It enforces rules that prevent other firms from offering television services. We show demand (weekly rate of output and price per unit), revenues, costs, and other data in panel (a) of Figure 25-4. In column 3, we see total revenues for this TV service monopolist, and in column 4, we see total costs. We can transfer these two columns to panel (b). The fundamental difference between the total revenue and total cost diagram in panel (b) and the one we showed for a perfect competitor in Chapter 24 is that the total revenue line is no longer straight. Rather, it curves. For any given demand curve, in order to sell more, the monopolist must lower the price. This reflects the fact that the basic difference between a monopolist and a perfect competitor has to do with the demand curve for the two types of firms. The monopolist faces a downward-sloping demand curve.

Profit maximization involves maximizing the positive difference between total revenues and total costs. This occurs at an output rate of between 9 and 10 units per week.

The Marginal Revenue–Marginal Cost Approach

Profit maximization will also occur where marginal revenue equals marginal cost. This is as true for a monopolist as it is for a perfect competitor (but the monopolist will charge a price in excess of marginal revenue). When we transfer marginal cost and marginal revenue information from columns 6 and 7 in panel (a) of Figure 25-4 to panel (c), we see that marginal revenue equals marginal cost at a weekly quantity of satellite TV services of between 9 and 10 units. Profit maximization must occur at the same output as in panel (b).

FIGURE 25-4

Monopoly Costs, Revenues, and Profits

In panel (a), we give demand (weekly satellite television services and price), revenues, costs, and other relevant data. As shown in panel (b), the satellite TV monopolist maximizes profits where the positive difference between TR and TC is greatest. This is at an output rate of between 9 and 10 units per week. Put another way, profit maximization occurs where marginal revenue equals marginal cost, as shown in panel (c). This is at the same weekly service rate of between 9 and 10 units. (The MC curve must cut the MR curve from below.)

Panel (a)

(1) Output (units)	(2) Price per Unit	(3) Total Revenues (TR) (3) = (2) x (1)	(4) Total Costs (TC)	(5) Total Profit (5) = (3) − (4)	(6) Marginal Cost (MC)	(7) Marginal Revenue (MR)
0	$8.00	$ .00	$10.00	−$10.00		
					$4.00	$7.80
1	7.80	7.80	14.00	−6.20		
					3.50	7.40
2	7.60	15.20	17.50	−2.30		
					3.25	7.00
3	7.40	22.20	20.75	1.45		
					3.05	6.60
4	7.20	28.80	23.80	5.00		
					2.90	6.20
5	7.00	35.00	26.70	8.30		
					2.80	5.80
6	6.80	40.80	29.50	11.30		
					2.75	5.40
7	6.60	46.20	32.25	13.95		
					2.85	5.00
8	6.40	51.20	35.10	16.10		
					3.20	4.60
9	6.20	55.80	38.30	17.50		
					4.40	4.20
10	6.00	60.00	42.70	17.30		
					6.00	3.80
11	5.80	63.80	48.70	15.10		
					9.00	3.40
12	5.60	67.20	57.70	9.50		

Panel (b)

Panel (c)

WHY PRODUCE WHERE MARGINAL REVENUE EQUALS MARGINAL COST? If the monopolist produces past the point where marginal revenue equals marginal cost, marginal cost will exceed marginal revenue. That is, the incremental cost of producing any more units will exceed the incremental revenue. It just would not be worthwhile, as was true also in perfect competition. Furthermore, just as in the case of perfect competition, if the monopolist produces less than that, it is not making maximum profits. Look at output rate Q_1 in Figure 25-5. Here the monopolist's marginal revenue is at A, but marginal cost is at B. Marginal revenue exceeds marginal cost on the last unit sold; the profit for that *particular* unit, Q_1, is equal to the vertical difference between A and B, or the difference between marginal revenue and marginal cost. The monopolist would be foolish to stop at output rate Q_1 because if output is expanded, marginal revenue will still exceed marginal cost, and therefore total profits will be increased by selling more. In fact, the profit-maximizing monopolist will continue to expand output and sales until marginal revenue equals marginal cost, which is at output rate Q_m. The monopolist won't produce at rate Q_2 because here, as we see, marginal costs are C and marginal revenues are F. The difference between C and F represents the *reduction* in total profits from producing that additional unit. Total profits will rise as the monopolist reduces its rate of output back toward Q_m.

What Price to Charge for Output?

How does the monopolist set prices? We know the quantity is set at the point at which marginal revenue equals marginal cost. The monopolist then finds out how much can be charged—how much the market will bear—for that particular quantity, Q_m, in Figure 25-5.

THE MONOPOLY PRICE We know that the demand curve is defined as showing the *maximum* price for which a given quantity can be sold. That means that our monopolist knows that to sell Q_m, it can charge only P_m because that is the price at which that

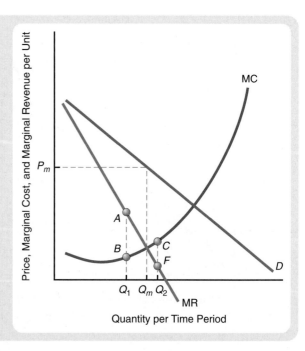

FIGURE 25-5

Maximizing Profits

The profit-maximizing production rate is Q_m, and the profit-maximizing price is P_m. The monopolist would be unwise to produce at the rate Q_1 because here marginal revenue would be Q_1A, and marginal cost would be Q_1B. Marginal revenue would exceed marginal cost. The firm will keep producing until the point Q_m, where marginal revenue just equals marginal cost. It would be foolish to produce at the rate Q_2, for here marginal cost exceeds marginal revenue. It would behoove the monopolist to cut production back to Q_m.

specific quantity, Q_m, is demanded. This price is found by drawing a vertical line from the quantity, Q_m, to the market demand curve. Where that line hits the market demand curve, the price is determined. We find that price by drawing a horizontal line from the demand curve over to the price axis; that gives us the profit-maximizing price, P_m.

In our numerical example, at a profit-maximizing quantity of satellite TV services of between 9 and 10 units in Figure 25-4 on page 649, the firm can charge a maximum price of about $6 and still sell all the services it provides, all at the same price.

The basic procedure for finding the profit-maximizing short-run price-quantity combination for the monopolist is first to determine the profit-maximizing rate of output, by either the total revenue–total cost method or the marginal revenue–marginal cost method, and then to determine by use of the demand curve, D, the maximum price that can be charged to sell that output.

REAL-WORLD INFORMATIONAL LIMITATIONS Don't get the impression that just because we are able to draw an exact demand curve in Figures 25-4 and 25-5, real-world monopolists have such perfect information. The process of price searching by a less-than-perfect competitor is just that—a process. A monopolist can only estimate the actual demand curve and therefore can make only an educated guess when it sets its profit-maximizing price. This is not a problem for the perfect competitor because price is given already by the intersection of market demand and market supply. The monopolist, in contrast, reaches the profit-maximizing output-price combination by trial and error.

Calculating Monopoly Profit

We have talked about the monopolist's profit. We have yet to indicate how much profit the monopolist makes, which we do in Figure 25-6.

FIGURE 25-6

Monopoly Profit

We find monopoly profit by subtracting total costs from total revenues at a quantity of satellite TV services of between 9 and 10 units per week, labeled Q_m, which is the profit-maximizing rate of output for the satellite TV monopolist. The profit-maximizing price is therefore about $6 per week and is labeled P_m. Monopoly profit is given by the green-shaded area, which is equal to total revenues ($P \times Q$) minus total costs (ATC $\times Q$). This diagram is similar to panel (c) of Figure 25-4 on page 649, with the short-run average total cost curve (ATC) added.

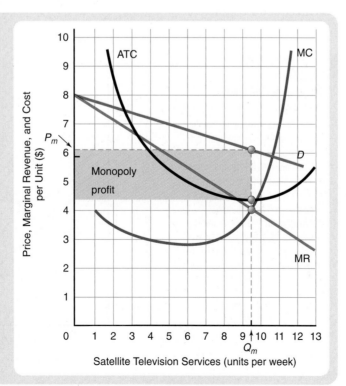

The Graphical Depiction of Monopoly Profits

We have actually shown total profits in column 5 of panel (a) in Figure 25-4 on page 649. We can also find total profits by adding an average total cost curve to panel (c) of that figure, as shown in Figure 25-6 on the preceding page. When we add the average total cost curve, we find that the profit that a monopolist makes is equal to the green-shaded area—or total revenues ($P \times Q$) minus total costs ($\text{ATC} \times Q$). Given the demand curve and a uniform pricing system (that is, all units sold at the same price), there is no way for a monopolist to make greater profits than those shown by the green-shaded area. The monopolist is maximizing profits where marginal cost equals marginal revenue. If the monopolist produces less than that, it will be forfeiting some profits. If the monopolist produces more than that, it will also be forfeiting some profits.

No Guarantee of Profits

The term *monopoly* conjures up the notion of a greedy firm ripping off the public and making exorbitant profits. The mere existence of a monopoly, however, does not guarantee high profits. Numerous monopolies have gone bankrupt. Figure 25-7 shows the monopolist's demand curve as D and the resultant marginal revenue curve as MR. It does not matter at what rate of output this particular monopolist operates; total costs cannot be covered. Look at the position of the average total cost curve. It lies everywhere above D (the average revenue curve). Thus, there is no price-output combination that will allow the monopolist even to cover costs, much less earn profits. This monopolist will, in the short run, suffer economic losses as shown by the red-shaded area. The graph in Figure 25-7, which applies to many inventions, depicts a situation of resulting monopoly. The owner of a patented invention or discovery has a pure legal monopoly, but the demand and cost curves are such that production is not profitable. Every year at inventors' conventions, one can see many inventions that have never been put into production because they were deemed "uneconomic" by potential producers and users.

FIGURE 25-7

Monopolies: Not Always Profitable

Some monopolists face the situation shown here. The average total cost curve, ATC, is everywhere above the average revenue, or demand, curve, D. In the short run, the monopolist will produce where MC = MR at point A. Output Q_m will be sold at price P_m, but average total cost per unit is C_1. Losses are the red-shaded rectangle. Eventually, the monopolist will go out of business.

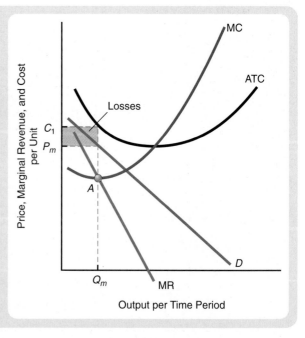

The basic difference between a monopolist and a perfect competitor is that a monopolist faces a _____ -sloping demand curve, and therefore marginal revenue is _____ than price.

The monopolist must choose the profit-maximizing price-output combination—the output at which _____ revenue equals _____ cost and the highest price possible as given by the _____ curve for that particular output rate.

Monopoly profits are found by looking at average _____ costs compared to price per unit. This difference multiplied by the _____ sold at that price determines monopoly profit.

A monopolist does not necessarily earn a profit. If the average _____ cost curve lies entirely _____ the demand curve for a monopoly, no production rate will be profitable.

On Making Higher Profits: Price Discrimination

In a perfectly competitive market, each buyer is charged the same price for every constant-quality unit of the particular commodity (corrected for differential transportation charges). Because the product is homogeneous and we also assume full knowledge on the part of the buyers, a difference in price cannot exist. Any seller of the product who tried to charge a price higher than the going market price would find that no one would purchase it from that seller.

In this chapter, we have assumed until now that the monopolist charged all consumers the same price for all units. A monopolist, however, may be able to charge different people different prices or different unit prices for successive units sought by a given buyer. When there is no cost difference, such strategies are called **price discrimination.** A firm will engage in price discrimination whenever feasible to increase profits. A price-discriminating firm is able to charge some customers more than other customers.

How do online retailers engage in price discrimination?

Price discrimination

Selling a given product at more than one price, with the price difference being unrelated to differences in marginal cost.

E-COMMERCE EXAMPLE
Online Retailers Are Watching

A Web site's price for an item that you express an interest in buying online may depend on your gender. Where you live may also influence the price, as may the time of day that you shop. Even the speed of your Internet connection may affect how much you have to pay.

Whenever you surf a seller's Web site, your computer's Internet connection automatically leaves a limited trail of information, including the location of your Internet service provider and the speed of your connection to the Internet. *Price-optimization software* utilized by the seller can directly access this information. It can also transmit small programs called "cookies" to your own computer, and these can gather additional information about how you search among the firm's

products. If you have already provided the seller with other information about yourself, such as your gender, a cookie will recognize your computer and relay that information to the software. Naturally, the software also logs the time of day that you are shopping. Using complex algorithms, price-optimization software estimates your price elasticity of demand for the item. Based on this estimate, the software then quotes you a price. This is the price that the software determines you are most likely to be willing to pay. If the software estimates that your price elasticity of demand is lower than that of another Web shopper, you will be quoted a higher price than that other individual. Hence, price-optimization software might more aptly be named "price-discrimination software."

E-COMMERCE EXAMPLE (cont.)

FOR CRITICAL ANALYSIS

Why might information about your location and the speed of your Internet connection provide information about your price elasticity of demand? (Hint: On average, someone in Beverly Hills, California, using an ultra-high-speed Internet connection is likely to have a higher income than someone in South Central Los Angeles using a phone dial-up connection. Price elasticity of demand depends, in part, on expenditures on an item as a share of total income.)

Price differentiation
Establishing different prices for similar products to reflect differences in marginal cost in providing those commodities to different groups of buyers.

It must be made clear at the outset that charging different prices to different people or for different units to reflect differences in the cost of service does not amount to price discrimination. This is **price differentiation:** differences in price that reflect differences in marginal cost.

We can also say that a uniform price does not necessarily indicate an absence of price discrimination. Charging all customers the same price when production costs vary by customer is actually a situation of price discrimination.

Necessary Conditions for Price Discrimination

Three conditions are necessary for price discrimination to exist:

1. The firm must face a downward-sloping demand curve.
2. The firm must be able to readily (and cheaply) identify buyers or groups of buyers with predictably different elasticities of demand.
3. The firm must be able to prevent resale of the product or service.

Has it ever occurred to you that most of the other students seated in your college classroom pay different overall tuition rates than you do because your college and others use financial aid packages to engage in price discrimination?

EXAMPLE
Why Students Pay Different Prices to Attend College

Out-of-pocket tuition rates for any two college students can differ by considerable amounts, even if the students happen to major in the same subjects and enroll in many of the same courses. The reason is that colleges offer students diverse financial aid packages depending on their "financial need."

To document their "need" for financial aid, students must provide detailed information about family income and wealth. This information, of course, helps the college determine the prices that different families are most likely to be willing and able to pay, so that it can engage in price discrimination. Figure 25-8 shows how this collegiate price-discrimination process works. The college charges the price P_7, which is the college's official posted "tuition rate," to students with families judged to be most willing and able to pay the highest price.

Students whose families have the lowest levels of income and wealth are judged to be willing and able to pay a much lower price, such as P_1. To charge these students this lower tuition rate, the college provides them with a financial aid package that reduces the price they pay by the difference between P_7, the full tuition price, and P_1. In this way, the actual price paid by these "neediest" students is only P_1.

Likewise, the college groups other, somewhat less "needy" students into a slightly higher income-and-wealth category and determines that they are likely to be willing to pay a somewhat higher price, P_2. Hence, it grants them a smaller financial aid package, equal to $P_7 - P_2$, so that the students actually pay the price P_2. The college continues this process for other groups, thereby engaging in price discrimination in its tuition charges.

EXAMPLE (cont.)

FIGURE 25-8

Toward Perfect Price Discrimination in College Tuition Rates

Students that a college determines to be "neediest" and least able to pay the full tuition price, P_7, receive a financial aid package equal to $P_7 - P_1$. These students effectively pay only the price P_1. The college groups the remaining students into categories on the basis of their willingness and ability to pay a higher price, and each group receives a progressively smaller financial aid package. Those students who are willing and able to pay the full price, P_7, receive no financial aid from the college.

FOR CRITICAL ANALYSIS

Does the educational product supplied by colleges satisfy all three conditions necessary for price discrimination?

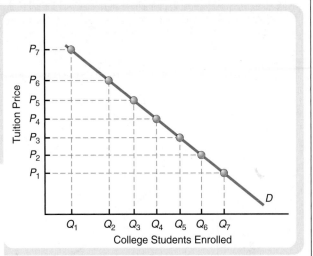

The Social Cost of Monopolies

Let's run a little experiment. We will start with a purely competitive industry with numerous firms, each one unable to affect the price of its product. The supply curve of the industry is equal to the horizontal sum of the marginal cost curves of the individual producers above their respective minimum average variable costs. In panel (a) of Figure 25-9 on the following page, we show the market demand curve and the market supply curve in a perfectly competitive situation. The perfectly competitive price in equilibrium is equal to P_e, and the equilibrium quantity at that price is equal to Q_e. Each individual perfect competitor faces a demand curve (not shown) that is coincident with the price line P_e. No individual supplier faces the market demand curve, D.

Comparing Monopoly with Perfect Competition

Now let's assume that a monopolist comes in and buys up every single perfect competitor in the industry. In so doing, we'll assume that monopolization does not affect any of the marginal cost curves or demand. We can therefore redraw D and S in panel (b) of Figure 25-9, exactly the same as in panel (a).

How does this monopolist decide how much to charge and how much to produce? If the monopolist is profit maximizing, it is going to look at the marginal revenue curve and produce at the output where marginal revenue equals marginal cost. But what is the marginal cost curve in panel (b) of Figure 25-9 on the next page? It is merely S, because we said that S was equal to the horizontal summation of the portions of the individual marginal cost curves above each firm's respective minimum average variable cost. The monopolist therefore produces quantity Q_m, and sells it at price P_m. Notice that Q_m is less than Q_e and that P_m is greater than P_e. A monopolist therefore produces a smaller quantity and sells it at a higher price. This is the reason usually given when economists criticize monopolists. Monopolists raise the

FIGURE 25-9

The Effects of Monopolizing an Industry

In panel (a), we show a perfectly competitive situation in which equilibrium is established at the intersection of D and S at point E. The equilibrium price is P_e and the equilibrium quantity is Q_e. Each individual perfectly competitive producer faces a demand curve that is perfectly elastic at the market clearing price, P_e. What happens if the industry is suddenly monopolized? We assume that the costs stay the same; the only thing that changes is that the monopolist now faces the entire downward-sloping demand curve. In panel (b), we draw the marginal revenue curve. Marginal cost is S because that is the horizontal summation of all the individual marginal cost curves. The monopolist therefore produces at Q_m and charges price P_m. This price P_m in panel (b) is higher than P_e in panel (a), and Q_m is less than Q_e.

Panel (a)

Panel (b)

price and restrict production, compared to a perfectly competitive situation. For a monopolist's product, consumers pay a price that exceeds the marginal cost of production. Resources are misallocated in such a situation—too few resources are being used in the monopolist's industry, and too many are used elsewhere. (See Appendix F at the end of this chapter.)

Implications of Higher Monopoly Prices

Notice from Figure 25-9 that by setting MR = MC, the monopolist produces at a rate of output where $P >$ MC (compare P_m to MC_m). The marginal cost of a commodity (MC) represents what society had to give up in order to obtain the last unit produced. Price, by contrast, represents what buyers are willing to pay to acquire that last unit. Thus, the price of a good represents society's valuation of the last unit produced. The monopoly outcome of $P >$ MC means that the value to society of the last unit produced is greater than its cost (MC); hence, not enough of the good is being produced. As we have pointed out before, these differences between monopoly and perfect competition arise not because of differences in costs but rather because of differences in the demand curves the individual firms face. The monopolist faces a downward-sloping demand curve. The individual perfect competitor faces a perfectly elastic demand curve.

Before we leave the topic of the cost to society of monopolies, we must repeat that our analysis is based on a heroic assumption. That assumption is that the monopolization of the perfectly competitive industry does not change the cost structure. If monopolization results in higher marginal cost, the net cost of monopoly to society is even greater.

Conversely, if monopolization results in cost savings, the net cost of monopoly to society is less than we infer from our analysis. Indeed, we could have presented a hypothetical example in which monopolization led to such a dramatic reduction in cost that society actually benefited. Such a situation is a possibility in industries in which economies of scale exist for a very great range of outputs.

QUICK QUIZ

See page 663 for the answers. Review concepts from this section in MyEconLab.

Three conditions are necessary for price discrimination: (1) The firm must face a _____-sloping demand curve, (2) the firm must be able to identify buyers with predictably different price _____ of demand, and (3) _____ of the product or service must be preventable.

Price _____ should not be confused with price _____, which occurs when differences in price reflect differences in marginal cost.

Monopoly tends to result in a _____ quantity being sold, because the price is _____ than it would be in an ideal perfectly competitive industry in which the cost curves were essentially the same as the monopolist's.

You Are There

Why Pouring Vegetable Oil into a Car Is Illegal in Illinois

David and Eileen Wetzel were surprised when two well-dressed men who had knocked on the door of their home in Decatur, Illinois, pulled out badges indicating that they were from the Illinois Department of Revenue. The Wetzels were even more surprised when the state revenue agents threatened them with felony charges and asked them to post a $2,500 bond to avoid arrest.

What was the elderly couple's crime? They were driving a 1986 Volkswagen Golf that Mr. Wetzel, a retired chemist and food plant manager, had converted to operate on a mixture of diesel fuel and vegetable oil. Illinois law prohibits acting as either a "special fuel supplier" or a "special fuel receiver" without a license. After getting information about the Wetzels' car, the Illinois Department of Revenue had determined that the Wetzels had both illegally supplied themselves with fuel and illegally received it. Thus, the couple had illegally entered the vehicle fuel industry.

CRITICAL ANALYSIS QUESTIONS

1. Why do producers of a government-licensed product, such as fuel for motor vehicles, have an incentive to report all others who try to produce similar products without a license?

2. Why do you suppose that many economists worry that government restraints on competition can impede innovation in markets?

The Predictable Consequences
of European State Religion Monopolies

CONCEPTS APPLIED

- Monopolist
- Social Cost of Monopoly
- Comparing Monopoly with Perfect Competition

For years, the Church of Sweden, a Christian religious denomination affiliated with the Lutheran Church, was an official institution of the Swedish state. Today, about 75 percent of all Swedes, or nearly 7 million people, remain official members. Nevertheless, a recent Sunday service at Stockholm's Hedvig Eleonara Church is typical of the scene in most individual parishes of the Church of Sweden. About 40 people, nearly all of them elderly, gathered beneath a huge, beautifully decorated dome in pews designed to hold more than 1,000 churchgoers. As this scene plays out at Church of Sweden parishes throughout the nation, one might be tempted to conclude that the bulk of Swedes are atheists. To an economist, however, the key to understanding low attendance by members of the Church of Sweden is its traditional status as a state monopoly.

The Usual Monopoly Outcome: Lower Output

Even though the Church of Sweden's state monopoly status formally ended in 2000, its 1,800 congregations continue to receive substantial subsidies from the state. For instance, the Hedvig Eleonara Church receives more than $2 million each year in funds raised from special taxes. Although most other European nations officially dethroned formal "state churches" many years ago, a number of governments continue to favor specific churches. In Italy, for instance, the government offers taxpayers a slate of churches to which they can direct the proceeds of a special "religious tax," of which the Catholic Church typically receives about 87 percent, or approximately $1 billion per year. Yet attendance rates in Italy's Catholic Church are nearly as low as those experienced by the Church of Sweden.

Economists who study the economics of religion have found that the Swedish and Italian pattern of low attendance holds true in all nations in which a single church predominates through state favors. The reason, they suggest, is that granting a religion a monopoly has a very predictable effect: restriction of religious output and higher-priced services. Consider the implied price of religious services at Stockholm's Hedvig Eleonara Church. Its $2 million in state subsidies translates into more than $38,000 per week. Yet the church has only three priests to provide spiritual support and guidance and other religious services to a membership of more than 1,000. Many members are offered low levels of religious output and hence do not attend church services regularly. Most do not attend at all. Indeed, the Hedvig Eleonara Church recently scrapped Sunday school because only five children were regularly attending.

The Effects of Increasing Religious Competition in Europe

On the Sundays when only about 40 members attend services at the Hedvig Eleonara Church, more than 100 young Swedes typically crowd into a small hall rented from Stockholm's Casino Theatre. These members of the nondenominational "Passion Church" attend evangelical religious services that include rock music blared out by a high-decibel band. Together, this church and a number of other small evangelical churches that operate outside the Church of Sweden have only about 31,000 members. Yet their facilities are packed every Sunday. Their per-member religious output is much higher than the output produced by the Church of Sweden.

Religious competition gradually is developing across Europe. Much of this competition is in the form of independent "market entrants," such as the nondenominational evangelical churches spreading through Sweden. But some of it comes from traditionally U.S.-based Christian denominations, the Islamic faith, and other world religions. Although Europe is hardly experiencing a competitive free-for-all in the "religious marketplace," competition does now exist and is growing. For this reason, a number of economists predict that religious output is likely to increase in Europe in the coming years.

Test your understanding of this chapter by going online to **MyEconLab**.
In the Study Plan for this chapter, select Section N: News.

For Critical Analysis

1. Why might economists disagree about the appropriateness of using rates of church attendance as a proxy measure of "religious output"?

2. What is the shape of the demand curve for religious services faced by a monopoly church?

Web Resources

1. For a discussion of how economics can be applied to religious institutions, go to www.econtoday.com/chapter25.

2. To download a study indicating lower levels of social spending by U.S. churches that are more nearly monopolies in their local areas, go to www.econtoday.com/chapter25.

Research Project

Based on this discussion, is there any evidence that the price of religious output is higher under a religious monopoly than it would be in a perfectly competitive religious marketplace? (Hint: Compare the price paid in member taxes to support the limited activities of Stockholm's Hedvig Eleonara Church with the likely price paid, undoubtedly in the form of private donations, by members of the Stockholm Passion Church.)

Here is what you should know after reading this chapter. **MyEconLab** will help you identify what you know, and where to go when you need to practice.

WHAT YOU SHOULD KNOW		WHERE TO GO TO PRACTICE

Why Monopoly Can Occur Monopoly, a situation in which a single firm produces and sells a good or service that has no close substitute, can occur when there are significant barriers to market entry by other firms. Examples of barriers to entry include (1) ownership of important resources for which there are no close substitutes; (2) economies of scale for ever-larger ranges of output, or natural monopoly conditions; and (3) legal or governmental restrictions.

monopolist, 640
natural monopoly, 642
tariffs, 644

- **MyEconLab** Study Plans 25.1, 25.2
- Audio introduction to Chapter 25
- Video: Barriers to Entry
- ABC News Video: Optometrists as Monopolists?
- ABC News Video: Tradeoffs to Higher-Priced Cancer Drugs

Demand and Marginal Revenue Conditions a Monopolist Faces Because a monopolist constitutes the entire industry, it faces the entire market demand curve. When it reduces the price of its product, it is able to sell more units at the new price, which pushes up its revenues, but it also sells other units at this lower price, which pushes its revenues down somewhat. Thus, the monopolist's marginal revenue at any given quantity is less than the price at which it sells that quantity. Its marginal revenue curve slopes downward and lies below the demand curve it faces.

KEY FIGURES
Figure 25-2, 646
Figure 25-3, 647

- **MyEconLab** Study Plans 25.3, 25.4
- Video: The Demand Curve Facing a Monopoly Is Not Vertical
- Animated Figures 25-2, 25-3

How a Monopolist Determines How Much Output to Produce and What Price to Charge A monopolist is a price searcher, meaning that it seeks to charge the price consistent with the production level that maximizes its economic profits. It maximizes its profits by producing to the point at which marginal revenue equals marginal cost. The monopolist then charges the maximum price for this amount of output, which is the price that consumers are willing to pay for that quantity of output.

price searcher, 648
KEY FIGURES
Figure 25-4, 649
Figure 25-5, 650

- **MyEconLab** Study Plan 25.5
- Animated Figures 25-4, 25-5

A Monopolist's Profits The profits earned by a monopolist equal the difference between the price it charges and its average production cost times the quantity it sells. The monopolist's price is at the point on the demand curve corresponding to the profit-maximizing output rate, and its average total cost of producing this output rate is at the corresponding point on the average total cost curve. A monopolist commonly earns positive economic profits, but situations can arise in which average total cost exceeds the profit-maximizing price, yielding negative profits.

KEY FIGURES
Figure 25-6, 651
Figure 25-7, 652

- **MyEconLab** Study Plan 25.6
- Animated Figures 25-6, 25-7

(continued)

(continued)

WHAT YOU SHOULD KNOW		WHERE TO GO TO PRACTICE
Price Discrimination If a monopolist engages in price discrimination, it sells its product at more than one price, with the price difference being unrelated to differences in production costs. To be able to engage successfully in price discrimination, a monopolist must be able to identify and separate buyers with different price elasticities of demand. If the monopolist can prevent those with more elastic demand from reselling its product to those with less elastic demand, it can sell some of its output at higher prices to consumers with less elastic demand.	price discrimination, 653 price differentiation, 654	• **MyEconLab** Study Plan 25.7 • Video: Price Discrimination
Social Cost of Monopolies Because a monopoly is a price searcher, it is able to charge the highest price that people are willing to pay for the amount of output it produces. This price exceeds the marginal cost of producing the output. In addition, if the monopolist's marginal cost curve corresponds to the sum of the marginal cost curves for the number of firms that would exist if the industry were perfectly competitive instead, then the monopolist produces and sells less output than perfectly competitive firms would have produced and sold.	**KEY FIGURE** Figure 25-9, 656	• **MyEconLab** Study Plan 25.8 • Animated Figure 25-9

Log in to MyEconLab, take a chapter test, and get a personalized Study Plan that tells you which concepts you understand and which ones you need to review. From there, MyEconLab will give you further practice, tutorials, animations, videos, and guided solutions.
Log in to www.myeconlab.com

PROBLEMS

All problems are assignable in . *Answers to odd-numbered problems appear at the back of the book.*

25-1. Under federal law, only the U.S. Postal Service has the right to deliver first-class mail. Thus, a consumer can either send a letter via the U.S. Postal Service for just over 40 cents or pay FedEx, UPS, or DHL $10 or more to deliver it. What is the shape of the demand curve faced by the U.S. Postal Service in the market for first-class mail?

25-2. Recently, a top constitutional law expert who had been licensed to practice law in Massachusetts and was under consideration for nomination to the California Supreme Court failed the California bar examination. In doing so, she joined a long list of accomplished lawyers who have failed to pass the notoriously difficult examination, including a former governor who required four attempts to pass and a Los Angeles mayor who gave up after four tries. In the legal industry, what is a key economic function of the California bar examination?

25-3. Suppose that it is the year 2038. Exclusive ownership of a resource found to be required for the production of fusion power has given a firm monopoly power in the provision of this good. What is true of the relationship between the price of this resource and the marginal revenue the firm receives?

25-4. Consider the resource owner and seller discussed in Problem 25-3. Discuss what would have been true of the price elasticity of demand facing this firm if the firm had been a perfectly competitive seller of this resource. Contrast this with the price elasticity of demand for this firm in its actual role as monopoly provider. Explain why the price elasticities in the two situations are different.

25-5. The following table depicts the daily output, price, and costs of a monopoly dry cleaner located near the campus of a remote college town.

Output (suits cleaned)	Price per Suit ($)	Total Costs ($)
0	8.00	3.00
1	7.50	6.00
2	7.00	8.50
3	6.50	10.50
4	6.00	11.50
5	5.50	13.50
6	5.00	16.00
7	4.50	19.00
8	4.00	24.00

   a. Compute revenues and profits at each output rate.

   b. What is the profit-maximizing rate of output?

   c. Calculate the dry cleaner's marginal revenue and marginal cost at each output level. What is the profit-maximizing level of output?

25-6. A manager of a monopoly firm notices that the firm is producing output at a rate at which average total cost is falling but is not at its minimum feasible point. The manager argues that surely the firm must not be maximizing its economic profits. Is this argument correct?

25-7. Use the graph at the top of the next column to answer the following questions.

   a. What is the monopolist's profit-maximizing output?

   b. At the profit-maximizing output rate, what are average total cost and average revenue?

   c. At the profit-maximizing output rate, what are the monopolist's total cost and total revenue?

   d. What is the maximum profit?

   e. Suppose that the marginal cost and average total cost curves in the diagram also illustrate the horizontal summation of the firms in a perfectly com-

petitive industry in the long run. What would the equilibrium price and output be if the market were perfectly competitive? Explain the economic cost to society of allowing a monopoly to exist.

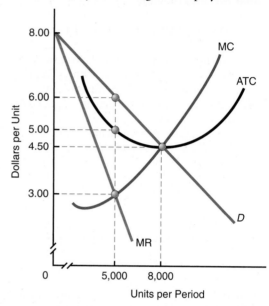

25-8. The marginal revenue curve of a monopoly crosses its marginal cost curve at $30 per unit and an output of 2 million units. The price that consumers are willing to pay for this output is $40 per unit. If it produces this output, the firm's average total cost is $43 per unit, and its average fixed cost is $8 per unit. What is the profit-maximizing (loss-minimizing) output? What are the firm's economic profits (or economic losses)?

25-9. Consider the revenue and cost conditions for a monopolist that are depicted in the figure below.

a. What is this producer's profit-maximizing (or loss-minimizing) output?

b. What are the firm's economic profits (or losses)?

25-10. For each of the following examples, explain how and why a monopoly would try to price discriminate.

a. Air transport for businesspeople and tourists

b. Serving food on weekdays to businesspeople and retired people. (Hint: Which group has more flexibility during a weekday to adjust to a price change and, hence, a higher price elasticity of demand?)

c. A theater that shows the same movie to large families and to individuals and couples. (Hint: For which set of people will the overall expense of a movie be a larger part of their budget, so that demand is more elastic?)

25-11. A monopolist's revenues vary directly with price. Is it maximizing its economic profits? Why or

why not? (Hint: Recall that the relationship between revenues and price depends on price elasticity of demand.)

25-12. A new competitor enters the industry and competes with a second firm, which had been a monopolist. The second firm finds that although demand is not perfectly elastic, it is now relatively more elastic. What will happen to the second firm's marginal revenue curve and to its profit-maximizing price?

25-13. A monopolist's marginal cost curve has shifted upward. What is likely to happen to the monopolist's price, output rate, and economic profits?

25-14. Demand has fallen. What is likely to happen to the monopolist's price, output rate, and economic profits?

ECONOMICS ON THE NET

Patents, Trademarks, and Intellectual Property This Internet application explores a firm's view on legal protections.

Title: Intellectual Property

Navigation: Follow the link at **www.econtoday.com/chapter25** to the GlaxoSmithKline Web site. Select *Investors*, then *Annual Reports and Reviews*. View the PDF of Annual Report 2007. Scroll down to Intellectual Property (page 28).

Application Read the statement and table; then answer the following questions.

1. How do patents, trademarks, and registered designs and copyrights differ?

2. What are GlaxoSmithKline's intellectual property goals? Do patents or trademarks seem to be more important?

For Group Discussion and Analysis In 1969, GlaxoSmith Kline developed Ventolin, a treatment for asthma symptoms. Though the patent and trademark have long expired, the company still retains over a third of the annual market sales of this treatment. Explain, in economic terms, the source of GlaxoSmithKline's strength in this area. Discuss whether patents and trademarks are beneficial for the development and discovery of new treatments.

ANSWERS TO QUICK QUIZZES

p. 644: (i) close; (ii) ownership . . . scale
p. 648: (i) change . . . total; (ii) marginal . . . marginal; (iii) elasticity . . . elasticity
p. 653: (i) downward . . . less; (ii) marginal . . . marginal . . . demand; (iii) total . . . quantity; (iv) total . . . above
p. 657: (i) downward . . . elasticities . . . resale; (ii) discrimination . . . differentiation; (iii) lower . . . higher

Appendix F

Consumer Surplus and the Losses Resulting from Monopoly

You have learned that a monopolist produces fewer units than would otherwise be produced in a perfectly competitive market and that it sells these units at a higher price. It seems that consumers surely must be worse off under monopoly than they would be under perfect competition. This appendix shows that, in fact, consumers are harmed by the existence of a monopoly in a market that otherwise could be perfectly competitive.

Consumer Surplus

Let's first examine how economists measure the benefits that consumers gain from engaging in market transactions. Consider Figure F-1, which displays a market demand curve, D. We assume that at the present time consumers face a per-unit price of this item given by P_A. Thus, the quantity demanded of this particular product is equal to Q_A at point A on the demand curve.

Typically, we visualize the market demand curve indicating the quantities that all consumers are willing to purchase at each possible price. In addition, however, the demand curve tells us the price that consumers are willing to pay for a unit of output at various possible quantities. For instance, if consumers were to buy Q_1 units of this good, they would be willing to pay a price equal to P_1 for the last unit purchased. If they only have to pay the price P_A for each unit they buy, however, consumers gain an amount equal to $P_1 - P_A$ for the last of the Q_1 units purchased. This benefit to consumers equals the vertical distance between the demand curve and the level of the market clearing price. Economists call this vertical distance a *surplus* value to consumers from being able to consume the last of the Q_1 units at the lower, market clearing price.

FIGURE F-1

Consumer Surplus

If the per-unit price is P_A, then at point A on the demand curve D, consumers desire to purchase Q_A units. To purchase Q_1 units of this item, consumers would have been willing to pay the price P_1 for the last unit purchased but only have to pay the per-unit price P_A, so they gain a surplus equal to $P_1 - P_A$ for the last of the Q_1 units purchased. Likewise, to buy Q_2 units, consumers would have been willing to pay P_2 for the last unit purchased but only have to pay P_A, so they gain the surplus $P_2 - P_A$ for the last of the Q_2 units purchased. Summing these and all other surpluses consumers receive from purchasing all Q_A units at the price P_A yields the total consumer surplus at this price, shown by the blue-shaded area.

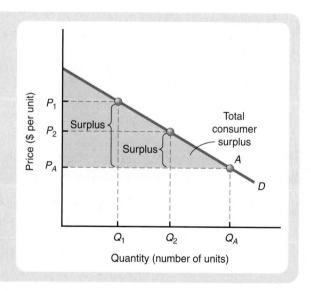

Likewise, if consumers were to purchase Q_2 units of this good, they would be willing to pay a price equal to P_2 for the last unit. Nevertheless, because they only have to pay the price P_A for each unit purchased, consumers gain an amount equal to $P_2 - P_A$. Hence, this is the surplus value associated with the last of the Q_2 units that consumers buy.

Of course, when they pay the same per-unit price P_A for every unit of this product that they purchase at point A, consumers obtain Q_A units. Thus, consumers gain surplus values—vertical distances between the demand curve and the level of the market clearing price—for each unit consumed, up to the total of Q_A units. Graphically, this is equivalent to the *entire blue-shaded area under the demand curve* but above the market clearing price. This entire area equals the total **consumer surplus,** which is the difference between the total amount that consumers *would have been willing to pay* for an item and the total amount that they *actually pay.*

Consumer surplus
The difference between the total amount that consumers would have been willing to pay for a good or service and the total amount that they actually pay.

Consumer Surplus in a Perfectly Competitive Market

Now let's consider the determination of consumer surplus in a perfectly competitive market. Take a look at the market diagram depicted in Figure F-2. In the figure, we assume that all firms producing in this market incur no fixed costs. We also assume that each firm faces the same marginal cost that does not vary with its output. These assumptions imply that the marginal cost curve is horizontal and that marginal cost is the same as average total cost at any level of output. Thus, if many perfectly competitive firms operate in this market, the horizontal summation of all firms' marginal cost curves, which is the market supply curve, is this same horizontal curve, labeled MC = ATC.

Under perfect competition, the point at which this market supply curve crosses the market demand curve, D, determines the equilibrium quantity, Q_{pc}, and the market clearing price, P_{pc}. Thus, in a perfectly competitive market, consumers obtain Q_{pc} units at the same per-unit price of P_{pc}. Consumers gain surplus values—vertical

FIGURE F-2

Consumer Surplus in a Perfectly Competitive Market

If all firms in this market incur no fixed costs and face the same, constant marginal costs, then the marginal cost curve, MC, and the average total cost curve, ATC, are equivalent and horizontal. Under perfect competition, the horizontal summation of all firms' marginal cost curves is this same horizontal curve, which is the market supply curve, so the market clearing price is P_{pc}, and the equilibrium quantity is Q_{pc}. The total consumer surplus in a perfectly competitive market is the striped area.

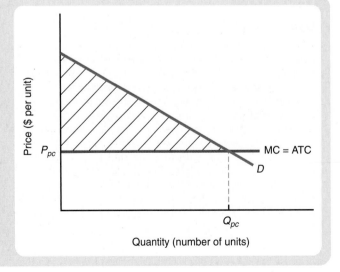

distances between the demand curve and the level of the market clearing price—for each unit consumed, up to the total of Q_{pc} units. This totals to the entire striped area under the demand curve above the market clearing price. Consumer surplus is the difference between the total amount that consumers would have been willing to pay and the total amount that they actually pay, given the market clearing price that prevails in the perfectly competitive market.

How Society Loses from Monopoly

Now let's think about what happens if a monopoly situation arises in this market, perhaps because a government licenses the firms to conduct joint operations as a single producer. These producers respond by acting as a single monopoly firm, which searches for the profit-maximizing quantity and price.

In this altered situation, which is depicted in Figure F-3, the new monopolist (which we assume is unable to engage in price discrimination—see pages 653 to 655) will produce to the point at which marginal revenue equals marginal cost. This rate of output is Q_m units. The demand curve indicates that consumers are willing to pay a price equal to P_m for this quantity of output. Consequently, as you learned in this chapter, the monopolist will produce fewer units of output than the quantity, Q_{pc}, that firms would have produced in a perfectly competitive market. The monopolist also charges a higher price than the market clearing price, P_{pc}, that would have prevailed under perfect competition.

Recall that the monopolist's maximized economic profits equal its output times the difference between price and average total cost, or the yellow-shaded rectangular area equal to $Q_m \times (P_m - \text{ATC})$. By setting its price at P_m, therefore, the monopolist is able to transfer this portion of the competitive level of consumer surplus to itself in the form of monopoly profits. Consumers are still able to purchase Q_m units of output at a per-unit price, P_m, below the prices they would otherwise have been willing to pay. Hence, the blue-shaded triangular area above this monopoly-profit rectangle is consumer surplus that remains in the new monopoly situation.

FIGURE F-3

Losses Generated by Monopoly

If firms are able to act as a single monopoly, then the monopolist will produce only Q_m units at the point at which marginal revenue equals marginal cost and charge the price P_m. Economic profits, $Q_m \times (P_m - \text{ATC})$, equal the yellow-shaded rectangular area, which is a portion of the competitive level of consumer surplus (the original striped area) transferred to the monopolist. Consumers can now purchase Q_m units of output at a per-unit price, P_m, below the prices they otherwise would have been willing to pay, so the blue-shaded triangular area above this monopoly-profit rectangle is remaining consumer surplus. The green-shaded triangular area is lost consumer surplus that results from the monopoly producing Q_m units instead of the Q_{pc} units that would have been produced under perfect competition. This is called a *deadweight loss* because it is a portion of the competitive level of consumer surplus that no one in society can obtain under monopoly.

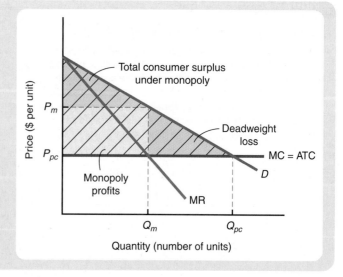

Once the monopoly is formed, what happens to the green-shaded portion of the competitive consumer surplus? The answer is that this portion of consumer surplus is lost to society. The monopolist's failure to produce the additional $Q_{pc} - Q_m$ units of output that would have been forthcoming in a perfectly competitive market eliminates this portion of the original consumer surplus. This lost consumer surplus resulting from monopoly production and pricing is called a **deadweight loss** because it is a portion of the competitive level of consumer surplus that no one in society can obtain in a monopoly situation.

Thus, as a result of monopoly, consumers are worse off in two ways. First, the monopoly profits that result constitute a transfer of a portion of consumer surplus away from consumers to the monopolist. Second, the failure of the monopoly to produce as many units as would have been produced under perfect competition eliminates consumer surplus that otherwise would have been a benefit to consumers. No one in society, not even the monopoly, can obtain this deadweight loss.

Deadweight loss
The portion of consumer surplus that no one in society is able to obtain in a situation of monopoly.

26

Monopolistic Competition

A fter spending an afternoon on the lots of auto dealers, you still can't decide among the available vehicle models. Should you go with one firm's MDX, or should you contemplate a competitor's MKX? One company's RSX has a nice look, but what about the RX brand offered elsewhere? The Q7 on one dealer's lot has a nice feel, but the Q45 at the dealer of a competing firm also has a number of desirable features. One company's M3 may be worth another look, but the M35 sold by another company is also attractive. Plus there are two different firms' LS models to consider. How do automakers selling similarly named yet slightly different brands determine how many vehicles to produce and what prices to charge? To find out the answer to this question, you must learn about the market structure in which today's auto producers interact, known as *monopolistic competition*.

LEARNING OBJECTIVES

After reading this chapter, you should be able to:

➤ Discuss the key characteristics of a monopolistically competitive industry

➤ Contrast the output and pricing decisions of monopolistically competitive firms with those of perfectly competitive firms

➤ Explain why brand names and advertising are important features of monopolistically competitive industries

➤ Describe the fundamental properties of information products and evaluate how the prices of these products are determined under monopolistic competition

? DID YOU KNOW THAT only one out of every three new soft drinks that sellers introduce ultimately remains in production longer than a few years? Every new product entry into the soft-drink market is introduced with advertising aimed at helping consumers find that they have a taste for an innovative flavor that is slightly different from every other. Nevertheless, two-thirds of soft drinks that sellers introduce into the market ultimately are withdrawn from production.

Product heterogeneity and advertising did not show up in our analysis of perfect competition. They play large roles, however, in industries that cannot be described as perfectly competitive but cannot be described as pure monopolies, either. A combination of consumers' preferences for variety and competition among producers has led to similar but *differentiated* products in the marketplace. This situation has been described as *monopolistic competition*, the subject of this chapter.

Monopolistic Competition

In the 1920s and 1930s, economists became increasingly aware that there were many industries for which both the perfectly competitive model and the pure monopoly model did not apply and did not seem to yield very accurate predictions. Theoretical and empirical research was instituted to develop some sort of middle ground. Two separately developed models of **monopolistic competition** resulted. At Harvard, Edward Chamberlin published *Theory of Monopolistic Competition* in 1933. The same year, Britain's Joan Robinson published *The Economics of Imperfect Competition*. In this chapter, we will outline the theory as presented by Chamberlin.

Monopolistic competition
A market situation in which a large number of firms produce similar but not identical products. Entry into the industry is relatively easy.

Chamberlin defined monopolistic competition as a market structure in which a relatively large number of producers offer similar but differentiated products. Monopolistic competition therefore has the following features:

1. Significant numbers of sellers in a highly competitive market
2. Differentiated products
3. Sales promotion and advertising
4. Easy entry of new firms in the long run

Even a cursory look at the U.S. economy leads to the conclusion that monopolistic competition is an important form of market structure in the United States. Indeed, that is true of all developed economies.

Number of Firms

In a perfectly competitive industry, there is an extremely large number of firms; in pure monopoly, there is only one. In monopolistic competition, there is a large number of firms, but not as many as in perfect competition. This fact has several important implications for a monopolistically competitive industry.

1. *Small share of market*. With so many firms, each firm has a relatively small share of the total market.
2. *Lack of collusion*. With so many firms, it is very difficult for all of them to get together to collude—to cooperate in setting a pure monopoly price (and output). Collusive pricing in a monopolistically competitive industry is virtually impossible. Also, barriers to entry are minor, and the flow of new firms into the industry makes collusive agreements less likely. The large number of firms makes the monitoring

and detection of cheating very costly and extremely difficult. This difficulty is compounded by differentiated products and high rates of innovation; collusive agreements are easier for a homogeneous product than for heterogeneous ones.

3. *Independence.* Because there are so many firms, each one acts independently of the others. No firm attempts to take into account the reaction of all of its rival firms—that would be impossible with so many rivals. Thus, an individual producer does not try to take into account possible reactions of rivals to its own output and price changes.

Follow the link at www.econtoday.com/chapter26 to *Wall Street Journal* articles about real-world examples of monopolistic competition.

Product Differentiation

Perhaps the most important feature of the monopolistically competitive market is **product differentiation.** We can say that each individual manufacturer of a product has an absolute monopoly over its own product, which is slightly differentiated from other similar products. This means that the firm has some control over the price it charges. Unlike the perfectly competitive firm, it faces a downward-sloping demand curve.

Product differentiation
The distinguishing of products by brand name, color, and other minor attributes. Product differentiation occurs in other than perfectly competitive markets in which products are, in theory, homogeneous, such as wheat or corn.

Consider the abundance of brand names for toothpaste, soap, gasoline, vitamins, shampoo, and most other consumer goods and a great many services. We are not obliged to buy just one type of television set, just one type of jeans, or just one type of footwear. We can usually choose from a number of similar but differentiated products. The greater a firm's success at product differentiation, the greater the firm's pricing options.

How is a tombstone producer using a high-tech approach to product differentiation?

EXAMPLE
Differentiation at the Graveyard—High-Definition RIP

For centuries, graveyard operators have explored the limits of product differentiation. In most graveyards, tombstones come in all manner of shapes, sizes, and colors. In the latest twist on tombstone differentiation, one producer, Vidstone, offers tombstones that come equipped with solar-powered speaker systems and flat-panel screens. At a mourner's touch, a tombstone will display a photo slideshow of the deceased individual and play back audio commentaries, including recordings of the individual's voice. For situations when quiet visitations are desired, the tombstones are equipped with headphone jacks.

FOR CRITICAL ANALYSIS
What does a seller of grave markers gain from product differentiation?

Each separate differentiated product has numerous similar substitutes. This clearly has an impact on the price elasticity of demand for the individual firm. Recall that one determinant of price elasticity of demand is the availability of substitutes: The greater the number and closeness of substitutes available, other things being equal, the greater the price elasticity of demand. If the consumer has a vast array of alternatives that are just about as good as the product under study, a relatively small increase in the price of that product will lead many consumers to switch to one of the many close substitutes. Thus, the ability of a firm to raise the price above the price of *close* substitutes is very small. At a given price, the demand curve is highly elastic compared to a monopolist's demand curve. In the extreme case, with perfect competition, the substitutes are perfect because we are dealing with only one particular undifferentiated product. In that case, the individual firm has a perfectly elastic demand curve.

Sales Promotion and Advertising

Monopolistic competition differs from perfect competition in that no individual firm in a perfectly competitive market will advertise. A perfectly competitive firm, by definition, can sell all that it wants to sell at the going market price anyway. Why, then, would it spend even one penny on advertising? Furthermore, by definition, the perfect competitor is selling a product that is identical to the product that all other firms in the industry are selling. Any advertisement that induces consumers to buy more of that product will, in effect, be helping all the competitors too. A perfect competitor therefore cannot be expected to incur any advertising costs (except when all firms in an industry collectively agree to advertise to urge the public to buy more beef or drink more milk, for example).

The monopolistic competitor, however, has at least *some* monopoly power. Because consumers regard the monopolistic competitor's product as distinguishable from the products of the other firms, the firm can search for the price consumers are willing to pay for its differentiated product. Advertising, therefore, may result in increased profits. Advertising is used to increase demand and to differentiate one's product. How much advertising should be undertaken? It should be carried to the point at which the additional revenue from one more dollar of advertising just equals that one dollar of additional cost.

How are companies increasingly using odors to advertise their products?

EXAMPLE
Firms Sell with Smell

A booming new approach to advertising is to sell with smell. Increasingly, companies are developing new ways to advertise products on the basis of odor differentiation. A chain of gasoline stations in California now wafts coffee aroma at the pumps to inform consumers about the quality of the brand of coffee sold inside the stations. Similarly, Westin Hotels & Resorts now pumps the fragrance of a white tea it sells at its gift shops into the lobbies of more than 100 of its hotels. Procter & Gamble, the manufacturer of numerous household products, is experimenting with fragrance-enhanced product displays at retail outlets. Thus, firms are using product odors to try to induce consumers to discover a preference for their fragrance-differentiated products.

FOR CRITICAL ANALYSIS
How will successful advertising affect the demand for a monopolistically competitive firm's differentiated product?

Ease of Entry

For any current monopolistic competitor, potential competition is always lurking in the background. The easier—that is, the less costly—entry is, the more a current monopolistic competitor must worry about losing business.

A good example of a monopolistic competitive industry is the computer software industry. Many small firms provide different programs for many applications. The fixed capital costs required to enter this industry are small; all you need are skilled programmers. In addition, there are few legal restrictions. The firms in this industry also engage in extensive advertising in more than 150 computer publications.

Price and Output for the Monopolistic Competitor

Now that we are aware of the assumptions underlying the monopolistic competition model, we can analyze the price and output behavior of each firm in a monopolistically competitive industry. We assume in the analysis that follows that the desired product type and quality have been chosen. We further assume that the budget and the type of promotional activity have already been chosen and do not change.

The Individual Firm's Demand and Cost Curves

Because the individual firm is not a perfect competitor, its demand curve slopes downward, as in all three panels of Figure 26-1. Hence, it faces a marginal revenue curve that is also downward sloping and below the demand curve. To find the profit-maximizing rate of output and the profit-maximizing price, we go to the output where the marginal cost (MC) curve intersects the marginal revenue (MR) curve from below. That gives us the profit-maximizing output rate. Then we draw a vertical line up to the demand curve. That gives us the price that can be charged to sell exactly that quantity produced. This is what we have done in Figure 26-1. In each panel, a marginal cost curve intersects the marginal revenue curve at A. The profit-maximizing rate of output is q, and the profit-maximizing price is P.

Short-Run Equilibrium

In the short run, it is possible for a monopolistic competitor to make economic profits—profits over and above the normal rate of return or beyond what is necessary to keep that firm in that industry. We show such a situation in panel (a) of Figure 26-1. The average total cost (ATC) curve is drawn below the demand curve, d, at the profit-maximizing rate of output, q. Economic profits are shown by the blue-shaded rectangle in that panel.

Losses in the short run are clearly also possible. They are presented in panel (b) of Figure 26-1. Here the average total cost curve lies everywhere above the individual firm's demand curve, d. The losses are indicated by the red-shaded rectangle.

Just as with any market structure or any firm, in the short run it is possible to observe either economic profits or economic losses. In either case, the price does not equal marginal cost but rather is above it.

FIGURE 26-1

Short-Run and Long-Run Equilibrium with Monopolistic Competition

In panel (a), the typical monopolistic competitor is shown making economic profits. In this situation, there would be entry into the industry, forcing the demand curve for the individual monopolistic competitor leftward. Eventually, firms would find themselves in the situation depicted in panel (c), where zero *economic* profits are being made. In panel (b), the typical firm is in a monopolistically competitive industry making economic losses. In this situation, firms would leave the industry. Each remaining firm's demand curve would shift outward to the right. Eventually, the typical firm would find itself in the situation depicted in panel (c).

The Long Run: Zero Economic Profits

The long run is where the similarity between perfect competition and monopolistic competition becomes more obvious. In the long run, because so many firms produce substitutes for the product in question, any economic profits will disappear with competition. They will be reduced to zero either through entry by new firms seeing a chance to make a higher rate of return than elsewhere or by changes in product quality and advertising outlays by existing firms in the industry. (Profitable products will be imitated by other firms.) As for economic losses in the short run, they will disappear in the long run because the firms that suffer them will leave the industry. They will go into another business where the expected rate of return is at least normal. Panels (a) and (b) of Figure 26-1 therefore represent only short-run situations for a monopolistically competitive firm. In the long run, the individual firm's demand curve *d* will just touch the average total cost curve at the particular price that is profit maximizing for that particular firm. This is shown in panel (c) of Figure 26-1.

A word of warning: This is an idealized, long-run equilibrium situation for each firm in the industry. It does not mean that even in the long run we will observe every single firm in a monopolistically competitive industry making *exactly* zero economic profits or *just* a normal rate of return. We live in a dynamic world. All we are saying is that if this model is correct, the rate of return will *tend toward* normal—economic profits will *tend toward* zero.

Comparing Perfect Competition with Monopolistic Competition

If both the monopolistic competitor and the perfect competitor make zero economic profits in the long run, how are they different? The answer lies in the fact that the demand curve for the individual perfect competitor is perfectly elastic. Such is not the case for the individual monopolistic competitor; its demand curve is less than perfectly elastic. This firm has some control over price. Price elasticity of demand is not infinite.

We see the two situations in Figure 26-2. Both panels show average total costs just touching the respective demand curves at the particular price at which the firm is selling the product. Notice, however, that the perfect competitor's average total costs are at a minimum. This is not the case with the monopolistic competitor. The equilibrium rate of output is to the left of the minimum point on the average total cost curve where price is greater than marginal cost. The monopolistic competitor cannot expand output to the point of minimum costs without lowering price, and then marginal cost would exceed marginal revenue. A monopolistic competitor at profit maximization charges a price that exceeds marginal cost. In this respect it is similar to the monopolist.

It has consequently been argued that monopolistic competition involves *waste* because minimum average total costs are not achieved and price exceeds marginal cost. There are too many firms, each with excess capacity, producing too little output. According to critics of monopolistic competition, society's resources are being wasted.

FIGURE 26-2

Comparison of the Perfect Competitor with the Monopolistic Competitor

In panel (a), the perfectly competitive firm has zero economic profits in the long run. The price is set equal to marginal cost, and the price is P_1. The firm's demand curve is just tangent to the minimum point on its average total cost curve. With the monopolistically competitive firm in panel (b), there are also zero economic profits in the long run. The price is greater than marginal cost. The monopolistically competitive firm does not find itself at the minimum point on its average total cost curve. It is operating at a rate of output to the left of the minimum point on the ATC curve.

Panel (a)
Perfect Competition

Panel (b)
Monopolistic Competition

Chamberlin had an answer to this criticism. He contended that the difference between the average cost of production for a monopolistically competitive firm in an open market and the minimum average total cost represented what he called the cost of producing "differentness." Chamberlin did not consider this difference in cost between perfect competition and monopolistic competition a waste. In fact, he argued that it is rational for consumers to have a taste for differentiation; consumers willingly accept the resultant increased production costs in return for more choice and variety of output.

QUICK QUIZ | *See page 688 for the answers. Review concepts from this section in MyEconLab.*

In the _____ run, it is possible for monopolistically competitive firms to make economic profits or economic losses.

In the _____ run, monopolistically competitive firms will make _____ economic profits—that is, they will make a _____ rate of return.

Because the monopolistic competitor faces a downward-sloping demand curve, it does not produce at the minimum point on its average _____ cost curve. Hence, we say that a monopolistic competitor has higher average _____ costs per unit than a perfect competitor would have.

Chamberlin argued that the difference between the _____ _____ cost of production for a monopolistically competitive firm and the _____ average total cost at which a perfectly competitive firm would produce is the cost of producing "differentness."

Brand Names and Advertising

Because "differentness" has value to consumers, monopolistically competitive firms regard their brand names as valuable. Firms use trademarks—words, symbols, and logos—to distinguish their product brands from goods or services sold by other firms. Consumers associate these trademarks with the firms' products. Thus, companies regard their brands as valuable private (intellectual) property, and they engage in advertising to maintain the differentiation of their products from those of other firms.

Why do firms consider their brand names to be valuable?

Brand Names and Trademarks

A firm's ongoing sales generate current profits and, as long as the firm is viable, the prospect of future profits. A company's value in the marketplace, or its purchase value, depends largely on its current profitability and perceptions of its future profitability.

Table 26-1 on the following page gives the market values of the world's most valuable product brands. Each valuation depends on the market prices of shares of stock in a company times the number of shares traded. Brand names, symbols, and logos relate to consumers' perceptions of product differentiation and hence to the market values of firms. Companies protect their trademarks from misuse by registering them with the U.S. Patent and Trademark Office. Once its trademark application is approved, a company has the right to seek legal damages if someone makes unauthorized use of its brand name, spreads false rumors about the company, or engages in other underhanded activities that can reduce the value of its brand.

You Are There

Contemplate how a company seeks economic profits by creating a variety of trademarked brands of clothing and accessories in **Trademarked Differentiation at Polo Ralph Lauren Corporation,** on pages 682 and 683.

Advertising

To help ensure that consumers differentiate their product brands from those of other firms, monopolistically competitive firms commonly engage in advertising. Advertising

TABLE 26-1

Values of the Top Ten Brands

The market value of a company is equal to the number of shares of stock ownership issued by the company times the market price of each share. To a large extent, the company's value reflects the value of its brand.

Brand	Market Value ($ billions)
Coca-Cola	65.3
Microsoft	58.7
International Business Machines (IBM)	57.1
General Electric (GE)	51.6
Nokia	33.7
Toyota	32.1
Intel	31.0
McDonald's	29.4
Disney	29.2
Mercedes-Benz	23.6

Source: Interbrand Annual Survey, 2008.

comes in various forms, and the nature of advertising can depend considerably on the types of products that firms wish to distinguish from competing brands.

METHODS OF ADVERTISING Figure 26-3 shows the current distribution of advertising expenses among the various advertising media. Today, as in the past, firms primarily rely on two approaches to advertising their products. One is **direct marketing,** in which firms engage in personalized advertising using postal mailings, phone calls, and e-mail messages (excluding so-called banner and pop-up ads on Web sites). The other is **mass marketing,** in which firms aim advertising messages at as many consumers as possible via media such as television, newspapers, radio, and magazines.

A third advertising method is called **interactive marketing.** This advertising approach allows a consumer to respond directly to an advertising message; often the consumer is able to search for more detailed information and place an order as part of the response. Sales booths and some types of Internet advertising, such as banner ads with links to sellers' Web pages, are forms of interactive marketing.

How has the Internet search engine company Google found a way to use interactive marketing to create real-time connections between potential buyers and product sellers?

Direct marketing
Advertising targeted at specific consumers, typically in the form of postal mailings, telephone calls, or e-mail messages.

Mass marketing
Advertising intended to reach as many consumers as possible, typically through television, newspaper, radio, or magazine ads.

Interactive marketing
Advertising that permits a consumer to follow up directly by searching for more information and placing direct product orders.

E-COMMERCE EXAMPLE
Clicking a Phone Connection

Google, Inc., the operator of the Internet search engine, has developed a way to make interactive marketing nearly instantaneous. Called "click to call," the new feature is a small telephone-handset icon that appears with some merchant ads on search pages. For an immediate connection to the seller of a product, a Web surfer can type in his or her phone number and click on the icon. Then both the individual's phone and the seller's phone ring simultaneously after Google establishes a connection.

FOR CRITICAL ANALYSIS
Why do you suppose that Internet sellers often agree to pay search engines an extra commission when interactive marketing generates a sale to a Web surfer?

FIGURE 26-3

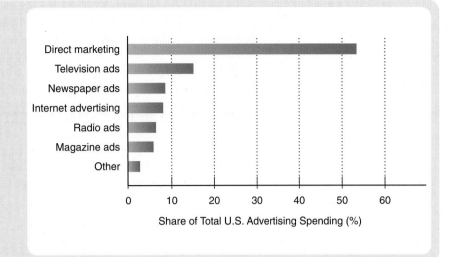

Distribution of U.S. Advertising Expenses
Direct marketing accounts for more than half of advertising expenses in the United States.

Sources: Advertising Today; Direct Marketing Today; and Internet Advertising Bureau.

INFORMATIONAL VERSUS PERSUASIVE ADVERTISING Some ads provide considerable information about products, while others seem designed mainly to attract a consumer's attention. The qualities and characteristics of a product determine how the firm should advertise that product. Some types of products, known as **search goods,** possess qualities that are relatively easy for consumers to assess in advance of their purchase. Clothing and music are common examples of items that have features that a consumer may assess, or perhaps even sample, before purchasing. Other products, known as **experience goods,** are products that people must actually consume before they can determine their qualities. Soft drinks, restaurant meals, and haircutting services are examples of experience goods. A third category of products, called **credence goods,** includes goods and services with qualities that might be difficult for consumers lacking expertise to assess without assistance. Products such as pharmaceuticals and services such as health care and legal advice are examples of credence goods.

The forms of advertising that firms use to market a search good are likely to be considerably different from those employed in marketing an experience good. If the item is a search good, a firm is more likely to use **informational advertising** that emphasizes the features of its product. An audio or video ad for the latest CD by a pop star is likely to include snippets of songs that are featured on the CD, which helps potential buyers assess the quality of the music. In contrast, if the product is an experience good, a firm is more likely to engage in **persuasive advertising** intended to induce a consumer to try the product and, as a consequence, discover a previously unknown taste for it. For example, a soft-drink ad is likely to depict happy people drinking the clearly identified product during breaks from enjoyable outdoor activities on a hot day. If a product is a credence good, producers commonly use a mix of informational and persuasive advertising. For instance, an ad for a pharmaceutical product commonly provides both detailed information about the product's curative properties and side effects and suggestions to consumers to ask physicians to help them assess the drug.

ADVERTISING AS SIGNALING BEHAVIOR Recall from Chapter 24 that *signals* are compact gestures or actions that convey information. For example, high profits in an industry are signals that resources should flow to that industry. Individual companies

Search good
A product with characteristics that enable an individual to evaluate the product's quality in advance of a purchase.

Experience good
A product that an individual must consume before the product's quality can be established.

Credence good
A product with qualities that consumers lack the expertise to assess without assistance.

Informational advertising
Advertising that emphasizes transmitting knowledge about the features of a product.

Persuasive advertising
Advertising that is intended to induce a consumer to purchase a particular product and discover a previously unknown taste for the item.

can explicitly engage in signaling behavior. A firm can do so by establishing brand names or trademarks and then promoting them heavily. This is a signal to prospective consumers that this is a company that plans to stay in business. Before the modern age of advertising, U.S. banks needed a way to signal their soundness. To do this, they constructed large, imposing bank buildings using marble and granite. Stone structures communicated permanence. The effect was to give bank customers confidence that they were not doing business with fly-by-night operations.

When Toyota advertises its brand name heavily, it incurs substantial costs. The only way it can recoup those costs is by selling many Toyota vehicles over a long period of time. Heavy advertising in the company's brand name thereby signals to car buyers that Toyota intends to stay in business a long time and wants to develop a loyal customer base—because loyal customers are repeat customers.

QUICK QUIZ *See page 688 for the answers. Review concepts from this section in MyEconLab.*

_____ such as words, symbols, and logos distinguish firms' products from those of other firms. Firms seek to differentiate their brands through advertising, via _____ marketing, _____ marketing, or _____ marketing.

A firm is more likely to use _____ advertising that emphasizes the features of its product if the item is a **search good** with features that consumers can assess in advance.

A firm is more likely to use _____ advertising to affect consumers' tastes and preferences if it sells an **experience good.** This is an item that people must actually consume before they can determine its qualities.

A firm that sells a _____ good, which is an item possessing qualities that consumers lack the expertise to fully assess, typically uses a combination of informational and persuasive advertising.

Information Products and Monopolistic Competition

Information product
An item that is produced using information-intensive inputs at a relatively high fixed cost but distributed for sale at a relatively low marginal cost.

A number of industries sell **information products,** which entail relatively high fixed costs associated with the use of knowledge and other information-intensive inputs as key factors of production. Once the first unit has been produced, however, it is possible to produce additional units at a relatively low per-unit cost. Most information products can be put into digital form. Good examples are computer games, computer operating systems, digital music and videos, educational and training software, electronic books and encyclopedias, and office productivity software.

Special Cost Characteristics of Information Products

Creating the first copy of an information product often entails incurring a relatively sizable up-front cost. Once the first copy is created, however, making additional copies can be very inexpensive. For instance, a firm that sells a computer game can simply make properly formatted copies of the original digital file of the game on a CD-ROM or DVD. Alternatively, the firm might make the game available for consumers to download, at a price, via the Internet.

COSTS OF PRODUCING INFORMATION PRODUCTS To think about the cost conditions faced by the seller of an information product, consider the production and sale of a computer game. The company that creates a computer game must devote many hours of labor to developing and editing its content. Each hour of labor and each unit of other resources devoted to performing this task entail an opportunity cost. The sum of all these up-front costs constitutes a relatively sizable *fixed cost* that the company must incur to generate the first copy of the computer game.

Once the company has developed the computer game in a form that is readable by personal computers, the marginal cost of making and distributing additional copies is very low. In the case of a computer game, it is simply a matter of incurring a minuscule cost to place the required files on a CD, on a DVD, or on the company's Web site.

COST CURVES FOR AN INFORMATION PRODUCT Suppose that a manufacturer decides to produce and sell a computer game. Creating the first copy of the game requires incurring a total fixed cost equal to $250,000. The marginal cost that the company incurs to place the computer game on a CD, on a DVD, or in downloadable format is a constant amount equal to $2.50 per computer game.

Figure 26-4 displays the firm's cost curves for this information product. By definition, average fixed cost is total fixed cost divided by the quantity produced and sold. Hence, the average fixed cost of the first computer game is $250,000. But if the company sells 5,000 copies, the average fixed cost drops to $50 per game. If the total quantity sold is 50,000, average fixed cost declines to $5 per game. The average fixed cost (AFC) curve slopes downward over the entire range of possible quantities of computer games.

Average variable cost equals total variable cost divided by the number of units of a product that a firm sells. If this company sells only one copy, then the total variable cost it incurs is the per-unit cost of $2.50, and this is also the average variable cost of producing one unit. Because the per-unit cost of producing the computer game is a

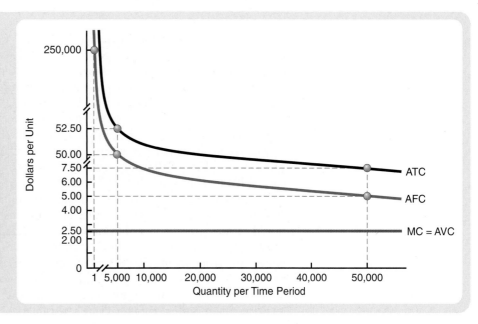

FIGURE 26-4

Cost Curves for a Producer of an Information Product

The total fixed cost of producing a computer game is $250,000. If the producer sells 5,000 copies, average fixed cost falls to $50 per copy. If quantity sold rises to 50,000, average fixed cost decreases to $5 per copy. Thus, the producer's average fixed cost (AFC) curve slopes downward. If the per-unit cost of producing each copy of the game is $2.50, then both the marginal cost (MC) and average variable cost (AVC) curves are horizontal at $2.50 per copy. Adding the AFC and AVC curves yields the ATC curve. Because the ATC curve slopes downward, the producer of this information product experiences short-run economies of operation.

constant \$2.50, producing two games entails a total variable cost of \$5.00, and the average variable cost of producing two games is \$5.00 ÷ 2 = \$2.50. Thus, as shown in Figure 26-4, the average variable cost of producing and selling this computer game is always equal to the constant marginal cost of \$2.50 per game that the company incurs. The average variable cost (AVC) curve is the same as the marginal cost (MC) curve, which for this company is the horizontal line depicted in Figure 26-4.

SHORT-RUN ECONOMIES OF OPERATION By definition, average total cost equals the sum of average fixed cost and average variable cost. The average total cost (ATC) curve for this computer game company slopes downward over its entire range.

Recall from Chapter 23 that along the downward-sloping range of an individual firm's *long-run* average cost curve, the firm experiences *economies of scale*. For the producer of an information product such as a computer game, the *short-run* average total cost curve slopes downward. Consequently, sellers of information products typically experience **short-run economies of operation.** The average total cost of producing and selling an information product declines as more units of the product are sold. Short-run economies of operation are a distinguishing characteristic of information products that sets them apart from most other goods and services.

Short-run economies of operation
A distinguishing characteristic of an information product arising from declining short-run average total cost as more units of the product are sold.

Monopolistic Competition and Information Products

In the example depicted in Figure 26-4 on the preceding page, the information product is a computer game. There are numerous computer games among which consumers can choose. Hence, there are many products that are close substitutes in the market for computer games. Yet no two computer games are exactly the same. This means that the particular computer game product sold by the company in our example is distinguishable from other competing products.

For the sake of argument, therefore, let's suppose that this company participates in a monopolistically competitive market for this computer game. Panels (a) and (b) of Figure 26-5 display a possible demand curve for the computer game manufactured and sold by this particular company.

MARGINAL COST PRICING AND INFORMATION PRODUCTS What if the company making this particular computer game were to behave *as if* it were a perfectly competitive firm by setting the price of its product equal to marginal cost? Panel (a) of Figure 26-5 provides the answer to this question. If the company sets the price of the computer game equal to marginal cost, it will charge only \$2.50 per game it sells. Naturally, a larger number of people desire to purchase computer games at this price, and given the demand curve in the figure, the company could sell 20,000 copies of this game.

The company would face a problem, however. At a price of \$2.50 per computer game, it would earn \$50,000 in revenues on sales of 20,000 copies. The average fixed cost of 20,000 copies equals \$250,000/20,000, or \$12.50 per computer game. Adding this to the constant \$2.50 average variable cost implies an average total cost of selling 20,000 copies of \$15 per game. Under marginal cost pricing, therefore, the company would earn an average loss of \$12.50 (price − average total cost = \$2.50 − \$15.00 = −\$12.50) per computer game for all 20,000 copies sold. The company's total economic loss from selling 20,000 computer games at a price equal to marginal cost would amount to \$250,000. Hence, the company would fail to recoup the \$250,000 total fixed cost of producing the computer game. If the company had planned to set its price equal to the computer game's marginal cost, it would never have sought to produce the computer game in the first place!

FIGURE 26-5

The Infeasibility of Marginal Cost Pricing of an Information Product

In panel (a), if the firm with the average total cost and marginal cost curves shown in Figure 26-4 on page 679 sets the price of the computer game equal to its constant marginal cost of $2.50 per copy, then consumers will purchase 20,000 copies. This yields $50,000 in revenues. The firm's average total cost of 20,000 games is $15 per copy, so its total cost of selling that number of copies is $15 × 20,000 = $300,000. Marginal cost pricing thereby entails a $250,000 loss, which is the total fixed cost of producing the computer game.

Panel (b) illustrates how the price of the game is ultimately determined under monopolistic competition. Setting a price of $27.50 per game induces consumers to buy 10,000 copies, and the average total cost of producing this number of copies is also $27.50. Consequently, total revenues equal $275,000, which just covers the sum of the $250,000 in total fixed costs and $25,000 (the 10,000 copies times the constant $2.50 average variable cost) in total variable costs. The firm earns zero economic profits.

The failure of marginal cost pricing to allow firms selling information products to cover the fixed costs of producing those products is intrinsic to the nature of such products. In the presence of short-run economies of operation in producing information products, marginal cost pricing is simply not feasible in the marketplace.

Recall that marginal cost pricing is associated with perfect competition. An important implication of this example is that markets for information products cannot function as perfectly competitive markets. Imperfect competition is the rule, not the exception, in the market for information products.

THE CASE IN WHICH PRICE EQUALS AVERAGE TOTAL COST Panel (b) of Figure 26-5 illustrates how the *price* of the computer game is ultimately determined in a monopolistically competitive market. After all entry or exit from the market has occurred, the price of the computer game will equal the producer's average cost of production, including all implicit opportunity costs. The price charged for the game generates total revenues sufficient to cover all explicit and implicit costs and therefore is consistent with earning a normal return on invested capital.

Given the demand curve depicted in Figure 26-5, at a price of $27.50 per computer game, consumers are willing to purchase 10,000 copies. The company's average total cost of offering 10,000 copies for sale is also equal to $27.50 per computer game. Consequently, the price of each copy equals the average total cost of producing the game.

At a price of $27.50 per computer game, the company's revenues from selling 10,000 copies equal $275,000. This amount of revenues is just sufficient to cover the company's total fixed cost (including the opportunity cost of capital) of $250,000 and the $25,000 total variable cost it incurs in producing 10,000 copies at an average variable cost of $2.50 per game. Thus, the company earns zero economic profits.

LONG-RUN EQUILIBRIUM FOR AN INFORMATION PRODUCT INDUSTRY When the price of an information product equals average total cost, sellers charge the minimum price required to cover their production costs, including the relatively high initial costs they must incur to develop their products in the first place. Consumers thereby pay the lowest price necessary to induce sellers to provide the item.

The situation illustrated in panel (b) of Figure 26-5 on the previous page corresponds to a long-run equilibrium for this particular firm in a monopolistically competitive market for computer games. If this and other companies face a situation such as the diagram depicts, there is no incentive for additional companies to enter or leave the computer game industry. Consequently, the product price naturally tends to adjust to equality with average total cost as a monopolistically competitive industry composed of sellers of information products moves toward long-run equilibrium.

QUICK QUIZ See page 688 for the answers. Review concepts from this section in MyEconLab.

Firms that sell **information products** experience relatively _____ fixed costs, but once they have produced the first unit, they can sell additional units at a relatively _____ per-unit cost. Consequently, the manufacturer of an information product experiences short-run _____ of _____.

If a firm sets the price of an information product equal to marginal cost, it earns only sufficient revenues to cover its

_____ costs. Engaging in marginal cost pricing, therefore, fails to cover the relatively high fixed costs of making an information product.

In a long-run equilibrium outcome under monopolistic competition, the price of an information product equals _____ _____ cost. The seller's total revenues exactly cover _____ costs, including the opportunity cost of capital.

 You Are There

Trademarked Differentiation at Polo Ralph Lauren Corporation

Some call him a master of product differentiation. Ralph Lauren, chair and chief executive of Polo Ralph Lauren Corporation, offers a brand of clothing and accessories to fit every possible product niche. At one end are his Black Label collections, which are shown on New York fashion runways twice each year and feature $250 shirts and $3,000 suede jackets. His Polo brand offers accessories that include $14,000 alligator handbags.

At the other end are Lauren's Chaps clothing brands. The Chaps brands feature men's dress shirts at less than $50 and linen trousers at less than $80. They commonly are

sold at outlets of discount retailers such as Kohl and Belk. Recently, Lauren began offering moderately priced apparel and accessories at J.C. Penney under the American Label brand name. Lauren's company also operates nearly 150 Polo Ralph Lauren Factory Stores that generate about $750 million in annual sales of discounted clothing.

Between these extremes are a host of other differentiated brands: Lauren by Ralph Lauren, RRL, RLX, Polo Sport, and Rugby. The total market value of Lauren's fashion empire of brand trademarks amounts to more than $4 billion.

You Are There (cont.)

CRITICAL ANALYSIS QUESTIONS

1. How is it possible that Polo Ralph Lauren Corporation can earn short-run economic profits each time it creates a slightly differentiated brand?

2. Why do you suppose that Polo Ralph Lauren uses mass marketing that draws consumers' attention to high-priced brands when promoting the company's discount brands but primarily uses direct marketing to advertise the high-priced brands?

Issues and Applications

What's in a Name? The Auto Name Game Heats Up

T he world's auto companies now offer more than 80 different groups of automobile brands. In addition, within each group, there typically are several different models from which consumers can choose. All of this product differentiation is creating a problem for automakers, however. They are running out of names to differentiate their vehicles from the pack.

CONCEPTS APPLIED

➤ Product Differentiation

➤ Monopolistic Competition

➤ Trademarks

The Monopolistically Competitive Auto Industry

In the auto industry, brand name groups now range across nearly the entire alphabet, from Honda's Acura model and Alfa Romeo Automobiles to Ford Motor Company's Volvo and Zimmer Motor Cars. In between, of course, are well-known brand groups such as Audi, BMW, Chevrolet, Dodge, Fiat, Isuzu, Jaguar, Land Rover, Mitsubishi, Saab, and Volkswagen. Others, such as Aston Martin Lagonda Limited, Bugatti, Holden, Morgan Motor Company, and Škoda, offer their own particularly differentiated brands.

Today's auto industry possesses all of the classic features of monopolistic competition: numerous producers, differentiated products, and considerable use of advertising. Furthermore, technological improvements in recent decades have reduced the costs of industry entry and exit. Thus, manufacturers now come and go with regularity. So do product names, as automakers continually seek to differentiate their vehicles from the similar but slightly different brands marketed by their competitors.

The Naming of Names

For decades, automakers have struggled to come up with vehicle names that differentiate their products in the minds of consumers. Henry Ford began with plain vanilla names such as "Model 1" and "Model A," but his company soon switched to more comprehensible names such as "Edsel," after a Ford family member, and the prestigious sounding "Lincoln Town Car." More recently, scientists have offered a helping hand in vehicle naming. Physicists have contributed vehicle names such as "Ion" and "Proton." Auto-naming consultants lately have been looking beyond earth to the planetary moons in our solar system for names, such as "Io," after Jupiter's volcanic moon, and "Hyperion," from Saturn's heavily crater-pockmarked moon.

In recent years, however, car companies have especially favored combinations of letters and numbers, such as the BMW X5 or the Lexus LS 450, which they have found resonate with consumers of their brands. The difficulty is that as more manufacturers have jumped on the letter-number combination bandwagon, effective product differentiation has become increasingly problematic. Currently, at least 22 of the 26 letters of the alphabet are used in the names of luxury cars. The letters L, M, S, and Z are particularly popular, although no letter tops X, which automakers now use to designate about two dozen different vehicles. Least popular is the letter O, which looks "empty" and, of course, is easily confused with zero.

A Trademark War Begins

The limited set of letters creates an additional problem when manufacturers begin combining letters and numbers. Consider, for instance, the following pairings of vehicle groups: Acura MDX and Lincoln MKX, Acura RSX and Lexus RX, Audi Q7/Q5 and Infiniti Q45, BMW M3/M5 and Infiniti M35/M45, and Lexus LS and Lincoln LS. In addition, among broad groups of vehicles, there are the Audi S Series, the Jaguar S Type, and the Mercedes S-Class.

Of course, every manufacturer seeks to build brand images in the minds of consumers and hence obtains a trademark for names of vehicle groups and models. Growing similarities among letter-number name combinations have set off a trademark free-for-all. When Infiniti ran ads in Canada announcing the arrival of a "new M," BMW charged that a trademark violation had occurred. The decision by Volkswagen's Audi to name its sport utility vehicle the Q7, taking the letter from its "quattro" all-wheel drive technology, prompted Nissan to allege that the act was a trademark violation. And when Ford's Lincoln division decided to use the MKX name, Acura's management suggested that the name infringed on its MDX trademark. Thus, as the naming wars heat up, so does the pace at which new quibbles over trademarks are erupting throughout the auto industry.

Test your understanding of this chapter by going online to **MyEconLab**.
In the Study Plan for this chapter, select Section N: News.

For Critical Analysis

1. What is the economic objective behind automakers' efforts to come up with new vehicle names on a regular basis?

2. Why do you suppose names of products such as vehicles sometimes become similar but not quite the same, just as the actual products share analogous but not quite identical features?

Web Resources

1. For links to information about the various vehicle brands marketed by the world's many auto companies, go to www.econtoday.com/chapter26.

2. Learn about how a branding consulting firm called Gravity Branding goes about helping automakers and other firms select brand names at www.econtoday.com/chapter26.

Research Project

Consider a monopolistically competitive auto company that is in an initial long-run equilibrium. What are two ways that identifying a new name for a slightly altered version of a vehicle might succeed in boosting the firm's economic profits? (Hint: What two changes in a product demand curve can enable the producer to boost the product's price?) Why are these economic profits likely to disappear in the long run?

Here is what you should know after reading this chapter. **MyEconLab** will help you identify what you know, and where to go when you need to practice.

WHAT YOU SHOULD KNOW		WHERE TO GO TO PRACTICE
The Key Characteristics of a Monopolistically Competitive Industry A monopolistically competitive industry consists of a large number of firms that sell differentiated products that are close substitutes. Firms can easily enter or exit a monopolistically competitive industry. Because monopolistically competitive firms can increase their profits if they can successfully distinguish their products from those of their rivals, they have an incentive to engage in sales promotions and advertising.	monopolistic competition, 669 product differentiation, 670	• **MyEconLab** Study Plan 26.1 • Audio introduction to Chapter 26 • Video: Characteristics of Monopolistic Competition
Contrasting the Output and Pricing Decisions of Monopolistically Competitive Firms with Those of Perfectly Competitive Firms In the short run, a monopolistically competitive firm produces output to the point at which marginal revenue equals marginal cost. The price it charges for this output can exceed both marginal cost and average total cost in the short run. The resulting economic profits induce new firms to enter the industry. In the long run, therefore, monopolistically competitive firms, like perfectly competitive firms, earn zero economic profits. In contrast to perfectly competitive firms, however, price exceeds marginal cost in the long-run equilibrium.	**KEY FIGURES** Figure 26-1, 673 Figure 26-2, 674	• **MyEconLab** Study Plans 26.2, 26.3 • Animated Figures 26-1, 26-2
Why Brand Names and Advertising Are Important Features of Monopolistically Competitive Industries Monopolistically competitive firms use product differentiation to boost the demand for their products. They engage in advertising, in the form of direct marketing, mass marketing, or interactive marketing. If the product is a search good with features that consumers can evaluate prior to purchase, the seller is more likely to use advertising to transmit information about product features. If the firm sells an experience good, with features that are apparent only when consumed, it is more likely to use persuasive advertising to induce consumers to discover unknown tastes. If the product is a credence good with characteristics that consumers cannot readily assess unaided, then the firm often uses a mix of informational and persuasive advertising.	direct marketing, 676 mass marketing, 676 interactive marketing, 676 search good, 677 experience good, 677 credence good, 677 informational advertising, 677 persuasive advertising, 677	• **MyEconLab** Study Plan 26.4

(continued)

(continued)

PROBLEMS

All problems are assignable in myeconlab. *Answers to odd-numbered problems appear at the back of the book.*

26-1. Explain why the following are examples of monopolistic competition.

    a. There are a number of fast-food restaurants in town, and they compete fiercely. Some restaurants cook their hamburgers over open flames. Others fry their hamburgers. In addition, some serve broiled fish sandwiches, while others serve fried fish sandwiches. A few serve ice cream cones for dessert, while others offer frozen ice cream pies.

    b. There is a vast number of colleges and universities across the country. Each competes for top students. All offer similar courses and programs, but some have better programs in business, while others have stronger programs in the arts and humanities. Still others are academically stronger in the sciences.

26-2. Consider the diagram at the right depicting the revenue and cost conditions faced by a monopolistically competitive firm.

    a. What are the total revenues, total costs, and economic profits experienced by this firm?

    b. Is this firm more likely in short- or long-run equilibrium? Explain.

26-3. The following table depicts the prices and total costs a local used-book store faces. The bookstore competes with a number of similar stores, but it capitalizes on its location and the word-of-mouth reputation of the coffee it serves to its customers. Calculate the store's total revenue, total profit, marginal revenue, and marginal cost at each level of output, beginning with the first unit. Based on marginal analysis, what is the approximate profit-maximizing level of output for this business?

Output	Price per Book ($)	Total Costs ($)
0	6.00	2.00
1	5.75	5.25
2	5.50	7.50
3	5.25	9.60
4	5.00	12.10
5	4.75	15.80
6	4.50	20.00
7	4.00	24.75

26-4. Calculate total average costs for the bookstore in Problem 26-3. Illustrate the store's short-run equilibrium by plotting demand, marginal revenue, average total costs, and marginal costs. What is its total profit?

26-5. Suppose that after long-run adjustments take place in the used-book market, the business in Problem 26-3 ends up producing 4 units of output. What are the market price and economic profits of this monopolistic competitor in the long run?

26-6. It is a typical Christmas electronics shopping season, and makers of flat-panel TVs are marketing the latest available models through their own Web sites as well as via retailers such as Best Buy, Wal-Mart, and Circuit City. Each manufacturer offers its own unique versions of flat-panel TVs in differing arrays of shapes and sizes. As usual, each is hoping to maintain a stream of economic profits earned since it first introduced these most recent models late last year or perhaps just a few months before Christmas. Nevertheless, as sales figures arrive at the headquarters of companies such as Dell, Samsung, Sharp, and Sony, it is clear that most of the companies will end up earning only a normal rate of return this year.

    a. How can makers of flat-panel TVs earn economic profits during the first few months after the introduction of new models?

    b. What economic forces result in the dissipation of economic profits earned by manufacturers of flat-panel TVs?

26-7. Classify each of the following as an example of direct, interactive, and/or mass marketing.

    a. The sales force of a pharmaceutical company visits physicians' offices to promote new medications and to answer physicians' questions about treatment options and possible side effects.

    b. A mortgage company targets a list of specific low-risk borrowers for a barrage of e-mail messages touting its low interest rates and fees.

    c. An online bookseller pays fees to an Internet search engine to post banner ads relating to each search topic chosen by someone conducting a search; in part, this helps promote the bookseller's brand, but clicking on the banner ad also directs the person to a Web page displaying books on the topic that are available for purchase.

    d. A national rental car chain runs advertisements on all of the nation's major television networks.

26-8. Classify each of the following as an example of direct, interactive, and/or mass marketing.

    a. A cosmetics firm pays for full-page display ads in a number of top women's magazines.

    b. A magazine distributor mails a fold-out flyer advertising its products to the addresses of all individuals it has identified as possibly interested in magazine subscriptions.

    c. An online gambling operation arranges for pop-up ads to appear on the computer screen every time a person uses a media player to listen to digital music or play video files, and clicking on the ads directs an individual to its Web gambling site.

    d. A car dealership places advertisements in newspapers throughout the region where potential customers reside.

26-9. Categorize each of the following as an experience good, a search good, or a credence good or service, and justify your answer.

    a. A heavy-duty filing cabinet

    b. A restaurant meal

    c. A wool overcoat

    d. Psychotherapy

26-10. Categorize each of the following as an experience good, a search good, or a credence good or service, and justify your answer.

 a. Services of a carpet cleaning company

 b. A new cancer treatment

 c. Athletic socks

 d. A silk necktie

26-11. In what ways do credence goods share certain characteristics of both experience goods and search goods? How do credence goods differ from both experience goods and search goods? Why does advertising of credence goods commonly contain both informational and persuasive elements? Explain your answers.

26-12. Is each of the following items more likely to be the subject of an informational or a persuasive advertisement? Why?

 a. An office copying machine

 b. An automobile loan

 c. A deodorant

 d. A soft drink

26-13. Discuss the special characteristics of an information product, and explain the implications for a producer's short-run average and marginal cost curves. In addition, explain why having a price equal to marginal cost is not feasible for the producer of an information product.

26-14. A firm that sells e-books—books in digital form downloadable from the Internet—sells all e-books relating to do-it-yourself topics (home plumbing, gardening, and the like) at the same price. At present, the company can earn a maximum annual profit of $25,000 when it sells 10,000 copies within a year's time. The firm incurs a 50-cent expense each time a consumer downloads a copy, but the company must spend $100,000 per year developing new editions of the e-books. The company has determined that it would earn zero economic profits if price were equal to average total cost, and in this case it could sell 20,000 copies. Under marginal cost pricing, it could sell 100,000 copies.

 a. In the short run, what is the profit-maximizing price of e-books relating to do-it-yourself topics?

 b. At the profit-maximizing quantity, what is the average total cost of producing e-books?

ECONOMICS ON THE NET

Legal Services on the Internet A number of legal firms now offer services on the Internet, and in this application you contemplate features of the market for Web-based legal services.

Title: Nolo.com—Law for All

Navigation: Link to the Nolo.com site via **www.econtoday.com/chapter26.**

Application Answer the following questions.

 1. In what respects does the market for legal services, such as those provided online by Nolo.com, have the characteristics of a monopolistically competitive industry?

 2. How can providers of legal services differentiate their products? How does Nolo.com attempt to do this?

For Group Discussion and Analysis Assign groups to search the Web for at least three additional online legal firms and compare the services these firms offer. Reconvene the entire class and discuss whether it is reasonable to classify the market for online legal services as monopolistically competitive.

ANSWERS TO QUICK QUIZZES

p. 672: (i) large . . . highly; (ii) differentiated; (iii) easy
p. 675: (i) short; (ii) long . . . zero . . . normal; (iii) total . . . total; (iv) average total . . . minimum
p. 678: (i) Trademarks . . . direct . . . mass . . . interactive; (ii) informational; (iii) persuasive; (iv) credence
p. 682: (i) high . . . low . . . economies . . . operation; (ii) variable; (iii) average total . . . total

Oligopoly and Strategic Behavior

27

As your jet taxis its way around the airport, you begin to notice a pattern. One company's wide-bodied airliners were manufactured by Boeing. Another company's were built by Airbus, while a third airline's jets were built by Boeing. The jet in which you happen to be seated was made by Airbus. In fact, during the past several years, these two firms—Airbus and Boeing—have been the only manufacturers of large commercial passenger jets. You might ask yourself, "How do quantities and prices get determined in a market with so few firms competing with each other?" In this chapter, you will learn the answer to this question.

LEARNING OBJECTIVES

MyEconLab helps you master each objective and study more efficiently. See end of chapter for details.

After reading this chapter, you should be able to:

➤ Outline the fundamental characteristics of oligopoly

➤ Understand how to apply game theory to evaluate the pricing strategies of oligopolistic firms

➤ Identify features of an industry that help or hinder efforts to form a cartel that seeks to restrain output and earn economic profits

➤ Illustrate how network effects and market feedback can explain why some industries are oligopolies

➤ Explain why multiproduct firms selling complementary sets of products may or may not want their products to be compatible with those of their competitors

? **DID YOU KNOW THAT** Google, Inc., the operator of the well-known Internet search engine, recently paid almost $1 billion to serve as the exclusive provider of search technology and text-based advertisements on the social networking site MySpace? This enabled Google to replace Yahoo as the search engine utilized by visitors to the MySpace Web site. Google hoped that this move would enable it to share in the bandwagon effect that MySpace is experiencing as more people join that site's network of users and begin communicating with each other about shared interests. In this way, Google anticipated that it would gain an advantage over Yahoo in attracting more visitors to its own Web site. In this chapter, you will learn about how firms in industries containing just a few competitors can benefit— or lose out—when a consumer's willingness to purchase their products is influenced by other consumers' decisions about whether to buy them.

Oligopoly

An important market structure that we have yet to discuss involves a situation in which a few large firms comprise essentially an entire industry. They are not perfectly competitive in the sense that we have used the term. They are not even monopolistically competitive. And because there are several of them, a pure monopoly does not exist. We call such a situation an **oligopoly,** which consists of a small number of *interdependent* sellers. Each firm in the industry knows that other firms will react to its changes in prices, quantities, and qualities. An oligopoly market structure can exist for either a homogeneous or a differentiated product.

Characteristics of Oligopoly

Oligopoly is characterized by a small number of interdependent firms that constitute the entire market.

SMALL NUMBER OF FIRMS How many is "a small number of firms"? More than two but less than a hundred? The question is not easy to answer. Basically, though, oligopoly exists when the top few firms in the industry account for an overwhelming percentage of total industry output.

Oligopolies often involve three to five big companies that produce the bulk of industry output. Between World War II and the 1970s, three firms—General Motors, Chrysler, and Ford—produced and sold nearly all the output of the U.S. automobile industry. Among manufacturers of chewing gum and coin-operated amusement games, four large firms produce and sell essentially the entire output of each industry.

INTERDEPENDENCE All markets and all firms are, in a sense, interdependent. But only when a few large firms produce most of the output in an industry does the question of **strategic dependence** of one on the others' actions arise. In this situation, when any one firm changes its output, its product price, or the quality of its product, other firms notice the effects of its decisions. The firms must recognize that they are interdependent and that any action by one firm with respect to output, price, quality, or product differentiation will cause a reaction by other firms. A model of such mutual interdependence is difficult to build, but examples of such behavior are not hard to find in the real world. Oligopolists in the cigarette industry, for example, are constantly reacting to each other.

Recall that in the model of perfect competition, each firm ignores the behavior of other firms because each firm is able to sell all that it wants at the going market price.

Oligopoly
A market structure in which there are very few sellers. Each seller knows that the other sellers will react to its changes in prices, quantities, and qualities.

Strategic dependence
A situation in which one firm's actions with respect to price, quality, advertising, and related changes may be strategically countered by the reactions of one or more other firms in the industry. Such dependence can exist only when there are a limited number of major firms in an industry.

At the other extreme, the pure monopolist does not have to worry about the reaction of current rivals because there are none. In an oligopolistic market structure, the managers of firms are like generals in a war: *They must attempt to predict the reaction of rival firms.* It is a strategic game.

Why Oligopoly Occurs

Why are some industries composed chiefly of a few large firms? What causes an industry that might otherwise be competitive to tend toward oligopoly? We can provide some partial answers here.

Follow the link at **www.econtoday.com/chapter27** to *Wall Street Journal* articles about real-world examples involving oligopoly.

ECONOMIES OF SCALE Perhaps the most common reason that has been offered for the existence of oligopoly is economies of scale. Recall that economies of scale exist when a doubling of output results in less than a doubling of total costs. When economies of scale exist, the firm's long-run average total cost curve will slope downward as the firm produces more and more output. Average total cost can be reduced by continuing to expand the scale of operation to the *minimum efficient scale,* or the output rate at which long-run average cost is minimized. Smaller firms in a situation in which the minimum efficient scale is relatively large will have average total costs greater than those incurred by large firms. Little by little, they will go out of business or be absorbed into larger firms.

BARRIERS TO ENTRY It is possible that certain barriers to entry have prevented more competition in oligopolistic industries. They include legal barriers, such as patents, and control and ownership of critical supplies. Indeed, we can find periods in the past when firms were able not only to erect a barrier to entry but also to keep it in place year after year. In principle, the chemical, electronics, and aluminum industries have been at one time or another either monopolistic or oligopolistic because of the ownership of patents and the control of strategic inputs by specific firms.

OLIGOPOLY BY MERGER Another reason that oligopolistic market structures may sometimes develop is that firms merge. A merger is the joining of two or more firms under single ownership or control. The merged firm naturally becomes larger, enjoys greater economies of scale as output increases, and may ultimately have a greater ability to influence the market price for the industry's output.

There are two key types of mergers, vertical and horizontal. A **vertical merger** occurs when one firm merges with either a firm from which it purchases an input or a firm to which it sells its output. Vertical mergers occur, for example, when a coal-using electrical utility purchases a coal-mining firm or when a shoe manufacturer purchases retail shoe outlets.

Vertical merger
The joining of a firm with another to which it sells an output or from which it buys an input.

Obviously, vertical mergers cannot create oligopoly as we have defined it. But that can indeed occur via a **horizontal merger,** which involves firms selling a similar product. If two shoe manufacturing firms merge, that is a horizontal merger. If a group of firms, all producing steel, merge into one, that is also a horizontal merger.

Horizontal merger
The joining of firms that are producing or selling a similar product.

So far we have been talking about oligopoly in a theoretical manner. Now it is time to look at the actual oligopolies in the United States.

Measuring Industry Concentration

As we have stated, oligopoly is a market structure in which a few interdependent firms produce a large part of total output in an industry. This situation is often called one of

TABLE 27-1

Computing the Four-Firm Concentration Ratio

Firm	Annual Sales ($ millions)		
1	150 ⎫		
2	100 ⎬ = 400	Total number of firms in industry = 25	
3	80		
4	70 ⎭		
5 through 25	50		
Total	450		

Four-firm concentration ratio = 400/450 = 88.9%

high *industry concentration*. Before we show the concentration statistics in the United States, let's determine how industry concentration can be measured.

CONCENTRATION RATIO The most common way to compute industry concentration is to determine the percentage of total sales or production accounted for by the top four or top eight firms in an industry. This gives the four- or eight-firm **concentration ratio,** also known as the *industry concentration ratio.* An example of an industry with 25 firms is given in Table 27-1. We can see in that table that the four largest firms account for almost 90 percent of total output in the hypothetical industry. This is an example of an oligopoly because a few firms will recognize the interdependence of their output, pricing, and quality decisions.

Concentration ratio
The percentage of all sales contributed by the leading four or leading eight firms in an industry; sometimes called the *industry concentration ratio.*

U.S. CONCENTRATION RATIOS Table 27-2 shows the four-firm *domestic* concentration ratios for various industries. Is there any way that we can show or determine which industries to classify as oligopolistic? There is no definite answer. If we arbitrarily picked a four-firm concentration ratio of 75 percent, we could infer that tobacco products and breakfast cereals were oligopolistic. But we would always be dealing with an arbitrary definition.

How concentrated is the personal computer industry?

E-COMMERCE EXAMPLE

Market Concentration in the Personal Computer Industry

The personal computer industry generated a total of $201.1 billion in worldwide revenues in a recent year. Hewlett-Packard received $35.0 billion of those revenues, Dell received $27.9 billion, Lenovo received $14.1 billion, and Acer received $13.7 billion. These figures imply that Hewlett-Packard's market share was 17.4 percent, Dell's was 13.9 percent, Levnovo's was 7.0 percent, and Acer's was 6.8 percent. Consequently, the four-firm concentration ratio for the personal computer industry was 45.1 percent.

FOR CRITICAL ANALYSIS
In light of the fact that Toshiba earned the fifth-largest amount of revenues, about $7.6 billion, from selling personal computers during this particular year, what was the five-firm concentration ratio in the computer industry?

TABLE 27-2		
Four-Firm Domestic Concentration Ratios for Selected U.S. Industries	Industry	Share of Total Sales Accounted for by the Top Four Firms (%)
	Tobacco products	99
	Breakfast cereals	83
	Household vacuum cleaners	69
	Primary aluminum	59
	Soft drinks	47
	Computers	45
	Printing and publishing	34
	Commercial banking	29.5

Source: U.S. Bureau of the Census.

The four-firm concentration ratio in the computer industry is about 45 percent. Is the computer industry therefore an oligopoly?

Oligopoly, Efficiency, and Resource Allocation

Although oligopoly is not the dominant form of market structure in the United States, oligopolistic industries do exist. To the extent that oligopolists have *market power*—the ability to *individually* affect the *market* price for the industry's output—they lead to resource misallocations, just as monopolies do. Oligopolists charge prices that exceed marginal cost. But what about oligopolies that occur because of economies of scale? Consumers might actually end up paying lower prices than if the industry were composed of numerous smaller firms.

All in all, there is no definite evidence of serious resource misallocation in the United States because of oligopolies. In any event, *the more U.S. firms face competition from the rest of the world, the less any current oligopoly will be able to exercise market power.*

QUICK QUIZ   *See page 713 for the answers. Review concepts from this section in MyEconLab.*

An **oligopoly** is a market situation in which there is a _____ number of _____ sellers.

Oligopoly may result from _____ of scale, barriers to entry, and _____.

_____ mergers involve the merging of one firm with either the supplier of an input or the purchaser of its output.

_____ mergers involve the joining of firms selling a similar product.

Industry concentration can be measured by the combined _____ of total _____ accounted for by the top four or top eight firms in the industry.

Strategic Behavior and Game Theory

At this point, we would like to be able to show oligopoly price and output determination in the way we showed it for perfect competition, pure monopoly, and monopolistic competition, but we cannot. Whenever there are relatively few firms competing in an industry, each can and does react to the price, quantity, quality, and product innovations that the others undertake. In other words, each oligopolist has a **reaction function.** Oligopolistic competitors are interdependent. Consequently, the decision makers in such firms must employ strategies. And we must be able to model

Reaction function
The manner in which one oligopolist reacts to a change in price, output, or quality made by another oligopolist in the industry.

Game theory

A way of describing the various possible outcomes in any situation involving two or more interacting individuals when those individuals are aware of the interactive nature of their situation and plan accordingly. The plans made by these individuals are known as *game strategies*.

their strategic behavior if we wish to predict how prices and outputs are determined in oligopolistic market structures. In general, we can think of reactions of other firms to one firm's actions as part of a *game* that is played by all firms in the industry. Economists have developed **game theory** models to describe firms' rational interactions. Game theory is the analytical framework in which two or more individuals, companies, or nations compete for certain payoffs that depend on the strategy that the others employ. Poker is such a game situation because it involves a strategy of reacting to the actions of others.

Why do many businesses have their managers engage in mock "war games"?

EXAMPLE
War Games Catch on at Firms

According to a sixth-century BC Chinese general named Sun Tzu, "To know your enemy, you must become your enemy." Dozens of businesses operating in markets in which their own outcomes depend on what other firms do have been taking Sun Tzu's dictum to heart. To do so, they periodically have their managers participate in computer-guided corporate war games.

These corporate war games involve several rounds and typically take a full day to play to completion. In the war game at Xerox, the office-equipment company, one team remains the "Xerox team." Another team acts as customers of Xerox. Remaining teams take on the roles of Xerox's competitors in the office-equipment industry, such as Canon, Hewlett-Packard, and Ricoh. These competing teams draw not just on their own strategies but also on the strategies currently

employed by Xerox. At the end of each round, the teams learn the combined effects of all teams' strategies on the computer-simulated market and team outcomes. Each team then adapts in subsequent rounds in an effort to improve its performance. One of Xerox's objectives in conducting corporate war games is to encourage its managers to think more carefully about how their own real-world actions influence outcomes. Another goal is to help the managers view Xerox from the perspective of competing firms, so that they can better foresee and react to the actions of their industry competitors.

FOR CRITICAL ANALYSIS
In any given industry, what types of factors might cause a firm's current reaction function to differ from its reaction function in a previous year?

Cooperative game

A game in which the players explicitly cooperate to make themselves better off. As applied to firms, it involves companies colluding in order to make higher than perfectly competitive rates of return.

Noncooperative game

A game in which the players neither negotiate nor cooperate in any way. As applied to firms in an industry, this is the common situation in which there are relatively few firms and each has some ability to change price.

Zero-sum game

A game in which any gains within the group are exactly offset by equal losses by the end of the game.

Negative-sum game

A game in which players as a group lose during the process of the game.

Some Basic Notions About Game Theory

Games can be either cooperative or noncooperative. If firms work together to obtain a jointly shared objective, such as maximizing profits for the industry as a whole, then they participate in a **cooperative game.** Whenever it is too costly for firms to coordinate their actions to obtain cooperative outcomes, they are in a **noncooperative game** situation. Most strategic behavior in the marketplace is best described as a noncooperative game.

Games can be classified by whether the payoffs are negative, zero, or positive. In a **zero-sum game,** one player's losses are offset by another player's gains. If two retailers have an absolutely fixed total number of customers, for example, the customers that one retailer wins over are exactly equal to the customers that the other retailer loses. In a **negative-sum game,** players as a group lose during the process of the game (although one perhaps by more than the other, and it's possible for one or more players to win). In a **positive-sum game,** players as a group end up better off. Some economists describe all voluntary exchanges as positive-sum games. After an exchange, both the buyer and the seller are better off than they were prior to the exchange.

STRATEGIES IN NONCOOPERATIVE GAMES Players, such as decision makers in oligopolistic firms, have to devise a **strategy,** which is defined as a rule used to make a choice. The goal of the decision maker is to devise a strategy that is more successful than alternative strategies. Whenever a firm's decision makers can come up with certain strategies that are generally successful no matter what actions competitors take, these are called **dominant strategies.** The dominant strategy always yields the unique best action for the decision maker no matter what action the other "players" undertake. Relatively few business decision makers over a long period of time have successfully devised dominant strategies. We know this by observation: Few firms in oligopolistic industries have maintained relatively high profits consistently over time.

How can a real-world situation faced by two captured bank robbers help to illustrate basic principles of game theory?

Positive-sum game

A game in which players as a group are better off at the end of the game.

Strategy

Any rule that is used to make a choice, such as "Always pick heads."

Dominant strategies

Strategies that always yield the highest benefit. Regardless of what other players do, a dominant strategy will yield the most benefit for the player using it.

EXAMPLE
The Prisoners' Dilemma

A real-world example of game theory occurs when two people involved in a bank robbery are caught. What should they do when questioned by police? Their situation has been called the **prisoners' dilemma.** The two suspects, Sam and Carol, are interrogated separately (they cannot communicate with each other) and are given various alternatives. The interrogator indicates separately to Sam and Carol the following:

1. If both confess to the bank robbery, they will both go to prison for five years.
2. If neither confesses, they will each be given a sentence of two years on a lesser charge.
3. If one prisoner turns state's evidence and confesses, that prisoner goes free and the other one, who did not confess, will serve 10 years on bank robbery charges.

You can see the prisoners' alternatives in the **payoff matrix** in Figure 27-1. The two possibilities for each prisoner are "confess" and "don't confess." There are four possibilities:

1. Both confess.
2. Neither confesses.
3. Sam confesses (turns state's evidence) but Carol doesn't.
4. Carol confesses (turns state's evidence) but Sam doesn't.

In Figure 27-1, all of Sam's possible outcomes are shown on the upper half of each rectangle, and all of Carol's possible outcomes are shown on the lower half.

By looking at the payoff matrix, you can see that if Carol confesses, Sam's best strategy is to confess also—he'll get

Prisoners' dilemma

A famous strategic game in which two prisoners have a choice between confessing and not confessing to a crime. If neither confesses, they serve a minimum sentence. If both confess, they serve a longer sentence. If one confesses and the other doesn't, the one who confesses goes free. The dominant strategy is always to confess.

Payoff matrix

A matrix of outcomes, or consequences, of the strategies available to the players in a game.

FIGURE 27-1

The Prisoners' Dilemma Payoff Matrix

Regardless of what the other prisoner does, each prisoner is better off if he or she confesses. So confessing is the dominant strategy, and each ends up behind bars for five years.

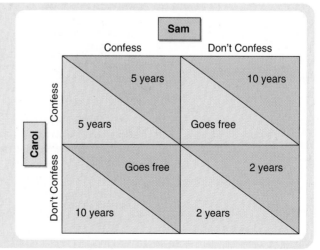

only 5 years instead of 10. Conversely, if Sam confesses, Carol's best strategy is also to confess—she'll get 5 years instead of 10. Now let's say that Sam is being interrogated and Carol doesn't confess. Sam's best strategy is still to confess, because then he goes free instead of serving two years. Conversely, if Carol is being interrogated, her best strategy is still to confess even if Sam hasn't. She'll go free instead of serving 10 years. To confess is a dominant strategy for Sam. To confess is also a dominant strategy for Carol. The situation is exactly symmetrical. So this is the prisoners' dilemma. The

prisoners know that both of them will be better off if neither confesses. Yet it is in each individual prisoner's interest to confess, even though the *collective* outcome of each prisoner's pursuit of his or her own interest is inferior for both.

FOR CRITICAL ANALYSIS

Can you apply the prisoners' dilemma to the firms in a two-firm industry that agree to share market sales equally? (Hint: Think about the payoff to cheating on the market-sharing agreement.)

Applying Game Theory to Pricing Strategies

We can apply game strategy to two firms—oligopolists—that have to decide on their pricing strategy. Each can choose either a high or a low price. Their payoff matrix is shown in Figure 27-2. If they both choose a high price, each will make $6 million, but if they both choose a low price, each will make only $4 million. If one sets a high price and the other a low one, the low-priced firm will make $8 million, but the high-priced firm will make only $2 million. As in the prisoners' dilemma, in the absence of collusion, they will end up choosing low prices.

Opportunistic Behavior

Opportunistic behavior
Actions that focus solely on short-run gains because long-run benefits of cooperation are perceived to be smaller.

In the prisoners' dilemma, it is clear that cooperative behavior—both parties standing firm without admitting to anything—leads to the best outcome for both players. But each prisoner (player) stands to gain by cheating. Such action is called **opportunistic behavior.** Our daily economic activities involve the potential for the prisoners' dilemma all the time. We could engage in opportunistic behavior. You could write a check for a purchase knowing that it is going to bounce because you have just closed

FIGURE 27-2

Game Theory and Pricing Strategies

This payoff matrix shows that if both oligopolists choose a high price, each makes $6 million. If they both choose a low price, each makes $4 million. If one chooses a low price and the other doesn't, the low-priced firm will make $8 million. Unless they collude, they will end up at the low-priced solution, because charging a low price is the dominant strategy.

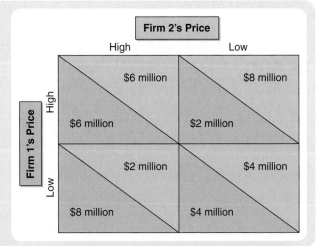

that bank account. When you agree to perform a specific task for pay, you could perform your work in a substandard way. When you go to buy an item, the seller might be able to cheat you by selling you a defective item.

In short, if all of us—sellers and buyers—engaged in opportunistic behavior all of the time, we would constantly be acting in a world of noncooperative behavior. That is not the world in which most of us live, however. Why not? Because most of us engage in *repeat transactions*. Manufacturers would like us to keep purchasing their products. Sellers would like us to keep coming back to their stores. As sellers of labor services, we all would like to keep our jobs, get promotions, or be hired away by another firm at a higher wage rate. Therefore, we engage in **tit-for-tat strategic behavior.** A consumer using a tit-for-tat strategy may, for instance, continue to purchase items from a firm each period as long as the firm provides products of the same quality and abides by any guarantees. If the firm fails in any period to provide high-quality products and honor its product guarantees, the consumer purchases items elsewhere.

Tit-for-tat strategic behavior
In game theory, cooperation that continues as long as the other players continue to cooperate.

QUICK QUIZ   *See page 713 for the answers. Review concepts from this section in MyEconLab.*

Each oligopolist has a _____ function because oligopolistic competitors are interdependent. They must therefore engage in _____ behavior. One way to model this behavior is to use **game theory.**

Games can be either **cooperative** or **noncooperative.** In a _____-sum game, one player's losses are exactly offset by

another player's gains. In a _____-sum game, all players collectively lose, perhaps one player more than the others. In a _____-sum game, the players as a group end up better off.

Decision makers in oligopolistic firms must devise a strategy. A _____ strategy is one that is generally successful no matter what actions competitors take.

The Cooperative Game: A Collusive Cartel

According to Adam Smith (1723–1790), "People of the same trade seldom meet together, even for merriment and diversion, but the conversation ends in a conspiracy against the public, or in some contrivance to raise prices." Why can firms profit from engaging in a "conspiracy against the public"? How can firms work together to create a "contrivance to raise prices"? Why does accomplishing this task turn out to be a feat only occasionally achieved by certain industries? Let's consider each of these questions in turn.

The Rationale for a Cartel and the Seeds of Its Undoing

If all the firms in an industry can find a way to cooperatively determine how much to produce to maximize their combined profits, then they can form a **cartel** and jointly act as a single producer. This means that they must *collude*. They must act together to attain the same outcome that a monopoly firm would aim to achieve: producing to the point at which marginal revenue derived from the *market* demand curve is equal to marginal cost. To do so, they must set common prices and output quotas for their members. If the firms are able to accomplish this task, they can all charge the same profit-maximizing price that a monopoly would have charged. Then they can share in the maximized monopoly profits.

Cartel
An association of producers in an industry that agree to set common prices and output quotas to prevent competition.

CUTTING BACK ON PRODUCTION Although the prospect of monopoly profits provides a strong incentive to collude, a fledgling cartel faces two fundamental problems. First, recall that a monopoly producer maximizes economic profits by restraining its production to a rate below the competitive output rate. Thus, the first problem for the members of the cartel is to determine how much each producer will restrain its output.

Once the first problem is solved, another immediately appears. As soon as all producers in the cartel begin restraining production and charging a higher price, each individual member could increase its revenues and profits by charging a slightly lower price, raising production, and selling more units. Hence, if all other cartel members honor their agreement to reduce production, one member could boost its economic profits by reneging on its promise to the rest of the cartel and increasing its production.

Enforcing a Cartel Agreement

Go to www.econtoday.com/chapter27 to find out from WTRG Economics how effective the Organization of Petroleum Exporting Countries has been in acting as an oil market cartel.

You Are There

To consider how cartel enforcement can affect even a small realty company, read **A Real Estate Cartel Corrals a "Cheater,"** on page 707.

There are four conditions that make it more likely that firms will be able to coordinate their efforts to restrain output and detect cheating, thereby reducing the temptation for participating firms to cheat:

1. *A small number of firms in the industry.* If an industry consists of only a few firms, it is easier to assess how much each firm should restrain production to yield the monopoly output and hence maximum industry profits. In addition, it is easier for each cartel member to monitor other firms' output rates for signs of cheating. For instance, when a cartel has only a few members, they might agree to keep their sales a certain percentage below pre-cartel levels. Failure to do so could be regarded as evidence of cheating.

2. *Relatively undifferentiated products.* If cartel members sell nearly homogeneous products, it is easier for them to agree on how much each firm should reduce its production. In contrast, if each firm sells a highly differentiated product, then some members can reasonably claim that the prices of their products should differ from the prices of other firms' products to reflect differences in costs of production. Thus, a firm with a differentiated product can reasonably claim that it is selling at a lower price for its differentiated good because its good is less valued by consumers—when in fact the firm may simply be using this as an excuse to cheat on the cartel agreement.

3. *Easily observable prices.* Naturally, one way to make sure that a producer is abiding by a cartel agreement is to look at the prices at which it actually sells its output. If the terms of industry transactions are publicly available, cartel members can more readily spot a firm's efforts to cheat.

4. *Little variation in prices.* If the industry's market is susceptible to frequent shifts in demand for firms' products or in prices of key inputs, the firms' prices will tend to fluctuate. Establishing a cartel agreement and monitoring cheating consequently will be more difficult. Hence, stable demand and cost conditions help a cartel form and continue to operate effectively.

Sometimes cartels use mechanisms for preventing cheating on prices that masquerade as contracts that are favorable to buyers. For example, all members of a cartel might agree to offer buyers contracts that permit a buyer to switch to another seller if that seller offers the product at a lower price. Naturally, if a customer can

Why has the Organization of Petroleum Exporting Countries (OPEC) been a successful long-term cartel?

provide evidence that a lower price is available from another firm claiming to participate in the cartel, this would constitute evidence that the other firm is cheating. In this way, cartel members use their customers to police other cartel participants!

Why Cartel Agreements Usually Break Down

Studies have shown that most cartel agreements do not last for more than 10 years. In many cases, cartel agreements break down more quickly than that. Even industries that usually satisfy the four conditions listed above have difficulty keeping cartels together over time.

One reason that cartels tend to break down is that the economic profits that existing firms obtain from holding prices above competitive levels provide an incentive for new firms to enter the market. Effectively, market entrants can earn profits by acting as a cheating cartel firm would behave. Their entry then provides incentives to cartel members to reduce their own prices and boost their production, and ultimately the cartel unravels.

Variations in overall economic activity also tend to make cartels unsustainable. During general business downturns, market demands tend to decline across all industries as consumers' incomes fall. So do profits of firms participating in a cartel. This increases the incentive for individual firms to cheat on a cartel agreement.

How are thousands of potato farmers attempting to organize a cartel?

EXAMPLE
Trying to Coordinate a Potato Cartel

Under the Capper-Volstead Act of 1922, U.S. farmers are permitted to form cooperative organizations aimed at influencing aggregate production and market prices of their crops. Today, many of the nation's 10,000 potato farmers are aiming to expand the United Potato Growers of America (UPGA), an organization dedicated to restricting potato production, pushing up potato prices, and boosting profits. The UPGA includes farmers from California, Colorado, Idaho, Oregon, Texas, Washington, and Wisconsin. Members sign an agreement to restrict their production of potatoes. The UPGA uses satellite photography and global-positioning-system technology to enforce the agreement and fines members who are caught cheating.

FOR CRITICAL ANALYSIS
Based on the discussion of the factors favoring the organization and enforcement of a cartel, what aspects of U.S. potato farming make the ultimate success of the UPGA's potato cartel more or less likely?

QUICK QUIZ   See page 713 for the answers. Review concepts from this section in MyEconLab.

A _____ is a group of firms in an industry that agree to set common prices and output quotas to restrict competition.

Characteristics of an industry that make it more likely that firms can coordinate efforts to restrain output and earn economic profits are a _____ number of firms,

relatively _____ products, easily _____ prices, and little _____ in prices.

Factors that contribute to the breakdown of a cartel are the _____ of firms seeking the economic profits earned by the cartel members and _____ in economic activity.

Network Effects

Network effect
A situation in which a consumer's willingness to purchase a good or service is influenced by how many others also buy or have bought the item.

A feature sometimes present in oligopolistic industries is **network effects,** or situations in which a consumer's willingness to use an item depends on how many others use it. Commonplace examples are telephones and fax machines. Ownership of a phone or fax machine is not particularly useful if no one else has one, but once a number of people own a phone or fax machine, the benefits that others gain from consuming these devices increases.

In like manner, people who commonly work on joint projects within a network of fellow employees, consultants, or clients naturally find it useful to share computer files. Trading digital files is an easier process if all use common word processing and office productivity software. The benefit that each person receives from using word processing and office productivity software increases when others also use the same software.

Network Effects and Market Feedback

Industries in which firms produce goods or services subject to network effects can experience sudden surges in growth, but the fortunes of such industries can also undergo significant and sometimes sudden reversals.

Positive market feedback
A tendency for a good or service to come into favor with additional consumers because other consumers have chosen to buy the item.

POSITIVE MARKET FEEDBACK   When network effects are an important characteristic of an industry's product, an industry can experience **positive market feedback.** This is the potential for a network effect to arise when an industry's product catches on with consumers. Increased use of the product by some consumers then induces other consumers to purchase the product.

Positive market feedback can affect the prospects of an entire industry. The market for Internet service provider (ISP) servers is an example. The growth of this industry has roughly paralleled the rapid growth of Internet servers worldwide. Undoubtedly, positive market feedback resulting from network effects associated with Internet communications and interactions resulted in additional people desiring to obtain access to the Internet.

Negative market feedback
A tendency for a good or service to fall out of favor with more consumers because other consumers have stopped purchasing the item.

NEGATIVE MARKET FEEDBACK   Network effects can also result in **negative market feedback,** in which a speedy downward spiral of product sales occurs for a product subject to network effects. If a sufficient number of consumers cut back on their use of the product, others are induced to reduce their consumption as well, and the product can rapidly become a "has-been."

An example of an industry that has experienced negative market feedback of late is the telecommunications industry. Traditional telecommunications firms such as AT&T, WorldCom, and Sprint experienced positive market feedback during the late 1980s and early 1990s as cellphones and fax machines proliferated and individuals and firms began making long-distance phone calls from cellphones or via fax machines. Since the mid-1990s, as more people have acquired Internet access via cable and satellite Internet service providers, e-mail communications and e-mail document attachments have supplanted large volumes of phone and fax communications. For the telecommunications industry, the greater use of e-mail and e-mail attachments by some individuals induced others to follow suit. This resulted in negative market feedback that reduced the overall demand for traditional long-distance phone services.

Network Effects and Industry Concentration

In some industries, a few firms can potentially reap most of the benefits of positive market feedback. Suppose that firms in an industry sell differentiated products that are subject to network effects. If the products of two or three firms catch on, these firms will capture the bulk of the sales due to industry network effects.

A good example is the market for online auction services. An individual is more likely to use the services of an auction site if there is a significant likelihood that many other potential buyers or sellers also trade items at that site. Hence, there is a network effect present in the online auction industry, in which eBay, Amazon, and Overstock account for more than 80 percent of total sales. eBay in particular has experienced positive market feedback, and its share of sales of online auction services has increased to more than 50 percent.

Consequently, in an industry that produces and sells products subject to network effects, a small number of firms may be able to secure the bulk of the payoffs resulting from positive market feedback. In such an industry, oligopoly is likely to emerge as the prevailing market structure.

QUICK QUIZ   *See page 713 for the answers. Review concepts from this section in MyEconLab.*

_____ effects exist when a consumer's demand for an item depends in part on how many other consumers also use the product.

_____ market feedback arises if consumption of a product by a sufficient number of individuals induces others to purchase it. _____ market feedback can take place if

a falloff in usage of a product by some consumers causes others to stop purchasing the item.

In an industry with differentiated products subject to **network effects,** an oligopoly may arise if a few firms can reap most of the sales _____ resulting from _____ market feedback.

Product Compatibility in Multiproduct Oligopolies Facing Network Effects

In addition to helping make industries more concentrated, network effects influence decisions that firms make regarding **product compatibility.** That is, firms must take into account the longer-term implications of network effects when deciding whether to offer products that function when used together with complementary products of competitors.

Product compatibility
The capability of a product sold by one firm to function together with another firm's complementary product.

Why Firms Face Product Compatibility Issues

Should a company share the computer code for its new office productivity software program with another software producer so that consumers will be able to use either firm's program, separately or together? Is the answer to this question altered if both companies sell hardware products that consumers regard as complements to their software products? How does the potential existence of network effects further complicate the issue? In today's information-technology-intensive economy, a growing number of firms must address these kinds of questions regularly.

THE BETA-VHS BATTLE Questions about product compatibility are not new. More than two decades ago, when the possibility of recording television shows and renting and selling movies for home viewing was a new idea, firms battled over two video-cassette formats known as Beta and VHS. The Beta format was the brainchild of Sony, which also offered a line of videocassette recorders and players compatible only with the Beta videocassette format. In the meantime, another firm, JVC, developed the rival VHS format, a bulkier videocassette that could hold more videotape. VHS videocassettes had room for longer movies and more recorded programming than Beta videocassettes.

Soon people were sharing lengthy VHS videotapes of children at play, complete sporting events, and the like with friends and relatives—as long as they had access to VHS players, which other consumer electronics firms were willing to produce. Within a few years, Sony realized that it had erred by opting to make its products compatible only with Beta videocassettes. Sony's decision had harmed its sales of video recorders and players and, ultimately, its sales of videocassettes. Eventually, Sony discontinued the production of all Beta-format products and switched to the VHS format.

Multiproduct firm
A firm that produces and sells two or more different items.

WHY PRODUCT COMPATIBILITY MATTERS The Beta-VHS format battle involved three key economic features. First, the products involved—lines of videocassettes, recorders, players, and related accessories—were items that consumers regarded as *complementary*. Second, these complementary goods were manufactured and sold by **multiproduct firms,** or firms that produce more than one product. Third, network effects were present. Because people shared their videotapes, the fact that most people preferred the VHS longer-play format led others to prefer VHS over Beta as well.

These features figure in many interactions in oligopolistic industries today, as new information technologies have led to the development of many complementary products sold by multiproduct firms and subject to network effects. In such situations, firms face a crucial product compatibility issue. Should a firm that produces two or more products that consumers regard as complements sell each one in a form that allows consumers to use the products only as a set? Or should the firm sell the items in a form that permits consumers to utilize each product individually, perhaps in conjunction with a complementary product offered by a competing firm?

While VHS videocassettes won the format war over Beta cassettes and machines, what happened with respect to a similar "war" between HD-DVDs and Blu-ray formats?

DIFFERENT COMPATIBILITY DECISIONS, DIFFERENT PAYOFFS In the battle between Beta and VHS formats, Sony opted for incompatibility with an intent to earn higher economic profits. What actually happened was that the demand for its VHS-incompatible products eventually disappeared as consumers substituted away from Beta videocassettes into VHS videocassettes. Consequently, Sony's profits from its video-related businesses plummeted, and the firm ultimately had to completely abandon its Beta-format video product line.

Does this mean that multiproduct firms should always make complementary products compatible with those of other firms? The answer is no. Sometimes firms lose, as Sony did, from making complementary products incompatible with those offered by other firms. Other times, however, firms reap exactly the same types of gains that Sony sought. Consider, for instance, Apple's experience with its iPod products during the 2000s. Apple offered a number of complementary products, such as iTunes downloadable music products, downloadable videos, and various accessories, in forms that were incompatible with products sold by other firms. In contrast to Sony, Apple boosted its profits by making its complementary products incompatible with those of its competitors.

Product Compatibility and Network Effects

The fact that Sony and Apple experienced such different outcomes indicates that multiproduct firms could experience either losses or gains by offering their products in forms that are incompatible with those sold by competing firms. Before we consider how firms' product compatibility choices affect oligopoly outcomes, let's consider why network effects matter to individual firms.

HOW A FIRM CAN GAIN FROM OPTING FOR INCOMPATIBILITY To see how a multiproduct firm might gain from making the complementary products it sells incompatible with those of competitors, again consider Apple's strategy of intentionally making its iPod-related product line incompatible with many other items sold by competitors. Alongside the iPod, Apple—or firms that paid Apple licensing royalties—offered a variety of complementary speaker systems, memory storage devices, and accessories.

For Apple, the main objective of opting for incompatibility was to sharply differentiate its own line of products. This tended to reduce price elasticities of demand for Apple's complementary product set. In addition, when its iPod-related products experienced positive market feedback, demand for these products increased. Consequently, Apple was able to charge higher prices for its entire line of complementary iPod products, and the firm's profits soared.

HOW A FIRM CAN LOSE FROM MAKING INCOMPATIBLE PRODUCTS Given how well product incompatibility turned out for Apple, why did things go wrong for Sony back in the days of videocassettes? After all, Sony also sought to differentiate its complementary Beta video products by making them incompatible with the products offered by competing firms.

The answer is that whereas Apple experienced positive market feedback in the downloadable-media industry, Sony's Beta-format video products suffered *negative* market feedback in the videocassette industry. Sony certainly succeeded in differentiating its products by making them incompatible with those offered by competitors. As more consumers opted for the larger-capacity VHS videocassettes, however, a bandwagon effect led other consumers to choose VHS as well, which led to a wave of substitutions away from Sony's Beta-format video products.

Why is Comcast developing what amounts to its own separate Internet?

E-COMMERCE EXAMPLE
Comcast Builds a Mini Internet for Its Online Programming

During the past two decades, the cable TV industry has been the predominant format for transmitting TV programming into homes and offices. Today, however, new formats for TV transmission have emerged. Telephone companies have begun offering TV transmissions on high-speed DSL lines, and TV networks such as CBS have begun experimenting with online services that transmit programming via the Internet.

One cable TV operator, Comcast, has responded by seeking to make its TV programming format incompatible with those of competitors. It has employed 400 software engineers to construct what amounts to a walled-off, TV version of the Internet. Within

this exclusive "mini Internet" of TV programming, Comcast is placing movies, archived TV programs, and various interactive features including a search engine. Thus, Comcast is hoping that if there are network effects in the provision of TV programming, it will be able to internalize those effects with its own customers via positive market feedback within its own "mini Internet."

FOR CRITICAL ANALYSIS

Why do you suppose that some Comcast stockholders have expressed concern that the company's strategy might ultimately expose it to negative market feedback?

Product Compatibility, Oligopolies, and Prices

Of course, oligopolistic multiproduct firms cannot make choices about product compatibility in isolation from the decisions of their competitors. In light of their strategic dependence, they must also take into account the reactions of other firms.

HOW INDUSTRY PRODUCT INCOMPATIBILITY CAN EMERGE To see how *industry* outcomes with regard to product compatibility can differ, begin by taking a look at Figure 27-3. This figure displays a payoff matrix for an industry composed of two multiproduct firms, "Firm 1" and "Firm 2," which are contemplating offering sets of complementary products in one of two incompatible formats, "Format A" or "Format B." We also assume that, at the outset, neither firm believes that network effects are likely to prove to be important to the industry in which they operate.

If both firms offer their products in Format A, each firm anticipates that the resulting homogeneity of their product lines will yield only $1 million in profits during the relevant period. If both firms offer their products in Format B, each expects to earn only $2 million in profits. If Firm 1 differentiates its product set by offering it in Format B while Firm 2 selects Format A, then each firm anticipates earning $3 million in profits. If Firm 1 uses Format A while Firm 2 selects Format B, then each firm expects to earn $4 million in profits. Firm 1, therefore, will opt for Format A, and Firm 2 will opt for Format B. Thus, the firms favor mutual incompatibility that differentiates their product sets and yields the highest anticipated profits. Each firm opts to go its separate way with its own different format, which is why in game theory the configuration of payoffs depicted in Figure 27-3 is often known as the *Tweedle Dee–Tweedle Dum game*.

THE COMPLICATING IMPACTS OF NETWORK EFFECTS If both of the firms with the payoffs depicted in Figure 27-3 are correct in assuming that network effects are minuscule in their industry, then they can achieve anticipated profit levels. What happens if their shared supposition about network effects is incorrect? Once the presence of network effects is discovered, Firm 1 will fight for Format A to be the industry standard, and Firm 2 will battle for Format B. That is, *after* opting for an incompatible format, each firm actually is likely to expend more resources than previously anticipated to promote its format and achieve positive market feedback.

For instance, suppose that Firms 1 and 2 manufacture videogame systems and various complementary accessories. After the firms have opted for incompatible formats,

FIGURE 27-3

Payoffs Yielding a Product Format Conflict

If two firms face the depicted payoff matrix, known as a *Tweedle Dee–Tweedle Dum game* situation, Firm 1 expects to earn the highest profits if it adopts Format A, and Firm 2 anticipates earning the highest profits if it opts for Format B. Hence, the firms choose these incompatible product formats.

consumers unexpectedly develop an interest in remote multiplayer gaming via the Internet. Each firm may respond by offering inducements to creators of multiplayer games to produce games compatible only with its selected format. Each may also "pre-announce" forthcoming complementary products in its selected format that allow multi-player gaming in an effort to discourage consumers from purchasing items in the other firm's product line. Either of these actions would push up each firm's operating costs. In addition, the firms may try to induce consumers to opt for their product formats by cutting prices, which would reduce the competitors' revenues. Thus, during the current period, both firms likely will earn lower profits than they anticipated when they selected their formats. If one firm ultimately loses the battle to become the industry standard, its profits likely will plummet, much as Sony's did when it lost the Beta-VHS battle. The profits of its competitor will then rise, much as Apple's profits soared when its iPod product line became a predominant downloadable-media system during the 2000s.

WHY PRODUCT COMPATIBILITY MIGHT BE AN INDUSTRY OUTCOME Now consider a different industry situation, depicted by the payoff matrices in Figure 27-4, in which Firm 1 and Firm 2 recognize in advance that network effects will result in one of the two formats winning out over the other with consumers. Panel (a) displays the simplest possible outcome, in which Firm 1 and Firm 2 each anticipate earning the most profits if both choose the same format. In this example, both firms earn the highest profits, $4 million during the relevant period, by mutually adopting the compatible Format A.

Panel (b) of Figure 27-4 depicts a more complicated situation. It is still true that both firms earn the most profits if they each choose the same format. Nevertheless, Firm 1 earns the highest profits if the firms mutually adopt the compatible Format A, but Firm 2 earns the most profits if the firms agree to choose Format B. The fact that

FIGURE 27-4

Payoffs Inducing Firms to Seek to Coordinate Product Formats

If two firms face the payoff matrix in panel (a), then both firms earn the highest profits by utilizing Format A, and they will gain by coordinating their choice of this compatible product format. In panel (b), both firms earn greater profits if their products have the same formats. Nevertheless, Firm 1 earns the highest profits if both firms opt for Format A, while Firm 2 earns the highest profits if both agree to use Format B. Hence, both parties wish to coordinate but may not agree on how to do so, which is why this game situation is called the *Battle of the Sexes*.

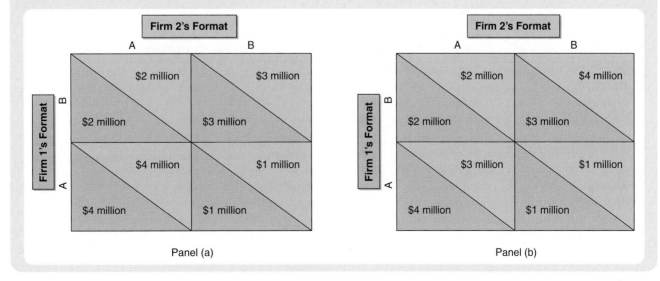

each party desires to coordinate with the other but agreement is not immediately forthcoming is why in game theory this payoff configuration is often referred to as the *Battle of the Sexes*.

As with the payoff matrix in Figure 27-3 on page 704, one result could be a battle between the firms over which format to adopt. Another possible result, given that both firms recognize the role of network effects, is that the firms might work together to develop one common format and arrange to share the profits.

QUICK QUIZ   *See page 713 for the answers. Review concepts from this section in MyEconLab.*

Product compatibility is the capability of an item sold by one firm to function with another firm's _____ product.

Product compatibility is an industrywide issue for _____ firms selling two or more complementary products subject to _____ effects.

An industry battle between incompatible product formats can occur if competing firms selling sets of _____ products fail to take into account _____ effects.

Comparing Market Structures

Now that we have looked at perfect competition, pure monopoly, monopolistic competition, and oligopoly, we are in a position to compare the attributes of these four different market structures. We do this in summary form in Table 27-3, in which we compare the number of sellers, their ability to set price, and the degree of product differentiation and also give some examples of each of the four market structures.

TABLE 27-3

Comparing Market Structures

Market Structure	Number of Sellers	Unrestricted Entry and Exit	Ability to Set Price	Long-Run Economic Profits Possible	Product Differentiation	Nonprice Competition	Examples
Perfect competition	Numerous	Yes	None	No	None	None	Agriculture, roofing nails
Monopolistic competition	Many	Yes	Some	No	Considerable	Yes	Toothpaste, toilet paper, soap, retail trade
Oligopoly	Few	Partial	Some	Yes	Frequent	Yes	Recorded music, college textbooks
Pure monopoly	One	No (for entry)	Considerable	Yes	None (product is unique)	Yes	Some electric companies, some local telephone companies

You Are There A Real Estate Cartel Corrals a "Cheater"

Sharon Jebavy, owner of HomeWise Real Estate Services in Columbus, Ohio, recently offered to include listings of homes for sale on the main Ohio real estate database. Customers had to pay a flat fee of $500 to be listed.

Although the number of Jebavy's customers nearly tripled, she soon found herself in hot water with the group of Ohio real estate brokers that operates the database. According to this group, Jebavy and other "discount real estate agents" fail to provide the "minimum services" required of real estate agents, who typically receive commission rates of 2 to 3 percent. Jebavy's offense, according to the brokers' group, was that she charged her customers a flat $500 fee to list their homes on the database even though these home sellers were not utilizing any additional services from Jebavy. Thus, Jebavy was charging a price for a key service that was "too low"—and profiting from the increase in customers that her low price attracted. In short, the brokers' group felt that Jebavy had cheated on the agreement under which she obtained access to the database—which in classic cartel

fashion required her to charge a predetermined price and restrict her service output. In the end, to maintain access to the database, Jebavy had to pay $6,250 in fines to the brokers' group and restrict the range of services she offered to home sellers.

CRITICAL ANALYSIS QUESTIONS

1. Why do you suppose that the Ohio real estate brokers' group was unhappy when Jebavy set her price to a flat fee of $500 and nearly tripled the volume of customers she served as a result?

2. Demand for real estate brokers' services in Ohio had declined sharply in the months preceding Jebavy's price cut and increase in customer volume. Why does this help explain why she had an increased incentive to "cheat" on the real estate cartel agreement governing use of the Ohio real estate database?

Issues and Applications

Oligopoly in the Global Commercial Aircraft Industry

CONCEPTS APPLIED

➤ Oligopoly

➤ Strategic Dependence

➤ Reaction Function

There are a large number of aircraft manufacturers around the globe. Nevertheless, only two firms—the European firm Airbus and the U.S. company Boeing—produce large commercial aircraft used by airline companies to transport more than 140 people at a time. Thus, the industry specializing in production of this type of aircraft is only one firm short of being a monopoly and hence is unambiguously oligopolistic.

The "Duopoly" in the Market for Large Commercial Aircraft

When only two firms comprise an industry, economists call the industry a *duopoly*. Figure 27-5 displays the market shares of Airbus and Boeing since 1996. As the figure indicates, because these two firms constitute the entire industry, a rise in the market share of one firm comes directly at the expense of the other firm.

Strategic dependence is as pronounced as it can possibly be in a duopoly setting. One firm's decisions unmistakably affect the outcomes experienced by the other firm. Thus, in the market for large commercial aircraft, Boeing's reaction function depends solely on the decisions made by managers at Airbus. Likewise, the reaction function for Airbus reflects managerial choices made only at Boeing.

Dimensions of Strategic Dependence: Airbus versus Boeing

In light of the one-on-one nature of the strategic dependence between Airbus and Boeing, the reaction functions of the two firms involve more than just the prices of their products. Considerable nonprice competition occurs as well. Key choices for both firms involve features of the jet aircraft that they produce, which each company adjusts to distinguish its planes from those of the other firm.

In recent years, Airbus and Boeing have even competed to top one another in the efficiency with which their planes can be recycled when they become obsolete. In light of increased global efforts to deplete fewer nonrenewable resources, each company is striving to convince customers that it is more adept at transforming aged aircraft into reusable materials. In 2007, Boeing claimed that more than 90 percent of the components in its old jets could be reclaimed for reuse. Airbus scoffed at that figure, arguing that available technology permitted only 60 percent of any large commercial aircraft to be recycled. Nevertheless, Airbus has launched its own effort to be able to recycle 95 percent of its obsolete jetliners by 2015. Thus, recycling capabilities have become one of a long list of nonprice elements of competition as each firm constantly vies to boost its market share at the other firm's expense.

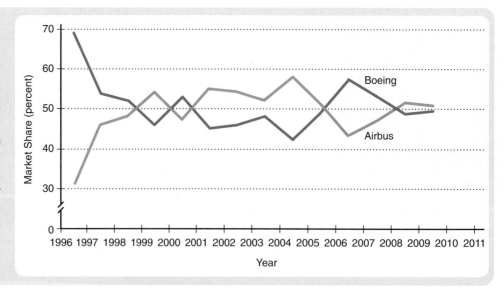

FIGURE 27-5

Market Shares in Global Sales of Large Commercial Airliners

For more than a decade, Airbus and Boeing have been the only producers of large commercial aircraft for use by airline companies, so each year the sum of the two companies' market shares equals 100 percent.

Source: U.S. Department of Transportation.

Test your understanding of this chapter by going online to **MyEconLab**.
In the Study Plan for this chapter, select Section N: News.

For Critical Analysis

1. In the most recent year for which data are plotted in Figure 27-5, what was the approximate one-firm concentration ratio in the large-commercial-aircraft industry, and what was this industry's two-firm concentration ratio?

2. Why are oligopolists more likely to engage in nonprice competition when their products are differentiated?

Web Resources

1. For a discussion of recent ways in which Airbus and Boeing have sought to differentiate their products, go to www.econtoday.com/chapter27.

2. To learn about the potential entry of new competitors that might end the duopoly situation in the market for large commercial aircraft, go to www.econtoday.com/chapter27.

Research Project

Suppose that Airbus and Boeing were to enter into secret discussions to form a cartel in the market for large commercial aircraft. Assuming that the two companies could find a way to hide their collusion, evaluate whether the features of their industry make formation and enforcement of a cartel agreement relatively easy or relatively difficult.

---

myeconlab

Here is what you should know after reading this chapter. MyEconLab will help you identify what you know, and where to go when you need to practice.

WHAT YOU SHOULD KNOW		WHERE TO GO TO PRACTICE
The Fundamental Characteristics of Oligopoly Economies of scale, certain barriers to entry, and horizontal mergers among firms that sell similar products can result in an oligopoly, a situation in which a few firms produce the bulk of an industry's total output. To measure the extent to which a few firms account for an industry's production and sales, economists calculate concentration ratios, which are the percentages of total sales or total production by the top handful of firms in an industry. Strategic dependence is an important characteristic of oligopoly. One firm's decisions concerning price, product quality, or advertising can bring about responses by other firms. Thus, one firm's choices can affect the prices charged by other firms in the industry.	oligopoly, 690 strategic dependence, 690 vertical merger, 691 horizontal merger, 691 concentration ratio, 692	• **MyEconLab** Study Plan 27.1 • Audio introduction to Chapter 27
Applying Game Theory to Evaluate the Pricing Strategies of Oligopolistic Firms Game theory is the analytical framework that economists apply to evaluate how two or more individuals, companies, or nations compete for payoffs that depend on the strategies that others employ. When firms work together for a common objective such as maximizing industry profits, they participate in cooperative games, but when they cannot work together, they engage in noncooperative games. One important type of game often applied to oligopoly situations is the prisoners' dilemma, in which the inability to cooperate in determining prices of their products can cause firms to choose lower prices than they otherwise would prefer.	reaction function, 693 game theory, 694 cooperative game, 694 noncooperative game, 694 zero-sum game, 694 negative-sum game, 694 positive-sum game, 695 strategy, 695 dominant strategies, 695 prisoners' dilemma, 695 payoff matrix, 695	• **MyEconLab** Study Plan 27.2 • Video: Opportunistic Behavior • Animated Figures 27-1, 27-2

(continued)

(continued)

WHAT YOU SHOULD KNOW		WHERE TO GO TO PRACTICE
	opportunistic behavior, 696 tit-for-tat strategic behavior, 697 **KEY FIGURES** Figure 27-1, 695 Figure 27-2, 696	
Industry Features That Contribute to or Detract from Efforts to Form a Cartel A cartel is an organization of firms in an industry that collude to earn economic profits by producing a combined output consistent with monopoly profit maximization. Four conditions make a collusive cartel agreement easier to create and enforce: (1) a small number of firms in the industry, (2) relatively undifferentiated products, (3) easily observable prices, and (4) little variation in prices. Even when these conditions are satisfied, economic profits earned by a cartel attract entry by competing firms, which tends to undermine the cartel. In addition, downturns in general economic conditions can place pressure on cartel members to expand output beyond agreed levels. This also tends to destabilize a cartel agreement.	cartel, 697	• **MyEconLab** Study Plan 27.3
Why Network Effects and Market Feedback Encourage Oligopoly Network effects arise when a consumer's demand for a good or service is affected by how many other consumers also use the item. There is positive market feedback when enough people consume a product to induce others to purchase it as well. Negative market feedback occurs when decreased purchases of a good or service by some consumers give others an incentive to stop buying the item. Oligopoly can develop in an industry with differentiated products subject to network effects because a few firms may be able to capture most of the growth in demand induced by positive market feedback.	network effect, 700 positive market feedback, 700 negative market feedback, 700	• **MyEconLab** Study Plans 27.4 • Video: Price Leadership and Price Wars
Why Multiproduct Firms Selling Complementary Sets of Products May or May Not Wish for Their Products to Be Compatible with Those of Competitors Product compatibility refers to the capability of an item sold by one firm to function with another firm's complementary product. A multiproduct firm selling two or more complementary products may opt for incompatibility with competing firms' products if it anticipates that lack of compatibility will differentiate its product set and maximize its profits. If network effects are important in the	product compatibility, 701 multiproduct firm, 702 **KEY TABLE** Table 27-3, 706	• **MyEconLab** Study Plans 27.5, 27.6 • Animated Table 27-3

(continued)

(continued)

WHAT YOU SHOULD KNOW	WHERE TO GO TO PRACTICE

industry, however, and firms choose product incompatibility, the result could be a battle of competing formats in which firms earn lower profits than they had anticipated. When network effects are present and firms recognize them, firms may choose to coordinate their decisions regarding the format of their products. Nevertheless, a format battle could still ensue if firms cannot agree on which format to produce.

Log in to MyEconLab, take a chapter test, and get a personalized Study Plan that tells you which concepts you understand and which ones you need to review. From there, MyEconLab will give you further practice, tutorials, animations, videos, and guided solutions. Log in to www.myeconlab.com

PROBLEMS

All problems are assignable in **X myeconlab** *. Answers to odd-numbered problems appear at the back of the book.*

27-1. Suppose that the distribution of sales within an industry is as shown in the table.

Firm	Share of Total Market Sales
A	15%
B	14
C	12
D	11
E	10
F	10
G	8
H	7
All others	13
Total	100%

a. What is the four-firm concentration ratio for this industry?

b. What is the eight-firm concentration ratio for this industry?

27-2. The table at the right shows recent worldwide market shares of producers of inkjet printers.

a. In this year, what was the four-firm concentration ratio in the inkjet-printer industry?

b. In this year, what was the seven-firm concentration ratio in the inkjet-printer industry?

Firm	Share of Worldwide Market Sales
Brother	3%
Canon	17
Dell	6
Epson	18
Hewlett-Packard	41
Lexmark	13
Samsung	1
Other	1

27-3. Characterize each of the following as a positive-sum game, a zero-sum game, or a negative-sum game.

a. Office workers contribute $10 each to a pool of funds, and whoever best predicts the winners in a professional sports playoff wins the entire sum.

b. After three years of fighting with large losses of human lives and materiél, neither nation involved in a war is any closer to its objective than it was before the war began.

c. Two collectors who previously owned incomplete and nearly worthless sets of trading cards exchange several cards, and as a result both end up with completed sets with significant market value.

27-4. Characterize each of the following as a positive-sum game, a zero-sum game, or a negative-sum game.

    a. You play a card game in your dorm room with three other students. Each player brings $5 to the game to bet on the outcome, winner take all.

    b. Two nations exchange goods in a mutually beneficial transaction.

    c. A thousand people buy $1 lottery tickets with a single payoff of $800.

27-5. Last weekend, Bob attended the university football game. At the opening kickoff, the crowd stood up. Bob therefore realized that he would have to stand up as well to see the game. For the crowd (not the football team), explain the outcomes of a cooperative game and a noncooperative game. Explain what Bob's "tit-for-tat strategic behavior" would be if he wished to see the game.

27-6. Consider two strategically dependent firms in an oligopolistic industry, Firm A and Firm B. Firm A knows that if it offers extended warranties on its products but Firm B does not, it will earn $6 million in profits, and Firm B will earn $2 million. Likewise, Firm B knows that if it offers extended warranties but Firm A does not, it will earn $6 million in profits, and Firm A will earn $2 million. The two firms know that if they both offer extended warranties on their products, each will earn $3 million in profits. Finally, the two firms know that if neither offers extended warranties, each will earn $5 million in profits.

    a. Set up a payoff matrix that fits the situation faced by these two firms.

    b. What is the dominant strategy for each firm in this situation? Explain.

27-7. Take a look back at the data regarding the inkjet-printer industry in Problem 27-2, and answer the following questions.

    a. Suppose that consumer demands for inkjet printers, the prices of which are readily observable in office supply outlets and at Internet sites, are growing at a stable pace. Discuss whether circumstances are favorable to an effort by firms in this industry to form a cartel.

    b. If the firms successfully establish a cartel, why will there naturally be pressures for the cartel to break down, either from within or from outside?

27-8. Consider the following payoff matrix. Firm 1 and Firm 2 are seeking to choose between Format A and Format B for their products, under the assumption that there are *not* any network effects. Will they desire to produce and sell compatible product formats?

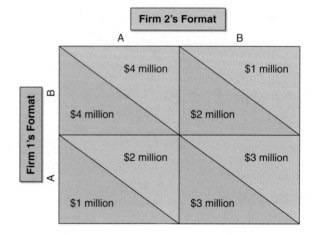

27-9. Consider the payoff matrix below, in which Firm 1 and Firm 2 seek to choose between product Format A and product Format B, under the assumption that there *are* network effects. Will they desire to produce and sell compatible product formats?

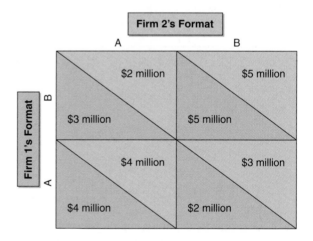

27-10. Explain why network effects can cause the demand for a product *either* to expand *or* to contract relative to what it would be if there were no network effects.

27-11. List three products that you think are subject to network effects. For each product, indicate whether, in your view, all or just a few firms within the industry that produces each product experience market feedback effects. In your view, are any market feedback effects in these industries currently positive or negative?

ECONOMICS ON THE NET

Current Concentration Ratios in U.S. Manufacturing Industries As you learned in this chapter, economists sometimes use concentration ratios to evaluate whether industries are oligopolies. In this application, you will make your own determination using the most recent data available.

Title: Concentration Ratios in Manufacturing

Navigation: Follow the link at **www.econtoday.com/ chapter27** to get to the U.S. Census Bureau's report on Concentration Ratios in Manufacturing.

Application Answer the following questions.

1. Select the report for the most recent year. Find the four-firm concentration ratios for the following industries: fluid milk (311511), women's and girls' cut & sew dresses (315233), envelopes (322232), electronic computers (334111).

2. Which industries are characterized by a high level of competition? Which industries are characterized by a low level of competition? Which industries qualify as oligopolies?

3. Name some of the firms that operate in the industries that qualify as oligopolies.

For Group Study and Analysis Discuss whether the four-firm concentration ratio is a good measure of competition. Consider some of the firms you named in item 3. Do you consider these firms to be "competitive" in their pricing and output decisions? Consider the four-firm concentration ratio for ready-mix concrete (327320). Do you think that on a local basis, this industry is competitive? Why or why not?

ANSWERS TO QUICK QUIZZES

p. 693: (i) small . . . interdependent; (ii) economies . . . mergers; (iii) Vertical; (iv) Horizontal; (v) percentage . . . sales
p. 697: (i) reaction . . . strategic; (ii) zero . . . negative . . . positive; (iii) dominant
p. 699: (i) cartel; (ii) small . . . undifferentiated . . . observable . . . variation; (iii) entry . . . variations
p. 701: (i) Network; (ii) Positive . . . Negative; (iii) gains . . . positive
p. 706: (i) complementary; (ii) multiproduct . . . network; (iii) complementary . . . network

28

Regulation and Antitrust Policy in a Globalized Economy

The term *sticker shock* has come into widespread use to describe consumers' surprise and dismay about higher-than-anticipated prices for an item. Of course, the term originally referred to consumers' surprise when confronted with prices listed on stickers attached to the windows of new and used vehicles on the lots of auto dealers. Today, after consumers have agreed on a final purchase price for a vehicle, they often experience another surprise: document-fee shock. In Nevada, auto dealers regularly charge $400 or more to process the documents required to finalize the sale of a vehicle. In Florida and Georgia, document fees range upward from $600. Why are document fees so high? As you will learn in this chapter, auto dealers' document fees are just one example of a cost of government regulation. In the auto market, an increased regulatory burden on sellers has boosted this cost of purchasing a vehicle.

LEARNING OBJECTIVES

After reading this chapter, you should be able to:

➤ Distinguish between economic regulation and social regulation

➤ Recognize the practical difficulties in regulating the prices charged by natural monopolies

➤ Explain the main rationales for regulation of industries that are not inherently monopolistic

➤ Identify alternative theories aimed at explaining the behavior of regulators

➤ Understand the foundations of antitrust laws and regulations

➤ Discuss basic issues in enforcing antitrust laws

? **DID YOU KNOW THAT** a recent estimate indicates that the gross costs of complying with government rules regulating U.S. health care are about $339 billion per year? The estimated dollar value of the benefits from these regulations is $170 billion. If correct, these estimates indicate that health care regulations generate a net cost to society of $169 billion, or about $1,500 per U.S. household.

Certainly, firms in the U.S. health care industry are highly regulated. So are firms in many other industries in the United States and throughout the world. Consequently, how regulations and other forms of government oversight *should act* to promote greater economic efficiency and how they *actually act* are important topics for understanding how every economy works. Nevertheless, before you can begin your study of the economic effects of regulation, it is important to understand the various ways in which the government oversees the activities of U.S. businesses.

Forms of Industry Regulation

The U.S. government began regulating social and economic activity early in the nation's history. The amount of government regulation began increasing in the twentieth century and has grown considerably since 1970. Figure 28-1 displays two common measures of regulation in the United States. Panel (a) shows that regulatory spending

---

FIGURE 28-1

Regulation on the Rise

Panel (a) shows that federal government regulatory spending is now more than $40 billion per year. State and local spending is not shown. As panel (b) shows, the number of pages in the *Federal Register* per year rose sharply in the 1970s, dropped off somewhat in the 1980s, and then began to rise once more.

Sources: Institute for University Studies; *Federal Register,* various issues.

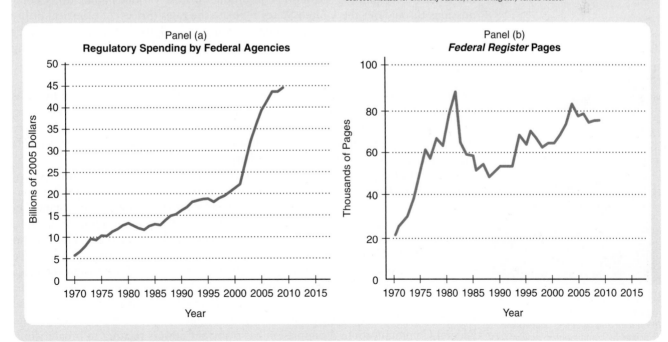

by federal agencies (in 2005 dollars) has generally trended upward since 1970 and has risen considerably during the 2000s. New national security regulations following the 2001 terrorist attacks in New York City and Washington, D.C., have fueled a significant portion of this growth. The remainder of the increase in spending is related to a general upswing in regulatory enforcement by the federal government during this period. Panel (b) on Figure 28-1 on the previous page depicts the number of pages in the *Federal Register*, a government publication that lists all new regulatory rules. According to this measure, the scope of new federal regulations increased sharply during the 1970s, dropped off in the 1980s, and has generally increased since then.

There are two basic types of government regulation. One is *economic regulation* of natural monopolies and of specific nonmonopolistic industries. For instance, some state commissions regulate the prices and quality of services provided by electric power companies, which are considered natural monopolies that experience lower long-run average costs as their output increases. Financial services industries and interstate transportation industries are examples of nonmonopolistic industries that are subjected to considerable government regulation. The other form of government regulation is *social regulation*, which covers all industries. Examples include various occupational, health, and safety rules that federal and state governments impose on most businesses.

Economic Regulation

Initially, most economic regulation in the United States was aimed at controlling prices in industries considered to be natural monopolies. Over time, federal and state governments have also sought to influence the characteristics of products or processes of firms in a variety of industries without inherently monopolistic features.

REGULATION OF NATURAL MONOPOLIES The regulation of natural monopolies has tended to emphasize restrictions on product prices. Various public utility commissions throughout the United States regulate the rates (prices) of electrical utility companies and some telephone operating companies. This *rate regulation*, as it is usually called, officially has been aimed at preventing such industries from earning monopoly profits.

REGULATION OF NONMONOPOLISTIC INDUSTRIES The prices charged by firms in many other industries that do not have steadily declining long-run average costs, such as financial services industries, have also been subjected to regulations. Every state in the United States, for instance, has a government agency devoted to regulating the prices that insurance companies charge.

More broadly, government regulations establish rules pertaining to production, product (or service) features, and entry and exit within a number of specific nonmonopolistic industries. The federal government is heavily involved, for instance, in regulating the securities, banking, transportation, and communications industries. The Securities and Exchange Commission regulates securities markets. The Federal Reserve, Office of the Comptroller of the Currency, and Federal Deposit Insurance Corporation regulate commercial banks. The Office of Thrift Supervision regulates savings banks, and the National Credit Union Administration supervises credit unions. The Federal Aviation Administration supervises the airline industry, and the Federal Motor Carrier Safety Administration regulates the trucking industry. The Federal Communications Commission has oversight powers relating to broadcasting and telephone and communications services.

What is the reason given for the regulation by state commissions of the prices and qualities of services provided by some electric power companies?

TABLE 28-1

Federal Agencies Engaged in Social Regulation

Agency	Jurisdiction	Date Formed	Major Regulatory Functions
Federal Trade Commission (FTC)	Product markets	1914	Responsible for preventing businesses from engaging in misleading advertising, unfair trade practices, and monopolistic actions, as well as for protecting consumer rights.
Food and Drug Administration (FDA)	Food and pharmaceuticals	1938	Regulates the quality and safety of foods, health and medical products, pharmaceuticals, cosmetics, and animal feed.
Equal Employment Opportunity Commission (EEOC)	Labor markets	1964	Investigates complaints of discrimination based on race, religion, gender, or age in hiring, promotion, firing, wages, testing, and all other conditions of employment.
Environmental Protection Agency (EPA)	Environment	1970	Develops and enforces environmental standards for air, water, waste, and noise.
Occupational Safety and Health Administration (OSHA)	Health and safety	1970	Regulates workplace safety and health conditions.
Consumer Product Safety Commission (CPSC)	Consumer product safety	1972	Responsible for protecting consumers from products posing fire, electrical, chemical, or mechanical hazards or dangers to children.

Social Regulation

In contrast to economic regulation, which covers only particular industries, social regulation applies to all firms in the economy. In principle, the aim of social regulation is a better quality of life through improved products, a less polluted environment, and better working conditions. Since the 1970s, an increasing array of government resources has been directed toward regulating product safety, advertising, and environmental effects. Table 28-1 lists some major federal agencies involved in these broad regulatory activities.

The *possible* benefits of social regulations are many. For example, the water supply in some cities is known to be contaminated with potentially hazardous chemicals, and air pollution contributes to many illnesses. Society might well benefit from cleaning up these pollutants. As we shall discuss, however, broad social regulations also entail costs that we all pay, and not just as taxpayers who fund the regulatory activities of agencies such as those listed in Table 28-1.

QUICK QUIZ   *See page 740 for the answers. Review concepts from this section in MyEconLab.*

_____ regulation applies to specific industries, whereas _____ regulation applies to businesses throughout the economy.

Governments commonly regulate the prices and quality of services provided by electric, gas, and other utilities, which traditionally have been considered _____ monopolies.

Governments also single out various nonmonopolistic industries, such as the financial and transportation industries, for special forms of _____ regulation.

Among the common forms of _____ regulation covering all industries are the occupational, health, and safety rules that federal and state governments impose on producers.

Regulating Natural Monopolies

At one time, much government regulation of business purportedly aimed to solve the so-called monopoly problem. Of particular concern was implementing appropriate regulations for natural monopolies.

The Theory of Natural Monopoly Regulation

Recall from Chapter 25 that a natural monopoly arises whenever a single firm can produce all of an industry's output at a lower per-unit cost than other firms attempting to produce less than total industry output. In a natural monopoly, therefore, economies of large-scale production exist, leading to a single-firm industry.

THE UNREGULATED NATURAL MONOPOLY Like any other firm, an unregulated natural monopolist will produce to the point at which marginal revenue equals marginal cost. Panel (a) of Figure 28-2 depicts a situation in which a monopolist faces the market demand curve, D, and the marginal revenue curve, MR. The monopolist searches along the demand curve for the profit-maximizing price and quantity. The

FIGURE 28-2

Profit Maximization and Regulation Through Marginal Cost Pricing

The profit-maximizing natural monopolist here would produce at the point in panel (a) at which marginal costs equal marginal revenue—that is, at point A, which gives the quantity of production Q_m. The per-unit price charged would be P_m at point F, which is the price consumers would be willing to pay for the quantity produced. If a regulatory commission attempted to regulate natural monopolies so that price equaled long-run marginal cost, the commission would make the monopolist set production at the point where the long-run marginal cost (LMC) curve intersects the demand schedule. This is shown in panel (b). The quantity produced would be Q_1, and the per-unit price would be P_1. Average costs at output rate Q_1 are equal to AC_1, however. Losses would ensue, equal to the red-shaded area. It would be self-defeating for a regulatory commission to force a natural monopolist to produce at an output rate at which MC $= P$ without subsidizing some of its costs because losses would eventually drive the natural monopolist out of business.

profit-maximizing quantity is at point A, at which the marginal revenue curve crosses the long-run marginal cost curve, LMC, and the unregulated monopolist maximizes profits by producing the quantity Q_m. Consumers are willing and able to pay the price per unit P_m for this quantity at point F. This price is above marginal cost, so it leads to a socially inefficient allocation of resources by restricting production to a rate below that at which price equals marginal cost.

THE IMPRACTICALITY OF MARGINAL COST PRICING What would happen if the government were to require the monopolist in Figure 28-2 to produce to the point at which price equals marginal cost, which is point B in panel (b)? Then it would produce a larger output rate, Q_1. Consumers, however, would pay only the price per unit P_1 for this quantity, which would be less than the average cost of producing this output rate, AC_1. Consequently, requiring the monopolist to engage in marginal cost pricing would yield a loss for the firm equal to the shaded rectangular area in panel (b). The profit-maximizing monopolist would go out of business rather than face such regulation.

AVERAGE COST PRICING Regulators cannot practically force a natural monopolist to engage in marginal cost pricing. Thus, regulation of natural monopolies has often taken the form of allowing the firm to set price at the point at which the long-run average cost (LAC) curve intersects the demand curve. In panel (b) of Figure 28-2, this is point C. In this situation, the regulator forces the firm to engage in *average cost pricing*, with average cost including what the regulators deem a "fair" rate of return on investment. For instance, a regulator might impose **cost-of-service regulation,** which requires a natural monopoly to charge only prices that reflect the actual average cost of providing products to consumers. Alternatively, although in a similar vein, a regulator might use **rate-of-return regulation,** which allows firms to set prices that ensure a normal return on investment.

Could the way in which cost-of-service and rate-of-return regulations are implemented be contributing to electrical power failures and fires?

Cost-of-service regulation
Regulation that allows prices to reflect only the actual average cost of production and no monopoly profits.

Rate-of-return regulation
Regulation that seeks to keep the rate of return in an industry at a competitive level by not allowing prices that would produce economic profits.

POLICY EXAMPLE
How Keeping Costs Low to Maintain Low Electricity Rates Creates Social Spillovers

In 2003, an old high-power line comes into contact with overgrown trees in Ohio. Then a computer software error in an aging computer system fails to alert technicians to a resulting power surge. The result: Power failures cascade across several eastern U.S. states. Now fast-forward to 2007. A power line falls from a tower into some dry brush in a remote location in Southern California. The result: Sparks fly, and soon a huge fire fanned by high winds engulfs thousands of acres.

These are only two of the more dramatic examples of costly accidents resulting from the use of worn-out equipment by electric utilities. Although U.S. electric utilities spend more than $18 billion every year on their power networks, most of this spending pays for stringing wire to *new* housing developments and commercial structures. To deal with obsolete and corroded *old* equipment,

utilities would have to spend roughly $10 billion more every year, which estimates indicate would boost electricity rates for the average U.S. consumer by about 5 percent. The problem that utilities face is that it is easier to convince regulators that expenditures on network *expansions* fueled by new consumer demand justify rate increases. Convincing regulators to authorize rate increases to cover replacing worn-out equipment is a harder sell, and many utilities do not even try. Thus, the nation's electrical networks continue to age, resulting in recurring power failures and fires.

FOR CRITICAL ANALYSIS
How could utility regulators adjust their practices to allow for replacement of obsolete power-generating equipment while ensuring average cost pricing?

Natural Monopolies No More?

For years, the electricity, natural gas, and telecommunications industries have been subjected to regulations intended to induce firms in these industries to engage in average cost pricing. Traditionally, a feature common to all three industries has been that they utilize large networks of wires or pipelines to transmit their products to consumers. Federal, state, and local governments concluded that the average costs of providing electricity, natural gas, and telecommunications declined as the output rates of firms in these industries increased. Consequently, governments treated these industries as natural monopolies and established regulatory commissions to subject the industries to forms of cost-of-service and rate-of-return regulation.

ELECTRICITY AND NATURAL GAS: SEPARATING PRODUCTION FROM DELIVERY

Today, 15 different companies provide electricity to homes, office buildings, and factories in Houston. Eight different firms compete to sell electricity in New York City, and six companies provide electricity in Philadelphia. Similarly, various producers of natural gas vie to market their product in a number of cities across the country. In nearly half of the U.S. states, there is active competition in the production of electricity and natural gas.

What circumstances led to this transformation? The answer is that regulators of electricity and natural gas companies figured out that the function of *producing* electricity or natural gas did not necessarily have to be combined with the *delivery* of the product. Until the mid-1980s, producers of natural gas and electricity had exclusive ownership of the pipeline and wire networks that provided energy for homes, office buildings, and factories. Since then, various regulators have gradually implemented policies that have separated production of electricity and natural gas from the distribution of these items to consumers.

Thus, in a growing number of U.S. locales, multiple producers now pay to use wire and pipeline networks to get their products to buyers. Economies of scale still exist in these distribution networks, and regulatory commissions impose cost-of-service or rate-of-return regulations on the network owners. Individual producers of electricity and natural gas openly compete, nonetheless, in the markets for the products that consumers actually utilize in their homes and businesses. The market clearing rates that consumers pay to consume electricity and natural gas reflect both the costs of producing these items and the transportation costs that producers pay to deliver them via regulated distribution networks.

TELECOMMUNICATIONS SERVICES MEET THE INTERNET

As the production and sale of electricity and natural gas began to become more competitive undertakings, regulators started to apply the same principles to telecommunications services. In the 1980s, the Federal Communications Commission (FCC) required AT&T to open its existing phone networks to competing providers of long-distance phone services. Gradually, during the 1990s and 2000s, federal, state, and local regulators applied the same principles to local telecommunications services. Today, many U.S. cities and towns are served by two or more competing producers of wired phone services.

At the same time, other forces reshaped the cost structure of the telecommunications industry. First, during the 1990s, significant technological advances drastically reduced the costs of providing wireless telecommunications. Most individuals and businesses regarded cellphone services as imperfect substitutes for wire-based telecommunications. Nevertheless, the growing use of cellphones slowed growth in the demand for services delivered over traditional wire networks.

Second, during the 2000s, Internet phone service became more widely available. Most cable television companies that provide Internet access now offer Web-based telephone services as well. Many other companies also offer Web phone services for purchase by anyone who already has access to the Internet.

ARE NATURAL MONOPOLIES RELICS OF THE PAST? Clearly, the scope of the government's role as regulator of natural monopolies has decreased with the unraveling of conditions that previously created this market structure. In many U.S. electricity and natural gas markets, government agencies now apply traditional cost-of-service or rate-of-return regulations primarily to wire and pipeline owners. Otherwise, the government's main role in many regional markets is to serve as a "traffic cop," enforcing property rights and rules governing the regulated networks that serve competing electricity and natural gas producers.

How has the increased use of cellular phone services and Internet phone services affected the demand for traditional land-line telecommunication services?

In telecommunications, any natural monopoly rationale for a governmental regulator role is rapidly dissipating as more and more households and businesses substitute cellular and Web-based phone services for wired phone services. Since 2000, consumers have stopped using more than 30 million land phone lines. At present, phone signals stop flowing on an additional 3 percent of existing lines each year. Telecommunications has become a technology-driven, competitive free-for-all. This industry is now far from being a natural monopoly.

QUICK QUIZ   *See page 740 for the answers. Review concepts from this section in MyEconLab.*

A **natural monopoly** arises when one firm can produce all of an industry's output at a _____ per-unit cost than other firms. A profit-maximizing natural monopolist produces to the point at which marginal _____ equals long-run marginal _____ and charges the price that people are willing to pay for the quantity produced.

Because a natural monopolist that is required to set price equal to long-run marginal cost will sustain long-run losses and shut down, regulators typically allow natural monopolists to charge prices that just cover _____

costs. Traditionally, regulators have done this through **cost-of-service regulation**, in which prices are based on actual production costs, or **rate-of-return regulation**, in which prices are set to yield a rate of return consistent with _____ economic profits.

Technological and regulatory innovations have made the concept of natural monopoly less relevant. In the electricity, natural gas, and telecommunications industries, production increasingly is accomplished by numerous competing firms that _____ their products through regulated _____.

Regulating Nonmonopolistic Industries

Traditionally, one of the fundamental purposes of governments has been to provide a coordinated system of safeguarding the interests of their citizens. Not surprisingly, protecting consumer interests is the main rationale offered for governmental regulatory functions.

Rationales for Consumer Protection in Nonmonopolistic Industries

The Latin phrase *caveat emptor*, or "let the buyer beware," was once the operative principle in most consumer dealings with businesses. The phrase embodies the idea that the buyer alone is ultimately responsible for assessing a producer and the quality of the items it sells before agreeing to purchase the firm's product. Today, various federal agencies require companies to meet specific minimal standards in their dealings with consumers. For instance, a few years ago, the U.S. Federal Trade Commission assessed monetary penalties on Toys "Я" Us and KB Toys because they failed to ship goods sold on their Web sites in time for a pre-Christmas delivery. Such a government action would have been unheard of a few decades ago.

In some industries, federal agencies dictate the rules of the game for firms' interactions with consumers. The Federal Aviation Administration (FAA), for example, oversees virtually every aspect of the delivery of services by airline companies. The FAA regulates the process by which tickets for flights are sold and distributed, oversees all flight operations, and even establishes rules governing the procedures for returning luggage after flights are concluded.

REASONS FOR GOVERNMENT-ORCHESTRATED CONSUMER PROTECTION Two rationales are commonly advanced for heavy government involvement in overseeing and supervising nonmonopolistic industries. One, which you encountered in Chapter 5, is the possibility of *market failures*. For example, the presence of negative externalities such as pollution may induce governments to regulate industries that create such externalities.

The second common rationale is *asymmetric information*. In the context of many producer-consumer interactions, this term refers to situations in which a producer has information about a product that the consumer lacks. For instance, administrators of your college or university may know that another school in your vicinity offers better-quality degree programs in certain fields. If so, it would not be in your college or university's interest to transmit this information to applicants who are interested in pursuing degrees in those fields.

For certain products, asymmetric information problems can pose special difficulties for consumers trying to assess product quality in advance of purchase. In unregulated financial markets, for example, individuals contemplating buying a company's stock, a municipality's bond, or a bank's certificate of deposit might struggle to assess the associated risks of financial loss. If the air transportation industry were unregulated, a person might have trouble determining if one airline's planes were less safe than those of competing airlines. In an unregulated market for pharmaceuticals, parents might worry about whether one company's childhood-asthma medication could have more dangerous side effects than medications sold by other firms.

ASYMMETRIC INFORMATION AND PRODUCT QUALITY In extreme cases, asymmetric information can create situations in which most of the available products are of low quality. A commonly cited example is the market for used automobiles. Current owners of cars that *appear* to be in good condition know the autos' service records. Some owners know that their cars have been well maintained and really do run great. Others, however, have not kept their autos in good repair and thus are aware that they will be susceptible to greater-than-normal mechanical or electrical problems.

Suppose that in your local used-car market, half of all used cars offered for sale are high-quality autos. The other half are low-quality cars, commonly called "lemons," that are likely to break down within a few months or perhaps even weeks. In addition, suppose that a consumer is willing to pay $20,000 for a particular car model if it is in excellent condition but is willing to pay only $10,000 if it is a lemon. Finally, suppose that people who own truly high-quality used cars are only willing to sell at a price of at least $20,000, but people who own lemons are willing to sell at any price at or above $10,000.

Because there is a 50–50 chance that a given car up for sale is of either quality, the average amount that a prospective buyer is willing to pay equals $(\frac{1}{2} \times \$20{,}000) + (\frac{1}{2} \times \$10{,}000) = \$15{,}000$. Owners of low-quality used cars are willing to sell them at this price, but owners of high-quality used cars are not. In this example, only lemons will be traded, at a price of $10,000, because owners of cars in excellent condition will not sell their cars at a price that prospective buyers are willing to pay.

THE LEMONS PROBLEM Economists refer to the possibility that asymmetric information can lead to a general reduction in product quality in an industry as the **lemons problem.** This problem does not apply only to the used-car industry. In principle, any product with qualities that are difficult for consumers to fully assess is susceptible to the same problem. *Credence goods*, which as you learned in Chapter 26 are items such as pharmaceuticals, health care, and professional services, also may be particularly vulnerable to the lemons problem.

Lemons problem
The potential for asymmetric information to bring about a general decline in product quality in an industry.

MARKET SOLUTIONS TO THE LEMONS PROBLEM Firms offering truly high-quality products for sale can address the lemons problem in a variety of ways. They can offer product guarantees and warranties. In addition, to help consumers separate high-quality producers from incompetent or unscrupulous competitors, the high-quality producers may work together to establish industry standards.

In some cases, firms in an industry may even seek external product certification. They may, for example, solicit scientific reports supporting proposed industry standards and bearing witness that products of certain firms in the industry meet those standards. To legitimize a product-certification process, firms may hire outside companies or groups to issue such reports.

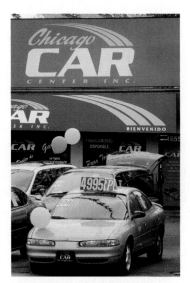

Implementing Consumer Protection Regulation

Governments offering asymmetric information and lemons problems as rationales for regulation presumably have concluded that private market solutions such as warranties, industry standards, and product certification are insufficient. To address asymmetric information problems, governments may offer legal remedies to consumers or enforce licensing requirements in an effort to provide minimum product standards. In some cases, governments go well beyond simple licensing requirements by establishing a regulatory apparatus for overseeing all aspects of an industry's operations.

Why might it be difficult to be sure that you are purchasing a high-quality used car?

Go to **www.econtoday.com/chapter28** to see how the Federal Trade Commission imposes regulations intended to protect consumers.

LIABILITY LAWS AND GOVERNMENT LICENSING Sometimes liability laws, which specify penalties for product failures, provide consumers with protections similar to guarantees and warranties. When the Federal Trade Commission (FTC) charged Toys "Я" Us and KB Toys with failing to meet pre-Christmas delivery dates for Internet toy orders, it operated under a mail-order statute Congress passed in the early 1970s. The mail-order law effectively made the toy companies' delivery guarantees legally enforceable. Although the FTC applied the law in this particular case, any consumer could have filed suit for damages under the terms of the statute.

Federal and state governments also get involved in consumer protection by issuing licenses granting only qualifying firms the legal right to produce and sell certain products. For instance, governments of nearly half of the states give the right to sell caskets only to people who have a mortuary or funeral director's license, allegedly to ensure that bodies of deceased individuals are handled with care and dignity.

Although government licensing may successfully limit the sale of low-quality goods, licensing requirements also often limit the number of providers. As you learned in Chapter 25, this can ease efforts by established firms to act as monopolists. In addition, if governments rely on the expertise of established firms for assistance in drafting licensing requirements, these firms may have strong incentives to recommend low standards for themselves but high standards for prospective entrants.

DIRECT ECONOMIC AND SOCIAL REGULATION In some instances, governments determine that liability laws and licensing requirements are insufficient to protect the interests of consumers. A government may decide that lemons problems in banking are so severe that without an extensive banking regulatory apparatus, consumers will lose confidence in banks, and bank runs may ensue. It may rely on similar rationales to establish economic regulation of other financial services industries. Eventually, it may apply consumer protection rationales to justify the economic regulation of additional industries such as trucking or air transportation.

The government may establish an oversight authority to make certain that consumers are protected from incompetent producers of foods and pharmaceuticals. Eventually, the government may determine that a host of other products should meet government consumer protection standards. It may also decide that the people who produce the products also require government agencies to ensure workplace safety. In this way, widespread social regulation emerges, as it has in the United States and most other developed nations.

Can two government regulations sometimes come into apparent conflict?

POLICY EXAMPLE
Trying to Satisfy One Regulation Can Violate Another Regulation

Under federal transportation laws, drivers of trucks with weights exceeding 10,000 pounds must be able to hear. Nevertheless, a federal appeals court recently supported an Equal Employment Opportunity Commission (EEOC) claim that United Parcel Service's refusal to allow a deaf individual to drive a 20,000-pound truck violated the 1990 Americans with Disabilities Act. Separately, the EEOC is also citing age discrimination regulations in trying to force

some firms to permit people over the age of 60 to fly airplanes. The EEOC is pursuing this claim even though a federal law prohibits people over 60 from piloting commercial passenger planes. Clearly, regulations can come into conflict.

FOR CRITICAL ANALYSIS
Are rules governing the characteristics of truck drivers and airplane pilots examples of economic or social regulations?

QUICK QUIZ   *See page 740 for the answers. Review concepts from this section in MyEconLab.*

Governments tend to regulate industries in which they think market _____ and _____ information problems are most severe.

A common justification for government regulation is to protect consumers from adverse effects of _____ information.

To address the _____ problem, or the potential for _____-quality products to predominate when asymmetric information is widespread, governments often supplement private firms' guarantees, warranties, and certification standards with liability laws and licensing requirements.

Incentives and Costs of Regulation

Abiding by government regulations is a costly undertaking for firms. Consequently, businesses engage in a number of activities intended to avoid the true intent of regulations or to bring about changes in the regulations that government agencies establish.

Creative Response and Feedback Effects: Results of Regulation

Sometimes individuals and firms respond to a regulation in a way that conforms to the letter of the law but undermines its spirit. When they do so, they engage in **creative response** to regulations.

One type of creative response has been labeled a *feedback effect*. Individuals' behaviors may change after a regulation has been put into effect. If a regulation requires fluoridated water, then parents know that their children's teeth have significant protection against tooth decay. Consequently, the feedback effect is that parents become less concerned about how many sweets their children eat.

What feedback effect sometimes occurs when products are almost covered with warning labels?

Creative response
Behavior on the part of a firm that allows it to comply with the letter of the law but violate the spirit, significantly lessening the law's effects.

POLICY EXAMPLE
The Feedback Effect of Warning-Label Overkill

At the behest of the Consumer Product Safety Commission, warning labels appear on many common products. For instance, stamped onto a standard ladder purchased at a hardware store are warnings that typically contain about 600 words, including a warning not to place the ladder in front of a swinging door. The labels that many toy makers attach to every toy include the blanket warning, "Small parts may cause a choking risk," even though a hammer would be required to break some toys into parts small enough to cause choking.

Studies indicate that consumers typically read a single, short warning that offers guidance about the key safety risks associated with using a product. When confronted with numerous and lengthy warning labels, however, consumers do not take the time to read *any* of the warnings, including the label most relevant to the main risks of using an item. Thus, a feedback effect of requiring labels warning of every conceivable risk is that consumers fail to read warnings about those risks most likely to matter for their safety.

FOR CRITICAL ANALYSIS
Why do you suppose that consumers are more likely to read a single safety label than to read multiple safety labels?

Explaining Regulators' Behavior

Those charged with enforcing government regulations operate outside the market, so their decisions are determined by nonmarket processes. A number of theories have emerged to describe the behavior of regulators. These theories explain how regulation can harm consumers by generating higher prices and fewer product choices while benefiting producers by reducing competitive forces and allowing higher profits. Two of the best-known theories of regulatory behavior are the *capture hypothesis* and the *share-the-gains, share-the-pains theory*.

THE CAPTURE HYPOTHESIS Regulators often end up becoming champions of the firms they are charged with regulating. According to the **capture hypothesis,** regardless of why a regulatory agency was originally established, eventually special interests of the

Capture hypothesis
A theory of regulatory behavior that predicts that regulators will eventually be captured by special interests of the industry being regulated.

industry it regulates will capture it. After all, the people who know the most about a regulated industry are the people already in the industry. Thus, people who have been in the industry and have allegiances and friendships with others in the industry will most likely be asked to regulate the industry.

According to the capture hypothesis, individual consumers of a regulated industry's products and individual taxpayers who finance a regulatory agency have interests too diverse to be greatly concerned with the industry's actions. In contrast, special interests of the industry are well organized and well defined. These interests also have more to offer political entrepreneurs within a regulatory agency, such as future employment with one of the regulated firms. Therefore, regulators have a strong incentive to support the position of a well-organized special-interest group within the regulated industry.

Share-the-gains, share-the-pains theory
A theory of regulatory behavior that holds that regulators must take account of the demands of three groups: legislators, who established and oversee the regulatory agency; firms in the regulated industry; and consumers of the regulated industry's products.

"SHARE THE GAINS, SHARE THE PAINS" The **share-the-gains, share-the-pains theory** offers a somewhat different view of regulators' behavior. This theory focuses on the specific aims of regulators. It proposes that a regulator's main objective is simply to keep his or her job as a regulator. To do so, the regulator must obtain the approval of both the legislators who originally established and continue to oversee the regulatory agency and the regulated industry. The regulator must also take into account the views of the industry's customers.

In contrast to the capture hypothesis, which holds that regulators must take into account only industry special interests, the share-the-gains, share-the-pains theory contends that regulators must worry about legislators and consumers as well. After all, if industry customers who are hurt by improper regulation complain to legislators, the regulators might lose their jobs. Whereas the capture theory predicts that regulators will quickly allow electric utilities to raise their rates in the face of higher fuel costs, the share-the-gains, share-the-pains theory predicts a slower, more measured regulatory response. Ultimately, regulators will permit an increase in utility rates, but the allowed adjustment will not be as speedy or complete as predicted by the capture hypothesis. The regulatory agency is not completely captured by the industry. It also has to consider the views of consumers and legislators.

The Benefits and Costs of Regulation

As noted earlier, regulation offers many *potential* benefits. *Actual* benefits, however, are difficult to measure. Putting a dollar value on safer products, a cleaner environment, and better working conditions is a difficult proposition. Furthermore, the benefits of most regulations accrue to society over a long time.

You Are There

To contemplate why the benefits of enforcing regulations might be hard to measure in relation to known regulatory costs, take a look at **Regulation of U.S. Currency Moves into the Court System,** on pages 733 and 734.

THE DIRECT COSTS OF REGULATION TO TAXPAYERS Measuring the costs of regulation is also a challenging undertaking. After all, about 5,000 new federal regulations are issued each year. One cost, though, is certain: U.S. taxpayers pay more than $40 billion per year to staff regulatory agencies with more than 250,000 employees and to fund their various activities. Figure 28-3 displays the distribution of total federal government outlays for economic and social regulation of various areas of the economy.

The *total* cost of regulation is much higher than just the explicit government outlays to fund the administration of various regulations, however. After all, businesses must expend resources complying with regulations, developing creative responses to regulations, and funding special-interest lobbying efforts directed at legislators and regulatory officials. Sometimes companies find that it is impossible to comply with one regulation without violating another, and determining how to avoid the resulting legal entanglements can entail significant expenditures.

How have lawmakers in the European Union (EU) exempted—at least temporarily—EU firms from costly regulations that have already been imposed on U.S. competitors?

INTERNATIONAL POLICY EXAMPLE
The Long Arm of Europe's REACH Slaps U.S. Firms

The European Union (EU) recently put into place a regulatory system for products containing chemicals. The system is called REACH, which is an acronym for "registration, evaluation, and authorization of chemicals." The nearly 2,000-page body of rules applies to more than 30,000 chemicals. Before a firm can sell any chemical-containing product in any of the 27 EU nations, the product must satisfy numerous testing requirements. The REACH regulations went into effect on June 1, 2008—but only for non-EU firms, including

U.S. manufacturers. EU lawmakers gave firms based in EU nations until 2010 to satisfy the regulations. Hence, U.S. firms were saddled immediately with REACH-related costs, but EU firms were granted additional time to comply.

FOR CRITICAL ANALYSIS
Why do you suppose that U.S. critics suggest that by implementing the REACH rules in this manner, the EU intended, at least in part, to protect EU firms from competition?

FIGURE 28-3

The Distribution of Federal Regulatory Spending

This figure shows the areas of the economy to which more than $40 billion of taxpayer-provided funds are distributed to finance economic and social regulation.

Source: Office of Management and Budget.

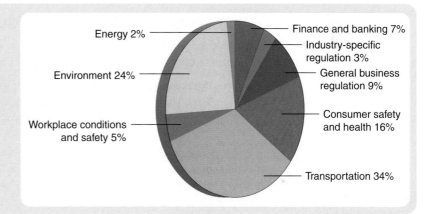

Energy 2% · Finance and banking 7% · Industry-specific regulation 3% · Environment 24% · General business regulation 9% · Consumer safety and health 16% · Workplace conditions and safety 5% · Transportation 34%

THE TOTAL SOCIAL COST OF REGULATION According to the Office of Management and Budget, annual expenditures that U.S. businesses must make solely to comply with regulations issued by various federal agencies amount to between $500 billion and $600 billion per year. Nevertheless, this estimate encompasses only explicit costs of satisfying regulatory demands placed on businesses. It ignores relevant opportunity costs. After all, owners, managers, and employees of companies could be doing other things with their time and resources than complying with regulations. Economists estimate that the opportunity costs of complying with federal regulations may be as high as $270 billion per year.

All told, therefore, the total social cost associated with satisfying federal regulations in the United States is probably between $800 billion and $900 billion per year. This figure, of course, applies only to federal regulations. It does not include the explicit and implicit opportunity costs associated with regulations issued by 50 different state governments and thousands of municipalities. Undoubtedly, the annual cost of regulation throughout the United States exceeds $1 trillion per year.

QUICK QUIZ   *See page 740 for the answers. Review concepts from this section in MyEconLab.*

The **capture hypothesis** holds that regulatory agencies will eventually be captured by industry special interests because

_____ individually are not greatly influenced by regulation, whereas regulated _____ are directly affected.

Antitrust Policy

An expressed aim of the U.S. government is to foster competition. To this end, Congress has made numerous attempts to legislate against business practices it has perceived to be anticompetitive. This is the general idea behind antitrust legislation. If the courts can prevent collusion among sellers of a product, there will be no restriction of output, and monopoly prices will not result. Instead, prices of goods and services will be close to their marginal social opportunity costs.

Antitrust Policy in the United States

Congress has enacted four key antitrust laws, which Table 28-2 summarizes. The most important of these is the original U.S. antitrust law, called the Sherman Act.

THE SHERMAN ANTITRUST ACT OF 1890 The Sherman Antitrust Act, which was passed in 1890, was the first attempt by the federal government to control the growth of monopoly in the United States. The most important provisions of that act are as follows:

Section 1: Every contract, combination in the form of a trust or otherwise, or conspiracy, in restraint of trade or commerce among the several states, or with foreign nations, is hereby declared to be illegal.

TABLE 28-2

Key U.S. Antitrust Laws

Sherman Antitrust Act of 1890	Forbids any contract, combination, or conspiracy to restrain trade or commerce within the United States or across U.S. borders. Holds any person who attempts to monopolize trade or commerce criminally liable.
Clayton Act of 1914	Prohibits specific business practices deemed to restrain trade or commerce. Bans discrimination in prices charged to various purchasers when price differences are not due to actual differences in selling or transportation costs. Also forbids a company from selling goods on the condition that the purchaser must deal exclusively with that company. Finally, it prevents corporations from holding stock in other companies when this may lessen competition.
Federal Trade Commission Act of 1914 (and 1938 Amendment)	Outlaws business practices that reduce the extent of competition, such as alleged cutthroat pricing intended to drive rivals from the marketplace. Also established the Federal Trade Commission and empowered it to issue cease and desist orders in situations in which it determines "unfair methods of competition in commerce" exist. The 1938 amendment added deceptive business practices to the list of illegal acts.
Robinson-Patman Act of 1936	Bans selected discriminatory price cuts by chain stores that allegedly drive smaller competitors from the marketplace. In addition, forbids price discrimination through special concessions in the form of price or quantity discounts, free advertising, or promotional allowances granted to one buyer but not to others, if these actions substantially reduce competition.

Section 2: Every person who shall monopolize, or attempt to monopolize, or combine or conspire with any other person or persons to monopolize any part of the trade or commerce . . . shall be guilty of a misdemeanor [now a felony].

Notice how vague this act really is. No definition is given for the terms *restraint of trade* or *monopolize*. Despite this vagueness, however, the act was used to prosecute the infamous Standard Oil Trust of New Jersey. This company was charged with and convicted of violations of Sections 1 and 2 of the Sherman Antitrust Act in 1906. At the time it controlled more than 80 percent of the nation's oil-refining capacity. In addressing the company's legal appeal, the U.S. Supreme Court ruled that Standard Oil's predominance in the oil market created "a *prima facie* presumption of intent and purpose to control and maintain dominancy . . . not as a result from normal methods of industrial development, but by means of combinations." Here the word *combination* meant entering into associations and preferential arrangements with the intent of restraining competition. The Supreme Court forced Standard Oil of New Jersey to break up into many smaller companies that would have no choice but to compete.

The Sherman Act applies today just as it did more than a century ago. In June 2001, the federal Court of Appeals for the District of Columbia determined that Microsoft Corporation had violated the Sherman Act. The court ruled that Microsoft had engaged in anticompetitive conduct in an effort to monopolize the market for operating systems for personal computers. Initially, the U.S. Justice Department proposed a Standard Oil–style remedy: splitting Microsoft into several companies. Ultimately, however, Microsoft reached a settlement that kept the company intact but required it to alter many of its business practices.

Do admitted violations of the 1890 Sherman Act ever occur in our modern, high-tech world?

E-COMMERCE EXAMPLE
The Justice Department Focuses on Flash Memory Price Fixing

In the early 2000s, officials representing four companies—Elpida Memory, Hunix Semiconductor, Infineon Technologies, and Samsung—colluded in setting prices of dynamic random-access memory (DRAM) microchips. In 2006, the U.S. Justice Department secured convictions under the Sherman Antitrust Act. All four companies admitted that officials representing their firms conspired to restrain trade in the market for DRAM microchips.

DRAM microchips are inputs in devices such as personal computers, digital cameras, music players, and cellphones. So are static random-access memory (SRAM) microchips and flash memory chips. After the Justice Department first unearthed evidence of price fixing in DRAM microchips in the early 2000s, it began an investigation of potential Sherman Act violations by firms producing SRAM microchips. In addi-

tion, when prices of flash memory chips rose in the late 2000s, the Justice Department opened a preliminary investigation into possible price fixing of those newer-technology chips. Most market observers suggested that the prices of flash memory chips rose for a less sinister reason—an increased demand for the newer, faster chips by makers of all kinds of digital gadgets. Nevertheless, the Justice Department continues to investigate possible price fixing of computer chips.

FOR CRITICAL ANALYSIS

How does the fact that higher prices could result from either higher market demand or collusive efforts to monopolize a market complicate efforts to determine whether a Sherman Act violation may have occurred?

OTHER IMPORTANT ANTITRUST LEGISLATION Table 28-2 lists three other important antitrust laws. In 1914, Congress passed the Clayton Act to clarify some of the vague provisions of the Sherman Act by identifying specific business practices that were to be legally prohibited.

Congress also passed the Federal Trade Commission Act in 1914. In addition to establishing the Federal Trade Commission to investigate unfair trade practices, this law enumerated certain business practices that, according to Congress, involved overly aggressive competition. A 1938 amendment to this law expressly prohibited "unfair or deceptive acts or practices in commerce" and empowered the FTC to regulate advertising and marketing practices by U.S. firms.

The Robinson-Patman Act of 1936 amended the Clayton Act by singling out specific business practices, such as selected price cuts, aimed at driving smaller competitors out of business. The act is often referred to as the "Chain Store Act" because it was intended to protect *independent* retailers and wholesalers from "unfair competition" by chain stores.

EXEMPTIONS FROM ANTITRUST LAWS Numerous laws exempt the following industries and business practices from antitrust legislation:

- Labor unions
- Public utilities—electric, gas, and telephone companies
- Professional baseball
- Cooperative activities among U.S. exporters
- Hospitals
- Public transit and water systems
- Suppliers of military equipment
- Joint publishing arrangements in a single city by two or more newspapers

Thus, not all U.S. businesses are subject to antitrust laws.

International Discord in Antitrust Policy

What, if anything, should U.S. antitrust authorities do if AT&T decides that it wishes to merge with British Telecommunications or if Germany's Deutsche Telecom wants to acquire Sprint Nextel? What, if anything, should they do if Time Warner, the largest U.S. entertainment company, attempts to merge with London-based EMI, one of the world's largest recorded-music companies? These are not just rhetorical questions, as U.S. and European antitrust authorities learned in the 2000s when these issues actually surfaced. Growing international linkages among markets for many goods and services have increasingly made antitrust policy a global undertaking.

The international dimensions of antitrust pose a problem for U.S. antitrust authorities in the Department of Justice and the Federal Trade Commission. In the United States, the overriding goal of antitrust policies has traditionally been protecting the interests of consumers. This is also a formal objective of antitrust efforts of European Union (EU) antitrust authorities. In the EU, however, policymakers are also required to reject any business combination that "creates or strengthens a dominant position as a result of which effective competition would be significantly impeded."

This additional clause is creating tension between U.S. and EU policymaking. In the United States, increasing dominance of a market by a single firm arouses the concern of antitrust authorities. Nevertheless, U.S. authorities typically will remain passive if they determine that the larger market dominance arises from factors such as exceptional management and greater cost efficiencies that ultimately benefit consumers by reducing prices. In contrast, under EU rules antitrust authorities are obliged to block *any* business combination that increases the dominance of any producer. They must do so regardless of what factors might have caused the business's preeminence in the marketplace or whether the antitrust action might have adverse implications for consumers.

QUICK QUIZ   *See page 740 for the answers. Review concepts from this section in MyEconLab.*

The first national antitrust law was the _____ Antitrust Act of 1890, which made illegal every contract and combination in restraint of trade; it remains the single most important antitrust law in the United States.

The _____ Act of 1914 made illegal various specific business practices, such as price discrimination.

The _____ _____ _____ Act of 1914 and its 1938 amendment established the Federal Trade Commission and prohibited "unfair or deceptive acts or practices in commerce."

The _____-_____ Act of 1936 aimed to prevent large producers from driving out small competitors by means of selective discriminatory price cuts.

Antitrust Enforcement

How are antitrust laws enforced? In the United States, most enforcement continues to be based on the Sherman Act. The Supreme Court has defined the offense of **monopolization** as involving the following elements: "(1) the possession of monopoly power in the relevant market and (2) the willful acquisition or maintenance of that power, as distinguished from growth or development as a consequence of a superior product, business acumen, or historical accident."

Monopoly Power and the Relevant Market

The Sherman Act does not define monopoly. Monopoly need not be a single entity. Also, monopoly is not a function of size alone. For example a "mom and pop" grocery store located in an isolated town can function as a monopolist.

It is difficult to define and measure market power precisely. As a workable proxy, courts often look to the firm's percentage share of the "relevant market." This is the so-called **market share test.** A firm is generally considered to have monopoly power if its share of the relevant market is 70 percent or more. This is only a rule of thumb, however, not an absolute dictum. In some cases, a smaller share may be held to constitute monopoly power.

The relevant market consists of two elements: a relevant *product* market and a relevant *geographic* market. What should the relevant product market include? It must include all items produced by different firms that have identical attributes, such as sugar. Yet products that are not identical may sometimes be substituted for one another. Coffee may be substituted for tea, for example. In defining the relevant product market, the key issue is the degree to which products are interchangeable. If one product is sufficiently substitutable for another, then the two products are considered to be part of the same product market.

The second component of the relevant market is the geographic boundaries of the market. For items that are sold nationwide, the geographic boundaries of the market encompass the entire United States. If a producer and its competitors sell in only a limited area (one in which customers have no access to other sources of the product), the geographic market is limited to that area. A national firm may thus compete in several distinct areas and have monopoly power in one area but not in another.

Monopolization
The possession of monopoly power in the relevant market and the willful acquisition or maintenance of that power, as distinguished from growth or development as a consequence of a superior product, business acumen, or historical accident.

Market share test
The percentage of a market that a particular firm supplies; used as the primary measure of monopoly power.

Product Packaging and Antitrust Enforcement

A particular problem in U.S. antitrust enforcement is determining whether a firm has engaged in "willful acquisition or maintenance" of market power. Unfortunately, actions that appear to some observers to be good business look like antitrust violations to others. To illustrate why quandaries can arise in antitrust enforcement, let's consider two examples: *versioning* and *bundling*.

Versioning
Selling a product in slightly altered forms to different groups of consumers.

PRODUCT VERSIONING A firm engages in product **versioning** when it sells an item in slightly altered forms to different groups of consumers. A typical method of versioning is to remove certain features from an item and offer what remains as a somewhat stripped-down version of the product at a different price.

Consider an office-productivity software program, such as Adobe Acrobat or Microsoft Word. Firms selling such programs typically offer both a "professional" version containing a full range of features and a "standard" version providing only basic functions. One perspective on this practice regards it as a form of price discrimination, or selling essentially the same product at different prices to different consumers. People who desire to use the full range of features in Adobe Acrobat or Microsoft Word are likely to be computing professionals. Compared to most other consumers, their demand for the full-featured version of an office-productivity software program is likely to be less elastic. In principle, therefore, Adobe and Microsoft can earn higher profits by offering "professional" versions at higher prices and selling a "standard" version at a lower price.

Price discrimination—charging varying prices to different consumers when the price differences are not a result of different production or transportation costs—is illegal under the Clayton Act of 1914. Are Adobe, Microsoft, and other companies engaging in illegal price discrimination? Another perspective on versioning indicates that they are not. According to this point of view, consumers regard "professional" and "standard" versions of software packages as imperfect substitutes. Consequently, each version is a distinctive product sold in a unique market. If so, versioning increases overall consumer satisfaction because consumers who are not computing professionals are able to utilize certain features of software products at a lower price. So far, antitrust authorities in the United States and elsewhere have been inclined toward this view of the economic effects of versioning, rather than perceiving it as a form of price discrimination.

Bundling
Offering two or more products for sale as a set.

PRODUCT BUNDLING Antitrust authorities have been less tolerant of another form of product packaging, known as **bundling,** which involves the joint sale of two or more products as a set. Antitrust authorities usually are not concerned if a firm allows consumers to purchase the products either individually or as a set. They are more likely to investigate a firm's business practices, however, when it allows consumers to purchase one product only when it is bundled with another. Antitrust officials often view this form of bundling as a method of price discrimination known as **tie-in sales,** in which a firm requires consumers who wish to buy one of its products to purchase another item the firm sells as well.

Tie-in sales
Purchases of one product that are permitted by the seller only if the consumer buys another good or service from the same firm.

To understand their reasoning, consider a situation in which one group of consumers is willing to pay $200 for a computer operating system but only $100 for an Internet-browsing program. A second group of consumers is willing to pay only $100 for the same computer operating system but is willing to pay $200 for the same Internet-browsing program. If the same company that sells both types of software offers the operating system at a price above $100, then only consumers in the first group will buy this software. Likewise, if it sells the Internet-browsing program at a price above $100, then only the second group of consumers will purchase that program.

But if the firm sells both products as a bundled set, it can charge $300 and generate sales of both software products to both groups. One interpretation is that the first group pays $200 for the operating system, but for the second group, the operating system's price is $100. At the same time, the first group has paid $100 for the Internet-browsing program, while the second group perceives the price of the program to be $200. Effectively, bundling enables the software company to engage in price discrimination by charging different prices to different groups.

Antitrust enforcers in the Justice Department applied this interpretation in their prosecution of Microsoft, which for years had bundled its Internet-browsing program, Internet Explorer, together with its Windows operating system. Enforcement officials added another twist by contending that Microsoft also had monopoly power in the market for computer operating systems. By bundling the two products, they argued, Microsoft had sought both to price-discriminate and to extend its monopoly power to the market for Internet-browsing software. The remedy that the courts imposed was for Microsoft to alter some of its business practices. As part of this legal remedy, Microsoft was required to unbundle its Windows and Internet Explorer products.

QUICK QUIZ   *See page 740 for the answers. Review concepts from this section in MyEconLab.*

As part of the enforcement of antitrust laws, officials at the U.S. Department of Justice and the Federal Trade Commission often apply _____ _____ tests to determine if a few firms account for most of industry _____.

Antitrust enforcers must decide whether producers seek to monopolize the relevant market, which involves determining both the relevant _____ market and the relevant _____ market.

Antitrust authorities generally have not considered product _____, or offering different versions of essentially the same product for sale at different prices, to be illegal price discrimination. U.S. authorities have, however, raised antitrust concerns about product _____, which they view as a method of engaging in **tie-in sales** that require consumers to purchase one product in order to obtain another.

 You Are There   **Regulation of U.S. Currency Moves into the Court System**

Under the Federal Reserve Act of 1913, the Federal Reserve System (the "Fed") is responsible for determining the amount of currency to be distributed through the nation's banking system. The U.S. Treasury's Bureau of Engraving and Printing designs and prints this currency. For years, the Bureau's main goal has been to produce recognizable, sturdy bills that are hard to counterfeit. The Bureau's efforts have yielded a national currency that has long consisted of

uniform bills distinguished mainly by portraits of famous patriots and different numerical denominations printed in corners of the bills.

In 2006, U.S. District Court Judge James Robertson was asked to rule on whether the uniformity of the nation's currency violates antidiscrimination regulations established by the Rehabilitation Act of 1973. According to the American Council of the Blind (ACB), these regulations require the

You Are There (cont.)

U.S. government to avoid actions that discriminate against people suffering from disabilities. The ACB argued that the Bureau of Engraving and Printing designed the nation's currency without taking into account the difficulties that blind individuals might have in distinguishing currency denominations. Thus, it failed to abide by the Rehabilitation Act's regulations.

After studying the currencies of about 180 other nations, Judge Robertson found that the U.S. government is the only one that has not taken steps to make its currency denominations readily identifiable by blind individuals. Thus, he ruled that the U.S. government is consciously discriminating against the blind by illegally denying them "meaningful access" to the currency in violation of the Rehabilitation Act's regulations. In May 2008, a federal appeals court upheld Judge Robertson's decision. Even though redesigning the nation's currency and its production process could cost millions of dollars, a majority of the appeals court judges agreed with Judge Robertson that the costs would

not be an "undue burden" on the U.S. Treasury. A third judge disagreed with the majority's decision and pointed out that retooling vending machines so that they would accept the new currency would cost *billions* of dollars.

CRITICAL ANALYSIS QUESTIONS

1. The president of another group, the National Federation of the Blind, noted that "blind people transact business with paper money every day" and attacked Judge Robertson's decision as a "feel-good gimmick that misinforms the public." Given that two different organizations claiming to represent the interests of the blind disagree on the benefits of a currency redesign, why might it be hard to put a monetary value on the actual benefits?

2. If the U.S. Treasury decides not to pursue any further appeals, who will ultimately pay for the costs of a redesign of U.S. currency?

The Latest in Spiraling Regulation Costs: "Doc Fees"

Issues and Applications

CONCEPTS APPLIED

- Economic Regulation
- Lemons Problem
- Social Regulation

The costs of finalizing vehicle purchases have increased considerably in recent years. The reason is that fees for processing documents associated with these transactions, or, as auto dealers commonly refer to them, "doc fees," have ballooned as a variety of regulations have expanded the range of legally required documents.

Doc Fees Related to Economic Regulation of Vehicle Sales

The transferal of ownership of a vehicle has long required a number of legal documents. Vehicle sellers, such as auto dealers, must be certain that documents such as formal title of ownership and state vehicle registration for tax purposes meet requirements established by law. To comply with these requirements, they must pay attorneys, specially trained employees, and others.

Beginning in the 1980s, a number of auto sellers started to charge separate fees for the service they provided in documenting the transferal of vehicle ownership. Until the 1990s, document-processing fees associated with vehicle purchases rarely exceeded $50 per transaction. Then state governments became more concerned about asymmetric information and lemons problems in auto sales. Since the early 1990s, many state legislatures have established regulations requiring auto sellers to provide detailed documents to purchasers verifying features that are present or absent in their vehicles. In addition, newly enacted or amended federal laws mandate that dealers provide buyers with documents detailing the monthly costs they will face if they borrow to finance vehicle purchases. Finally, many states now require sellers to provide buyers with documents attesting to vehicle inspections and repairs.

As a consequence of these forms of economic regulation, more documents must be processed when a transfer of vehicle ownership takes place. In addition to charging title processing fees and vehicle registration fees, auto sellers began adding fees for reports on financing costs, inspection documents, and used-vehicle

certifications. Thus, within a few years, vehicle doc fees more than doubled in most states.

The Latest in Doc Fees: Social Regulation of Vehicle Sales

During the 2000s, a new wave of document requirements swept across auto dealers' lots, as state and federal governments began subjecting vehicle sales transactions to various mandates related to social regulation. For instance, in an effort to protect the safety of future vehicle occupants, occupants of other vehicles, and pedestrians, state governments began requiring more detailed evidence of carefully conducted safety inspections. Additionally, the federal Gramm-Leach-Bliley Act included privacy rules requiring documents attesting that an auto seller will safeguard a buyer's private information. Furthermore, among the many antiterrorism measures passed by Congress in recent years is a requirement that auto sellers check customers against federal lists of people suspected of terrorist activities. The auto dealer must provide a document attesting that this task has been completed.

These and other laws specifying new forms of social regulation have pushed up doc fees markedly in many states. According to the American Automobile Association, in 2001 the average doc fees for a U.S. vehicle transaction were less than $200. Today, at least in states without legal ceilings on doc fees, average doc fees are close to $500. In some states, doc fees can exceed $1,000. Hence, expanded economic and social regulations have generated significant costs associated with transferring vehicle ownership. As usual, the benefits of many of the regulations that have pushed up doc fees are harder to pin down.

Test your understanding of this chapter by going online to **MyEconLab.**
In the Study Plan for this chapter, select Section N: News.

For Critical Analysis

1. How does requiring an auto seller to prepare additional documents affect the marginal cost that the seller faces in completing a vehicle transaction?

2. Why does a requirement to document that a customer has been checked against terrorist watch lists constitute social regulation instead of economic regulation?

Web Resources

1. To read a review of vehicle doc fees, go to www. econtoday.com/chapter28.

2. For a list of various fees associated with transferal of ownership of a vehicle, go to www.econtoday.com/ chapter28.

Research Project

Under the Gramm-Leach-Bliley Act, in addition to documenting that a customer's private information has been protected, an auto seller must also develop and implement privacy-protection train-ing programs for all employees. Are the costs generated by this requirement more likely to be borne largely by auto sellers or by buyers of vehicles? Explain your reasoning.

myeconlab

Here is what you should know after reading this chapter. **MyEconLab** will help you identify what you know, and where to go when you need to practice.

WHAT YOU SHOULD KNOW		WHERE TO GO TO PRACTICE
Government Regulation of Business There are two basic forms of government regulation of business: economic regulation and social regulation. Economic regulation applies to specific industries; it includes the regulation of prices charged by natural monopolies and the regulation of certain activities of specific nonmonopolistic industries. Social regulations affect nearly all businesses and encompass a broad range of objectives concerning such issues as product safety, environmental quality, and working conditions.	**KEY FIGURE** Figure 28-1, 715	• **MyEconLab** Study Plan 28.1 • Audio introduction to Chapter 28 • Animated Figure 28-1
Practical Difficulties in Regulating the Prices Charged by Natural Monopolies To try to ensure that a monopolist charges a price consistent with marginal cost, a government regulator might contemplate requiring the firm to set price equal to marginal cost at the point where the demand curve crosses the marginal cost curve. For a natural monopoly, however, long-run marginal cost is typically less than long-run average total cost, so requiring marginal cost pricing forces the firm to incur an economic loss. Hence, regulators normally aim for a natural monopoly to charge a price equal to average total cost so that the firm earns zero economic profits. In recent years, uncoupling production of electricity, natural gas, and telecommunications from their distribution has enabled regulators to promote competition in these industries.	cost-of-service regulation, 719 rate-of-return regulation, 719 **KEY FIGURE** Figure 28-2, 718	• **MyEconLab** Study Plan 28.2 • Animated Figure 28-2
Rationales for Regulating Nonmonopolistic Industries The two most common rationales for regulation of nonmonopolistic industries relate to addressing market failures and protecting consumers from problems arising from information asymmetries they face in some markets. Asymmetric information can also create a lemons problem, which occurs when uncertainty about product quality leads to markets containing mostly low-quality	lemons problem, 723	• **MyEconLab** Study Plan 28.3

(continued)

WHAT YOU SHOULD KNOW

WHERE TO GO TO PRACTICE

items. Governments may seek to reduce the lemons problem by establishing liability laws and business licensing requirements.

Regulators' Incentives and the Costs of Regulation The capture theory of regulator behavior predicts that regulators will eventually find themselves supporting the positions of the firms that they regulate. An alternative view, called the share-the-gains, share-the-pains theory, predicts that a regulator will try to satisfy all constituencies, at least in part. The costs of regulation are easier to quantify in dollar terms than the benefits. These costs include both the direct costs to taxpayers of funding regulatory agencies and the explicit and implicit opportunity costs that businesses must incur to comply with regulations.

creative response, 725
capture hypothesis, 725
share-the-gains,
    share-the-pains
    theory, 726

KEY FIGURE
Figure 28-3, 727

- **MyEconLab** Study Plan 28.4
- Animated Figure 28-3
- Video: Creative Response and Feedback Effects: Results of Regulation

Foundations of Antitrust There are four key antitrust laws. The Sherman Act of 1890 forbids attempts to monopolize an industry. The Clayton Act of 1914 clarified antitrust law by prohibiting specific types of business practices that Congress determined were aimed at restraining trade. In addition, the Federal Trade Commission Act of 1914, as amended in 1938, seeks to prohibit deceptive business practices and to prevent "cutthroat pricing," which Congress felt could unfairly eliminate too many competitors. Finally, the Robinson-Patman Act of 1936 outlawed price cuts that Congress had determined to be discriminatory and predatory.

- **MyEconLab** Study Plan 28.5
- Video: Antitrust Laws

Issues in Enforcing Antitrust Laws Antitrust laws are vague, so enforcement of the laws is based on court interpretations of their meaning. The Supreme Court has defined monopolization as possessing or seeking monopoly pricing power in the "relevant market." Authorities charged with enforcing antitrust laws use a market share test, which involves determining the percentage of market production or sales supplied by a firm. A key issue in applying the market share test is defining the relevant market. In recent years, antitrust officials have raised questions about whether product packaging, either in the form of different versions or as bundled sets, is a type of price discrimination. Versioning generally is not considered to constitute price discrimination, so it has not attracted much antitrust attention. In contrast, U.S. antitrust authorities have charged that product bundling is a means of engaging in tie-in sales, in

monopolization, 731
market share test, 731
versioning, 732
bundling, 732
tie-in sales, 732

- **MyEconLab** Study Plan 28.6
- Video: Theory of Contestable Markets

(continued)

(continued)

WHAT YOU SHOULD KNOW

WHERE TO GO TO PRACTICE

which a firm price-discriminates by requiring consumers to purchase one product before being able to buy another item.

Log in to MyEconLab, take a chapter test, and get a personalized Study Plan that tells you which concepts you understand and which ones you need to review. From there, MyEconLab will give you further practice, tutorials, animations, videos, and guided solutions.
Log in to www.myeconlab.com

PROBLEMS

All problems are assignable in myeconlab. *Answers to odd-numbered problems appear at the back of the book.*

28-1. Local cable television companies are sometimes granted monopoly rights to service a particular territory of a metropolitan area. The companies typically pay special taxes and licensing fees to local municipalities. Why might a municipality give monopoly rights to a cable company?

28-2. A local cable company, the sole provider of cable television service, is regulated by the municipal government. The owner of the company claims that she is normally opposed to regulation by government, but asserts that regulation is necessary because local residents would not want a large number of different cables crisscrossing the city. Why do you think the owner is defending regulation by the city?

28-3. The table below depicts the cost and demand structure a natural monopoly faces.

Quantity	Price ($)	Long-Run Total Cost ($)
0	100	0
1	95	92
2	90	177
3	85	255
4	80	331
5	75	406
6	70	480

a. Calculate total revenues, marginal revenue, and marginal cost at each output level. If this firm is allowed to operate as a monopolist, what will be the quantity produced and the price charged by the firm? What will be the amount of monopoly profit?

b. If regulators require the firm to practice marginal cost pricing, what quantity will it produce, and what price will it charge? What is the firm's profit under this regulatory framework?

c. If regulators require the firm to practice average cost pricing, what quantity will it produce, and what price will it charge? What is the firm's profit under this regulatory framework?

28-4. As noted in the chapter, separating the *production* of electricity from its *delivery* has led to considerable deregulation of producers.

a. Briefly explain which of these two aspects of the sale of electricity remains susceptible to natural monopoly problems.

b. Suppose that the potential natural monopoly problem you identified in part (a) actually arises. Why is marginal cost pricing not a feasible solution? What makes average cost pricing a feasible solution?

c. Discuss two approaches that a regulator could use to try to implement an average-cost-pricing solution to the problem identified in part (a).

28-5. Are lemons problems likely to be more common in some industries and less common in others? Based on your answer to this question, should government regulatory activities designed to reduce the scope of lemons problems take the form of economic regulation or social regulation? Take a stand, and support your reasoning.

28-6. Research into genetically modified crops has led to significant productivity gains for countries such as the United States that employ these techniques. Countries such as the European Union's member nations, however, have imposed controls on the import of these products, citing concern for public health. Is the European Union's regulation of genetically modified crops social regulation or economic regulation?

28-7. Do you think that the regulation described in Problem 28-6 is more likely an example of the capture hypothesis or the share-the-gains, share-the-pains theory? Why?

28-8. Prices of tickets for seats on commercial passenger planes are typically in the hundreds of dollars, whereas trips can be made by automobile at much lower cost. Accident rates per person per trip in the airline industry are considerably lower than auto accident rates per person per trip. Based on these facts, discuss how regulatory costs and benefits may help to explain why government regulations require children to be placed in safety seats in automobiles but not on commercial passenger planes.

28-9. In 2003, the U.S. government created a "Do Not Call Registry" and forbade marketing firms from calling people who placed their names on this list. Today, an increasing number of companies are sending mail solicitations to individuals inviting them to send back an enclosed postcard for more information about the firms' products. What these solicitations fail to mention is that they are worded in such a way that someone who returns the postcard gives up protection from telephone solicitations, even if they are on the government's "Do Not Call Registry." In what type of behavior are these companies engaging? Explain your answer. (Hint: Are these firms meeting the letter of the law but violating its spirit?)

28-10. Suppose that a business has developed a very high-quality product and operates more efficiently in producing that product than any other potential competitor. As a consequence, at present it is the only seller of this product, for which there are few close substitutes. Is this firm in violation of U.S. antitrust laws? Explain.

28-11. Consider the following fictitious sales data (in thousands of dollars) for books sold both over the Internet and in physical retail establishments. Firms have numbers instead of names, and Firm 1 generates book sales only over the Internet. Antitrust authorities judge that a single firm possesses "monopoly power" if its share of sales in the relevant market exceeds 70 percent.

Internet Book Sales		Book Sales in Physical Stores		Combined Book Sales	
Firm	Sales	Firm	Sales	Firm	Sales
1	$ 750	2	$4,200	2	$ 4,250
2	50	3	2,000	3	2,050
3	50	4	1,950	4	2,000
4	50	5	450	1	750
5	50	6	400	5	500
6	50			6	450
Total	$1,000		$9,000		$10,000

a. Suppose that the antitrust authorities determine that bookselling in physical retail stores and Internet bookselling are individually separate relevant markets. Does any single firm have monopoly power, as defined by the antitrust authorities?

b. Suppose that in fact there is really only a single book industry, in which firms compete both in physical retail stores and via the Internet. According to the antitrust authorities' measure of monopoly power, is there actually cause for concern?

28-12. In recent years, the Internet auction firm eBay has sought to make its auction technology the favorite of software programmers, and it has begun licensing its technology to other Web sites. The company's managers have publicly stated that their goal is for eBay's auction system to become the dominant "operating system" of all auction applications on the Internet. Are there any potential antitrust issues related to the company's efforts?

28-13. Recently, the U.S. Justice Department initiated an antitrust investigation of Homestore.com, a Web site containing the property listings of thousands of real estate agents in the United States. In cities and in local communities, there is considerable rivalry among real estate agents. Nevertheless, nearly all belong to the National Association of Realtors (NAR), which is the majority owner of Homestore.com. In 2000, Homestore.com purchased a rival site, Move.com, and took its name. This left Homeadvisor.com as its only remaining key rival. Why do you suppose the Justice Department became concerned about the activities of the NAR? What factors are likely to affect its decision about whether the NAR violated any antitrust laws?

28-14. A package delivery company provides both overnight and second-day delivery services. It charges almost twice as much to deliver an overnight package to any world location as it does to deliver the same package to the same location in two days. Often, second-day packages arrive at company warehouses in destination cities by the next day, but drivers intentionally do not deliver these packages until the following day. What is this business practice called? Briefly summarize alternative perspectives concerning whether this activity should or should not be viewed as a form of price discrimination.

28-15. A firm that sells both Internet-security software and computer antivirus software will sell the antivirus software as a stand-alone product. It will only sell the Internet-security software to consumers in a combined package that also includes the antivirus software. What is this business practice called? Briefly explain why an antitrust authority might view this practice as a form of price discrimination.

28-16. Recently, a food retailer called Whole Foods sought to purchase Wild Oats, a competitor in the market for organic foods. When the Federal Trade Commission (FTC) sought to block this merger on antitrust grounds, FTC officials argued that such a merger would dramatically increase concentration in the market for "premium organic foods." Whole Foods' counterargument was that it considered itself to be part of the broadly defined supermarket industry that includes retailers such as Albertson's, Kroger, and Safeway. What key issue of antitrust regulation was involved in this dispute? Explain.

ECONOMICS ON THE NET

Guidelines for U.S. Antitrust Merger Enforcement How does the U.S. government apply antitrust laws to mergers? This application gives you the opportunity to learn about the standards applied by the Antitrust Division of the U.S. Department of Justice when it evaluates a proposed merger.

Title: U.S. Department of Justice Antitrust Merger Enforcement Guidelines

Navigation: Go to **www.econtoday.com/chapter28** to access the home page of the Antitrust Division of the U.S. Department of Justice.

Application Answer the following questions.

1. Click on *Horizontal Merger Guidelines*. In section 1, click on *Overview*, and read this section. What factors do U.S. antitrust authorities consider when evaluating the potential for a horizontal merger to "enhance

market power"—that is, to place the combination in a monopoly situation?

2. Back up to the page titled *Merger Enforcement Guidelines*, and click on *Non-Horizontal Merger Guidelines*. Read the guidelines. In what situations will the antitrust authorities most likely question a nonhorizontal merger?

For Group Study and Analysis Have three groups of students from the class examine sections 1, 2, and 3 of the *Horizontal Merger Guidelines* discussed in item 1. After each group reports on all the factors that the antitrust authorities consider when evaluating a horizontal merger, discuss why large teams of lawyers and many economic consultants are typically involved when the Antitrust Division of the Department of Justice alleges that a proposed merger would be "anticompetitive."

ANSWERS TO QUICK QUIZZES

p. 717: (i) Economic . . . social; (ii) natural . . . economic; (iii) social
p. 721: (i) lower . . . revenue . . . cost; (ii) average . . . zero; (iii) deliver . . . networks
p. 724: (i) failures . . . asymmetric; (ii) asymmetric; (iii) lemons . . . low
p. 727: (i) consumers . . . firms; (ii) industry . . . legislators . . . consumers; (iii) government . . . firms'
p. 731: (i) Sherman; (ii) Clayton; (iii) Federal Trade Commission; (iv) Robinson-Patman
p. 733: (i) market share . . . sales; (ii) product . . . geographic; (iii) versioning . . . bundling

The Labor Market: Demand, Supply, and Outsourcing

29

Ever since economists first began collecting data on wages to try to determine key factors influencing variations in earnings across different individuals, they have found that, on average, women consistently earn less than men. This differential between the average earnings of men and women, which is often called the "male-female wage gap," has narrowed in recent years. Nevertheless, the gap remains substantial. What factors account for the average pay gap between men and women? To be able to consider potential answers to this question, you must first learn about the determinants of labor demand and supply, which together determine the market clearing wages earned by both men and women.

 LEARNING OBJECTIVES **myeconlab**

MyEconLab helps you master each objective and study more efficiently. See end of chapter for details.

After reading this chapter, you should be able to:

► Understand why a firm's marginal revenue product curve is its labor demand curve

► Explain in what sense the demand for labor is a "derived" demand

► Identify the key factors influencing the elasticity of demand for inputs

► Describe how equilibrium wage rates are determined for perfectly competitive firms

► Explain what labor outsourcing is and how it is ultimately likely to affect U.S. workers' earnings and employment prospects

► Contrast the demand for labor and wage determination by a product market monopolist with outcomes that would arise under perfect competition

DID YOU KNOW THAT when European advocacy groups wish to hold a protest march but find themselves short on protesters, some of them turn to a German firm called Erento that specializes in renting demonstrators? The firm's Web site features about 300 demonstrators-for-hire and lists personal characteristics such as height, skin color, and ethnicity. The company charges a fee of nearly $190 per demonstrator for a six-hour day of protesting.

The demand for demonstrators-for-hire by advocacy groups or for any other inputs on the part of businesses can be studied in much the same manner as we studied the demand for output. Our analysis will always end with the same conclusion: A firm will hire employees up to the point beyond which it isn't profitable to hire any more. It will hire employees to the point at which the marginal benefit of hiring a worker will just equal the marginal cost. Indeed, in every profit-maximizing situation, it is most profitable to carry out an activity up to the point at which the marginal benefit equals the marginal cost. Remembering that guideline will help you in analyzing decision making at the firm level, which is where we will begin our discussion of the demand for labor.

Labor Demand for a Perfectly Competitive Firm

We will start our analysis under the assumption that the market for input factors is perfectly competitive. We will further assume that the output market is perfectly competitive. This provides a benchmark against which to compare other situations in which labor markets or product markets are not perfectly competitive.

Competition in the Product Market

Let's take as our example a firm that sells flash memory drives and is in competition with many companies selling the same kind of product. Assume that the laborers hired by this manufacturing firm do not need any special skills. This firm sells flash memory drives in a perfectly competitive market. It also buys labor (its variable input) in a perfectly competitive market. A firm that hires labor under perfectly competitive conditions hires only a minuscule proportion of all the workers who are potentially available to the firm. By "potentially available," we mean all the workers in a given geographic area who possess the skills demanded by our perfect competitor. In such a market, it is always possible for the individual firm to hire extra workers without having to offer a higher wage. Thus, the supply of labor to the firm is perfectly elastic at the going wage rate established by the forces of supply and demand in the entire labor market. The firm is a *price taker* in the labor market.

Marginal Physical Product

Look at panel (a) of Figure 29-1. In column 1, we show the number of workers per week that the firm can employ. In column 2, we show total physical product (TPP) per week, the total *physical* production of flash memory drives that different quantities of the labor input (in combination with a fixed amount of other inputs) will generate in a week's time. In column 3, we show the additional output gained when the company adds workers to its existing manufacturing facility. This column, the **marginal physical product (MPP) of labor,** represents the extra (additional) output attributed to employing additional units of the variable input factor. If this firm employs seven workers rather than six, the MPP is 118. The law of diminishing marginal product predicts that additional units of a variable factor will, after some point, cause the MPP to decline, other things held constant.

Marginal physical product (MPP) of labor

The change in output resulting from the addition of one more worker. The MPP of the worker equals the change in total output accounted for by hiring the worker, holding all other factors of production constant.

FIGURE 29-1

Marginal Revenue Product

In panel (a), column 4 shows marginal revenue product (MRP), which is the additional revenue the firm receives for the sale of that additional output. Marginal revenue product is simply the revenue the additional worker brings in—the combination of that worker's contribution to production and the revenue that that production will bring to the firm. For this perfectly competitive firm, marginal revenue is equal to the price of the product, or $10 per unit. At a weekly wage of $830, the profit-maximizing employer will pay for only 12 workers because then the marginal revenue product is just equal to the wage rate or weekly salary.

Panel (a)

(1) Labor Input (workers per week)	(2) Total Physical Product (TPP) (flash drives per week)	(3) Marginal Physical Product (MPP) (flash drives per week)	(4) Marginal Revenue (MR = P = $10) x MPP = Marginal Revenue Product (MRP) ($ per additional worker)	(5) Wage Rate ($ per week) = Marginal Factor Cost (MFC) = Change in Total Costs ÷ Change in Labor
6	882			
		118	$1,180	$830
7	1,000			
		111	1,110	830
8	1,111			
		104	1,040	830
9	1,215			
		97	970	830
10	1,312			
		90	900	830
11	1,402			
		83	830	830
12	1,485			
		76	760	830
13	1,561			

In panel (b), we find the number of workers the firm will want to hire by observing the wage rate that is established by the forces of supply and demand in the entire labor market. We show that this employer is hiring labor in a perfectly competitive labor market and therefore faces a perfectly elastic supply curve represented by *s* at a constant marginal factor cost (MFC) of $830 per week. As in other situations, we have a supply and demand model; in this example, the demand curve is represented by MRP, and the supply curve is *s*. Profit maximization occurs at their intersection, which is the point at which MRP = MFC.

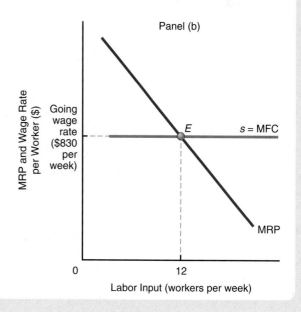

We are assuming that all other nonlabor factors of production are held constant. So, if our manufacturing firm wants to add one more worker to its production line, it has to crowd all the existing workers a little closer together because it does not increase its capital stock (the production equipment). Therefore, as we add more workers, each one has a smaller and smaller fraction of the available capital stock with which to work. If one worker uses one machine, adding another worker usually won't double the output because the machine can run only so fast and for so many hours per day. In other words, MPP declines because of the law of diminishing marginal product (see Chapter 23).

Marginal Revenue Product

Marginal revenue product (MRP)

The marginal physical product (MPP) times marginal revenue (MR). The MRP gives the additional revenue obtained from a one-unit change in labor input.

We now need to translate into a dollar value the physical product that results from hiring an additional worker. This is done by multiplying the marginal physical product by the marginal revenue of the firm. Because this firm sells flash memory drives in a perfectly competitive market, marginal revenue is equal to the price of the product. If employing seven workers rather than six yields an MPP of 118 and the marginal revenue is $10 per flash memory drive, the **marginal revenue product (MRP)** is $1,180 (118 × $10). The MRP is shown in column 4 of panel (a) of Figure 29-1 on the preceding page. *The marginal revenue product represents the incremental worker's contribution to the firm's total revenues.*

When a firm operates in a perfectly competitive product market, the marginal physical product times the product price is also referred to as the *value of marginal product (VMP)*. Because price and marginal revenue are the same for a perfectly competitive firm, the VMP is also the MRP for such a firm.

In column 5 of panel (a) of Figure 29-1, we show the wage rate, or *marginal factor cost*, of each worker. The marginal cost of workers is the extra cost incurred in employing an additional unit of that factor of production. We call that cost the **marginal factor cost (MFC).** Otherwise stated,

Marginal factor cost (MFC)

The cost of using an additional unit of an input. For example, if a firm can hire all the workers it wants at the going wage rate, the marginal factor cost of labor is the wage rate.

$$\text{Marginal factor cost} = \frac{\text{change in total cost}}{\text{change in amount of resource used}}$$

Because each worker is paid the same competitively determined wage of $830 per week, the MFC is the same for all workers. And because the firm is buying labor in a perfectly competitive labor market, the wage rate of $830 per week really represents the supply curve of labor to the firm. That supply curve is perfectly elastic because the firm can purchase all labor at the same wage rate, considering that it is a minuscule part of the entire labor-purchasing market. (Recall the definition of perfect competition.) We show this perfectly elastic supply curve as *s* in panel (b) of Figure 29-1.

GENERAL RULE FOR HIRING Virtually every optimizing rule in economics involves comparing marginal benefits with marginal cost. Because the benefit from added workers is extra output and consequently more revenues, the general rule for the hiring decision of a firm is this:

> *The firm hires workers up to the point at which the additional cost associated with hiring the last worker is equal to the additional revenue generated by hiring that worker.*

In a perfectly competitive market, this is the point at which the wage rate just equals the marginal revenue product. If the firm were to hire more workers, the additional wages would not be covered by additional increases in total revenue. If the firm were to hire fewer workers, it would be forfeiting the contributions that those workers otherwise could make to total profits.

Therefore, referring to columns 4 and 5 in panel (a) of Figure 29-1 on page 743, we see that this firm would certainly employ at least seven workers because the MRP is $1,180 while the MFC is only $830. The firm would continue to add workers up to the point at which MFC = MRP because as workers are added, those additional workers contribute more to revenue than to cost.

THE MRP CURVE: DEMAND FOR LABOR We can also use panel (b) of Figure 29-1 to find how many workers our firm should hire. First, we draw a line at the going wage rate, which is determined by demand and supply in the labor market. The line is labeled s to indicate that it is the supply curve of labor for the *individual* firm purchasing labor in a perfectly competitive labor market. That firm can purchase all the labor it wants of equal quality at $830 per worker. This perfectly elastic supply curve, s, intersects the marginal revenue product curve at 12 workers per week. At the intersection, E, the wage rate is equal to the marginal revenue product. The firm maximizes profits where its demand curve for labor, which turns out to be its MRP curve, intersects the firm's supply curve for labor, shown as s. The firm in our example would not hire the thirteenth worker, who would add only $760 to revenue but $830 to cost. If the price of labor should fall to, say, $760 per worker per week, the firm would hire an additional worker. Thus, the quantity of labor demanded increases as the wage decreases.

Derived Demand for Labor

We have identified an individual firm's demand for labor curve, which shows the quantity of labor that the firm will wish to hire at each wage rate, as its MRP curve. Under conditions of perfect competition in both product and labor markets, MRP is determined by multiplying MPP times the product's price. This suggests that the demand for labor is a **derived demand.** Factors of production are rented or purchased not because they give any intrinsic satisfaction to the firms' owners but because they can be used to manufacture output that is expected to be sold at a profit.

Derived demand
Input factor demand derived from demand for the final product being produced.

We know that an increase in the market demand for a given product raises the product's price (all other things held constant), which in turn increases the marginal revenue product, or demand for the resource. Figure 29-2 on the following page illustrates the effective role played by changes in product demand in a perfectly competitive product market. The MRP curve shifts whenever there is a change in the price of the final product that the workers are producing. Suppose, for example, that the market price of flash memory drives declines. In that case, the MRP curve will shift to the left from MRP_0 to MRP_1. We know that $MRP \equiv MPP \times MR$. If marginal revenue (here the output price) falls, so does the demand for labor. At the same going wage rate, the firm will hire fewer workers. This is because at various levels of labor use, the marginal revenue product of labor is now lower. At the initial equilibrium, therefore, the price of labor (here the MFC) becomes greater than MRP. Thus, the firm would reduce the number of workers hired. Conversely, if marginal revenue (the output price) rises, the demand for labor will also rise, and the firm will want to hire more workers at each and every possible wage rate.

We just pointed out that $MRP \equiv MPP \times MR$. Clearly, then, a change in marginal productivity, or in the marginal physical product of labor, will shift the MRP curve. If the marginal productivity of labor decreases, the MRP curve, or demand curve, for

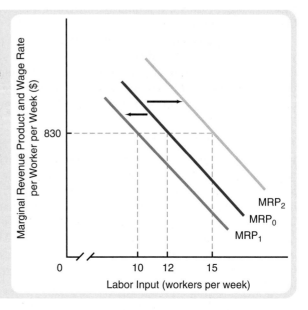

FIGURE 29-2

Demand for Labor, a Derived Demand

The demand for labor is derived from the demand for the final product being produced. Therefore, the marginal revenue product curve will shift whenever the price of the product changes. If we start with the marginal revenue product curve MRP_0 at the going wage rate of $830 per week, 12 workers will be hired. If the price of flash memory drives goes down, the marginal product curve will shift to MRP_1, and the number of workers hired will fall, in this case to 10. If the price of flash memory drives goes up, the marginal revenue product curve will shift to MRP_2, and the number of workers hired will increase, in this case to 15.

labor will shift inward to the left. Again, this is because at every quantity of labor used, the MRP will be lower. A lower quantity of labor will be demanded at every possible wage rate.

QUICK QUIZ | *See page 767 for the answers. Review concepts from this section in MyEconLab.*

The change in total _____ due to a one-unit change in one variable _____, holding all other _____ constant, is called the **marginal physical product (MPP).** When we multiply marginal physical product times _____ _____, we obtain the **marginal revenue product (MRP).**

A firm will hire workers up to the point at which the additional cost of hiring one more worker is equal to the additional revenue generated. For the individual firm, therefore, its MRP of labor curve is also its _____ _____ labor curve.

The demand for labor is a _____ demand, _____ from the demand for final output. Therefore, a change in the price of the final output will cause a _____ in the MRP curve (which is also the firm's demand for labor curve).

The Market Demand for Labor

The downward-sloping portion of each individual firm's marginal revenue product curve is also its demand curve for the one variable factor of production—in our example, labor. When we go to the entire market for a particular type of labor in a particular industry, we will also find that the quantity of labor demanded will vary inversely as the wage rate changes.

Constructing the Market Labor Demand Curve

Given that the market demand curve for labor is made up of the individual firms' downward-sloping demand curves for labor, we can safely infer that the market demand curve for labor will look like *D* in panel (b) of Figure 29-3: It will slope

FIGURE 29-3

Derivation of the Market Demand Curve for Labor

The market demand curve for labor is not simply the horizontal summation of each individual firm's demand curve for labor. If wage rates fall from $20 to $10, all 200 firms will increase employment and therefore output, causing the price of the product to fall. This causes the marginal revenue product curve of each firm to shift inward, from d_0 to d_1 in panel (a). The resulting market demand curve, D, in panel (b) is therefore less elastic around prices from $10 to $20 than it would be if the output price remained constant.

downward. That market demand curve for labor in the flash memory drive industry shows the quantities of labor demanded by all of the firms in the industry at various wage rates.

Nevertheless, the market demand curve for labor is *not* a simple horizontal summation of the labor demand curves of all individual firms. Remember that the demand for labor is a derived demand. Even if we hold labor productivity constant, the demand for labor still depends on both the wage rate and the price of the final output.

For instance, suppose that we start at a wage rate of $20 per hour and employment level 10 in panel (a) of Figure 29-3. If we sum all such employment levels—point *a* in panel (a)—across 200 firms, we get a market quantity demanded of 2,000, or point *A* in panel (b), at the wage rate of $20. A decrease in the wage rate to $10 per hour would induce individual firms' employment levels to increase toward a quantity demanded of 22 *if product price did not change.*

As all 200 firms simultaneously increase employment, total industry output also increases at the present price. Indeed, this would occur at *any* price, meaning that the industry product supply curve will shift rightward, and the market clearing price of the product must fall. The fall in the output price in turn causes a downward shift of each firm's MRP curve (d_0) to MRP_1 (d_1) in panel (a). Thus, each firm's employment of labor increases to 15 rather than to 22 at the wage rate of $10 per hour. A summation of all such 200 employment levels gives us 3,000—point *B*—in panel (b).

Determinants of Demand Elasticity for Inputs

Just as we were able to discuss the price elasticity of demand for different commodities in Chapter 20, we can discuss the price elasticity of demand for inputs. The price elasticity of demand for labor is defined in a manner similar to the price elasticity of demand for goods: the percentage change in quantity demanded divided by the percentage change in the price of labor. When the *numerical* (or absolute) value of this ratio is less than 1, demand is inelastic; when it is 1, demand is unit-elastic; and when it is greater than 1, demand is elastic.

There are four principal determinants of the price elasticity of demand for an input. The price elasticity of demand for a variable input will be greater:

1. The greater the price elasticity of demand for the final product
2. The easier it is to employ substitute inputs in production
3. The larger the proportion of total costs accounted for by the particular variable input
4. The longer the time period available for adjustment

FINAL PRODUCT PRICE ELASTICITY An individual radish farmer faces an extremely elastic demand for radishes, given the existence of many competing radish growers. If the farmer's laborers tried to obtain a significant wage increase, the farmer couldn't pass on the resultant higher costs to radish buyers. So any wage increase would lead to a large reduction in the quantity of labor demanded by the individual radish farmer.

EASE OF SUBSTITUTION Clearly, the easier it is for producers to switch to using another factor of production, the more responsive those producers will be to an increase in an input's price. If plastic can easily substitute for chrome plating in the production of, say, car bumpers, then a rise in the price of chrome plating will cause automakers to greatly reduce their quantity of chrome plating demanded.

PORTION OF TOTAL COST When a particular input's costs account for a very large share of total costs, any increase in that input's price will affect total costs relatively more. If labor costs are 80 percent of total costs, companies will cut back on employment more aggressively than if labor costs are only 8 percent of total costs, for any given wage increase.

ADJUSTMENT PERIOD Finally, over longer periods, firms have more time to figure out ways to economize on the use of inputs whose prices have gone up. Furthermore, over time, technological change will allow for easier substitution in favor of relatively cheaper inputs and against inputs whose prices went up. At first, a pay raise obtained by a strong telephone industry union may not result in many layoffs, but over time, the telephone companies will use new technology to replace many of the now more expensive workers.

QUICK QUIZ See page 767 for the answers. Review concepts from this section in MyEconLab.

Because the demand for labor is a derived demand that depends on both the _____ rate and the _____ of final output, the market demand curve for labor is not a simple horizontal summation of the labor demand curves of all individual firms. The market demand curve for labor does slope _____, however.

Input price elasticity of demand depends on the final product's _____ of demand, the ease of substituting other _____, the relative importance of the input's cost in total _____, and the time available for _____.

Wage Determination in a Perfectly Competitive Labor Market

Having developed the demand curve for labor (and all other variable inputs) in a particular industry, let's turn to the labor supply curve. By adding supply to the analysis, we can determine the equilibrium wage rate that workers earn in an industry. We can think in terms of a supply curve for labor that slopes upward in a particular industry. At higher wage rates, more workers will want to enter that particular industry. The individual firm, however, does not face the entire *market* supply curve. Rather, in a perfectly competitive case, the individual firm is such a small part of the market that it can hire all the workers that it wants at the going wage rate. We say, therefore, that the industry faces an upward-sloping supply curve but that the individual *firm* faces a perfectly elastic supply curve for labor.

Labor Market Equilibrium

The demand curve for labor in the flash memory drive industry is D in Figure 29-4, and the supply curve of labor is S. The equilibrium wage rate of $830 a week is established at the intersection of the two curves. The quantity of workers both supplied and demanded at that rate is Q_1. If for some reason the wage rate fell to $800 a week, in our hypothetical example, there would be an excess number of workers demanded at that wage rate. Conversely, if the wage rate rose to $900 a week, there would be an excess quantity of workers supplied at that wage rate. In either case, competition would quickly force the wage back to the equilibrium level.

We have just found the equilibrium wage rate for the entire flash memory drive industry. The individual firm must take that equilibrium wage rate as given in the perfectly competitive model used here because the individual firm is a very small part of the total demand for labor. Thus, each firm purchasing labor in a perfectly competitive market can purchase all of the input it wants at the going market price.

Shifts in the Market Demand for and the Supply of Labor

Just as we discussed shifts in the supply curve and the demand curve for various products in Chapter 3, we can discuss the effects of shifts in supply and demand in labor markets.

FIGURE 29-4

The Equilibrium Wage Rate and the Flash Memory Drive Industry

The industry demand curve for labor is D. We put in a hypothetical upward-sloping labor supply curve for the flash memory drive industry, S. The intersection is at point E, giving an equilibrium wage rate of $830 per week and an equilibrium quantity of labor demanded of Q_1. At a wage above $830 per week, there will be an excess quantity of workers supplied. At a wage below $830 per week, there will be an excess quantity of workers demanded.

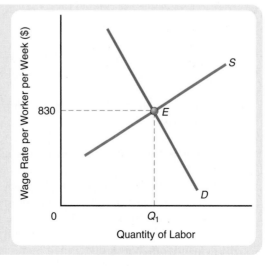

REASONS FOR LABOR DEMAND CURVE SHIFTS Many factors can cause the demand curve for labor to shift. We have already discussed a number of them. Clearly, because the demand for labor or any other variable input is a derived demand, the labor demand curve will shift if there is a shift in the demand for the final product. There are two other important determinants of the position of the demand curve for labor: changes in labor's productivity and changes in the price of related factors of production (substitute inputs and complementary inputs).

1. *Changes in the demand for the final product.* The demand for labor or any other variable input is derived from the demand for the final product. The marginal revenue product is equal to marginal physical product times marginal revenue. Therefore, any change in the demand for the final product will change its price and hence the MRP of the input. The rule of thumb is as follows:

   A change in the demand for the final product that labor (or any other variable input) is producing will shift the market demand curve for labor in the same direction.

   Why has the market demand for railcars increased during the 2000s?

EXAMPLE
The Derived Demand for Railcars

At present, U.S. railroads own about 595,000 railcars and lease an additional 717,000. The demand for rail freight services has increased markedly in recent years as the booming ethanol industry has sought rail transport of raw ingredients, by-products, and finished ethanol. The resulting rise in the price of rail freight services has increased railroads' marginal revenue product, so the demand for railcars has also increased. Manufacturers' average annual production of railcars has more than doubled since the early 2000s, to in excess of 60,000 railcars per year.

FOR CRITICAL ANALYSIS
What would likely happen to the demand for railcars if the ethanol boom were to go bust?

Because of the shift to the right in the demand for railcars, what has happened to the demand for railcar production employees?

2. *Changes in labor productivity.* The second part of the MRP equation is MPP, which relates to labor productivity. We can surmise, then, that, other things being equal:

   A change in labor productivity will shift the market labor demand curve in the same direction.

   Labor productivity can increase because labor has more capital or land to work with, because of technological improvements, or because labor's quality has improved. Such considerations explain why the real standard of living of workers in the United States is higher than in most other countries. U.S. workers generally work with a larger capital stock, have more natural resources, are in better physical condition, and are better trained than workers in many countries. Hence the demand for labor in the United States is, other things held constant, greater.

3. *Change in the price of related factors.* Labor is not the only resource that firms use. Some resources are substitutes and some are complements in the production process. If we hold output constant, we have the following general rule:

> **A change in the price of a substitute input will cause the demand for labor (or any other input) to change in the same direction.**

Thus, if the price of an input for which labor can substitute as a factor of production decreases, the demand for labor falls. For instance, if the price of mechanized ditch-digging equipment decreases, the demand for workers who, in contrast, can use shovels to dig ditches decreases.

In general, a fall in the price of an input generates a decline in demand for any substitute input. How are computer programs contributing to a reduction in the demand for the skills of performing musicians?

E-COMMERCE EXAMPLE
Why Hire an Orchestra When a Computer Program Will Do?

Today, when a composer wishes to record a six-minute musical composition written for an ensemble of 18 string instruments, one option is to pay about $50,000 for 18 musicians to produce a professional recording. Another option is to pay $800 to firms such as Fauxharmonic Orchestra to create a recording using a computer program that re-creates the tones of the required 18 instruments. For most composers, this is an easy decision to make. As the price of computer-generated musical recordings has decreased, the demand for human musicians has declined.

FOR CRITICAL ANALYSIS
What do you suppose has happened to the demand for string instruments used by performing musicians as a result of the decrease in the demand for musicians' services?

Suppose that a particular type of capital equipment and labor are complementary. In general, we predict the following:

> **A change in the price of a complementary input will cause the demand for labor to change in the opposite direction.**

If the price of machines goes up but they must be used with labor, fewer machines will be purchased and therefore fewer workers will be used.

DETERMINANTS OF THE SUPPLY OF LABOR Labor supply curves may shift in a particular industry for a number of reasons. For example, if wage rates for factory workers in the digital camera industry remain constant while wages for factory workers in the computer industry go up dramatically, the supply curve of factory workers in the digital camera industry will shift inward to the left as these workers move to the computer industry.

Why are highly trained divers supplying their labor to the nuclear power industry?

Many professional divers work for oil companies. They inspect oil rigs and sometimes engage in underwater repair work. Municipal governments also employ divers to repair aging bridges and water tanks and to perform lifesaving rescue missions.

Another line of work for trained divers is nuclear diving. Nuclear reactors range in size from 35 feet to 70 feet tall and 14 feet to 20 feet wide. During normal operations, reactors are partially filled with about 60,000 gallons of water to cool the nuclear fuel and to be transformed into steam to power turbines. When reactors are shut down for refueling and maintenance, primary and secondary pools are filled with

more than 500,000 gallons of water to cool them down. During these periods, divers are lowered into the pools to replace cylinders of fuel and to perform routine maintenance. Divers are attracted to nuclear diving because a diver who is certified for this specialized work earns as much as $100,000 per year, an annual salary that is higher than the salaries available in most other diving-related occupations.

FOR CRITICAL ANALYSIS
What happened to the labor supply curve in the market for nuclear divers when wages earned by divers in other industries fell relative to those available in the nuclear power industry?

Changes in working conditions in an industry can also affect its labor supply curve. If employers in the digital camera industry discover a new production technique that makes working conditions much more pleasant, the supply curve of labor to the digital camera industry will shift outward to the right.

Job flexibility also determines the position of the labor supply curve. For example, when an industry allows workers more flexibility, such as the ability to work at home via computer, the workers are likely to provide more hours of labor. That is to say, their supply curve will shift outward to the right. Some industries in which firms offer *job sharing*, particularly to people raising families, have found that the supply curve of labor has shifted outward to the right.

QUICK QUIZ   *See page 767 for the answers. Review concepts from this section in MyEconLab.*

The individual perfectly competitive firm faces a perfectly _____ labor supply curve—it can hire all the labor it wants at the going market wage rate. The industry supply curve of labor slopes _____.

By plotting an industrywide supply curve for labor and an industrywide demand curve for labor on the

same graph, we obtain the _____ wage rate in the industry.

The labor demand curve can shift because the _____ for the final product shifts, labor _____ changes, or the price of a related (_____ or _____) factor of production changes.

Labor Outsourcing, Wages, and Employment

In addition to making it easier for people to work at home, computer technology has made it possible for them to provide labor services to companies located in another country. Some companies based in Canada regularly transmit financial records—often via the Internet—to U.S. accountants so that they can process payrolls and compile income statements. Meanwhile, some U.S. manufacturers of personal computers and peripheral devices arrange for customers' calls for assistance to be directed to call centers in India, where English-speaking technical-support specialists help the customers with their problems.

A firm that employs labor located outside the country in which it is based engages in labor **outsourcing.** Canadian companies that hire U.S. accountants outsource accounting services to the United States. U.S. computer manufacturers that employ Indian call-center staff outsource technical-support services to India. How does outsourcing affect employment and wages in the United States? Who loses and who gains from outsourcing? Let's consider each of these questions in turn.

Outsourcing
A firm's employment of labor outside the country in which the firm is located.

Wage and Employment Effects of Outsourcing

Equilibrium wages and levels of employment in U.S. labor markets are determined by the demands for and supplies of labor in those markets. As you have learned, one of the determinants of the market demand for labor is the price of a substitute input. Availability of a lower-priced substitute, you also learned, causes the demand for labor to fall. Thus, the *immediate* economic effects of labor outsourcing are straightforward. When a home industry's firms can obtain *foreign* labor services that are a close substitute for *home* labor services, the demand for labor services provided by home workers will decrease. What this economic reasoning ultimately implies for U.S. labor markets, however, depends on whether we view the United States as the "home" country or the "foreign" country.

U.S. LABOR MARKET EFFECTS OF OUTSOURCING BY U.S. FIRMS To begin, let's view the United States as the home country. Suppose that initially all U.S. firms employ only U.S. workers. Then developments in computer, communications, and transportation technologies enable an increasing number of U.S. firms to regard the labor of foreign workers as a close substitute for labor provided by U.S. workers. Take a look at Figure 29-5 on the following page. Panel (a) depicts demand and supply curves in the U.S. market for workers who handle calls for technical support for U.S. manufacturers of personal computers. Suppose that before technological change makes foreign labor substitutable for U.S. labor, point E_1 is the initial equilibrium. At this point, the market wage rate in this U.S. labor market is $19 per hour.

Now suppose that improvements in communications technologies enable U.S. personal computer manufacturers to consider foreign labor as a substitute input for U.S. labor. Panel (b) displays demand and supply curves in a market for substitutable labor services in India. At the initial equilibrium point E_1, the wage rate denominated in U.S. dollars is $8 per hour. Firms in this U.S. industry will respond to the lower price of substitute labor in India by increasing their demand for labor services in that country and reducing their demand for U.S. labor. Thus, in panel (b), the market demand for the substitute labor services available in India rises. The market wage in India rises to $13 per hour, at point E_2, and Indian employment increases. In panel (a), the market demand for U.S. labor services decreases. At the new equilibrium point E_2, the U.S. market wage has fallen to $16 per hour, and equilibrium employment has decreased.

Consequently, when U.S. firms are the home firms engaging in labor outsourcing, the effects are lower wages and decreased employment in the relevant U.S. labor markets. In those nations where workers providing the outsourced labor reside, the effects are higher wages and increased employment.

How are U.S. educational tutoring services being outsourced? (See the next page.)

When U.S. firms employ the services of Indian call centers, what happens to the demand curve for suitable Indian labor and what happens to wage rates for this type of labor in India?

FIGURE 29-5

Outsourcing of U.S. Computer Technical-Support Services

Initially, the market wage for U.S. workers providing technical support for customers of U.S. computer manufacturers is $19 per hour at point E_1 in panel (a), while the market wage for Indian workers who provide the same service is $8 per hour in panel (b). Then, improvements in communications technologies enable U.S. firms to substitute away from U.S. workers in favor of Indian workers. The market demand for U.S. labor decreases in panel (a), generating a new equilibrium at point E_2 at a lower U.S. market wage and employment level. The market demand for Indian labor increases in panel (b), bringing about higher wages and employment at point E_2.

Panel (a)

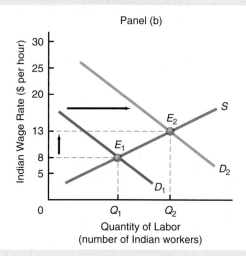

Panel (b)

To U.S. residents with access to a personal computer, a webcam, and the appropriate software, tutoring services are available from anyone willing to provide them via the Internet. Online tutoring firms based in India, such as Educomp, TutorVista, and Career Launcher, offer real-time, interactive video tutoring for students at levels ranging from elementary school through junior college. These firms charge as little as $150 per month, whereas a single session with a U.S. tutor might run as high as $100. Not surprisingly, an increasing number of U.S. parents are opting to outsource tutoring to these Indian tutoring companies.

FOR CRITICAL ANALYSIS
How does U.S. labor outsourcing help to fuel the demand for U.S. export products? (Hint: How does outsourcing by U.S. firms affect foreign workers' wage incomes, which they can use to buy items from other nations, including the United States?)

U.S. LABOR MARKET EFFECTS OF OUTSOURCING BY FOREIGN FIRMS U.S. firms are not the only companies that engage in outsourcing. Consider the Canadian companies that hire U.S. accountants to calculate their payrolls and maintain their financial records. Figure 29-6 shows the effects in the Canadian and U.S. markets for labor services provided by accountants before and after *Canadian* outsourcing of accountants' labor. At point E_1 in panel (a), before any outsourcing takes place, the initial market wage for qualified accountants in Canada is $29 per hour. In panel (b), the market wage for similarly qualified U.S. accountants is $21 per hour.

FIGURE 29-6

Outsourcing of Accounting Services by Canadian Firms

Suppose that the market wage for accounting services in Canada is initially $29 per hour, at point E_1 in panel (a), but in the United States accountants earn just $21 per hour at point E_1 in panel (b). Then, Internet access enables Canadian firms to substitute labor services provided by U.S. accountants for the services of Canadian accountants. The market demand for the services of

Canadian accountants decreases in panel (a), and at point E_2 fewer Canadian accountants are employed at a lower market wage. The market demand for U.S. accounting services increases in panel (b). This generates higher wages and employment for U.S. accountants at point E_2.

Panel (a)

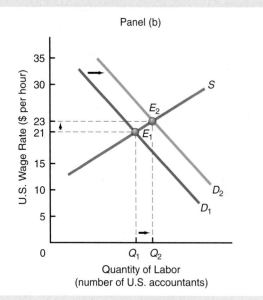

Panel (b)

After Internet access allows companies in Canada to transfer financial data electronically, the services of U.S. accountants become available as a less expensive substitute for those provided by Canadian accountants. When Canadian firms respond by seeking to outsource to U.S. accountants, the demand for U.S. accountants' labor services rises in panel (b). This causes the market wage earned by U.S. accountants to increase to $23 per hour. Canadian firms substitute away from the services of Canadian accountants, so in panel (a) the demand for the labor of accountants in Canada declines. Canadian accountants' wages decline to $26 per hour.

In contrast to the situation in which U.S. firms are the home firms engaging in labor outsourcing, when foreign firms outsource by hiring workers in the United States, wages and employment levels rise in the affected U.S. markets. In the nations where the firms engaging in outsourcing are located, the effects are lower wages and decreased employment.

Gauging the Net Effects of Outsourcing on the U.S. Economy

In the example depicted in Figure 29-5, the market wage and employment level for U.S. technical-support workers declined as a result of outsourcing by U.S. firms. In contrast, in the example shown in Figure 29-6, U.S. accountants earned higher wages and experienced increased employment as a result of outsourcing by Canadian firms. Together, these examples illustrate a fundamental conclusion concerning the short-run effects of global labor outsourcing in U.S. labor markets:

To read a Heritage Foundation lecture about the net effects of outsourcing on U.S. jobs, use the link at www.econtoday.com/chapter29.

Labor outsourcing by U.S. firms tends to reduce U.S. wages and employment. Whenever foreign firms engage in labor outsourcing in the United States, however, U.S. wages and employment increase.

Consequently, the immediate effects of increased worldwide labor outsourcing are lower wages and employment in some U.S. labor markets and higher wages and employment in others. In this narrow sense, some U.S. workers "lose" from outsourcing while others "gain," just as some Canadian workers "lose" while some Indian workers "gain."

SUMMING UP THE ECONOMIC IMPLICATIONS OF OUTSOURCING Even in the best of times, workers in labor markets experience short-run ups and downs in wages and jobs. In the United States, after all, about 4 million jobs come and go every month.

Certainly, various groups of U.S. workers earn lower pay or experience reduced employment opportunities, at least for a time, as a result of labor outsourcing. Nevertheless, outsourcing is a two-way street. Labor outsourcing does not just involve U.S. firms purchasing the labor services of residents located abroad. This phenomenon also entails the purchase of labor services from U.S. workers who provide outsourcing services to companies located in other nations.

Indeed, outsourcing really amounts to another way for residents of different nations to conduct trade with one another. As you learned in Chapter 2 (also see Chapter 33 for a more detailed look), trade allows nations' residents to specialize according to their *comparative advantages* and thereby obtain gains from exchanging items across country boundaries. To be sure, not all workers gain equally from the trade of outsourced labor services, and some people temporarily lose, in the form of either lower wages or reduced employment opportunities. Nevertheless, specialization and trade of labor services through outsourcing generate overall gains from trade for participating nations, such as India, Canada, and the United States.

You Are There

To learn about how U.S. jobs are already being created as a by-product of foreign outsourcing, read **"Reverse Outsourcing" Provides New Jobs in Ohio,** on page 761.

QUICK QUIZ *See page 767 for the answers. Review concepts from this section in MyEconLab.*

Advances in telecommunications and computer networking are making foreign labor more easily _____ for home labor, and home firms' _____ of foreign labor for home labor is known as labor **outsourcing.**

In the short run, outsourcing by U.S. firms _____ the demand for labor, market wages, and equilibrium employment in U.S. labor markets. Outsourcing by foreign firms

that hire U.S. labor _____ the demand for labor, market wages, and equilibrium employment in U.S. labor markets. The net short-run effects on U.S. wages and employment are mixed.

In the long run, outsourcing enables U.S. firms to operate more efficiently and this activity generates overall _____ _____ _____ for U.S. residents.

Monopoly in the Product Market

So far we've considered only perfectly competitive markets, both in selling the final product and in buying factors of production. We will continue our assumption that the firm purchases its factors of production in a perfectly competitive factor market. Now, however, we will assume that the firm sells its product in an *imperfectly* competitive output market. In other words, we are considering the output market structures of monopoly, oligopoly, and monopolistic competition. In all such cases, the firm, be it a monopolist, an oligopolist, or a monopolistic competitor, faces a downward-sloping demand curve for its product.

Throughout the rest of this chapter, we will simply refer to a monopoly situation for ease of analysis. The analysis holds for all industry structures that are less than perfectly competitive. In any event, the fact that our firm now faces a downward-sloping demand curve for its product means that if it wants to sell more of its product (at a uniform price), it has to lower the price, *not just on the last unit, but on all preceding units*. The *marginal revenue* received from selling an additional unit is continuously falling (and is less than price) as the firm attempts to sell more and more. This is certainly different from our earlier discussions in this chapter in which the firm could sell all it wanted at a constant price. Why? Because the firm we discussed until now was a perfect competitor.

Constructing the Monopolist's Input Demand Curve

In reconstructing our demand schedule for an input, we must account for the facts that (1) the marginal *physical* product falls because of the law of diminishing marginal product as more workers are added and (2) the price (and marginal revenue) received for the product sold also falls as more is produced and sold. That is, for the monopolist, we have to account for both the diminishing marginal physical product and the diminishing marginal revenue. Marginal revenue is always less than price for the monopolist. The marginal revenue curve always lies below the downward-sloping product demand curve.

MARGINAL REVENUE PRODUCT FOR A PERFECTLY COMPETITIVE FIRM Marginal revenue for the perfect competitor is equal to the price of the product because all units can be sold at the going market price. In our example involving the production of flash memory drives, we assumed that the perfect competitor could sell all it wanted at $10 per unit. A one-unit change in sales always led to a $10 change in total revenues. Hence, marginal revenue was always equal to $10 for that perfect competitor. Multiplying this unchanging marginal revenue by the marginal physical product of labor then yielded the perfectly competitive firm's marginal revenue product.

MARGINAL REVENUE PRODUCT FOR A MONOPOLY FIRM The monopolist, however, cannot simply calculate marginal revenue by looking at the price of the product. To sell the additional output from an additional unit of input, the monopolist has to cut prices on all previous units of output. As output is increasing, then, marginal revenue is falling. The underlying concept is, of course, the same for both the perfect competitor and the monopolist. We are asking exactly the same question in both cases: When an additional worker is hired, what is the benefit? In either case, the benefit is obviously the change in total revenues due to the one-unit change in the variable input, labor. In our discussion of the perfect competitor, we were able simply to look at the marginal physical product and multiply it by the *constant* per-unit price of the product because the price of the product never changed (for the perfect competitor, $P \equiv MR$).

A single monopolist ends up hiring fewer workers than would all of the perfectly competitive firms added together. To see this, we must consider the marginal revenue product for the monopolist, which varies with each one-unit change in the monopolist's labor input. This is what we do in panel (a) of Figure 29-7 on the next page, where

FIGURE 29-7

A Monopolist's Marginal Revenue Product

The monopolist hires just enough workers to make marginal revenue product equal to the going wage rate. If the going wage rate is $830 per week, as shown by the labor supply curve, s, in panel (b), the monopolist would want to hire approximately 10 workers per week. That is the profit-maximizing amount of labor. The labor demand curve for a perfectly competitive industry from Figure 29-4 on page 749 is also plotted (D). The monopolist's MRP curve will always be less elastic around the going wage rate than it would be if marginal revenue were constant.

Panel (a)

(1) Labor Input (workers per week)	(2) Marginal Physical Product (MPP) (flash drives per week)	(3) Price of Product (P)	(4) Marginal Revenue (MR)	(5) Marginal Revenue Product (MRP$_m$) = (2) x (4)
8	111	$11.60	$9.40	$1,043.40
9	104	11.40	9.00	936.00
10	97	11.20	8.60	834.20
11	90	11.00	8.20	738.00
12	83	10.80	7.80	647.40
13	76	10.60	7.40	562.40

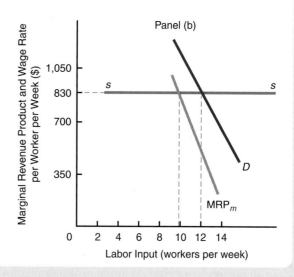

column 5, "Marginal Revenue Product," gives the monopolist a quantitative notion of how additional workers and additional production generate additional revenues. The marginal revenue product curve for this monopolist has been plotted in panel (b) of the figure. To emphasize the lower elasticity of the monopolist's MRP curve (MRP$_m$) around the wage rate $830, the labor demand curve for a perfectly competitive industry (labeled *D*) has been plotted on the same graph in Figure 29-7. Recall that this curve is not simply the sum of the marginal revenue product curves of all perfectly competitive firms, because when competitive firms together increase employment, their output expands and the product price declines. Nevertheless, at any given wage rate, the quantity of labor demanded by the monopoly is still less than the quantity of labor demanded by a perfectly competitive industry.

Why does MRP_m represent the monopolist's input demand curve? As always, our profit-maximizing monopolist will continue to hire labor as long as additional profits result. Profits are made as long as the additional cost of more workers is outweighed by the additional revenues made from selling the output of those workers. When the wage rate equals these additional revenues, the monopolist stops hiring. That is, the firm stops hiring when the wage rate is equal to the marginal revenue product because additional workers would add more to cost than to revenue.

Why the Monopolist Hires Fewer Workers

Because we have used the same numbers as in Figure 29-1 on page 743, we can see that the monopolist hires fewer workers per week than firms in a perfect competitive market would. That is to say, if we could magically change the flash memory drive industry in our example from one in which there is perfect competition in the output market to one in which there is monopoly in the output market, the amount of employment would fall. Why? Because the monopolist must take account of the declining product price that must be charged in order to sell a larger number of flash memory drives. Remember that every firm hires up to the point at which marginal benefit equals marginal cost. The marginal benefit to the monopolist of hiring an additional worker is not simply the additional output times the price of the product. Rather, the monopolist faces a reduction in the price charged on *all* units sold in order to be able to sell more.

So the monopolist ends up hiring fewer workers than all of the perfect competitors taken together, assuming that all other factors remain the same for the two hypothetical examples. But this should not come as a surprise. In considering product markets, by implication we saw that a monopolized flash memory drive industry would produce less output than a competitive one. Therefore, the monopolized industry would hire fewer workers.

The Utilization of Other Factors of Production

The analysis in this chapter has been given in terms of the demand for the variable input labor. The same analysis holds for any other variable factor input. We could have talked about the demand for fertilizer or the demand for the services of tractors by a farmer instead of the demand for labor and reached the same conclusions. The entrepreneur will hire or buy any variable input up to the point at which its price equals the marginal revenue product.

A further question remains: How much of each variable factor should the firm utilize when all the variable factors are combined to produce the product? We can answer this question by looking at either the cost-minimizing side of the question or the profit-maximizing side.

Cost Minimization and Factor Utilization

From the cost minimization point of view, how can the firm minimize its total costs for a given output? Assume that you are an entrepreneur attempting to minimize costs. Consider a hypothetical situation in which if you spend $1 more on labor, you would get 20 more units of output, but if you spend $1 more on machines, you would get only 10 more units of output. What would you want to do in such a situation? You would wish to hire more workers or sell off some of your machines, for you are not getting as much output per *last* dollar spent on machines as you are per *last* dollar spent on labor. You would want to employ factors of production so that the marginal products per last dollar spent on each are equal. Thus, the least-cost, or cost minimization, rule will be as follows:

> *To minimize total costs for a particular rate of production, the firm will hire factors of production up to the point at which the marginal physical product per last dollar spent on each factor of production is equalized.*

That is,

$$\frac{\text{MPP of labor}}{\text{price of labor}} = \frac{\text{MPP of capital}}{\text{price of capital (cost per}} = \frac{\text{MPP of land}}{\text{price of land (rental}}$$
$$\text{(wage rate)} \qquad \text{unit of service)} \qquad \text{rate per unit)}$$

All we are saying here is that the cost-minimizing firm will always utilize *all* resources in such combinations that cost will be minimized for any given output rate. This is commonly called the *least-cost combination of resources.*

What new variable resource is finding employment at hospitals?

EXAMPLE
Employing a New Nurse's Aide

Each year, the average 300-bed hospital spends about $3 million to pay employees for time they spend transporting medical instruments, medications, meals, and other items on carts along hallways and corridors. This is why hospitals are considering utilizing robots, such as the "Tug" produced by robotics firm Aethon, to perform some of these tasks. These robots wheel across floors; attach themselves to carts holding pumps, prescriptions, linen hampers, or other items; and transport the carts from one room to another according to preprogrammed sequences of steps. Currently, such robots can be leased for about $1,500 per month, so a hospital effectively pays just over $2 per hour for a robot's services. Not surprisingly, a number of hospitals are experimenting with investing in these capital resources as a way of attaining a new least-cost combination of resources.

FOR CRITICAL ANALYSIS
At the least-cost combination of hospital resources, what will be true of the marginal physical product of robot utilization divided by the hourly price of robots in relation to the marginal physical product of labor divided by the price of labor?

Profit Maximization Revisited

If a firm wants to maximize profits, how much of each factor should be hired (or bought)? As you have learned, the firm will never utilize a factor of production unless the marginal benefit from hiring that factor is at least equal to the marginal cost. What is the marginal benefit? As we have pointed out several times, the marginal benefit is the change in total revenues due to a one-unit change in utilization of the variable input. What is the marginal cost? In the case of a firm buying in a perfectly competitive market, it is the price of the variable factor—the wage rate if we are referring to labor.

The profit-maximizing combination of resources for the firm will be where, in a perfectly competitive market structure,

MRP of labor = price of labor (wage rates)

MRP of capital = price of capital (cost per unit of service)

MRP of land = price of land (rental rate per unit)

To attain maximum profits, the marginal revenue product of each of a firm's resources must be exactly equal to its price. If the MRP of labor is $20 and its price is only $15, the firm will expand its employment of labor.

There is an exact match between the profit-maximizing combination of resources and the least-cost combination of resources discussed above. In other words, either rule can be used to yield the same cost-minimizing rate of utilization of each variable resource.

QUICK QUIZ   *See page 767 for the answers. Review concepts from this section in MyEconLab.*

When a firm sells its output in a monopoly market, marginal revenue is _____ than price.

Just as the MRP is the perfectly competitive firm's input demand curve, the MRP is also the _____ input demand curve.

The profit-maximizing combination of factors will occur when each factor is used up to the point at which its MRP is equal to its unit _____.

To minimize total costs for a given output, the profit-maximizing firm will hire each factor of production up to the point at which the marginal _____ product per last dollar spent on each factor is equal to the marginal _____ product per last dollar spent on each of the other factors of production.

You Are There   "Reverse Outsourcing" Provides New Jobs in Ohio

Christy Rice has been designated senior team leader at a call center in Reno, Ohio. The call center, which employs 250 individuals to answer phones for clients such as the online travel agency Expedia, is owned by an outsourcing company called Tata Group, which is based in Mumbai, India. Although most of Tata Group's employees are based in India, it recently decided to outsource some of its operations to the United States. The company has found that many U.S. callers feel more comfortable talking to a fellow U.S. resident over the telephone. Furthermore, the outsourcing services that Tata Group provides for some U.S. firms such as Expedia require that employees have a firm grasp of U.S. geography. There is also one additional incentive. Market clearing wages for English-speaking Indian workers with skills that Tata Group and other outsourcing firms require have been increasing. Wages in Ohio, in contrast, have declined in recent years.

Rice and her co-workers are benefiting from a phenomenon called "reverse outsourcing." As wages of workers in other nations have risen, the demand for U.S. labor by outsourcing firms in those countries has increased. This is perhaps the most important reason why Tata Group and other outsourcing firms based in India have begun hiring workers located in the United States.

CRITICAL ANALYSIS QUESTIONS

1. If Indian and U.S. call center workers were equally skilled, what would you predict would gradually happen over time to the differential between the market clearing wages of call center workers in the two countries?

2. Can you think of any types of jobs that would be difficult to outsource to India?

The Narrowing Male-Female Wage Gap

CONCEPTS APPLIED

➤ Marginal Revenue Product (MRP)

➤ Derived Demand

➤ Labor Demand

Women have consistently earned lower average wages than men, even after taking into account differences in education and age, as shown in Figure 29-8. What accounts for the existence of this male-female wage gap? Even though it persists, why has it declined over time?

Explaining Why the Male-Female Pay Gap Exists

Economists have offered several rationales for the existence of a gap between the earnings of men and women. One possible reason is gender-based discrimination. Some employers may consciously choose to pay men more than women, despite laws prohibiting differential treatment of a man and a woman when both are equally qualified for a position. Another rationale is differences in skills. Suppose that men obtain more skills that generate higher marginal revenue product than women obtain. Then the derived demand for skills possessed by men will be higher, and so will men's wages, other things being equal. Furthermore, in years past, women have tended to be more likely than men to seek employment in traditionally lower-paying occupations. Indeed, to the extent that women have supplied more labor in lower-wage markets, the resulting increases in labor supply have tended to push those wages down even farther.

FIGURE 29-8

The Male-Female Wage Gap

Even after taking into account differences in education and age, there has been a persistent, albeit declining, differential between the average wages of men and women holding full-time positions.

Sources: U.S. Department of Labor; author's estimates.

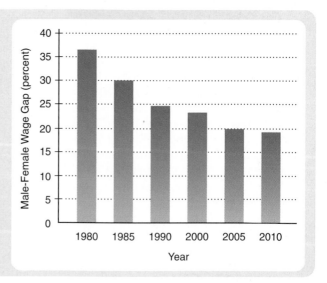

Economists have verified that an important factor accounting for the male-female wage gap is observed differences in men's and women's attachment to the labor force. On average, men are more likely than women to remain in the labor force and to be employed from year to year. As a consequence, men tend to obtain more on-the-job training and accumulate more human capital. If the growth in demand for labor in markets for high-skilled labor is greater than the growth in demand for labor in markets for lower-skilled positions, men will benefit from their more persistent involvement in the labor market by earning higher wages.

Why the Male-Female Wage Gap Has Narrowed

Although some discrimination against women undoubtedly exists in labor markets, economists argue that it should gradually dissipate over time. If firms hire men who are less qualified for positions than women, then those firms experience lower marginal revenue product and hence lower profits than firms that do not discriminate. In the long run, firms that discriminate against more highly qualified women will fail to survive in the marketplace. Hence, one possible explanation for the declining male-female wage gap is a reduction in discriminatory behavior by employers.

In all likelihood, a much more important factor, however, has been a steady increase in the skills obtained by women. Today, there are more young women than men graduating from colleges and universities. Furthermore, more young women are supplying labor in markets for traditionally higher-paying occupations, such as law and medicine. Finally, the average amount of time that women remain in the labor force has increased. Taken together, these factors explain why the male-female wage gap has continued to decline over time.

Test your understanding of this chapter by going online to **MyEconLab**.
In the Study Plan for this chapter, select Section N: News.

For Critical Analysis

1. How would a gradual increase in the percentage of fathers who stay home to care for young children while their wives continue working ultimately alter the male-female wage gap?

2. What is likely to eventually happen to the male-female wage gap if a higher percentage of college graduates continue to be women in future years?

Web Resources

1. For a detailed discussion of factors contributing to the male-female wage gap and its gradual decline, go to www.econtoday.com/chapter29.

2. To learn about the first major piece of legislation making it illegal to pay men and women differently for performing the same tasks on the job, go to www.econtoday.com/chapter29.

Research Project

Recently, officials at The Championships, Wimbledon, the annual tennis tournament, decided that their profit-maximizing strategy was to offer equal prizes to women and men. Evaluate what this decision implies about the marginal revenue products of male and female tennis players at Wimbledon. In light of your conclusion, what does this imply about tennis fans' demands for viewing tennis matches played by male and female players? (Hint: Keep in mind that the demand for the services of tennis players is derived from the fans' demand for tournament tickets.)

Here is what you should know after reading this chapter. **MyEconLab** will help you identify what you know, and where to go when you need to practice.

WHAT YOU SHOULD KNOW		WHERE TO GO TO PRACTICE
Why a Firm's Marginal Revenue Product Curve Is Its Labor Demand Curve The marginal revenue product of labor equals marginal revenue times the marginal physical product of labor. Because of the law of diminishing marginal product, for a perfectly competitive producer the marginal revenue product curve slopes downward. To maximize profits, a firm hires labor to the point where the marginal factor cost of labor—the addition to total input costs resulting from employing an additional unit of labor—equals the marginal revenue product. In a competitive labor market, the market wage rate is the marginal factor cost of labor, so profit maximization requires hiring labor to the point where the wage rate equals marginal revenue product.	marginal physical product (MPP) of labor, 742 marginal revenue product (MRP), 744 marginal factor cost (MFC), 744 **KEY FIGURES** Figure 29-1, 743 Figure 29-2, 746	• **MyEconLab** Study Plan 29.1 • Audio introduction to Chapter 29 • Animated Figures 29-1, 29-2 • ABC News Video: How Outsourcing Affects Our Lives
The Demand for Labor as a Derived Demand For firms that are perfect competitors in their product markets, marginal revenue equals the market price of their output, so the marginal revenue product of labor equals the product price times the marginal physical product of labor. As product-market conditions vary and cause the market price at which firms sell their output to change, their marginal revenue product curves shift. Hence, the demand for labor by perfectly competitive firms is derived from the demand for the final products these firms produce.	derived demand, 745	• **MyEconLab** Study Plan 29.2
Key Factors Affecting the Elasticity of Demand for Inputs The price elasticity of demand for an input, such as labor, is equal to the percentage change in the quantity of the input demanded divided by the percentage change in the price of the input, such as the wage rate. The price elasticity of demand for an input is relatively high when any one of the following is true: (1) the price elasticity of demand for the final product is relatively high; (2) it is relatively easy to substitute other inputs in production; (3) the proportion of total costs accounted for by the input is relatively large; or (4) the firm has a longer time period to adjust to the change in the input's price.	KEY FIGURE Figure 29-3, 747	• **MyEconLab** Study Plan 29.2 • Animated Figure 29-3 • Video: Determinants of Demand Elasticity for Inputs

(continued)

(continued)

WHAT YOU SHOULD KNOW		WHERE TO GO TO PRACTICE
How Equilibrium Wage Rates at Perfectly Competitive Firms Are Determined In a perfectly competitive labor market, at the equilibrium wage rate, the quantity of labor demanded by all firms is equal to the quantity of labor supplied by all workers in the marketplace. At this wage rate, each firm looks to its own labor demand curve to determine how much labor to employ.	KEY FIGURE Figure 29-4, 749	• **MyEconLab** Study Plan 29.3 • Animated Figure 29-4 • Video: Shifts in the Market Demand for Labor
U.S. Wage and Employment Effects of Labor Outsourcing Technological changes have made foreign labor more readily available as a cheaper substitute for home labor for firms that engage in labor outsourcing. The immediate, short-run effects on wages and employment in U.S. labor markets are mixed. Outsourcing by U.S. firms reduces the demand for labor in affected U.S. labor markets and thereby pushes down wages and employment. Outsourcing by foreign firms that hire U.S. labor, however, raises the demand for labor in related U.S. labor markets, which boosts U.S. wages and employment.	outsourcing, 753 KEY FIGURES Figure 29-5, 754 Figure 29-6, 755	• **MyEconLab** Study Plan 29.4 • Animated Figures 29-5, 29-6
Contrasting the Demand for Labor and Wage Determination Under Monopoly with Outcomes Under Perfect Competition If a firm that is a monopolist in its product market competes for labor in a competitive labor market, it takes the market wage rate as given. Its labor demand curve, however, lies to the left of the labor demand curve for the industry that would have arisen in a perfectly competitive industry. The reason is that marginal revenue is less than price for a monopolist, so the marginal revenue product of the monopolist is lower than under competition. Thus, at the competitively determined wage rate, a monopolized industry employs fewer workers than the industry otherwise would if it were perfectly competitive.	KEY FIGURE Figure 29-7, 758	• **MyEconLab** Study Plans 29.5, 29.6 • Animated Figure 29-7

Log in to MyEconLab, take a chapter test, and get a personalized Study Plan that tells you which concepts you understand and which ones you need to review. From there, MyEconLab will give you further practice, tutorials, animations, videos, and guided solutions.
Log in to www.myeconlab.com

PROBLEMS

All problems are assignable in ⊠ myeconlab . *Answers to the odd-numbered problems appear at the back of the book.*

29-1. The following table depicts the output of a firm that manufactures computer printers. The printers sell for $100 each.

Labor Input (workers per week)	Total Physical Output (printers per week)
10	200
11	218
12	234
13	248
14	260
15	270
16	278

Calculate the marginal physical product and marginal revenue product at each input level above 10 units.

29-2. Refer back to your answers to Problem 29-1 in answering the following questions.

   a. What is the maximum wage the firm will be willing to pay if it hires 15 workers?

   b. The weekly wage paid by computer printer manufacturers in a perfectly competitive market is $1,200. How many workers will the profit-maximizing employer hire?

   c. Suppose that there is an increase in the demand for personal computer systems. Explain the likely effects on marginal revenue product, marginal factor cost, and the number of workers hired by the firm.

29-3. Explain what happens to the elasticity of demand for labor in a given industry after each of the following events.

   a. A new manufacturing technique makes capital easier to substitute for labor.

   b. There is an increase in the number of substitutes for the final product that labor produces.

   c. After a drop in the prices of capital inputs, labor accounts for a larger portion of a firm's factor costs.

29-4. Explain how the following events would affect the demand for labor.

   a. A new education program administered by the company increases labor's marginal product.

   b. The firm completes a new plant with a larger workspace and new machinery.

29-5. The following table depicts the product market and labor market an MP3 player manufacturer faces.

Labor Input (workers per day)	Total Physical Product	Product Price ($)
10	100	50
11	109	49
12	116	48
13	121	47
14	124	46
15	125	45

   a. Calculate the firm's marginal physical product, total revenue, and marginal revenue product at each input level above 10 units.

   b. The firm competes in a perfectly competitive labor market, and the market wage it faces is $100 per worker per day. How many workers will the profit-maximizing employer hire?

29-6. Recently, there has been an increase in the market demand for products of firms in manufacturing industries. The production of many of these products requires the skills of welders. Because welding is a dirty and dangerous job compared with other occupations, in recent years fewer people have sought employment as welders. Draw a diagram of the market for the labor of welders. Use this diagram to explain the likely implications of these recent trends for the market clearing wage earned by welders and the equilibrium quantity of welding services hired.

29-7. During most of the 2000s, there was a significant increase in the price of corn-based ethanol.

   a. A key input in the production of corn-based ethanol is corn. Use an appropriate diagram to explain what likely occurred in the market for corn.

   b. In light of your answer to part (a), explain why many hog farmers, who in the past used corn as the main feed input in hog production, switched to cookies, licorice, cheese curls, candy bars, and other human snack foods instead of corn as food for their hogs.

29-8. A firm hires labor in a perfectly competitive labor market. Its current profit-maximizing hourly output is 100 units, which the firm sells at a price of $5 per unit. The marginal physical product of the last unit of labor employed is 5 units per hour. The firm pays each worker an hourly wage of $15.

    a. What marginal revenue does the firm earn from sale of the output produced by the last worker employed?

    b. Does this firm sell its output in a perfectly competitive market?

29-9. Explain why the short-term effects of outsourcing on U.S. wages and employment tend to be more ambiguous than the long-term effects.

29-10. A profit-maximizing monopolist hires workers in a perfectly competitive labor market. Employing the last worker increased the firm's total weekly output from 110 units to 111 units and caused the firm's weekly revenues to rise from $25,000 to $25,750. What is the current prevailing weekly wage rate in the labor market?

29-11. A monopoly firm hires workers in a perfectly competitive labor market in which the market wage rate is $20 per day. If the firm maximizes profit, and if the marginal revenue from the last unit of output produced by the last worker hired equals $10, what is the marginal physical product of that worker?

29-12. The current market wage rate is $10, the rental rate of land is $1,000 per unit, and the rental rate of capital is $500. Production managers at a firm find that under their current allocation of factors of production, the marginal physical product of labor is 100, the marginal physical product of land is 10,000, and the marginal physical product of capital is 4,000. Is the firm minimizing costs? Why or why not?

29-13. The current wage rate is $10, and the rental rate of capital is $500. A firm's marginal physical product of labor is 200, and its marginal physical product of capital is 20,000. Is the firm maximizing profits for the given cost outlay? Why or why not?

ECONOMICS ON THE NET

Current Trends in U.S. Labor Markets The Federal Reserve's "Beige Book," which summarizes regional economic conditions around the United States, provides a wealth of information about the current status of U.S. labor markets. This Internet application helps you assess developments in employment and wages in the United States.

Title: The Beige Book—Summary

Navigation: Go to **www.econtoday.com/chapter29** to access the home page of the Federal Reserve's Board of Governors. Click on *Monetary Policy*, and then click on *Beige Book*. Then select the report for the most recent period.

Application Read the section entitled "Prices and Wages," and answer the following questions.

1. Has overall employment been rising or falling during the most recent year? Based on what you learned in this chapter, what factors might account for this pattern? Does the Beige Book summary bear our any of these explanations for changes in U.S. employment?

2. Have U.S. workers' wages been rising or falling during the most recent year?

For Group Study and Analysis The left-hand margin of the Beige Book site lists the reports of the 12 Federal Reserve districts. Divide the class into two groups, and have each group develop brief summaries of the main conclusions of one district's report concerning employment and wages within that district. Reconvene and compare the reports. Are there pronounced regional differences?

ANSWERS TO QUICK QUIZZES

p. 746: (i) output . . . input . . . inputs . . . marginal revenue; (ii) demand for; (iii) derived . . . derived . . . shift
p. 748: (i) wage . . . price . . . downward; (ii) elasticity . . . inputs . . . costs . . . adjustment
p. 752: (i) elastic . . . upward; (ii) equilibrium; (iii) demand . . . productivity . . . substitute . . . complementary
p. 756: (i) substitutable . . . substitution; (ii) reduces . . . increases; (iii) gains from trade
p. 761: (i) less; (ii) monopolist's; (iii) price; (iv) physical . . . physical

30

Unions and Labor Market Monopoly Power

From the 1930s, Chrysler employed thousands of workers at its plant in New Castle, Indiana, and the union wages it paid them fueled the town's economy—until 2003 when Chrysler closed the plant, putting hundreds out of work. Since then, Chrysler retirees residing in the town have been worrying about whether their pension and health benefits will continue. The town's school board has even dropped "Chrysler" from the high school's name, to which it had been added in 1958 in honor of the company's founder. The experience of this town is indicative of the sea change taking place in relations between U.S. auto companies and their unionized workers. U.S. automakers have been unprofitable, and the United Auto Workers union has been struggling to maintain workers' wages and retirees' benefits. To understand the transformation under way in the U.S. auto industry, you must first learn about the economic role of unions, which is a key topic of this chapter.

After reading this chapter, you should be able to:

▶ Outline the essential history of the labor union movement

▶ Discuss the current status of labor unions

▶ Describe the basic economic goals and strategies of labor unions

▶ Evaluate the potential effects of labor unions on wages and productivity

▶ Explain how a monopsonist determines how much labor to employ and what wage rate to pay

▶ Compare wage and employment decisions by a monopsonistic firm with the choices made by firms in industries with alternative market structures

? **DID YOU KNOW THAT** the average civilian employee of the federal government receives two times the annual earnings and benefits earned by the average private worker? In 1950, the average federal government worker earned 19 percent more than a private worker, and by 1990 the differential was 50 percent. Now, the differential is 100 percent. One factor helping to boost wages earned by employees of the federal government is that an increasing percentage of them belong to **labor unions**—organizations that seek to secure economic improvements for their members. In the early 1960s, only about 10 percent of all government employees in the United States belonged to unions. Now nearly 40 percent of government workers are union members, and 46 percent of *all* U.S. union members work in the public sector.

Clearly, the labor landscape is shifting in the United States. Traditionally, one rationale for forming a union was that members might be able to earn more than they would in a competitive labor market by obtaining a type of monopoly power. Because the entire supply of a particular group of workers is controlled by a single source when a union bargains as a single entity with management, a certain monopoly element enters into the determination of employment. We can no longer talk about a perfectly competitive supply of labor. Later in the chapter, we will examine the converse—a single employer who is the sole employer of a particular group of workers.

Labor unions
Worker organizations that seek to secure economic improvements for their members; they also seek to improve the safety, health, and other benefits (such as job security) of their members.

Industrialization and Labor Unions

In most parts of the world, labor movements began with local **craft unions.** These were groups of workers in individual trades, such as shoemaking, printing, or baking. Beginning around the middle of the eighteenth century, new technologies permitted reductions in unit production costs through the formation of larger-scale enterprises that hired dozens or more workers. By the late 1790s, workers in some British craft unions began trying to convince employers to engage in **collective bargaining,** in which business management negotiates with representatives of all union members about wages and hours of work.

In 1799 and 1800, the British Parliament passed laws called the Combination Acts aimed at prohibiting the formation of unions. In 1825, Parliament enacted a replacement Combination Act allowing unions to exist and to engage in limited collective bargaining. Unions on the European continent managed to convince most governments throughout Europe to enact similar laws during the first half of the nineteenth century.

Craft unions
Labor unions composed of workers who engage in a particular trade or skill, such as baking, carpentry, or plumbing.

Collective bargaining
Negotiation between the management of a company or of a group of companies and the management of a union or a group of unions for the purpose of reaching a mutually agreeable contract that sets wages, fringe benefits, and working conditions for all employees in all the unions involved.

Unions in the United States

The development of unions in the United States lagged several decades behind events in Europe. In the years between the Civil War and World War I (1861–1914), the Knights of Labor, an organized group of both skilled and unskilled workers, pushed for an eight-hour workday and equal pay for women and men. In 1886, a dissident group split from the Knights of Labor to form the American Federation of Labor (AFL) under the leadership of Samuel Gompers. During World War I, union membership increased to more than 5 million. But after the war, the government decided to stop protecting labor's right to organize. Membership began to fall.

THE FORMATION OF INDUSTRIAL UNIONS The Great Depression was a landmark event in U.S. labor history. Franklin Roosevelt's National Industrial Recovery Act of 1933 gave labor the federal right to bargain collectively, but that act was declared

Industrial unions
Labor unions that consist of workers from a particular industry, such as automobile manufacturing or steel manufacturing.

unconstitutional. The 1935 National Labor Relations Act (NLRA), otherwise known as the Wagner Act, took its place. The NLRA guaranteed workers the right to form unions, to engage in collective bargaining, and to be members of any union.

In 1938, the Congress of Industrial Organizations (CIO) was formed by John L. Lewis, the president of the United Mine Workers. Prior to the formation of the CIO, most labor organizations were craft unions. The CIO was composed of **industrial unions,** which drew their membership from an entire industry such as steel or automobiles. In 1955, the CIO and the AFL merged because the leaders of both associations thought a merger would help organized labor grow faster.

CONGRESSIONAL CONTROL OVER LABOR UNIONS Since the Great Depression, Congress has occasionally altered the relationship between labor and management through significant legislation. One of the most important pieces of legislation was the Taft-Hartley Act of 1947 (the Labor Management Relations Act). In general, the Taft-Hartley Act outlawed certain labor practices of unions, such as imposing make-work rules and forcing unwilling workers to join a particular union. Among other things, it allowed individual states to pass their own **right-to-work laws.** A right-to-work law makes it illegal for union membership to be a requirement for continued employment in any establishment.

Right-to-work laws
Laws that make it illegal to require union membership as a condition of continuing employment in a particular firm.

Closed shop
A business enterprise in which employees must belong to the union before they can be hired and must remain in the union after they are hired.

The Taft-Hartley Act also made a **closed shop** illegal; a closed shop requires union membership before employment can be obtained. A **union shop,** however, is legal. A union shop does not require membership as a prerequisite for employment, but it can, and usually does, require that workers join the union after a specified amount of time on the job. (Even a union shop is illegal in states with right-to-work laws.)

Union shop
A business enterprise that may hire nonunion members, conditional on their joining the union by some specified date after employment begins.

Jurisdictional disputes, sympathy strikes, and secondary boycotts were also made illegal by the Taft-Hartley Act. A **jurisdictional dispute** involves two or more unions fighting (and striking) over which should have control in a particular jurisdiction. For example, should carpenters working for a steel manufacturer be members of the steelworkers' union or the carpenters' union? A **sympathy strike** occurs when one union strikes in sympathy with another union's cause or strike. For example, if the retail clerks' union in an area is striking grocery stores, Teamsters union members may refuse to deliver products to those stores in sympathy with the retail clerks' demands for higher wages or better working conditions. A **secondary boycott** is a boycott of a company that deals with a struck company. For example, if union workers strike a baking company, the boycotting of grocery stores that continue to sell that company's products is a secondary boycott. A secondary boycott brings pressure on third parties to force them to stop dealing with an employer who is being struck.

Jurisdictional dispute
A disagreement involving two or more unions over which should have control of a particular jurisdiction, such as a particular craft or skill or a particular firm or industry.

Sympathy strike
A work stoppage by a union in sympathy with another union's strike or cause.

Secondary boycott
A refusal to deal with companies or purchase products sold by companies that are dealing with a company being struck.

Perhaps the most famous aspect of the Taft-Hartley Act is its provision allowing the president to obtain a court injunction that will stop a strike for an 80-day cooling-off period if the strike is expected to imperil the nation's safety or health.

The Current Status of U.S. Labor Unions

As Figure 30-1 shows, union membership has been declining in the United States since the 1960s. At present, only about 12 percent of U.S. workers are union members. Only about 9 percent of workers in the private sector belong to unions.

A DECLINE IN MANUFACTURING EMPLOYMENT A large part of the explanation for the decline in union membership has to do with the shift away from manufacturing. In 1948, workers in manufacturing industries, transportation, and utilities, which traditionally have been among the most heavily unionized industries, constituted

Go to www.econtoday.com/chapter30 to link to the Legal Information Institute's review of all the key U.S. labor laws.

FIGURE 30-1

Decline in Union Membership

Numerically, union membership in the United States has increased dramatically since the 1930s, but as a percentage of the labor force, union membership peaked around 1960 and has been falling ever since. Most

recently, the absolute number of union members has also diminished.

Sources: L. Davis et al., *American Economic Growth* (New York: HarperCollins, 1972), p. 220; U.S. Department of Labor, Bureau of Labor Statistics.

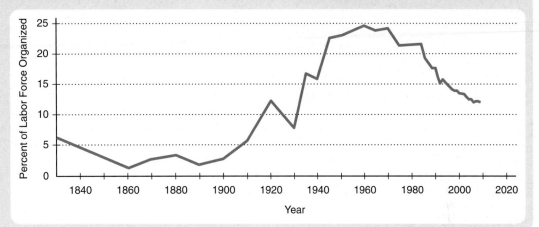

more than half of private nonagricultural employment. Today, that fraction is less than one-fifth.

The relative decline in manufacturing employment helps explain why most of the largest U.S. unions now draw their members primarily from workers in service industries and governments. As you can see in Table 30-1, five of the ten largest unions now represent workers in these areas. The remaining five largest unions represent the manufacturing industries, transportation, and utilities that once dominated the U.S. union movement.

TABLE 30-1

The Ten Largest Unions in the United States

Half of the top ten U.S. unions have members who work in service and government occupations.

Union	Industry	Members
National Education Association	Education	2,731,000
Service Employees International Union	Health care, public, and janitorial services	1,505,000
American Federation of State, County, and Municipal Employees	Government services	1,405,000
International Brotherhood of Teamsters	Trucking, delivery	1,396,000
United Food and Commercial Workers International Union	Food and grocery services	1,312,000
American Federation of Teachers	Education	829,000
United Steelworkers of America	Steel	755,000
International Brotherhood of Electrical Workers	Electrical	705,000
Laborers' International Union of North America	Construction, utilities	670,000
International Association of Machinists and Aerospace Workers	Machine and aerospace	654,000

Source: U.S. Department of Labor.

DEREGULATION AND IMMIGRATION Although the trend away from manufacturing is the main reason for the decline in unionism, the deregulation of certain industries, such as airlines and trucking, has also contributed, as has increased global competition. In addition, immigration has weakened the power of unions. Much of the unskilled and typically nonunionized work in the United States is done by foreign-born workers, and immigrant workers who are undocumented cannot legally join a union.

CHANGES IN THE STRUCTURE OF THE U.S. UNION MOVEMENT After its founding in 1955, the AFL-CIO remained the predominant labor union organization for 50 years. In 2005, however, seven unions with more than 45 percent of total AFL-CIO membership broke off to form a separate union organization called Change to Win. More recently, two construction industry unions also left the AFL-CIO and joined with ironworkers and bricklayers unions to form the National Construction Alliance.

Unions in these new umbrella groups, which represent mainly workers in growing service industries, had become frustrated because they felt that the AFL-CIO was not working hard enough to expand union membership. In addition, some of these unions were more interested than the AFL-CIO in pursuing boycotts against companies viewed as anti-union, such as Wal-Mart, and strikes against industries trying to slow the growth of union membership, such as the hotel industry.

QUICK QUIZ | *See page 790 for the answers. Review concepts from this section in MyEconLab.*

The _____ _____ of _____, composed of **craft unions**, was formed in 1886 under the leadership of Samuel Gompers. Membership increased until after World War I, when the government temporarily stopped protecting labor's right to organize.

During the Great Depression, legislation was passed that allowed for **collective bargaining**. The _____ _____ _____ Act of 1935 guaranteed workers

the right to form unions. The Congress of Industrial Organizations (CIO), composed of _____ unions, was formed during the Great Depression. The AFL and the CIO merged in 1955.

In the United States, union membership as a percentage of the labor force peaked at nearly _____ percent in 1960 and has declined since then to only about _____ percent.

Union Goals and Strategies

Through collective bargaining, unions establish the wages below which no individual worker may legally offer his or her services. Each year, union representatives and management negotiate collective bargaining contracts covering wages as well as working conditions and fringe benefits for about 6 million workers. If approved by the members, a union labor contract sets wage rates, maximum workdays, working conditions, fringe benefits, and other matters, usually for the next two or three years.

Strike: The Ultimate Bargaining Tool

Whenever union-management negotiations break down, union negotiators may turn to their ultimate bargaining tool, the threat or the reality of a strike. Strikes make headlines, but a strike occurs in less than 2 percent of all labor-management disputes before the contract is signed. In the other 98 percent, contracts are signed without much public fanfare.

The purpose of a strike is to impose costs on recalcitrant management to force it to accept the union's proposed contract terms. Strikes disrupt production and interfere with a company's or an industry's ability to sell goods and services. The strike works both ways, though, because workers receive no wages while on strike (though they may be partly compensated out of union strike funds). Striking union workers may also be eligible to draw state unemployment benefits.

The impact of a strike is closely related to the ability of striking unions to prevent nonstriking (and perhaps nonunion) employees from continuing to work for the targeted company or industry. Therefore, steps are usually taken to prevent others from working for the employer. **Strikebreakers** can effectively destroy whatever bargaining power rests behind a strike. Numerous methods have been used to prevent strikebreakers from breaking strikes. Violence has been known to erupt, almost always in connection with union attempts to prevent strikebreaking.

In recent years, companies have had less incentive to hire strikebreakers, because work stoppages have become much less common. From 1945 until 1990, on average more than 200 union strikes took place in the United States each year. Since 1990, however, the average has been closer to 25 strikes per year.

Can strikes occur in any organization whose workers are unionized? As the Brazilian central bank has learned, the answer to this question is yes.

Strikebreakers
Temporary or permanent workers hired by a company to replace union members who are striking.

Why would these Hollywood screenwriters choose to strike?

INTERNATIONAL EXAMPLE
No Pay Raise, No Data!

A recent strike by workers at the Brazilian central bank shut down many of the institution's operations for more than a month. Although a skeleton staff of nonunionized supervisors continued to perform the central bank's day-to-day monetary policy responsibilities, its regulatory and data-processing departments experienced significant slowdowns. Production of weekly and monthly statistical reports halted, leaving those seeking the latest information about the state of Brazil's financial system and economy in the dark. When workers settled for a 10 percent pay increase spread over two years instead of the 15 percent raise they had been demanding, financial and economic data began to flow once more.

FOR CRITICAL ANALYSIS
Why do you suppose that Brazil's central bank and most other unionized organizations always make sure that their nonunionized personnel are trained to operate their organizations' core functions?

Union Goals with Direct Wage Setting

We have already pointed out that one of the goals of unions is to set minimum wages. The effects of setting a wage rate higher than a competitive market clearing wage rate can be seen in Figure 30-2 on the next page. The market for labor is perfectly competitive. The market demand curve is D, and the market supply curve is S. The market clearing wage rate is W_e. The equilibrium quantity of labor is Q_e. If the union establishes by collective bargaining a minimum wage rate that exceeds W_e, an excess quantity of labor will be supplied (assuming no change in the labor demand schedule). If the minimum wage established by union collective bargaining is W_U, the quantity supplied will be Q_S. The quantity demanded will be Q_D. The difference is the excess quantity supplied, or surplus. Hence, the following point becomes clear:

One of the major roles of a union that establishes a wage rate above the market clearing wage rate is to ration available jobs among the excess number of workers who wish to work in the unionized industry.

FIGURE 30-2

Unions Must Ration Jobs

The market clearing wage rate is W_e, at point E, at which the equilibrium quantity of labor is Q_e. If the union succeeds in obtaining wage rate W_U, the quantity of labor demanded will be Q_D, at point A on the labor demand curve, but the quantity of labor supplied will be Q_S, at point B on the labor supply curve. The union must ration a limited number of jobs among a greater number of workers; the surplus of labor is equivalent to a shortage of jobs at that wage rate.

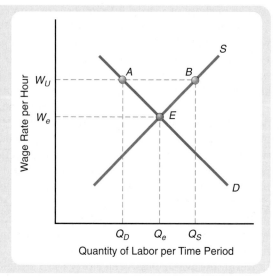

Note also that the surplus of labor is equivalent to a shortage of jobs at wage rates above equilibrium.

To ration jobs, the union may use a seniority system, lengthen the apprenticeship period to discourage potential members from joining, or institute other rationing methods. This has the effect of shifting the supply of labor curve to the left in order to support the higher wage, W_U.

There is a trade-off here that any union's leadership must face: Higher wages inevitably mean a reduction in total union employment—fewer union positions. When facing higher wages, management may replace part of the workforce with machinery or may even seek to hire nonunion workers.

If we view unions as monopoly sellers of a service, we can identify three different types of goals that they may pursue: ensuring employment for all members of the union, maximizing aggregate income of workers, and maximizing wage rates for some workers.

EMPLOYING ALL MEMBERS IN THE UNION Assume that the union has Q_1 workers. If it faces a labor demand curve such as D in Figure 30-3, the only way it can "sell" all of those workers' services is to accept a wage rate of W_1. This is similar to any other market. The demand curve tells the maximum price that can be charged to sell any particular quantity of a good or service. Here the service happens to be labor.

MAXIMIZING MEMBER INCOME If the union is interested in maximizing the gross income of its members, it will normally want a smaller membership than Q_1—namely, Q_2 workers, all employed and paid a wage rate of W_2. The aggregate income to all members of the union is represented by the wages of only the ones who work. Total income earned by union members is maximized where the price elasticity of demand is numerically equal to 1. That occurs where marginal revenue equals zero. In Figure 30-3, marginal revenue equals zero at a quantity of labor Q_2. So we know that if the union obtains a wage rate equal to W_2, and therefore Q_2 workers are demanded, the total income to the union membership will be maximized. In other words, $Q_2 \times W_2$ (the blue-shaded area) will be greater than any other combination of

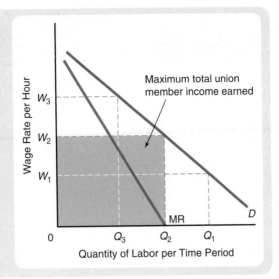

FIGURE 30-3

What Do Unions Maximize?

Assume that the union wants to employ all its Q_1 members. It will attempt to get wage rate W_1. If the union wants to maximize total wage receipts (income) of members who have jobs in this industry, it will do so at wage rate W_2, where the elasticity of the demand for labor is equal to 1. (The blue-shaded area represents the maximum total income that the union membership would earn at W_2.) If the union wants to maximize the wage rate for a given number of workers, say, Q_3, it will set the wage rate at W_3.

wage rates and quantities of union workers demanded. It is, for example, greater than $Q_1 \times W_1$. Note that in this situation, if the union started out with Q_1 members, there would be $Q_1 - Q_2$ members out of *union* work at the wage rate W_2. (Those out of union work either remain unemployed or go to other industries. Such actions have a depressing effect on wages in nonunion industries due to the increase in supply of workers there.)

MAXIMIZING WAGE RATES FOR CERTAIN WORKERS Assume that the union wants to maximize the wage rates for some of its workers—perhaps those with the most seniority. If it wants to maximize the wage rate for a given quantity of workers, Q_3, it will seek to obtain a wage rate of W_3. This will require deciding which workers should be unemployed and which workers should work and for how long each week or each year they should be employed.

Union Strategies to Raise Wages Indirectly

One way or another, unions seek above-market wages for some or all of their members. Sometimes unions try to achieve this goal without making wage increases direct features of contract negotiations.

LIMITING ENTRY OVER TIME One way to raise wage rates without specifically setting wages is for a union to limit the size of its membership to the size of its employed workforce at the time the union was first organized. No workers are put out of work when the union is formed. Over time, as the demand for labor in the industry increases, the union prevents any net increase in membership, so larger wage increases are obtained than would otherwise be the case. We see this in Figure 30-4 on the following page. In this example, union members freeze entry into their union, thereby obtaining a wage rate of $21 per hour instead of allowing a wage rate of $20 per hour with no restriction on labor supply.

How have longshoremen's unions used their control over key technologies to restrict the supply of labor at U.S. ports?

EXAMPLE
Longshoremen's Unions Win Control over Key Technologies

Recently, two longshoremen's unions, the International Longshoremen's Association on the U.S. East Coast and the International Longshore and Warehouse Union on the West Coast, won an important negotiation victory. The unions received authorization to develop and implement software that governs the filling of shipping containers and the use of global positioning systems for tracking cargoes. Through their control over this technology, they can determine who receives training in its use and thereby effectively control entry into workforces at most U.S. port facilities.

FOR CRITICAL ANALYSIS
Why does the ability to restrict the supply of labor tend to push up the wages of employed members of longshoremen's unions?

FIGURE 30-4

Restricting Supply over Time

When the union was formed, it didn't affect wage rates or employment, which remained at $19 and Q_1 (the equilibrium wage rate and quantity at point E_1). However, as demand increased—that is, as the demand schedule shifted outward from D_1 to D_2 —the union restricted membership to its original level of Q_1. The new supply curve is S_1S_2, which intersects D_2 at E_2, or at a wage rate of $21. Without the union, equilibrium would be at E_3, with a wage rate of $20 and employment of Q_2.

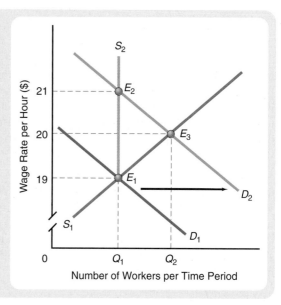

ALTERING THE DEMAND FOR UNION LABOR Another way that unions can increase wages is to shift the demand curve for labor outward to the right. This approach has the advantage of increasing both wage rates and the employment level. The demand for union labor can be increased by increasing worker productivity, increasing the demand for union-made goods, and decreasing the demand for non-union-made goods.

1. *Increasing worker productivity.* Supporters of unions have argued that unions provide a good system of industrial jurisprudence. The presence of unions may induce workers to feel that they are working in fair and just circumstances. If so, they work harder, increasing labor productivity. Productivity is also increased when unions resolve differences and reduce conflicts between workers and management, thereby providing a more peaceful administrative environment.

2. *Increasing demand for union-made goods.* Because the demand for labor is a derived demand, a rise in the demand for products produced by union labor will increase the demand for union labor itself. One way that unions attempt to increase the

demand for goods produced by union labor is by advertising "Look for the union label."

3. *Decreasing the demand for non-union-made goods.* When the demand for goods that are competing with (or are substitutes for) union-made goods is reduced, consumers shift to union-made goods, increasing the demand. The campaigns of various unions against buying foreign imports are a good example. The result is greater demand for goods "made in the USA," which in turn presumably increases the demand for U.S. union (and nonunion) labor.

How is a union trying to reduce the demand for products sold by nonunionized Wal-Mart?

EXAMPLE
Advertising Against Wal-Mart

The United Food and Commercial Workers union operates a Web site called WakeUpWal-Mart.com, through which it seeks to dissuade consumers from shopping at Wal-Mart, which hires nonunion labor. Recently, the union took its anti-Wal-Mart efforts a step farther by financing television ads criticizing the retailer's more than $35 billion in annual purchases of goods from China as "just not American." The union hoped that identifying

Wal-Mart as a company that buys non-U.S.-made goods would discourage people from shopping at the retailer's nonunion stores.

FOR CRITICAL ANALYSIS
What does the United Food and Commercial Workers union seek to gain from trying to convince people to stop shopping at Wal-Mart?

Economic Effects of Labor Unions

Today, the most heavily unionized occupations are government service, transportation and material moving, and construction. Do union members in these and other occupations earn higher wages? Are they more or less productive than nonunionized workers in their industries? What are the broader economic effects of unionization? Let's consider each of these questions in turn.

Unions and Wages

You have learned that unions are able to raise the wages of their members if they can successfully limit the supply of labor in a particular industry. Unions are also able to raise wages if they can induce increases in the demand for union labor.

Economists have extensively studied the differences between union wages and nonunion wages. They have found that the average *hourly* wage earned by a typical private-sector union worker is about $2.25 higher than the hourly wage earned by a typical worker who is not a union member. Adjusted for inflation, this union-nonunion hourly wage differential is only about half as large as it was two decades ago, however.

Comparisons of the *annual* earnings of union and nonunion workers indicate that in recent years, unions have not succeeded in raising the annual incomes of their members. In 1985, workers who belonged to unions earned nearly 7 percent more per year than nonunion workers, even though union workers worked fewer hours per week. Today, a typical nonunion employee still works slightly longer each week, but the average nonunion worker also has a higher annual income than the average union worker.

Even the $2.25 hourly wage differential already mentioned is somewhat misleading because it is an average across *all* U.S. workers. In the private sector, union workers earn only about 4 percent more than nonunion workers, or a little less than 60 cents per hour. The hourly wage gain for government workers is more than six times higher at about $3.55 per hour. A state government employee who belongs to a union currently earns an hourly wage more than 20 percent higher than a state government worker who is not a union member.

Unions and Labor Productivity

A traditional view of union behavior is that unions decrease productivity by artificially shifting the demand curve for union labor outward through excessive staffing and make-work requirements. For example, some economists have traditionally argued that unions tend to bargain for excessive use of workers, as when an airline union requires an engineer on all flights. This is called **featherbedding.** Many painters' unions, for example, resisted the use of paint sprayers and required that their members use only brushes. They even specified the maximum width of the brush. Moreover, whenever a union strikes, productivity drops, and this reduction in productivity in one sector of the economy can spill over into other sectors.

Featherbedding
Any practice that forces employers to use more labor than they would otherwise or to use existing labor in an inefficient manner.

Economic Benefits and Costs of Labor Unions

As should be clear by now, there are two opposing views of unions. One sees them as monopolies whose main effect is to raise the wage rate of high-seniority members at the expense of low-seniority members (and nonunion workers). The other contends that unions can increase labor productivity by promoting safer working conditions and generally better work environments and that they contribute to workforce stability by providing arbitration and grievance procedures.

Critics point out that the positive view of unionism overlooks the fact that many of the benefits that unions provide do not require that unions engage in restrictive labor practices, such as the closed shop. Unions could still provide benefits for their members without restricting the labor market.

Consequently, a key issue that economists seek to assess when judging the social costs of unions is the extent to which their existence has a negative effect on employment growth. Most evidence indicates that while unions do significantly reduce employment in some of the most heavily unionized occupations, the overall effects on U.S. employment are modest. On the whole, therefore, the social costs of unions in the U.S. private sector are probably relatively low.

QUICK QUIZ   *See page 790 for the answers. Review concepts from this section in MyEconLab.*

When unions set wage rates _____ market clearing prices, they face the problem of _____ a restricted number of jobs to workers who desire to earn the higher wages.

Unions may pursue any one of three goals: (1) to employ _____ union members, (2) to maximize total _____ of the union's members, or (3) to _____ wages for certain, usually high-seniority, workers.

Unions can increase the wage rate of members by engaging in practices that shift the union labor supply curve _____ or shift the demand curve for union labor _____ (or both).

Some economists believe that unions can increase _____ by promoting safer working conditions and generally better work environments.

Monopsony: A Buyer's Monopoly

Let's assume that a firm is a perfect competitor in the product market. The firm cannot alter the price of the product it sells, and it faces a perfectly elastic demand curve for its product. We also assume that the firm is the only buyer of a particular input. Although this situation may not occur often, it is useful to consider. Let's think in terms of a factory town, like those dominated by textile mills or those in the mining industry. One company not only hires the workers but also owns the businesses in the community, owns the apartments that workers live in, and hires the clerks, waiters, and all other personnel. This buyer of labor is called a **monopsonist,** the only buyer in the market.

What does this situation mean to a monopsonist in terms of the costs of hiring extra workers? It means that if the monopsonist wants to hire more workers, it has to offer higher wages. Our monopsonist firm cannot hire all the labor it wants at the going wage rate. Instead, it faces an upward-sloping supply curve. If it wants to hire more workers, it has to raise wage rates, including the wages of all its current workers (assuming a non-wage-discriminating monopsonist). It therefore has to take account of these increased costs when deciding how many more workers to hire.

Monopsonist
The only buyer in a market.

You Are There

To learn about how Chinese consumers regularly band together in an effort to act as a single monopsony buyer, read **In China, Consumers Seek to Act Together as a Monopsonist,** on page 784.

Marginal Factor Cost

The monopsonist faces an upward-sloping supply curve of the input in question because as the only buyer, it faces the entire market supply curve. Each time the monopsonist buyer of labor, for example, wishes to hire more workers, it must raise wage rates. Thus, the marginal cost of another unit of labor is rising. In fact, the marginal cost of increasing its workforce will always be greater than the wage rate. This is because the monopsonist must pay the same wage rate to everyone in order to obtain another unit of labor; thus, the higher wage rate has to be offered not only to the last worker but also to *all* its other workers. We call the additional cost to the monopsonist of hiring one more worker the marginal factor cost (MFC).

The marginal factor cost of hiring the last worker is therefore that worker's wages plus the increase in the wages of all other existing workers. As we pointed out in Chapter 29, marginal factor cost is equal to the change in total variable costs due to a one-unit change in the one variable factor of production—in this case, labor. In Chapter 29, marginal factor cost was simply the competitive wage rate because the employer could hire all workers at the same wage rate.

Derivation of a Marginal Factor Cost Curve

Panel (a) of Figure 30-5 on the following page shows the quantity of labor purchased, the wage rate per hour, the total cost of the quantity of labor supplied per hour, and the marginal factor cost per hour for the additional labor bought.

We translate the columns from panel (a) to the graph in panel (b) of the figure. We show the supply curve as *S*, which is taken from columns 1 and 2. (Note that this is the same as the *average* factor cost curve. Hence, you can view Figure 30-5 as showing the relationship between average factor cost and marginal factor cost.) The marginal factor cost curve (MFC) is taken from columns 1 and 4. The MFC curve must be above the supply curve whenever the supply curve is upward sloping. If the supply curve is upward sloping, the firm must pay a higher wage rate in order to attract a larger amount of labor. This higher wage rate must be paid to all workers; thus, the increase in total costs due to an increase in the labor input will exceed the wage rate.

FIGURE 30-5

Derivation of a Marginal Factor Cost Curve

The supply curve, *S*, in panel (b) is taken from columns 1 and 2 of panel (a). The marginal factor cost curve (MFC) is taken from columns 1 and 4. It is the increase in the total wage bill resulting from a one-unit increase in labor input.

Panel (a)

(1) Quantity of Labor Supplied to Management	(2) Required Hourly Wage Rate	(3) Total Wage Bill (3) = (1) x (2)	(4) Marginal Factor Cost (MFC) = Change in (3) / Change in (1)
0	—	—	
			$12
1	$12	$12	
			16
2	14	28	
			20
3	16	48	
			24
4	18	72	
			28
5	20	100	
			32
6	22	132	

(Recall from Chapter 29 that in a perfectly competitive input market, the supply curve facing the firm is perfectly elastic and the marginal factor cost curve is identical to the supply curve.)

Employment and Wages Under Monopsony

To determine the number of workers that a monopsonist desires to hire, we compare the marginal benefit to the marginal cost of each hiring decision. The marginal cost

FIGURE 30-6

Wage and Employment Determination for a Monopsonist

The monopsonist firm looks at a marginal cost curve, MFC, that slopes upward and lies above its labor supply curve, S. The marginal benefit of hiring additional workers is given by the firm's MRP curve (its demand-for-labor curve). The intersection of MFC with MRP, at point A, determines the number of workers hired. The firm hires Q_m workers but has to pay them only W_m in order to attract them.

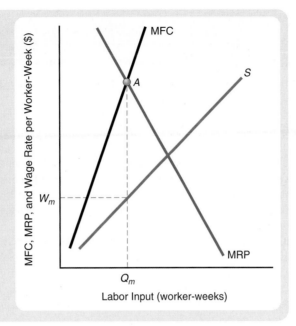

is the marginal factor cost (MFC) curve, and the marginal benefit is the marginal revenue product (MRP) curve. In Figure 30-6, we assume competition in the output market and monopsony in the input market. A monopsonist finds its profit-maximizing quantity of labor demanded at A, where the marginal revenue product is just equal to the marginal factor cost. The monopsonist will therefore desire to hire exactly Q_m workers.

THE INPUT PRICE PAID BY A MONOPSONY How much is the firm going to pay these workers? The monopsonist sets the wage rate so that it will get exactly the quantity, Q_m, supplied to it by its "captive" labor force. We find that wage rate is W_m. There is no reason to pay the workers any more than W_m because at that wage rate, the firm can get exactly the quantity it wants. The actual quantity used is determined by the intersection of the marginal factor cost curve and the marginal revenue product curve for labor—that is, at the point at which the marginal revenue from expanding employment just equals the marginal cost of doing so (point A in Figure 30-6).

Notice that the profit-maximizing wage rate paid to workers (W_m) is lower than the marginal revenue product. That is to say, workers are paid a wage that is less than their contribution to the monopsonist's revenues. This is sometimes referred to as **monopsonistic exploitation** of labor.

You learned in Chapter 4 that in a perfectly competitive labor market, establishing a minimum wage rate above the market clearing wage rate causes employers to reduce the quantity of labor demanded, resulting in a decline in employment. What happens if a minimum wage rate is established above the wage rate that a *monopsony* would otherwise pay its workers?

Monopsonistic exploitation
Paying a price for the variable input that is less than its marginal revenue product; the difference between marginal revenue product and the wage rate.

POLICY EXAMPLE
Can Minimum Wage Laws Ever Boost Employment?

How does a monopsony respond to a minimum wage law that sets a wage floor above the wage rate it otherwise would pay its workers? Figure 30-7 provides the answer to this question. In the figure, the entire upward-sloping curve labeled S is the labor supply curve in the absence of a minimum wage. Given the associated MFC curve and the firm's MRP curve, Q_m is the quantity of labor hired by a monopsony in the absence of a minimum wage law. The profit-maximizing wage rate is W_m. If the government establishes a minimum wage equal to W_{min}, however, then the supply of labor to the firm becomes horizontal at the minimum wage and includes only the upward-sloping portion of the curve S above this legal minimum. In addition, the wage rate W_{min} becomes the monopsonist's marginal factor cost along the horizontal portion of this new labor supply curve, because when the firm hires one more unit of labor, it must pay each unit of labor the same wage rate, W_{min}.

To maximize its economic profits under the minimum wage, the monopsony equalizes the minimum wage rate with marginal revenue product and hires Q_{min} units of labor. This quantity exceeds the amount of labor, Q_m, that the monopsony would have hired in the absence of the minimum wage law. Thus, establishing a minimum wage can generate a rise in employment at a monopsony firm.

FOR CRITICAL ANALYSIS
If a government establishes a minimum wage law covering all firms within its jurisdiction, including firms operating in both perfectly competitive and monopsonistic labor markets, will overall employment necessarily increase?

FIGURE 30-7

A Monopsony's Response to a Minimum Wage

In the absence of a minimum wage law, a monopsony faces the upward-sloping labor supply curve, S, and the marginal factor cost curve, MFC. To maximize its profits, the monopsony hires Q_m units of labor, at which MFC is equal to MRP, and it pays the wage rate W_m. Once the minimum wage rate, W_{min}, is established, the supply of labor becomes horizontal at the minimum wage and includes only the upward-sloping portion of the labor supply curve above this legal minimum. Because the monopsony must pay the same wage rate W_{min} for each unit of labor along this horizontal portion of the new labor supply curve, its marginal factor cost is also equal to the minimum wage rate, W_{min}. Thus, the monopsony hires Q_{min} units of labor. Employment at the monopsony firm increases.

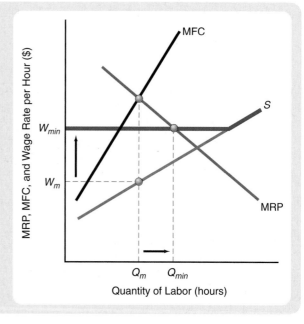

BILATERAL MONOPOLY We have studied the pricing of labor in various situations, including perfect competition in both the output and input markets and monopoly in both the output and input markets. Figure 30-8 shows four possible situations graphically.

The organization of workers into a union normally creates a monopoly supplier of labor, which gives the union some power to bargain for higher wages. What happens when a monopsonist meets a monopolist? This situation is called **bilateral monopoly,** defined as a market structure in which a single buyer faces a single seller. An example of bilateral monopoly is a county education employer facing a single teachers' union

Bilateral monopoly
A market structure consisting of a monopolist and a monopsonist.

FIGURE 30-8

Pricing and Employment Under Various Market Conditions

In panel (a), the firm operates in perfect competition in both the input and output markets. It purchases labor up to the point where the going rate W_e is equal to MRP_c. It hires quantity Q_e of labor. In panel (b), the firm is a perfect competitor in the input market but has a monopoly in the output market. It purchases labor up to the point where W_e is equal to MRP_m. In panel (c), the firm is a monopsonist in the input market and a perfect competitor in the output market. It hires labor up to the point where $MFC = MRP_c$. It will hire quantity Q_1 and pay wage rate W_c. Panel (d) shows a situation in which the firm is both a monopolist in the market for its output and a monopsonist in its labor market. It hires the quantity of labor Q_2 at which $MFC = MRP_m$ and pays the wage rate W_m.

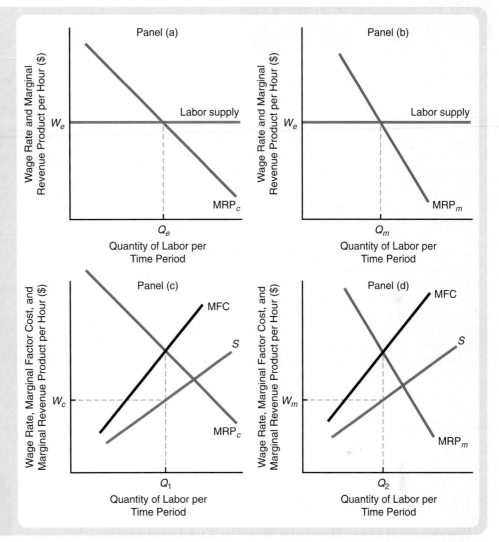

in that labor market. Another example is a players' union facing an organized group of team owners, as has occurred in professional baseball and football. To analyze bilateral monopoly, we would have to look at the interaction of both sides, buyer and seller. The price outcome turns out to be indeterminate.

QUICK QUIZ   *See page 790 for the answers. Review concepts from this section in MyEconLab.*

A **monopsonist** is the _____ _____ in a market. The monopsonist faces an _____-sloping supply curve of labor.

Because the monopsonist faces an _____-sloping supply curve of labor, the marginal factor cost of increasing the labor input by one unit is _____ than the wage

rate. Thus, the marginal factor cost curve always lies _____ the supply curve.

A monopsonist will hire workers up to the point at which marginal _____ cost equals marginal _____ product. Then the monopsonist will find the lowest necessary wage to attract that number of workers, as indicated by the supply curve.

You Are There

In China, Consumers Seek to Act Together as a Monopsonist

Zhang Qinyong, the owner of a kitchen-cabinetry shop in Suzhou, China, a city not far from Shanghai, finds himself cornered against his display cabinets by an organized team of about 20 shoppers. For more than an hour, he tries to convince the group that the products in his store are worth the tagged prices. "Forget quality. Let's talk about price," one member of the team snaps, and others join in, demanding 35 percent off the ticketed prices.

Haggling over prices is a tradition in China. Now, many Chinese consumers have taken the practice to a new level by engaging in *tuangou*, or "team buying." Via Internet chat rooms or organized Web sites such as 51tuangou.com and Teambuy.com, they organize mobs of people to descend, sometimes unannounced, on retail establishments that sell items such as kitchen appliances. These large groups often spend hours in retailers' stores. Sometimes the presence of a mob of *tuangou* members scares away other shoppers, but at other times the regular shoppers join forces with the buying team. Either outcome makes the buying team the

retailer's only shoppers for an extended period, and the team members join together in calling for group price cuts on items on display. In this way, the buying team members seek to act as a single buyer and obtain a lower price for items sold by the retailer. The buying teams often secure discounts ranging from 10 percent to 30 percent on kitchen gadgets, ovens, and other goods that the teams regard as inputs in household production.

CRITICAL ANALYSIS QUESTIONS

1. During the period of time that the only shoppers in a retail store are the members of a buying team, what is true of the marginal factor cost curve in relation to the supply curve for an item offered for sale by the retailer?

2. In what respects is the behavior of a monopsonistic buying team in China analogous to the behavior of a cartel, as discussed in Chapter 27?

Can the U.S. Auto Industry and the United Auto Workers Union Remain Viable Enterprises?

Issues and Applications

CONCEPTS APPLIED

- Industrial Unions
- Collective Bargaining
- Union Goals and Strategies

For the past several years, U.S. automakers have struggled to remain profitable. Beginning in the late 1990s, General Motors, Ford, and Chrysler have all experienced prolonged intervals of U.S. losses punctuated by a few promising but short-lived bursts of profitability. By the mid-2000s, it was clear to all in the auto industry, including its industrial union, the United Auto Workers (UAW), that significant changes would be necessary if U.S. automakers were to survive.

The Good Old Days for the UAW

From the 1950s through the 1970s, collective bargaining between the three major U.S. automakers and the UAW produced negotiated agreements that were the envy of most other U.S. unions. Before health and dental insurance became commonplace in numerous U.S. industries, the auto industry led the way in offering such benefits. U.S. auto companies and the UAW also negotiated generous pension plans for employees.

By the mid-1970s, UAW members received pay and benefits packages that ranked among the best available to U.S. unskilled and semiskilled workers. Very few U.S. workers who were members of other unions had negotiated packages that came close to those of UAW members.

Foreign Competition Becomes Domestic Competition

Starting in the 1980s, however, competitive pressures on automakers began to build. Quality improvements by foreign automakers induced U.S. consumers to substitute away from U.S.-manufactured vehicles in favor of imported vehicles manufactured by foreign firms such as Toyota, Honda, and BMW.

Then, in the 1990s, these and other foreign automakers, such as Mercedes and Subaru, began opening production facilities in the United States. In contrast to their U.S. competitors, foreign firms hired mostly nonunion labor to produce their vehicles.

Mounting "Legacy Costs" Associated with Union Workforces

Soon, the wage and benefits packages received by UAW workers translated into a competitive disadvantage for U.S. automakers. For instance, the higher average wages paid to UAW workers caused per-vehicle production costs to be nearly $300 higher for U.S. automakers than for Toyota. In addition, the average UAW worker received at least 10 more days of vacation than a worker in a U.S. Toyota plant, adding another $140 to U.S. firms' per-vehicle costs relative to those incurred by Toyota. A UAW worker even had about 16 minutes more break time per vehicle produced, pushing U.S. automakers' costs an additional $20 per vehicle above Toyota's.

Expenses related to all those UAW health and pension benefits, however, accounted for U.S. automakers' primary cost disadvantage relative to foreign firms. These benefits, which automakers call "legacy costs," were so generous that they increased the per-vehicle cost differential between U.S. automakers and Toyota by about $600. When other factors, such as inefficient production techniques, were taken into account, U.S. firms spent about $1,700 more to produce a vehicle than Toyota did.

A Period of Readjustment Commences

By the mid-2000s, following several years of meager or negative profitability in the United States, General Motors, Ford, and Chrysler were all experiencing severe financial difficulties. All three companies had responded by slashing slow-selling vehicle brands, closing plants, and terminating the employment of thousands of workers. When the time came for the UAW to renegotiate new four-year contracts with these U.S. firms, the issue was not how much more the UAW could achieve. It was which wage and benefit advantages the UAW could successfully retain for remaining autoworkers and for retirees who outnumbered active workers by nearly three to one. Faced with a dwindling demand for its membership, the UAW had to plot new strategies in light of its two-part goal to retain current working members while protecting the benefits of retired members.

In the end, the UAW showed that it valued job retention more highly than wages. It agreed to nearly 50 percent wage reductions for newly hired workers in exchange for maintaining the wage levels of senior employees. The most significant aspect of the new UAW contracts, however, was an agreement by U.S. automakers to transmit lump sums amounting to tens of billions of dollars to health care trusts. These trusts, managed by the UAW, will use interest earnings from all the funds set aside by automakers to provide health care benefits to retired workers. Thus, the UAW saved jobs for current workers—albeit at lower wages in the future—and protected the benefits of its retired members. At the same time, U.S. automakers accepted higher costs in the present in exchange for lower costs in the future that they hope will enable them to better compete with foreign firms.

Test your understanding of this chapter by going online to **MyEconLab.**
In the Study Plan for this chapter, select Section N: News.

For Critical Analysis

1. To U.S. automakers, are costs of retiree benefits variable costs or fixed costs?

2. How will the lower negotiated wages of newly employed autoworkers likely affect future employment at U.S. automakers, other things being equal?

Web Resources

1. To find out more about the United Auto Workers, go to www.econtoday.com/chapter30.

2. To learn more about the specifics of the current UAW agreement with Ford Motor Company, go to www.econtoday.com/chapter30.

Research Project

Do the UAW's objectives appear to correspond to any single goal discussed in this chapter? Or has the union sought to satisfy more than one goal as well as it could under the circumstances? Take a stand, and support your answer.

Here is what you should know after reading this chapter. **MyEconLab** will help you identify what you know, and where to go when you need to practice.

WHAT YOU SHOULD KNOW

Labor Unions The first labor unions were craft unions, representing workers in specific trades. In the United States, the American Federation of Labor (AFL) emerged in the late nineteenth century. In 1935, the National Labor Relations Act (or Wagner Act) granted workers the right to form unions and bargain collectively. Industrial unions, which represent workers of specific industries, formed the Congress of Industrial Organizations (CIO) in 1938, and in 1955 a merger formed the AFL-CIO. The Taft-Hartley Act of 1947 placed limitations on unions' rights to organize, strike, and boycott.

labor unions, 769
craft unions, 769
collective bargaining, 769
industrial unions, 770
right-to-work laws, 770
closed shop, 770
union shop, 770
jurisdictional dispute, 770
sympathy strike, 770
secondary boycott, 770

The Current Status of Labor Unions In recent years, overall U.S. union membership has decreased. A key reason for the decline in U.S. union membership rates is undoubtedly the relative decline in manufacturing jobs as a share of total employment. In addition, in less skilled occupations that would otherwise be attractive to union organizers, many workers are undocumented and foreign-born (i.e., illegal immigrants). Greater domestic and global competition has probably also had a part in bringing about a decline in unions in the United States.

WHERE TO GO TO PRACTICE

- **MyEconLab** Study Plan 30.1
- Audio introduction to Chapter 30

- **MyEconLab** Study Plan 30.1

(continued)

(continued)

WHAT YOU SHOULD KNOW		WHERE TO GO TO PRACTICE

Basic Goals and Strategies of Labor Unions A key goal of most unions is to achieve higher wages. Often this entails bargaining for wages above competitive levels, which produces surplus labor. Thus, a major task of many unions is to ration available jobs among the excess number of individuals who desire to work at the wages established by collective bargaining agreements. One strategy that unions often use to address this trade-off between wages and the number of jobs is to maximize the total income of members. If the focus of union objectives is the well-being of current members only, the union may bargain for limits on entry of new workers and seek to maximize the wages of current union members only. Another way for unions to try to push up wages is to try to increase worker productivity and lobby consumers to increase their demands for union-produced goods and reduce their demands for goods produced by nonunionized industries.

strikebreakers, 773

KEY FIGURES
Figure 30-2, 774
Figure 30-3, 775
Figure 30-4, 776

- **MyEconLab** Study Plan 30.2
- Video: Union Goals
- Animated Figures 30-2, 30-3, 30-4

Effects of Labor Unions on Wages and Productivity Economists have found that hourly wages of unionized workers are typically higher than those of workers who are not union members. On average, union hourly wages are about $2.25 higher than wages of nonunionized workers. Because unionized employees typically work fewer hours per year, however, their average annual earnings are lower than those of nonunionized employees. It is less clear how unions affect worker productivity. On the one hand, some collective bargaining rules specifying how jobs are performed appear to reduce productivity. On the other hand, unionization promotes generally better work environments, which may enhance productivity.

featherbedding, 778

- **MyEconLab** Study Plan 30.3
- Video: The Benefits of Labor Unions

How a Monopsonist Determines How Much Labor to Employ and What Wage Rate to Pay A monopsony is the only firm that buys a particular input, such as labor, in a specific market. For a monopsonist in a labor market, paying a higher wage to attract an additional unit of labor increases its total factor costs for all other labor employed. For this reason, the marginal factor cost of labor is always higher than the wage rate, so the marginal factor cost schedule lies above the labor supply schedule. The labor market monopsonist employs labor to the point at which the marginal factor cost of labor equals the marginal revenue product of labor. It then pays the workers it hires the wage at which they are willing to work, as determined by the labor supply curve, which lies below the marginal factor cost curve. As a result, the monopsonist pays workers a wage that is less than their marginal revenue product.

monopsonist, 779
monopsonistic exploitation, 781
bilateral monopoly, 782

KEY FIGURES
Figure 30-5, 780
Figure 30-6, 781
Figure 30-7, 782

- **MyEconLab** Study Plan 30.4
- Video: The Buyer's Monopoly—Monopsony
- Animated Figures 30-5, 30-6, 30-7

(continued)

(continued)

WHAT YOU SHOULD KNOW		WHERE TO GO TO PRACTICE
Comparing a Monopsonist's Wage and Employment Decisions with Choices by Firms in Industries with Other Market Structures Firms that are perfect competitors or monopolies in their product markets but hire workers in perfectly competitive labor markets take the wage rate as market determined, meaning that their individual actions are unable to influence the market wage rate. A product market monopolist tends to employ fewer workers than would be employed if the monopolist's industry were perfectly competitive, but the product market monopolist nonetheless cannot affect the market wage rate. In contrast, a monopsonist is the only employer of labor, so it searches for the wage rate that maximizes its profit. This wage rate is less than the marginal revenue product of labor. In a situation in which a firm is both a product market monopolist and a labor market monopsonist, the firm's demand for labor is also lower than it would be if the firm's product market were competitive, and hence the firm hires fewer workers as well.	**KEY FIGURE** Figure 30-8, 783	• **MyEconLab** Study Plan 30.4 • Animated Figure 30-8

Log in to MyEconLab, take a chapter test, and get a personalized Study Plan that tells you which concepts you understand and which ones you need to review. From there, MyEconLab will give you further practice, tutorials, animations, videos, and guided solutions.
Log in to www.myeconlab.com

PROBLEMS

All problems are assignable in myeconlab *. Answers to the odd-numbered problems appear at the back of the book.*

30-1. Discuss three aspects of collective bargaining that society might deem desirable.

30-2. Give three reasons why a government might seek to limit the power of a union.

30-3. Recently, the Writers Guild of America (WGA), which represents TV and film screenwriters, called for a strike, and most screenwriters stopped working. Nevertheless, writers for certain TV soap operas, such as *The Young and Restless*—which have had shrinking audiences for years, draw small numbers of viewers for repeat shows, and rarely sell on DVDs—opted to drop their WGA memberships and tried to continue working during the strike. Why do you suppose that the WGA posted on its Web site a phone number for union members to report "strike-breaking activities and 'scab writing'" to the union's 12-person Strike Rules

Compliance Committee? What effect do strike-breakers have on the collective bargaining power of a union?

30-4. Suppose that the objective of a union is to maximize the total dues paid to the union by its membership. Explain the union's strategy, in terms of the wage level and employment level, under the following two scenarios.

a. Union dues are a percentage of total earnings of the union membership.

b. Union dues are paid as a flat amount per union member employed.

30-5. Explain why, in economic terms, the total income of union membership is maximized when marginal revenue is zero. (Hint: How much more revenue is forthcoming when marginal revenue is equal to zero?)

30-6. Explain the impact of each of the following events on the market for union labor.

  a. Union-produced TV and radio commercials convince consumers to buy domestically manufactured clothing instead of imported clothing.

  b. The union sponsors periodic training programs that instruct union laborers about the most efficient use of machinery and tools.

30-7. Why are unions in industries in which inputs such as machines are poor substitutes for labor more likely to be able to bargain for wages higher than market levels?

30-8. How is it possible for the average annual earnings of nonunionized workers to exceed those of unionized workers even though unionized workers' hourly wages are more than $2 higher?

30-9. In the short run, a tool manufacturer has a fixed amount of capital. Labor is a variable input. The cost and output structure that the firm faces is depicted in the following table:

Labor Supplied	Total Physical Product	Hourly Wage Rate ($)
10	100	5
11	109	6
12	116	7
13	121	8
14	124	9
15	125	10

Derive, at each level of labor supplied, the firm's total wage costs and marginal factor cost.

30-10. Suppose that for the firm in Problem 30-9, the goods market is perfectly competitive. The market price of the product the firm produces is $4 at each quantity supplied by the firm. What is the amount of labor that this profit-maximizing firm will hire, and what wage rate will it pay?

30-11. The price and wage structure that a firm faces is depicted in the following table.

Labor Supplied	Total Physical Product	Hourly Wage Rate ($)	Product Price ($)
10	100	5	3.11
11	109	6	3.00
12	116	7	2.95
13	121	8	2.92
14	124	9	2.90
15	125	10	2.89

The firm finds that the price of its product changes with the rate of output. In addition, the wage it pays its workers varies with the amount of labor it employs. This firm maximizes profits. How many units of labor will it hire? What wage will it pay?

30-12. What is the amount of monopsonistic exploitation that takes place at the firm examined in Problem 30-11?

30-13. A profit-maximizing clothing producer in a remote area is the only employer of people in that area. It sells its clothing in a perfectly competitive market. The firm pays each worker the same weekly wage rate. The last worker hired raised the firm's total weekly wage expenses from $105,600 to $106,480. What is the marginal revenue product of the last worker hired by this firm if it is maximizing profits?

30-14. A single firm is the only employer in a labor market. The marginal revenue product, labor supply, and marginal factor cost curves that it faces are displayed in the diagram below. Use this information to answer the following questions.

  a. How many units of labor will this firm employ in order to maximize its economic profits?

  b. What hourly wage rate will this firm pay its workers?

  c. What is the total amount of wage payments that this firm will make to its workers each hour?

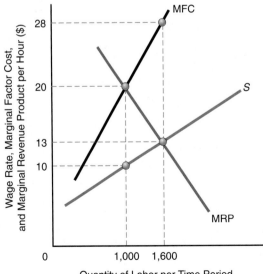

ECONOMICS ON THE NET

Evaluating Union Goals As discussed in this chapter, unions can pursue any of a number of goals. The AFL-CIO's home page provides links to the Web sites of several unions, and reviewing these sites can help you determine the objectives these unions have selected.

Title: American Federation of Labor–Congress of Industrial Organizations

Navigation: Go to **www.econtoday.com/chapter30** to visit the AFL-CIO's home page.

Application Perform the indicated operations, and answer the following questions.

1. Click on *About Us*, then click on *This Is the AFL-CIO*, and finally click on *Mission Statement*. Does the AFL-CIO claim to represent the interests of all workers or just workers in specific firms or industries? Can you discern what broad wage and employment strategy the AFL-CIO pursues?

2. Click on *Unions of the AFL-CIO*. Explore two or three of these Web sites. Do these unions appear to represent the interests of all workers or just workers in specific firms or industries? What general wage and employment strategies do these unions appear to pursue?

For Group Study and Analysis Divide up all the unions affiliated with the AFL-CIO among groups, and have each group explore the Web sites listed under *Unions of the AFL-CIO* at the AFL-CIO Web site. Have each group report on the wage and employment strategies that appear to prevail for the unions it examined.

ANSWERS TO QUICK QUIZZES

p. 772: (i) American Federation . . . Labor; (ii) National Labor Relations . . . industrial; (iii) 25 . . . 12

p. 778: (i) above . . . rationing; (ii) all . . . income . . . maximize; (iii) inward . . . outward; (iv) productivity

p. 783: (i) only buyer . . . upward; (ii) upward . . . greater . . . above; (iii) factor . . . revenue

Income, Poverty, and Health Care

31

Like many studies with provocative implications, a recent study by economists at the Brookings Institution and the Federal Reserve has been the topic of a number of media reports. The study found that a measure of the variability of household incomes had generally increased since the early 1970s, from an index value of 18 to a value of more than 22, or by about 23 percent. The authors' conclusion was that today's households tend to experience more sudden increases in income than households did more than three decades ago. Households also face more risk of unexpected income declines. What factors determine households' income levels and their stability over time? How much do incomes vary *across* households? These are key questions considered in this chapter.

LEARNING OBJECTIVES

 myeconlab

MyEconLab helps you master each objective and study more efficiently. See end of chapter for details.

After reading this chapter, you should be able to:

➤ Describe how to use a Lorenz curve to represent a nation's income distribution

➤ Identify the key determinants of income differences across individuals

➤ Discuss theories of desired income distribution

➤ Distinguish among alternative approaches to measuring and addressing poverty

➤ Recognize the major reasons for rising health care costs

➤ Describe alternative approaches to paying for health care

? **DID YOU KNOW THAT** additional education that culminates with a bachelor's degree is worth an average of about $24,000 per year in additional income? The average income of a college graduate is now more than $55,000 per year, whereas the average high school graduate earns just under $31,000 per year. Furthermore, not only does more education push up average earnings even farther, but less education yields even lower earnings. The average annual income of someone who obtains a graduate degree exceeds $80,000, but those who fail to graduate from high school earn average annual incomes of only a little more than $20,000.

Clearly, education must play an important role in determining the **distribution of income,** which is the way that income is allocated among the population. What other factors influence the distribution of income? Economists have devised various theories to explain income distribution. We will present some of these theories in this chapter. We will also present some of the more obvious institutional reasons why income is not distributed equally in the United States. In addition, we will examine what might be done about health care problems confronting individuals in all income groups.

Distribution of income
The way income is allocated among the population.

Why is this couple on an island vacation likely to be college or graduate-school graduates?

Lorenz curve
A geometric representation of the distribution of income. A Lorenz curve that is perfectly straight represents complete income equality. The more bowed a Lorenz curve, the more unequally income is distributed.

Income

Income provides each of us with the means of consuming and saving. Income can be the result of a payment for labor services or a payment for ownership of one of the other factors of production besides labor—land, physical capital, or entrepreneurship. In addition, individuals obtain spendable income from gifts and government transfers. (Some individuals also obtain income by stealing, but we will not treat this matter here.) Right now, let us examine how money income is distributed across classes of income earners within the United States.

Measuring Income Distribution: The Lorenz Curve

We can represent the distribution of money income graphically with what is known as the **Lorenz curve,** named after a U.S.-born statistician, Max Otto Lorenz, who proposed it in 1905. The Lorenz curve shows what share of total money income is accounted for by different proportions of the nation's households. Look at Figure 31-1. On the horizontal axis, we measure the *cumulative* percentage of households, lowest-income households first. Starting at the left corner, there are zero households; at the right corner, we have 100 percent of households; and in the middle, we have 50 percent of households. The vertical axis represents the cumulative percentage of money income. The 45-degree line represents complete equality: 50 percent of the households obtain 50 percent of total income, 60 percent of the households obtain 60 percent of total income, and so on. Of course, in no real-world situation is there such complete equality of income; no actual Lorenz curve would be a straight line. Rather, it would be some curved line, like the one labeled "Actual money income distribution" in Figure 31-1. For example, the bottom 50 percent of households in the United States receive about 28 percent of total money income.

In Figure 31-2, we again show the actual money income distribution Lorenz curve for the United States, and we also compare it to the distribution of money income in 1929. Since that year, the Lorenz curve has generally become less bowed; that is, it has moved closer to the line of complete equality.

CRITICISMS OF THE LORENZ CURVE In recent years, economists have placed less and less emphasis on the shape of the Lorenz curve as an indication of the degree of

FIGURE 31-1

The Lorenz Curve

The horizontal axis measures the cumulative percentage of households, with lowest-income households first, from 0 to 100 percent. The vertical axis measures the cumulative percentage of money income from 0 to 100. A straight line at a 45-degree angle cuts the box in half and represents a line of complete income equality, along which 25 percent of the families get 25 percent of the money income, 50 percent get 50 percent, and so on. The observed Lorenz curve, showing the actual U.S. money income distribution, is not a straight line but rather a curved line as shown. The difference between complete money income equality and the Lorenz curve is the inequality gap.

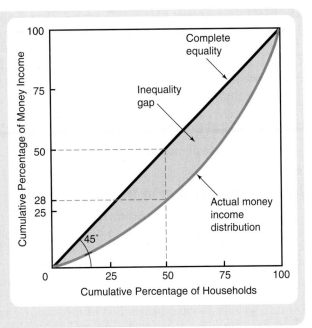

income inequality in a country. There are five basic reasons why the Lorenz curve has been criticized:

1. The Lorenz curve is typically presented in terms of the distribution of *money* income only. It does not include **income in kind,** such as government-provided food stamps, education, medical care, or housing aid, and goods or services produced and consumed in the home or on the farm.

2. The Lorenz curve does not account for differences in the size of households or the number of wage earners they contain.

Income in kind
Income received in the form of goods and services, such as housing or medical care; to be contrasted with money income, which is simply income in dollars, or general purchasing power, that can be used to buy *any* goods and services.

FIGURE 31-2

Lorenz Curves of Income Distribution, 1929 and 2009

Since 1929, the Lorenz curve has moved inward toward the straight line of perfect income equality.

Source: U.S. Department of Commerce.

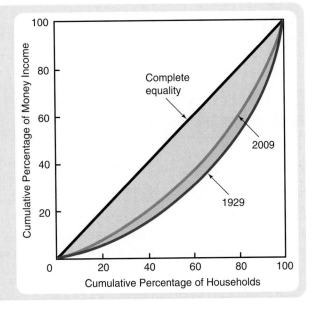

3. It does not account for age differences. Even if all families in the United States had exactly the same *lifetime* incomes, chances are that young families would have modest incomes, middle-aged families would have relatively high incomes, and retired families would have low incomes. Because the Lorenz curve is drawn at a moment in time, it can never tell us anything about the inequality of *lifetime* income.

4. The Lorenz curve ordinarily reflects money income *before* taxes.

5. It does not measure unreported income from the underground economy, a substantial source of income for some individuals.

Income Distribution in the United States

Go to www.econtoday/chapter31 to view the U.S. Census Bureau's most recent data on the U.S. income distribution. Click on the most recent year next to "Money Income in the United States."

We could talk about the percentage of income earners within specific income classes—those earning between $20,001 and $30,000 per year, those earning between $30,001 and $40,000 per year, and so on. The problem with this type of analysis is that we live in a growing economy. Income, with infrequent exceptions, is going up all the time. If we wish to compare the relative shares of total income going to different income classes, we cannot look at specific amounts of money income. Instead, we talk about a distribution of income over five groups. Then we can talk about how much the bottom fifth (or quintile) makes compared with the top fifth, and so on.

In Table 31-1, we see the percentage share of income for households before direct taxes. The table groups households according to whether they are in the lowest 20 percent of the income distribution, the second lowest 20 percent, and so on. We see that in 2009, the lowest 20 percent had an estimated combined money income of 3.4 percent of the total money income of the entire population. This is less than the lowest 20 percent had at the end of World War II. Accordingly, some have concluded that the distribution of money income has become slightly more unequal. *Money* income, however, understates *total* income for individuals who receive in-kind transfers from the government in the form of food stamps, public housing, education, and the like. In particular, since World War II, the share of *total* income—money income plus in-kind benefits—going to the bottom 20 percent of households has more than doubled.

How has the distribution of income in China changed in recent decades?

INTERNATIONAL EXAMPLE
Evidence of a More Unequal Distribution of Income in China

In addition to using Lorenz curves to measure the degree of income inequality, economists sometimes calculate an index measure of inequality known as the *Gini coefficient*, which has a value varying between 0 and 1. A Gini-coefficient value of 0 represents complete equality of income, and a value of 1 represents complete income inequality in which one person receives all income. In the late 1970s, the value of the Gini coefficient for China was 0.15, indicating considerable income equality. Today, it is estimated to be closer to 0.60, indicating that income in China has become much more unequal during the past three decades.

FOR CRITICAL ANALYSIS
Based on the change in value of the Gini coefficient since the late 1970s, has the Lorenz curve for China likely become more or less outward bowed?

TABLE 31-1

Percentage Share of Money Income for Households Before Direct Taxes

Income Group	2009	1975	1960	1947
Lowest fifth	3.4	4.4	4.8	5.1
Second fifth	8.6	10.5	12.2	11.8
Third fifth	14.6	17.1	17.8	16.7
Fourth fifth	23.0	24.8	24.0	23.2
Highest fifth	50.4	43.2	41.3	43.3

Note: Figures may not sum to 100 percent due to rounding.
Sources: U.S. Bureau of the Census; author's estimates.

The Distribution of Wealth

When referring to the distribution of income, we must realize that income—a flow—can be viewed as a return on wealth (both human and nonhuman)—a stock. A discussion of the distribution of income is not necessarily the same thing as a discussion of the distribution of wealth, however. A complete concept of wealth would include not only tangible objects, such as buildings, machinery, land, cars, and houses—nonhuman wealth—but also people who have skills, knowledge, initiative, talents, and the like—human wealth. The total of human and nonhuman wealth in the United States makes up our nation's capital stock.

Figure 31-3 shows that the richest 10 percent of U.S. households hold more than two-thirds of all measured wealth. The problem with those data, gathered by the Federal Reserve System, however, is that they do not include many important assets. One of these is workers' claims on private pension plans, which equal at least $6 trillion. If you add the value of these pensions, household wealth increases by almost 25 percent and reveals that many more U.S. households are middle-wealth households (popularly known as the *middle class*). Another asset excluded from the data is anticipated claims on the Social Security system, which tend to comprise a larger share of the wealth of lower-income individuals.

FIGURE 31-3

Measured Total Wealth Distribution

The top 10 percent of households have 71 percent of all *measured* wealth. This distribution changes dramatically if other nonmeasured components of wealth, such as claims on private pension plans and on government-guaranteed Social Security commitments, are taken into account.

Source: Board of Governors of the Federal Reserve.

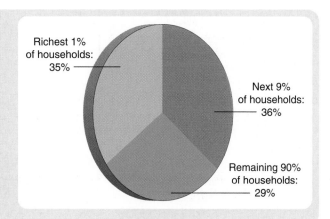

Richest 1% of households: 35%

Next 9% of households: 36%

Remaining 90% of households: 29%

The **Lorenz curve** graphically represents the distribution of _____. If it is a straight line, there is complete _____ of income. The more it is bowed, the more _____ income is distributed.

The distribution of wealth is not the same as the distribution of income. Wealth includes _____ such as

houses, stocks, and bonds. Although the apparent distribution of wealth seems to be _____ concentrated at the top than income, the data used are not very accurate, and most summary statistics fail to take account of workers' claims on private and public pensions, which are substantial.

Determinants of Income Differences

We know that there are income differences—that is not in dispute. A more important question is why these differences in income occur. We will look at four determinants of income differences: age, marginal productivity, inheritance, and discrimination.

Age

Age turns out to be a determinant of income because with age come, usually, more education, more training, and more experience. It is not surprising that within every class of income earners, there seem to be regular cycles of earning behavior. Most individuals earn more when they are middle-aged than when they are younger or older. We call this the **age-earnings cycle.**

Age-earnings cycle
The regular earnings profile of an individual throughout his or her lifetime. The age-earnings cycle usually starts with a low income, builds gradually to a peak at around age 50, and then gradually curves down until it approaches zero at retirement.

THE AGE-EARNINGS CYCLE Every occupation has its own age-earnings cycle, and every individual will probably experience some variation from the average. Nonetheless, we can characterize the typical age-earnings cycle graphically in Figure 31-4. Here we see that at age 18, earnings from wages are relatively low. As a person's productivity increases through more training and experience, earnings gradually rise until they peak at about age 50. Then they fall until retirement, when they become zero (that is, currently earned wages become zero, although retirement payments may then commence).

FIGURE 31-4

Typical Age-Earnings Profile
Within every class of income earners there is usually a typical age-earnings profile. Earnings from wages are lowest when starting work at age 18, reach their peak at around age 50, and then taper off until retirement around age 65, when they become zero for most people. The rise in earnings up to age 50 is usually due to increased experience, longer working hours, and better training and schooling. (We abstract from economywide productivity changes that would shift the entire curve upward.)

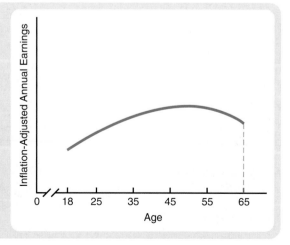

Note that general increases in overall productivity for the entire workforce will result in an upward shift in the typical age-earnings profile depicted in Figure 31-4. Thus, even at the end of the age-earnings cycle, when just about to retire, the worker would receive a relatively high wage compared with the starting wage 45 years earlier. The wage would be higher due to factors that contribute to rising real wages for everyone, regardless of the stage in the age-earnings cycle.

In light of the shape of the age-earnings profile, how do you suppose that U.S. households' assets are distributed by age group?

EXAMPLE
Higher Incomes Imply More Assets for the Older Set

Because people's incomes typically rise as they reach their fifties, so does their saving and hence their accumulation of assets. People over the age of 60 currently comprise 30 percent of U.S. individuals aged 18 and older, but they own more than 41 percent of all assets held by adult individuals. Roughly another 30 percent of adults are between the ages of 18 and 41, but they own less than 20 percent of assets.

FOR CRITICAL ANALYSIS
What is likely to happen to the share of assets of those currently aged 18 to 41 as they grow older?

Now we have some idea why specific individuals earn different incomes at different times in their lives, but we have yet to explain why different people are paid different amounts for their labor. One way to explain this is to recall the marginal productivity theory developed in Chapter 29.

Marginal Productivity

When trying to determine how many workers a firm would hire, we had to construct a marginal revenue product curve. We found that as more workers were hired, the marginal revenue product fell due to diminishing marginal product. If the forces of demand and supply established a certain wage rate, workers would be hired until their marginal physical product times marginal revenue (which equals the market price under perfect competition) was equal to the going wage rate. Then the hiring would stop. This analysis suggests what workers can expect to be paid in the labor market: As long as there are low-cost information flows and the labor and product markets are competitive, each worker can expect to be paid his or her marginal revenue product.

DETERMINANTS OF MARGINAL PRODUCTIVITY According to marginal revenue product theory, if people can increase their marginal physical product, they can expect to earn higher incomes. Key determinants of marginal physical product are talent, experience, and training.

Talent. Talent is the easiest factor to explain, but it is difficult to acquire if you don't have it. Innate abilities and attributes can be very strong, if not overwhelming, determinants of a person's potential productivity. Strength, coordination, and mental alertness are facets of nonacquired human capital and thus have some bearing on the ability to earn income. Someone who is tall and agile has a better chance of being a basketball player than someone who is short and unathletic. A person born with a superior talent for abstract thinking has a better chance of earning a relatively high income as a mathematician or a physicist than someone who is not born with that capability.

Experience. Additional experience at particular tasks is another way to increase productivity. Experience can be linked to the well-known *learning curve* that applies when the same task is done over and over. The worker repeating a task becomes more efficient: The worker can do the same task in less time or in the same amount of time but better. Take an example of a person going to work on an automobile assembly line. At first she is able to fasten only three bolts every two minutes. Then the worker becomes more adept and can fasten four bolts in the same time plus insert a rubber guard on the bumper. After a few more weeks, another task can be added. Experience allows this individual to improve her productivity. The more effectively people learn to do something, the more productive they are.

Training. Training is similar to experience but is more formal. Much of a person's increased productivity is due to on-the-job training. Many companies have training programs for new workers.

INVESTMENT IN HUMAN CAPITAL Investment in human capital is just like investment in anything else. If you invest in yourself by going to college, rather than going to work after high school and earning more current income, you will presumably be rewarded in the future with a higher income or a more interesting job (or both). This is exactly the motivation that underlies the decision of many college-bound students to obtain a formal higher education.

As with other investments, we can determine the rate of return on an investment in a college education. To do so, we first have to figure out the marginal cost of going to school. A major cost is not simply what you have to pay for books, fees, and tuition but rather the income you forgo. *A key cost of education is the income forgone—the opportunity cost of not working.* In addition, the direct expenses of college must be paid for. Certainly, not all students forgo all income during their college years. Many work part time. Taking account of those who work part time and those who are supported by tuition grants and other scholarships, the average rate of return on going to college ranges between 6 and 8 percent per year.

Inheritance

It is not unusual to inherit cash, jewelry, stocks, bonds, homes, or other real estate. Yet only about 10 percent of income inequality in the United States can be traced to differences in inherited wealth. If for some reason the government confiscated all property that had been inherited, the immediate result would be only a modest change in the distribution of income in the United States. In any event, at both federal and state levels substantial inheritance taxes are levied on the estates of relatively wealthy deceased Americans (although there are some legally valid ways to avoid certain estate taxes).

Discrimination

Economic discrimination occurs whenever workers with the same marginal revenue product receive unequal pay due to some noneconomic factor such as their race, gender, or age. It is possible—and indeed quite obvious—that discrimination affects the distribution of income. Certain groups in our society are not paid wages at rates comparable to those received by other groups, even when we correct for productivity.

Differences in income remain between whites and nonwhites and between men and women. For example, the median income of black families is about 65 percent that of white families. The median wage rate of women is about 80 percent that of men. Some people argue that all of these differences are due to discrimination against non-whites and against women.

We cannot simply accept *any* differences in income as due to discrimination, though. What we need to do is discover why differences in income between groups exist and then determine if factors other than discrimination in the labor market can explain them. The unexplained part of income differences can rightfully be considered the result of discrimination.

ACCESS TO EDUCATION African Americans and other minorities have faced discrimination in the acquisition of human capital. The amount and quality of schooling offered black U.S. residents has generally been inferior to that offered whites. As a result, among other things, African Americans and certain other minority groups, such as Hispanics, suffer from reduced investment in human capital. Even when this difference in human capital is taken into account, however, there still appears to be an income differential that cannot be explained.

The unexplained income differential between whites and blacks is often attributed to discrimination in the labor market. Because no better explanation is offered, we will infer that discrimination in the labor market does indeed still exist.

Theories of Desired Income Distribution

We have talked about the factors affecting the distribution of income, but we have not yet mentioned the normative issue of how income *ought* to be distributed. This, of course, requires a value judgment. We are talking about the problem of economic justice. We can never completely resolve this problem because there are always going to be conflicting values. It is impossible to give all people what each thinks is just. Nonetheless, two particular normative standards for the distribution of income have been popular with economists. These are income distribution based on productivity and income distribution based on equality.

Productivity

The *productivity standard* for the distribution of income can be stated simply as "To each according to what he or she produces." This is also called the *contributive standard* because it is based on the principle of rewarding according to the contribution to society's total output. It is also sometimes referred to as the *merit standard* and is one of the oldest concepts of justice. People are rewarded according to merit, and merit is judged by one's ability to produce what is considered useful by society.

We measure a person's productive contribution in a capitalist system by the market value of that person's output. We have already referred to this as the marginal revenue product theory of wage determination.

Equality

The *egalitarian principle* of income distribution is simply "To each exactly the same." Everyone would have exactly the same amount of income. This criterion of income distribution has been debated as far back as biblical times. This system of income distribution has been considered equitable, meaning that presumably everybody is dealt with fairly and equally. There are problems, however, with an income distribution that is completely equal.

Some jobs are more unpleasant or more dangerous than others. Should the people undertaking these jobs be paid exactly the same as everyone else? Indeed, under an equal distribution of income, what incentive would there be for individuals to take risky, hazardous, or unpleasant jobs at all? What about overtime? Who would be willing to work overtime without additional pay? There is another problem: If everyone earned the same income, what incentive would there be for individuals to invest in their own human capital—a costly and time-consuming process?

Just consider the incentive structure within a corporation. Within corporations, much of the differential between, say, the pay of the CEO and the pay of all of the vice presidents is meant to create competition among the vice presidents for the CEO's job. The result is higher productivity. If all incomes were the same, much of this competition would disappear, and productivity would fall.

There is some evidence that differences in income lead to higher rates of economic growth. Future generations are therefore made better off. Elimination of income differences may reduce the rate of economic growth and cause future generations to be poorer than they otherwise might have been.

QUICK QUIZ   *See page 817 for the answers. Review concepts from this section in MyEconLab.*

Most people follow an _____-_____ cycle in which they earn relatively small incomes when they first start working, increase their incomes until about age 50, and then slowly experience a decrease in their real incomes as they approach retirement.

According to the marginal _____ theory of wages, workers can expect to be paid their marginal _____ product.

Marginal physical productivity depends on _____, _____, _____, and _____.

Going to school and receiving on-the-job training can be considered an investment in _____ capital. A key cost of education is the _____ cost of not working.

Two normative standards for income distribution are income distribution based on _____ and income distribution based on _____.

Poverty and Attempts to Eliminate It

Throughout the history of the world, mass poverty has been accepted as inevitable. This nation and others, particularly in the Western world, however, have sustained enough economic growth in the past several hundred years so that *mass* poverty can no longer be said to be a problem for these fortunate countries. As a matter of fact, the residual of poverty in the United States strikes us as bizarre, an anomaly. How can there still be so much poverty in a nation of such abundance? Having talked about the determinants of the distribution of income, we now have at least some ideas of why some people are destined to remain low-income earners throughout their lives.

Income can be transferred from the relatively well-to-do to the relatively poor by various methods, and as a nation we have been using them for a long time. Today, we have a vast array of welfare programs set up for the purpose of redistributing income.

As we know, however, these programs have not been entirely successful. Are there alternatives to our current welfare system? Is there a better method of helping the poor? Before we answer these questions, take a look at Figure 31-5, which displays the percentage of the U.S. population determined to be in a state of poverty by the U.S. government. This percentage, called the *poverty rate*, has varied between roughly 11 percent and 16 percent since 1965.

Defining Poverty

The threshold income level, which is used to determine who falls into the poverty category, was originally based on the cost of a nutritionally adequate food plan designed by the U.S. Department of Agriculture. The threshold was determined by multiplying the food plan cost by 3 on the assumption that food expenses comprise approximately one-third of a poor family's income. Annual revisions of the threshold level were based only on price changes in the food budget. In 1969, a federal interagency committee looked at the calculations of the threshold and decided to set new standards, with adjustments made on the basis of changes in the Consumer Price Index. For example, in 2009, the official poverty level for an urban family of four was around $22,000. It goes up each year to reflect whatever inflation has occurred.

Absolute Poverty

Because the low-income threshold is an absolute measure, we know that if it never changes in real terms, we will reduce poverty even if we do nothing. How can that be? The reasoning is straightforward. Real incomes in the United States have been growing at a compounded annual rate of almost 2 percent per capita for at least the past century and at about 2.5 percent since World War II. If we define the poverty line at a specific real income level, more and more individuals will make incomes that exceed that poverty line. Thus, in absolute terms, we will eliminate poverty (assuming continued per capita growth and no change in income distribution).

Go to **www.econtoday.com/chapter31** to learn about the World Bank's programs intended to combat global poverty.

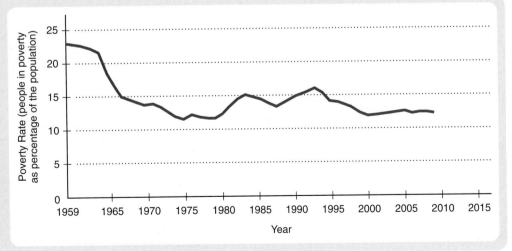

FIGURE 31-5

The Official Poverty Rate in the United States

The official poverty rate, or the number of people in poverty as a percentage of the U.S. population, has remained in a range of roughly 11 to 16 percent since 1965.

Source: U.S. Department of Labor.

Relative Poverty

Be careful with this analysis, however. Poverty can also be defined in relative terms, that is, in terms of the income levels of individuals or families relative to the rest of the population. As long as the distribution of income is not perfectly equal, there will always be some people who make less income than others, even if their relatively low income is high by historical standards. Thus, in a relative sense, the problem of poverty will always exist.

Transfer Payments as Income

The official poverty level is based on pretax income, including cash but not in-kind subsidies—food stamps, housing vouchers, and the like. If we correct poverty levels for such benefits, the percentage of the population that is below the poverty line drops dramatically. Some economists argue that the way the official poverty level is calculated makes no sense in a nation that redistributed more than $1.4 trillion in cash and noncash transfers in 2008.

Furthermore, some of the nation's official poor partake in the informal, or underground, sectors of the economy without reporting their income from these sources. And some of the officially defined poor obtain benefits from owning their own home (40 percent of all poor households do own their own homes). Look at Figure 31-6 for two different views of what has happened to the relative position of this nation's poor. The graph shows the ratio of the top fifth of the nation's households to the bottom fifth of the nation's households. If we look only at measured income, it appears that the poor are getting relatively poorer compared to the rich (the top line). If we compare household spending (consumption), however, a different picture emerges. The nation's poorest households are in fact holding their own in relative terms.

FIGURE 31-6

Relative Poverty: Comparing Household Income and Household Spending

This graph shows on the vertical axis the ratio of the top 20 percent of income-earning households to the bottom 20 percent. If measured household income is used, there appears to be increasing income inequality. If we look at household *spending*, though, inequality is more nearly constant.

Sources: U.S. Bureau of Labor Statistics; U.S. Bureau of the Census.

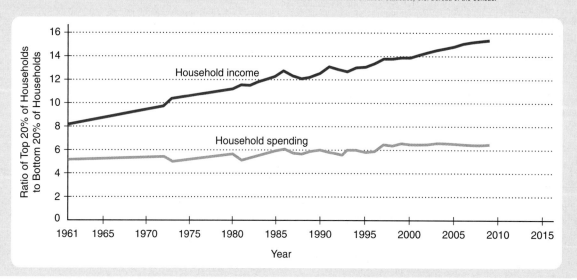

Attacks on Poverty: Major Income Maintenance Programs

There are a variety of income maintenance programs designed to help the poor. We examine a few of them here.

SOCIAL SECURITY For the retired, the unemployed, and the disabled, social insurance programs provide income payments in prescribed situations. The best known is Social Security, which includes what has been called old-age, survivors', and disability insurance (OASDI). As discussed in Chapter 6, this was originally supposed to be a program of compulsory saving financed from payroll taxes levied on both employers and employees. Workers pay for Social Security while working and receive the benefits after retirement. The benefit payments are usually made to people who have reached retirement age. When the insured worker dies, benefits accrue to the survivors, including widows and children. Special benefits provide for disabled workers. Over 90 percent of all employed persons in the United States are covered by OASDI. Today, Social Security is an intergenerational income transfer that is only vaguely related to past earnings. It transfers income from U.S. residents who work—the young through the middle-aged—to those who do not work—older retired persons.

In 2009, more than 50 million people were receiving OASDI checks averaging about $1,000 a month. Benefit payments from OASDI redistribute income to some degree. Benefit payments, however, are not based on recipient need. Participants' contributions give them the right to benefits even if they would be financially secure without them. Social Security is not really an insurance program because people are not guaranteed that the benefits they receive will be in line with the "contributions" they have made. It is not a personal savings account. The benefits are legislated by Congress. In the future, Congress may not be as sympathetic toward older people as it is today. It could (and probably will have to) legislate for lower real levels of benefits instead of higher ones.

SUPPLEMENTAL SECURITY INCOME AND TEMPORARY ASSISTANCE TO NEEDY FAMILIES Many people who are poor but do not qualify for Social Security benefits are assisted through other programs. The federally financed and administered Supplemental Security Income (SSI) program was instituted in 1974. The purpose of SSI is to establish a nationwide minimum income for the aged, the blind, and the disabled. SSI has become one of the fastest-growing transfer programs in the United States. Whereas in 1974 less than $8 billion was spent, the prediction for 2010 is $47 billion. U.S. residents currently eligible for SSI include children and individuals with mental disabilities, including drug addicts and alcoholics.

Temporary Assistance to Needy Families (TANF) is a state-administered program, financed in part by federal grants. The program provides aid to families in need. TANF replaced Aid to Families with Dependent Children (AFDC) in 1996. TANF payments are intended to be temporary. Projected expenditures for TANF are $20 billion in 2009.

FOOD STAMPS Food stamps are government-issued coupons (or, increasingly, electronic debit cards) that can be used to purchase food. In 1964, some 367,000 Americans were receiving food stamps. In 2009, the estimate is over 29 million recipients. The annual cost has jumped from $860,000 to more than $36 billion. In 2009, almost one in every nine citizens (including children) was using food stamps.

THE EARNED INCOME TAX CREDIT PROGRAM In 1975, the Earned Income Tax Credit (EITC) Program was created to provide rebates of Social Security taxes to low-income workers. Over one-fifth of all tax returns claim an earned income tax credit; each year the federal government grants more than $43 billion in these credits. In some states, such as Mississippi, nearly half of all families are eligible for an EITC. The program works as follows: Single-income households with two children that report income of about $39,000 (exclusive of welfare payments) receive EITC benefits up to about $5,000. There is a catch, though. Those with earnings up to a threshold of about $13,000 receive higher benefits as their incomes rise. But families earning more than this threshold income are penalized about 18 cents for every dollar they earn above the income threshold. Thus, on net the EITC discourages work by low- or moderate-income earners more than it rewards work. In particular, it discourages low-income earners from taking on second jobs. The Government Accounting Office estimates that hours worked by working wives in EITC-beneficiary households have consequently decreased by 15 percent. The average EITC recipient works 1,700 hours a year compared to a normal work year of about 2,000 hours.

No Apparent Reduction in Poverty Rates

In spite of the numerous programs in existence and the trillions of dollars transferred to the poor, the officially defined rate of poverty in the United States has shown no long-run tendency to decline. From 1945 until the early 1970s, the percentage of U.S. residents in poverty fell steadily every year. As Figure 31-5 on page 801 shows, it reached a low of around 11 percent in 1974, shot back up beyond 15 percent in 1983, fell to 13.1 percent in 1990, and has since fallen to near 12 percent. Why this pattern has emerged is a real puzzle. Since the War on Poverty was launched under President Lyndon B. Johnson in 1965, more than $13 trillion has been transferred to the poor, and yet more U.S. residents are poor today than ever before. This fact created the political will to pass the Welfare Reform Act of 1996, putting limits on people's use of welfare. The law's goal has been to get people off welfare and into jobs.

QUICK QUIZ *See page 817 for the answers. Review concepts from this section in MyEconLab.*

If poverty is defined in _____ terms, economic growth eventually decreases the number of officially defined poor. If poverty is defined in _____ terms, however, we will never eliminate it.

Although the relative position of the _____ measured by household _____ seems to have worsened, household spending by the bottom 20 percent of households

compared to that of the top 20 percent has shown little change since the 1960s.

Major attacks on poverty have been made through social insurance programs, including _____ Security, _____ Security Income (SSI), Temporary Assistance to Needy Families, the _____ _____ tax credit, and _____ stamps.

Health Care

It may seem strange to be reading about health care in a chapter on the distribution of income and poverty. Yet health care is intimately related to those two topics. For example, sometimes people become poor because they do not have adequate health insurance (or have none at all), fall ill, and deplete all of their wealth in obtaining medical care. Moreover, some individuals remain in certain jobs simply because their employer's health care package seems so good that they are afraid to change jobs and risk not being covered by health insurance in the process. Finally, as you will see, much of the cause of the increased health care spending in the United States can be attributed to a change in the incentives that U.S. residents face.

The U.S. Health Care Situation

Spending for health care is estimated to account for about 16 percent of U.S. real GDP. You can see from Figure 31-7 that in 1965, about 6 percent of annual income was spent on health care, but that percentage has been increasing ever since.

WHY HAVE HEALTH CARE COSTS RISEN SO MUCH? There are numerous explanations for why health care costs have risen so much. At least one has to do with changing demographics: The U.S. population is getting older.

The Age–Health Care Expenditure Equation. The top 5 percent of health care users incur over 50 percent of all health costs. The bottom 70 percent of health care users account for only 10 percent of health care expenditures. Not surprisingly, the elderly make up most of the top users of health care services. Nursing home expenditures are made primarily by people older than 70. The use of hospitals is also dominated by the aged.

The U.S. population is aging steadily. More than 13 percent of the 300 million U.S. residents are over 65. It is estimated that by the year 2035, senior citizens will comprise about 22 percent of our population. This aging population stimulates the demand for health care. The elderly consume more than four times as much per capita health care services as the rest of the population. In short, whatever the demand for health care services is today, it is likely to be considerably higher in the future as the U.S. population ages.

New Technologies. Another reason that health care costs have risen so dramatically is advancing technology. Each CT (computerized tomography) scanner costs at least $100,000. An MRI (magnetic resonance imaging) scanner can cost over $2 million.

FIGURE 31-7

Percentage of Total National Income Spent on Health Care in the United States

The portion of total national income spent on health care has risen steadily since 1965.

Sources: U.S. Department of Commerce; U.S. Department of Health and Human Services; Deloitte and Touche LLP; VHA, Inc.

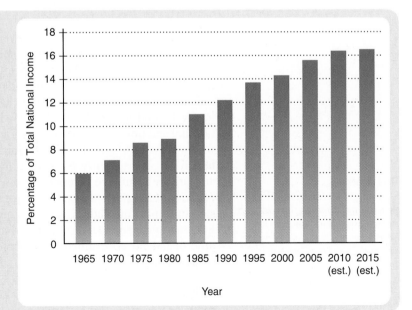

A PET (positron emission tomography) scanner costs around $4 million. All of these machines have become increasingly available in recent decades and are desired throughout the country. Typical fees for procedures using them range from $300 to $400 for a CT scan to as high as $2,000 for a PET scan. The development of new technologies that help physicians and hospitals prolong human life is an ongoing process in an ever-advancing industry. New procedures at even higher prices can be expected in the future.

What new pill technologies promise to boost health care costs?

E-COMMERCE EXAMPLE

High-Priced Pills and Future Health Care Costs

Several new pill technologies have emerged in the past few years. For instance, one new pill, called the accordion pill, releases medication slowly, thereby reducing the side effects of medications that currently must be taken several times per day. The accordion pill unfolds inside the stomach and remains anchored there for up to 20 hours. Each pill costs a little less than $10.

Other pills are much more high tech. One, called Smart-Pill, transmits data wirelessly via a radio frequency identification system to a receiver worn around the patient's neck or waist. The pill transmits information about acidity, pressure, temperature, and digestive activity. Each pill costs $500. A complete SmartPill monitoring system marketed to hospitals—including laptop, software, docking station, data

receiver, activation device, and a set of 10 pills—is priced at $20,000.

Clearly, average pill prices will be on the upswing in the short run if physicians begin prescribing many of these and other high-tech pills. In the long run, however, new pill technologies could succeed in reducing costs of other forms of health care. Thus, medical technologies that appear to raise costs in the short run may well offer hope for lower costs in the future.

FOR CRITICAL ANALYSIS

Are high-priced health care technologies necessarily inefficient simply because they currently have high relative prices? Why or why not?

Third parties

Parties who are not directly involved in a given activity or transaction. For example, in the relationship between caregivers and patients, fees may be paid by third parties (insurance companies, government).

Third-Party Financing. Currently, government spending on health care constitutes over 40 percent of total health care spending (of which the *federal* government pays about 70 percent). Private insurance accounts for a little over 35 percent of payments for health care. The remainder—less than 20 percent—is paid directly by individuals. Figure 31-8 shows the change in the payment scheme for medical care in the United States since 1930. Medicare and Medicaid are the main sources of hospital and other medical benefits for more than 40 million U.S. residents, most of whom are over 65. Medicaid—the joint state-federal program—provides long-term health care, particularly for people living in nursing homes. Medicare, Medicaid, and private insurance companies are considered **third parties** in the medical care equation. Caregivers and patients are the two primary parties. When third parties step in to pay for medical care, the quantity demanded of those services increases. For example, when Medicare and Medicaid went into effect in the 1960s, the volume of federal government–reimbursed medical services increased by more than 65 percent.

PRICE, QUANTITY DEMANDED, AND THE QUESTION OF MORAL HAZARD Although some people may think that the demand for health care is insensitive to price

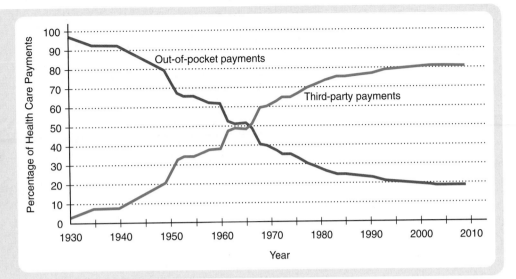

FIGURE 31-8

Third-Party versus Out-of-Pocket Health Care Payments

Out-of-pocket payments for health care services have been falling steadily since the 1930s. In contrast, third-party payments for health care have risen to the point that they account for over 80 percent of all such outlays today.

Sources: Health Care Financing Administration; U.S. Department of Health and Human Services.

changes, theory clearly indicates otherwise. Look at Figure 31-9 on the following page. There you see a hypothetical demand curve for health care services. To the extent that third parties—whether government or private insurance—pay for health care, the out-of-pocket cost, or net price, to the individual decreases. If all medical expenses were paid for by third parties, dropping the price to zero in Figure 31-9, the quantity demanded would increase.

One of the issues here has to do with the problem of *moral hazard*. Consider two individuals with two different health insurance policies. The first policy pays for all medical expenses, but under the second, the individual has to pay the first $1,000 a year (this amount is known as the *deductible*). Will the behavior of the two individuals be different? Generally, the answer is yes. The individual with no deductible is more likely to seek treatment for health problems after they develop rather than try to avoid them and will generally seek medical attention on a more regular basis. In contrast, the individual who faces the first $1,000 of medical expenses each year will tend to engage in more wellness activities and will be less inclined to seek medical care for minor problems. The moral hazard here is that the individual with the zero deductible for medical care expenses will tend to engage in a less healthful lifestyle than will the individual with the $1,000 deductible.

MORAL HAZARD AS IT AFFECTS PHYSICIANS AND HOSPITALS The issue of moral hazard also has a direct effect on the behavior of physicians and hospital administrators. Due to third-party payments, patients rarely have to worry about the expense of operations and other medical procedures. As a consequence, both physicians and hospitals order more procedures. Physicians are typically reimbursed on the basis of medical procedures. Thus, they have no financial interest in trying to keep hospital costs down. Indeed, many have an incentive to raise costs.

Such actions are most evident with terminally ill patients. A physician may order a CT scan and other costly procedures for a terminally ill patient. The physician knows that Medicare or some other type of insurance will pay. Then the physician can charge a fee for analyzing the CT scan. Fully 30 percent of Medicare expenditures are for U.S. residents who are in the last six months of their lives.

You Are There

To read about why moral hazard concerns associated with health insurance posed a practical problem for a West Virginia clinic, consider **The New Experimental Therapy: Prepaid Clinics,** on pages 810 and 811.

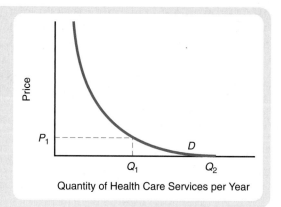

FIGURE 31-9

The Demand for Health Care Services

At price P_1, the quantity of health care services demanded per year would hypothetically be Q_1. If the price fell to zero (third-party payment with zero deductible), the quantity demanded would expand to Q_2.

Rising Medicare expenditures are one of the most serious problems facing the federal government today. The number of beneficiaries has increased from 19.1 million in 1966 (first year of operation) to more than 40 million in 2009. Figure 31-10 shows that federal spending on Medicare has been growing at an average of about 10 percent per year, adjusted for inflation. The rate of growth in Medicare spending will be even higher in the future as a result of the Medicare prescription drug benefit that was implemented in 2006.

Is National Health Insurance the Answer?

Proponents of a national health care system believe that the current system relies too heavily on private insurers. They argue in favor of a Canadian-style system. In Canada, the government sets the fees that are paid to each physician for seeing a patient and prohibits most private practice. The Canadian government also imposes a cap on the income that any physician can receive in a given year. The Canadian federal

FIGURE 31-10

Federal Medicare Spending

Federal spending on Medicare has increased about 10 percent per year, *after adjusting for inflation*, since its inception in 1966. (All figures expressed in constant 2005 dollars per year.)

Sources: Economic Report of the President; U.S. Bureau of Labor Statistics.

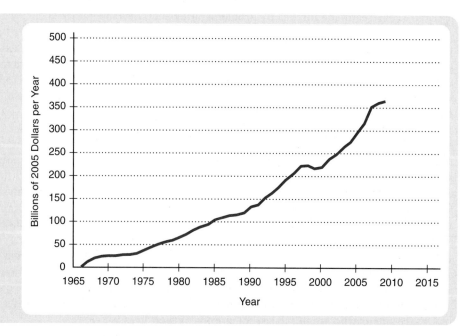

government provides a specified amount of funding to hospitals, leaving it to them to decide how to allocate the funds. If we were to follow the Canadian model, the average U.S. resident would receive considerably fewer health services than at present. Hospital stays would be longer, but there would be fewer tests and procedures.

Alternatives to a national health care policy involve some type of national health insurance, perhaps offered only to people who qualify on the basis of low annual income. A number of politicians have offered variations on such a program. The more than 40 million U.S. residents who have no health insurance at some time during each year might benefit. The share of annual national income that goes to health care expenditures would rise, however. Also, federal government spending might increase by another $60 billion to $100 billion (or more) per year to pay for the program.

How is care rationed under most national health insurance programs?

INTERNATIONAL EXAMPLE
A Symptom of National Health Plans—Long Queues

Most national health plans fix prices for a long period. Thus, when the market clearing price of a health care service rises above the government price, alternative rationing mechanisms arise to address the resulting shortage. In most nations, rationing by queues—that is, waiting in line—is the primary rationing mechanism. For instance, in Canada, the average wait time to see a specialist upon the recommendation of a general physician is nearly 18 weeks. In the United Kingdom (UK), long wait times prevail even to see general practitioners. Wait times are so lengthy to see UK National Health Center dentists that some British residents have resorted to pulling their own teeth or to repairing broken teeth or replacing crowns with Super Glue.

FOR CRITICAL ANALYSIS
Why do you suppose that when the state of Massachusetts implemented a universal-coverage health plan for state residents, the average wait time to see a physician jumped by nearly 60 percent, to more than seven weeks?

Countering the Moral Hazard Problem: A Health Savings Account

As an alternative to completely changing the U.S. health care industry, in 2003 Congress authorized **health savings accounts (HSAs).** These accounts replaced experimental *medical savings accounts* that Congress had previously permitted in only a limited number nationwide. Anyone with a relatively high health insurance deductible—a minimum level of out-of-pocket expenses of slightly more than $1,000 for an individual or just over $2,000 for a family—can open an HSA at a financial institution offering such accounts. Individuals younger than 55 can make annual deposits of up to about $3,000 per person per year, and families can deposit as much as about $6,000 per year. Once a person reaches the age of 55, allowable deposits can be even higher, but contributions must end once the person reaches 65 and becomes eligible for Medicare.

People with HSAs may use deposited funds and tax-free interest earnings to cover any out-of-pocket health care expenses. In addition, they can draw on HSAs to pay health insurance premiums if they become unemployed or to cover medical expenses they incur after they have retired. There is a 10 percent penalty for most withdrawals

Health savings account (HSA)
A tax-exempt health care account into which individuals can pay on a regular basis and out of which medical expenses can be paid.

used for nonmedical purposes before retirement, but when a person retires, funds in an HSA may be used to supplement other sources of income. A single person depositing the maximum amount each year with no withdrawals will have hundreds of thousands of dollars in the account after 40 years.

COMBATING MORAL HAZARD A major benefit of an HSA is that the moral hazard problem is reduced. Individuals ultimately pay for their own *minor* medical expenses. They do not have the incentive to seek medical care as frequently for minor problems. In addition, they have an incentive to engage in wellness activities. Finally, for those using an HSA, the physician-patient relationship remains intact because third parties (insurance companies or the government) do not intervene in paying or monitoring medical expenses. Patients with HSAs usually will not allow physicians to routinely order expensive tests for every minor ache or pain because they get to keep any funds saved in the HSA.

CRITICS' RESPONSES Some critics argue that because individuals get to keep whatever they don't spend from their HSAs, they will forgo necessary visits to medical care facilities and may develop more serious medical problems as a consequence. Other critics argue that HSAs will sabotage managed care plans. Under managed care plans, deductibles are either reduced or eliminated completely. In exchange, managed health care plan participants are extremely limited in physician choice. Just the opposite is true with HSAs—high deductibles and unlimited choice of physicians.

QUICK QUIZ *See page 817 for the answers. Review concepts from this section in MyEconLab.*

Health care costs have risen because (1) our population has been getting older and the elderly use _____ health care services, (2) new technologies and medicines cost more, and (3) _____-_____ financing (private and government-sponsored health insurance) _____ the incentive for individuals to decrease their spending on health care services.

_____ health insurance has been proposed as an answer to our current problems, but it does little

to alter the reasons why health care costs continue to rise.

In 2003, Congress authorized _____ _____ accounts, which allow individuals to set aside funds that are tax-exempt and can be used only for medical care. Whatever is left over becomes a type of _____ account.

You Are There ► The New Experimental Therapy: Prepaid Clinics

Vic Wood's clinic in Wheeling, West Virginia, is open 11 hours per day, six days per week. At the clinic, Wood, another physician, and four physician assistants treat people seeking care for problems ranging from cold symptoms to severe chest pains. Many of them do so under a prepaid-care plan offered by the clinic, in which individuals pay less

than $90 per month and families pay about $125 per month for unlimited primary health care. More than one in five of the clinic's patients have no health insurance, and many of them have opted for the clinic's prepaid plan. Others who had employer-provided health insurance plans with high deductibles—spending levels that must be met out of

You Are There (cont.)

pocket before insurance payments begin—have dropped those plans in favor of Wood's prepaid plan.

Not too long ago, Wood hit a major roadblock to his prepaid-care arrangement. When he began advertising the plan, West Virginia's state insurance commissioner argued that his clinic was operating as an unlicensed insurer and would have to obtain approval of the prices it was charging. In the commissioner's view, the clinic's prices were "too low" and gave people an incentive to switch from regular health insurance plans to Wood's lower-priced plan. The commissioner worried that Wood's plan might be underfunded in light of the moral hazard problem associated with health insurance.

At a chance meeting with the state's governor, Wood was able to argue successfully for a law authorizing an experiment in prepaid health plans in West Virginia. Now Wood is

signing up about a dozen additional patients to the clinic's prepaid plan every month. He estimates that about 1,200 enrollees will provide sufficient monthly funding to keep the clinic in operation.

CRITICAL ANALYSIS QUESTIONS

1. How might it be possible for a health insurance plan to set its prices too low to remain viable for a long period? (Hint: Insurers always keep reserves of cash to handle claims by policyholders, but how do they build up those reserves?)

2. Why do you suppose that some small employers in Wheeling have opted to offer their employees prepaid plans at Wood's clinic instead of traditional health insurance plans?

Issues and Applications

The Volatility of U.S. Households' Incomes

CONCEPTS APPLIED

➤ Income

➤ Distribution of Income

➤ Age-Earnings Cycle

A recent study by Douglas Elmendorf of the Brookings Institution and Federal Reserve economists Karen Dynan and Daniel Sichel found that a measure of U.S. household income volatility has risen by almost one-fourth since the early 1970s. The study attracted considerable media attention. Even though the authors cautioned against interpreting their findings as evidence that U.S. households face more risk of hardship than before, that conclusion is exactly the one that the media reported. Were the media reports justified? Do households today face a much greater potential for sudden drops in their incomes than in years past?

The Two-Sided Implication of Greater Income Variability

By emphasizing only downside income risks faced by households, media reports on the study by Dynan, Elmendorf, and Sichel overlooked an important fact. Any measure of income variability applies to the potential for both downward *and* upward movements in income.

Certainly, the media reports were correct that a general increase in the variability of household incomes implies a greater risk of income declines. Indeed, based on the rise in income variability found in their study, the authors calculated that the probability that a family will experience a decline in income of 50 percent or more in one year, in relation to their income three years earlier, nearly tripled between the early 1970s and the late 2000s. Nevertheless, a rise in income variability also implies an increased probability of unexpected *increases* in incomes of similar magnitude. When income is more volatile, households can receive sudden bursts of income as well as experience abrupt income declines. The media, however, chose not to emphasize this positive aspect of the rise in income volatility.

Has the Share of Households with Large Income Drops Risen?

A 50 percent decline in household income is not as rare as you might think. Figure 31-11 indicates that in the years since 1981, between 12 percent and just over 20 percent of households have experienced an earnings decline of at least 50 percent during the previous year. Thus, in a given year, many households in the United States experience sharp drops in their incomes.

Note, however, that the *actual* share of households experiencing annual income declines of at least 50 percent generally decreased between 1982 and 2000. Although the actual percentage of households with income drops of 50 percent or more has increased slightly during the 2000s, this percentage remains lower than during the 1980s, a fact that the media ignored.

Gender-Based Income Distribution Aspects of Income Volatility

Figure 31-11 also displays percentages for males and females. In every year, more men than women experienced a drop in their incomes of 50 percent or more in relation to the preceding year. This is consistent with

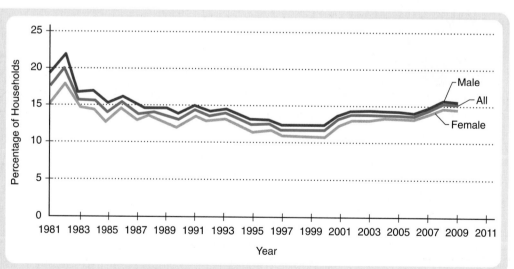

FIGURE 31-11

Percentage of U.S. Households Experiencing at Least a 50 Percent Decline in Earnings

In recent years, nearly 15 percent of households in the United States have experienced earnings reductions of at least 50 percent. Men are more likely than women to experience significant decreases in earnings.

Sources: U.S. Department of Labor; author's estimates.

conclusions that Dynan, Elmendorf, and Sichel reported in their study. Thus, men face a greater risk of sudden drops in income than do women. Because men typically earn more than women, in married households this implies greater income volatility overall. Consequently, couples and families more dependant on a male's income face a higher risk of income reductions.

Nevertheless, there is potentially good news as well as bad news in the greater income variability experienced by men. Sudden *increases* in men's incomes can also occur. The higher male income risks are on the upside as well as on the downside. Once again, however, this is an implication of the study that the media chose not to emphasize.

Test your understanding of this chapter by going online to **MyEconLab**.
In the Study Plan for this chapter, select Section N: News.

For Critical Analysis

1. If the variability of men's incomes were to decline, why might this change be regarded as either "good news" or "bad news" for males?

2. If the variability of men's incomes were to decline without any change taking place in the volatility of women's incomes, what would be the net effect on the income variability of all households?

Web Resources

1. To read the study of household income volatility by Dynan, Elmendorf, and Sichel, go to www.econtoday .com/chapter31.

2. To learn about why increased male income volatility might increase the probability of divorce, go to www.econtoday .com/chapter31.

Research Project

Could differences in the variability of incomes for high-, middle-, and low-income households affect the distribution of income? If not, why not? If so, would the distribution of income necessarily become more or less equal? Explain.

 Here is what you should know after reading this chapter. **MyEconLab** will help you identify what you know, and where to go when you need to practice.

WHAT YOU SHOULD KNOW

Using a Lorenz Curve to Represent a Nation's Income Distribution A Lorenz curve is a diagram that illustrates the distribution of income geometrically by measuring the percentage of households in relation to the cumulative percentage of income earnings. A perfectly straight Lorenz curve depicts perfect income equality because at each percentage of households measured along a straight-line Lorenz curve, those households earn exactly the same percentage of income. The more bowed a Lorenz curve is, the more unequally income is distributed.

distribution of income, 792
Lorenz curve, 792
income in kind, 793

KEY FIGURES
Figure 31-1, 793
Figure 31-2, 793

WHERE TO GO TO PRACTICE

- **MyEconLab** Study Plan 31.1
- Audio introduction to Chapter 31
- Animated Figures 31-1, 31-2
- ABC News Video: Tradeoffs to High-Priced Cancer Drugs

(continued)

(continued)

WHAT YOU SHOULD KNOW		WHERE TO GO TO PRACTICE
Key Determinants of Income Differences Across Individuals Because of the age-earnings cycle, in which people typically begin working at relatively low incomes when young, age is an important factor influencing income differences. So are marginal productivity differences, which arise from differences in talent, experience, and training due to different investments in human capital. Discrimination likely plays a role as well, and economists attribute some of the unexplained portions of income differences across people to factors related to discrimination.	age-earnings cycle, 796 **KEY FIGURE** Figure 31-4, 796	• **MyEconLab** Study Plan 31.2 • Video: The Determinants of Income Differences • Animated Figure 31-4
Theories of Desired Income Distribution Economists agree that determining how income ought to be distributed is a normative issue influenced by alternative notions of economic justice. Nevertheless, two theories of desired income distribution receive considerable attention. One is the productivity standard (also called the contributive or merit standard), according to which each person receives income according to the value of what the person produces. The other is the egalitarian principle of income distribution, which proposes that each person should receive exactly the same income.		• **MyEconLab** Study Plan 31.3
Alternative Approaches to Measuring and Addressing Poverty One approach to measuring poverty is to define an absolute poverty standard, such as a specific and unchanging income level. If an absolute measure of poverty is used and the economy experiences persistent real growth, poverty will eventually disappear. Another approach defines poverty in terms of income levels relative to the rest of the population. Under this definition, poverty exists as long as the distribution of incomes is unequal. Official poverty measures are often based on pretax income and fail to take transfer payments into account. Currently, the U.S. government seeks to address poverty via income maintenance programs such as Social Security, Supplemental Security Income, Temporary Assistance to Needy Families, food stamps, and the Earned Income Tax Credit Program.	**KEY FIGURES** Figure 31-5, 801 Figure 31-6, 802	• **MyEconLab** Study Plan 31.4 • Video: Defining Poverty • Animated Figure 31-5, 31-6
Major Reasons for Rising Health Care Costs Spending on health care as a percentage of total U.S. national income has increased during recent decades. One reason is that the U.S. population is aging, and older people typically experience more health problems. Another contributing factor is the adoption of higher-quality but also higher-priced technologies for diagnosing and treating health problems. In addition, third-party financing of health care expenditures by private and government	third parties, 806 **KEY FIGURES** Figure 31-7, 805 Figure 31-8, 807 Figure 31-9, 808	• **MyEconLab** Study Plan 31.5 • Animated Figures 31-7, 31-8, 31-9

(continued)

myeconlab *(continued)*

WHAT YOU SHOULD KNOW		WHERE TO GO TO PRACTICE
insurance programs gives covered individuals an incentive to purchase more health care than they would if they paid all expenses out of pocket. Moral hazard problems can also arise because consumers may be more likely to seek treatment for insured health problems after they develop instead of trying to avoid them, and physicians and hospitals may order more procedures than they otherwise would require.		
Alternative Approaches to Paying for Health Care An alternative approach to funding health care would be to rely less on private insurers and more on governmental funding of care for all citizens. Under such a system, the government typically sets fees and establishes limits on access to care. Another approach would be to establish an income-based national health insurance program, in which only lower-income people would qualify for government assistance in meeting their health care expenses. Another option, which Congress authorized in 2003, is to provide incentives for people to save some of their income in health savings accounts, from which they can draw funds to pay for health care expenses in the future.	health savings account (HSA), 809	• **MyEconLab** Study Plan 31.5

Log in to MyEconLab, take a chapter test, and get a personalized Study Plan that tells you which concepts you understand and which ones you need to review. From there, MyEconLab will give you further practice, tutorials, animations, videos, and guided solutions.
Log in to www.myeconlab.com

PROBLEMS

All problems are assignable in myeconlab. *Answers to the odd-numbered problems appear at the back of the book.*

31-1. Consider the graph at the right, which depicts Lorenz curves for countries X, Y, and Z.

    a. Which country has the least income inequality?

    b. Which country has the most income inequality?

    c. Countries Y and Z are identical in all but one respect: population distribution. The share of the population made up of children below working age is much higher in country Z. Recently, however, birthrates have declined in country Z and risen in country Y. Assuming that the countries remain identical in all other respects, would you expect that in 20 years the Lorenz curves for the two countries will be

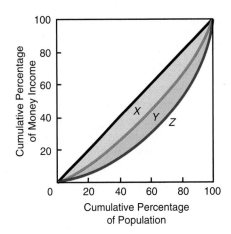

closer together or farther apart? (Hint: According to the age-earnings cycle, what typically happens to income as an individual begins working and ages?)

31-2. Consider the following estimates from the mid-2000s of shares of income to each group. Use graph paper or a hand-drawn diagram to draw rough Lorenz curves for each country. Which has the most nearly equal distribution, based on your diagram?

Country	Poorest 40%	Next 30%	Next 20%	Richest 10%
Bolivia	13	21	26	40
Chile	13	20	26	41
Uruguay	22	26	26	26

31-3. Suppose that the 20 percent of people with the highest incomes decide to increase their annual giving to charities, which pass nearly all the funds on to the 20 percent of people with the lowest incomes. What is the effect on the shape of the Lorenz curve?

31-4. Suppose that a nation has implemented a system for applying a tax rate of 2 percent to the incomes earned by the 10 percent of its residents with the highest incomes. All funds collected are then transferred directly to the 10 percent of the nation's residents with the lowest incomes.

    a. What is the general effect on the shape of a Lorenz curve based on incomes prior to collection and redistribution of the tax?

    b. What is the general effect on the shape of a Lorenz curve based on after-tax, post-redistribution incomes?

31-5. Estimates indicate that during the mid-2000s, the poorest 40 percent of the population earned about 15 percent of total income in Argentina. In Brazil, the poorest 40 percent earned about 10 percent of total income. The next-highest 30 percent of income earners in Argentina received roughly 25 percent of total income. By contrast, in Brazil, the next-highest 30 percent of income earners received approximately 20 percent of total income. Can you determine, without drawing a diagram (though you can if you wish), which country's Lorenz curve was bowed out farther to the right?

31-6. Explain why the productivity standard for the distribution of income entails rewarding people based on their contribution to society's total output. Why does the productivity standard typically fail to yield an equal distribution of income?

31-7. Identify whether each of the following proposed poverty measures is an absolute or relative measure of poverty, and discuss whether poverty could ever be eliminated if that measure were utilized.

    a. An inflation-adjusted annual income of $25,000 for an urban family of four

    b. Individuals with annual incomes among the lowest 15 percent

    c. An inflation-adjusted annual income of $10,000 per person

31-8. Some economists have argued that if the government wishes to subsidize health care, it should instead provide predetermined sums of payments (based on the type of health care problems experienced) directly to patients, who then would be free to choose their health care providers. Whether or not you agree, can you give an economic rationale for this approach to governmental health care funding?

31-9. Suppose that a government agency guarantees to pay all of an individual's future health care expenses after the end of this year, so that the effective price of health care for the individual will be zero from that date onward. In what ways might this well-intended policy induce the individual to consume "excessive" health care services in future years?

31-10. Suppose that a group of physicians establishes a joint practice in a remote area. This group provides the only health care available to people in the local community, and its objective is to maximize total economic profits for the group's members. Draw a diagram illustrating how the price and quantity of health care will be determined in this community. (Hint: How does a single producer of any service determine its output and price?)

31-11. A government agency determines that the entire community discussed in Problem 31-10 qualifies for a special program in which the government will pay for a number of health care services that most residents previously had not consumed. Many residents immediately make appointments with the community physicians' group. Given the information in Problem 31-10, what is the likely effect on the profit-maximizing price and the equilibrium quantity of health care services provided by the physicians' group in this community?

31-12. A government agency notifies the physicians' group in Problem 31-10 that to continue providing services in the community, the group must document its activities. The resulting paperwork expenses raise the cost of each unit of health care services that the group provides. What is the likely effect on the profit-maximizing price and the equilibrium quantity of health care services provided by the physicians' group in this community?

31-13. As discussed in this chapter, interest-bearing health savings accounts (HSAs) allow individuals with qualifying health insurance plans to use deposited funds to pay out-of-pocket medical expenses. Subject to penalties and taxation, holders of HSAs can use funds in the accounts and tax-free interest earnings to pay non-health-related expenses if they wish. Many people, however, participate in optional *health reimbursement accounts (HRAs)* offered alongside employer-provided health insurance plans. HRAs, into which people typically make payments via tax-free deductions from their weekly or monthly earnings, are non-interest-bearing and can be used only to pay medical expenses. In most plans, any funds in HRAs that individuals fail to use for medical expenses within a calendar year revert to the employer at the end of the year. Is an HSA or an HRA more likely to create moral hazard problems? Explain your reasoning.

ECONOMICS ON THE NET

Measuring Poverty In this application, you will learn why poverty can be difficult to measure.

Title: World Bank PovertyNet: Understanding Poverty

Navigation: Go to **www.econtoday.com/chapter31** to visit the World Bank's home page. Click on *Topics* and then *Poverty Analysis*. Then click on *Measuring Poverty*.

Application Perform the indicated operations, and answer the following questions.

1. Click on "Defining welfare measures." Why does this discussion suggest that measures of consumption are more useful to use in measuring poverty than income measures? Does the U.S. government's use of income thresholds for its official definition of poverty accord with this discussion?

2. Click on "Choose and estimate a poverty line." What alternative absolute poverty definitions are discussed? If the U.S. government were to adopt any of these absolute measures for its official poverty definition, what would happen to the U.S. poverty rate as real incomes and living standards rise over time?

For Group Study and Analysis Click on "Choose and estimate poverty indicators." What are the advantages and disadvantages of the poverty indicators that are discussed? Which indicator does the U.S. government utilize?

ANSWERS TO QUICK QUIZZES

p. 796: (i) income . . . equality . . . unequally; (ii) assets . . . more
p. 800: (i) age-earnings; (ii) productivity . . . revenue; (iii) talent . . . education . . . experience . . . training; (iv) human . . . opportunity; (v) productivity . . . equality
p. 804: (i) absolute . . . relative; (ii) poor . . . income; (iii) Social . . . Supplemental . . . earned income . . . food
p. 810: (i) more . . . third-party . . . reduces; (ii) National; (iii) health savings . . . retirement

32

Environmental Economics

Market activities in China currently generate about 200 million tons of solid waste annually. Estimates indicate that this flow of trash is rising by about 12 million additional tons with each passing year. Yet only about 30 percent of China's solid waste is incinerated or buried in sequestered landfills, as compared with 90 percent in the United States. Much of China's solid waste contains harmful chemicals, which have contaminated the water supplies of an estimated 90 percent of the nation's cities. Why are residents of China apparently willing to tolerate so much pollution? Will ongoing economic growth contribute to even more pollution in China, or can we anticipate efforts to engage in more pollution abatement in the future? After reading this chapter, you will be prepared to contemplate these questions.

LEARNING OBJECTIVES

myeconlab

MyEconLab helps you master each objective and study more efficiently. See end of chapter for details.

After reading this chapter, you should be able to:

➤ Distinguish between private costs and social costs

➤ Understand market externalities and possible ways to correct externalities

➤ Explain how economists can conceptually determine the optimal quantity of pollution

➤ Contrast the roles of private and common property rights in alternative approaches to addressing the problem of pollution

➤ Describe how many of the world's governments are seeking to reduce pollution by capping and controlling the use of pollution-generating resources

➤ Discuss how the assignment of property rights may influence the fates of endangered species

? **DID YOU KNOW THAT** the Portland, Oregon–based Bonneville Power Administration, an agency of the U.S. Department of Energy, has spent more than $9 billion over the past three decades trying to increase the U.S. salmon population? These fish travel from the mountain streams of their birth to the Pacific Ocean and then back again to lay eggs in their home streams. As part of their trek, they must navigate several human-made dams administered by the Bonneville Power Administration. To help the salmon along, the agency has created artificial waterways to enable the salmon to traverse its dams. It has even used barges to give the salmon rides around the dams. To try to learn why salmon populations remain low despite these efforts, agency employees attached tracking equipment to fish. They discovered that salmon are succumbing to several dangers in addition to the dams. Key threats include predatory birds and sea lions, whose numbers have increased in recent years—in part because other government agencies have spent millions of dollars to boost populations of these salmon predators.

The economic way of thinking about potentially endangered species, including certain fish species such as salmon, requires considering the costs of protecting endangered species. Likewise, the economic way of thinking about nonrenewable resources or the environment requires taking into account the costs of resource conservation and environmental protection. What additional portion of your weekly wages are you willing to give up to take measures to protect declining populations of species such as salmon? To some people, framing questions in terms of the dollars-and-cents costs of environmental improvement sounds anti-ecological. But this is not so. Economists want to help citizens and policymakers opt for informed policies that have the maximum possible *net* benefits (benefits minus costs). As you will see, every decision made in favor of "the environment" involves a trade-off.

Private versus Social Costs

Human actions often give rise to unwanted side effects—the destruction of our environment is one. Human actions generate pollutants that go into the air and the water. The question that is often asked is, Why do individuals and businesses continue to create pollution without necessarily paying directly for the negative consequences?

Until now, we've been dealing with settings in which the costs of an individual's actions are borne directly by the individual. When a business has to pay wages to workers, it knows exactly what its labor costs are. When it has to buy materials or build a plant, it knows quite well what these will cost. An individual who has to pay for car repairs or a theater ticket knows exactly what the cost will be. These costs are what we term *private costs*. **Private costs** are borne solely by the individuals who incur them. They are *internal* in the sense that the firm or household must explicitly take account of them.

Private costs
Costs borne solely by the individuals who incur them. Also called *internal costs*.

What about a situation in which a business dumps the waste products from its production process into a nearby river or an individual litters a public park or beach? Obviously, a cost is involved in these actions. When the firm pollutes the water, people downstream suffer the consequences. They may not want to swim in or drink the polluted water. They may also be unable to catch as many fish as before because of the pollution. In the case of littering, the people who come along after the litterer has cluttered the park or the beach are the ones who bear the costs. The cost of these actions is borne by people other than those who commit the actions. The creator of the cost is not the sole bearer. The costs are not internalized by the individual or firm; they are external. When we add *external* costs to *internal*, or private, costs, we get **social costs.** Pollution problems—indeed, all problems pertaining to the environment—may be

Social costs
The full costs borne by society whenever a resource use occurs. Social costs can be measured by adding external costs to private, or internal, costs.

viewed as situations in which social costs exceed private costs. Because some economic participants pay only the smaller private costs of their actions, not the full social costs, their actions ultimately contribute to higher external costs on the rest of society. In such situations in which social and private costs diverge, we therefore see "too much" steel production, automobile driving, and beach littering, to pick only a few of the many possible examples.

The Costs of Polluted Air

Why is the air in cities so polluted from automobile exhaust fumes? When automobile drivers step into their cars, they bear only the private costs of driving. That is, they must pay for the gas, maintenance, depreciation, and insurance on their automobiles. But they cause an additional cost, that of air pollution, which they are not forced to take into account when they make the decision to drive. Air pollution is a cost because it causes harm to individuals—burning eyes, respiratory ailments, and dirtier clothes, cars, and buildings—and adds to accumulations of various gases that may contribute to global warming. The air pollution created by automobile exhaust is a cost that individual operators of automobiles do not yet bear directly. The social cost of driving includes all the private costs plus at least the cost of air pollution, which society bears. Decisions made only on the basis of private costs lead to too much automobile driving. Clean air is a scarce resource used by automobile drivers free of charge. They will use more of it than they would if they had to pay the full social costs.

Externalities

Externality

A situation in which a private cost (or benefit) diverges from a social cost (or benefit); a situation in which the costs (or benefits) of an action are not fully borne (or gained) by the decision makers engaging in a scarce-resource-using activity.

When a private cost differs from a social cost, we say that there is an **externality** because individual decision makers are not paying (internalizing) all the costs. (We briefly covered this topic in Chapter 5.) Some of these costs remain external to the decision-making process. Remember that the full cost of using a scarce resource is borne one way or another by all who live in the society. That is, members of society must pay the full opportunity cost of any activity that uses scarce resources. The individual decision maker is the firm or the customer, and external costs and benefits will not enter into that individual's or firm's decision-making processes.

We might want to view the problem as it is presented in Figure 32-1. Here we have the market demand curve, D, for product X and the supply curve, S_1, for product X. The supply curve, S_1, includes only internal, or private, costs, which for simplicity are assumed to be identical for each producer. The intersection of the demand and supply curves as drawn will be at price P_1 and quantity Q_1 (at E_1). We now assume that the production of good X involves externalities that the private firms did not take into account. Those externalities could be air pollution, water pollution, scenery destruction, or anything of that nature.

We know that the social costs of producing product X exceed the private costs. We show this by drawing curve S_2. It is above the original supply curve S_1 because it includes the full social costs of producing the product. If firms could be made to bear these costs, their willingness to supply the good would be reduced, so the price would be P_2 and the quantity Q_2 (at E_2). The inclusion of external costs in the decision-making process would lead to a higher-priced product and a decline in quantity produced. Thus, we see that when social costs are not being fully borne by the creators of those costs, the quantity produced is "excessive" because the price to consumers is too low.

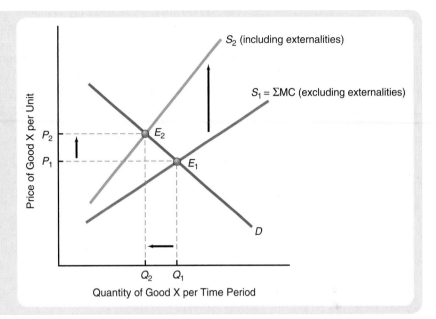

Reckoning with Full Social Costs

The supply curve, S_1, is equal to the horizontal summation (represented by the capital Greek letter Σ) of the individual marginal cost curves above the respective minimum average variable costs of all the firms producing good X. These individual marginal cost curves include only internal, or private, costs, assumed to be identical for all producers. If the external costs were included and added to the private costs, we would have social costs. The supply curve would shift upward to S_2. In the uncorrected situation, the equilibrium price is P_1, and the equilibrium quantity is Q_1. In the corrected situation, the equilibrium price would rise to P_2, and the equilibrium quantity would fall to Q_2.

Correcting for Externalities

We can see here a method for reducing pollution and environmental degradation. Somehow the signals in the economy must be changed so that decision makers will take into account *all* the costs of their actions. In the case of automobile pollution, we might want to devise some method of taxing motorists according to the amount of pollution they cause. In the case of a firm, we might want to devise a system of taxing businesses according to the amount of pollution for which they are responsible. They might then have an incentive to install pollution abatement equipment.

The Polluters' Choice

Facing an additional private cost for polluting, firms will be induced to (1) install pollution abatement equipment or otherwise change production techniques so as to reduce the amount of pollution, (2) reduce pollution-causing activity, or (3) simply pay the price and reduce its pollution-generating activities. The relative costs and benefits of each option for each polluter will determine which one or combination will be chosen. Allowing the choice is the efficient way to decide who pollutes and who doesn't. In principle, just as with the use of all other scarce resources, each polluter faces the full social cost of its actions and makes a production decision accordingly.

Is a Uniform Tax Appropriate?

It may not be appropriate to levy a *uniform* tax according to physical quantities of pollution. After all, we're talking about external costs. Such costs are not necessarily the same everywhere in the United States for the same action.

Essentially, we must establish the amount of the *economic damages* rather than the amount of the physical pollution. A polluting electrical plant in New York City will cause much more damage than the same plant in Montana. There are already innumerable demands on the air in New York City, so the pollution from smokestacks will not be cleansed away naturally. Millions of people will breathe the polluted air and thereby incur the costs of sore throats, sickness, emphysema, and even early death. Buildings will become dirtier faster because of the pollution, as will cars and clothes. A given quantity of pollution will cause more harm in concentrated urban environments than it will in less dense rural environments. If we were to establish some form of taxation to align private costs with social costs and to force people to internalize externalities, we would somehow have to come up with a measure of *economic* costs instead of *physical* quantities. But the tax, in any event, would fall on the private sector and modify individuals' and firms' behavior. Therefore, because the economic cost for the same physical quantity of pollution would be different in different locations depending on population density, natural formations of mountains and rivers, and the like, so-called optimal taxes on pollution would vary from location to location. (Nonetheless, a uniform tax might make sense when administrative costs, particularly the cost of ascertaining the actual economic costs, are relatively high.)

Could raising uniform taxes on cigarettes be more effective than outright bans on public smoking in protecting nonsmokers from harmful effects of cigarette smoke?

POLICY EXAMPLE
Passive Smoking Effects of Smoking Bans versus Cigarette Taxes

By studying data on concentrations of *cotinine*, a by-product of nicotine that shows up in people's blood samples, economists have found that bans on public cigarette smoking have mixed effects. On the one hand, such bans certainly cut down on the amount of cigarette smoke inhaled by nonsmokers in public places. On the other hand, the bans encourage more cigarette smoking at home, thereby exposing nonsmokers who live with smokers, such as children and other relatives, to even more smoke. Economists have found that nonsmoking family members' exposure to cigarette smoke increases significantly, particularly in lower-income households, in cities where smoking bans are in effect.

In contrast, economists have found evidence that higher cigarette taxes reduce exposure to smoke among *all* nonsmokers,

including family members of smokers. Every 10 percent increase in the excise tax on cigarettes is associated with a 3 to 4 percent reduction in nonsmokers' exposure to cigarette smoke. One possible explanation is that when smokers cut back on cigarette consumption in response to higher excise taxes, they smoke the smaller number of cigarettes alone, rather than in the presence of nonsmokers. Thus, imposing higher uniform taxes on cigarettes may be more effective at shielding nonsmokers from cigarette smoke than bans on public smoking.

FOR CRITICAL ANALYSIS
Where does the post-tax cigarette supply curve lie in relation to the pre-tax cigarette supply curve?

QUICK QUIZ
See page 837 for the answers. Review concepts from this section in MyEconLab.

_____ costs are costs that are borne directly by consumers and producers when they engage in any resource-using activity.

Social costs are _____ costs plus any other costs that are external to the decision maker. For example, the social

costs of driving include all the _____ costs plus, at a minimum, any pollution caused.

When _____ costs differ from social costs, _____ exist because individual decision makers are not internalizing all the costs that society is bearing.

Pollution

The term *pollution* is used quite loosely and can refer to a variety of by-products of any activity. Industrial pollution involves mainly air and water but can also include noise and even aesthetic pollution, as when a landscape is altered in a negative way. For the most part, we will be analyzing the most common forms—air and water pollution.

Assessing the Appropriate Amount of Pollution

When asked how much pollution there should be in the economy, many people will respond, "None." But if we ask those same people how much starvation or deprivation of consumer products should exist in the economy, many will again say, "None." Growing and distributing food or producing consumer products creates pollution, however. There is no correct answer to how much pollution should be in an economy because when we ask how much pollution there *should* be, we are entering the realm of normative economics. We are asking people to express values. There is no way to disprove somebody's value system scientifically.

One way we can approach a discussion of the "correct" amount of pollution is to set up the same type of marginal analysis we used in our discussion of a firm's employment and output decisions. That is to say, we can consider pursuing measures to reduce pollution only up to the point at which the marginal benefit from pollution reduction equals the marginal cost of pollution reduction.

Go to **www.econtoday.com/chapter32** to see a review by the ACCF Center for Policy Research of possible economic effects of efforts to reduce pollution.

THE MARGINAL BENEFIT OF A LESS POLLUTED ENVIRONMENT Look at Figure 32-2. On the horizontal axis, we show the degree of air cleanliness. A vertical line is drawn at 100 percent cleanliness—the air cannot become any cleaner. Consider the benefits of obtaining a greater degree of air cleanliness. The benefits of obtaining cleaner air are represented by the marginal benefit curve, which slopes downward.

FIGURE 32-2

The Optimal Quantity of Air Pollution

As we attempt to get a greater degree of air cleanliness, the marginal cost rises until trying to increase air cleanliness even slightly leads to a very high marginal cost, as can be seen at the upper right of the graph. Conversely, the marginal benefit curve slopes downward: The more pure air we have, the less we value an additional unit of pure air. Marginal cost and marginal benefit intersect at point E. The optimal degree of air cleanliness is something less than 100 percent at Q_0. The price that we should pay for the last unit of air cleanup is no greater than P_0, for that is where marginal cost equals marginal benefit.

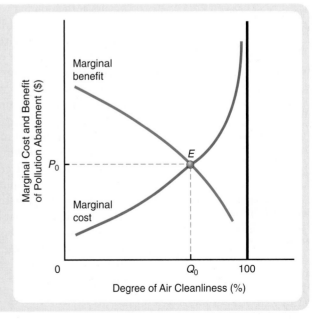

When the air is very dirty, the marginal benefit from air that is a little cleaner appears to be relatively high, as shown on the vertical axis. As the air becomes cleaner, however, the marginal benefit of a little bit more air cleanliness falls.

THE MARGINAL COST OF POLLUTION ABATEMENT Consider the marginal cost of pollution abatement—that is, the marginal cost of obtaining cleaner air. In the 1960s, automobiles had no pollution abatement devices. Eliminating only 20 percent of the pollutants emitted by internal-combustion engines entailed a relatively small cost per unit of pollution removed. The per-unit cost of eliminating the next 20 percent increased, though. Finally, as we now get to the upper limits of removal of pollutants from the emissions of internal-combustion engines, we find that the elimination of one more percentage point of the amount of pollutants becomes astronomically expensive. In the short run, moving from 97 percent cleanliness to 98 percent cleanliness involves a marginal cost that is many times greater than the marginal cost of going from 10 percent cleanliness to 11 percent cleanliness.

It is realistic, therefore, to draw the marginal cost of pollution abatement as an upward-sloping curve, as shown in Figure 32-2 on the preceding page. (The marginal cost curve slopes up because of the law of diminishing marginal product.)

The Optimal Quantity of Pollution

Optimal quantity of pollution

The level of pollution for which the marginal benefit of one additional unit of pollution abatement just equals the marginal cost of that additional unit of pollution abatement.

The **optimal quantity of pollution** is defined as the level of pollution at which the marginal benefit equals the marginal cost of pollution abatement. This occurs at the intersection of the marginal benefit curve and the marginal cost curve in Figure 32-2, at point E. This solution is analytically exactly the same as for every other economic activity. If we increased pollution control by one unit beyond Q_0, the marginal cost of that small increase in the degree of air cleanliness would be greater than the marginal benefit to society.

As is usually the case in economic analysis, the optimal quantity occurs when marginal cost equals marginal benefit. That is, the optimal quantity of pollution occurs at the point at which the marginal cost of reducing (or abating) pollution is just equal to the marginal benefit of doing so. The marginal cost of pollution abatement rises as more and more abatement is achieved (as the environment becomes cleaner and cleaner, the *extra* cost of cleansing rises). Early units of pollution abatement are easily achieved (at low cost), but attaining higher and higher levels of environmental quality becomes progressively more difficult (as the extra cost rises to prohibitive levels). At the same time, the marginal benefits of an increasingly cleaner environment fall; the marginal benefit of pollution abatement declines as our notion of a cleaner environment moves from sustenance of human life to recreation to beauty to a perfectly pure environment. The point at which the increasing marginal cost of pollution abatement equals the decreasing marginal benefit of pollution abatement defines the optimal quantity of pollution.

Go to www.econtoday.com/chapter32 to learn from the National Center for Policy Analysis about a market-oriented government program for reducing pollution.

Recognizing that the optimal quantity of pollution is not zero becomes easier when we realize that it takes scarce resources to reduce pollution. A trade-off exists between producing a cleaner environment and producing other goods and services. In that sense, environmental cleanliness is a good that can be analyzed like any other good, and a cleaner environment must take its place with other human wants.

QUICK QUIZ *See page 837 for the answers. Review concepts from this section in MyEconLab.*

The marginal cost of cleaning up the environment _____ as we get closer to 100 percent cleanliness. Indeed, it _____ at an _____ rate.

The marginal benefit of environmental cleanliness _____ as we have more of it.

The **optimal quantity of pollution** is the quantity at which the _____ _____ of cleanup equals the _____ _____ of cleanup.

Pollution abatement is a trade-off. We trade off _____ and _____ for cleaner air and water, and vice versa.

Common Property

In most cases, you do not have **private property rights**, or exclusive ownership rights, to the air surrounding you, nor does anyone else. Air is a **common property**, or a nonexclusive resource. Therein lies the crux of the problem. When no one owns a particular resource, no one has any incentive (conscience aside) to consider externality spillovers associated with that resource. If one person decides not to add to externality spillovers and avoids polluting the air, normally there will not be any significant effect on the total level of pollution. If one person decides not to pollute the ocean, there will still be approximately the same amount of ocean pollution—provided, of course, that the individual was previously responsible for only a small part of the total amount of ocean pollution.

Basically, pollution and other activities that create spillovers occur when we have poorly defined private property rights, as in air and common bodies of water. We do not, for example, have a visual pollution problem in people's attics. That is their own property, which they choose to keep as clean as they want, depending on their preferences for cleanliness weighed against the costs of keeping the attic neat and tidy.

When private property rights exist, individuals have legal recourse for any damages sustained through the use of their property. When private property rights are well defined, the use of property—that is, the use of resources—will generally involve contracting between the owners of those resources. If you own land, you might contract with another person who wants to use your land for raising cattle. The contract would most likely take the form of a written lease agreement.

Voluntary Agreements and Transaction Costs

Is it possible for externalities to be internalized via voluntary agreement? Take a simple example. You live in a house with a nice view of a lake. The family living below you plants a tree. The tree grows so tall that it eventually starts to cut off your view. In most cities, no one has property rights to views; therefore, you usually cannot go to court to obtain relief. You do have the option of contracting with your neighbors, however.

VOLUNTARY AGREEMENTS: CONTRACTING You have the option of paying your neighbors (contracting) to cut back the tree. You could start out by offering a small amount and keep going up until your neighbors agree or until you reach your limit. Your limit will equal the value you place on having an unobstructed view of the lake. Your neighbors will be willing if the payment is at least equal to the reduction in

Private property rights
Exclusive rights of ownership that allow the use, transfer, and exchange of property.

Common property
Property that is owned by everyone and therefore by no one. Air and water are examples of common property resources.

> **You Are There**
>
> For practice thinking about why private versus common property matters when considering how to limit pollution spillovers, contemplate **A U.S. Senator Finds the Largest U.S. Carbon Footprint,** on page 831.

their intrinsic property value due to a stunted tree. Your offer of the payment makes your neighbors aware of the social cost of their actions. The social cost here is equal to the care of the tree plus the cost suffered by you from an impeded view of the lake.

In essence, then, your offer of money income to your neighbors indicates to them that there is an opportunity cost to their actions. If they don't comply, they forfeit the payments that you are offering them. The point here is that *opportunity cost always exists, no matter who has property rights*. Therefore, we would expect that under some circumstances voluntary contracting will occur to internalize externalities. The question is, When will voluntary agreements occur?

Transaction costs
All costs associated with making, reaching, and enforcing agreements.

TRANSACTION COSTS One major condition for the outcome just outlined is that the **transaction costs**—all costs associated with making and enforcing agreements—must be low relative to the expected benefits of reaching an agreement. (We already looked at this topic briefly in Chapter 4.) If we expand our example to a much larger one such as air pollution, the transaction costs of numerous homeowners trying to reach agreements with the individuals and companies that create the pollution are relatively high. Consequently, people may not always engage in voluntary contracting, even though it can be an effective way to internalize the externality of air pollution.

What prevents the homeowners surrounding this polluting manufacturing plant from paying the plant to reduce pollution?

Changing Property Rights

We can approach the problem of property rights by assuming that initially in a society, many property rights to resources are not defined. But this situation does not cause a problem as long as no one cares to use the resources for which there are no property rights or resources are available in desired quantities at a zero price. Only if and when a use is found for a resource at a zero price does a problem develop. Unless some decision then is made about property rights, the resource will be wasted and possibly even destroyed. Property rights can be assigned to individuals who will then assert control; or they may be assigned to government, which can maintain and preserve the resource, charge for its use, or implement some other rationing device. With common property such as air and water, governments have indeed attempted to take over the control of those resources so that they cannot be wasted or destroyed.

Another way of viewing the problem of pollution spillovers is to argue that it cannot continue to arise if a way can be found to assign private property rights for all resources. We can then say that each individual does not have the right to act on anything that is not his or her property. Hence, no individual has the right to create pollution spillovers on property that the individual does not specifically own.

Clearly, we must fill the gap between private costs and social costs in situations in which property rights are not well defined or assigned. There are three ways to fill this gap: taxation, subsidization, and regulation. Government is involved in all three. Unfortunately, government does not have perfect information and may not pick the appropriate tax, subsidy, or type of regulation. Furthermore, in some situations, it may be difficult to enforce taxes or direct subsidies to "worthy" recipients. In such cases, outright prohibition of the polluting activity may be the optimal solution to a particular pollution spillover. For example, if it is difficult to monitor the level of a particular type of pollution that even in small quantities can cause severe environmental damage, outright prohibition of activities that cause such pollution may be the best alternative.

Reducing Humanity's Carbon Footprint: Restraining Pollution-Causing Activities

In light of the costs arising from spillovers that polluting activities create, one solution might seem to be for governments to try to stop them from taking place. Why don't more governments simply *require* businesses and households to cut back on pollution-causing activities?

How the European Union Mixes Government Controls and Market Processes

In fact, many governments are implementing schemes aimed at capping and controlling the use of pollution-generating resources. In recent years, certain scientific research has suggested that emissions of carbon dioxide, sulfur dioxide, and various other so-called *greenhouse gases* might be contributing to atmospheric warming. The result, some scientists fear, might be global climate changes harmful to people inhabiting various regions of the planet. In response, the governments of more than three dozen nations agreed to participate in the *Kyoto Protocol* of a broader set of international treaties called the Framework Convention on Climate Change. Under this 1997 agreement, the governments of participating nations agreed to reduce their overall emissions of greenhouse gases by 2020 to as much as 20 percent below 1990 levels.

To what lengths are the members of the European Union (EU) going to fight emissions of greenhouse gases?

INTERNATIONAL POLICY EXAMPLE
EU Governments Get Serious About Emissions—Or Do They?

The governments of the EU's member nations appear to have become quite serious about inducing average citizens to cut back on activities that yield greenhouse gas emissions (the so-called carbon footprint). In Wallonia, a French-speaking region in Belgium, the government charges a fee of more than $30 to people who desire to use barbecue grills that

emit about 100 grams of carbon dioxide per cooked meal. It enforces the policy by using helicopters with thermal sensors. In London, a local government uses light aircraft fitted with military spy technology to identify homes that are wasting energy. Government officials place the images on the Internet in an effort to shame people with poorly insulated homes into doing better.

INTERNATIONAL POLICY EXAMPLE (cont.)

EU governments are also using taxpayer funds to finance projects aimed at reducing worldwide methane gas emissions created by growing rice, a staple food for an estimated 2 billion people.

Nevertheless, some observers question the depth of the EU governments' commitment to reducing their countries' carbon emissions. Because the EU governments insist on having meetings in both France and Belgium, thousands of legislators and their staff assistants fly between the two countries each month. The exhaust from jet engines used to transport all of these officials creates an estimated 20,000 *tons* of additional carbon dioxide emissions each year.

FOR CRITICAL ANALYSIS
Given that a short helicopter flight typically generates at least 50,000 grams of carbon dioxide emissions, is the Wallonian effort to regulate the use of barbecue grills likely to generate a net reduction in carbon dioxide emissions?

EMISSIONS CAPS AND PERMITS TRADING The members of the European Union are among the key participants in the Kyoto Protocol. In January 2005, the EU established a set of rules called the *Emissions Trading Scheme*. Under this program, each nation in the EU seeks to cap its aggregate greenhouse gas emissions at a level consistent with its target under the Kyoto Protocol. Thus, for instance, the French government specified limits on aggregate emissions of carbon dioxide and other greenhouse gases that would enable France to meet its Kyoto target.

Once an overall national cap was set, each EU nation established an *allowance* of metric tons of a gas, such as carbon dioxide, that a company is permitted to release. If a company's emissions of carbon dioxide exceed its allowance—that is, if its "carbon footprint" in the atmosphere is too large—then the company must buy more allowances through a trading system. These allowances can be obtained, at the current market clearing price, from companies that are emitting less carbon dioxide than their permitted amounts and therefore have unutilized allowances.

THEORY CONFRONTS EUROPEAN POLICY AND MARKET REALITIES In theory, if EU governments had set the national emissions caps low enough to force companies to reduce greenhouse gases, the market clearing price of emissions allowances should have reflected this constraint. In addition, as governments continue to tighten the caps to meet the Kyoto limits that require greenhouse gas emissions to be reduced to 20 percent below 1990 levels by 2020, more firms should respond by purchasing allowances. Then the market clearing price of allowances would rise. Rather than paying a higher price for emissions allowances, many firms would instead opt to develop methods of reducing their emissions. In this way, this market-based mechanism established by the Emissions Trading Scheme would induce firms to reduce their emissions, and the EU nations would achieve the targets set under the Kyoto Protocol.

In fact, in the spring of 2006, the market clearing price of EU emissions allowances dropped by more than 60 percent. The reason that prices dropped, many economists agree, is that most EU governments issued more allowances than were consistent with capping emissions at the Kyoto target levels. Indeed, the price drop was consistent with an initial surplus of more than 200 million allowances.

Most observers suspect that the Emissions Trading Scheme's fundamental weakness was that each nation's government was permitted to establish the emissions target and allowances for its own country. Each government feared making its own nation's firms less cost-competitive than those in other nations, so every government inflated its estimate of its mid-2000s emissions of greenhouse gases. Doing so allowed each government to set its overall emissions cap at a level that actually failed to constrain emissions. One result was the big drop in prices of emissions allowances, which have remained substantially lower than when the Emissions Trading Scheme was first established. Another outcome is that instead of declining, greenhouse gas emissions by companies based in the EU actually *increased* during the late 2000s.

Are There Alternatives to Pollution-Causing Resource Use?

Some people cannot understand why, if pollution is bad, we still use pollution-causing resources such as coal and oil to generate electricity. Why don't we forgo the use of such polluting resources and opt for one that apparently is pollution-free, such as solar energy? The plain fact is that the cost of generating solar power in many circumstances is much higher than generating that same power through conventional means. We do not yet have the technology that allows us the luxury of driving solar-powered cars. Moreover, with current technology, the solar panels necessary to generate the electricity for the average town would cover massive sections of the countryside, and the manufacturing of those solar panels would itself generate pollution.

Wild Species, Common Property, and Trade-Offs

One common property problem that receives considerable media attention involves endangered species, usually in the wild. Few are concerned about not having enough dogs, cats, cattle, sheep, and horses. The reason is that virtually all of those species are private property. People have economic incentives—satisfaction from pet ownership, desire for food products, or preference for animal-borne transport—to protect members of these species. Spotted owls, bighorn mountain sheep, condors, and the like are typically common property. Therefore, no one has a vested interest in making sure that they perpetuate in good health.

In 1973, the federal government passed the Endangered Species Act in an attempt to prevent species from dying out. Initially, few individuals were affected by the rulings of the Interior Department regarding which species were listed as endangered. Eventually, however, as more and more species were put on the endangered list, a trade-off became apparent. Nationwide, the trade-off was brought to the public's attention when the snail darter was declared an endangered species in the Tennessee Valley. Ultimately, thousands of construction jobs were lost when the courts halted completion of a dam in the snail darter's habitat. Then two endangered small birds, the spotted owl and marbled murrelet, were found in the Pacific Northwest, inducing lumber companies to cut back their logging practices. In 1995, the U.S. Supreme Court ruled that the federal government has the right to regulate activities on private land in order to save endangered species.

Why do we generate such a small percentage of America's electricity using wind turbines?

Go to **www.econtoday.com/chapter32** to contemplate the issue of endangered species via a link to the National Center for Policy Analysis.

The issues are not straightforward. Today, the earth has only 0.02 percent of all of the species that have ever lived, and nearly all the 99.98 percent of extinct species became extinct before humans appeared. Every year, 1,000 to 3,000 new species are discovered and classified. Estimates of how many species are actually dying out range from a high of 50,000 a year (based on the assumption that undiscovered insect species are dying off before being discovered) to a low of one every four years.

Why does determining whether one species differs from another become a dollars-and-cents issue when it comes to enforcing laws protecting endangered species?

POLICY EXAMPLE
Determining Whether Species Are Distinct Can Have a Dollar Value

Every once in a while, scientists cannot agree on whether one species is different from another. For instance, in the mid-2000s, biologists studying jungle life in Southeast Asia announced that they had found a new species of "rock rat." When some paleontologists who study long-extinct creatures such as dinosaurs took a look at the animal, which has a face like a rat and a body like a skinny squirrel, they realized that it was already known to scientists. Until the biologists came across living specimens in Southeast Asia, however, paleontologists had recorded the animal as having been extinct for more than 11 million years. Now the biologists are attempting to determine if this rare, multi-million-years-old species qualifies for taxpayer-funded protection by Southeast Asian governments.

In Colorado, a slightly different issue has arisen regarding the status of a rodent called the Preble's meadow jumping mouse. Studies have shown that this mouse is 99.5 percent genetically identical to other mice. Thus, some biologists have concluded that it is basically a run-of-the-mill field mouse, untold millions of which populate planet Earth. Nevertheless, the U.S. government has classified the Colorado mouse as an endangered species. The U.S. Fish and Wildlife Service estimates that the opportunity cost to those forced to quarantine lands they own from development in an effort to protect the mouse from human encroachment is probably at least $180 million.

FOR CRITICAL ANALYSIS
Why do you suppose that there is a growing demand for the skills of biologists who can help prove or disprove whether a group of distinguishable animals is a subset of a broad species or constitutes its own narrow, endangered species?

QUICK QUIZ   See page 837 for the answers. Review concepts from this section in MyEconLab.

The more than three dozen countries that participated in the 1997 Kyoto Protocol of the Framework Convention on Climate Change agreed to reduce their emissions of greenhouse gases by the year _____ to at least _____ percent below the levels that prevailed in the year _____.

Under a program called the Emissions Trading Scheme, the governments of European Union member nations establish overall targets for greenhouse gas emissions and issue _____, or permits, authorizing companies to emit certain amounts. In theory, an increase in the market clearing price of _____ should induce firms to develop methods of _____ their emissions of greenhouse gases.

In contrast to domesticated animals that are _____ property, most endangered species are _____ property. Consequently, there is a problem in perpetuating these species that the federal government has sought to address through legislation governing use of lands where such species reside.

You Are There A U.S. Senator Finds the Largest U.S. Carbon Footprint

Senator Barbara Boxer of California, head of the Senate Environment and Public Works Committee, has been searching for ways to cut electricity consumption in an effort to reduce sources of atmospheric carbon pollutants, such as coal burning. After considerable study, her staff has discovered the consumer of the most energy in the United States.

The single largest U.S. energy consumer, it turns out, is neither a large corporation such as General Motors nor a huge concentration of households in a city such as Los Angeles. The entity consuming the most energy in the United States, and hence contributing the largest carbon footprint, is the U.S. government. All told, the federal government consumes an average of 32 percent more energy per square foot of space than the total building stock of the private sector. Estimated explicit costs to taxpayers generated by inefficiencies in government energy consumption are at least $1 billion per year. According to the staff of

Boxer's committee, the spillover effect of the government's energy waste to the nation's pollution levels is more difficult to estimate. Nevertheless, staff members agree that it probably accounts for a substantial fraction of the spillovers. Boxer suggests to her committee that it would be a good idea for heads of government departments to ask employees to use more efficient light bulbs and to turn off their computers at night.

CRITICAL ANALYSIS QUESTIONS

1. Are pollution-generating activities of governments included among private costs in markets in which governments operate?

2. How might efforts to reduce the U.S. government's contribution to the nation's pollution levels encounter a common property problem?

Issues and Applications

The Economics of Pollution in China—Present and Future

CONCEPTS APPLIED

- Common Property
- Social Costs
- Private Property Rights

According to estimates, arsenic taints groundwater that serves as the source of drinking water for more than 2 million people in China. There is excess fluorine in the water supplies of 63 million Chinese residents. All told, about 300 million people in China drink contaminated water.

China's air is also experiencing pollution problems. Air quality is unhealthful in more than 350 of the nation's cities. Winds carry pollution to Hong Kong, where levels of particulate matter—tiny flakes of soot, dust, and ash considered to be the most harmful form of air pollution—average more than *250 percent* higher than recommended safe levels. Some of China's air pollution makes its way to Korea and Japan, and even as far as the United States.

What accounts for the high pollution levels experienced by residents of China? Does economic theory offer any hope that pollution spillovers will eventually level off or even decline in this rapidly growing nation?

The Obvious and Less Visible Contributors to China's Pollution

The most apparent factor contributing to China's growing pollution problem is the nation's striking rate of economic growth, which has exceeded 8 percent annually for most of the past 30 years. Accompanying this growth have been spillover effects onto the environment. Since 2000, annual emissions of sulfur dioxide into the air have risen by about 30 percent. Total wastewater discharges from industries now exceed 55 billion tons, up almost one-third since 2000. The nation currently experiences more than 100 major water-pollution incidents every year as firms, in their haste to rush chemical-laden products to customers, inadvertently spill portions of them into rivers and lakes.

Another, less obvious factor has also contributed to China's pollution problems. This is a common property problem. China's government owns, either in part or in full, many of the nation's businesses. The government also owns large shares of its land and other resources. Because so many businesses and resources are owned by everyone, no readily identifiable parties must shoulder responsibility for internalizing the social costs of economic activities that create pollution. Thus, China's pollution problem continues to grow, seemingly unabated.

Hope for Pollution Containment and Abatement in China

Is China's environmental future likely to be literally darkened by escalating pollution? There is good economic reason to suspect that the answer ultimately must be no. The reason is that in recent years, China's government has adopted new guarantees of property rights for its residents. Although the government remains Communist from a political point of view, private ownership of resources is becoming much more commonplace. The government is also actively trying to disengage itself from its ownership of many of the nation's industries.

As more individuals become property owners, it will be easier to assign responsibility for activities that create spillover costs for others. Hence, the potential for voluntary agreements to help reduce pollution will broaden over time. As more and more of China's pollution-generating activities are covered by agreements that internalize pollution externalities, the scope of the nation's pollution problem should level off. Eventually, it may even begin to shrink as the private owners of resources seek to bring the marginal benefit of pollution abatement into alignment with its marginal cost.

Test your understanding of this chapter by going online to **MyEconLab**.
In the Study Plan for this chapter, select Section N: News.

For Critical Analysis

1. In your own words, explain in a sentence how the Chinese government's ownership of so many of the nation's resources contributes to the nation's pollution problem.

2. Recently, an increasing number of people who had done business in the most heavily polluted cities of China have decided to move their operations to Korea, Japan, and Australia in order to avoid the health risks caused by

China's air pollution. How might this trend influence the interplay between marginal costs and benefits of pollution abatement and alter the optimal quantity of pollution in China?

Web Resources

1. For a detailed discussion of the scope of China's pollution difficulties, go to www.econtoday.com/chapter32.
2. To read a World Bank assessment of the social costs of pollution in China, go to www.econtoday.com/chapter32.

Research Project

Recently, some government leaders in China have expressed the view that the nation's pollution problem is not the government's fault. In their view, the fault lies with consumers in other nations who import Chinese products manufactured using pollution-generating processes. Thus, they conclude, the costs of abating at least part of the air and water pollution in China should be borne by other countries' governments—that is, foreign taxpayers who are also the consumers of Chinese products. Based on this argument, these Chinese government officials suggest that Chinese firms (many of which are at least partly government owned) should not be expected to bear the costs of pollution abatement. Evaluate this argument from an economic standpoint. If China's firms were to incur the costs of cutting back on pollution-generating activities, would their owners (including the Chinese government) really bear *all* of the abatement costs? In light of your answer, are the government officials necessarily seeking to insulate private residents of China from bearing pollution abatement costs, or are they mainly promoting the government's own interest? Explain your reasoning. (Hint: Recall the effects that *any* costly pollution abatement efforts in China will have on market supply curves and prices, and consider will who pay these prices both inside and outside China.)

myeconlab

Here is what you should know after reading this chapter. MyEconLab will help you identify what you know, and where to go when you need to practice.

WHAT YOU SHOULD KNOW		WHERE TO GO TO PRACTICE
Private Costs versus Social Costs Private, or internal, costs are borne solely by individuals who use resources. Social costs are the full costs that society bears whenever resources are used. Problems related to the environment arise when individuals take into account only private costs instead of the broader social costs arising from their use of resources.	private costs, 819 social costs, 819	• **MyEconLab** Study Plan 32.1 • Audio introduction to Chapter 32 • ABC News Video: Coca-Cola in India
Market Externalities and Ways to Correct Them A market externality is a situation in which a private cost (or benefit) differs from the social cost (or benefit) associated with a market transaction between two parties or from the use of a scarce resource. Correcting an externality arising from differences between private and social costs, such as pollution, requires forcing individuals to take all the social costs of their actions into account. This might be accomplished by taxing those who create externalities, such as polluters.	externality, 820 KEY FIGURE Figure 32-1, 821	• **MyEconLab** Study Plan 32.2 • Video: Correcting for Externalities • Animated Figure 32-1

(continued)

(continued)

WHAT YOU SHOULD KNOW		WHERE TO GO TO PRACTICE
Determining the Optimal Amount of Pollution The marginal benefit of pollution abatement, or the additional benefit to society from reducing pollution, declines as the quality of the environment improves. At the same time, however, the marginal cost of pollution abatement, or the additional cost to society from reducing pollution, increases as more and more resources are devoted to bringing about an improved environment. The optimal quantity of pollution is the amount of pollution for which the marginal benefit of pollution abatement just equals the marginal cost of pollution abatement. Beyond this level of pollution, the additional cost of cleaning the environment exceeds the additional benefit.	optimal quantity of pollution, 824 KEY FIGURE Figure 32-2, 823	• **MyEconLab** Study Plan 32.3 • Animated Figure 32-2
Private and Common Property Rights and the Pollution Problem Private property rights are exclusive individual rights of ownership that permit the use and exchange of a resource. Common property is owned by everyone and therefore by no single individual. A pollution problem often arises because air and many water resources are common property, and private property rights relating to them are not well defined. Therefore, no one has an individual incentive to take the long-run pernicious effects of excessive pollution into account. This is a common rationale for using taxes, subsidies, or regulations to address the pollution problem.	private property rights, 825 common property, 825 transaction costs, 826	• **MyEconLab** Study Plan 32.4
Restraining Pollution-Causing Activities Through Caps and Allowances Under the terms of the Kyoto Protocol, a number of countries have agreed to reduce their emissions of greenhouse gases, such as carbon dioxide and sulfur dioxide, which some scientists suggest could harm the planet's climate. Toward this end, the European Union (EU) has established a program called the Emissions Trading Scheme. Each EU nation's government establishes an overall target level of greenhouse gas emissions and distributes allowances, or permits, granting companies the right to emit a certain amount of gases. If a firm's greenhouse gas emissions exceed its allowances, it must purchase a sufficient number of allowances from firms emitting less than the allowances they possess. In theory, the market clearing price of allowances will increase, giving EU companies incentives to develop methods of restraining their emissions of greenhouse gases.		• **MyEconLab** Study Plan 32.5
Endangered Species and the Assignment of Property Rights Many members of such species as dogs, pigs, and horses are the private property of human beings. Thus, people have economic		• **MyEconLab** Study Plan 32.6

(continued)

(continued)

WHAT YOU SHOULD KNOW	WHERE TO GO TO PRACTICE

incentives—satisfaction derived from pet ownership, the desire for pork as a food product, a preference for animal-borne transport—to protect members of these species. In contrast, most members of species such as spotted owls, condors, or tigers are common property, so no specific individuals have incentives to keep these species in good health. A possible way to address the endangered species problem is government involvement via regulations.

Log in to MyEconLab, take a chapter test, and get a personalized Study Plan that tells you which concepts you understand and which ones you need to review. From there, MyEconLab will give you further practice, tutorials, animations, videos, and guided solutions.
Log in to www.myeconlab.com

PROBLEMS

All problems are assignable in myeconlab. *Answers to the odd-numbered problems appear at the back of the book.*

32-1. The market price of insecticide is initially $10 per unit. To address a negative externality in this market, the government decides to charge producers of insecticide for the privilege of polluting during the production process. A fee that fully takes into account the social costs of pollution is determined, and once it is put into effect, the market supply curve for insecticide shifts upward by $4 per unit. The market price of insecticide also increases, to $12 per unit. What fee is the government charging insecticide manufacturers?

32-2. One possible method for reducing emissions of greenhouse gases such as carbon dioxide is to inject the gases into deep saltwater-laden rock formations where they would be trapped for thousands of years. Suppose that the federal government provides a fixed per-unit subsidy to firms that utilize this technology in West Virginia and other locales where such rock formations are known to exist.

    a. Use an appropriate diagram to examine the effects of the government subsidy on the production and sale of equipment that injects greenhouse gases into underground rock formations. What happens to the market clearing price of such pollution abatement equipment?

    b. Who pays to achieve the results discussed in part (a)?

32-3. Examine the following marginal costs and marginal benefits associated with water cleanliness in a given locale:

Quantity of Clean Water (%)	Marginal Cost ($)	Marginal Benefit ($)
0	3,000	200,000
20	15,000	120,000
40	50,000	90,000
60	85,000	85,000
80	100,000	40,000
100	Infinite	0

    a. What is the optimal degree of water cleanliness?

    b. What is the optimal degree of water pollution?

    c. Suppose that a company creates a food additive that offsets most of the harmful effects of drinking polluted water. As a result, the marginal benefit of water cleanliness declines by $40,000 at each degree of water cleanliness at or less than 80 percent. What is the optimal degree of water cleanliness after this change?

32-4. Consider the diagram below, which displays the marginal cost and marginal benefit of water pollution abatement in a particular city, and answer the following questions.

  a. What is the optimal percentage degree of water cleanliness?

  b. When the optimal percentage degree of water cleanliness has been attained, what price will be paid for the last unit of water cleanup?

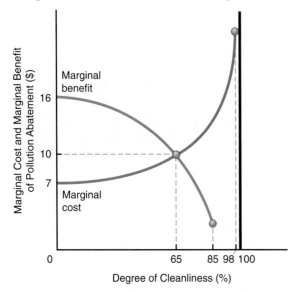

32-5. Consider the diagram in Problem 32-4, and answer the following questions.

  a. Suppose that a new technology for reducing water pollution generates a reduction in the marginal cost of pollution abatement at every degree of water cleanliness. After this event occurs, will the optimal percentage degree of water cleanliness rise or fall? Will the cost incurred for the last unit of water cleanup increase or decrease? Provide a diagram to assist in your explanation.

  b. Suppose that the event discussed in part (a) occurs and that, in addition, medical studies determine that the marginal benefit from water pollution abatement is higher at every degree of water cleanliness. Following *both* events, will the optimal percentage degree of water cleanliness increase or decrease? In comparison with the *initial* optimum, can you determine whether the price paid for the last unit of water cleanup will increase or decrease? Use a new diagram to assist in explaining your answers.

32-6. Under an agreement with U.S. regulators, American Electric Power Company of Columbus, Ohio, has agreed to offset part of its 145 million metric tons of carbon dioxide emissions by paying another company to lay plastic tarps. These tarps cover farm lagoons holding rotting livestock wastes that emit methane gas 21 times more damaging to the atmosphere than carbon dioxide. The annual methane produced by a typical 1,330-pound cow translates into about 5 metric tons of carbon dioxide emissions per year.

  a. How many cows' worth of manure would have to be covered to offset the carbon dioxide emissions of this single electric utility?

  b. Given that there are about 9 million cows in the United States in a typical year, what percentage of its carbon dioxide emissions could this firm offset if it paid for all cow manure in the entire nation to be covered with tarps?

32-7. The following table displays hypothetical annual total costs and total benefits of conserving wild tigers at several possible worldwide tiger population levels.

Population of Wild Tigers	Total Cost ($ millions)	Total Benefit ($ millions)
0	0	40
2,000	25	90
4,000	35	130
6,000	50	160
8,000	75	185
10,000	110	205
12,000	165	215

  a. Calculate the marginal costs and benefits.

  b. Given the data, what is the socially optimal world population of wild tigers?

  c. Suppose that tiger farming is legalized and that this has the effect of reducing the marginal cost of tiger conservation by $15 million for each 2,000-tiger population increment in the table. What is the new socially optimal population of wild tigers?

32-8. The following table gives hypothetical annual total costs and total benefits of maintaining alternative populations of Asian elephants.

Population of Asian Elephants	Total Cost ($ millions)	Total Benefit ($ millions)
0	0	0
7,500	20	100
15,000	45	185
22,500	90	260
30,000	155	325
37,500	235	375
45,000	330	410

a. Calculate the marginal costs and benefits, and draw marginal benefit and cost schedules.

b. Given the data, what is the socially optimal world population of Asian elephants?

c. Suppose that two events occur simultaneously. Technological development allows machines to do more efficiently much of the work that elephants once did, which reduces by $10 million the marginal benefit of maintaining the elephant population for each 7,500 increment in the elephant population. In addition, new techniques for breeding, feeding, and protecting elephants reduce the marginal cost by $40 million for each 7,500 increment in the elephant population. What is the new socially optimal population of Asian elephants?

ECONOMICS ON THE NET

Economic Analysis at the Environmental Protection Agency In this chapter, you learned how to use economic analysis to think about environmental problems. Does the U.S. government use economic analysis? This application helps you learn the extent to which the government uses economics in its environmental policymaking.

Title: National Center for Environmental Economics (NCEE)

Navigation: Go to **www.econtoday.com/chapter32** to visit the NCEE's home page. Click on *Publications*. Under *related publications*, select *Plain English*. Click on "Environmental Protection: Is It Bad for the Economy? A Non-Technical Summary of the Literature," and view the table of contents. Read "What Do We Spend on Environmental Protection?"

Application Read this section of the article; then answer the following questions.

1. According to the article, what are the key objectives of the EPA? What role does cost-benefit analysis appear to play in the EPA's efforts? Does the EPA appear to take other issues into account in its policymaking?

2. Back up to Table of Contents, and click on "Regardless of the Cost of Environmental Protection, Is It Still Money Well Spent?" In what ways does this discussion help clarify your answers in Question 1?

For Group Study and Analysis Have a class discussion of the following question: Should the EPA apply economic analysis in all aspects of its policymaking? If not, why not? If so, in what manner should economic analysis be applied?

ANSWERS TO QUICK QUIZZES

p. 822: (i) Private; (ii) private . . . private; (iii) private . . . externalities
p. 825: (i) rises . . . rises . . . increasing; (ii) falls; (iii) marginal cost . . . marginal benefit; (iv) goods . . . services
p. 827: (i) no one . . . everyone; (ii) private property; (iii) social . . . contract
p. 830: (i) 2020 . . . 20 . . . 1990; (ii) allowances . . . allowances . . . reducing; (iii) private . . . common

33

Comparative Advantage and the Open Economy

The costs of shipping, trucking, or flying physical goods exported from one nation to another have increased dramatically during the past few years. Indeed, since 2006 the per-unit cost of transporting internationally traded items has nearly tripled. A number of policymakers have expressed concern that this upswing in transport costs will eventually bring about a reduction in international trade. Why is international trade important to the world's people? Is it likely that rising costs of moving goods from exporting nations to importing countries really will slow or even halt the growth of international trade? By the time you have finished reading this chapter, you will be able to evaluate these questions.

LEARNING OBJECTIVES

After reading this chapter, you should be able to:

➤ Discuss the worldwide importance of international trade

➤ Explain why nations can gain from specializing in production and engaging in international trade

➤ Understand common arguments against free trade

➤ Describe ways that nations restrict foreign trade

➤ Identify key international agreements and organizations that adjudicate trade disputes among nations

? DID YOU KNOW THAT each year, U.S. residents spend more than $5 million on U.S. flags manufactured outside the United States? This figure may fall somewhat in future years, however, if some state governments have their way. Arizona requires public schools and colleges to buy only U.S. flags manufactured in the United States. Tennessee requires all publicly funded purchases of the U.S. flag to be limited to U.S.-manufactured versions. In Minnesota, it is illegal for anyone to sell any U.S. flag that was not manufactured within the United States. The Minnesota restriction is the toughest in the land, with violations punishable by a maximum fine of $1,000 and a jail sentence of up to 90 days.

What effects do restrictions on imports have on quantities and prices of domestically produced goods and services? You will learn the answer to this question in this chapter. First, however, you must learn more about international trade.

The Worldwide Importance of International Trade

Look at panel (a) of Figure 33-1 on the following page. Since the end of World War II, world output of goods and services (world real gross domestic product, or world real GDP) has increased almost every year; it is now almost nine times what it was then. Look at the top line in panel (a). World trade has increased to more than 28 times what it was in 1950.

The United States figured prominently in this expansion of world trade. In panel (b) of Figure 33-1, you see imports and exports expressed as a percentage of total annual yearly income (GDP). Whereas imports added up to barely 4 percent of annual U.S. GDP in 1950, today they account for more than 17 percent. International trade has definitely become more important to the economy of the United States, and it may become even more so as other countries loosen their trade restrictions.

How do you and others take advantage of international trade when you order certain types of seafood at restaurants?

Go to **www.econtoday.com/chapter33** for the World Trade Organization's most recent data on world trade.

INTERNATIONAL EXAMPLE
Have Seafood, Will Travel

Increasingly, U.S. restaurants strive to offer fresh seafood, which often requires some kinds of seafood to be shipped long distances. For instance, a number of the live lobsters caught each day in Nova Scotia take a 30-hour truck ride to Louisville, Kentucky. There, they are placed in 25,000-gallon saltwater pools. When restaurant orders arrive, United Parcel Service, which operates a major shipping center in Louisville, transports lobsters directly to restaurants.

Some types of seafood travel even farther to reach your plate. Every day, in Uganda, Nile perch from Africa's Lake Victoria are processed and chilled to near-freezing tempera-

tures. The fish are added to cargo freight transported by British Airways passenger planes to San Francisco. From there, the fish make their way to restaurants across the land, in some cases as much as 8,000 miles distant from their original location in Africa.

FOR CRITICAL ANALYSIS
Some critics claim that international trade causes nations to "lose jobs." Why do you suppose that hundreds of workers in Uganda's Nile perch industry might disagree with this statement?

The Growth of World Trade

In panel (a), you can see the growth in world trade in relative terms because we use an index of 100 to represent real world trade in 1950. By the late 2000s, that index had increased to over 2,800. At the same time, the index of world real GDP (annual world real income) had gone up to only around 900. World trade is clearly on the rise: In the United States, both imports and exports, expressed as a percentage of annual national income (GDP) in panel (b), have generally been rising since 1950.

Sources: Steven Husted and Michael Melvin, *International Economics*, 3d ed. (New York: HarperCollins, 1995), p. 11, used with permission; World Trade Organization; Federal Reserve System; U.S. Department of Commerce.

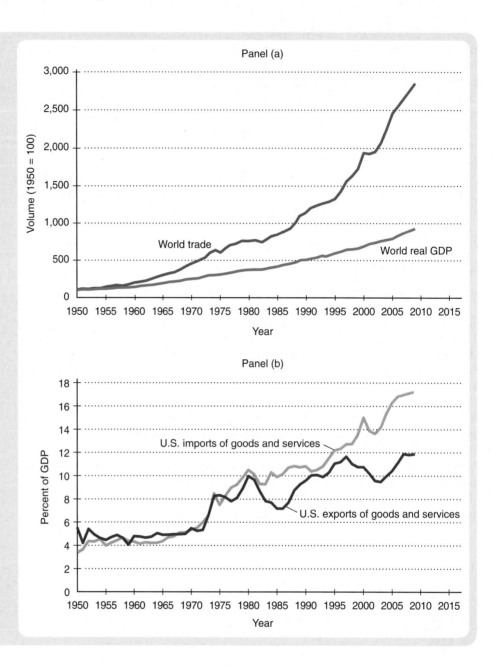

Why We Trade: Comparative Advantage and Mutual Gains from Exchange

You have already been introduced to the concept of specialization and mutual gains from trade in Chapter 2. These concepts are worth repeating because they are essential to understanding why the world is better off because of more international trade. The best way to understand the gains from trade among nations is first to understand the output gains from specialization between individuals.

The Output Gains from Specialization

Suppose that a creative advertising specialist can come up with two pages of ad copy (written words) an hour or generate one computerized art rendering per hour. At the same time, a computer artist can write one page of ad copy per hour or complete one computerized art rendering per hour. Here the ad specialist can come up with more pages of ad copy per hour than the computer specialist and seemingly is just as good as the computer specialist at doing computerized art renderings. Is there any reason for the creative specialist and the computer specialist to "trade"? The answer is yes because such trading will lead to higher output.

Consider the scenario of no trading. Assume that during each eight-hour day, the ad specialist and the computer whiz devote half of their day to writing ad copy and half to computerized art rendering. The ad specialist would create eight pages of ad copy (4 hours × 2) and four computerized art renderings (4 × 1). During that same period, the computer specialist would create four pages of ad copy (4 hours × 1) and four computerized art renderings (4 × 1). Each day, the combined output for the ad specialist and the computer specialist would be 12 pages of ad copy and eight computerized art renderings.

Go to www.econtoday.com/chapter33 for data on U.S. trade with all other nations of the world.

If the ad specialist specialized only in writing ad copy and the computer whiz specialized only in creating computerized art renderings, their combined output would rise to 16 pages of ad copy (8 × 2) and eight computerized art renderings (8 × 1). Overall, production would increase by four pages of ad copy per day with no decline in art renderings.

Note that this example implies that to create one additional computerized art rendering during a day, the ad specialist has to sacrifice creating two pages of ad copy. The computer specialist, however, only has to give up creating one page of ad copy to create one more computerized art rendering. Thus, the creative advertising employee has a comparative advantage in writing ad copy, and the computer specialist has a comparative advantage in doing computerized art renderings. **Comparative advantage** is simply the ability to produce something at a lower opportunity cost than other producers, as we pointed out in Chapter 2.

Why do you suppose that countries in Africa and the Middle East have a comparative advantage in producing a specific type of milk?

Comparative advantage
The ability to produce a good or service at a lower opportunity cost than other producers.

INTERNATIONAL EXAMPLE
The Comparative Advantage of Desert Dairies

Research has found that camel's milk contains 10 times more iron per unit than cow's milk. Camel's milk also has antibodies that could help fight cancer and potentially even forestall Alzheimer's disease. There are more than 20 million camels in the world. The bulk of these camels are located in the desert lands of Africa and the Middle East, which enables residents of nations in those regions to produce camel's milk at a lower opportunity cost than residents of other nations. In addition to cartons of camel's milk, companies in nations such as Kenya are now producing ice cream and chocolate candies made from camel's milk, which they recently have begun exporting to other parts of the world.

FOR CRITICAL ANALYSIS

If residents of nations in regions other than Africa and the Middle East were to develop methods of raising camels and producing camel's milk, would African and Middle Eastern residents necessarily lose their comparative advantage?

Specialization Among Nations

To demonstrate the concept of comparative advantage for nations, let's consider a simple two-country, two-good world. As a hypothetical example, let's suppose that the nations in this world are India and the United States.

PRODUCTION AND CONSUMPTION CAPABILITIES IN A TWO-COUNTRY, TWO-GOOD WORLD In Table 33-1, we show maximum feasible quantities of computer software and personal computers (PCs) that may be produced during an hour using all resources—labor, capital, land, and entrepreneurship—available in the United States and in India. As you can see from the table, U.S. residents can utilize all their resources to produce either 90 units of software per hour or 225 PCs per hour. Residents of India are able to utilize all their resources to produce either 100 units of software per hour or 50 PCs per hour.

COMPARATIVE ADVANTAGE Suppose that in each country, there are constant opportunity costs of producing software and PCs. Table 33-1 implies that allocating all available resources to production of 50 PCs would require residents of India to sacrifice the production of 100 units of software. Thus, the opportunity cost in India of producing 1 PC is equal to 2 units of software. At the same time, the opportunity cost of producing 1 unit of software in India is 0.5 PC.

In the United States, allocating all available resources to production of 225 PCs would require U.S. residents to give up producing 90 units of software. This means that the opportunity cost in the United States of producing 1 PC is equal to 0.4 unit of software. Alternatively, we can say that the opportunity cost to U.S. residents of producing 1 unit of software is 2.5 PCs.

The opportunity cost of producing a PC is lower in the United States than in India. At the same time, the opportunity cost of producing software is lower in India than in the United States. Thus, the United States has a comparative advantage in manufacturing PCs, and India has a comparative advantage in producing software.

PRODUCTION WITHOUT TRADE Table 33-2 tabulates two possible production choices in a situation in which U.S. and Indian residents choose not to engage in international trade. Let's suppose that in the United States, residents choose to produce and

---

TABLE 33-1

Maximum Feasible Hourly Production Rates of Either Commercial Software or Personal Computers Using All Available Resources

This table indicates maximum feasible rates of production of software and personal computers if all available resources are allocated to producing either one item or the other. If U.S. residents allocate all resources to producing a single good, they can produce either 90 units of software per hour or 225 PCs per hour. If residents of India allocate all resources to manufacturing one good, they can produce either 100 units of software per hour or 50 PCs per hour.

Product	United States	India
Units of software	90	100
Personal computers	225	50

TABLE 33-2

U.S. and Indian Production and Consumption Without Trade

This table indicates two possible hourly combinations of production and consumption of software and personal computers in the absence of trade in a "world" encompassing the United States and India. U.S. residents produce 30 units of software, and residents of India produce 25 units of software, so the total amount of software that can be consumed worldwide is 55 units. In addition, U.S. residents produce 150 PCs, and Indian residents produce 37.5 PCs, so worldwide production and consumption of PCs amount to 187.5 PCs per hour.

Product	United States	India	Actual World Output
Units of software (per hour)	30	25	55
Personal computers (per hour)	150	37.5	187.5

consume 30 units of software. To produce this amount of software requires producing 75 fewer PCs (30 units of software times 2.5 PCs per unit of software) than the maximum feasible PC production of 225 PCs, or 150 PCs. Thus, in the absence of trade, 30 units of software and 150 PCs are produced and consumed in the United States.

Table 33-2 indicates that during an hour's time in India, residents choose to produce and consume 37.5 PCs. Obtaining this amount of PCs entails producing 75 fewer units of software (37.5 PCs times 2 units of software per PC) than the maximum of 100 units, or 25 units of software. Thus, in the absence of trade, 37.5 PCs and 25 units of software are produced and consumed in India.

Finally, Table 33-2 displays production of software and PCs for this two-country world given the nations' production (and, implicitly, consumption) choices in the absence of trade. In an hour's time, U.S. software production is 30 units, and Indian software production is 25 units, so total world software production is 55 units. Thus, the total amount of software available for world consumption is also 55 units. Hourly U.S. PC production is 150 PCs, and Indian PC production is 37.5 PCs, so total world production is 187.5 PCs per hour. Consequently, the total number of PCs available for consumption in this two-country world is 187.5 PCs per hour.

SPECIALIZATION IN PRODUCTION More realistically, residents of the United States will choose to specialize in the activity for which they experience a lower opportunity cost. In other words, U.S. residents will specialize in the activity in which they have a comparative advantage, which is the production of personal computers, which they can offer in trade to residents of India. Likewise, residents of India will specialize in the area of manufacturing in which they have a comparative advantage, which is the production of commercial software, which they can offer in trade to residents of the United States.

By specializing, the two countries can gain from engaging in international trade. To see why, suppose that U.S. residents allocate all available resources to producing 225 PCs, the good in which they have a comparative advantage. In addition, residents of India utilize all resources they have on hand to produce 100 units of commercial software, the good in which they have a comparative advantage.

CONSUMPTION WITH SPECIALIZATION AND TRADE U.S. residents will be willing to buy a unit of Indian commercial software as long as they must provide in exchange no more than 2.5 PCs, which is the opportunity cost of producing 1 unit of software at home. At the same time, residents of India will be willing to buy a U.S. PC as long as they must provide in exchange no more than 2 units of software, which is their opportunity cost of producing a PC.

For instance, suppose that residents of both countries agree to trade at a rate of exchange of 1 PC for 1 unit of software and that U.S. residents agree with Indian residents to trade 75 PCs for 75 units of software. Table 33-3 displays the outcomes that result in both countries. By specializing in PC production and engaging in trade, U.S. residents can continue consuming 150 PCs. In addition, U.S. residents are also able to import and consume 75 units of software produced in India. At the same time, specialization and exchange allow residents of India to continue to consume 25 units of software. Producing 75 more units of software for export to the United States allows India to import 75 PCs.

GAINS FROM TRADE Table 33-4 summarizes the rates of consumption of U.S. and Indian residents with and without trade. Column 1 displays U.S. and Indian software and PC consumption rates with specialization and trade from Table 33-3, and it sums these to determine total consumption rates in this two-country world. Column 2 shows U.S., Indian, and worldwide consumption rates without international trade from Table 33-2. Column 3 gives the differences between the two columns.

Table 33-4 indicates that by producing 75 additional PCs for export to India in exchange for 75 units of software, U.S. residents are able to expand their software consumption from 30 units to 75 units. Thus, the U.S. gain from specialization and trade is 45 units of software. This is a net gain in software consumption for the two-country world as a whole, because neither country had to give up consuming any PCs for U.S. residents to realize this gain from trade.

TABLE 33-3

U.S. and Indian Production and Consumption with Specialization and Trade

In this table, U.S. residents produce 225 personal computers and no software, and Indian residents produce 100 units of software and no PCs. Residents of the two nations then agree to a rate of exchange of 1 PC for 1 unit of software and proceed to trade 75 U.S. PCs for 75 units of Indian software. Specialization and trade allow U.S. residents to consume 75 units of software imported from India and to consume 150 PCs produced at home. By specializing and engaging in trade, Indian residents consume 25 units of software produced at home and import 75 PCs from the United States.

Product	U.S. Production and Consumption with Trade		Indian Production and Consumption with Trade	
Units of software (per hour)	U.S. production	0	Indian production	100
	+Imports from India	75	−Exports to U.S.	75
	Total U.S. consumption	75	Total Indian consumption	25
Personal computers (per hour)	U.S. production	225	Indian production	0
	−Exports to India	75	+Imports from U.S.	75
	Total U.S. consumption	150	Total Indian consumption	75

TABLE 33-4

National and Worldwide Gains from Specialization and Trade

This table summarizes the consumption gains experienced by the United States, India, and the two-country world. U.S. and Indian software and PC consumption rates with specialization and trade from Table 33-3 are listed in column 1, which sums the national consumption rates to determine total worldwide consumption with trade. Column 2 shows U.S., Indian, and worldwide consumption rates without international trade, as reported in Table 33-2. Column 3 gives the differences between the two columns, which are the resulting national and worldwide gains from international trade.

Product	(1) National and World Consumption with Trade		(2) National and World Consumption without Trade		(3) Worldwide Consumption Gains from Trade	
Units of software (per hour)	U.S. consumption +Indian consumption World consumption	75 25 100	U.S. consumption +Indian consumption World consumption	30 25 55	Change in U.S. consumption Change in Indian consumption **Change in world consumption**	+45 +0 **+45**
Personal computers (per hour)	U.S. consumption +Indian consumption World consumption	150 75 225	U.S. consumption +Indian consumption World consumption	150 37.5 187.5	Change in U.S. consumption Change in Indian consumption **Change in world consumption**	+0 +37.5 **+37.5**

In addition, without trade residents of India could have used all resources to produce and consume only 37.5 PCs and 25 units of software. By using all resources to specialize in producing 100 units of software and engaging in trade, residents of India can consume 37.5 *more* PCs than they could have produced and consumed alone without reducing their software consumption. Thus, the Indian gain from trade is 37.5 PCs. This represents a worldwide gain in PC consumption, because neither country had to give up consuming any PCs for Indian residents to realize this gain from trade.

SPECIALIZATION IS THE KEY This example shows that when nations specialize in producing goods for which they have a comparative advantage and engage in international trade, considerable consumption gains are possible for those nations and hence for the world. Why is this so? The answer is that specialization and trade enable Indian residents to obtain each PC at an opportunity cost of 1 unit of software instead of 2 units of software and permit U.S. residents to obtain each unit of software at an opportunity cost of 1 PC instead of 2.5 PCs. Indian residents effectively experience a gain from trade of 1 unit of software for each PC purchased from the United States, and U.S. residents experience a gain from trade of 1.5 PCs for each unit of software purchased from India. Thus, specializing in producing goods for which the two nations have a comparative advantage allows both nations to produce more efficiently. As a consequence, worldwide production capabilities increase. This makes greater worldwide consumption possible through international trade.

Of course, not everybody in our example is better off when free trade occurs. In our example, the U.S. software industry and Indian computer industry have disappeared. Thus, U.S. software makers and Indian computer manufacturers are worse off.

Some people are worried that the United States (or any country, for that matter) might someday "run out of exports" because of overaggressive foreign competition. The analysis of comparative advantage tells us the contrary. No matter how much

FIGURE 33-2

World Trade Flows

International merchandise trade amounts to more than $15.6 trillion worldwide. The percentage figures show the proportion of trade flowing in the various directions throughout the globe.

Sources: World Trade Organization and author's estimates (data are for 2009).

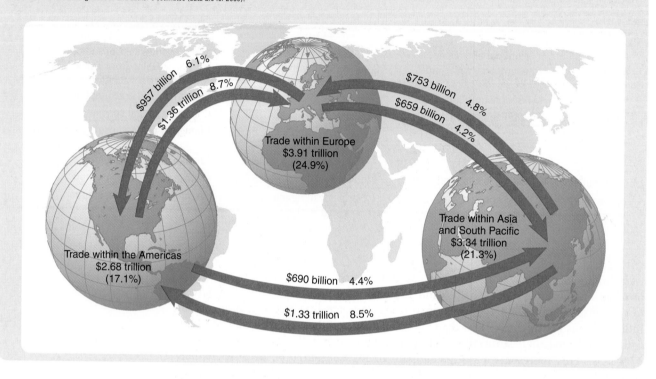

other countries compete for our business, the United States (or any other country) will always have a comparative advantage in something that it can export. In 10 or 20 years, that something may not be what we export today, but it will be exportable nonetheless because we will have a comparative advantage in producing it. Consequently, the significant flows of world trade shown in Figure 33-2 will continue because the United States and other nations will retain comparative advantages in producing various goods and services.

Can nations ever lose their comparative advantages in producing certain types of items to trade with other countries?

INTERNATIONAL EXAMPLE
China Discovers a New Comparative Advantage

From the 1950s until the 1990s, companies based in Japan made that nation a major exporter of electronic devices, including radios, stereo equipment, and televisions. In the 1990s, U.S. companies elbowed out Japanese firms by developing music players, videogame consoles, handheld devices, and digital cameras. Then, in the 2000s, Chinese firms developed comparative advantages in many of those same products. During the decade, China's trade in

INTERNATIONAL EXAMPLE (cont.)

information-technology (IT) products grew at an annual rate exceeding 30 percent. In 2003, China's IT exports passed those of both the European Union and Japan. By the late 2000s, China had also passed the United States and had become the world's top exporter of IT products. Today, the United States is the destination for 30 percent of China's IT exports.

FOR CRITICAL ANALYSIS

If firms in China have a comparative advantage in producing certain types of IT products, what must be true of the opportunity cost of producing these items in China compared with the opportunity cost elsewhere?

Other Benefits from International Trade: The Transmission of Ideas

Beyond the fact that comparative advantage results in an overall increase in the output of goods produced and consumed, there is another benefit to international trade. International trade bestows benefits on countries through the international transmission of ideas. According to economic historians, international trade has been the principal means by which new goods, services, and processes have spread around the world. For example, coffee was initially grown in Arabia near the Red Sea. Around AD 675, it began to be roasted and consumed as a beverage. Eventually, it was exported to other parts of the world, and the Dutch started cultivating it in their colonies during the seventeenth century and the French in the eighteenth century. The lowly potato is native to the Peruvian Andes. In the sixteenth century, it was brought to Europe by Spanish explorers. Thereafter, its cultivation and consumption spread rapidly. It became part of the North American agricultural scene in the early eighteenth century.

New processes have also been transmitted through international trade. An example is the Japanese manufacturing innovation that emphasized redesigning the system rather than running the existing system in the best possible way. Inventories were reduced to just-in-time levels by reengineering machine setup methods.

In addition, international trade has enabled *intellectual property* to spread throughout the world. New music, such as rock and roll in the 1950s and 1960s and hip-hop in the 1990s and 2000s, has been transmitted in this way, as have the software applications and computer communications tools that are common for computer users everywhere.

To what extent has international trade been responsible for the world-wide spread of spices and coffee?

The Relationship Between Imports and Exports

The basic proposition in understanding all of international trade is this:

In the long run, imports are paid for by exports.

The reason that imports are ultimately paid for by exports is that foreign residents want something in exchange for the goods that are shipped to the United States. For the most part, they want U.S.-made goods. From this truism comes a remarkable corollary:

Any restriction of imports ultimately reduces exports.

How has international trade benefited the music industry?

This is a shocking revelation to many people who want to restrict foreign competition to protect domestic jobs. Although it is possible to "protect" certain U.S. jobs by restricting foreign competition, it is impossible to make *everyone* better off by imposing import restrictions. Why? The reason is that ultimately such restrictions lead to a reduction in employment and output—and hence incomes—in the export industries of the nation.

International Competitiveness

"The United States is falling behind." "We need to stay competitive internationally." Statements such as these are often heard in government circles when the subject of international trade comes up. There are two problems with such talk. The first has to do with a simple definition. What does "global competitiveness" really mean? When one company competes against another, it is in competition. Is the United States like one big corporation, in competition with other countries? Certainly not. The standard of living in each country is almost solely a function of how well the economy functions *within that country*, not relative to other countries.

Another point relates to real-world observations. According to the Institute for Management Development in Lausanne, Switzerland, the United States continues to lead the pack in overall productive efficiency, ahead of Japan, Germany, and the rest of the European Union. According to the report, the top ranking of the United States has been due to widespread entrepreneurship, more than a decade of economic restructuring, and information-technology investments. Other factors include the open U.S. financial system and large investments in scientific research.

How have new efficiencies in transporting imported goods and domestic goods intended for export helped the United States maintain its international competitiveness?

EXAMPLE
How "Transfer Points" Contribute to U.S. Competitiveness

During the early 2000s, U.S. railroads suffered significant bottlenecks in moving imported goods and domestic goods to be exported between ports and distribution centers. In response to increasing congestion on the tracks, trucking firms and railroad companies, including Union Pacific and Burlington Northern Santa Fe, created "transfer points." These are inland rail yards located on the outer fringes of metropolitan rail networks near cities such as Chicago and San Francisco. Instead of sending freight cars carrying shipping containers directly to cities and adding to rail congestion, railroad companies route trains to transfer points near Rochelle, Illinois, Meridian, Mississippi, and other small communities.

There, the containers are transferred to trucks for transport. Containers filled with imported goods go to distribution centers serving the metropolitan centers, and those with items for export are trucked to ports for shipment abroad. In this way, a cost-efficient flow of internationally traded goods proceeds unabated, day and night, throughout the United States.

FOR CRITICAL ANALYSIS
Why do you suppose that it is often more efficient to offload items from trains at transfer points and truck them to final destination cities than it would be to leave all the goods on trains bound for those cities?

Arguments Against Free Trade

Numerous arguments are raised against free trade. They mainly focus on the costs of trade; they do not consider the benefits or the possible alternatives for reducing the costs of free trade while still reaping benefits.

The Infant Industry Argument

A nation may feel that if a particular industry is allowed to develop domestically, it will eventually become efficient enough to compete effectively in the world market. Therefore, the nation may impose some restrictions on imports in order to give domestic producers the time they need to develop their efficiency to the point where they can compete in the domestic market without any restrictions on imports. In graphic terminology, we would expect that if the protected industry truly does experience improvements in production techniques or technological breakthroughs toward greater efficiency in the future, the supply curve will shift outward to the right so that the domestic industry can produce larger quantities at each and every price. National policymakers often assert that this **infant industry argument** has some merit in the short run. They have used it to protect a number of industries in their infancy around the world.

Such a policy can be abused, however. Often the protective import-restricting arrangements remain even after the infant has matured. If other countries can still produce more cheaply, the people who benefit from this type of situation are obviously the stockholders (and specialized factors of production that will earn economic rents) in the industry that is still being protected from world competition. The people who lose out are the consumers, who must pay a price higher than the world price for the product in question. In any event, it is very difficult to know beforehand which industries will eventually survive making it possible, perhaps even likely, that policymakers will choose to protect industries that have no reasonable chance of competing on their own in world markets. Note that when we speculate about which industries "should" be protected, we are in the realm of *normative economics*. We are making a value judgment, a subjective statement of what *ought to be*.

After years of operations, what industry is still regarded as an infant industry in Canada? See the following page.

Infant industry argument
The contention that tariffs should be imposed to protect from import competition an industry that is trying to get started. Presumably, after the industry becomes technologically efficient, the tariff can be lifted.

E-COMMERCE EXAMPLE

Canadian Consumers Cheat to Watch U.S. TV Programming

In Canada, TV viewers cannot watch ESPN, HBO, MTV, Nickelodeon, Showtime, and a number of other popular U.S. channels. Very little of this U.S. programming is available via Canadian cable systems. To view U.S. TV programming, perhaps as many as 1 million residents of Canada pay monthly bills for satellite TV services using U.S. addresses or convince U.S. satellite-TV companies that they reside in the United States. Alternatively, they intercept U.S. satellite signals without paying for the right to do so.

Why do Canadians have to go to such lengths to see U.S. TV programs? The Canadian government still regards Canada's decades-old TV industry as an infant industry. Thus, there are laws prohibiting Canadian residents from receiving signals transmitting U.S. TV programming. The Canadian government actively enforces the laws, as evidenced by recent high-profile prosecutions of individuals who allegedly broke the law by selling satellite systems capable of capturing U.S. TV programs.

FOR CRITICAL ANALYSIS

What is the likely effect of laws excluding U.S. TV programming on the prices Canadians must pay to watch programming produced by Canadian firms?

Countering Foreign Subsidies and Dumping

Go to www.econtoday.com/chapter33 for a Congressional Budget Office review of antidumping actions in the United States and around the world.

Another common argument against unrestricted foreign trade has to do with countering other nations' subsidies to their own producers. When a foreign government subsidizes its producers, our producers claim that they cannot compete fairly with these subsidized foreign producers. To the extent that such subsidies fluctuate, it can be argued that unrestricted free trade will seriously disrupt domestic producers. They will not know when foreign governments are going to subsidize their producers and when they are not. Our competing industries will be expanding and contracting too frequently.

The phenomenon called *dumping* is also used as an argument against unrestricted trade. **Dumping** is said to occur when a producer sells its products abroad below the price that is charged in the home market or at a price below its cost of production. Often, when a foreign producer is accused of dumping, further investigation reveals that the foreign nation is in the throes of a recession. The foreign producer does not want to slow down its production at home. Because it anticipates an end to the recession and doesn't want to hold large inventories, it dumps its products abroad at prices below home prices. U.S. competitors may also allege that it sells its output at prices below its full costs in an effort to cover variable costs of production.

Dumping

Selling a good or a service abroad below the price charged in the home market or at a price below its cost of production.

Protecting Domestic Jobs

Perhaps the argument used most often against free trade is that unrestrained competition from other countries will eliminate jobs in the United States because other countries have lower-cost labor than we do. (Less restrictive environmental standards in other countries might also lower their private costs relative to ours.) This is a compelling argument, particularly for politicians from areas that might be threatened by foreign competition. For example, a representative from an area with shoe factories would certainly be upset about the possibility of constituents' losing their jobs because of competition from lower-priced shoe manufacturers in Brazil and Italy. But, of course, this argument against free trade is equally applicable to trade between the states within the United States.

Economists David Gould, G. L. Woodbridge, and Roy Ruffin examined the data on the relationship between increases in imports and the rate of unemployment. Their conclusion was that there is no causal link between the two. Indeed, in half the cases they studied, when imports increased, unemployment fell.

Another issue has to do with the cost of protecting U.S. jobs by restricting international trade. The Institute for International Economics examined just the restrictions on foreign textiles and apparel goods. U.S. consumers pay $9 billion a year more than they would otherwise pay for those goods to protect jobs in those industries. That comes out to $50,000 *a year* for each job saved in an industry in which the average job pays only $20,000 a year. Similar studies have yielded similar results: Restrictions on imports of Japanese cars have cost $160,000 *per year* for every job saved in the auto industry. Every job preserved in the glass industry has cost $200,000 each and every year. Every job preserved in the U.S. steel industry has cost an astounding $750,000 per year.

How does a charitable U.S. government program aimed at saving millions of people from hunger also seek to protect domestic jobs from foreign competition?

POLICY EXAMPLE
Paying More for U.S.-Grown Charitable Food Donations

Since 1954, the U.S. government's Food for Peace program has worked with about 50 charities and foreign government organizations to donate food to other countries. In recent years, this program has coordinated the annual delivery of more than 3 million metric tons of food aid to about 80 nations at a cost of $1.2 billion in taxpayer funds per year. If the government could use these funds to buy less expensive foods grown in countries located close to recipient nations, assistance could be provided to hundreds of thousands more people. Nevertheless, the law governing the Food for Peace program requires virtually all food items to be produced in the United States. Thus, instead of paying Ugandan farmers $180 per ton of corn used for African food donations, the U.S. government spends nearly $450 per ton purchasing corn from U.S. farmers and shipping the U.S.-grown corn to Africa.

FOR CRITICAL ANALYSIS
Who benefits from rules requiring the Food for Peace program to purchase only U.S.-grown corn?

Emerging Arguments Against Free Trade

In recent years, two new antitrade arguments have been advanced. One of these focuses on environmental and safety concerns. For instance, many critics of free trade have suggested that genetic engineering of plants and animals could lead to accidental production of new diseases and that people, livestock, and pets could be harmed by tainted foods imported for human and animal consumption. These worries have induced the European Union to restrain trade in such products.

Another argument against free trade arises from national defense concerns. Major espionage successes by China in the late 1990s and early 2000s led some U.S. strategic experts to propose sweeping restrictions on exports of new technology.

Free trade proponents counter that at best these are arguments for the judicious regulation of trade. They continue to argue that, by and large, broad trade restrictions mainly harm the interests of the nations that impose them.

Ways to Restrict Foreign Trade

International trade can be stopped or at least stifled in many ways. These include quotas and taxes (the latter are usually called *tariffs* when applied to internationally traded items). Let's talk first about quotas.

Quotas

Quota system

A government-imposed restriction on the quantity of a specific good that another country is allowed to sell in the United States. In other words, quotas are restrictions on imports. These restrictions are usually applied to one or several specific countries.

Under a **quota system,** individual countries or groups of foreign producers are restricted to a certain amount of trade. An import quota specifies the maximum amount of a commodity that may be imported during a specified period of time. For example, the government might allow no more than 200 million barrels of foreign crude oil to enter the United States in a particular month.

Consider the example of quotas on textiles. Figure 33-3 presents the demand and supply curves for imported textiles. In an unrestricted import market, the equilibrium quantity imported is 900 million yards at a price of $1 per yard (expressed in

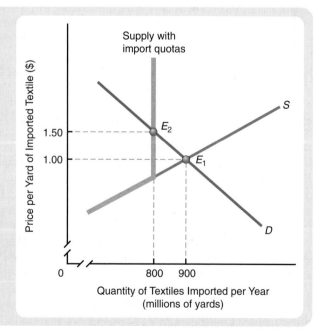

FIGURE 33-3

The Effect of Quotas on Textile Imports

Without restrictions, at point E_1, 900 million yards of textiles would be imported each year into the United States at the world price of $1.00 per yard. If the federal government imposes a quota of only 800 million yards, the effective supply curve becomes vertical at that quantity. It intersects the demand curve at point E_2, so the new equilibrium price is $1.50 per yard.

constant-quality units). When an import quota is imposed, the supply curve is no longer *S*. Instead, the supply curve becomes vertical at some amount less than the equilibrium quantity—here, 800 million yards per year. The price to the U.S. consumer increases from $1.00 to $1.50.

Clearly, the output restriction generated by a quota on foreign imports of a particular item has the effect of raising the domestic price of the imported item. Two groups benefit. One group is importers that are able to obtain the rights to sell imported items domestically at the higher price, which raises their revenues and boosts their profits. The other group is domestic producers. Naturally, a rise in the price of an imported item induces an increase in the demand for domestic substitutes. Thus, the domestic prices of close substitutes for the item subject to the import restriction also increase, which generates higher revenues and profits for domestic producers.

VOLUNTARY QUOTAS Quotas do not have to be explicit and defined by law. They can be "voluntary." Such a quota is called a **voluntary restraint agreement (VRA)**. In the early 1980s, Japanese automakers voluntarily restrained exports to the United States. These restraints stayed in place into the 1990s. Today, there are VRAs on machine tools and textiles.

The opposite of a VRA is a **voluntary import expansion (VIE)**. Under a VIE, a foreign government agrees to have its companies import more foreign goods from another country. The United States almost started a major international trade war with Japan in 1995 over just such an issue. The U.S. government wanted Japanese automobile manufacturers to voluntarily increase their imports of U.S.-made automobile parts. Ultimately, Japanese companies did make a token increase in their imports of U.S. auto parts.

Tariffs

We can analyze tariffs by using standard supply and demand diagrams. Let's use as our commodity laptop computers, some of which are made in Japan and some of which are made domestically. In panel (a) of Figure 33-4 on the following page, you see the demand for and supply of Japanese laptops. The equilibrium price is $1,000 per constant-quality unit, and the equilibrium quantity is 10 million per year. In panel (b), you see the same equilibrium price of $1,000, and the *domestic* equilibrium quantity is 5 million units per year.

Now a tariff of $500 is imposed on all imported Japanese laptops. The supply curve shifts upward by $500 to S_2. For purchasers of Japanese laptops, the price increases to $1,250. The quantity demanded falls to 8 million per year. In panel (b), you see that at the higher price of imported Japanese laptops, the demand curve for U.S.-made laptops shifts outward to the right to D_2. The equilibrium price increases to $1,250, and the equilibrium quantity increases to 6.5 million units per year. So the tariff benefits domestic laptop producers because it increases the demand for their products due to the higher price of a close substitute, Japanese laptops. This causes a redistribution of income from Japanese producers and U.S. consumers of laptops to U.S. producers of laptops.

TARIFFS IN THE UNITED STATES In Figure 33-5 on page 855, we see that tariffs on all imported goods have varied widely. The highest rates in the twentieth century occurred with the passage of the Smoot-Hawley Tariff in 1930.

CURRENT TARIFF LAWS The Trade Expansion Act of 1962 gave the president the authority to reduce tariffs by up to 50 percent. Subsequently, tariffs were reduced by

You Are There

To consider how laws affecting the ability of people to move internationally can protect certain domestic industries from foreign competition, read **How Visa Rules Protect U.S. Pop Stars from a British Invasion**, on page 857.

Voluntary restraint agreement (VRA)
An official agreement with another country that "voluntarily" restricts the quantity of its exports to the United States.

Voluntary import expansion (VIE)
An official agreement with another country in which it agrees to import more from the United States.

Go to www.econtoday.com/chapter33 to take a look at the U.S. State Department's reports on economic policy and trade practices.

FIGURE 33-4

The Effect of a Tariff on Japanese-Made Laptop Computers

Without a tariff, the United States buys 10 million Japanese laptops per year at an average price of $1,000, at point E_1 in panel (a). U.S. producers sell 5 million domestically made laptops, also at $1,000 each, at point E_1 in panel (b). A $500-per-laptop tariff will shift the Japanese import supply curve to S_2 in panel (a), so that the new equilibrium is at E_2 with price increased to $1,250 and quantity sold reduced to 8 million per year. The demand curve for U.S.-made laptops (for which there is no tariff) shifts to D_2, in panel (b). Domestic sales increase to 6.5 million per year, at point E_2.

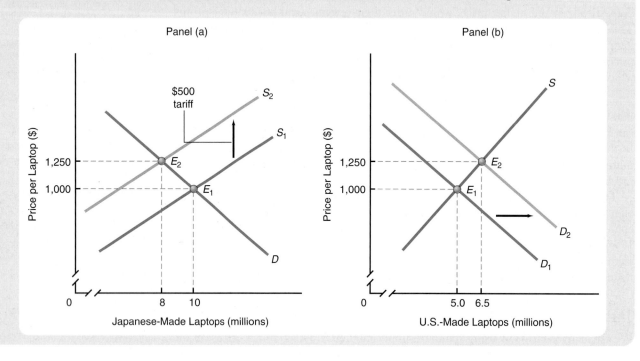

about 35 percent. In 1974, the Trade Reform Act allowed the president to reduce tariffs further. In 1984, the Trade and Tariff Act resulted in the lowest tariff rates ever. All such trade agreement obligations of the United States were carried out under the auspices of the **General Agreement on Tariffs and Trade (GATT),** which was signed in 1947. Member nations of the GATT account for more than 85 percent of world trade. As you can see in Figure 33-5, U.S. tariff rates have declined since the early 1960s, when several rounds of negotiations under the GATT were initiated. In 2002, the U.S. government proposed eliminating all tariffs on manufactured goods by 2015.

General Agreement on Tariffs and Trade (GATT)
An international agreement established in 1947 to further world trade by reducing barriers and tariffs. The GATT was replaced by the World Trade Organization in 1995.

International Trade Organizations

The widespread effort to reduce tariffs around the world has generated interest among nations in joining various international trade organizations. These organizations promote trade by granting preferences in the form of reduced or eliminated tariffs, duties, or quotas.

The World Trade Organization (WTO)

World Trade Organization (WTO)
The successor organization to the GATT that handles trade disputes among its member nations.

The most important international trade organization with the largest membership is the **World Trade Organization (WTO),** which was ratified by the final round of negotiations of the General Agreement on Tariffs and Trade at the end of 1993. The

FIGURE 33-5

Tariff Rates in the United States Since 1820

Tariff rates in the United States have bounced around like a football; indeed, in Congress, tariffs are a political football. Import-competing industries prefer high tariffs. In the twentieth century, the highest tariff was the

Smoot-Hawley Tariff of 1930, which was about as high as the "tariff of abominations" in 1828.

Source: U.S. Department of Commerce.

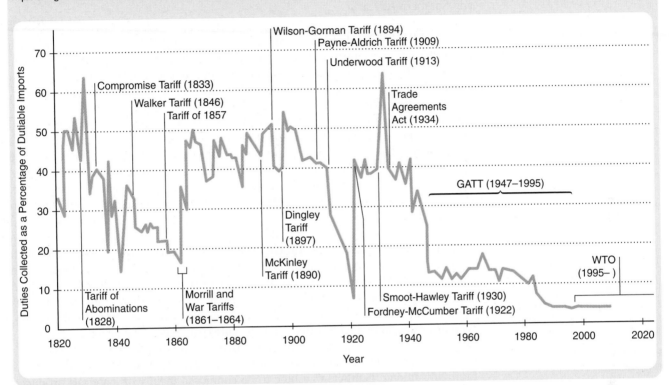

WTO, which as of 2009 had 153 member nations and included 30 observer governments, began operations on January 1, 1995. WTO decisions have concerned such topics as special U.S. steel tariffs imposed in the early 2000s, which the U.S. government removed after the WTO determined that they violated its rules. The WTO also adjudicated the European Union's "banana wars" and determined that the EU's policies unfairly favored many former European colonies in Africa, the Caribbean, and the Pacific at the expense of banana-exporting countries in Latin America. Now those former colonies no longer have a privileged position in European markets.

On a larger scale, the WTO fostered the most important and far-reaching global trade agreement ever covering financial institutions, including banks, insurers, and investment companies. The more than 100 signatories to this new treaty have legally committed themselves to giving foreign residents more freedom to own and operate companies in virtually all segments of the financial services industry.

Regional Trade Agreements

Numerous other international trade organizations exist alongside the WTO. Sometimes known as **regional trade blocs,** these organizations are created by special deals among groups of countries that grant trade preferences only to countries within their groups. Currently, more than 230 bilateral or regional trade agreements are in effect

Regional trade bloc
A group of nations that grants members special trade privileges.

around the globe. Examples include groups of industrial powerhouses, such as the European Union, the North American Free Trade Agreement, and the Association of Southeast Asian Nations. Nations in South America with per capita real GDP nearer the world average have also formed regional trade blocs called Mercosur and the Andean Community. Less developed nations have also formed regional trade blocs, such as the Economic Community of West African States and the Community of East and Southern Africa.

DO REGIONAL TRADE BLOCS SIMPLY DIVERT TRADE? Figure 33-6 shows that the formation of regional trade blocs, in which the European Union and the United States are often key participants, is on an upswing. An average African nation participates in four separate regional trading agreements. A typical Latin American country belongs to eight different regional trade blocs.

In the past, economists worried that the formation of regional trade blocs could mainly result in **trade diversion,** or the shifting of trade from countries outside a regional trade bloc to nations within a bloc. Indeed, a study by Jeffrey Frankel of the University of California at Berkeley found evidence that some trade diversion does take place. Nevertheless, Frankel and other economists have concluded that the net effect of regional trade agreements has been to boost overall international trade, in some cases considerably.

THE TRADE DEFLECTION ISSUE Today, the primary issue associated with regional trade blocs is **trade deflection.** This occurs when a company located in a nation outside a regional trade bloc moves goods that are not quite fully assembled into a member country, completes assembly of the goods there, and then exports them to other nations in the bloc. To try to reduce incentives for trade deflection, regional trade agreements often include **rules of origin,** which are regulations carefully defining categories of products that are eligible for trading preferences under the agreements. Some rules of origin, for instance, require any products trading freely among members of a bloc to be composed mainly of materials produced within a member nation.

Trade diversion
Shifting existing international trade from countries outside a regional trade bloc to nations within the bloc.

Trade deflection
Moving partially assembled products into a member nation of a regional trade bloc, completing assembly, and then exporting them to other nations within the bloc, so as to benefit from preferences granted by the trade bloc.

Rules of origin
Regulations that nations in regional trade blocs establish to delineate product categories eligible for trading preferences.

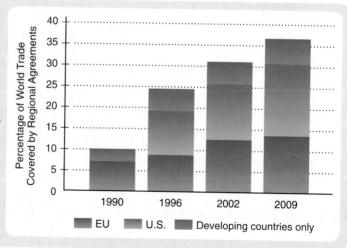

FIGURE 33-6

The Percentage of World Trade Within Regional Trade Blocs

As the number of regional trade agreements has increased since 1990, the share of world trade undertaken among nations that are members of regional trade blocs—involving the European Union (EU), United States, and developing nations—has also increased.

Source: World Bank.

Proponents of free trade worry, however, about the potential for parties to regional trade agreements to use rules of origin to create barriers to trade. Sufficiently complex rules of origin, they suggest, can provide disincentives for countries to utilize the trade-promoting preferences that regional trade agreements ought to provide. Indeed, some free trade proponents applaud successful trade deflection. They contend that it helps to circumvent trade restrictions and thus allows nations within regional trade blocs to experience additional gains from trade.

QUICK QUIZ | *See page 862 for the answers. Review concepts from this section in MyEconLab.*

One means of restricting foreign trade is an import quota, which specifies a _____ amount of a good that may be imported during a certain period. The resulting increase in import prices benefits those who gain the right to sell the imported item and domestic _____ that receive higher prices resulting from substitution to domestic goods.

Another means of restricting imports is a **tariff,** which is a _____ on imports only. An import tariff _____ import-competing industries and harms consumers by raising prices.

The main international institution created to improve trade among nations was the General Agreement on Tariffs and Trade (GATT). The last round of trade talks under the GATT led to the creation of the _____ _____ _____.

_____ _____ agreements among numerous nations of the world have established more than 230 _____ _____ blocs, which grant special trade privileges such as reduced tariff barriers and quota exemptions to member nations.

 You Are There ◀ **How Visa Rules Protect U.S. Pop Stars from a British Invasion**

For weeks, rising British pop singer Lily Allen has been set to perform at the MTV Video Music Awards in Las Vegas. Her itinerary included a trip to the West Coast to perform at sold-out concerts. Instead, she now finds herself at home in London.

Like many recent musical splashes from the United Kingdom, including singers such as James Blunt and Holly Golightly and bands such as Coldplay and Klaxons, Allen is unable to meet U.S. visa rules for foreign music acts. To obtain a P-1 class visitor's visa required for foreign musicians seeking to perform in the United States, Allen had to prove that she has been "internationally recognized" for a "sustained and substantial" period of time. Last week, her manager offered considerable proof that her rapid rise in the popular music world is evidence of international recognition. Nevertheless, a U.S. visa adjudications supervisor

ruled that her recognition has been too short lived to qualify for U.S. entry.

Allen watches on TV as a U.S. performer fills her time slot at the MTV Video Music Awards. As she watches, she finds herself wondering what U.S. musical act will be booked in her place for the West Coast concert tour.

CRITICAL ANALYSIS QUESTIONS

1. How do visa requirements shutting out the musical performers mentioned here, plus numerous other British performers, such as M.I.A., Mysterious Jets, and New Model Army, affect the demand for performances by U.S. musicians?

2. How do restrictions on the entry of British musical performers affect the price that U.S. musicians receive for concert performances?

Higher Shipping Costs: A Barrier to Trade or a By-Product of Its Growth?

CONCEPTS APPLIED

- Tariffs and Quotas
- Gains from Trade
- Comparative Advantage

Recently, some observers have suggested that the most significant barrier to international trade today may not be protectionism. In their view, tariffs and quotas are becoming a minor hindrance to global trade growth. Instead, these observers argue, increased costs of transporting exported items and delivering the items to the nations that import them may be the chief obstacle to the growth of international trade.

Sharp Rises in Global Freight Costs

The costs of physically moving exported goods have jumped significantly. Since 2006, the Baltic Dry Index, which tracks the cost of shipping "dry" goods such as iron ore, coal, and grains around the world, has increased by about 170 percent.

One reason for the rise in shipping costs faced by exporting and importing firms has been that the world has too few cargo ships to handle all the traded goods. New flotillas of cargo ships, some of which can carry as many as 9,000 shipping containers, are either under construction or being launched. Nevertheless, the world's current fleet of cargo ships already has difficulty finding sufficient space to dock at existing ports. Thus, the cost of transporting goods via the sea-lanes promises to remain relatively high for years to come.

Another factor pushing up global trade costs has been the expansion of trade across Asia. Although ships handle much of the trade along Asia's southern and eastern tier, there has been a significant increase in the flow of exports across overland routes in Europe, the Americas, Africa, and Asia. Trucks transporting items across Asia's vast expanse struggle to maintain average speeds as high as 25 miles per hour. As global oil and gasoline prices have continued to climb, so have the costs of this overland trading. Many companies have opted to cut transport times by using cargo jets to fly export goods, but higher oil prices have also pushed up jet fuel expenses considerably.

Trade Barrier or a Symptom of Trade's Popularity?

Undoubtedly, increases in transportation costs discourage some businesses and individuals from opting to export goods to other nations or to import goods from other countries. Higher transportation costs cut into realized gains from trade. In some countries, the resulting reductions in net gains from trade can translate into a reduced incentive to specialize in production and to engage in international trade.

Nevertheless, a key factor underlying the increase in global costs of using ships, overland trucking, and air transit to transport exported goods is a rise in the demand for such services as nations have pursued gains from trade. Nations around the globe have discovered new sources of comparative advantage throughout the past two decades, and efforts to exploit these advantages are a key source of the rising demand for sea, land, and air transportation services. For most businesses throughout much of the world, the higher prices of these services arguably are a symptom of the quest for gains from trade, not a fundamental hindrance to trade.

Test your understanding of this chapter by going online to **MyEconLab**.
In the Study Plan for this chapter, select Section N: News.

For Critical Analysis

1. How do you suppose that higher shipping and air freight costs might be contributing to the increased use of overland transportation in Asia and the resulting increase in overland transport prices? (Hint: Overland transport is a substitute for services provided by cargo ships and air freight businesses.)

2. Why are net gains from trade—gains from trade minus costs of transporting traded goods—what really matter for determining how much international trade actually takes place?

Web Resources

1. To view trends in the Baltic Dry Index and the latest variations in global freight transport rates, go to www .econtoday.com/chapter33.

2. To see how importing and exporting firms calculate shipping rates, go to www.econtoday.com/chapter33.

Research Project

Draw a diagram of an initial equilibrium in the market for export transportation services, in which the demand and supply curves have their normal slopes. When increased growth in trade fuels a rise in demand for these services, does the equilibrium quantity of services provided change by the amount of the rise in demand? Why or why not? Does the equilibrium quantity of transportation services rise on net, however? How does your answer help support the argument that higher transportation costs generated by greater trade undoubtedly discourage some international exchange yet may be a symptom of trade rather than a threat? Explain.

Here is what you should know after reading this chapter. **MyEconLab** will help you identify what you know, and where to go when you need to practice.

WHAT YOU SHOULD KNOW		WHERE TO GO TO PRACTICE
The Worldwide Importance of International Trade Total trade among nations has been growing faster than total world GDP. The growth of U.S. exports and imports relative to U.S. GDP parallels this global trend. Today, exports constitute 12 percent of total national production. In some countries, trade accounts for a much higher share of total economic activity.	KEY FIGURE Figure 33-1, 840	• **MyEconLab** Study Plan 33.1 • Audio introduction to Chapter 33 • Animated Figure 33-1 • ABC News Video: How Outsourcing Affects Our Lives
Why Nations Can Gain from Specializing in Production and Engaging in Trade A country has a comparative advantage in producing a good if it can produce that good at a lower opportunity cost, in terms of forgone production of a second good, than another nation. Because the other nation has a comparative	comparative advantage, 841 KEY FIGURE Figure 33-2, 846	• **MyEconLab** Study Plan 33.2 • Animated Figure 33-2 • Video: The Gains from Trade

(continued)

WHAT YOU SHOULD KNOW		WHERE TO GO TO PRACTICE

advantage in producing the second good, both nations can gain by specializing in producing the goods in which they have a comparative advantage and engaging in international trade. Together, they can then produce and consume more than they would have produced and consumed in the absence of specialization and trade.

Arguments Against Free Trade One argument against free trade is that temporary import restrictions might permit an "infant industry" to develop to the point at which it could compete without such restrictions. Another argument concerns dumping, in which foreign companies allegedly sell some of their output in domestic markets at prices below the prices in the companies' home markets or even below the companies' costs of production. In addition, some environmentalists contend that nations should restrain foreign trade to prevent exposing their countries to environmental hazards to plants, animals, or even humans. Finally, some contend that countries should limit exports of technologies that could pose a threat to their national defense.

infant industry
  argument, 849
dumping, 850

- **MyEconLab** Study Plans 33.3, 33.4, 33.5
- Video: Arguments Against Free Trade

Ways That Nations Restrict Foreign Trade One way to restrain trade is to impose a quota, or a limit on imports of a good. This action restricts the supply of the good in the domestic market, thereby pushing up the equilibrium price of the good. Another way to reduce trade is to place a tariff on imported goods. This reduces the supply of foreign-made goods and increases the demand for domestically produced goods, thereby bringing about a rise in the price of the good.

quota system, 852
voluntary restraint
  agreement (VRA), 853
voluntary import
  expansion (VIE), 853
General Agreement
  on Tariffs and Trade
  (GATT), 854

KEY FIGURES
Figure 33-3, 852
Figure 33-4, 854

- **MyEconLab** Study Plan 33.6
- Animated Figures 33-3, 33-4

Key International Trade Agreements and Organizations From 1947 to 1995, nations agreed to abide by the General Agreement on Tariffs and Trade (GATT), which laid an international legal foundation for relaxing quotas and reducing tariffs. Since 1995, the World Trade Organization (WTO) has adjudicated trade disputes that arise between or among nations. Now there are also more than 230 regional trade blocs, including the North American Free Trade Agreement and the European Union, that provide special trade preferences to member nations.

World Trade
  Organization, 854
regional trade bloc, 855
trade diversion, 856
trade deflection, 856
rules of origin, 856

KEY FIGURE
Figure 33-5, 855

- **MyEconLab** Study Plan 33.7
- Animated Figure 33-5

Log in to MyEconLab, take a chapter test, and get a personalized Study Plan that tells you which concepts you understand and which ones you need to review. From there, MyEconLab will give you further practice, tutorials, animations, videos, and guided solutions.
Log in to www.myeconlab.com

PROBLEMS

All problems are assignable in myeconlab *. Answers to the odd-numbered problems appear at the back of the book.*

33-1. To answer the questions that follow, consider the following table for the neighboring nations of Northland and West Coast. The table lists maximum feasible hourly rates of production of pastries if no sandwiches are produced and maximum feasible hourly rates of production of sandwiches if no pastries are produced. Assume that the opportunity costs of producing these goods are constant in both nations.

Product	Northland	West Coast
Pastries (per hour)	50,000	100,000
Sandwiches (per hour)	25,000	200,000

   a. What is the opportunity cost of producing pastries in Northland? Of producing sandwiches in Northland?

   b. What is the opportunity cost of producing pastries in West Coast? Of producing sandwiches in West Coast?

33-2. Based on your answers to Problem 33-1, which nation has a comparative advantage in producing pastries? Which nation has a comparative advantage in producing sandwiches?

33-3. Suppose that the two nations in Problems 33-1 and 33-2 choose to specialize in producing the goods for which they have a comparative advantage. They agree to trade at a rate of exchange of 1 pastry for 1 sandwich. At this rate of exchange, what are the maximum possible numbers of pastries and sandwiches that they could agree to trade?

33-4. Residents of the nation of Border Kingdom can forgo production of digital televisions and utilize all available resources to produce 300 bottles of high-quality wine per hour. Alternatively, they can forgo producing wine and instead produce 60 digital TVs per hour. In the neighboring country of Coastal Realm, residents can forgo production of digital TVs and use all resources to produce 150 bottles of high-quality wine per hour, or they can forgo wine production and produce 50 digital TVs per hour. In both nations, the opportunity costs of producing the two goods are constant.

   a. What is the opportunity cost of producing digital TVs in Border Kingdom? Of producing bottles of wine in Border Kingdom?

   b. What is the opportunity cost of producing digital TVs in Coastal Realm? Of producing bottles of wine in Coastal Realm?

33-5. Based on your answers to Problem 33-4, which nation has a comparative advantage in producing digital TVs? Which nation has a comparative advantage in producing bottles of wine?

33-6. Suppose that the two nations in Problem 33-4 decide to specialize in producing the good for which they have a comparative advantage and to engage in trade. Will residents of both nations agree to trade wine for digital TVs at a rate of exchange of 4 bottles of wine for 1 digital TV? Why or why not?

To answer Problems 33-7 and 33-8, refer to the following table, which shows possible combinations of hourly outputs of modems and flash memory drives in South Shore and neighboring East Isle, in which opportunity costs of producing both products are constant.

South Shore		East Isle	
Modems	Flash Drives	Modems	Flash Drives
75	0	100	0
60	30	80	10
45	60	60	20
30	90	40	30
15	120	20	40
0	150	0	50

33-7. Consider the above table and answer the questions that follow.

   a. What is the opportunity cost of producing modems in South Shore? Of producing flash memory drives in South Shore?

   b. What is the opportunity cost of producing modems in East Isle? Of producing flash memory drives in East Isle?

   c. Which nation has a comparative advantage in producing modems? Which nation has a comparative advantage in producing flash memory drives?

33-8. Refer to your answers to Problem 33-7 when answering the following questions.

    a. Which *one* of the following rates of exchange of modems for flash memory drives will be acceptable to *both* nations: (i) 3 modems for 1 flash drive; (ii) 1 modem for 1 flash drive; or (iii) 1 flash drive for 2.5 modems? Explain.

    b. Suppose that each nation decides to use all available resources to produce only the good for which it has a comparative advantage and to engage in trade at the single feasible rate of exchange you identified in part (a). Prior to specialization and trade, residents of South Shore chose to produce and consume 30 modems per hour and 90 flash drives per hour, and residents of East Isle chose to produce and consume 40 modems per hour and 30 flash drives per hour. Now, residents of South Shore agree to export to East Isle the same quantity of South Shore's specialty good that East Isle residents were consuming prior to engaging in international trade.

How many units of East Isle's specialty good does South Shore import from East Isle?

    c. What is South Shore's hourly consumption of modems and flash drives after the nation specializes and trades with East Isle? What is East Isle's hourly consumption of modems and flash drives after the nation specializes and trades with South Shore?

    d. What consumption gains from trade are experienced by South Shore and East Isle?

33-9. Critics of the North American Free Trade Agreement (NAFTA) suggest that much of the increase in exports from Mexico to the United States now involves goods that Mexico otherwise would have exported to other nations. Mexican firms choose to export the goods to the United States, the critics argue, solely because the items receive preferential treatment under NAFTA tariff rules. What term describes what these critics are claiming is occurring with regard to U.S.-Mexican trade as a result of NAFTA? Explain your reasoning.

ECONOMICS ON THE NET

How the World Trade Organization Settles Trade Disputes A key function of the WTO is to adjudicate trade disagreements that arise among nations. This application helps you learn about the process that the WTO follows when considering international trade disputes.

Title: The World Trade Organization: Settling Trade Disputes

Navigation: Go to **www.econtoday.com/chapter33** to access the WTO's Web page titled *Dispute Settlement*. Under "Introduction to dispute settlement in the WTO," click on *How does the WTO settle disputes?*

Application Read the article; then answer the following questions.

1. As the article discusses, settling trade disputes often takes at least a year. What aspects of the WTO's dispute settlement process take the longest time?

2. Does the WTO actually "punish" a country it finds has broken international trading agreements? If not, who does impose sanctions?

For Group Study and Analysis Go to the WTO's main site at **www.econtoday.com/chapter33**, and click on *About the WTO*. Divide the class into groups, and have the groups explore this information on areas of WTO involvement. Have a class discussion of the pros and cons of WTO involvement in these areas. Which are most important for promoting world trade? Which are least important?

ANSWERS TO QUICK QUIZZES

p. 849: (i) lower; (ii) comparative advantage . . . consume; (iii) Gains . . . consume

p. 852: (i) infant . . . protected; (ii) dumping . . . dumping

p. 857: (i) maximum . . . producers; (ii) tax . . . benefits; (iii) World Trade Organization; (iv) Regional trade . . . regional trade

Exchange Rates and the Balance of Payments

34

In the mid-1990s, the world's developed nations together exported more goods and services to other countries than they imported. Since then, however, they have become net importers of goods and services. During the same period, so-called emerging countries—primarily a number of previously less developed nations in Asia—experiencing rapid rates of economic growth have observed the opposite trend. They began as net importers of goods and services in the mid-1990s, but today they export significantly more than they import. In this chapter, you will learn how economists keep track of nations' exports and imports of goods and services. By the time you have finished reading the chapter, you will also understand why emerging countries have become net exporters at the same time that developed nations have switched to being net importers.

LEARNING OBJECTIVES

myeconlab

MyEconLab helps you master each objective and study more efficiently. See end of chapter for details.

After reading this chapter, you should be able to:

- Distinguish between the balance of trade and the balance of payments
- Identify the key accounts within the balance of payments
- Outline how exchange rates are determined in the markets for foreign exchange
- Discuss factors that can induce changes in equilibrium exchange rates
- Understand how policymakers can go about attempting to fix exchange rates
- Explain alternative approaches to limiting exchange rate variability

?**DID YOU KNOW THAT** since 1980, in years when the U.S. *trade deficit*—the excess of imports of physical goods over exports of such goods—decreased, U.S. real GDP growth was much lower than in years when the trade deficit increased? Over this time interval, in years of a decrease, the trade deficit has declined an average of about 1.4 percent, and during those years average annual U.S. real GDP growth has been just under 1.9 percent. In contrast, in years of a trade deficit increase, the average increase has been approximately 2.7 percent, and in those years average annual real GDP growth has been about 3.5 percent. Trade deficits also are not necessarily associated with lower job growth. The United States has experienced a trade deficit in every year since 2001, while the European Union has experienced a *trade surplus*—more exports of goods than imports. U.S. job growth, however, has been more than twice as high as European Union job growth.

Clearly, experiencing a trade deficit is not necessarily "bad news" for a nation. In this chapter, you will learn how the U.S. trade deficit is measured, and you will also learn that the trade deficit is just a part of an international accounting system called the *balance of payments*.

The Balance of Payments and International Capital Movements

Governments typically keep track of each year's economic activities by calculating the gross domestic product—the total of expenditures on all newly produced final domestic goods and services—and its components. A summary information system has also been developed for international trade. It covers the balance of trade and the balance of payments. The **balance of trade** refers specifically to exports and imports of physical goods, or merchandise, as discussed in Chapter 33. When international trade is in balance, the value of exports equals the value of imports. When the value of imports exceeds the value of exports, we are running a deficit in the balance of trade. When the value of exports exceeds the value of imports, we are running a surplus.

The **balance of payments** is a more general concept that expresses the total of all economic transactions between a nation and the rest of the world, usually for a period of one year. Each country's balance of payments summarizes information about that country's exports and imports of services as well as physical goods, earnings by domestic residents on assets located abroad, earnings on domestic assets owned by foreign residents, international capital movements, and official transactions by central banks and governments. In essence, then, the balance of payments is a record of all the transactions between households, firms, and the government of one country and the rest of the world. Any transaction that leads to a *payment* by a country's residents (or government) is a deficit item, identified by a negative sign (−) when the actual numbers are given for the items listed in the second column of Table 34-1. Any transaction that leads to a *receipt* by a country's residents (or government) is a surplus item and is identified by a plus sign (+) when actual numbers are considered. Table 34-1 gives a listing of the surplus and deficit items on international accounts.

Accounting Identities

Accounting identities—definitions of equivalent values—exist for financial institutions and other businesses. We begin with simple accounting identities that must hold for families and then go on to describe international accounting identities.

Balance of trade
The difference between exports and imports of physical goods.

Balance of payments
A system of accounts that measures transactions of goods, services, income, and financial assets between domestic households, businesses, and governments and residents of the rest of the world during a specific time period.

Accounting identities
Values that are equivalent by definition.

TABLE 34-1 Surplus (+) and Deficit (−) Items on the International Accounts	

Surplus Items (+)	Deficit Items (−)
Exports of merchandise	Imports of merchandise
Private and governmental gifts from foreign residents	Private and governmental gifts to foreign residents
Foreign use of domestically operated travel and transportation services	Use of foreign-operated travel and transportation services
Foreign tourists' expenditures in this country	U.S. tourists' expenditures abroad
Foreign military spending in this country	Military spending abroad
Interest and dividend receipts from foreign entities	Interest and dividends paid to foreign residents
Sales of domestic assets to foreign residents	Purchases of foreign assets
Funds deposited in this country by foreign residents	Funds placed in foreign depository institutions
Sales of gold to foreign residents	Purchases of gold from foreign residents
Sales of domestic currency to foreign residents	Purchases of foreign currency

If a family unit is spending more than its current income, such a situation necessarily implies that the family unit must be doing one of the following:

1. Reducing its money holdings or selling stocks, bonds, or other assets
2. Borrowing
3. Receiving gifts from friends or relatives
4. Receiving public transfers from a government, which obtained the funds by taxing others (a transfer is a payment, in money or in goods or services, made without receiving goods or services in return)

We can use this information to derive an identity: If a family unit is currently spending more than it is earning, it must draw on previously acquired wealth, borrow, or receive either private or public aid. Similarly, an identity exists for a family unit that is currently spending less than it is earning: It must be increasing its money holdings or be lending and acquiring other financial assets, or it must pay taxes or bestow gifts on others. When we consider businesses and governments, each unit in each group faces its own identities or constraints. Ultimately, net lending by households must equal net borrowing by businesses and governments.

DISEQUILIBRIUM Even though our individual family unit's accounts must balance, in the sense that the identity discussed previously must hold, sometimes the item that brings about the balance cannot continue indefinitely. *If family expenditures exceed family income and this situation is financed by borrowing, the household may be considered to be in disequilibrium because such a situation cannot continue indefinitely.* If such a deficit is financed by drawing on previously accumulated assets, the family may also be in disequilibrium because it cannot continue indefinitely to draw on its wealth. Eventually, it will become impossible for that family to continue such a lifestyle. (Of course, if the family members are retired, they may well be in equilibrium by drawing on previously acquired assets to finance current deficits. This example illustrates that it is necessary to understand circumstances fully before pronouncing an economic unit in disequilibrium.)

EQUILIBRIUM Individual households, businesses, and governments, as well as the entire group of households, businesses, and governments, must eventually reach equilibrium. Certain economic adjustment mechanisms have evolved to ensure equilibrium. Deficit households must eventually increase their income or decrease their expenditures. They will find that they have to pay higher interest rates if they wish to borrow to finance their deficits. Eventually, their credit sources will dry up, and they will be forced into equilibrium. Businesses, on occasion, must lower costs or prices—or go bankrupt—to reach equilibrium.

AN ACCOUNTING IDENTITY AMONG NATIONS When people from different nations trade or interact, certain identities or constraints must also hold. People buy goods from people in other nations; they also lend to and present gifts to people in other nations. If residents of a nation interact with residents of other nations, an accounting identity ensures a balance (but not necessarily an equilibrium, as will soon become clear). Let's look at the three categories of balance of payments transactions: current account transactions, capital account transactions, and official reserve account transactions.

Current Account Transactions

Current account
A category of balance of payments transactions that measures the exchange of merchandise, the exchange of services, and unilateral transfers.

During any designated period, all payments and gifts that are related to the purchase or sale of both goods and services constitute the **current account** in international trade. Major types of current account transactions include the exchange of merchandise, the exchange of services, and unilateral transfers.

MERCHANDISE TRADE EXPORTS AND IMPORTS The largest portion of any nation's balance of payments current account is typically the importing and exporting of merchandise. During 2009, for example, as can be seen in lines 1 and 2 of Table 34-2, the United States exported an estimated $1,334.8 billion of merchandise and imported $2,221.4 billion. The balance of merchandise trade is defined as the difference between the value of merchandise exports and the value of merchandise imports. For 2009, the United States had a balance of merchandise trade deficit because the value of its merchandise imports exceeded the value of its merchandise exports. This deficit was about $886.6 billion (line 3).

SERVICE EXPORTS AND IMPORTS The balance of (merchandise) trade has to do with tangible items—things you can feel, touch, and see. Service exports and imports have to do with invisible or intangible items that are bought and sold, such as shipping, insurance, tourist expenditures, and banking services. Also, income earned by foreign residents on U.S. investments and income earned by U.S. residents on foreign investments are part of service imports and exports. As can be seen in lines 4 and 5 of Table 34-2, in 2009, estimated service exports were $457.3 billion, and service imports were $332.2 billion. Thus, the balance of services was about $125.1 billion in 2009 (line 6). Exports constitute receipts or inflows into the United States and are positive; imports constitute payments abroad or outflows of money and are negative.

When we combine the balance of merchandise trade with the balance of services, we obtain a balance on goods and services equal to –$761.5 billion in 2009 (line 7).

UNILATERAL TRANSFERS U.S. residents give gifts to relatives and others abroad, the federal government makes grants to foreign nations, foreign residents give gifts to U.S. residents, and in the past some foreign governments have granted funds to the U.S. government. In the current account, we see that net unilateral transfers—the total amount of gifts given by U.S. residents and the government minus the total

TABLE 34-2

U.S. Balance of Payments Account, 2009 (in billions of dollars)

Current Account

(1) Exports of merchandise goods	+1,334.8	
(2) Imports of merchandise goods	−2,221.4	
(3) Balance of merchandise trade		−886.6
(4) Exports of services	+457.3	
(5) Imports of services	−332.2	
(6) Balance of services		+125.1
(7) Balance on goods and services [(3) + (6)]		−761.5
(8) Net unilateral transfers	−132.1	
(9) Balance on current account		−893.6

Capital Account

(10) U.S. private capital going abroad	−1,361.9	
(11) Foreign private capital coming into the United States	+1,815.4*	
(12) Balance on capital account [(10) + (11)]		+453.5
(13) Balance on current account plus balance on capital account [(9) + (12)]		−440.1

Official Reserve Transactions Account

(14) Official transactions balance		+440.1
(15) Total (balance)		0

Sources: U.S. Department of Commerce, Bureau of Economic Analysis; author's estimates.
*Includes an approximately $28 billion statistical discrepancy, probably uncounted capital inflows, many of which relate to the illegal drug trade.

amount received from abroad by U.S. residents and the government—came to an estimated −$132.1 billion in 2009 (line 8). The fact that there is a minus sign before the number for unilateral transfers means that U.S. residents gave more to foreign residents than foreign residents gave to U.S. residents.

BALANCING THE CURRENT ACCOUNT The balance on current account tracks the value of a country's exports of goods and services (including military receipts plus income on investments abroad) and transfer payments (private and government) relative to the value of that country's imports of goods and services and transfer payments (private and government). In 2009, it was estimated to be −$893.6 billion (line 9).

Go to www.econtoday.com/chapter34 for the latest U.S. balance of payments data from the Bureau of Economic Analysis.

If the sum of net exports of goods and services plus net unilateral transfers plus net investment income exceeds zero, a **current account surplus** *is said to exist; if this sum is negative, a* **current account deficit** *is said to exist. A* **current account deficit** *means that we are importing more goods and services than we are exporting. Such a deficit must be paid for by the export of financial assets.*

Capital Account Transactions

In world markets, it is possible to buy and sell not only goods and services but also real (e.g., real estate) and financial assets. These are the international transactions measured in the **capital account.** Capital account transactions occur because of foreign investments—either by foreign residents investing in the United States or by

Capital account
A category of balance of payments transactions that measures flows of real and financial assets.

U.S. residents investing in other countries. The purchase of shares of stock in British firms on the London stock market by a U.S. resident causes an outflow of funds from the United States to Britain. The construction of a Japanese automobile factory in the United States causes an inflow of funds from Japan to the United States. Any time foreign residents buy U.S. government securities, there is an inflow of funds from other countries to the United States. Any time U.S. residents buy foreign government securities, there is an outflow of funds from the United States to other countries. Loans to and from foreign residents cause outflows and inflows.

Line 10 of Table 34-2 on the preceding page indicates that in 2009, the value of private capital going out of the United States was an estimated −$1,361.9 billion, and line 11 shows that the value of private capital coming into the United States (including a statistical discrepancy) was $1,815.4 billion. U.S. capital going abroad constitutes payments or outflows and is therefore negative. Foreign capital coming into the United States constitutes receipts or inflows and is therefore positive. Thus, there was a positive net capital movement of $453.5 billion into the United States (line 12). This net private flow of capital is also called the balance on capital account.

There is a relationship between the current account balance and the capital account balance, assuming no interventions by the finance ministries or central banks of nations.

> *In the absence of interventions by finance ministries or central banks, the current account balance and the capital account balance must sum to zero. Stated differently, the current account deficit must equal the capital account surplus when governments or central banks do not engage in foreign exchange interventions. In this situation, any nation experiencing a current account deficit, such as the United States, must also be running a capital account surplus.*

This basic relationship is apparent in the United States, as you can see in Figure 34-1. As the figure shows, U.S. current account deficits experienced since the early 1980s have largely been balanced by private capital inflows, but there are exceptions, for reasons that we explain in the next section.

Official Reserve Account Transactions

The third type of balance of payments transaction concerns official reserve assets, which consist of the following:

Special drawing rights (SDRs)
Reserve assets created by the International Monetary Fund for countries to use in settling international payment obligations.

International Monetary Fund
An agency founded to administer an international foreign exchange system and to lend to member countries that had balance of payments problems. The IMF now functions as a lender of last resort for national governments.

1. Foreign currencies

2. Gold

3. **Special drawing rights (SDRs),** which are reserve assets that the **International Monetary Fund** created to be used by countries to settle international payment obligations

4. The reserve position in the International Monetary Fund

5. Financial assets held by an official agency, such as the U.S. Treasury Department

To consider how official reserve account transactions occur, look again at Table 34-2 on the previous page. The surplus in the U.S. capital account was $453.5 billion. But the deficit in the U.S. current account was −$893.6 billion, so the United States had a net deficit on the combined accounts (line 13) of −$440.1 billion. In other words, the United States obtained less in foreign funds in all its international transactions than it used. How is this deficiency made up? By foreign central banks and governments adding to their U.S. funds, shown by the +$440.1 billion in official transactions on line 14 in Table 34-2. There is a plus sign on line 14 because this represents an *inflow* of foreign exchange in our international transactions.

FIGURE 34-1

The Relationship Between the Current Account and the Capital Account

To a large extent, the capital account is the mirror image of the current account. We can see this in most years since 1970. Typically, when the current account was in surplus, the capital account was in deficit. When the current account was in deficit, the capital account was in surplus. There are exceptions, such as the 1996–1998 and 2005–2007 intervals, during which the current account balance and capital account balance declined at the same time. During these periods, the official reserve transactions balance increased significantly as a result of particularly large purchases of U.S. financial assets by foreign governments and central banks.

Sources: International Monetary Fund; *Economic Indicators.*

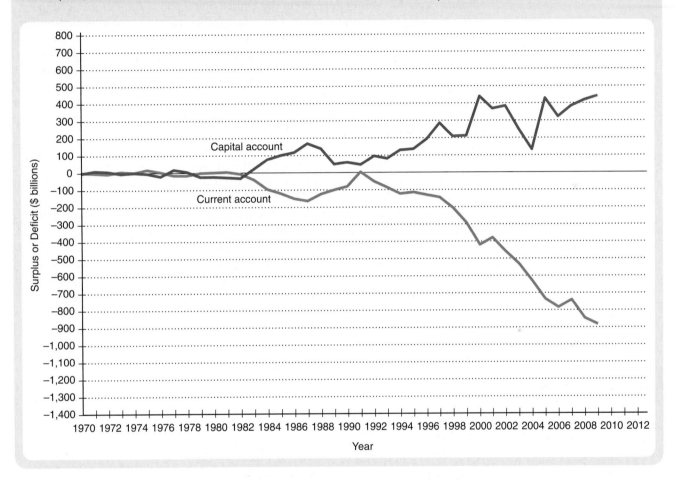

The balance (line 15) in Table 34-2 is zero, as it must be with double-entry bookkeeping. The U.S. balance of payments deficit is measured by the official transactions figure on line 14.

The official reserve account transactions also explain why the movements in the current account balance and the capital account balance in Figure 34-1 are not exact mirror images. This is because the official reserve transactions balance has also varied over time. In recent years, there have been significant surpluses in the official reserve transactions balance. Foreign governments and central banks have purchased large volumes of U.S. financial assets, and these official capital inflows have also offset U.S. current account deficits within the overall balance of payments account.

For instance, between 1996 and 1998 and again between 2005 and 2007, the current account balance and the capital account balance declined simultaneously. During these periods, foreign governments and central banks purchased particularly large quantities of U.S. financial assets. Thus, the official reserve transactions balance increased significantly during these intervals.

What Affects the Distribution of Account Balances Within the Balance of Payments?

A major factor affecting the distribution of account balances within any nation's balance of payments is its rate of inflation relative to that of its trading partners. Assume that the rates of inflation in the United States and in the European Monetary Union (EMU)—the nations that use the euro as their currency—are equal. Now suppose that all of a sudden, the U.S. inflation rate increases. EMU residents will find that U.S. products are becoming more expensive, and U.S. firms will export fewer of them to EMU nations. At the current dollar-euro exchange rate, U.S. residents will find EMU products relatively cheaper, and they will import more. The reverse will occur if the U.S. inflation rate suddenly falls relative to that of the EMU. All other things held constant, whenever the U.S. rate of inflation exceeds that of its trading partners, we expect to see a larger deficit in the U.S. balance of merchandise trade and in the U.S. current account balance. Conversely, when the U.S. rate of inflation is less than that of its trading partners, other things being constant, we expect to see a smaller deficit in the U.S. balance of merchandise trade and in the U.S. current account balance.

Another important factor that sometimes influences account balances within a nation's balance of payments is its relative political stability. Political instability causes *capital flight*. Owners of capital in countries anticipating or experiencing political instability will often move assets to countries that are politically stable, such as the United States. Hence, the U.S. capital account balance is likely to increase whenever political instability looms in other nations in the world.

QUICK QUIZ See page 890 for the answers. Review concepts from this section in MyEconLab.

The _____ of _____ reflects the value of all transactions in international trade, including goods, services, financial assets, and gifts.

The merchandise trade balance gives us the difference between exports and imports of _____ items.

Included in the _____ account along with merchandise trade are service exports and imports relating to commerce in intangible items, such as shipping, insurance, and tourist expenditures. The _____ account also includes income earned by foreign residents on U.S. investments and income earned by U.S. residents on foreign investments.

_____ _____ involve international private gifts and federal government grants or gifts to foreign nations.

When we add the balance of merchandise trade and the balance of services and take account of net unilateral transfers and net investment income, we come up with the balance on the _____ account, a summary statistic.

There are also _____ account transactions that relate to the buying and selling of financial and real assets. Foreign capital is always entering the United States, and U.S. capital is always flowing abroad. The difference is called the balance on the _____ account.

Another type of balance of payments transaction concerns the _____ _____ assets of individual countries, or what is often simply called official transactions. By standard accounting convention, official transactions are exactly equal to but opposite in sign from the sum of the current account balance and the capital account balance.

Account balances within a nation's balance of payments can be affected by its relative rate of _____ and by its _____ stability relative to other nations.

Determining Foreign Exchange Rates

When you buy foreign products, such as European pharmaceuticals, you have dollars with which to pay the European manufacturer. The European manufacturer, however, cannot pay workers in dollars. The workers are European, they live in Europe, and they must have euros to buy goods and services in nations that are members of the European Monetary Union (EMU) and use the euro as their currency. There must therefore be some way of exchanging dollars for euros that the pharmaceuticals manufacturer will accept. That exchange occurs in a **foreign exchange market,** which in this case involves the exchange of euros and dollars.

The particular **exchange rate** between euros and dollars that prevails—the dollar price of the euro—depends on the current demand for and supply of euros and dollars. In a sense, then, our analysis of the exchange rate between dollars and euros will be familiar, for we have used supply and demand throughout this book. If it costs you $1.50 to buy 1 euro, that is the foreign exchange rate determined by the current demand for and supply of euros in the foreign exchange market. The European person going to the foreign exchange market would need 0.67 euro to buy 1 dollar.

Now let's consider what determines the demand for and supply of foreign currency in the foreign exchange market. We will continue to assume that the only two regions in the world are the EMU and the United States.

Demand for and Supply of Foreign Currency

You wish to purchase European-produced pharmaceuticals directly from a manufacturer located in an EMU nation. To do so, you must have euros. You go to the foreign exchange market (or your U.S. bank). Your desire to buy the pharmaceuticals therefore causes you to offer (supply) dollars to the foreign exchange market. Your demand for EMU euros is equivalent to your supply of U.S. dollars to the foreign exchange market.

> *Every U.S. transaction involving the importation of foreign goods constitutes a supply of dollars and a demand for some foreign currency, and the opposite is true for export transactions.*

In this case, the import transaction constitutes a demand for EMU euros.

In our example, we will assume that only two goods are being traded, European pharmaceuticals and U.S. computer printers. The U.S. demand for European pharmaceuticals creates a supply of dollars and a demand for euros in the foreign exchange market. Similarly, the European demand for U.S. computer printers creates a supply of euros and a demand for dollars in the foreign exchange market. Under a system of **flexible exchange rates,** the supply of and demand for dollars and euros in the foreign exchange market will determine the equilibrium foreign exchange rate. The equilibrium exchange rate will tell us how many euros a dollar can be exchanged for—that is, the euro price of dollars—or how many dollars a euro can be exchanged for—the dollar price of euros.

The Equilibrium Foreign Exchange Rate

To determine the equilibrium foreign exchange rate, we have to find out what determines the demand for and supply of foreign exchange. We will ignore for the moment any speculative aspect of buying foreign exchange. That is, we assume that there are no individuals who wish to buy euros simply because they think that their price will go up in the future.

The idea of an exchange rate is no different from the idea of paying a certain price for something you want to buy. If you like coffee, you know you have to pay about $1.50 a cup. If the price went up to $2.50, you would probably buy fewer cups. If the price went

Foreign exchange market
A market in which households, firms, and governments buy and sell national currencies.

Exchange rate
The price of one nation's currency in terms of the currency of another country.

Flexible exchange rates
Exchange rates that are allowed to fluctuate in the open market in response to changes in supply and demand. Sometimes called *floating exchange rates*.

Go to www.econtoday.com/chapter34 for recent data from the Federal Reserve Bank of St. Louis on the exchange value of the U.S. dollar relative to the major currencies of the world.

down to 50 cents, you would likely buy more. In other words, the demand curve for cups of coffee, expressed in terms of dollars, slopes downward following the law of demand. The demand curve for euros slopes downward also, and we will see why.

Let's think more closely about the demand schedule for euros. Let's say that it costs you $1.35 to purchase 1 euro; that is the exchange rate between dollars and euros. If tomorrow you had to pay $1.50 for the same euro, the exchange rate would have changed. Looking at such a change, we would say that there has been an **appreciation** in the value of the euro in the foreign exchange market. But another way to view this increase in the value of the euro is to say that there has been a **depreciation** in the value of the dollar in the foreign exchange market. The dollar used to buy 0.74 euro; tomorrow, the dollar will be able to buy only 0.67 euro at a price of $1.50 per euro. If the dollar price of euros rises, you will probably demand fewer euros. Why? The answer lies in the reason you and others demand euros in the first place.

Why is an appreciating currency good news for some residents of a country but bad news for other residents?

Appreciation
An increase in the exchange value of one nation's currency in terms of the currency of another nation.

Depreciation
A decrease in the exchange value of one nation's currency in terms of the currency of another nation.

INTERNATIONAL EXAMPLE
Going Loony over an Appreciating Loonie

One face of a Canadian dollar coin displays an image of a bird called the loon, so the Canadian dollar is informally known as the "loonie." In the mid-2000s, the loonie was worth only about 75 U.S. cents. In the late 2000s, however, its value soared to over 1 U.S. dollar. For Canadians who enjoy making sightseeing-shopping trips to the United States, the loonie's significant appreciation was a bonanza. These Canadians could use their loonies to obtain about a third more U.S. dollars than before, so U.S. travel expenses and goods were more than 30 percent cheaper.

Nevertheless, for Canadian export firms and their employees, the loonie's considerable appreciation rapidly made their products more expensive to U.S. residents. Hence, U.S. purchases of Canadian products plummeted, and Canadian profits and job opportunities declined. In addition, U.S. residents cut back on visits to Canada, because prices of touring Canada and buying its goods and services increased. This only intensified the bad news for Canadian retailers who had already lost considerable business when Canadian shoppers headed south to grab U.S. bargains.

FOR CRITICAL ANALYSIS
Which groups in the United States gained and which lost when the loonie appreciated?

Which Canadians have been hurt by the rise in the U.S. dollar value of the Canadian "loonie."

APPRECIATION AND DEPRECIATION OF EUROS Recall that in our example, you and others demand euros to buy European pharmaceuticals. The demand curve for European pharmaceuticals follows the law of demand and therefore slopes downward. If it costs more U.S. dollars to buy the same quantity of European pharmaceuticals, presumably you and other U.S. residents will not buy the same quantity; your quantity demanded will be less. We say that your demand for euros is *derived from* your demand for European pharmaceuticals. In panel (a) of Figure 34-2 we present the hypothetical demand schedule for packages of European pharmaceuticals by a representative set of U.S. consumers during a typical week. In panel (b), we show graphically the U.S. demand curve for European pharmaceuticals in terms of U.S. dollars taken from panel (a).

AN EXAMPLE OF DERIVED DEMAND Let us assume that the price of a package of European pharmaceuticals in Europe is 100 euros. Given that price, we can find the

Panel (a)
Demand Schedule for Packages of European Pharmaceuticals in the United States per Week

Price per Package	Quantity Demanded
$155	100
150	300
145	500
140	700

Panel (b)
U.S. Demand Curve for European Pharmaceuticals

Panel (c)
Euros Required to Purchase Quantity Demanded
(at *P* = 100 euros per package of pharmaceuticals)

Quantity Demanded	Euros Required
100	10,000
300	30,000
500	50,000
700	70,000

Panel (d)
Derived Demand Schedule for Euros in the United States with Which to Pay for Imports of Pharmaceuticals

Dollar Price of One Euro	Dollar Price of Pharmaceuticals	Quantity of Pharmaceuticals Demanded	Quantity of Euros Demanded per Week
$1.55	$155	100	10,000
1.50	150	300	30,000
1.45	145	500	50,000
1.40	140	700	70,000

FIGURE 34-2

Deriving the Demand for Euros

In panel (a), we show the demand schedule for European pharmaceuticals in the United States, expressed in terms of dollars per package of pharmaceuticals. In panel (b), we show the demand curve, *D*, which slopes downward. In panel (c), we show the number of euros required to purchase up to 700 packages of pharmaceuticals. If the price per package of pharmaceuticals is 100 euros, we can now find the quantity of euros needed to pay for the various quantities demanded. In panel (d), we see the derived demand for euros in the United States in order to purchase the various quantities of pharmaceuticals given in panel (a). The resultant demand curve, D_1, is shown in panel (e). This is the U.S. derived demand for euros.

Panel (e)
U.S. Derived Demand for Euros

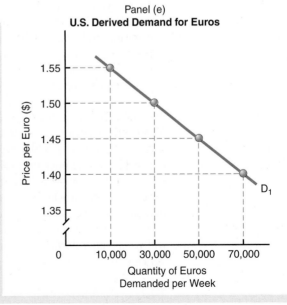

number of euros required to purchase 500 packages of European pharmaceuticals. That information is given in panel (c) of Figure 34-2. If purchasing one package of European pharmaceuticals requires 100 euros, 500 packages require 50,000 euros. Now we have enough information to determine the derived demand curve for euros. If 1 euro costs $1.45, a package of pharmaceuticals would cost $145 (100 euros per package × $1.45 per euro = $145 per package). At $145 per package, the representative group of U.S. consumers would, we see from panel (a) of Figure 34-2, demand 500 packages of pharmaceuticals.

From panel (c), we see that 50,000 euros would be demanded to buy the 500 packages of pharmaceuticals. We show this quantity demanded in panel (d). In panel (e), we draw the derived demand curve for euros. Now consider what happens if the price of euros goes up to $1.50. A package of European pharmaceuticals priced at 100 euros in Europe would now cost $150. From panel (a), we see that at $150 per package, 300 packages of pharmaceuticals will be imported from Europe into the United States by our representative group of U.S. consumers. From panel (c), we see that 300 packages of pharmaceuticals would require 30,000 euros to be purchased; thus, in panels (d) and (e), we see that at a price of $1.50 per euro, the quantity demanded will be 30,000 euros.

We continue similar calculations all the way up to a price of $1.55 per euro. At that price, a package of European pharmaceuticals costing 100 euros in Europe would cost $155, and our representative U.S. consumers would import only 100 packages of pharmaceuticals.

DOWNWARD-SLOPING DERIVED DEMAND As can be expected, as the price of the euro rises, the quantity demanded will fall. The only difference here from the standard demand analysis developed in Chapter 3 and used throughout this text is that the demand for euros is derived from the demand for a final product—European pharmaceuticals in our example.

SUPPLY OF EUROS Assume that European pharmaceutical manufacturers buy U.S. computer printers. The supply of euros is a derived supply in that it is derived from the European demand for U.S. computer printers. We could go through an example similar to the one for pharmaceuticals to come up with a supply schedule of euros in Europe. It slopes upward. Obviously, Europeans want dollars to purchase U.S. goods. European residents will be willing to supply more euros when the dollar price of euros goes up, because they can then buy more U.S. goods with the same quantity of euros. That is, the euro would be worth more in exchange for U.S. goods than when the dollar price for euros was lower.

AN EXAMPLE Let's take an example. Suppose a U.S.-produced computer printer costs $200. If the exchange rate is $1.45 per euro, a European resident will have to come up with 137.93 euros (= $200 at $1.45 per euro) to buy one computer printer. If, however, the exchange rate goes up to $1.50 per euro, a European resident must come up with only 133.33 euros (= $200 at $1.50 per euro) to buy a U.S. computer printer. At this lower price (in euros) of U.S. computer printers, Europeans will demand a larger quantity. In other words, as the price of euros goes up in terms of dollars, the quantity of U.S. computer printers demanded will go up, and hence the quantity of euros supplied will go up. Therefore, the supply schedule of euros, which is derived from the European demand for U.S. goods, will slope upward, as seen in Figure 34-3 on the following page.

TOTAL DEMAND FOR AND SUPPLY OF EUROS Let us now look at the total demand for and supply of euros. We take all U.S. consumers of European pharma-

FIGURE 34-3

The Supply of Euros

If the market price of a U.S.-produced computer printer is $200, then at an exchange rate of $1.45 per euro, the price of the printer to a European consumer is 137.93 euros. If the exchange rate rises to $1.50 per euro, the European price of the printer falls to 133.33 euros. This induces an increase in the quantity of printers demanded by European consumers and consequently an increase in the quantity of euros supplied in exchange for dollars in the foreign exchange market. In contrast, if the exchange rate falls to $1.40 per euro, the European price of the printer rises to 142.86 euros. This causes a decrease in the quantity of printers demanded by European consumers. As a result, there is a decline in the quantity of euros supplied in exchange for dollars in the foreign exchange market.

ceuticals and all European consumers of U.S. computer printers and put their demands for and supplies of euros together into one diagram. Thus, we are showing the total demand for and total supply of euros. The horizontal axis in Figure 34-4 represents the quantity of foreign exchange—the number of euros per year. The vertical axis represents the exchange rate—the price of foreign currency (euros) expressed in dollars (per euro). The foreign currency price of $1.50 per euro means it will cost you $1.50 to buy 1 euro. At the foreign currency price of $1.45 per euro, you know that it will cost you $1.45 to buy 1 euro. The equilibrium, E, is again established at $1.45 for 1 euro.

In our hypothetical example, assuming that there are only representative groups of pharmaceutical consumers in the United States and computer printer consumers in Europe, the equilibrium exchange rate will be set at $1.45 per euro.

FIGURE 34-4

Total Demand for and Supply of Euros

The market supply curve for euros results from the total European demand for U.S. computer printers. The demand curve, D, slopes downward like most demand curves, and the supply curve, S, slopes upward. The foreign exchange price, or the U.S. dollar price of euros, is given on the vertical axis. The number of euros is represented on the horizontal axis. If the foreign exchange rate is $1.50—that is, if it takes $1.50 to buy 1 euro—U.S. residents will demand 20 billion euros. The equilibrium exchange rate is at the intersection of D and S, or point E. The equilibrium exchange rate is $1.45 per euro. At this point, 30 billion euros are both demanded and supplied each year.

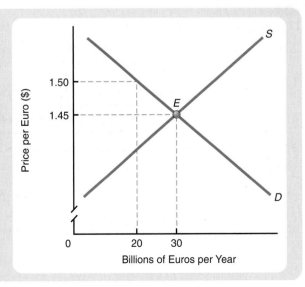

This equilibrium is not established because U.S. residents like to buy euros or because Europeans like to buy dollars. Rather, the equilibrium exchange rate depends on how many computer printers Europeans want and how many European pharmaceuticals U.S. residents want (given their respective incomes, their tastes, and, in our example, the relative prices of pharmaceuticals and computer printers).

A SHIFT IN DEMAND Assume that a successful advertising campaign by U.S. pharmaceutical importers has caused U.S. demand for European pharmaceuticals to rise. U.S. residents demand more pharmaceuticals at all prices. Their demand curve for European pharmaceuticals has shifted outward to the right.

The increased demand for European pharmaceuticals can be translated into an increased demand for euros. All U.S. residents clamoring for European pharmaceuticals will supply more dollars to the foreign exchange market while demanding more euros to pay for the pharmaceuticals. Figure 34-5 presents a new demand schedule, D_2, for euros; this demand schedule is to the right of the original demand schedule. If Europeans do not change their desire for U.S. computer printers, the supply schedule for euros will remain stable.

A new equilibrium will be established at a higher exchange rate. In our particular example, the new equilibrium is established at an exchange rate of $1.50 per euro. It now takes $1.50 to buy 1 euro, whereas formerly it took $1.45. This will be translated into an increase in the price of European pharmaceuticals to U.S. residents and into a decrease in the price of U.S. computer printers to Europeans. For example, a package of European pharmaceuticals priced at 100 euros that sold for $145 in the United States will now be priced at $150. Conversely, a U.S. printer priced at $200 that previously sold for 137.93 euros will now sell for 133.33 euros.

A SHIFT IN SUPPLY We just assumed that the U.S. demand for European pharmaceuticals had shifted due to a successful ad campaign. Because the demand for euros is derived from the demand by U.S. residents for pharmaceuticals, this is translated into a shift in the demand curve for euros. As an alternative exercise, we might assume that the supply curve of euros shifts outward to the right. Such a supply shift could occur

FIGURE 34-5

A Shift in the Demand Schedule

The demand schedule for European pharmaceuticals shifts to the right, causing the derived demand schedule for euros to shift to the right also. We have shown this as a shift from D_1 to D_2. We have assumed that the supply schedule for euros has remained stable—that is, European demand for U.S. computer printers has remained constant. The old equilibrium foreign exchange rate was $1.45 per euro. The new equilibrium exchange rate will be E_2. It will now cost $1.50 to buy 1 euro. The higher price of euros will be translated into a higher U.S. dollar price for European pharmaceuticals and a lower euro price for U.S. computer printers.

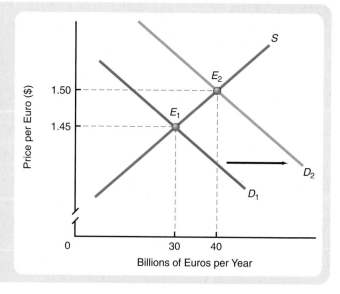

FIGURE 34-6

A Shift in the Supply of Euros

There has been a shift in the supply curve for euros. The new equilibrium will occur at E_1, meaning that $1.40, rather than $1.45, will now buy 1 euro. After the exchange rate adjustment, the annual amount of euros demanded and supplied will increase from 30 billion to 60 billion.

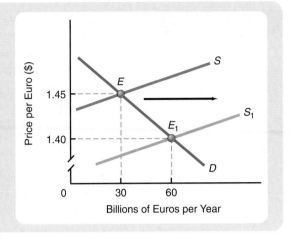

for many reasons, one of which is a relative rise in the European price level. For example, if the prices of all European-manufactured computer peripherals went up 20 percent in euros, U.S. computer printers would become relatively cheaper. That would mean that European residents would want to buy more U.S. computer printers. But remember that when they want to buy more U.S. printers, they supply more euros to the foreign exchange market.

Thus, we see in Figure 34-6 that the supply curve of euros moves from S to S_1. In the absence of restrictions—that is, in a system of flexible exchange rates—the new equilibrium exchange rate will be $1.40 equals 1 euro. The quantity of euros demanded and supplied will increase from 30 billion per year to 60 billion per year. We say, then, that in a flexible international exchange rate system, shifts in the demand for and supply of foreign currencies will cause changes in the equilibrium foreign exchange rates. Those rates will remain in effect until world supply or demand shifts.

Market Determinants of Exchange Rates

The foreign exchange market is affected by many other variables in addition to changes in relative price levels, including the following:

- *Changes in real interest rates.* Suppose that the U.S. interest rate, corrected for people's expectations of inflation, increases relative to the rest of the world. Then international investors elsewhere seeking the higher returns now available in the United States will increase their demand for dollar-denominated assets, thereby increasing the demand for dollars in foreign exchange markets. An increased demand for dollars in foreign exchange markets, other things held constant, will cause the dollar to appreciate and other currencies to depreciate.

- *Changes in consumer preferences.* If Germany's citizens suddenly develop a taste for U.S.-made automobiles, this will increase the derived demand for U.S. dollars in foreign exchange markets.

- *Perceptions of economic stability.* As already mentioned, if the United States looks economically and politically more stable relative to other countries, more foreign residents will want to put their savings into U.S. assets than in their own domestic assets. This will increase the demand for dollars.

QUICK QUIZ   *See page 890 for the answers. Review concepts from this section in MyEconLab.*

The foreign _____ _____ is the rate at which one country's currency can be exchanged for another's.

The _____ for foreign exchange is a derived _____; it is derived from the demand for foreign goods and services (and financial assets). The _____ of foreign exchange is derived from foreign residents' demands for U.S. goods and services.

The demand curve of foreign exchange slopes _____, and the supply curve of foreign exchange slopes

_____. The equilibrium foreign exchange rate occurs at the intersection of the demand and supply curves for a currency.

A _____ in the demand for foreign goods will result in a shift in the _____ for foreign exchange, thereby changing the equilibrium foreign exchange rate. A shift in the supply of foreign currency will also cause a change in the equilibrium exchange rate.

The Gold Standard and the International Monetary Fund

The current system of more or less freely floating exchange rates is a relatively recent development. In the past, we have had periods of a gold standard, fixed exchange rates under the International Monetary Fund, and variants of the two.

The Gold Standard

Until the 1930s, many nations were on a gold standard. The value of their domestic currency was fixed, or *pegged*, in units of gold. Nations operating under this gold standard agreed to redeem their currencies for a fixed amount of gold at the request of any holder of that currency. Although gold was not necessarily the means of exchange for world trade, it was the unit to which all currencies under the gold standard were pegged. And because all currencies in the system were pegged to gold, exchange rates between those currencies were fixed. Indeed, the gold standard has been offered as the prototype of a fixed exchange rate system. The heyday of the gold standard was from about 1870 to 1914.

There was (and always is) a relationship between the balance of payments and changes in domestic money supplies throughout the world. Under a gold standard, the international financial market reached equilibrium through the effect of gold flows on each country's money supply. When the sum of a nation's current account balance and its capital account balance was negative, more gold would flow out than in. Because the domestic money supply was based on gold, an outflow of gold to foreign residents caused an automatic reduction in the domestic money supply. This caused several things to happen. Interest rates rose, thereby attracting foreign capital and pushing the sum of the current account balance and the capital account balance back toward zero. At the same time, the reduction in the money supply was equivalent to a restrictive monetary policy, which caused national output and prices to fall. Imports were discouraged and exports were encouraged, thereby again increasing net exports.

Two problems plagued the gold standard. One was that by fixing the value of its currency in relation to the amount of gold, a nation gave up control of its domestic monetary policy. Another was that the world's commerce was at the mercy of gold discoveries. Throughout history, each time new veins of gold were found, desired domestic expenditures on goods and services increased. If production of goods and services failed to increase proportionately, inflation resulted.

Bretton Woods and the International Monetary Fund

In 1944, as World War II was ending, representatives from the world's capitalist countries met in Bretton Woods, New Hampshire, to create a new international payment system to replace the gold standard, which had collapsed during the 1930s. The Bretton Woods Agreement Act was signed on July 31, 1945, by President Harry Truman. It created a new permanent institution, the International Monetary Fund (IMF). The IMF's task was to administer the agreement and to lend to member countries for which the sum of the current account balance and the capital account balance was negative, thereby helping them maintain an offsetting surplus in their official reserve transactions accounts. The arrangements thus provided are now called the old IMF system or the Bretton Woods system.

Member governments agreed to maintain the value of their currencies within 1 percent of the declared **par value**—the officially determined value. The United States, which owned most of the world's gold stock, was similarly obligated to maintain gold prices within a 1 percent margin of the official rate of $35 an ounce. Except for a transitional arrangement permitting a onetime adjustment of up to 10 percent in par value, members could alter exchange rates thereafter only with the approval of the IMF.

On August 15, 1971, President Richard Nixon suspended the convertibility of the dollar into gold. On December 18, 1971, the United States officially devalued the dollar—that is, lowered its official value—relative to the currencies of 14 major industrial nations. Finally, on March 16, 1973, the finance ministers of the European Economic Community (now the European Union) announced that they would let their currencies float against the dollar, something Japan had already begun doing with its yen. Since 1973, the United States and most other trading countries have had either freely floating exchange rates or managed ("dirty") floating exchange rates, in which their governments or central banks intervene from time to time to try to influence world market exchange rates.

Par value
The officially determined value of a currency.

Fixed versus Floating Exchange Rates

The United States went off the Bretton Woods system of fixed exchange rates in 1973. As Figure 34-7 indicates, many other nations of the world have been less willing to permit the values of their currencies to vary in the foreign exchange markets.

FIGURE 34-7

Current Foreign Exchange Rate Arrangements

Today, 22 percent of the member nations of the International Monetary Fund have an independent float, and just over 22 percent have a managed float exchange rate arrangement. Slightly over 21 percent of all nations use the currencies of other nations instead of issuing their own currencies.

Source: International Monetary Fund.

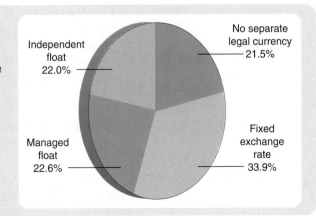

FIGURE 34-8

A Fixed Exchange Rate

This figure illustrates how the Central Bank of Bahrain could fix the dollar-dinar exchange rate in the face of an increase in the supply of dinars caused by a rise in the demand for U.S. goods by Bahraini residents. In the absence of any action by the Central Bank of Bahrain, the result would be a movement from point E_1 to point E_2. The dollar value of the dinar would fall from $2.66 to $2.00. The Central Bank of Bahrain can prevent this exchange rate change by purchasing dinars with dollars in the foreign exchange market, thereby raising the demand for dinars. At the new equilibrium point, E_3, the dinar's value remains at $2.66.

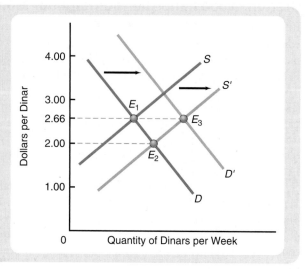

Fixing the Exchange Rate

How did nations fix their exchange rates in years past? How do many countries accomplish this today? Figure 34-8 shows the market for dinars, the currency of Bahrain. At the initial equilibrium point E_1, U.S. residents had to give up $2.66 to obtain 1 dinar. Suppose now that there is an increase in the supply of dinars for dollars, perhaps because Bahraini residents wish to buy more U.S. goods. Other things being equal, the result would be a movement to point E_2 in Figure 34-8. The dollar value of the dinar would fall to $2.00.

To prevent a dinar depreciation from occurring, however, the Central Bank of Bahrain could increase the demand for dinars in the foreign exchange market by purchasing dinars with dollars. The Central Bank of Bahrain can do this using dollars that it has on hand as part of its *foreign exchange reserves*. All central banks hold reserves of foreign currencies. Because the U.S. dollar is a key international currency, the Central Bank of Bahrain and other central banks typically hold billions of dollars in reserve so that they can make transactions such as the one in this example. Note that a sufficiently large purchase of dinars could, as shown in Figure 34-8, cause the demand curve to shift rightward to achieve the new equilibrium point E_3, at which the dinar's value remains at $2.66. Provided that it has enough dollar reserves on hand, the Central Bank of Bahrain could maintain—effectively fix—the exchange rate in the face of the rise in the supply of dinars.

The Central Bank of Bahrain has maintained the dollar-dinar exchange rate in this manner since 2001. This basic approach—varying the amount of the national currency demanded at any given exchange rate in foreign exchange markets when necessary—is also the way that *any* central bank seeks to keep its nation's currency value unchanged in light of changing market forces.

> *Central banks can keep exchange rates fixed as long as they have enough foreign exchange reserves to deal with potentially long-lasting changes in the demand for or supply of their nation's currency.*

Pros and Cons of a Fixed Exchange Rate

Why might a nation such as Bahrain wish to keep the value of its currency from fluctuating? One reason is that changes in the exchange rate can affect the market values of assets that are denominated in foreign currencies. This can increase the financial risks that a nation's residents face, thereby forcing them to incur costs to avoid these risks.

FOREIGN EXCHANGE RISK   The possibility that variations in the market value of assets can take place due to changes in the value of a nation's currency is the **foreign exchange risk** that residents of a country face because their nation's currency value can vary. For instance, if companies in Bahrain had many loans denominated in dollars but earned nearly all their revenues in dinars from sales within Bahrain, a decline in the dollar value of the dinar would mean that Bahraini companies would have to allocate a larger portion of their earnings to make the same *dollar* loan payments as before. Thus, a fall in the dinar's value would increase the operating costs of these companies, thereby reducing their profitability and raising the likelihood of eventual bankruptcy.

Foreign exchange risk
The possibility that changes in the value of a nation's currency will result in variations in the market value of assets.

Limiting foreign exchange risk is a classic rationale for adopting a fixed exchange rate. Nevertheless, a country's residents are not defenseless against foreign exchange risk. In what is known as a **hedge,** they can adopt strategies intended to offset the risk arising from exchange rate variations. For example, a company in Bahrain that has significant euro earnings from sales in Germany but sizable loans from U.S. investors could arrange to convert its euro earnings into dollars via special types of foreign exchange contracts called *currency swaps.* The Bahraini company could likewise avoid holdings of dinars and shield itself—*hedge*—against variations in the dinar's value.

Hedge
A financial strategy that reduces the chance of suffering losses arising from foreign exchange risk.

What do currency traders do when a nation's currency value is so volatile that it is difficult to determine the current market exchange rate?

INTERNATIONAL EXAMPLE
Measuring the Value of Zimbabwe's Dollar

For years, Zimbabwe's government has stated that the "official" value of its currency has been a few hundred Zimbabwe dollars per U.S. dollar. Nevertheless, for some time the actual market rates of exchange have been in *millions* of Zimbabwe dollars per U.S. dollar. Recently, the value of the Zimbabwe dollar went through numerous gyrations, mostly in a downward direction. Foreign exchange market trades in Zimbabwe dollars are relatively infrequent, so currency traders experienced difficulties in assessing a true market rate of exchange.

Then traders found out that prices of shares of an insurance company called Old Mutual are traded in both Zimbabwe and the United Kingdom. Each share in the company is worth the same after adjusting for valuation in the different currencies. Thus, dividing the Zimbabwe dollar price of a share in Old Mutual by the British pound price in London markets yields a market measure of the exchange rate in Zimbabwe dollars per British pound. Multiplying this exchange rate by the market exchange rate of British pounds per U.S. dollar then yields the market rate of exchange of Zimbabwe dollars per U.S. dollar.

FOR CRITICAL ANALYSIS
Why might the fact that Zimbabwe's annual inflation rate has exceeded 2.5 million percent help to explain why the nation's currency has experienced sudden depreciations?

THE EXCHANGE RATE AS A SHOCK ABSORBER   If fixing the exchange rate limits foreign exchange risk, why do so many nations allow the exchange rates to float? The answer must be that there are potential drawbacks associated with fixing exchange rates. One is that exchange rate variations can actually perform a valuable service for a

You Are There

To think about how even individual households in some nations can face foreign exchange risks, consider **Literally Betting the House on an Exchange Rate,** on page 884.

Is this resident of Zimbabwe rich because he has local currency that shows 10,000,000 on each bill?

Dirty float

Active management of a floating exchange rate on the part of a country's government, often in cooperation with other nations.

nation's economy. Consider a situation in which residents of a nation speak only their own nation's language. As a result, the country's residents are very *immobile*: They cannot trade their labor skills outside their own nation's borders.

Now think about what happens if this nation chooses to fix its exchange rate. Imagine a situation in which other countries begin to sell products that are close substitutes for the products its people specialize in producing, causing a sizable drop in worldwide demand for the nation's goods. If wages and prices do not instantly and completely adjust downward, the result will be a sharp decline in production of goods and services, a falloff in national income, and higher unemployment. Contrast this situation with one in which the exchange rate floats. In this case, a sizable decline in outside demand for the nation's products will cause it to experience a trade deficit, which will lead to a significant drop in the demand for that nation's currency. As a result, the nation's currency will experience a sizable depreciation, making the goods that the nation offers to sell abroad much less expensive in other countries. People abroad who continue to consume the nation's products will increase their purchases, and the nation's exports will increase. Its production will begin to recover somewhat, as will its residents' incomes. Unemployment will begin to fall.

This example illustrates how exchange rate variations can be beneficial, especially if a nation's residents are relatively immobile. It can be difficult, for example, for a Polish resident who has never studied Portuguese to move to Lisbon, even if she is highly qualified for available jobs there. If many residents of Poland face similar linguistic or cultural barriers, Poland could be better off with a floating exchange rate even if its residents must incur significant costs hedging against foreign exchange risk as a result.

Splitting the Difference: Dirty Floats and Target Zones

In recent years, national policymakers have tried to soften the choice between adopting a fixed exchange rate and allowing exchange rates full flexibility in the foreign exchange markets by "splitting the difference" between the two extremes.

A DIRTY FLOAT One way to split the difference is to let exchange rates float most of the time but "manage" exchange rate movements part of the time. U.S. policymakers have occasionally engaged in what is called a **dirty float,** the active management of flexible exchange rates. The management of flexible exchange rates has usually come about through international policy cooperation.

Is it possible for nations to "manage" foreign exchange rates? Some economists do not think so. For example, economists Michael Bordo and Anna Schwartz studied the foreign exchange intervention actions coordinated by the Federal Reserve and the U.S. Treasury during the second half of the 1980s. Besides showing that such interventions were sporadic and variable, Bordo and Schwartz came to an even more compelling conclusion: Exchange rate interventions were trivial relative to the total trading of foreign exchange on a daily basis. For example, in April 1989, total foreign exchange trading amounted to $129 billion per day, yet the U.S. central bank purchased only $100 million in deutsche marks and yen during that entire month (and did so on a single day). For all of 1989, Fed purchases of marks and yen were only $17.7 billion, or the equivalent of less than 13 percent of the amount of an average *day's* trading in April of that year. Their conclusion is that foreign exchange market interventions by the U.S. central bank or the central banks of other nations do not influence exchange rates in the long run.

CRAWLING PEGS Another approach to splitting the difference between fixed and floating exchange rates is called a **crawling peg.** This is an automatically adjusting target for the value of a nation's currency. For instance, a central bank might announce that it wants the value of its currency relative to the U.S. dollar to decline at an annual rate of 5 percent, a rate of depreciation that it feels is consistent with long-run market forces. The central bank would then try to buy or sell foreign exchange reserves in sufficient quantities to be sure that the currency depreciation takes place gradually, thereby reducing the foreign exchange risk faced by the nation's residents. In this way, a crawling peg functions like a floating exchange rate in the sense that the exchange rate can change over time. But it is like a fixed exchange rate in the sense that the central bank always tries to keep the exchange rate close to a target value. In this way, a crawling peg has elements of both kinds of exchange rate systems.

Crawling peg
An exchange rate arrangement in which a country pegs the value of its currency to the exchange value of another nation's currency but allows the par value to change at regular intervals.

TARGET ZONES A third way to try to split the difference between fixed and floating exchange rates is to adopt an exchange rate **target zone.** Under this policy, a central bank announces that there are specific upper and lower *bands*, or limits, for permissible values for the exchange rate. Within those limits, which define the exchange rate target zone, the central bank permits the exchange rate to move flexibly. The central bank commits itself, however, to intervene in the foreign exchange markets to ensure that its nation's currency value will not rise above the upper band or fall below the lower band. For instance, if the exchange rate measured in units of foreign currency per unit of domestic currency approaches the upper band, the central bank must sell foreign exchange reserves in sufficient quantities to prevent additional depreciation of its nation's currency. If the exchange rate approaches the lower band, the central bank must purchase sufficient amounts of foreign exchange reserves to halt any further currency appreciation.

Target zone
A range of permitted exchange rate variations between upper and lower exchange rate bands that a central bank defends by selling or buying foreign exchange reserves.

In 1999, officials from the European Union attempted to get the U.S. and Japanese governments to agree to target zones for the exchange rate between the newly created euro, the dollar, and the yen. So far, however, no target zones have been created, and the euro has floated freely.

QUICK QUIZ   *See page 890 for the answers. Review concepts from this section in MyEconLab.*

The International Monetary Fund was developed after World War II as an institution to maintain _____ exchange rates in the world. Since 1973, however, _____ exchange rates have disappeared in most major trading countries. For these nations, exchange rates are largely determined by the forces of demand and supply in foreign exchange markets.

Many other nations, however, have tried to fix their exchange rates, with varying degrees of success. Although fixing the exchange rate helps protect a nation's residents from foreign exchange _____, this policy makes less mobile residents susceptible to greater volatility in income and employment.

Countries have experimented with exchange rate systems between the extremes of fixed and floating exchange rates. Under a _____ float, a central bank permits the value of its nation's currency to float in foreign exchange markets but intervenes from time to time to influence the exchange rate. Under a _____ peg, a central bank tries to push the value of its nation's currency in a desired direction. Pursuing a _____ _____ policy, a central bank aims to keep the exchange rate between upper and lower bands, intervening only when the exchange rate approaches either limit.

You Are There   Literally Betting the House on an Exchange Rate

When Tamas Bencze, a resident of Budapest, Hungary, opened a recent statement from his bank regarding his mortgage loan, he received an unpleasant surprise: His monthly payment had gone up 10 percent. The interest rate and other terms of the loan had not been altered, but the exchange rate had changed. Bencze, like about half of all homeowners in Hungary, has a mortgage denominated in a currency other than the Hungarian currency, called the *forint*. Bencze's mortgage is valued in Swiss francs, but he makes his mortgage payments in Hungarian forint. Thus, every time the forint depreciates in relation to the Swiss franc, he has to pay more forint.

Why do Bencze and so many other residents of Hungary arrange to borrow Swiss francs instead of Hungarian forint when they finance purchases of their homes? The answer is that market interest rates on loans denominated in the Hungarian forint are more than twice as high as rates on Swiss franc loans. Of course, one reason Hungarian rates are higher than Swiss rates is that most individuals anticipate that the Hungarian currency will tend to depreciate in relation to the Swiss franc. Consequently, they require a higher interest return on Hungarian assets—such as mortgage loans—to induce them to hold the assets alongside Swiss assets.

Bencze and other Hungarian residents who have their mortgages denominated in Swiss francs have made a choice. They have opted for the certainty of a lower loan interest rate, but in doing so they have taken on a foreign exchange risk: the potential for sudden exchange rate changes such as the one that has just occurred. Now that this risk has been realized and pushed up his mortgage payments, while his annual forint-denominated income has barely changed, Bencze can only hope that the forint will not lose even more value in relation to the Swiss franc. After all, he has literally bet his house on the hope that the value of the forint will not experience a significant decline.

CRITICAL ANALYSIS QUESTIONS

1. Do you suppose that Bencze and others with foreign-currency-denominated loans would prefer for Hungary's central bank to opt for a floating exchange rate or a fixed exchange rate?

2. How might Bencze shield himself from the foreign exchange risk exposure he faces through his mortgage loan arrangement?

The Current Account Deficit for One Group of Nations Is the Current Account Surplus for Another

Issues and Applications

CONCEPTS APPLIED

- Current Account
- Balance of Payments
- Capital Account

As you have learned in this chapter, the United States has been experiencing a significant current account deficit in recent years. It is not the only developed nation with a deficit in the current account of its balance of payments. All told, the United States and othe highly developed nations are experiencing a combined current account deficit of close to $1 trillion per year. Who is financing these current account deficits? The answer must be the so-called *emerging countries*—nations with previously less developed economies, such as China and India, that are now experiencing significant growth. Let's see why this is so and contemplate the implications.

Mirror Image Current Account Balances for Developed and Developing Countries

Figure 34-9 displays the combined current account balances of the world's most developed nations since 1996. Until 1997, developed nations were operating with a combined current account surplus, but then they fell into a deficit position that has widened dramatically in recent years.

The figure also shows the combined current account balances of emerging countries. Until 1997, emerging countries experienced a combined current account deficit. Since then, they have operated with current account surpluses that have steadily increased in magnitude. The fact that emerging countries' combined current account surpluses have been nearly the mirror image of the deficits of developed nations is no accident. After all, in the long run net imports of goods, services, and gifts from abroad by developed nations must correspond to net exports of goods, services, and gifts by the rest of the world—which means primarily emerging countries.

Implications for Capital Account Balances

Recall that because surplus and deficit items cancel out in the balance of payments, any nation's current account deficit will be associated with a capital account surplus. Hence, the recent combined current account deficit experienced by the world's developed nations closely

FIGURE 34-9

Combined Current Account Balances of Developed Nations and of Emerging Countries

Since 1997, developed nations have experienced higher combined current account deficits. During the same time, emerging nations have had increasing combined current account surpluses that have been nearly a mirror image of the developed nations' current account deficits.

Sources: International Monetary Fund; author's estimates.

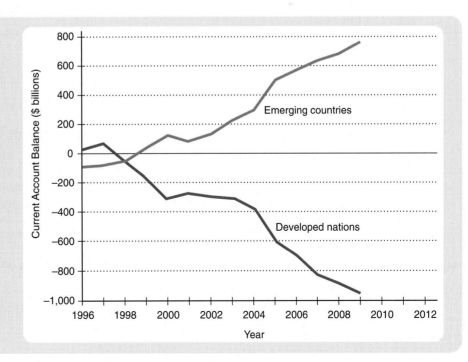

corresponds to a combined capital account surplus. Conversely, the combined current account surpluses recently experienced by emerging countries imply a combined capital account deficit for these countries.

This means that residents of developed nations have been financing their imports and thus their current account deficits by obtaining funds from emerging countries. As funds have flowed out of emerging countries, their capital accounts have experienced deficits. As the funds have flowed into developed nations, their capital accounts have experienced surpluses. Effectively, emerging countries have provided developed nations with the funds required to buy the emerging countries' exports.

Two Contrasting Scenarios for the Future

Some observers look at Figure 34-9 and see the potential for major balance of payments readjustments in the future. In their view, residents of emerging countries are likely to tire of financing the current account deficits of developed nations by purchasing the latter's

stocks and bonds. Once this occurs, according to this view, residents of developed nations will no longer be able to finance their spending on goods and services imported from emerging countries. If this happens all at once, these observers worry, the world may experience significant difficulties: Residents of emerging countries will be unable to find buyers for their exports, and residents of developed nations will be unable to pay their debts.

Others examine Figure 34-9 and see only evidence of the gains from trade discussed in Chapter 33. In their view, emerging countries are willing to invest in developed nations because the latter offer high rates of return on investments. The emerging countries gain because residents of developed nations buy their exports. Residents of developed nations, in turn, expand their consumption of items imported from emerging countries and thereby gain from trade. From this perspective, the relationship shown in Figure 34-9 is a "win-win situation" for both sets of nations—and hence is likely to continue for years to come.

Test your understanding of this chapter by going online to **MyEconLab**.
In the Study Plan for this chapter, select Section N: News.

For Critical Analysis

1. If the current account balances of the world's least developed nations—those outside the sets of developed nations and emerging countries—were added to the combined current account surplus of emerging countries, would the result exactly mirror the current account deficit of the world's developed nations? Why or why not?

2. If combined capital account, current account, and official reserve transactions balances were computed for all the nations of the world, what should the sum of all three turn out to be? Explain.

Web Resources

1. To see a typical example of the view that the current account deficits of the United States and other developed nations pose a threat to the world economy, go to www.econtoday.com/chapter34.

2. For a discussion of the size of the U.S. current account deficit in relation to the current account deficits of other developed nations, go to www.econtoday.com/chapter34.

Research Project

If the capital account balances of the world's least developed nations—those outside the sets of developed nations and emerging countries—were added to the combined capital account deficit of emerging countries, would the result exactly mirror the capital account surplus of the world's developed nations? Why or why not? Explain your reasoning. (Hint: Recall that another financial account in every country's balance of payments is its official reserve transactions account.)

Here is what you should know after reading this chapter. **MyEconLab** will help you identify what you know, and where to go when you need to practice.

WHAT YOU SHOULD KNOW		WHERE TO GO TO PRACTICE
The Balance of Trade versus the Balance of Payments The balance of trade is the difference between exports and imports of physical goods, or merchandise, during a given period. The balance of payments is a system of accounts for all transactions between a nation's residents and the residents of other countries of the world. In addition to exports and imports, therefore, the balance of payments includes cross-border exchanges of services and financial assets within a given time interval.	balance of trade, 864 balance of payments, 864 accounting identities, 864	• **MyEconLab** Study Plan 34.1 • Audio introduction to Chapter 34
The Key Accounts Within the Balance of Payments There are three important accounts within the balance of payments. The current account measures net exchanges of goods and services, transfers, and income flows across a nation's borders. The capital account measures net flows of financial assets. The official reserve transactions account tabulates cross-border exchanges of financial assets involving the home nation's government and central bank as well as foreign governments and central banks. Because each international exchange generates both an inflow and an outflow, the sum of the balances on all three accounts must equal zero.	current account, 866 capital account, 867 special drawing rights (SDRs), 868 International Monetary Fund, 868 **KEY FIGURE** Figure 34-1, 869	• **MyEconLab** Study Plan 34.1 • Animated Figure 34-1
Exchange Rate Determination in the Market for Foreign Exchange From the perspective of the United States, the demand for a nation's currency by U.S. residents is derived largely from the demand for imports from that nation. Likewise, the supply of a nation's currency is derived mainly from the supply of U.S. exports to that country. The equilibrium exchange rate is the rate of exchange between the dollar and the other nation's currency at which the quantity of the currency demanded is equal to the quantity supplied.	foreign exchange market, 871 exchange rate, 871 flexible exchange rates, 871 appreciation, 872 depreciation, 872 **KEY FIGURES** Figure 34-2, 873 Figure 34-3, 875 Figure 34-4, 875 Figure 34-5, 876	• **MyEconLab** Study Plan 34.2 • Animated Figures 34-2, 34-3, 34-4, 34-5 • Video: Market Determinants of Foreign Exchange Rates
Factors That Can Induce Changes in Equilibrium Exchange Rates The equilibrium exchange rate changes in response to changes in the demand for or supply of another nation's currency. Changes in desired flows of exports or imports, real interest rates, tastes and preferences of consumers, and perceptions of economic stability are key factors that can affect the positions of the demand and supply curves in foreign exchange markets. Thus, changes in these factors can induce variations in equilibrium exchange rates.	**KEY FIGURES** Figure 34-6, 877	• **MyEconLab** Study Plan 34.2 • Animated Figures 34-6 • Video: Market Determinants of Foreign Exchange Rates

(continued)

(continued)

WHAT YOU SHOULD KNOW		WHERE TO GO TO PRACTICE
How Policymakers Can Attempt to Keep Exchange Rates Fixed If the current price of the home currency in terms of another nation's currency starts to fall below the level where the home country wants it to remain, the home country's central bank can use reserves of the other nation's currency to purchase the home currency in foreign exchange markets. This raises the demand for the home currency and thereby pushes up the currency's value in terms of the other nation's currency. In this way, the home country can keep the exchange rate fixed at a desired value, as long as it has sufficient reserves of the other currency to use for this purpose.	par value, 879 foreign exchange risk, 881 hedge, 881 **KEY FIGURE** Figure 34-8, 880	• **MyEconLab** Study Plans 34.3, 34.4 • Animated Figure 34-8 • Video: Pros and Cons of a Fixed Exchange Rate
Alternative Approaches to Limiting Exchange Rate Variability Today, many nations permit their exchange rates to vary in foreign exchange markets. Others pursue policies that limit the variability of exchange rates. Some engage in a dirty float, in which they manage exchange rates, often in cooperation with other nations. Some establish crawling pegs, in which the target value of the exchange rate is adjusted automatically over time. And some establish target zones, with upper and lower limits on the extent to which exchange rates are allowed to vary.	dirty float, 882 crawling peg, 883 target zone, 883	• **MyEconLab** Study Plan 34.4

Log in to MyEconLab, take a chapter test, and get a personalized Study Plan that tells you which concepts you understand and which ones you need to review. From there, MyEconLab will give you further practice, tutorials, animations, videos, and guided solutions.
Log in to www.myeconlab.com

PROBLEMS

All problems are assignable in **myeconlab**. *Answers to the odd-numbered problems appear at the back of the book.*

34-1. Over the course of a year, a nation tracked its foreign transactions and arrived at the following amounts:

Merchandise exports	500
Service exports	75
Net unilateral transfers	10
Domestic assets abroad (capital outflows)	−200
Foreign assets at home (capital inflows)	300
Changes in official reserves	−35
Merchandise imports	600
Service imports	50

What are this nation's balance of trade, current account balance, and capital account balance?

34-2. Identify whether each of the following items creates a surplus item or a deficit item in the current account of the U.S. balance of payments.

a. A Central European company sells products to a U.S. hobby-store chain.

b. Japanese residents pay a U.S. travel company to arrange hotel stays, ground transportation, and tours of various U.S. cities, including New York, Chicago, and Orlando.

c. A Mexican company pays a U.S. accounting firm to audit its income statements.

d. U.S. churches and mosques send relief aid to Pakistan following a major earthquake in that nation.

e. A U.S. microprocessor manufacturer purchases raw materials from a Canadian firm.

34-3. Explain how the following events would affect the market for the Mexican peso, assuming a floating exchange rate.

a. Improvements in Mexican production technology yield superior guitars, and many musicians around the world buy these guitars.

b. Perceptions of political instability surrounding regular elections in Mexico make international investors nervous about future business prospects in Mexico.

34-4. Explain how the following events would affect the market for South Africa's currency, the rand, assuming a floating exchange rate.

a. A rise in U.S. inflation causes many U.S. residents to seek to buy gold, which is a major South African export good, as a hedge against inflation.

b. Major discoveries of the highest-quality diamonds ever found occur in Russia and Central Asia, causing a significant decline in purchases of South African diamonds.

34-5. Suppose that the following two events take place in the market for China's currency, the yuan: U.S. parents are more willing than before to buy action figures and other Chinese toy exports, and China's government tightens restrictions on the amount of U.S. dollar–denominated financial assets that Chinese residents may legally purchase. What happens to the dollar price of the yuan? Does the yuan appreciate or depreciate relative to the dollar?

34-6. On Wednesday, the exchange rate between the Japanese yen and the U.S. dollar was $0.0125 per yen. On Thursday, it was $0.0110. Did the dollar appreciate or depreciate against the yen? By how much, expressed as a percentage change?

34-7. On Wednesday, the exchange rate between the euro and the U.S. dollar was $1.45 per euro, and the exchange rate between the Canadian dollar and the U.S. dollar was U.S. $0.94 per Canadian dollar. What is the exchange rate between the Canadian dollar and the euro?

34-8. Suppose that signs of an improvement in the Japanese economy lead international investors to resume lending to the Japanese government and businesses. Policymakers, however, are worried about how this will influence the yen. How would this event affect the market for the yen? How should the central bank, the Bank of Japan, respond to this event if it wants to keep the value of the yen unchanged?

34-9. Briefly explain the differences between a flexible exchange rate system, a fixed exchange rate system, a dirty float, and the use of target zones.

34-10. Suppose that under a gold standard, the U.S. dollar is pegged to gold at a rate of $35 per ounce and the pound sterling is pegged to gold at a rate of £17.50 per ounce. Explain how the gold standard constitutes an exchange rate arrangement between the dollar and the pound. What is the exchange rate between the U.S. dollar and the pound sterling?

34-11. Suppose that under the Bretton Woods system, the dollar is pegged to gold at a rate of $35 per ounce and the pound sterling is pegged to the dollar at a rate of $2 = £1. If the dollar is devalued against gold and the pegged rate is changed to $40 per ounce, what does this imply for the exchange value of the pound in terms of dollars?

34-12. Suppose that the People's Bank of China wishes to peg the rate of exchange of its currency, the yuan, in terms of the U.S. dollar. In each of the following situations, should it add to or subtract from its dollar foreign exchange reserves? Why?

a. U.S. parents worrying about safety begin buying fewer Chinese-made toys for their children.

b. U.S. interest rates rise relative to interest rates in China, so Chinese residents seek to purchase additional U.S. financial assets.

c. Chinese furniture manufacturers produce high-quality early American furniture and successfully export large quantities of the furniture to the United States.

ECONOMICS ON THE NET

Daily Exchange Rates It is an easy matter to keep up with changes in exchange rates every day using the Web site of the Federal Reserve Bank of New York. In this application, you will learn how hard it is to predict exchange rate movements, and you will get some practice thinking about what factors can cause exchange rates to change.

Title: The Federal Reserve Bank of New York: Foreign Exchange 12 PM Rates

Navigation: Go to **www.econtoday.com/chapter34** to visit the Federal Reserve Bank of New York's Statistics home page. Click on *Foreign Exchange 12 PM Rates*.

Application Answer the following questions.

1. For each currency listed, how many dollars does it take to purchase a unit of the currency in the spot foreign exchange market?

2. For each day during a given week (or month), choose a currency from those listed and keep track of its value relative to the dollar. Based on your tabulations, try to predict the value of the currency at the end of the week *following* your data collections. Use any information you may have, or just do your best without any additional information. How far off did your prediction turn out to be?

For Group Study and Analysis Each day, you can also click on a report titled "Foreign Exchange 10 AM Rates," which shows exchange rates for a subset of countries listed in the noon report. Assign each country in the 10 AM report to a group. Ask the group to determine whether the currency's value appreciated or depreciated relative to the dollar between 10 AM and noon. In addition, ask each group to discuss what kinds of demand or supply shifts could have caused the change that occurred during this interval.

ANSWERS TO QUICK QUIZZES

p. 870: (i) balance . . . payments; (ii) physical; (iii) current . . . current; (iv) Unilateral transfers; (v) current; (vi) capital . . . capital; (vii) official reserve; (viii) inflation . . . political

p. 878: (i) exchange rate; (ii) demand . . . demand . . . supply; (iii) downward . . . upward; (iv) shift . . . demand

p. 883: (i) fixed . . . fixed; (ii) risk; (iii) dirty . . . crawling . . . target zone

Answers to Odd-Numbered Problems

Chapter 1

1-1. Economics is the study of how individuals allocate limited resources to satisfy unlimited wants.

a. Among the factors that a rational, self-interested student will take into account are her income, the price of the textbook, her anticipation of how much she is likely to study the textbook, and how much studying the book is likely to affect her grade.

b. A rational, self-interested government official will, for example, recognize that higher taxes will raise more funds for mass transit while making more voters, who have limited resources, willing to elect other officials.

c. A municipality's rational, self-interested government will, for instance, take into account that higher hotel taxes will produce more funds if as many visitors continue staying at hotels, but that the higher taxes will also discourage some visitors from spending nights at hotels.

1-3. Because wants are unlimited, the phrase applies to very high-income households as well as low- and middle-income households. Consider, for instance, a household with a low income and unlimited wants at the beginning of the year. The household's wants will still remain unlimited if it becomes a high-income household later in the year.

1-5. Sally is displaying rational behavior if all of these activities are in her self-interest. For example, Sally likely derives intrinsic benefit from volunteer and extracurricular activities and may believe that these activities, along with good grades, improve her prospects of finding a job after she completes her studies. Hence, these activities are in her self-interest even though they reduce some available study time.

1-7. The rationality assumption states that people do not intentionally make choices that leave them worse off. The bounded rationality hypothesis suggests that people are *almost*, but not completely, rational.

1-9. Suppose that there is a change in the environment that a person faces, and the person adjusts to this change as predicted by the rationality assumption. If the new environment becomes predictable, then the individual who actually behaves as predicted by the traditional rationality assumption may settle into behavior that *appears* to involve repetitive applications of a rule of thumb.

1-11. a. The model using prices from the Iowa Electronic Market is more firmly based on the rationality assumption, because people who trade assets on this exchange based on poor forecasts actually experience losses. This gives them a strong incentive to make the best possible forecasts. Unpaid respondents to opinion polls have less incentive to give truthful answers about whether and how they will vote.

b. An economist would develop a means of evaluating whether prices in the Iowa Electronic Market or results of opinion polls did a better job of matching actual electoral outcomes.

1-13. a. Positive
   b. Normative
   c. Normative
   d. Positive

APPENDIX A

A-1. a. Independent: price of a notebook; Dependent: quantity of notebooks
   b. Independent: work-study hours; Dependent: credit hours
   c. Independent: hours of study; Dependent: economics grade

A-3. a. above x axis; left of y axis
   b. below x axis, right of y axis
   c. on x axis; to right of y axis

A-5.

y	x
−20	−4
−10	−2
0	0
10	2
20	4

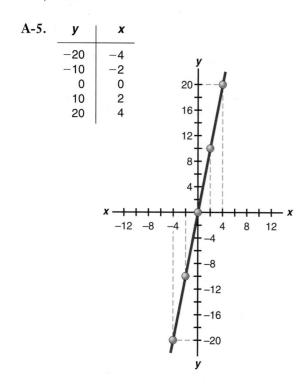

A-7. Each one-unit increase in *x* yields a 5-unit increase in *y*, so the slope given by the change in *y* corresponding to the change in *x* is equal to 5.

Chapter 2

2-1. The opportunity cost of attending a class at 11:00 A.M. is the next-best use of that hour of the day. Likewise, the opportunity cost of attending an 8:00 A.M. class is the next-best use of that particular hour of the day. If you are an early riser, it is arguable that the opportunity cost of the 8:00 A.M. hour is lower, because you will already be up at that time but have fewer choices compared with the 11:00 A.M. hour when shops, recreation centers, and the like are open. If you are a late riser, it may be that the opportunity cost of the 8:00 A.M. hour is higher, because you place a relatively high value on an additional hour of sleep in the morning.

2-3. The bank apparently determined that the net gain that it anticipated receiving from trying to sell the house to someone else, taking into account the opportunity cost of resources that the bank would have had to devote to renovating the house, was less than $10.

2-5. If the student allocates additional study time to economics in order to increase her score from 90 to 100, her biology score declines from 50 to 40, so the opportunity cost of earning 10 additional points in economics is 10 fewer points in biology.

2-7.

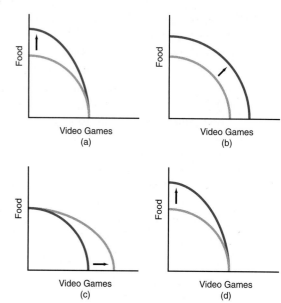

2-9. D

2-11. a. If the nation's residents increase production of consumption goods from 0 units to 10 units, the opportunity cost is 3 units of human capital forgone. If the nation's residents increase production of consumption goods from 0 units to 60 units, the opportunity cost is 100 units of human capital.
b. Yes, because successive 10-unit increases in production of consumption goods generate larger sacrifices of human capital, equal to 3, 7, 15, 20, 25, and 30.

2-13. Because it takes you less time to do laundry, you have an absolute advantage in laundry. Neither you nor your roommate has an absolute advantage in meal preparation. You require 2 hours to fold a basket of laundry, so your opportunity cost of folding a basket of laundry is 2 meals. Your roommate's opportunity cost of folding a basket of laundry is 3 meals. Hence, you have a comparative advantage in laundry, and your roommate has a comparative advantage in meal preparation.

2-15. It may be that the professor is very proficient at doing yard work relative to teaching and research activities, so in fact the professor may have a comparative advantage in doing yard work.

Chapter 3

3-1. The equilibrium price is $21 per DVD, and the equilibrium quantity is 80 million DVDs. At a price of $20 per DVD, the quantity of DVDs demanded is 90 million, and the quantity of DVDs supplied is 60 million. Hence, there is a shortage of 30 million DVDs at a price of $20 per DVD.

3-3. a. DSL and cable Internet access services are substitutes, so a reduction in the price of cable Internet access services causes a decrease in the demand for DSL high-speed Internet access services.

   b. A decrease in the price of DSL Internet access services generates an increase in the quantity of these services demanded.

   c. DSL high-speed Internet access services are a normal good, so a fall in the incomes of consumers reduces the demand for these services.

   d. If consumers expect that the price of DSL high-speed Internet services will fall in the future, then the demand for these services will tend to decrease today.

3-5. a. Complement: eggs; Substitute: sausage

   b. Complement: tennis balls; Substitute: racquetball racquets

   c. Complement: cream; Substitute: tea

   d. Complement: gasoline; Substitute: city bus

3-7. a. At the $1,000 rental rate, the quantity of one-bedroom apartments supplied is 8,500 per month, but the quantity demanded is only 7,000 per month. Thus, there is an excess quantity of one-bedroom apartments supplied equal to 1,500 apartments per month.

   b. To induce consumers to lease unrented one-bedroom apartments, some landlords will reduce their rental rates. As they do so, the quantity demanded will increase. In addition, some landlords will choose not to offer apartments for rent at lower rates, and the quantity supplied will decrease. At the equilibrium rental rate of $800 per month, there will be no excess quantity supplied.

   c. At the $600 rental rate, the quantity of one-bedroom apartments demanded is 8,000 per month, but the quantity supplied is only 6,500 per month. Thus, there is an excess quantity of one-bedroom apartments demanded equal to 1,500 apartments per month.

   d. To induce landlords to make more one-bedroom apartments available for rent, some consumers will offer to pay higher rental rates. As they do so, the quantity supplied will increase. In addition, some consumers will choose not to try to rent apartments at higher rates, and the quantity demanded will decrease. At the equilibrium rental rate of $800 per month, there will be no excess quantity demanded.

3-9. a. Because memory chips are an input in the production of laptop computers, a decrease in the price of memory chips causes an increase in the supply of laptop computers. The market supply curve shifts to the right, which causes the market price of laptop computers to fall and the equilibrium quantity of laptop computers to increase.

   b. Machinery used to produce laptop computers is an input in the production of these devices, so an increase in the price of machinery generates a decrease in the supply of laptop computers. The market supply curve shifts to the left, which causes the market price of laptop computers to rise and the equilibrium quantity of laptop computers to decrease.

   c. An increase in the number of manufacturers of laptop computers causes an increase in the supply of laptop computers. The market supply curve shifts rightward. The market price of laptop computers declines, and the equilibrium quantity of laptop computers increases.

d. The demand curve for laptop computers shifts to the left along the supply curve, so there is a decrease in the quantity supplied. The market price falls, and the equilibrium quantity declines.

3-11. The decline in the price of palladium, a substitute for platinum, will cause a decrease in the demand for platinum, so the platinum demand curve will shift leftward. Both the market clearing price and the equilibrium quantity of platinum will decrease.

3-13. Because processor chips are an input in the production of personal computers, a decrease in the price of processor chips generates an increase in the supply of personal computers. The market price of personal computers will decrease, and the equilibrium quantity will increase.

Chapter 4

4-1. The ability to produce music CDs at lower cost and the entry of additional producers shift the supply curve rightward, from S_1 to S_2. At the same time, reduced prices of substitute goods result in a leftward shift in the demand for music CDs, from D_1 to D_2. Consequently, the equilibrium price of music CDs declines, from P_1 to P_2. The equilibrium quantity may rise, fall, or, as shown in the diagram, remain unchanged.

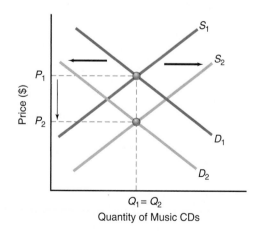

4-3. The market rental rate is $700 per apartment, and the equilibrium quantity of apartments rented to tenants is 2,000. At a ceiling price of $650 per month, the number of apartments students desire

to rent increases to 2,500 apartments. At the ceiling price, the number of apartments that owners are willing to supply decreases to 1,800 apartments. Thus, there is a shortage of 700 apartments at the ceiling price, and only 1,800 are rented at the ceiling price.

4-5. At the above-market price of sugar in the U.S. sugar market, U.S. chocolate manufacturers that use sugar as an input face higher costs. Thus, they supply less chocolate at any given price of chocolate, and the market supply curve shifts leftward. This pushes up the market price of chocolate products and reduces the equilibrium quantity of chocolate. U.S. sugar producers also sell surplus sugar in foreign sugar markets, which causes the supply curve for sugar in foreign markets to shift rightward. This reduces the market price of foreign sugar and raises the equilibrium quantity in the foreign market.

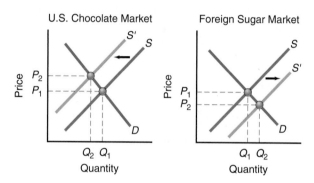

4-7. The market price is $400, and the equilibrium quantity of seats is 1,600. If airlines cannot sell tickets to more than 1,200 passengers, then passengers are willing to pay $600 per seat. Normally, airlines would be willing to sell each ticket for $200, but they will be able to charge a price as high as $600 for each of the 1,200 tickets they sell. Hence, the quantity of tickets sold declines from 1,600, and the price of a ticket rises from $400 to as high as $600.

4-9. a. Consumers buy 10 billion kilograms at the support price of $0.20 per kilogram and hence spend $2 billion on wheat.

b. The amount of surplus wheat at the support price is 8 billion kilograms, so at the $0.20-per-kilogram support price, the government must spend $1.6 billion to purchase this surplus wheat.

c. Pakistani wheat farmers receive a total of $3.6 billion for the wheat they produce at the support price.

4-11. a. At the present minimum wage of $9 per hour, the quantity of labor supplied is 102,000 workers, and the quantity of labor demanded by firms is 98,000. There is an excess quantity supplied of 4,000 workers, which is the number of people who are unemployed.

   b. At a minimum wage of $6 per hour, there would be nothing to prevent market forces from pushing the wage rate to the market clearing level of $8 per hour. This $8-per-hour wage rate would exceed the legal minimum and hence would prevail. There would be no unemployed workers.

   c. At a $10-per-hour minimum wage, the quantity of labor supplied would increase to 106,000 workers, and the quantity of labor demanded would decline to 96,000. There would be an excess quantity of labor supplied equal to 10,000 workers, which would then be the number of people unemployed.

4-13. a. The rise in the number of wheat producers causes the market supply curve to shift rightward, so more wheat is supplied at the support price.

   b. The quantity of wheat demanded at the same support price is unchanged.

   c. Because quantity demanded is unchanged while quantity supplied has increased, the amount of surplus wheat that the government must purchase has risen.

Chapter 5

5-1. In the absence of laws forbidding cigar smoking in public places, people who are bothered by the odor of cigar smoke will experience costs not borne by cigar producers. Because the supply of cigars will not reflect these costs, from society's perspective the market cigar supply curve will be in a position too far to the right. The market price of cigars will be too low, and too many cigars will be produced and consumed.

5-3. Imposing the tax on pesticides causes an increase in the price of pesticides, which are an input in the production of oranges. Hence, the supply curve in the orange market shifts leftward. The market price of oranges increases, and the equilibrium quantity of oranges declines. Hence, orange consumers indirectly help to pay for dealing with the spillover costs of pesticide production by paying more for oranges.

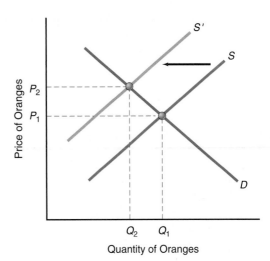

5-5. a. As shown in the figure below, if the social benefits associated with bus ridership were taken into account, the demand schedule would be D' instead of D, and the market price would be higher. The equilibrium quantity of bus rides would be higher.

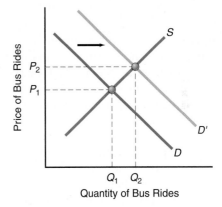

   b. The government could pay commuters a subsidy to ride the bus, thereby shifting the demand curve outward and to the right. This would increase the market price and equilibrium number of bus rides.

5-7. At present, the equilibrium quantity of residences with Internet access is 2 million. To take into account the external benefit of Internet access and boost the quantity of residences with access to 3 million, the demand curve would have to shift upward by $20 per month at any given quantity, to D_2 from the current position D_1. Thus, the government would have to offer a $20-per-month subsidy to raise the quantity of residences with Internet access to 3 million.

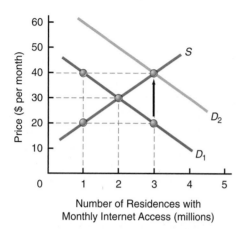

Number of Residences with
Monthly Internet Access (millions)

5-9. The problem is that although most people around the lighthouse will benefit from its presence, there is no incentive for people to voluntarily contribute if they believe that others ultimately will pay for it. That is, the city is likely to face a free-rider problem in its efforts to raise its share of the funds required for the lighthouse.

5-11. No, the outcome will be different. If the government had simply provided grants to attend private schools at the current market tuition rate, parents and students receiving the grants would have paid a price equal to the market valuation of the last unit of educational services provided. Granting a subsidy to private schools allows the private schools to charge parents and students a price less than the market price. Private schools thereby will receive a higher-than-market price for the last unit of educational services they provide. Consequently, they will provide a quantity of educational services in excess of the market equilibrium quantity. At this quantity, parents and students place a lower value on the services than the price received by the private schools.

5-13. a. $40 million
b. The effective price of a DVD drive to consumers will be lower after the government pays the subsidy, so people will purchase a larger quantity.
c. $60 million
d. $90 million

5-15. a. $60 − $50 = $10
b. Expenditures after the program expansion are $2.4 million. Before the program expansion, expenditures were $1 million. Hence, the increase in expenditures is $1.4 million.
c. At a per-unit subsidy of $50, the share of the per-unit $60 price paid by the government is 5/6, or 83.3 percent. Hence, this is the government's share of total expenditures on the 40,000 devices that consumers purchase.

Chapter 6

6-1. a. The average tax rate is the total tax of $40 divided by the $200 in income: $40/$200 = 0.2, or 20 percent.
b. The marginal tax rate for the last hour of work is the change in taxes, $3, divided by the change in income, $8: $3/$8 = 0.375, or 37.5 percent.

6-3. 2001: $300 million; 2003: $350 million; 2005: $400 million; 2007: $400 million; 2009: $420 million

6-5. During 2008, the income tax base was an amount of income equal to $20 million/0.05 = $400 million. During 2009, the income tax base was equal to $19.2 million/0.06 = $320 million. Although various factors could have contributed to the fall in taxable income, dynamic tax analysis suggests that the higher income tax rate induced people to reduce their reported income. For instance, some people might have earned less income subject to city income taxes, and others might have even moved outside the city to avoid paying the higher income tax rate.

6-7. a. The supply of tickets for flights into and out of London shifts upward by $154. The equilibrium quantity of flights in and out of London declines. The market clearing price of London airline tickets rises by an amount less than the tax.

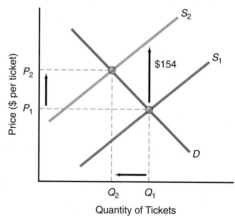

Quantity of Tickets

b. Tickets for flights into and out of London are substitutes for tickets for flights into and out of nearby cities. Thus, the demand for tickets for flights into and out of these cities will increase. This will cause an increase in the equilibrium quantities of these tickets and an increase in the market clearing prices.

6-9. As shown in the diagram, if the supply and demand curves have their normal shapes, then the $2-per-month tax on DSL Internet access services shifts the market supply curve upward by $2. The equilibrium quantity of DSL access services produced and consumed declines. In addition, the monthly market price of DSL access increases by an amount less than $2 per month. Consequently, consumers and producers share in paying the tax on each unit.

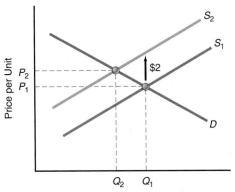

6-11. If the market price of DSL access for businesses does not change, then as shown in the diagram, over the relevant range the demand for Internet access services by businesses is horizontal. The quantity of services demanded by businesses is very highly responsive to the tax, so DSL access providers must bear the tax in the form of higher costs. Providers of DSL access services pay all of the tax.

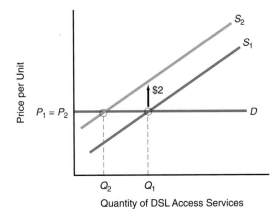

6-13. a. 50 percent
 b. −20 percent

Chapter 20

20-1. −[(200 − 150)/(350/2)]/[(9 − 10)/(19/2)], which is approximately equal to −2.7. Thus, the absolute price elasticity of demand equals 2.7.

20-3. a. −[(90 − 80)/(85)]/[(0.20 − 0.40)/(0.30)], which is approximately equal to −0.18. Consequently, the absolute price elasticity of demand is 0.18, so demand is inelastic over this range.
 b. −[(60 − 40)/(50)]/[(0.80 − 1.20)/(1.00)] = −1.00. The absolute price elasticity of demand, therefore, equals 1.00, which implies that demand is unit-elastic over this range.
 c. −[(20 − 10)/(15)]/[(1.60 − 1.80)/(1.70)], which is approximately equal to −5.67. Thus, the absolute price elasticity of demand is 5.67, so demand is elastic over this range.

20-5. −[(80 − 120)/(200/2)]/[($22.50 − $17.50)/($40/2)] = −1.6. Hence, the absolute price elasticity of demand equals 1.6. Demand is elastic over this range.

20-7. Because price and total revenue move in the same direction, then over this range of demand, the demand for handmade guitars is inelastic.

20-9. a. More inelastic, because it represents a smaller portion of the budget
 b. More elastic, because there are many close substitutes
 c. More elastic, because there are a number of substitutes
 d. More inelastic, because there are few close substitutes
 e. More inelastic, because it represents a small portion of the budget

20-11. Let X denote the percentage change in the quantity of bacon. Then $X/10$ percent = −0.5. X, therefore, is −5 percent.

20-13. [(125,000 − 75,000)/(200,000/2)]/[($35,000 − $25,000)/($60,000/2)] = 1.5. Supply is elastic.

20-15. The short-run price elasticity of supply is 10 percent/20 percent = 0.5, and the long-run price elasticity of supply is 40 percent/20 percent = 2.0.

Chapter 21

21-1. The campus pizzeria indicates by its pricing policy that it recognizes the principle of diminishing marginal utility. As shown in Figure 21-1 on page 528, a customer's marginal utility for the second pizza is typically lower than for the first. Thus, the customer is likely to value the second pizza less and, therefore, only be willing to pay less for it.

21-3. The total utility of the third, fourth, and fifth cheeseburgers is 48, 56, and 60, respectively. The marginal utility of the first and second cheeseburgers is 20 and 16, respectively. The total utility of the first, second, and third bags of french fries is 10, 18, and 20, respectively. The marginal utility of the fourth and fifth bags of french fries is 1 and 0, respectively.

21-5. The new utility-maximizing combination is four cheeseburgers and two orders of french fries, at which the marginal utility per dollar spent is 2 units per dollar and the entire $6 is spent.

21-7. Other things being equal, when the price of soft drinks rises, the substitution effect comes into play, and the individual tends to consume less of the more expensive item, soft drinks, and more of the item with the unchanged price, tacos. Hence, the marginal utility of soft drinks rises, and the marginal utility of tacos falls.

21-9. **a.** Of all the possible one-unit increases in consumption displayed, the movement from point A to point B generates the highest marginal utility. Total utility rises by 5 units between these points, so the marginal utility of the first unit consumed is 5 units.

b. Between points E and F, a one-unit increase in the quantity consumed leaves total utility unchanged at 11 units, so marginal utility is equal to zero.

c. Between points F and G, a one-unit increase in the quantity consumed causes total utility to decline from 11 units to 10 units, so marginal utility is negative and equal to -1 unit.

21-11. For this consumer, at these prices the marginal utility per dollar spent on 2 fudge bars is 500 units of utility per dollar, and the marginal utility per dollar spent on 5 popsicles is also 500 units of utility per dollar. In addition, the entire budget of $9 is spent at this combination, which is the consumer optimum.

21-13. The marginal utility per dollar spent is equalized at 2.50 if 5 hot dogs and 3 baseball games are consumed, and this consumption combination just exhausts the now-available $190 in income.

21-15. The marginal utility of good Y is three times the marginal utility of good X, or 3×3 utils = 9 utils.

APPENDIX E

E-1. The indifference curve is convex to the origin because of a diminishing marginal rate of substitution. As an individual consumes more and more of an item, the less the individual is willing to forgo of the other item. The diminishing marginal rate of substitution is due to diminishing marginal utility.

E-3. Sue's marginal rate of substitution is calculated below:

Combination of Bottled Water and Soft Drinks	Bottled Water per Month	Soft Drinks per Month	MRS
A	5	11	
B	10	7	5:4
C	15	4	5:3
D	20	2	5:2
E	25	1	5:1

The diminishing marginal rate of substitution of soft drinks for water shows Sue's diminishing marginal utility of bottled water. She is willing to forgo fewer and fewer soft drinks to get an additional five bottles of water.

E-5. Given that water is measured along the horizontal axis and soft drinks are measured along the vertical axis, the slope of Sue's budget constraint is the price of water divided by the price of soft drinks, or $P_W/P_S = \frac{1}{2}$. The only combination of bottled water and soft drinks that is on Sue's indifference curve and budget constraint is combination C. For this combination, total expenditures on water and soft drinks equal ($15 \times \$1$) + ($4 \times \$2$) = $15 + \$8 = \$23$.

E-7. With the quantity of bottled water measured along the horizontal axis and the quantity of soft drinks measured along the vertical axis, the slope of Sue's budget constraint is the price of water divided by the price of soft drinks. This ratio equals $\frac{1}{2}$. The only combination of bottled water and soft drinks that is on Sue's indifference curve and budget constraint is combination C, where expenditures on water and soft drinks total $23.

E-9. Yes, Sue's revealed preferences indicate that her demand for soft drinks obeys the law of demand. When the price of soft drinks declines from $2 to $1, her quantity demanded rises from 4 to 8.

Chapter 22

22-1. **a.** Bob earns a high economic rent. Because he has a specialized skill that is in great demand, his income is likely to be high, and his opportunity cost relatively low.

b. Sally earns a high economic rent. Because she is a supermodel, her income is likely to be relatively high, and, without any education, her opportunity cost is likely to be relatively low.

c. If Tim were to leave teaching, not a relatively high-paying occupation, he could sell insurance full time. Hence, his opportunity cost is high relative to his income, and his economic rent is low.

22-3. The economic rents that Michael Jordan was able to earn as a basketball player relative to those he could earn as a baseball player surely played a large role in his decision to return to basketball. Hence, they helped direct his resources (athletic talents) to their most efficient uses.

22-5. A sole proprietorship is a business entity owned by a single individual, whereas a partnership is a business entity jointly owned by more than one individual. A corporation, in contrast, is a legal entity that is owned by shareholders, who own shares of the profits of the entity. Sole proprietorships and partnerships do not face double taxation, but corporations do. The owners of corporations, however, enjoy limited liability, whereas the sole proprietor or partner does not.

22-7. Accounting profit is total revenue, $77,250, minus explicit costs, $37,000, for a total of $40,250. Economic profit is total revenue, $77,250, less explicit costs, $37,000, and implicit costs, $40,250, for a total equal to zero.

22-9. **a.** Physical capital
b. Financial capital
c. Financial capital
d. Physical capital

22-11. **a.** The owner of WebCity faces both tax rates if the firm is a corporation, but if it is a proprietorship, the owner faces only the 30 percent personal income tax rate. Thus, it should choose to be a proprietorship.

b. If WebCity is a corporation, the $100,000 in corporate earnings is taxed at a 20 percent rate, so after-tax dividends are $80,000, and these are taxed at the personal income tax rate of 30 percent, leaving $56,000 in after-tax income for the owner. Hence, the firm should be organized as a proprietorship, with after-tax earnings $70,000, or a value advantage of $14,000.

c. Yes. In this case, incorporation raises earnings to $150,000, which are taxed at a rate of 20 percent, yielding after-tax dividends of $120,000 that are taxed at the personal rate of 30 percent. This leaves an after-tax income for the owner of $84,000, which is higher than the after-tax earnings of $70,000 if WebCity is a proprietorship that earns lower pre-tax income taxed at the personal rate.

d. After-tax profits rise from $56,000 to $84,000, or by $28,000.

e. This policy change would only increase the incentive to incorporate.

f. A corporate structure provides limited liability for owners, which can be a major advantage. Furthermore, owners may believe that the corporate structure will yield higher pre-tax earnings, as in the above example.

22-13. The real rate of interest in Japan is 2% − 0.5% = 1.5%. The real rate of interest in the United States is 4% − 3% = 1%. Japan, therefore, has the higher *real* rate of interest.

22-15. Ownership of common stock provides voting rights within the firm but also entails immediate loss if assets fall below the value of the firm's liabilities. Preferred stockholders are repaid prior to owners of common stock, but preferred stockholders do not have voting rights.

22-17. You should point out to your classmate that stock prices tend to drift upward following a random walk. That is, yesterday's price plus any upward drift is the best guide to today's price. Therefore, there are no predictable trends that can be used to "beat" the market.

Chapter 23

23-1. The short run is a time period during which the professor cannot enter the job market and find employment elsewhere. This is the nine-month period from August 15 through May 15. The professor can find employment elsewhere after the contract has been fulfilled, so the short run is nine months and the long run is greater than nine months.

23-3. Total variable costs are equal to total costs, $5 million, less total fixed costs, $2 million, which equals $3 million. Average variable costs are equal to total variable costs divided by the number of units produced. Average variable costs, therefore, equal $3 million divided by 10,000, or $300.

23-5. **a.** Total fixed costs equal average fixed costs, $10 per LCD screen, times the quantity produced per day, 100 LCD screens, which equals $1,000 per day.

b. The total variable costs of producing 100 LCD screens equal average variable costs, $10 per unit, times the quantity produced per day, 100 LCD screens, which equals $1,000 per day.

c. The total costs of producing 100 LCD screens equal total fixed costs plus the total variable costs of producing 100 LCD screens, or $1,000 per day plus $1,000 per day, which equals $2,000 per day.

d. The average total costs of producing 99 LCD screens equal the average fixed costs of $10.101 plus the average variable costs of $10.070, or $20.171 per LCD screen. Thus, the total cost of producing 99 LCD screens equals $20.171 times 99, or $1,996.929. The marginal cost of producing the hundredth LCD screen equals the change in total costs from increasing production from 99 to 100, or $2,000 − $1,996.929, or $3.071 per LCD screen.

23-7. **a.** Average total costs are $20 per unit plus $30 per unit, or $50 per unit, and total costs divided by average total costs equal output, which therefore is $2,500/$50 per unit, or 50 units.

b. TVC = AVC × Q = $20 per unit × 50 units = $1,000.

c. TFC = AFC × Q = $30 per unit × 50 units = $1,500; or TFC = TC − TVC = $2,500 − $1,000 = $1,500.

23-9. **a.** The expense incurred in cutting back trees on a regular basis would be unrelated to the quantity of rail services provided on the tracks and hence would represent a fixed cost.

b. The expense of dumping sand on the slippery tracks in advance of trains would vary with the number of trains that run on the tracks and hence would constitute a variable cost.

23-11. Hiring 1 more unit of labor at a wage rate of $20 to increase output by 1 unit causes total costs to rise by $20, so the marginal cost of the 251st unit is $20.

23-13. **a.** AVC = $2 million/1 million units = $2 per unit.

b. APP = 1 million units/1,000 units of labor = 1,000 units of output per unit of labor.

c. Wage rate = $2 million/1,000 units of labor = $2,000 per unit of labor.

23-15. **a.** plant size E, because this is the minimum output scale at which LRATC is at a minimum level

b. leftward movement, because the functioning plant size for the firm would decrease

Chapter 24

24-1. **a.** The single firm producing much of the industry's output can affect price. Therefore, this is currently not a perfectly competitive industry.

b. The output of each firm is not homogeneous, so this is not a perfectly competitive industry.

c. Firms must obtain government permission to enter the industry and hence cannot easily enter, so this is not a perfectly competitive industry.

24-3. **a.** For a perfectly competitive firm, marginal revenue and average revenue are equal to the market clearing price. Hence, average revenue equals $20 per unit at each possible output rate.

b. At the present output of 10,000 units per week, the firm's total revenues equal price times output, or $20 per unit times 10,000 units per week, which equals $200,000 per week. The firm's total costs equal ATC times output, or $15.75 per unit times 10,000 units per week, which equals $157,500 per week. Weekly economic profits equal total revenues minus total costs, or $200,000 − $157,500 = $42,500. The firm is maximizing economic profits, because it is producing the output rate at which marginal revenue equals marginal cost.

c. If the market clearing price were to fall to $12.50 per unit, the marginal revenue curve would shift down to this level. Average total costs would exceed the price at this output rate, but in the short run the firm would minimize its short-run economic losses by producing 8,100 units per week.

d. If the market clearing price were to fall to $7.50 per unit, the marginal revenue curve would shift down to this level. Average variable costs at an output rate of 5,000 units per week would exceed the market clearing price, so total variable costs of producing 5,000 units per week would exceed total revenues. The firm should cease production if this event takes place.

24-5. Even though the price of pizzas, and hence marginal revenue, falls to only $5, this covers average variable costs. Thus, the shop should stay open.

24-7. Because price is less than average variable cost at this rate of output, the firm's total revenues ($5 per unit × 1,500 units = $7,500) fail to cover its total variable costs ($5.50 per unit × 1,500 units = $8,250). Thus, in the short run the firm should shut down and incur only its fixed costs, which equal AVC × Q, or $0.50 per unit × 1,500 units = $750.

24-9. In the described situation, the firm is producing an output rate at a point on the marginal cost curve below the average total cost curve. Marginal revenue is above the minimum point of the average total cost curve, however. Hence, marginal cost at the current rate of production is less than marginal revenue. The firm is not maximizing profit, and it should increase its rate of production.

24-11. a. There was a significant increase in market supply as more firms entered the industry. A consequence for the typical firm was that the market price fell below the minimum average total cost, resulting in negative economic profits.

b. Firms will consider leaving the industry, and some firms probably will leave the industry.

Chapter 25

25-1. The alternatives are not close substitutes for first-class mail, so the U.S. Postal Service faces a downward-sloping demand curve for first-class mail.

25-3. The demand curve faced by the firm is the downward-sloping market demand curve, so price exceeds marginal revenue at all quantities beyond the first unit produced.

25-5. a. The total revenue and total profits of the dry cleaner are as follows.

Output (suits cleaned)	Price ($ per unit)	Total Costs ($)	Total Revenue ($)	Total Profit ($)
0	8.00	3.00	0	−3.00
1	7.50	6.00	7.50	1.50
2	7.00	8.50	14.00	5.50
3	6.50	10.50	19.50	9.00
4	6.00	11.50	24.00	12.50
5	5.50	13.50	27.50	14.00
6	5.00	16.00	30.00	14.00
7	4.50	19.00	31.50	12.50
8	4.00	24.00	32.00	8.00

b. The profit-maximizing rate of output is between 5 and 6 units.

c. The marginal cost and marginal revenue of the dry cleaner are as follows. The profit-maximizing rate of output is 6 units.

Output (suits cleaned)	Price ($ per unit)	Total Costs ($)	Total Revenue ($)	Total Profit ($)	Marginal Cost ($ per unit)	Marginal Revenue ($ per unit)
0	8.00	3.00	0	−3.00	—	—
1	7.50	6.00	7.50	1.50	3.00	7.50
2	7.00	8.50	14.00	5.50	2.50	6.50
3	6.50	10.50	19.50	9.00	2.00	5.50
4	6.00	11.50	24.00	12.50	1.00	4.50
5	5.50	13.50	27.50	14.00	2.00	3.50
6	5.00	16.00	30.00	14.00	2.50	2.50
7	4.50	19.00	31.50	12.50	3.00	1.50
8	4.00	24.00	32.00	8.00	4.00	0.50

25-7. a. The profit-maximizing output rate is 5,000 units.

b. Average total cost is $5 per unit. Average revenue is $6 per unit.

c. Total costs equal $5 per unit × 5,000 units = $25,000. Total revenue equals $6 per unit × 5,000 units = $30,000.

d. ($6 per unit − $5 per unit) × 5,000 units = $5,000.

e. In a perfectly competitive market, price would equal marginal cost at $4.50 unit, at which the quantity is 8,000 units. Because the monopolist produces less and charges a higher price than under perfect competition, price exceeds marginal cost at the profit-maximizing level of output. The difference between the price and marginal cost is the per-unit cost to society of a monopolized industry.

25-9. **a.** The monopoly maximizes economic profits or minimizes economic losses by producing to the point at which marginal revenue is equal to marginal cost, which is 1 million units of output per month.

b. The profit-maximizing or loss-minimizing price of 1 million units per month is $30 per unit, so total revenues equal $30 million per month. The average total cost of producing 1 million units per month is $33 per unit, so total costs equal $33 million per month. Hence, in the short run, producing 1 million units minimizes the monopoly's loss at $3 million per month.

25-11. If price varies positively with total revenue, then the monopolist is operating on the inelastic portion of the demand curve. This corresponds to the range where marginal revenue is negative. The monopolist cannot, therefore, be at the point where its profits are maximized. In other words, the monopolist is not producing where marginal cost equals marginal revenue.

25-13. Because marginal cost has risen, the monopolist will be operating at a lower rate of output and charging a higher price. Economic profits are likely to decline because even though the price is higher, its output will be more than proportionately lower.

Chapter 26

26-1. **a.** There are many fast-food restaurants producing and selling differentiated products. Both of these features of this industry are consistent with the theory of monopolistic competition.

b. There are numerous colleges and universities, but each specializes in different academic areas and hence produces heterogeneous products, as in the theory of monopolistic competition.

26-3. The values for marginal cost and marginal revenue appear below. Marginal revenue equals marginal cost at approximately the fifth unit of output, so marginal analysis indicates that 5 units is the profit-maximizing production level.

Output	Price ($ per unit)	Total Costs ($)	Total Revenue ($)	Marginal Cost ($ per unit)	Marginal Revenue ($ per unit)	Total Profit ($)
0	6.00	2.00	0	—	—	−2.00
1	5.75	5.25	5.75	3.25	5.75	0.00
2	5.50	7.50	11.00	2.25	5.25	3.50
3	5.25	9.60	15.75	2.10	4.75	6.15
4	5.00	12.10	20.00	2.50	4.25	7.90
5	4.75	15.80	23.75	3.70	3.75	7.95
6	4.50	20.00	27.00	4.20	3.25	7.00
7	4.00	24.75	28.00	4.75	1.00	3.25

26-5. After these long-run adjustments have occurred, the demand curve will have shifted to tangency with the average total cost curve at 4 units of output. At this production level, average total cost is $3.03, so this will be the long-run equilibrium price. Because price and average total cost will be equal, the firm will earn zero economic profits.

26-7. **a.** interactive
b. direct
c. mass and interactive
d. mass

26-9. **a.** search good. Given the knowledge that it is a heavy-duty filing cabinet, a photo and description providing features such as dimensions are sufficient to evaluate the characteristics of a filing cabinet.

b. experience good. A meal must be eaten for its characteristics to be determined.

c. search good. Given the knowledge that the coat is made of wool, a photo and description providing size information are sufficient to evaluate the characteristics of the coat.

d. credence good. Psychotherapy services have characteristics that are likely to be difficult for consumers lacking expertise to assess without assistance from another health care provider, such as a general practitioner who guides someone experiencing depression in seeking psychotherapy treatment from a psychiatrist.

26-11. Consumers may be able to assess certain features of a credence good in advance of purchase, so in this sense a credence good is similar to a search good. Consumers lack expertise to evaluate the full qualities of a credence good until after they have purchased it, which is somewhat analogous to the characteristics of an experience good. Nevertheless, the fact that consumers cannot fully evaluate a credence good's qualities in advance of purchase makes it different from a search good. Likewise, the inability to be certain, without assistance, of the qualities of a credence good following purchase of the good also distinguishes a credence good from an experience good. The fact that consumers can evaluate certain aspects of a credence good in advance of purchase, as in the case of a search good, explains why ads for credence goods, such as pharmaceuticals, often have informational elements. At the same time, however, the fact that consumers cannot truly evaluate credence goods until after purchase, and even then only with assistance, explains why ads for credence goods also commonly include persuasive elements.

26-13. Typically, the fixed costs of producing an information product are relatively high, while average variable cost is equal to a very small per-unit amount. As a consequence, the average total cost curve slopes downward with increased output, and average variable cost equals marginal cost at a low, constant amount irrespective of the quantity produced. For an information product, marginal cost is always below average total cost. Consequently, if price were equal to marginal cost, it would always be less than average total cost, so the producer would always earn short-run economic losses.

Chapter 27

27-1. **a.** 15 percent + 14 percent + 12 percent + 11 percent = 52 percent.
  b. 52 percent + 10 percent + 10 percent + 8 percent + 7 percent = 87 percent; or 100 percent − 13 percent = 87 percent.

27-3. **a.** zero-sum game
  b. negative-sum game
  c. positive-sum game

27-5. Bob is currently a participant in a noncooperative game, in which some people stand and block his view of the football game. His tit-for-tat strategy is to stand up as well. If he stands, however, he will block the view of another spectator. In a cooperative game, all would sit or stand up simultaneously, so that no individual's view is blocked.

27-7. **a.** The fact that prices are growing at a stable rate and readily observable favor enforcing a cartel agreement So does the fact that there are only seven firms of significant size in the

inkjet-printer industry, which is a relatively small number. Therefore, much depends on degree of heterogeneity of inkjet printers; if these products are relatively homogeneous, then taken together these characteristics of the industry would generally support an effort to form a cartel.
  b. Once the cartel is formed, any one of the firms that produce inkjet printers could enlarge its profits by expanding production at the higher cartel price, so there is always an incentive to cheat. In addition, the presence of positive economic profits in the industry could induce firms outside the industry cartel to begin manufacturing and selling inkjet printers.

27-9. If Firm 2 opts for Format A, Firm 1 also prefers Format A, and if Firm 2 opts for Format B, Firm 1 prefers Format A. At the same time, if Firm 1 opts for Format A, Firm 2 prefers Format B, and if Firm 1 opts for Format B, Firm 2 prefers Format A. Thus, both firms will wish to produce compatible formats, although they will have to find a mechanism for settling on a format.

27-11. Possible examples include office productivity software, online auction services, telecommunications services, and Internet payment services. In each case, more people are likely to choose to consume the item when others do, because the inherent usefulness of consuming the item for each person increases as the number of consumers rises.

Chapter 28

28-1. If cable service is an industry that experiences diminishing long-run average total costs, then the city may determine that it is more efficient to have a single, large firm that produces at a lower long-run average cost. The city could then regulate the activity of the firm.

28-3. **a.** As the table indicates, long-run average cost and long-run marginal cost decline with greater output. If the firm were allowed to operate as a monopolist, it would produce to the point at which marginal cost equals marginal revenue, which is 2 units of output. The price that consumers are willing to pay for this quantity is $90 per unit, and maximum economic profits are $180 − $175 = $5.

Quantity	Price ($ per unit)	Long-Run Total Cost ($)	LRAC ($ per unit)	LRMC ($ per unit)	MR ($ per unit)
0	$100	$ 0	—	—	
1	95	92	$92.00	$92	$95
2	90	177	88.50	85	85
3	85	255	85.00	78	75
4	80	331	82.75	76	65
5	75	406	81.20	75	55
6	70	480	80.00	74	45

    b. Long-run marginal cost and price both equal $75 per unit at 5 units of output. At a price of $75 per unit, the firm experiences economic losses equal to $375 − $407 = −$32.

    c. Long-run average cost and price both equal $85 per unit at 3 units of output. At a price of $80 per unit, the firm's economic profits equal $255 − $255 = $0.

28-5. Lemons problems are likely to be more common in industries in which evaluating the characteristics of goods or services by simple inspection is difficult, as is true of the credence goods discussed in Chapter 26. Unaddressed lemons problems tend to depress the prices that sellers of high-quality items can obtain, which induces them to refrain from selling their high-quality items, resulting in sales of only lower-quality items. The main concern of economic regulation is to balance the trade-off between service and price, with economic regulation aiming to keep price lower than the price a profit-maximizing monopolist would charge. Social regulation seeks to improve working conditions and minimize adverse spillovers of production. The adverse incentives resulting from lemons problems are a form of market spillover, so it is arguable that social regulation is most appropriate for addressing lemons problems.

28-7. If European regulation is designed to protect domestic industries, then this is an example of the capture hypothesis. If, on the other hand, there are legitimate health concerns, then this is an example of the share-the-pain, share-the-gain hypothesis.

28-9. This is a creative response to the do-not-call legislation, in which firms are legally satisfying the terms of the regulation but evading the regulation's intent.

28-11. a. In this case, Firm 1 makes 75.0 percent of the sales in the Internet book market, and Firm 2 makes 46.7 percent of the sales in physical retail stores. By the antitrust authority's definition, there is a monopoly situation in the Internet book market.

    b. In the combined market, Firm 2 accounts for 42.5 percent of all sales, and Firm 1's share drops to 7.5 percent, so under this alternative definition there is no cause for concern about monopoly.

28-13. If the Justice Department viewed Internet Realtor listing services as a "relevant market" for antitrust policy, then the growing concentration of ownership within this single retailing association might be a concern. Control over Internet listings by this group could help promote cartel-type behavior. A key issue is whether the Internet marketplace for Realtor listings is separate from the physical market.

28-15. This is an example of bundling. Because consumers who purchase the bundled product perceive that they have effectively paid different prices for the bundled products based on their willingness to pay, an antitrust authority might view this practice as charging consumers different prices for the same products, or price discrimination.

Chapter 29

29-1.

Labor Input (workers per week)	Total Physical Output (printers per day)	Marginal Physical Product	Marginal Revenue Product ($)
10	200	—	—
11	218	18	1,800
12	234	16	1,600
13	248	14	1,400
14	260	12	1,200
15	270	10	1,000
16	278	8	800

29-3. a. The greater the substitutability of capital, the more elastic is the demand for labor.

    b. Because the demand for labor is a derived demand, the greater the elasticity of demand for the final product, the greater is the elasticity of demand for labor.

c. The larger the portion of factor costs accounted for by labor, the larger is the price elasticity of demand for labor.

29-5. a.

Labor Input (workers per week)	Total Physical Product	Product Price ($ per unit)	Marginal Physical Product	Total Revenue ($)	Marginal Revenue Product ($)
10	100	50	—	5,000	—
11	109	49	9	5,341	341
12	116	48	7	5,568	227
13	121	47	5	5,687	119
14	124	46	3	5,704	17
15	125	45	1	5,625	−79

b. The profit-maximizing firm would hire 13 workers, which is the quantity of labor beyond which the marginal revenue product of labor falls below the marginal factor cost.

29-7. a. The rise in the price of ethanol results in an increase in the marginal revenue product of corn, the key input in the production of ethanol. Thus, each ethanol producer's marginal revenue product curve shifts rightward, which ultimately translates into an increase in the demand for corn, from D_1 to D_2. The market clearing price of corn increases, from P_1 to P_2, and the equilibrium quantity of corn rises, from Q_1 to Q_2.

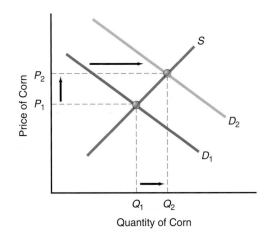

b. Human snack foods are a substitute input in the production of hogs, so the increase in the price of corn induced farmers to substitute in favor of snack foods.

29-9. Labor outsourcing by U.S. firms tends to push down market wages and employment in affected U.S. labor markets, but labor outsourcing by foreign firms that hire U.S. workers tends to push up market wages and employment in affected U.S. labor markets. Consequently, the overall wage and employment effects are ambiguous in the short run. In the long run, however, outsourcing enables U.S. and foreign firms to specialize in producing and trading the goods and services that they can produce most efficiently. The resulting resource saving ultimately expands the ability of U.S. residents to consume more goods and services than they could have otherwise.

29-11. The wage rate, $20 per unit of labor, equals marginal revenue product, so the marginal physical product of labor is $20 per unit of labor divided by the marginal revenue, $10 per unit of output, or 2 units of output per unit of labor.

29-13. In order to maximize profits, the firm should hire inputs up to the point at which the marginal physical product per dollar spent on the input is equalized across all inputs. This is not the case in this example. The marginal physical product of labor per dollar spent on wages is 200/$10 = 20 units of output per dollar spent on labor, which is less than the marginal physical product of capital per dollar spent on capital, which is 20,000/$500 or 40 units of output per dollar spent on capital. Thus, the firm should increase the additional output per dollar spent on labor by reducing the number of labor units it hires, and it should reduce the additional output per dollar spent on capital by increasing its use of capital, to the point where these amounts are equalized.

Chapter 30

30-1. Individual workers can air grievances to the collective voice who then takes the issue to the employer. The individual does not run the risk of being singled out by an employer. The individual employee does not waste work time trying to convince the employer that changes are needed in the workplace.

30-3. The reporting system probably was intended to provide information to union officials charged with seeking to impede strikebreaking activities by nonunion workers such as the soap opera writers. Strikebreakers can replace union employees, so they diminish the collective bargaining power of a union.

30-5. When marginal revenue is zero, demand for labor is unit-elastic, and total revenue is neither rising nor falling. No additional revenues can be earned by altering the quantity of labor, so the union's total wage revenues are maximized.

30-7. When unions in these industries attempt to bargain for higher-than-market levels of wages, the firms that employ members of these unions will not be able to readily substitute to alternative inputs. Hence, these unions are more likely to be able to achieve their wage objectives.

30-9.

Quantity of Labor Supplied	Total Physical Product	Required Hourly Wage Rate ($ per unit of labor)	Total Wage Bill ($)	Marginal Factor Cost ($ per unit of labor)
10	100	5	50	—
11	109	6	66	16
12	116	7	84	18
13	121	8	104	20
14	124	9	126	22
15	125	10	150	24

30-11. At 11 units of labor, the marginal revenue product of labor equals $16. This is equal to the marginal factor cost at this level of employment. The firm, therefore, will hire 11 units of labor and pay a wage of $6 an hour.

Quantity of Labor Supplied	Required Hourly Wage Rate ($ per unit of labor)	Total Factor Cost ($)	Marginal Factor Cost ($ per unit of labor)	Total Physical Product	Product Price ($ per unit)	Total Revenue ($)	Marginal Revenue Product ($ per unit of labor)
10	5	50	—	100	3.11	311.00	—
11	6	66	16.00	109	3.00	327.00	16.00
12	7	84	18.00	116	2.95	342.20	15.20
13	8	104	20.00	121	2.92	353.32	11.12
14	9	126	22.00	124	2.90	359.60	6.28
15	10	150	24.00	125	2.89	361.25	1.65

30-13. The marginal factor cost of the last worker hired was $106,480 − $105,600 = $880, so this is the marginal product of this worker if the firm is maximizing its profits.

Chapter 31

31-1. **a.** X, because for this country the Lorenz curve implies complete income equality.

b. Z, because this country's Lorenz curve is bowed farthest away from the case of complete income equality.

c. Closer, because if all other things including aggregate income remain unchanged, when more people in country Y are children below working age the share of income to people this age will decline, while the reverse will occur in country Z as more of its people reach working age and begin to earn incomes.

31-3. If the Lorenz curve is based on incomes net of transfer payments, then the Lorenz curve will become less bowed. But if the Lorenz curve does not account for transfer payments, its shape will remain unaffected.

31-5. Brazil

31-7. **a.** Absolute. If economic growth ultimately led to inflation-adjusted annual incomes for all urban families of four rising above $25,000 per year, then by this definition poverty would be ended.

b. Relative. By this definition, the lowest 15 percent of income earners will always be classified as being in a state of poverty.

c. Absolute. If economic growth eventually raised inflation-adjusted annual incomes of all individuals above $10,000, then by this definition poverty would cease to exist.

31-9. First, a moral hazard problem will exist, because government action would reduce the individual's incentive to continue a healthful lifestyle, thereby increasing the likelihood of greater health problems that will require future treatment. Second, an individual who currently has health problems will have an incentive to substitute future care that will be available at a zero price for current care that the individual must purchase at a positive price. Finally, in future years the patient will no longer have an incentive to contain health care expenses, and health care providers will have no incentive to minimize their costs.

31-11. The demand for health care will increase, and the marginal revenue curve will shift rightward. Hence, the profit-maximizing price and equilibrium quantity of health care services will increase.

31-13. Because funds in HRAs earn no interest, can be used to pay only medical expenses, and revert back to the employer at the end of the year if unused, an individual faces incentives to spend all these funds on every possible health care expense. In contrast, because funds in HSAs earn interest and can be used (subject to penalties and taxation) for other types of expenses, an individual has at least some incentive to try not to spend all the funds on health care expenses. Consequently, moral hazard problems are greater with HRAs than with HSAs.

Chapter 32

32-1. $4 per unit, which exactly accounts for the per-unit social cost of pollution.

32-3. a. 60 percent
   b. 40 percent
   c. 40 percent

32-5. a. There is a downward shift in the position of the marginal cost curve. The optimal degree of water cleanliness will rise above 65 percent, to a level such as 70 percent, and the cost incurred for the last unit of water clean-up will decrease to less than $10, such as a per-unit cost of $7.

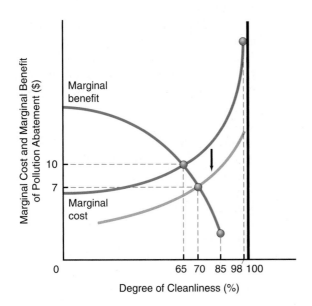

b. The second event induces an upward shift in the marginal benefit curve. Taken together, as shown in the diagram below, the two events unambiguously indicate that the optimal degree of water cleanliness increases above 65 percent, such as a level of 85 percent. The cost incurred for the last unit of water clean-up may rise or fall, however, and could end up at the initial level, which is the situation illustrated in the diagram.

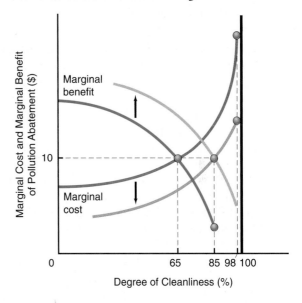

32-7. a. The marginal costs and benefits are tabulated below:
   b. 8,000
   c. 10,000

Population of Wild Tigers	Marginal Cost ($)	Marginal Benefit ($)
0	—	—
2,000	25	50
4,000	10	40
6,000	15	30
8,000	25	25
10,000	35	20
12,000	50	10

Chapter 33

33-1. a. The opportunity cost of pastries in Northland is 0.5 sandwich per pastry. The opportunity cost of sandwiches in Northland is 2 pastries per sandwich.

b. The opportunity cost of pastries in West Coast is 2 sandwiches per pastry. The opportunity cost of sandwiches in West Coast is 0.5 pastries per sandwich.

33-3. If Northland specializes in producing pastries, the maximum number of pastries it can produce and trade to West Coast is 50,000 pastries. Hence, the maximum number of units of each good that the two countries can trade at a rate of exchange of 1 pastry for 1 sandwich is 50,000.

33-5. Coastal Realm has a comparative advantage in producing digital TVs, and Border Kingdom has a comparative advantage in wine production.

33-7. a. The opportunity cost of modems in South Shore is 2 flash drives per modem. The opportunity cost of flash drives in South Shore is 0.5 modem per flash drive.

b. The opportunity cost of modems in East Isle is 0.5 flash drive per modem. The opportunity cost of flash drives in East Isle is 2 modems per flash drive.

c. Residents of South Shore have a comparative advantage in producing flash drives, and residents of East Isle have a comparative advantage in producing modems.

33-9. The critics are suggesting that Mexican exporters are shifting exports that would have gone to other nations to the United States, a nation within NAFTA, which would constitute trade diversion.

Chapter 34

34-1. The trade balance is merchandise exports minus merchandise imports, which equals $500 - 600 = -100$, or a deficit of 100. Adding service exports of 75 and subtracting net unilateral transfers of 10 and service imports of 50 yields $-100 + 75 - 10 - 50 = -85$, or a current account balance of -85. The capital account balance equals the difference between capital inflows and capital outflows, or $300 - 200 = +100$, or a capital account surplus of 100.

34-3. a. The increase in demand for Mexican-made guitars increases the demand for Mexican pesos, and the peso appreciates.

b. International investors will remove some of their financial capital from Mexico. The increase in the supply of pesos in the foreign exchange market will cause the peso to depreciate.

34-5. The demand for Chinese yuan increases, and the supply of yuan decreases. The dollar-yuan exchange rate rises, so the yuan appreciates.

34-7. The Canadian dollar–euro exchange rate is found by dividing the U.S. dollar–euro exchange rate by the U.S. dollar–Canadian dollar exchange rate, or (1.45 \$US/euro)/(0.94 \$US/\$C) = 1.54 \$C/euro, or 1.54 Canadian dollars per euro.

34-9. A flexible exchange rate system allows the exchange value of a currency to be determined freely in the foreign exchange market with no intervention by the government. A fixed exchange rate pegs the value of the currency, and the authorities responsible for the value of the currency intervene in foreign exchange markets to maintain this value. A dirty float involves occasional intervention by the exchange authorities. A target zone allows the exchange rate to fluctuate, but only within a given range of values.

34-11. When the dollar is pegged to gold at a rate of \$35 and the pound is pegged to the dollar at \$2 = £1, an implicit value between gold and the pound is established at £17.50 = 1 ounce of gold. If the dollar falls in value relative to gold, yet the pound is still valued to the dollar at \$2 = £1, the pound become undervalued relative to gold. The exchange rate between the dollar and the pound will have to be adjusted to 2.29 \$/£.

Glossary

A

Absolute advantage The ability to produce more units of a good or service using a given quantity of labor or resource inputs. Equivalently, the ability to produce the same quantity of a good or service using fewer units of labor or resource inputs.

Accounting identities Values that are equivalent by definition.

Accounting profit Total revenues minus total explicit costs.

Action time lag The time between recognizing an economic problem and implementing policy to solve it. The action time lag is quite long for fiscal policy, which requires congressional approval.

Active (discretionary) policymaking All actions on the part of monetary and fiscal policymakers that are undertaken in response to or in anticipation of some change in the overall economy.

Ad valorem taxation Assessing taxes by charging a tax rate equal to a fraction of the market price of each unit purchased.

Adverse selection The likelihood that individuals who seek to borrow may use the funds that they receive for high-risk projects.

Age-earnings cycle The regular earnings profile of an individual throughout his or her lifetime. The age-earnings cycle usually starts with a low income, builds gradually to a peak at around age 50, and then gradually curves down until it approaches zero at retirement.

Aggregate demand The total of all planned expenditures in the entire economy.

Aggregate demand curve A curve showing planned purchase rates for all final goods and services in the economy at various price levels, all other things held constant.

Aggregate demand shock Any event that causes the aggregate demand curve to shift inward or outward.

Aggregate supply The total of all planned production for the economy.

Aggregate supply shock Any event that causes the aggregate supply curve to shift inward or outward.

Aggregates Total amounts or quantities; aggregate demand, for example, is total planned expenditures throughout a nation.

Anticipated inflation The inflation rate that we believe will occur; when it does, we are in a situation of fully anticipated inflation.

Antitrust legislation Laws that restrict the formation of monopolies and regulate certain anticompetitive business practices.

Appreciation An increase in the exchange value of one nation's currency in terms of the currency of another nation.

Asset demand Holding money as a store of value instead of other assets such as certificates of deposit, corporate bonds, and stocks.

Assets Amounts owned; all items to which a business or household holds legal claim.

Asymmetric information Information possessed by one party in a financial transaction but not by the other party.

Automatic, or built-in, stabilizers Special provisions of certain federal programs that cause changes in desired aggregate expenditures without the action of Congress and the president. Examples are the federal progressive tax system and unemployment compensation.

Autonomous consumption The part of consumption that is independent of (does not depend on) the level of disposable income. Changes in autonomous consumption shift the consumption function.

Average fixed costs Total fixed costs divided by the number of units produced.

Average physical product Total product divided by the variable input.

Average propensity to consume (APC) Real consumption divided by real disposable income; for any given level of real income, the proportion of total real disposable income that is consumed.

Average propensity to save (APS) Real saving divided by real disposable income; for any given level of real income, the proportion of total real disposable income that is saved.

Average tax rate The total tax payment divided by total income. It is the proportion of total income paid in taxes.

Average total costs Total costs divided by the number of units produced; sometimes called *average per-unit total costs*.

Average variable costs Total variable costs divided by the number of units produced.

B

Balance of payments A system of accounts that measures transactions of goods, services, income, and financial assets between domestic households, businesses, and governments and residents of the rest of the world during a specific time period.

Balance of trade The difference between exports and imports of physical goods.

Balance sheet A statement of the assets and liabilities of any business entity, including financial institutions and the Federal Reserve System. Assets are what is owned; liabilities are what is owed.

Balanced budget A situation in which the government's spending is exactly equal to the total taxes and other revenues it collects during a given period of time.

Bank runs Attempts by many of a bank's depositors to convert transactions and time deposits into currency out of fear that the bank's liabilities may exceed its assets.

Barter The direct exchange of goods and services for other goods and services without the use of money.

Base year The year that is chosen as the point of reference for comparison of prices in other years.

Base-year dollars The value of a current sum expressed in terms of prices in a base year.

Behavioral economics An approach to the study of consumer behavior that emphasizes psychological limitations and complications that potentially interfere with rational decision making.

Bilateral monopoly A market structure consisting of a monopolist and a monopsonist.

Black market A market in which goods are traded at prices above their legal maximum prices or in which illegal goods are sold.

Bond A legal claim against a firm, usually entitling the owner of the bond to receive a fixed annual coupon payment, plus a lump-sum payment at the bond's maturity date. Bonds are issued in return for funds lent to the firm.

Bounded rationality The hypothesis that people are *nearly*, but not fully, rational, so that they cannot examine every possible choice available to them but instead use simple rules of thumb to sort among the alternatives that happen to occur to them.

Budget constraint All of the possible combinations of goods that can be purchased (at fixed prices) with a specific budget.

Bundling Offering two or more products for sale as a set.

Business fluctuations The ups and downs in business activity throughout the economy.

C

Capital account A category of balance of payments transactions that measures flows of real and financial assets.

Capital consumption allowance Another name for depreciation, the amount that businesses would have to save in order to take care of deteriorating machines and other equipment.

Capital gain A positive difference between the purchase price and the sale price of an asset. If a share of stock is bought for $5 and then sold for $15, the capital gain is $10.

Capital goods Producer durables; nonconsumable goods that firms use to make other goods.

Capital loss A negative difference between the purchase price and the sale price of an asset.

Capture hypothesis A theory of regulatory behavior that predicts that regulators will eventually be captured by

special interests of the industry being regulated.

Cartel An association of producers in an industry that agree to set common prices and output quotas to prevent competition.

Central bank A banker's bank, usually an official institution that also serves as a country's treasury's bank. Central banks normally regulate commercial banks.

Certificate of deposit (CD) A time deposit with a fixed maturity date offered by banks and other financial institutions.

Ceteris paribus **[KAY-ter-us PEAR-uh-bus] assumption** The assumption that nothing changes except the factor or factors being studied.

Ceteris paribus **conditions** Determinants of the relationship between price and quantity that are unchanged along a curve; changes in these factors cause the curve to shift.

Closed shop A business enterprise in which employees must belong to the union before they can be hired and must remain in the union after they are hired.

Collective bargaining Negotiation between the management of a company or of a group of companies and the management of a union or a group of unions for the purpose of reaching a mutually agreeable contract that sets wages, fringe benefits, and working conditions for all employees in all the unions involved.

Collective decision making How voters, politicians, and other interested parties act and how these actions influence nonmarket decisions.

Common property Property that is owned by everyone and therefore by no one. Air and water are examples of common property resources.

Comparative advantage The ability to produce a good or service at a lower opportunity cost than other producers.

Complements Two goods are complements when a change in the price of one causes an opposite shift in the demand for the other.

Concentration ratio The percentage of all sales contributed by the leading four or leading eight firms in an industry; sometimes called the *industry concentration ratio*.

Constant dollars Dollars expressed in terms of real purchasing power using a particular year as the base or standard of comparison, in contrast to current dollars.

Constant returns to scale No change in long-run average costs when output increases.

Constant-cost industry An industry whose total output can be increased without an increase in long-run per-unit costs; its long-run supply curve is horizontal.

Consumer optimum A choice of a set of goods and services that maximizes the level of satisfaction for each consumer, subject to limited income.

Consumer Price Index (CPI) A statistical measure of a weighted average of prices of a specified set of goods and services purchased by typical consumers in urban areas.

Consumer surplus The total difference between the total amount that consumers would have been willing to pay for a good or service and the total amount that they actually pay.

Consumption Spending on new goods and services to be used up out of a household's current income. Whatever is not consumed is saved. Consumption includes such things as buying food and going to a concert.

Consumption function The relationship between amount consumed and disposable income. A consumption function tells us how much people plan to consume at various levels of disposable income.

Consumption goods Goods bought by households to use up, such as food and movies.

Contraction A business fluctuation during which the pace of national economic activity is slowing down.

Cooperative game A game in which the players explicitly cooperate to make themselves better off. As applied to firms, it involves companies colluding in order to make higher than perfectly competitive rates of return.

Corporation A legal entity that may conduct business in its own name just as an individual does; the owners of a corporation, called shareholders, own shares of the firm's profits and enjoy the protection of limited liability.

Cost-of-living adjustments (COLAs) Clauses in contracts that allow for increases in specified nominal values to take account of changes in the cost of living.

Cost-of-service regulation Regulation that allows prices to reflect only the actual average cost of production and no monopoly profits.

Cost-push inflation Inflation caused by decreases in short-run aggregate supply.

Craft unions Labor unions composed of workers who engage in a particular trade or skill, such as baking, carpentry, or plumbing.

Crawling peg An exchange rate arrangement in which a country pegs the value of its currency to the exchange value of another nation's currency but allows the par value to change at regular intervals.

Creative response Behavior on the part of a firm that allows it to comply with the letter of the law but violate the spirit, significantly lessening the law's effects.

Credence good A product with qualities that consumers lack the expertise to assess without assistance.

Cross price elasticity of demand (E_{xy}) The percentage change in the demand for one good (holding its price constant) divided by the percentage change in the price of a related good.

Crowding-out effect The tendency of expansionary fiscal policy to cause a decrease in planned investment or planned consumption in the private sector; this decrease normally results from the rise in interest rates.

Current account A category of balance of payments transactions that measures the exchange of merchandise, the exchange of services, and unilateral transfers.

Cyclical unemployment Unemployment resulting from business recessions that occur when aggregate (total) demand is insufficient to create full employment.

D

Dead capital Any capital resource that lacks clear title of ownership.

Deadweight loss The portion of consumer surplus that no one in society is able to obtain in a situation of monopoly.

Decreasing-cost industry An industry in which an increase in output leads to a reduction in long-run per-unit costs, such that the long-run industry supply curve slopes downward.

Deflation A sustained decrease in the average of all prices of goods and services in an economy.

Demand A schedule showing how much of a good or service people will purchase at any price during a specified time period, other things being constant.

Demand curve A graphical representation of the demand schedule; a negatively sloped line showing the inverse relationship between the price and the quantity demanded (other things being equal).

Demand-pull inflation Inflation caused by increases in aggregate demand not matched by increases in aggregate supply.

Dependent variable A variable whose value changes according to changes in the value of one or more independent variables.

Depository institutions Financial institutions that accept deposits from savers and lend funds from those deposits out at interest.

Depreciation A decrease in the exchange value of one nation's currency in terms of the currency of another nation.

Depression An extremely severe recession.

Derived demand Input factor demand derived from demand for the final product being produced.

Development economics The study of factors that contribute to the economic growth of a country.

Diminishing marginal utility The principle that as more of any good or service is consumed, its extra benefit declines. Otherwise stated, increases in total utility from the consumption of a good or service become smaller and smaller as more is consumed during a given time period.

Direct expenditure offsets Actions on the part of the private sector in spending income that offset government fiscal policy actions. Any increase in government spending in an area that competes with the private sector will have some direct expenditure offset.

Direct marketing Advertising targeted at specific consumers, typically in the form of postal mailings, telephone calls, or e-mail messages.

Direct relationship A relationship between two variables that is positive, meaning that an increase in one variable is associated with an increase in the other and a decrease in one variable is associated with a decrease in the other.

Dirty float Active management of a floating exchange rate on the part of a country's government, often in cooperation with other nations.

Discount rate The interest rate that the Federal Reserve charges for reserves that it lends to depository institutions. It is sometimes referred to as the *rediscount rate* or, in Canada and England, as the *bank rate*.

Discounting The method by which the present value of a future sum or a future stream of sums is obtained.

Discouraged workers Individuals who have stopped looking for a job because they are convinced that they will not find a suitable one.

Diseconomies of scale Increases in long-run average costs that occur as output increases.

Disposable personal income (DPI) Personal income after personal income taxes have been paid.

Dissaving Negative saving; a situation in which spending exceeds income. Dissaving can occur when a household is able to borrow or use up existing assets.

Distribution of income The way income is allocated among the population.

Dividends Portion of a corporation's profits paid to its owners (shareholders).

Division of labor The segregation of resources into different specific tasks; for example, one automobile worker puts on bumpers, another doors, and so on.

Dominant strategies Strategies that always yield the highest benefit. Regardless of what other players do, a dominant strategy will yield the most benefit for the player using it.

Dumping Selling a good or a service abroad below the price charged in the home market or at a price below its cost of production.

Durable consumer goods Consumer goods that have a life span of more than three years.

Dynamic tax analysis Economic evaluation of tax rate changes that recognizes that the tax base eventually declines with ever-higher tax rates, so that tax revenues may eventually decline if the tax rate is raised sufficiently.

E

Economic freedom The rights to own private property and to exchange goods, services, and financial assets with minimal government interference.

Economic goods Goods that are scarce, for which the quantity demanded exceeds the quantity supplied at a zero price.

Economic growth Increases in per capita real GDP measured by its rate of change per year.

Economic profits Total revenues minus total opportunity costs of all inputs used, or the total of all implicit and explicit costs.

Economic rent A payment for the use of any resource over and above its opportunity cost.

Economics The study of how people allocate their limited resources to satisfy their unlimited wants.

Economies of scale Decreases in long-run average costs resulting from increases in output.

Effect time lag The time that elapses between the implementation of a policy and the results of that policy.

Efficiency The case in which a given level of inputs is used to produce the maximum output possible. Alternatively, the situation in which a given output is produced at minimum cost.

Effluent fee A charge to a polluter that gives the right to discharge into the air or water a certain amount of pollution; also called a *pollution tax*

Elastic demand A demand relationship in which a given percentage change in price will result in a larger percentage change in quantity demanded.

Empirical Relying on real-world data in evaluating the usefulness of a model.

Endowments The various resources in an economy, including both physical resources and such human resources as ingenuity and management skills.

Entitlements Guaranteed benefits under a government program such as Social Security, Medicare, or Medicaid.

Entrepreneurship The component of human resources that performs the functions of raising capital, organizing, managing, and assembling other factors of production, making basic business policy decisions, and taking risks.

Equation of exchange The formula indicating that the number of monetary units (M_s) times the number of times each unit is spent on final goods and services (V) is identical to the price level (P) times real GDP (Y).

Equilibrium The situation when quantity supplied equals quantity demanded at a particular price.

Excess reserves The difference between actual reserves and required reserves.

Exchange rate The price of one nation's currency in terms of the currency of another country.

Excise tax A tax levied on purchases of a particular good or service.

Expansion A business fluctuation in which the pace of national economic activity is speeding up.

Expenditure approach Computing GDP by adding up the dollar value at current market prices of all final goods and services.

Experience good A product that an individual must consume before the product's quality can be established.

Explicit costs Costs that business managers must take account of because they must be paid; examples are wages, taxes, and rent.

Externality A consequence of an economic activity that spills over to affect third parties. Pollution is an externality.

F

Featherbedding Any practice that forces employers to use more labor than they would otherwise or to use existing labor in an inefficient manner.

Federal Deposit Insurance Corporation (FDIC) A government agency that insures the deposits held in banks and most other depository institutions; all U.S. banks are insured this way.

Federal funds market A private market (made up mostly of banks) in which banks can borrow reserves from other banks that want to lend them. Federal funds are usually lent for overnight use.

Federal funds rate The interest rate that depository institutions pay to borrow reserves in the interbank federal funds market.

Fiduciary monetary system A system in which money is issued by the government and its value is based uniquely on the public's faith that the currency represents command over goods and services.

Final goods and services Goods and services that are at their final stage of production and will not be transformed into yet other goods or services. For example, wheat ordinarily is not considered a final good because it is usually used to make a final good, bread.

Financial capital Funds used to purchase physical capital goods, such as buildings and equipment, and patents and trademarks.

Financial intermediaries Institutions that transfer funds between ultimate lenders (savers) and ultimate borrowers.

Financial intermediation The process by which financial institutions accept savings from businesses, households, and governments and lend the savings to other businesses, households, and governments.

Firm A business organization that employs resources to produce goods or services for profit. A firm normally owns and operates at least one "plant" or facility in order to produce.

Fiscal policy The discretionary changing of government expenditures or taxes to achieve national economic goals, such as high employment with price stability.

Fixed costs Costs that do not vary with output. Fixed costs typically include such expenses as rent on a building. These costs are fixed for a certain period of time (in the long run, though, they are variable).

Fixed investment Purchases by businesses of newly produced producer durables, or capital goods, such as production machinery and office equipment.

Flexible exchange rates Exchange rates that are allowed to fluctuate in the open market in response to changes in supply and demand. Sometimes called *floating exchange rates.*

Flow A quantity measured per unit of time; something that occurs over time, such as the income you make per week or per year or the number of individuals who are fired every month.

FOMC Directive A document that summarizes the Federal Open Market Committee's general policy strategy, establishes near-term objectives for the federal funds rate, and specifies target ranges for money supply growth.

Foreign direct investment The acquisition of more than 10 percent of the shares of ownership in a company in another nation.

Foreign exchange market A market in which households, firms, and governments buy and sell national currencies.

Foreign exchange rate The price of one currency in terms of another.

Foreign exchange risk The possibility that changes in the value of a nation's currency will result in variations in the market value of assets.

45-degree reference line The line along which planned real expenditures equal real GDP per year.

Fractional reserve banking A system in which depository institutions hold reserves that are less than the amount of total deposits.

Free-rider problem A problem that arises when individuals presume that others will pay for public goods so that, individually, they can escape paying for their portion without causing a reduction in production.

Frictional unemployment Unemployment due to the fact that workers must search for appropriate job offers. This takes time, and so they remain temporarily unemployed.

Full employment An arbitrary level of unemployment that corresponds to "normal" friction in the labor market. In 1986, a 6.5 percent rate of unemployment was considered full employment. Today, it is assumed to be around 5 percent.

G

Game theory A way of describing the various possible outcomes in any situation involving two or more interacting individuals when those individuals are aware of the interactive nature of their situation and plan accordingly. The plans made by these individuals are known as *game strategies.*

GDP deflator A price index measuring the changes in prices of all new goods and services produced in the economy.

General Agreement on Tariffs and Trade (GATT) An international agreement established in 1947 to further world trade by reducing barriers and tariffs. The GATT was replaced by the World Trade Organization in 1995.

Goods All things from which individuals derive satisfaction or happiness.

Government budget constraint The limit on government spending and transfers imposed by the fact that every dollar the government spends, transfers, or uses to repay borrowed funds must ultimately be provided by the user charges and taxes it collects.

Government budget deficit An excess of government spending over government revenues during a given period of time.

Government budget surplus An excess of government revenues over government spending during a given period of time.

Government, or political, goods Goods (and services) provided by the public sector; they can be either private or public goods.

Government-inhibited good A good that has been deemed socially undesirable through the political process. Heroin is an example.

Government-sponsored good A good that has been deemed socially desirable through the political process. Museums are an example.

Gross domestic income (GDI) The sum of all income—wages, interest, rent, and profits—paid to the four factors of production.

Gross domestic product (GDP) The total market value of all final goods and services produced during a year by factors of production located within a nation's borders.

Gross private domestic investment The creation of capital goods, such as factories and machines, that can yield production and hence consumption in the future. Also included in this definition are changes in business inventories and repairs made to machines or buildings.

Gross public debt All federal government debt irrespective of who owns it.

H

Health savings account (HSA) A tax-exempt health care account into which individuals can pay on a regular basis and out of which medical expenses can be paid.

Hedge A financial strategy that reduces the chance of suffering losses arising from foreign exchange risk.

Horizontal merger The joining of firms that are producing or selling a similar product.

Human capital The accumulated training and education of workers.

I

Implicit costs Expenses that managers do not have to pay out of pocket and hence normally do not explicitly calculate, such as the opportunity cost of factors of production that are owned; examples are owner-provided capital and owner-provided labor.

Import quota A physical supply restriction on imports of a particular good, such as sugar. Foreign exporters are unable to sell in the United States more than the quantity specified in the import quota.

Incentive structure The system of rewards and punishments individuals face with respect to their own actions.

Incentives Rewards for engaging in a particular activity.

Income approach Measuring GDP by adding up all components of national income, including wages, interest, rent, and profits.

Income elasticity of demand (E_i) The percentage change in demand for any good, holding its price constant, divided by the percentage change in income; the responsiveness of demand to changes in income, holding the good's relative price constant.

Income in kind Income received in the form of goods and services, such as housing or medical care; to be contrasted with money income, which is simply income in dollars, or general purchasing power, that can be used to buy any goods and services.

Income velocity of money (V) The number of times per year a dollar is spent on final goods and services; identically equal to nominal GDP divided by the money supply.

Income-consumption curve The set of optimal consumption points that would occur if income were increased, relative prices remaining constant.

Increasing-cost industry An industry in which an increase in industry output is accompanied by an increase in long-run per-unit costs, such that the long-run industry supply curve slopes upward.

Independent variable A variable whose value is determined independently of, or outside, the equation under study.

Indifference curve A curve composed of a set of consumption alternatives, each of which yields the same total amount of satisfaction.

Indirect business taxes All business taxes except the tax on corporate profits. Indirect business taxes include sales and business property taxes.

Industrial unions Labor unions that consist of workers from a particular industry, such as automobile manufacturing or steel manufacturing.

Industry supply curve The locus of points showing the minimum prices at which given quantities will be forthcoming; also called the *market supply curve*.

Inefficient point Any point below the production possibilities curve, at which the use of resources is not generating the maximum possible output.

Inelastic demand A demand relationship in which a given percentage change in price will result in a less than proportionate percentage change in the quantity demanded.

Infant industry argument The contention that tariffs should be imposed to protect from import competition an industry that is trying to get started. Presumably, after the industry becomes technologically efficient, the tariff can be lifted.

Inferior goods Goods for which demand falls as income rises.

Inflation A sustained increase in the average of all prices of goods and services in an economy.

Inflation-adjusted return A rate of return that is measured in terms of real goods and services; that is, after the effects of inflation have been factored out.

Inflationary gap The gap that exists whenever equilibrium real GDP per year is greater than full-employment real GDP as shown by the position of the long-run aggregate supply curve.

Information product An item that is produced using information-intensive inputs at a relatively high fixed cost but distributed for sale at a relatively low marginal cost.

Informational advertising Advertising that emphasizes transmitting knowledge about the features of a product.

Innovation Transforming an invention into something that is useful to humans.

Inside information Information that is not available to the general public about what is happening in a corporation.

Interactive marketing Advertising that permits a consumer to follow up directly by searching for more information and placing direct product orders.

Interest The payment for current rather than future command over resources; the cost of obtaining credit.

Interest rate effect One of the reasons that the aggregate demand curve slopes downward: Higher price levels increase the interest rate, which in turn causes businesses and consumers to reduce desired spending due to the higher cost of borrowing.

Intermediate goods Goods used up entirely in the production of final goods.

International financial crisis The rapid withdrawal of foreign investments and loans from a nation.

International Monetary Fund An agency founded to administer an international foreign exchange system and to lend to member countries that had balance of payments problems. The IMF now functions as a lender of last resort for national governments.

Inventory investment Changes in the stocks of finished goods and goods in process, as well as changes in the raw materials that businesses keep on hand. Whenever inventories are decreasing, inventory investment is negative; whenever they are increasing, inventory investment is positive.

Inverse relationship A relationship between two variables that is negative, meaning that an increase in one variable is associated with a decrease in the other and a decrease in one variable is associated with an increase in the other.

Investment Any use of today's resources to expand tomorrow's production or consumption.

J

Job leaver An individual in the labor force who quits voluntarily.

Job loser An individual in the labor force whose employment was involuntarily terminated.

Jurisdictional dispute A disagreement involving two or more unions over which should have control of a particular jurisdiction, such as a particular craft or skill or a particular firm or industry.

K

Keynesian short-run aggregate supply curve The horizontal portion of the aggregate supply curve in which there is excessive unemployment and unused capacity in the economy.

L

Labor Productive contributions of humans who work.

Labor force Individuals aged 16 years or older who either have jobs or who are looking and available for jobs; the number of employed plus the number of unemployed.

Labor force participation rate The percentage of noninstitutionalized working-age individuals who are employed or seeking employment.

Labor productivity Total real domestic output (real GDP) divided by the number of workers (output per worker).

Labor unions Worker organizations that seek to secure economic improvements for their members; they also seek to improve the safety, health, and other benefits (such as job security) of their members.

Land The natural resources that are available from nature. Land as a resource includes location, original fertility and mineral deposits, topography, climate, water, and vegetation.

Law of demand The observation that there is a negative, or inverse, relationship between the price of any good or service and the quantity demanded, holding other factors constant.

Law of diminishing marginal product The observation that after some point, successive equal-sized increases in a variable factor of production, such as labor, added to fixed factors of production, will result in smaller increases in output.

Law of increasing relative cost The fact that the opportunity cost of additional units of a good generally increases as society attempts to produce more of that good. This accounts for the bowed-out shape of the production possibilities curve.

Law of supply The observation that the higher the price of a good, the more of that good sellers will make available over a specified time period, other things being equal.

Leading indicators Events that have been found to occur before changes in business activity.

Lemons problem The potential for asymmetric information to bring about a general decline in product quality in an industry.

Lender of last resort The Federal Reserve's role as an institution that is willing and able to lend to a temporarily illiquid bank that is otherwise in good financial condition to prevent the bank's illiquid position from leading to a general loss of confidence in that bank or in others.

Liabilities Amounts owed; the legal claims against a business or household by nonowners.

Limited liability A legal concept in which the responsibility, or liability, of the owners of a corporation is limited to the value of the shares in the firm that they own.

Liquidity The degree to which an asset can be acquired or disposed of without much danger of any intervening loss in *nominal* value and with small transaction costs. Money is the most liquid asset.

Liquidity approach A method of measuring the money supply by looking at money as a temporary store of value.

Long run The time period during which all factors of production can be varied.

Long-run aggregate supply curve A vertical line representing the real output of goods and services after full adjustment has occurred. It can also be viewed as representing the real GDP of the economy under conditions of full employment—the full-employment level of real GDP.

Long-run average cost curve The locus of points representing the minimum unit cost of producing any given rate of output, given current technology and resource prices.

Long-run industry supply curve A market supply curve showing the relationship between prices and quantities after firms have been allowed the time to enter into or exit from an industry, depending on whether there have been positive or negative economic profits.

Lorenz curve A geometric representation of the distribution of income. A Lorenz curve that is perfectly straight represents complete income equality. The more bowed a Lorenz curve, the more unequally income is distributed.

Lump-sum tax A tax that does not depend on income. An example is a $1,000 tax that every household must pay, irrespective of its economic situation.

M

M1 The money supply, measured as the total value of currency plus transactions deposits plus traveler's checks not issued by banks.

M2 M1 plus (1) savings and small-denomination time deposits at all depository institutions, (2) balances in retail money market mutual funds, and (3) money market deposit accounts (MMDAs).

Macroeconomics The study of the behavior of the economy as a whole, including such economywide phenomena as changes in unemployment, the general price level, and national income.

Majority rule A collective decision-making system in which group decisions are made on the basis of more than 50 percent of the vote. In other words, whatever more than half of the electorate votes for, the entire electorate has to accept.

Marginal cost pricing A system of pricing in which the price charged is equal to the opportunity cost to society of producing one more unit of the good or service in question. The opportunity cost is the marginal cost to society.

Marginal costs The change in total costs due to a one-unit change in production rate.

Marginal factor cost (MFC) The cost of using an additional unit of an input. For example, if a firm can hire all the workers it wants at the going wage rate, the marginal factor cost of labor is the wage rate.

Marginal physical product The physical output that is due to the addition of one more unit of a variable factor of production; the change in total product occurring when a variable input is increased and all other inputs are held constant; also called *marginal product*.

Marginal physical product (MPP) of labor The change in output resulting from the addition of one more worker. The MPP of the worker equals the change in total output accounted for by hiring the worker, holding all other factors of production constant.

Marginal propensity to consume (MPC) The ratio of the change in consumption to the change in disposable income. A marginal propensity to consume of 0.8 tells us that an additional $100 in take-home pay will lead to an additional $80 consumed.

Marginal propensity to save (MPS) The ratio of the change in saving to the change in disposable income. A marginal propensity to save of 0.2 indicates that out of an additional $100 in take-home pay, $20 will be saved. Whatever is not saved is consumed. The marginal propensity to save plus the marginal propensity to consume must always equal 1, by definition.

Marginal revenue The change in total revenues resulting from a one-unit change in output (and sale) of the product in question.

Marginal revenue product (MRP) The marginal physical product (MPP) times marginal revenue (MR). The MRP gives the additional revenue obtained from a one-unit change in labor input.

Marginal tax rate The change in the tax payment divided by the change in income, or the percentage of additional dollars that must be paid in taxes. The marginal tax rate is applied to the highest tax bracket of taxable income reached.

Marginal utility The change in total utility due to a one-unit change in the quantity of a good or service consumed.

Market All of the arrangements that individuals have for exchanging with one another. Thus, for example, we can speak of the labor market, the automobile market, and the credit market.

Market clearing, or equilibrium, price The price that clears the market, at which quantity demanded equals quantity supplied; the price where the demand curve intersects the supply curve.

Market demand The demand of all consumers in the marketplace for a particular good or service. The summation at each price of the quantity demanded by each individual.

Market failure A situation in which an unrestrained market operation leads to either too few or too many resources going to a specific economic activity.

Market share test The percentage of a market that a particular firm supplies; used as the primary measure of monopoly power.

Mass marketing Advertising intended to reach as many consumers as possible, typically through television, newspaper, radio, or magazine ads.

Medium of exchange Any item that sellers will accept as payment.

Microeconomics The study of decision making undertaken by individuals (or households) and by firms.

Minimum efficient scale (MES) The lowest rate of output per unit time at which long-run average costs for a particular firm are at a minimum.

Minimum wage A wage floor, legislated by government, setting the lowest hourly rate that firms may legally pay workers.

Models, or theories Simplified representations of the real world used as the basis for predictions or explanations.

Money Any medium that is universally accepted in an economy both by sellers of goods and services as payment for those goods and services and by creditors as payment for debts.

Money balances Synonymous with money, money stock, money holdings.

Money illusion Reacting to changes in money prices rather than relative prices. If a worker whose wages double when the price level also doubles thinks he or she is better off, that worker is suffering from money illusion.

Money market deposit accounts (MMDAs) Accounts issued by banks yielding a market rate of interest with a minimum balance requirement and a limit on transactions. They have no minimum maturity.

Money market mutual funds Funds obtained from the public that investment companies hold in common and use to acquire short-maturity credit instruments, such as certificates of deposit and securities sold by the U.S. government.

Money multiplier A number that, when multiplied by a change in reserves in the banking system, yields the resulting change in the money supply.

Money price The price that we observe today, expressed in today's dollars; also called the *absolute* or *nominal price*.

Money supply The amount of money in circulation.

Monopolist The single supplier of a good or service for which there is no close substitute. The monopolist therefore constitutes its entire industry.

Monopolistic competition A market situation in which a large number of firms produce similar but not identical products. Entry into the industry is relatively easy.

Monopolization The possession of monopoly power in the relevant market and the willful acquisition or maintenance of that power, as distinguished from growth or development as a consequence of a superior product, business acumen, or historical accident.

Monopoly A firm that can determine the market price of a good. In the extreme case, a monopoly is the only seller of a good or service.

Monopsonist The only buyer in a market.

Monopsonistic exploitation Paying a price for the variable input that is less than its marginal revenue product; the difference between marginal revenue product and the wage rate.

Moral hazard The possibility that a borrower might engage in riskier behavior after a loan has been obtained.

Multiplier The ratio of the change in the equilibrium level of real GDP to the change in autonomous real expenditures; the number by which a change in autonomous real investment or autonomous real consumption, for example, is multiplied to get the change in equilibrium real GDP.

Multiproduct firm A firm that produces and sells two or more different items.

N

National income (NI) The total of all factor payments to resource owners. It can be obtained from net domestic product (NDP) by subtracting indirect business taxes and transfers and adding net U.S. income earned abroad and other business income adjustments.

National income accounting A measurement system used to estimate national income and its components; one approach to measuring an economy's aggregate performance.

Natural monopoly A monopoly that arises from the peculiar production characteristics in an industry. It usually arises when there are large economies of scale relative to the industry's demand such that one firm can produce at a lower average cost than can be achieved by multiple firms.

Natural rate of unemployment The rate of unemployment that is estimated to prevail in long-run macroeconomic equilibrium, when all workers and employers have fully adjusted to any changes in the economy.

Negative market feedback A tendency for a good or service to fall out of favor with more consumers because other consumers have stopped purchasing the item.

Negative-sum game A game in which players as a group lose during the process of the game.

Net domestic product (NDP) GDP minus depreciation.

Net investment Gross private domestic investment minus an estimate of the wear and tear on the existing capital stock. Net investment therefore measures the change in the capital stock over a one-year period.

Net public debt Gross public debt minus all government interagency borrowing.

Net worth The difference between assets and liabilities.

Network effect A situation in which a consumer's willingness to purchase a good or service is influenced by how many others also buy or have bought the item.

Neutral federal funds rate A value of the interest rate on interbank loans at which the growth rate of real GDP tends neither to rise nor to fall relative to the rate of growth of potential, long-run, real GDP, given the expected rate of inflation.

New entrant An individual who has never held a full-time job lasting two weeks or longer but is now seeking employment.

New growth theory A theory of economic growth that examines the factors that determine why technology, research, innovation, and the like are undertaken and how they interact.

New Keynesian inflation dynamics In new Keynesian theory, the pattern of inflation exhibited by an economy with growing aggregate demand—initial sluggish adjustment of the price level in response to increased aggregate demand followed by higher inflation later.

Nominal rate of interest The market rate of interest expressed in today's dollars.

Nominal values The values of variables such as GDP and investment expressed in current dollars, also called *money values*; measurement in terms of the actual market prices at which goods and services are sold.

Nonaccelerating inflation rate of unemployment (NAIRU) The rate of unemployment below which the rate of inflation tends to rise and above which the rate of inflation tends to fall.

Noncontrollable expenditures Government spending that changes automatically without action by Congress.

Noncooperative game A game in which the players neither negotiate nor cooperate in any way. As applied to firms in an industry, this is the common situation in which there are relatively few firms and each has some ability to change price.

Nondurable consumer goods Consumer goods that are used up within three years.

Nonincome expense items The total of indirect business taxes and depreciation.

Nonprice rationing devices All methods used to ration scarce goods that are price-controlled. Whenever the price system is not allowed to work, nonprice rationing devices will evolve to ration the affected goods and services.

Normal goods Goods for which demand rises as income rises. Most goods are normal goods.

Normal rate of return The amount that must be paid to an investor to induce investment in a business; also known as the *opportunity cost of capital*.

Normative economics Analysis involving value judgments about economic policies; relates to whether things are good or bad. A statement of *what ought to be*.

Number line A line that can be divided into segments of equal length, each associated with a number.

O

Oligopoly A market structure in which there are very few sellers. Each seller knows that the other sellers will react to its changes in prices, quantities, and qualities.

Open economy effect One of the reasons that the aggregate demand curve slopes downward: Higher price levels result in foreign residents desiring to buy fewer U.S.-made goods, while U.S. residents now desire more foreign-made goods, thereby reducing net exports. This is equivalent to a reduction in the amount of real goods and services purchased in the United States.

Open market operations The purchase and sale of existing U.S. government securities (such as bonds) in the open private market by the Federal Reserve System.

Opportunistic behavior Actions that focus solely on short-run gains because long-run benefits of cooperation are perceived to be smaller.

Opportunity cost The highest-valued, next-best alternative that must be sacrificed to obtain something or to satisfy a want.

Opportunity cost of capital The normal rate of return, or the available return on the next-best alternative investment. Economists consider this a cost of production, and it is included in our cost examples.

Optimal quantity of pollution The level of pollution for which the marginal benefit of one additional unit of pollution abatement just equals the marginal cost of that additional unit of pollution abatement.

Origin The intersection of the *y* axis and the *x* axis in a graph.

Outsourcing A firm's employment of labor outside the country in which the firm is located.

P

Par value The officially determined value of a currency.

Partnership A business owned by two or more joint owners, or partners, who share the responsibilities and the profits of the firm and are individually liable for all the debts of the partnership.

Passive (nondiscretionary) policymaking Policymaking that is carried out in response to a rule. It is therefore not in response to an actual or potential change in overall economic activity.

Patent A government protection that gives an inventor the exclusive right to make, use, or sell an invention for a limited period of time (currently, 20 years).

Payment intermediaries Institutions that facilitate transfers of funds between depositors who hold transactions deposits with those institutions.

Payoff matrix A matrix of outcomes, or consequences, of the strategies available to the players in a game.

Perfect competition A market structure in which the decisions of *individual* buyers and sellers have no effect on market price.

Perfectly competitive firm A firm that is such a small part of the total *industry* that it cannot affect the price of the product it sells.

Perfectly elastic demand A demand that has the characteristic that even the slightest increase in price will lead to zero quantity demanded.

Perfectly elastic supply A supply characterized by a reduction in quantity supplied to zero when there is the slightest decrease in price.

Perfectly inelastic demand A demand that exhibits zero responsiveness to price changes; no matter what the price is, the quantity demanded remains the same.

Perfectly inelastic supply A supply for which quantity supplied remains constant, no matter what happens to price.

Personal Consumption Expenditure (PCE) Index A statistical measure of average prices that uses annually updated weights based on surveys of consumer spending.

Personal income (PI) The amount of income that households actually receive before they pay personal income taxes.

Persuasive advertising Advertising that is intended to induce a consumer to purchase a particular product and discover a previously unknown taste for the item.

Phillips curve A curve showing the relationship between unemployment and changes in wages or prices. It was long thought to reflect a trade-off between unemployment and inflation.

Physical capital All manufactured resources, including buildings, equipment, machines, and improvements to land that are used for production.

Planning curve The long-run average cost curve.

Planning horizon The long run, during which all inputs are variable.

Plant size The physical size of the factories that a firm owns and operates to produce its output. Plant size can be defined by square footage, maximum physical capacity, and other physical measures.

Policy irrelevance proposition The conclusion that policy actions have no real effects in the short run if the policy actions are anticipated and none in the

long run even if the policy actions are unanticipated.

Portfolio investment The purchase of less than 10 percent of the shares of ownership in a company in another nation.

Positive economics Analysis that is *strictly* limited to making either purely descriptive statements or scientific predictions; for example, "If A, then B." A statement of *what is.*

Positive market feedback A tendency for a good or service to come into favor with additional consumers because other consumers have chosen to buy the item.

Positive-sum game A game in which players as a group are better off at the end of the game.

Potential money multiplier The reciprocal of the required reserve ratio, assuming no leakages into currency and no excess reserves. It is equal to 1 divided by the required reserve ratio.

Precautionary demand Holding money to meet unplanned expenditures and emergencies.

Present value The value of a future amount expressed in today's dollars; the most that someone would pay today to receive a certain sum at some point in the future.

Price ceiling A legal maximum price that may be charged for a particular good or service.

Price controls Government-mandated minimum or maximum prices that may be charged for goods and services.

Price differentiation Establishing different prices for similar products to reflect differences in marginal cost in providing those commodities to different groups of buyers.

Price discrimination Selling a given product at more than one price, with the price difference being unrelated to differences in marginal cost.

Price elasticity of demand (E_p) The responsiveness of the quantity demanded of a commodity to changes in its price; defined as the percentage change in quantity demanded divided by the percentage change in price.

Price elasticity of supply (E_s) The responsiveness of the quantity supplied of a commodity to a change in its price; the

percentage change in quantity supplied divided by the percentage change in price.

Price floor A legal minimum price below which a good or service may not be sold. Legal minimum wages are an example.

Price index The cost of today's market basket of goods expressed as a percentage of the cost of the same market basket during a base year.

Price searcher A firm that must determine the price-output combination that maximizes profit because it faces a downward-sloping demand curve.

Price system An economic system in which relative prices are constantly changing to reflect changes in supply and demand for different commodities. The prices of those commodities are signals to everyone within the system as to what is relatively scarce and what is relatively abundant.

Price taker A perfectly competitive firm that must take the price of its product as given because the firm cannot influence its price.

Price-consumption curve The set of consumer-optimum combinations of two goods that the consumer would choose as the price of one good changes, while money income and the price of the other good remain constant.

Principle of rival consumption The recognition that individuals are rivals in consuming private goods because one person's consumption reduces the amount available for others to consume.

Principle of substitution The principle that consumers shift away from goods and services that become priced relatively higher in favor of goods and services that are now priced relatively lower.

Prisoners' dilemma A famous strategic game in which two prisoners have a choice between confessing and not confessing to a crime. If neither confesses, they serve a minimum sentence. If both confess, they serve a longer sentence. If one confesses and the other doesn't, the one who confesses goes free. The dominant strategy is always to confess.

Private costs Costs borne solely by the individuals who incur them. Also called *internal costs.*

Private goods Goods that can be consumed by only one individual at a time.

Private goods are subject to the principle of rival consumption.

Private property rights Exclusive rights of ownership that allow the use, transfer, and exchange of property.

Producer durables, or capital goods Durable goods having an expected service life of more than three years that are used by businesses to produce other goods and services.

Producer Price Index (PPI) A statistical measure of a weighted average of prices of goods and services that firms produce and sell.

Product compatibility The capability of a product sold by one firm to function together with another firm's complementary product.

Product differentiation The distinguishing of products by brand name, color, and other minor attributes. Product differentiation occurs in other than perfectly competitive markets in which products are, in theory, homogeneous, such as wheat or corn.

Production function The relationship between inputs and maximum physical output. A production function is a technological, not an economic, relationship.

Production possibilities curve (PPC) A curve representing all possible combinations of maximum outputs that could be produced assuming a fixed amount of productive resources of a given quality.

Production Any activity that results in the conversion of resources into products that can be used in consumption.

Profit-maximizing rate of production The rate of production that maximizes total profits, or the difference between total revenues and total costs; also, the rate of production at which marginal revenue equals marginal cost.

Progressive taxation A tax system in which, as income increases, a higher percentage of the additional income is paid as taxes. The marginal tax rate exceeds the average tax rate as income rises.

Property rights The rights of an owner to use and to exchange property.

Proportional rule A decision-making system in which actions are based on the proportion of the "votes" cast and are in proportion to them. In a market system, if 10 percent of the "dollar votes" are cast for blue cars, 10 percent of automobile output will be blue

Proportional taxation A tax system in which, regardless of an individual's income, the tax bill comprises exactly the same proportion.

Proprietorship A business owned by one individual who makes the business decisions, receives all the profits, and is legally responsible for the debts of the firm.

Public debt The total value of all outstanding federal government securities.

Public goods Goods for which the principle of rival consumption does not apply; they can be jointly consumed by many individuals simultaneously at no additional cost and with no reduction in quality or quantity. Also no one who fails to help pay for the good can be denied the benefit of the good.

Purchasing power The value of money for buying goods and services. If your money income stays the same but the price of one good that you are buying goes up, your effective purchasing power falls, and vice versa.

Purchasing power parity Adjustment in exchange rate conversions that takes into account differences in the true cost of living across countries.

Q

Quantity theory of money and prices The hypothesis that changes in the money supply lead to equiproportional changes in the price level.

Quota subscription A nation's account with the International Monetary Fund, denominated in special drawing rights.

Quota system A government-imposed restriction on the quantity of a specific good that another country is allowed to sell in the United States. In other words, quotas are restrictions on imports. These restrictions are usually applied to one or several specific countries.

R

Random walk theory The theory that there are no predictable trends in securities prices that can be used to "get rich quick."

Rate of discount The rate of interest used to discount future sums back to present value.

Rate of return The proportional annual benefit that results from making an investment.

Rate-of-return regulation Regulation that seeks to keep the rate of return in an industry at a competitive level by not allowing prices that would produce economic profits.

Rational expectations hypothesis A theory stating that people combine the effects of past policy changes on important economic variables with their own judgment about the future effects of current and future policy changes.

Rationality assumption The assumption that people do not intentionally make decisions that would leave them worse off.

Reaction function The manner in which one oligopolist reacts to a change in price, output, or quality made by another oligopolist in the industry.

Real disposable income Real GDP minus net taxes, or after-tax real income.

Real rate of interest The nominal rate of interest minus the anticipated rate of inflation.

Real values Measurement of economic values after adjustments have been made for changes in the average of prices between years.

Real-balance effect The change in expenditures resulting from a change in the real value of money balances when the price level changes, all other things held constant; also called the wealth effect.

Real-income effect The change in people's purchasing power that occurs when, other things being constant, the price of one good that they purchase changes. When that price goes up, real income, or purchasing power, falls, and when that price goes down, real income increases.

Recession A period of time during which the rate of growth of business activity is consistently less than its long-term trend or is negative.

Recessionary gap The gap that exists whenever equilibrium real GDP per year is less than full-employment real GDP as shown by the position of the long-run aggregate supply curve.

Recognition time lag The time required to gather information about the current state of the economy.

Reentrant An individual who used to work full-time but left the labor force and has now reentered it looking for a job.

Regional trade bloc A group of nations that grants members special trade privileges.

Regressive taxation A tax system in which as more dollars are earned, the percentage of tax paid on them falls. The marginal tax rate is less than the average tax rate as income rises.

Reinvestment Profits (or depreciation reserves) used to purchase new capital equipment.

Relative price The money price of one commodity divided by the money price of another commodity; the number of units of one commodity that must be sacrificed to purchase one unit of another commodity.

Rent control Price ceilings on rents.

Repricing, or menu, cost of inflation The cost associated with recalculating prices and printing new price lists when there is inflation.

Required reserve ratio The percentage of total transactions deposits that the Fed requires depository institutions to hold in the form of vault cash or deposits with the Fed.

Required reserves The value of reserves that a depository institution must hold in the form of vault cash or deposits with the Fed.

Reserves In the U.S. Federal Reserve System, deposits held by Federal Reserve district banks for depository institutions, plus depository institutions' vault cash.

Resources Things used to produce goods and services to satisfy people's wants.

Retained earnings Earnings that a corporation saves, or retains, for investment in other productive activities; earnings that are not distributed to stockholders.

Ricardian equivalence theorem The proposition that an increase in the government budget deficit has no effect on aggregate demand.

Right-to-work laws Laws that make it illegal to require union membership as a condition of continuing employment in a particular firm.

Rule of 70 A rule stating that the approximate number of years required for per capita real GDP to double is equal to 70 divided by the average rate of economic growth.

Rules of origin Regulations that nations in regional trade blocs establish to delineate product categories eligible for trading preferences.

S

Sales taxes Taxes assessed on the prices paid on most goods and services.

Saving The act of not consuming all of one's current income. Whatever is not consumed out of spendable income is, by definition, saved. *Saving* is an action measured over time (a flow), whereas *savings* are a stock, an accumulation resulting from the act of saving in the past.

Savings deposits Interest-earning funds that can be withdrawn at any time without payment of a penalty.

Say's law A dictum of economist J. B. Say that supply creates its own demand; producing goods and services generates the means and the willingness to purchase other goods and services.

Scarcity A situation in which the ingredients for producing the things that people desire are insufficient to satisfy all wants at a zero price.

Search good A product with characteristics that enable an individual to evaluate the product's quality in advance of a purchase.

Seasonal unemployment Unemployment resulting from the seasonal pattern of work in specific industries. It is usually due to seasonal fluctuations in demand or to changing weather conditions that render work difficult, if not impossible, as in the agriculture, construction, and tourist industries.

Secondary boycott A refusal to deal with companies or purchase products sold by companies that are dealing with a company being struck.

Secular deflation A persistent decline in prices resulting from economic growth in the presence of stable aggregate demand.

Securities Stocks and bonds.

Services Mental or physical labor or help purchased by consumers. Examples are the assistance of physicians, lawyers, dentists, repair personnel, housecleaners, educators, retailers, and wholesalers; items purchased or used by consumers that do not have physical characteristics.

Share of stock A legal claim to a share of a corporation's future profits. If it is *common stock*, it incorporates certain voting rights regarding major policy decisions of the corporation. If it is *preferred stock*, its owners are accorded preferential treatment in the payment of dividends but do not have any voting rights.

Share-the-gains, share-the-pains theory A theory of regulatory behavior that holds that regulators must take account of the demands of three groups: legislators, who established and oversee the regulatory agency; firms in the regulated industry; and consumers of the regulated industry's products.

Short run The time period during which at least one input, such as plant size, cannot be changed.

Shortage A situation in which quantity demanded is greater than quantity supplied at a price below the market clearing price.

Short-run aggregate supply curve The relationship between total planned economywide production and the price level in the short run, all other things held constant. If prices adjust incompletely in the short run, the curve is positively sloped.

Short-run break-even price The price at which a firm's total revenues equal its total costs. At the break-even price, the firm is just making a normal rate of return on its capital investment. (It is covering its explicit and implicit costs.)

Short-run economies of operation A distinguishing characteristic of an information product arising from declining short-run average total cost as more units of the product are sold.

Short-run shutdown price The price that covers average variable costs. It occurs just below the intersection of the marginal cost curve and the average variable cost curve.

Signals Compact ways of conveying to economic decision makers information needed to make decisions. An effective signal not only conveys information but also provides the incentive to react appropriately. Economic profits and economic losses are such signals.

Slope The change in the *y* value divided by the corresponding change in the *x* value of a curve; the "incline" of the curve.

Small menu costs Costs that deter firms from changing prices in response to demand changes—for example, the costs of renegotiating contracts or printing new price lists.

Social costs The full costs borne by society whenever a resource use occurs. Social costs can be measured by adding external costs to private, or internal, costs.

Social Security contributions The mandatory taxes paid out of workers' wages and salaries.

Special drawing rights (SDRs) Reserve assets created by the International Monetary Fund for countries to use in settling international payment obligations.

Specialization The organization of economic activity so that what each person (or region) consumes is not identical to what that person (or region) produces. An individual may specialize, for example, in law or medicine. A nation may specialize in the production of coffee, computers, or digital cameras.

Stagflation A situation characterized by lower real GDP, lower employment, and a higher unemployment rate during the same period that the rate of inflation increases.

Standard of deferred payment A property of an item that makes it desirable for use as a means of settling debts maturing in the future; an essential property of money.

Static tax analysis Economic evaluation of the effects of tax rate changes under the assumption that there is no effect on the tax base, meaning that there is an unambiguous positive relationship between tax rates and tax revenues.

Stock The quantity of something, measured at a given point in time—for example, an inventory of goods or a bank account. Stocks are defined independently of time, although they are assessed at a point in time.

Store of value The ability to hold value over time; a necessary property of money.

Strategic dependence A situation in which one firm's actions with respect to price, quality, advertising, and related changes may be strategically countered by the reactions of one or more other firms in the industry. Such dependence can exist only when there are a limited number of major firms in an industry.

Strategy Any rule that is used to make a choice, such as "Always pick heads."

Strikebreakers Temporary or permanent workers hired by a company to replace union members who are striking.

Structural unemployment Unemployment resulting from a poor match of workers' abilities and skills with current requirements of employers.

Subsidy A negative tax; a payment to a producer from the government, usually in the form of a cash grant per unit.

Substitutes Two goods are substitutes when a change in the price of one causes a shift in demand for the other in the same direction as the price change.

Substitution effects The tendency of people to substitute cheaper commodities for more expensive commodities.

Supply A schedule showing the relationship between price and quantity supplied for a specified period of time, other things being equal.

Supply curve The graphical representation of the supply schedule; a line (curve) showing the supply schedule, which generally slopes upward (has a positive slope), other things being equal.

Supply-side economics The suggestion that creating incentives for individuals and firms to increase productivity will cause the aggregate supply curve to shift outward.

Surplus A situation in which quantity supplied is greater than quantity demanded at a price above the market clearing price.

Sweep account A depository institution account that entails regular shifts of funds from transactions deposits that are subject to reserve requirements to savings deposits that are exempt from reserve requirements.

Sympathy strike A work stoppage by a union in sympathy with another union's strike or cause.

T

Target zone A range of permitted exchange rate variations between upper and lower exchange rate bands that a central bank defends by selling or buying foreign exchange reserves.

Tariffs Taxes on imported goods.

Tax base The value of goods, services, wealth, or incomes subject to taxation.

Tax bracket A specified interval of income to which a specific and unique marginal tax rate is applied.

Tax incidence The distribution of tax burdens among various groups in society.

Tax rate The proportion of a tax base that must be paid to a government as taxes.

Taylor rule An equation that specifies a federal funds rate target based on an estimated long-run real interest rate, the current deviation of the actual inflation rate from the Federal Reserve's inflation objective, and the gap between actual real GDP and a measure of potential real GDP.

Technology Society's pool of applied knowledge concerning how goods and services can be produced.

Terms of exchange The conditions under which trading takes place. Usually, the terms of exchange are equal to the price at which a good is traded.

The Fed The Federal Reserve System; the central bank of the United States.

Theory of public choice The study of collective decision making.

Third parties Parties who are not directly involved in a given activity or transaction. For example, in the relationship between caregivers and patients, fees may be paid by third parties (insurance companies, government).

Thrift institutions Financial institutions that receive most of their funds from the savings of the public; they include savings banks, savings and loan associations, and credit unions.

Tie-in sales Purchases of one product that are permitted by the seller only if the consumer buys another good or service from the same firm.

Time deposit A deposit in a financial institution that requires notice of intent to withdraw or must be left for an agreed period. Withdrawal of funds prior to the end of the agreed period may result in a penalty.

Tit-for-tat strategic behavior In game theory, cooperation that continues as long as the other players continue to cooperate.

Total costs The sum of total fixed costs and total variable costs.

Total income The yearly amount earned by the nation's resources (factors of production). Total income therefore includes wages, rent, interest payments, and profits that are received by workers, landowners, capital owners, and entrepreneurs, respectively.

Total revenues The price per unit times the total quantity sold.

Trade deflection Moving partially assembled products into a member nation of a regional trade bloc, completing assembly, and then exporting them to other nations within the bloc, so as to benefit from preferences granted by the trade bloc.

Trade diversion Shifting existing international trade from countries outside a regional trade bloc to nations within the bloc.

Trading Desk An office at the Federal Reserve Bank of New York charged with implementing monetary policy strategies developed by the Federal Open Market Committee.

Transaction costs All costs associated with making, reaching, and enforcing agreements.

Transactions approach A method of measuring the money supply by looking at money as a medium of exchange.

Transactions demand Holding money as a medium of exchange to make payments. The level varies directly with nominal GDP.

Transactions deposits Checkable and debitable account balances in commercial banks and other types of financial institutions, such as credit unions and savings banks; any accounts in financial institutions from which you can easily transmit debit-card and check payments.

Transfer payments Money payments made by governments to individuals for which no services or goods are rendered in return. Examples are Social Security old-age and disability benefits and unemployment insurance benefits.

Transfers in kind Payments that are in the form of actual goods and services, such as food stamps, subsidized public housing, and medical care, and for which no goods or services are rendered in return.

Traveler's checks Financial instruments obtained from a bank or a nonbanking organization and signed during purchase that can be used as cash upon a second signature by the purchaser.

U

Unanticipated inflation Inflation at a rate that comes as a surprise, either higher or lower than the rate anticipated.

Unemployment The total number of adults (aged 16 years or older) who are willing and able to work and who are actively looking for work but have not found a job.

Union shop A business enterprise that may hire nonunion members, conditional on their joining the union by some specified date after employment begins.

Unit elasticity of demand A demand relationship in which the quantity demanded changes exactly in proportion to the change in price.

Unit of accounting A measure by which prices are expressed; the common denominator of the price system; a central property of money.

Unit tax A constant tax assessed on each unit of a good that consumers purchase.

Unlimited liability A legal concept whereby the personal assets of the owner of a firm can be seized to pay off the firm's debts.

Util A representative unit by which utility is measured.

Utility The want-satisfying power of a good or service.

Utility analysis The analysis of consumer decision making based on utility maximization.

V

Value added The dollar value of an industry's sales minus the value of intermediate goods (for example, raw materials and parts) used in production.

Variable costs Costs that vary with the rate of production. They include wages paid to workers and purchases of materials.

Versioning Selling a product in slightly altered forms to different groups of consumers.

Vertical merger The joining of a firm with another to which it sells an output or from which it buys an input.

Voluntary exchange An act of trading, done on an elective basis, in which both parties to the trade expect to be better off after the exchange.

Voluntary import expansion (VIE) An official agreement with another country in which it agrees to import more from the United States.

Voluntary restraint agreement (VRA) An official agreement with another country that "voluntarily" restricts the quantity of its exports to the United States.

W

Wants What people would buy if their incomes were unlimited.

Wealth The stock of assets owned by a person, household, firm, or nation. For a household, wealth can consist of a house, cars, personal belongings, stocks, bonds, bank accounts, and cash.

World Bank A multinational agency that specializes in making loans to about 100 developing nations in an effort to promote their long-term development and growth.

World Trade Organization (WTO) The successor organization to the GATT that handles trade disputes among its member nations.

X

x **axis** The horizontal axis in a graph.

Y

y **axis** The vertical axis in a graph.

Z

Zero-sum game A game in which any gains within the group are exactly offset by equal losses by the end of the game.

Index

776–777; productivity and, 778; right-to-work laws and, 770; strategies of, 772–777; strikes and, 772–773. *See also* Strike(s); in U.S. *See* Union(s) in United States; wages and, 773–778

Union shop, 770

Union(s) in United States: current status of, 770–772; membership in, decline in, 771; ten largest, listed, 771

Union-made goods, 776–777

Unit elasticity of demand, 504

Unit tax, 146

United Auto Workers (UAW), 768, 784–785

United Food and Commercial Workers, 777

United Kingdom. *See also* Great Britain: emissions control efforts in, 827; long queues to see doctors in, 809; pop stars from, 857

United Mine Workers, 770

United Parcel Service, 724, 839

United Potato Growers of America, 699

United States: advertising expenses in, 677; agricultural subsidies in, 96–97; antitrust policy in, 728–730; China's air pollution reaches, 832; China's "voluntary" textile products quota and, 99; demonstration of comparative advantage in a two-country, two-good world and, 842–846; economy of, outsourcing's effects on, 755–756; income distribution in, 794–795; industry concentration ratios in, 692, 693; labor movement in, 769–770; participation in world trade and, 839, 840; poverty rate in, 801, 804; price of broadband Internet service in, 54; productive efficiency in, 848; tariffs in, 853–854, 855; trade deficit in, 864; trade within, 43; unions in. *See* Union(s) in United States

United States Bureau of the Census, 501

United States Constitution, Sixteenth Amendment to, 138–139

United States Department of Commerce, 640

United States Department of Energy, Bonneville Power Administration of, 819

United States Department of Homeland Security, 139

United States Department of the Interior, 829

United States Department of Justice, antitrust laws enforced by, 114, 729, 730, 733

United States Department of the Treasury, 868; Bureau of Engraving and Printing of, 733, 734; Internal Revenue Service of. *See* Internal Revenue Service

United States Fish and Wildlife Service, 830

United States government. *See* Federal government

United States Patent and Trademark Office, 675

United States Postal Service (USPS): incentive structure and, 123–124; rates decisions and, 513

Unit-elastic demand, 506

Unit-elastic supply, 516

Unlimited liability, 563

U.S. Telecommunications Act (1996), 122

User charges, 135

USPS. *See* United States Postal Service

Util, 527, 540

Utilitarianism, 526–527

Utility, 525; applying marginal analysis to, 527; defined, 526; marginal. *See* Marginal utility(ies); measuring, 540–541; total. *See* Total utility; utils and, 526–527

Utility analysis, 526

Utility theory, 526–527

V

Value(s): of forgone alternatives, 31; par, 879; present. *See* Present value(s)

Variable costs: average. *See* Average variable costs; defined, 590; total, 590

Variable factors of production, 584

Variable inputs, 584

Vending machines, newspaper versus candy, 530–531

Versioning, 732

Vertical merger, 691

Vidstone, 670

Volkswagen, 683, 684

Voluntary exchange, 83

Voluntary import expansion, 853

Voluntary quotas, 853

Voluntary restraint agreement, 853

Voting, spending versus, 124–125

W

Wage(s): male-female gap in, 741, 762–763; minimum. *See* Minimum wage; under monopsony, 780–783; outsourcing's effects on, 753–755; unions and, 773–778

Wage determination, in perfectly competitive labor market, 749–752

Wagner Act (National Labor Relations Act)(NLRA)(1935), 770

WakeUpWal-Mart.com, 777

Waldfogel, Joel, 6

Wal-Mart: advertising against, 777; radio-frequency identification (RFID) tags used by, 594; unions and, 772, 777

Wants: defined, 3; needs versus, 30

War on Poverty, 804

Warning labels, numerous and lengthy, 725

Waste, 674

Wealth: distribution of, 795; inherited, 798; measured, 795; more assets held by older set and, 797

Weather forecasts, price expectations and, 69

Web blogs, as businesses, 612

Weblogs, Inc., 612

Weiner, Claudia, 11–12

Welfare Reform Act (1996), 804

Wendy's, long run and, 584

Westin Hotels & Resorts, 671

Wetzel, David and Eileen, 657

Whirlpool, 541

Wild species, common property, trade-offs and, 829–830

Witherspoon, Reese, 560

Wood, Vic, 810–811

Woodbridge, G. L., 851

World Trade Organization (WTO), 854–855

World War II, government spending during, 118

WorldCom, 700

WTO (World Trade Organization), 854–855

X

X axis, 20

Xerox, war game competitions and, 694

Y

Y axis, 20

Yahoo, 690

Z

Zero-sum game, 694

Zhang Qinyong, 784

Zilinek, Steve, 44

Zimbabwe, depreciated currency in, 881

Zimmer Motor Cars, 683

Photo Credits